Foundations of
Programming Languages

Foundations of Programming Languages

Jacques Loeckx
Kurt Mehlhorn
Reinhard Wilhelm

Universität des Saarlandes
Saarbrücken
West Germany

JOHN WILEY & SONS
Chichester · New York · Brisbane · Toronto · Singapore

First published as *Grundlagen der Programmiersprachen*, by
Loeckx/Mehlhorn/Wilhelm, c 1986. This edition is published by
permission of Verlag B. G. Teubner, Stuttgart, and is the sole
authorized English translation of the original German edition.

British Library Cataloguing in Publication Data:

Loeckx, Jacques
    Foundations of programming languages.
    1. Computer systems. Programming languages.
    Theories
    I. Title II. Mehlhorn, Kurt III. Wilhelm,
    Reinhard
    005.13′01

ISBN 0 471 92139 4

Printed and Bound in Great Britain by Anchor Brendon Ltd, Tiptree, Essex

Preface to the German Edition

This book discusses principles of programming languages, their connection to actual computers and — by example — algorithms. The objective of this book is to provide a firm basis for the study of computer science. It is intended, in particular, for undergraduate students taking an introductory course in computer science.

A program is only useful when it correctly solves the given problem and does this with the desired efficiency. Assertions as to correctness and efficiency of a program are only possible if the programming language used is defined precisely, i.e. the set of programs (syntax) and their meaning (semantics) is fixed. Thus the definition of syntax and semantics plays an important role in this book. Formal definitions only come to life if they are based on a good intuitive understanding and when they lead to conclusions in the form of theorems. This book therefore contains a large number of examples, theorems and exercises.

The principles of programming languages are introduced by way of a specific programming language called PROSA (**PRO**gramming language **SA**arbrücken). PROSA is very similar to Pascal but deviates in some points (e.g. dynamic arrays, nested records) for didactic reasons. These deviations serve both to simplify and to illustrate some concepts not present in Pascal. Using Pascal in an accompanying programming practical, on the other hand, does not pose any problem.

Syntax and semantics of PROSA are formally defined. We have decided on attribute grammars (context-free grammars with attributes) to describe the syntax. The attributes express context conditions. Attribute grammars have, as a rule, the advantage of facilitating simple formulation of the context conditions. They also provide a method to check context conditions by a compiler for the programming language. When defining the semantics of PROSA we have, for many reasons, decided on operational semantics. Used in a suitable way, such semantics is simple, intuitively clear and thus also comprehensible for the beginner. Furthermore the operational approach directly leads to the concept of run-time. It is simple to derive axiomatic semantics which is the basis for the usual correctness proofs. Finally, operational semantics leads to compilation in a natural way.

The connection between programming languages and computers is illustrated by describing a compiler which translates PROSA into the machine language of a simple computer, called RESA (**RE**chner **SA**arbrücken). To this end the translation is split into manageable parts. Each part is proved correct.

This book aims at introducing the reader thoroughly to a typical higher programming language and the methods necessary to describe it. It should then be easy to acquire further programming languages independently. Numerous examples, presenting a first stock of interesting algorithms, enable the reader to get a good intuitive understanding of the concepts. A mathematical treatment leads to further familiarization and a thorough understanding. The reader gets to know and understand two large systems: the formal description of PROSA and the translation of PROSA into RESA. This provides an excellent training in an essential part of the activities of a computer scientist, i.e. the design of complex systems. In this book much emphasis has been placed on proving the given programs correct and on analysing their computation time. Hopefully this will promote a certain pattern of behaviour on the part of the reader.

The individual chapters are laid out as follows. The first chapter provides the foundation for a mathematical treatment of programming languages and programs. Firstly important concepts such as relation and function are introduced. Partial functions are considered to be the "normal case". Section 1.3 is dedicated to words (i.e. *strings*). Section 1.4 contains a detailed discussion of context-free grammars as a means of defining the syntax of formal languages. Semantics of formal languages is the subject of Sections 1.5 (recursively defined functions), 1.6 (attribute grammars) and 1.7 (mathematical machines). To be more precise, as the sentences of a formal language, defined by a grammar, bear a structure, it is obvious that this structure is employed in defining the semantics. Methods for doing so are provided in Sections 1.5 and 1.6. The algorithmic approach, as an alternative, is discussed in Section 1.7. The general concept of a mathematical machine is introduced here. It is the basis for the operational semantics given later. Sections 1.4, 1.5 and 1.7 can be studied in parallel to Chapter II, Section 1.6 is not needed until Chapter III.

In the second chapter we deal with arithmetic expressions using the mechanism introduced in the first chapter. Expressions represent one of the simplest examples which can be used to try out and practice all the concepts introduced in the first chapter. Not only classical notations such as those in elementary mathematics are considered, but also special forms such as fully parenthesised expressions and bracket-free notation, specially suited to mechanical processing.

We begin with fully parenthesised expressions. The brackets in these expressions determine exactly the order of the operations. Next we define their semantics, i.e. the value represented by the expression, in two ways, namely algebraically and algorithmically. In the algebraic definition the structure of an expression is used to define its meaning, i.e. the meaning of an expression is defined in terms of the meaning of its subexpressions. The algorithmic definition uses a simple mathematical machine which evaluates expressions. A central assertion of the chapter is the equivalence of both approaches. We also illustrate to what extent this machine recognises the syntactic structure of the expressions to be evaluated. The concept of translation or compilation is then introduced, i.e. the meaning preserving transformation of one formal language into another. We show how fully parenthesised expressions are transformed into a uniquely defined bracket-free notation. Finally, various approaches to the algorithmic definition are compared, and the concept of simulation is illustrated.

Fully parenthesised expressions are too restrictive to be of practical use. Partially parenthesised expressions with precedence are usually used, both in mathematics and in most programming languages. For this reason we repeat essential parts of the discussion for this practical important notation in Section 2.2.

Chapter III begins with the description of the programming language PROSA, and using it as an example, introduces the fundamental concepts of Algol-like programming languages. With respect to its language concepts and its syntax, PROSA is very similar to Pascal. We will indicate where in Chapters III, IV and VI we deviate from Pascal. In addition, similarities and differences to other widely used programming languages, such as Algol-60, PL/I and Ada, will be pointed out.

This chapter is structured as follows. Section 3.1 introduces the fundamental concepts of syntax, context-conditions and semantics and fixes notations for the rest of the chapter. Programs manipulate objects (data), they are introduced in Section 3.2. In 3.3 a first example of a PROSA program is given and, using this example, important aspects of algorithmic languages are discussed. In 3.4 we start defining the PROSA machine which we use to specify the operational semantics of PROSA. The PROSA machine is a mathematical machine (see 1.7) executing PROSA programs. Such a machine is usually called an interpreter. PROSA is formally defined in Sections 3.5 to 3.8, namely, the declaration section in 3.5, the statement section in 3.7 and the program in 3.6. Section 3.8 is a short summary. In Sections 3.9 and 3.10 we discuss correctness proofs and the analysis of computation time, making use of the formal definition of PROSA. From the semantics defined in terms of the PROSA machine we derive a so-called axiomatic semantics which is more suitable for correctness proofs of programs than operational semantics. Besides, the PROSA machine is the basis for analysing the efficiency of programs. Efficiency is measured in terms of the order of the number of execution steps required by the PROSA machine. In the course of these sections and again in Section 3.11 we illustrate PROSA using several nontrivial examples, and thus give the reader a first impression of algorithmic problem solving.

In the fourth chapter the simple programming language of Chapter III is enriched by complex data types, namely arrays, records and pointers. An array (*row*) is a collection of several variables of the same type and a record (*structure*) is a collection of several variables of arbitrary type. Pointers are a new set of variables. A pointer variable can have a record as a value.

This chapter is structured as follows. In the first section arrays are introduced and explained by some examples. In the second section the same is done for records and pointers. Finally, in the third section, the new concepts are formally described and the extended syntax and semantics of PROSA is given.

In order to formulate algorithms, programmers use higher programming languages such as Pascal and PROSA. Such programs are therefore easily read. However, they cannot be executed directly on a computer. Programs in higher programming languages must therefore be translated into the machine language of a computer before they can be processed by this computer.

The fifth chapter introduces the RESA computer and its machine language and shows how PROSA programs can be translated into RESA programs. RESA, together with its machine language, is introduced in Section 5.1. Neither its architecture nor its technical realisation will be discussed. The other sections describe the translation.

This chapter has two aims. Firstly, we show that PROSA can be translated into the machine language of RESA. The proof is constructive, i.e. an algorithm for this translation is given. This compiler is structured somewhat differently to actual compilers in order to facilitate proofs. For this reason we informally describe how actual compilers are constructed and how they function.

In Chapter VI we discuss a further language extension, procedures, which brings PROSA more in line with a practical programming language.

This chapter is structured as follows. Section 6.1 is an introduction. We present the most important new concepts informally, using different examples. The presentation is informal. Section 6.2 deals with these new concepts more precisely, again by way of many examples. These examples illustrate the – partly nontrivial – properties of procedures. They also deal with correctness proofs and analysis of computation time of programs with procedures. Section 6.3 contains a precise discussion of the syntax and Section 6.4 of the semantics.

Chapter VII describes the translation of PROSA with procedures into RESA. Two new problems are added to the compilation problem of Chapter V.

1) Procedures permit a more flexible control structure.

2) Procedures demand a more elaborate storage organisation.

Of the two, storage organisation is the bigger problem. It is discussed in detail in Section 7.1 where we specify how the binding stack and the storage state of the PROSA machine is reflected in the storage organisation of the RESA machine. In Section 7.2 we describe storage access, i.e. how applied occurrence of names are translated into RESA. Then, in Section 7.3, we give the translation proper and show which RESA statements must be generated from PROSA statements.

When this book was published Pascal had already reached the venerable old computer science age of 16 years. PROSA, because of its similarity to Pascal, shares its strength and weaknesses. Thus both PROSA and Pascal lack concepts developed for newer programming languages, conducive to the efficient construction of reliable programs. Some possible language extensions are briefly introduced in Chapter VIII. Section 8.1 describes a concept to support modular construction of programs. Section 8.2 introduces polymorphic functions and procedures. Such functions and procedures therefore have type parameters. Section 8.3 introduces some generalised control structures which prove to be very useful for formulating parallel processes in Section 8.4.

Figure 1 shows the logical dependency of the chapters. It indicates the order in which the different chapters or sections should be read. The book can also be read effectively without referring to this order. In particular, the informal introductions and detailed examples make it possible to do without the formal treatment when reading the book for the first time.

This book has evolved from introductory lectures held by the authors in the "Universität des Saarlandes" during the past years. In their first year our students attend the lectures *Principles of Programming Languages* and *Computer Architecture* . They also participate in programming practicals. We interweave the contents of both lecture series and discuss computers following Chapter IV or V. Alternatively, computers can be treated either before or after presenting the material of this book. The scope of this book exceeds that of a four hourly lecture series covering one semester. Therefore we assume that the student studies individual sections of the book independently, e.g. the informal introductions and larger examples.

We would like to thank our colleagues, in particular Günter Hotz and Wolfgang Wahlster, as well as numerous co-workers and critical students for many fruitful discussions and hints while writing this book. Kurt Sieber's experience with the semantics of programming languages has benefited the conception of operational semantics. Christian Uhrig formulated, collected and compiled part of the exercises and co-ordinated the editorial work. Meta Rebeck-Güttler proof-read the German version. Gabriele Jacquinot, Brigitte Kuhn, Anette Lucks, Michael Müller, Hans-J. Profitlich, Klaus-Dieter Rottmann and Nikola Truxa with the help of the two TEXnicians Dieter Maurer and Hans Rohnert produced the TEXmanuscript for the German edition. Georg Hickel and Michael Baston prepared the diagrams.

Saarbrücken, Summer 1986

Jacques Loeckx
Kurt Mehlhorn
Reinhard Wilhelm

Preface to the English Edition

We thank Peggy and Franz Geiselbrechtinger for a most careful translation and for the preparation of the TEXmanuscript. Klaus-Dieter Rottmann, Bernhard Weinelt TEXed most of the figures anew; together with Michael Müller they produced the final layout.

Many people have supplied comments and corrections to the German edition of this book. We would like to thank them all and in particular Jan Messerschmidt. Arno Schmitt very carefully proofread the English manuscript and incorporated the corrections.

Saarbrücken, Spring 1988

Jacques Loeckx
Kurt Mehlhorn
Reinhard Wilhelm

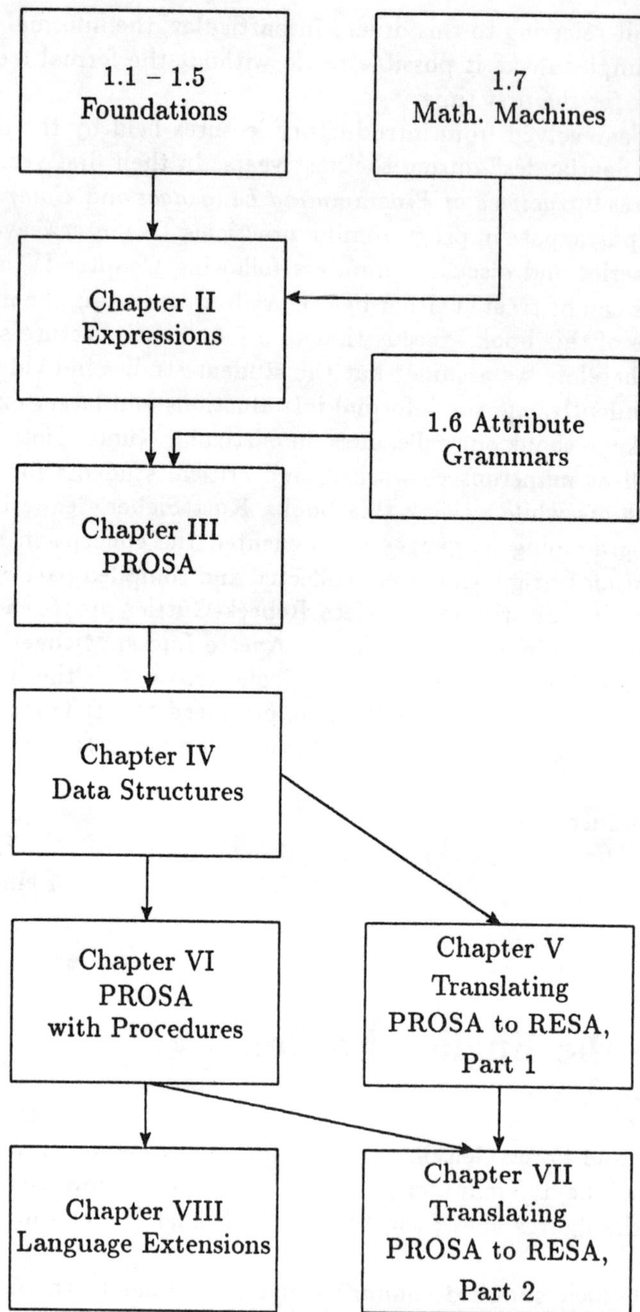

Fig. 1. Logical dependency of the chapters. Sections 1.4, 1.5 and 1.7 can be studied parallel to Chapter II. Section 1.7 is not required until Chapter II

Contents

Introduction: Programming Languages as a Tool

A programming language is an essential tool for the programmer and the software developer. In using the language he describes the objects with which his program should work, i.e. integers, strings, collections of such objects or files. Besides, he employs the language to formulate procedures which manipulate these objects, e.g. computing the trajectory of a rocket, booking sums of money onto a bank account or sorting the entries of account files in alphabetical order. Programming languages are used to determine how various programs co-operate in more complex systems. A bank's system for control of bank accounts, for example, communicates with similar programs in other banks by means of suitable data-processing in order to register incoming and outgoing transfers of money.

Similar to an engineer in other areas, a software developer "assembles" larger units from elementary units according to suitable methods to form a finished product. As in other fields, the product must satisfy requirements and be efficient. More frequently than in other areas of engineering, the end product is not a consumer article such as a television, a house or a car, but is itself a tool for engineers, business people, politicians or computer scientists. An **operating system**, for example, administrates the computer resources, such as the central processing unit, memory, disc storage and input and output devices. By allocating them to the actual users according to certain priorities and strategies it makes the computer effectively available for users. A problem-oriented language — as opposed to the machine language of a computer — is translated by a **compiler**, thus making it usable on a computer. A **data base system** enables a company to have a clear overview of its suppliers and customers and to record all parts and their specifications used in production. Indeed the state, too, can collect information about traffic offenders, stolen vehicles, etc. A **stock-control system** offers the business man at all times an overview of the actual state of his stock and automatically prints orders for articles no longer in stock in sufficient numbers.

The systems referred to, and indeed all complex programming systems, can only be developed if they have a suitable structure and are divided into clear and well structured subsystems. The term **programming in the large** is used for describing the structure of a programming system and the interaction of the different subsystems. The term **programming in the small** means the realisation of the subsystems and, in particular, the procedures used in them.

The programming language PASCAL by N. Wirth has been generally adopted for programming in the small, particularly in the field of education. In many ways it has been the model for the programming language PROSA which will be formally defined in this book. Since Chapters I and II provide the formal foundations for describing programming languages, we now first present some examples of programs written in stylised English as motivation. In the course of this discussion some important concepts of programming - correctness, efficiency, termination - are illustrated.

Some Program Examples

In the following programs "program variables" m, k, $count$, z etc. occur. They are used as names for "containers" which can hold precisely one integer, real number or symbol at any time during the execution of a program. Certain operations are possible on these containers. Four of these are:

"set i to 0"
>   meaning: The content of the container named i is replaced by the number 0. The previous content is thus lost.

"increment i by 1"
>   meaning: The content of i is increased by 1.

"swap i and j"
>   meaning: The contents of i and j are exchanged.

"$i < j$"
>   meaning: The contents of i and j are compared (they remain unchanged). The result of the comparison is "true", if the content of i is less than the content of j, otherwise it is false.

We shall now discuss four programs.

First example: Pattern Recognition

Problem specification:
Given two words, a "text" t and a "pattern" m, find the number of occurrences of m in t.

Example:

Text:　　$t =$ 'mondaymorning'
Pattern:　$m =$ 'mo'
Result:　twice

The following is a precise specification of the problem.

Given: A text $t = t_0 t_1 \ldots t_{r-1}$ and a pattern $m = m_0 m_1 \ldots m_{p-1}$, where $r \geq 1, p \geq$
　　1 and $t_0, \ldots, t_{r-1}, m_0, \ldots, m_{p-1}$ are symbols.
Problem: Determine the number of indices i, $0 \leq i \leq r - p$, for which $t_{i+j} = m_j$
　　for all j, $0 \leq j \leq p - 1$.

One method of solving the problem is to "move" a "pointer" z from left to
right through text t ($z = 0, 1, \ldots, r - p$) comparing the sections of the text starting
at pointer z with pattern m (see diagram). Every time they correspond the number
of occurrences is increased by 1.

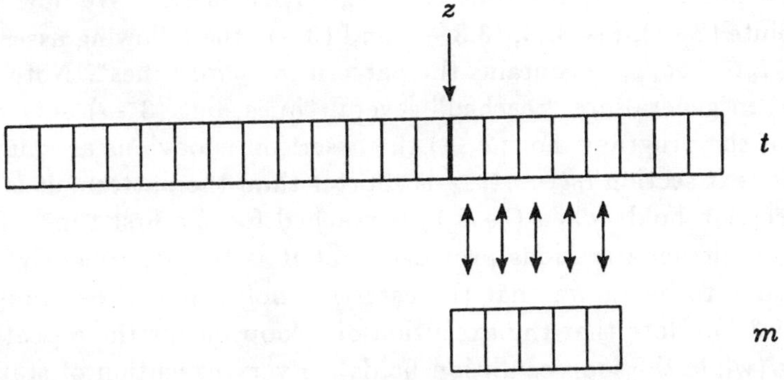

A program which works according to this method is

Program 1:

```
- set z to 0;                                          (1)

- set count to 0;                                      (2)

- while z ≤ r - p do                                   (3)

    - compare t_z t_{z+1} ... t_{z+p-1} and m_0 m_1 ... m_{p-1};   (3.1)

    - if identical then                                (3.2)

        - increment count by 1;                        (3.2.1)

    - increment z by 1;                                (3.3)
```

Program 1 comprises three statements. The first two statements set z and *count* to 0. The third statement is a **loop statement** (short **loop**). A loop consists of a **loop condition** (here $z \le r - p$) and a **loop body**. The loop body is a sequence of statements (here the sequence of statements (3.1), (3.2) and (3.3)). A loop is executed by performing the loop body as long as the loop condition holds. Thus in our example the body is executed for $z = 0, 1, 2, \ldots, r - p$. Observe that statement (3.3) increases z by one. Statement (3.1) is a comparison of the pattern with the text section starting at z. This statement will be developed into simpler statements later on. Statement (3.2) is a **conditional statement**. A conditional statement consists of a test (here "identical") and a statement (here (3.2.1)) which is only executed if the test succeeds. Finally, statement (3.3) shifts the pattern by one position relative to the text.

It seems intuitively clear that the program solves the problem on hand. It is therefore all the more instructive to prove it. We will then be equipped for more difficult problems. For the proof the concept "program point" is introduced. If (n) is a step then the program point $(\to n)$ represents the time before the execution of step (n) and program point $(n \to)$ the time after execution of (n). We now show that at program points $(2 \to)$, $(\to 3.1)$, $(3.3 \to)$ and $(3 \to)$ the following assertion holds: " text section $t_0 t_1 \ldots t_{z+p-2}$ contains the pattern m *count* times". Note that $(\to 3.1)$ and $(3.3 \to)$ in general are "reached" several times, but $(3 \to)$ only once, namely at the end of the program. For $(2 \to)$ the assertion is obvious as *count* is equal to zero and the text section $t_0 t_1 \ldots t_{p-2}$ is shorter than the pattern. It is also obvious that the assertion holds when $(\to 3.1)$ is reached for the first time. The assertion also holds for further iterations provided that it is true "previously" at $(3.3 \to)$. It thus remains to be shown that the assertion holds at $(3.3 \to)$ provided that it holds at $(\to 3.1)$. Note that the execution of a loop means the repeated execution of the body (while the loop condition holds). Every execution of statement (3.1), which is not the first, succeeds the execution of statement (3.3). Suppose the assertion is true at $(\to 3.1)$ for some $z = z_0$ and $count = count_0$, i.e. text section $t_0 \ldots t_{z_0+p-2}$ contains the pattern $count_0$ times. Now $t_z \ldots t_{z+p-1}$ and $m_0 \ldots m_{p-1}$ are compared. We distinguish between two cases:

Case 1:   If the words $t_z \ldots t_{z+p-1}$ and $m_0 \ldots m_{p-1}$ are identical, a new occurrence of the pattern has been found. The value $count_0$ of *count* Now the assertion holds at $(3.3 \to)$ with the new values of z and *count*, namely $z_0 + 1$ and $count_0 + 1$.

Case 2:   If the words are not identical then z is set to $z_0 + 1$. The assertion holds at $(3.3 \to)$ for the new values of z and *count*, namely $z_0 + 1$ and $count_0$.

We now consider the program point $(3 \to)$. When this point is reached the loop condition no longer holds, i.e. $z = r - p + 1$ or $z = 0$ and $p > r$. Furthermore, the previous program point was either $(2 \to)$ or $(3.3 \to)$ (in the first case the text is shorter than the pattern). In each case, therefore, *count* corresponds to the number of occurrences of patterns m in the text section $t_0 t_1 \ldots t_r$, i.e. in the whole text. When we reach the program point $(3 \to)$, *count* has the desired value. One says that the program is **partially correct**. Why only partially correct? Note that we have not yet shown that the program point $(3 \rightarrow)$ is actually reached. Only when we have shown (see below) that point $(3 \rightarrow)$ is indeed reached can we say that our program is **correct** (alternatively **totally correct**).

Not every programming language provides a direct test for equality of words such as $t_z \ldots t_{z+p-2}$ and $m_0 \ldots m_{p-1}$. For this reason we replace Program 1 by Program 2 which, instead, only has to test the equality of two symbols.

Program 2:

- set z to 0;

- set *count* to 0;

- while $z \leq r - p$ do

- set j to 0;

- while $j \leq p - 1$ and then $t_{z+j} = m_j$ do

  > - increment j by 1

- if $j = p$ (i.e. identical!) then

  > - increment *count* by 1

- increment z by 1;

If one is sure that the newly introduced "while-loop", together with the test "$j = p$", has the same effect as steps (3.1) and (3.2) in Program 1 then it is obvious that Program 2 also solves the problem. Note that it is **not** necessary to know which problem Program 1 solves but only that Program 1 and Program 2 solve the same problem. An important property for the user of a program is its **efficiency**, i.e. the use of resources (e.g. computation time, storage) during the execution of the program. The computation time of a program, i.e. the number of "elementary operations" performed (or at least the order of this number) is thus quite important. We now calculate the computation time for Program 2 depending on the length of the text and the pattern.

As already stated, the outer "while-loop" is executed exactly $r - p + 1$ times. Assuming that r is much greater than p, one says that the outer loop is executed in the order of r. "Within" the outer loop the "most expensive" step is the "while-loop". It requires at least two comparisons (if the first symbols of the pattern and the text section are not identical), but at most $2p$ comparisons and p increments (if an occurrence of the pattern is found). As we are only interested in the order of the number of elementary operations we ignore the steps which do not depend on p and r in the outer loop and those which do not depend on p in the inner loop. Thus the result is that the program (in the "worst" case) requires operations in the order of $r \cdot p$, i.e. its computation time is in the order of $r \cdot p$. (Note that it is possible to construct a program for the same problem whose computation time is in the order of $r + p$!)

Apart from correctness and efficiency there is a third question connected with programs, the question of their **termination**. Does the above program terminate for all texts t (of length r) and all patterns m (of length p)? The discussion of efficiency for this example program already provides an answer to this question. The computation time of the program is of the order $r \cdot p$. This implies that it terminates. Usually it is simpler to prove termination directly than to give a relevant estimate of the computation time (see fourth example).

Second example: Search for Minimum

Problem specification:

Given: A collection of n containers $a_1, \ldots, a_n, (n \geq 1)$, which hold n integers where any two are different.

Problem: Determine the index of the container which holds the smallest number.

One way of solving the problem is to examine the contents of the containers with indices in increasing order, retaining the index of the container holding the currently smallest element, for example *min*, (*min* can be considered as the name of an additional container). The content of the container currently investigated is compared with the content of a_{min}. If it is smaller then *min* is set to the index of the container under examination.

Program:

```
- set i to 1;                                              (1)

- set min to 1;                                            (2)

- while i < n do                                           (3)

- increment i by 1;                                        (3.1)

- if a_i < a_min, then   | - set min to i |               (3.2)
```

Prove that at program points $(2 \rightarrow)$, $(\rightarrow 3.1)$, $(3.2 \rightarrow)$, $(3 \rightarrow)$ the assertion "$1 \leq min \leq i$ and $a_{min} \leq a_j$ for all j with $1 \leq j \leq i$ " holds. The validity of this assertion at point $(3 \rightarrow)$, i.e. for $i = n$, shows that the program solves the problem correctly. Efficiency and termination are easily established in this program. The computation time is in the order of n.

Third example: Sorting

Problem specification:

Given: A collection of n containers $a_1, \ldots, a_n (n \geq 1)$ which hold n integers where any two are different.

Problem: Swap the existing contents such that
$$value(a_i) < value(a_{i+1}) \text{ for } 1 \leq i \leq n-1 .$$

To solve this sorting problem we proceed iteratively, i.e. we construct increasingly larger initial segments of the sorted array. Using our solution of Search for Minimum we first determine the smallest content, say $value(a_{min})$, of all containers and swap it with the content of a_1. Then we determine the second smallest content of all containers by searching for the minimum of the containers $a_2, \ldots, a_n$ and then swapping it for the content of a_2, and so on. In general, the list then consists of a sorted section, such as $a_1 a_2 \ldots a_k$, and a section, namely $a_{k+1} \ldots a_n$, which, in general, is not yet sorted. The following assertion holds:

$$\left. \begin{array}{ll} value(a_i) < value(a_{i+1}) & \text{for all } i,\ 1 \leq i < k \\[2mm] \text{and} & \\[2mm] value(a_k) < value(a_j) & \text{for all } j,\ k+1 \leq j \leq n \end{array} \right\} \quad (A)$$

The corresponding program is

Program:

```
- set k to 0;
- while k < n - 1 do

      - search for index min of the container with the smallest element
        of a_{k+1}, ..., a_n;
      - swap a_{k+1} and a_{min};
      - increment k by 1
```

For the statement "Search for the index of the container ..." the program Search for Minimum can be used after it has been modified such that it accepts an arbitrary given interval as an index range for the containers (instead of — as in the second example — a fixed interval $1 \ldots n$). The chapter on procedures and parameters provides for such possibilities.

The above assertion (A) can serve as the assertion for the correctness proof. It holds at the beginning of the program ($k = 0$) as the sorted section is empty. At the end of the program, i.e. for $k = n - 1$, the correctness of the program follows from assertion (A).

Let us consider the computation time of the program. As can be seen above, the computation time for the Search for Minimum for m containers is in the order of m. In our sorting program we determine successively the minimum of n, $n - 1$, ..., 2 numbers. Thus the total computation time is in the order of $n + (n - 1) + \ldots + 2 = n(n - 1)/2$, that is the square of n. The sorting problem can also be solved by programs whose computation time is only in the order of $n \log n$.

Fourth example: Greatest Common Divisor

Problem specification:

Given: Two natural numbers a and b.

Problem: Determine the greatest common divisor $gcd(a, b)$ of numbers a and b, i.e. the largest natural number which divides a and b.

To construct the program, the following properties of the greatest common divisor (gcd) are used.

- if $b = 0$ then $gcd(a, b) = a$
- if $b \neq 0$ then $gcd(a, b) = gcd(b, a \bmod b)$ where $a \bmod b$ stands for the remainder of the integer division of a by b.

Thus we arrive at the following solution, also called Euclidean algorithm.

$$gcd(a, b) = \begin{cases} a & \text{if } b = 0 \\ gcd(b, a \bmod b) & \text{otherwise} \end{cases}$$

This solution represents a so-called **recursive** program. When computing the values of gcd for arguments a and b we use the value of gcd for arguments b and $a \bmod b$. The case $b = 0$ serves as a "brake", so to speak, where this "referring" to subcases ends. Consider this program with input $a = 103\ 574$ and $b = 63\ 459$. We get

$$
\begin{aligned}
gcd(103\ 574, 63\ 459) &= gcd(63\ 459, 40\ 115) \\
= gcd(40\ 115, 23\ 344) &= gcd(23\ 344, 16\ 771) \\
= gcd(16\ 771, 6\ 573) &= gcd(6\ 573, 3\ 625) \\
= gcd(3\ 625, 2\ 948) &= gcd(2\ 948, 677) \\
= gcd(677, 240) &= gcd(240, 197) \\
= gcd(197, 43) &= gcd(43, 25) \\
= gcd(25, 18) &= gcd(18, 7) \\
= gcd(7, 4) &= gcd(4, 3) \\
= gcd(3, 1) &= gcd(1, 0) \\
= 1 &
\end{aligned}
$$

In general, the result is a (possibly infinite) sequence

$$
(x_0, y_0), (x_1, y_1), \ldots, (x_k, y_k), \ldots
$$

of pairs of natural numbers satisfying

a) $x_0 = a$, $y_0 = b$

b) if $y_k \neq 0$ then (x_{k+1}, y_{k+1}) exists and $x_{k+1} = y_k$ and $y_{k+1} = x_k \bmod y_k$

c) if $y_k = 0$ then (x_k, y_k) is the last element of the sequence and x_k is the result.

To show termination, we observe, since $y_{k+1} = (x_k \bmod y_k) < y_k$, that the second component of the elements of the sequence decreases monotonically. Thus $n \leq b+1$ with $y_n = 0$. Our program thus always stops, i.e. it terminates. We now show the correctness of our program, i.e. that the value at which the program stops is the greatest common divisor of a and b. To this end we show that $gcd(x_i, y_i) = gcd(a, b)$ by induction on i for all i, $0 \leq i \leq n$. For $i = 0$ as $x_0 = a$ and $y_0 = b$ this is obvious. For the induction step the second property of gcd is used; that is

$$
\begin{aligned}
gcd(x_{i+1}, y_{i+1}) \ &= gcd(y_i, x_i \bmod y_i), &&\text{def. of } x_{i+1} \text{ and } y_{i+1} \\
&= gcd(x_i, y_i), &&\text{property of } gcd \\
&= gcd(a, b), &&\text{induction hypothesis}
\end{aligned}
$$

In particular, for $i = n$ we have

$$
gcd(a, b) \ = \ gcd(x_n, y_n) \ = \ gcd(x_n, 0) \ = \ x_n
$$

What about efficiency? We have already shown above that $n \leq b+1$, i.e. computing $gcd(a, b)$ leads to a sequence of at most $b + 1$ elements. If an element of the sequence is created every second, we need at most 17.5 hours to compute $gcd(103\ 574, 63\ 459)$. Our example shows that the computation can be much shorter. We now prove that it is **always** much shorter by showing that the y_k decrease very quickly.

Claim 1. If $2 \leq k + 2 \leq n$ then $y_{k+2} \leq y_k/2$

Proof: First we note $x_{k+1} > y_{k+1}$. This follows immediately from $x_{k+1} = y_k$ and $y_{k+1} = x_k \bmod y_k$. Therefore $x_{k+1} = cy_{k+1} + (x_{k+1} \bmod y_{k+1})$ for $c \geq 1$ and thus $x_{k+1} \geq 2(x_{k+1} \bmod y_{k+1})$. The claim now follows from $y_k = x_{k+1}$ and $y_{k+2} = x_{k+1} \bmod y_{k+1}$. $\blacksquare$

Claim 1 is now used to derive an upper bound for n.

Claim 2. $n \leq 2 + 2 \log b$

Proof: Let $n = 2i + j$ for $j \in \{1, 2\}$. Then, according to Claim 1,

$$y_{2i} \leq y_{2(i-1)}/2 \leq y_{2(i-2)}/4 \leq \cdots \leq y_{2(i-l)}/2^l \leq \cdots \leq y_0/2^i$$

Because $y_{2i} \geq 1$ ((x_{2i}, y_{2i}) is not the last element of the sequence) we have $y_0 \geq y_{2i}2^i \geq 2^i$ and thus $i \leq \log y_0$. (Logarithms in this book are always to the base 2.) With the representation of n as a sum we obtain $n \leq 2 + 2 \log y_0$. $\blacksquare$

If we apply Claim 2 in our example we get

$$n \leq 2 + 2 \log 63\ 459 \leq 2 + 2 \cdot 16 = 34$$

Suppose one element of the sequence per second is generated, we are certain to be finished in 34 seconds at the latest. This shows that the Euclidean algorithm can also be used for very large numbers.

Exercises for the Introduction

1) Two integers n and m are given. Write a program which computes the product $n \cdot m$ by repeated addition, i.e. by adding number n m-times. Give assertions which are true before and after execution of the "while-loop" and thus prove the program correct.

2) Given a polynomial of the order n : $P_n(x) = a_n x^n + \ldots + a_1 x + a_0$. Write a program which computes the value of the polynomial at a given point x_0: $P_n(x_0) = a_n x_0^n + a_{n-1} x_0^{n-1} + a_1 x_0 + a_0$. This can be done in an obvious way. Compute x_0^n, multiply by a_n etc. $P_n(x)$ can also be written in the form $(\ldots((a_n \cdot x + a_{n-1}) \cdot x + a_{n-2}) \cdot x + \ldots)\ldots) + a_0$. This representation suggests another evaluation strategy. Your program should realise this strategy. Compare the number of multiplications necessary with respect to the two strategies.

3) Write two programs which compute $n!$ for a natural number n ($n! = n \cdot (n - 1) \cdot (n - 2) \cdot \ldots \cdot 2 \cdot 1$), namely

a) a "normal" program (loop-program)

b) a recursive program.

4) Consider the following program

What do you think of the assertion: z has the value 17 when program point (2→) is reached?

Chapter 1: Formal Foundations

This chapter introduces fundamental concepts such as relations and functions. Partial functions are considered to be the "normal case". Section 1.3 deals with strings (i.e. symbol sequences). In Section 1.4 we then discuss context-free grammars in detail as a means to define the syntax of formal languages. The semantics of formal languages is the subject matter of Sections 1.5 (recursively defined functions), 1.6 (attribute grammars) and 1.7 (mathematical machines). More precisely, since sentences of a formal language defined by a grammar bear a structure, it seems obvious to define their semantics based on this structure. Relevant methods are introduced in Sections 1.5 and 1.6. In Section 1.7 we discuss the algorithmic approach as an alternative.

The usual set theoretic concepts (like "union", "is element of") and notations (such as $\cup$, $\in$) are assumed to be known. In particular, $\mathbb{N}$ is the set of natural numbers and $\mathbb{N}_0$ the set of natural numbers with zero.

We recommend the reader to start reading only Sections 1.1 up to 1.4 and then to proceed directly to Chapter II. There we refer to Section 1.5 and then later to Section 1.7. These two sections should be studied in this context. The attribute grammars of Section 1.6 will be used first in Chapter III.

1.1 Relations

In this section we introduce the concept of relations and discuss special cases and properties which are important for our purposes.

Definition 1: Let A and B be sets. A subset $R \subseteq A \times B$ is called a **relation** from A to B. If $A = B$ we speak of a relation **on** A. ∎

Example 1:

(a) Let A be the set of EEC countries, B the set of cities in these countries. The relation "has-as-capital" is the following subset of $A \times B$, {(Belgium, Brussels), (Denmark, Copenhagen), (West Germany, Bonn), (France, Paris), (Greece, Athens), (Great Britain, London),...}.

(b) The relations "is equal", "is less than" and "is less than or equal", usually written as "$=$", "$<$" and "$\leq$", are relations on $\mathbb{N}$.

(c) "divides" is a relation on $\mathbb{N}$.

(d) The relations "is father of", "has the same father as" and "is brother of" are relations on the set of people. ∎

Definition 2: Let $R \subseteq A \times A$ be a relation on A.

(a) R is **reflexive** if $(a,a) \in R$ for all $a \in A$; R is **irreflexive** if $(a,a) \notin R$ for all $a \in A$.

(b) R is **symmetric** if $(a,b) \in R$ implies $(b,a) \in R$ for all $a, b \in A$.

(c) R is **antisymmetric** if for all $a, b \in A$: if $(a,b) \in R$ and $(b,a) \in R$ then $a = b$.

(d) R is **transitive** if for all $a, b, c \in A$: if $(a,b) \in R$ and $(b,c) \in R$ then $(a,c) \in R$.

(e) R is an **equivalence relation** if it is reflexive, symmetric and transitive.

(f) Let R be an equivalence relation and $a \in A$. The set $\{b \in A \mid (a,b) \in R \}$ is called the **equivalence class** of a, denoted as $[a]_R$ or short $[a]$.
$A/_R = \{[a] \mid a \in A\}$ denotes the set of equivalence classes of R. ∎

Example (continued):
The relation "$<$" on $\mathbb{N}$ is transitive, but neither reflexive nor symmetric.
"$\leq$" is reflexive, transitive and antisymmetric on $\mathbb{N}$.
"divides" is reflexive, transitive and antisymmetric on $\mathbb{N}$.
"is brother of" is transitive, but not reflexive and not symmetric.
"has the same father as" is reflexive, transitive and symmetric, i.e. it is an equivalence relation. ∎

The following theorem is an important conclusion of these definitions.

Theorem 1. *Let R be an equivalence relation on A and let $a, b \in A$. Then either $[a] = [b]$ or $[a] \cap [b] = \emptyset$, i.e. the equivalence classes form a partition of A.*

Proof: We first prove two auxiliary claims.

Auxiliary claim 1. If $x \in [y]$ then $[y] \subseteq [x]$.

Proof: With $d \in [y]$ arbitrary, we have $(y, d) \in R$ by definition. Since $x \in [y]$, $(y, x) \in R$ and so $(x, y) \in R$ (by symmetry of R). Because of transitivity of R, $(x, y) \in R$ and $(y, d) \in R$ implies $(x, d) \in R$ and therefore $d \in [x]$. Thus $[y] \subseteq [x]$. ∎

Auxiliary claim 2. If $c \in [a]$ then $[c] = [a]$.

Proof: By Auxiliary claim 1 with $x = c$ and $y = a$, we have $c \in [a]$ implies $[a] \subseteq [c]$. From $c \in [a]$ and therefore $(a, c) \in R$ it follows, by symmetry of R, that $(c, a) \in R$ and consequently $a \in [c]$. Hence by Auxiliary claim 1, $[c] \subseteq [a]$ and thus $[c] = [a]$. ∎

It is easy to prove Theorem 1 from Auxiliary claim 1. Let $[a] \cap [b] \neq \emptyset$, i.e. $c \in [a] \cap [b]$ for some $c \in A$. Auxiliary claim 2 yields $[c] = [a]$ and $[c] = [b]$ and therefore $[a] = [b]$. ∎

An arbitrary relation R on A can be extended to a relation with certain properties using the following construction.

Definition 3: Let $R \subseteq A \times A$ be a relation on A.
Let $R_0 = \{R' \mid R' \text{ is a reflexive and transitive relation on } A \text{ and } R \subseteq R'\}$.
The relation

$$R^* = \bigcap_{R' \in R_0} R'$$

is called **reflexive, transitive closure** of R. ∎

Before giving examples we will justify this naming by proving that R^* is indeed a reflexive and transitive relation. Furthermore we shall give a "constructive" characterisation of R^*.

Theorem 2.

(a) *Let $R \subseteq A \times A$ be a relation and let R^* be as in Definition 3. R^* is reflexive and transitive.*

(b) *Let $\hat{R} \subseteq A \times A$ be defined as follows. $(a, b) \in \hat{R}$ if and only if there is a sequence $a_0, a_1, \ldots, a_n$ of elements in A where $n \geq 0$, with $a = a_0$ and $(a_i, a_{i+1}) \in R$ for $0 \leq i < n$, and $a_n = b$. Then $\hat{R} = R^*$.*

Proof:

(a) First we show that R^* is reflexive. For arbitrary $a \in A$ we have $(a, a) \in R'$ for each $R' \in R_0$, since all elements of R_0 are reflexive. Hence $(a, a) \in R^*$.

To show transitivity of R^*, let $a, b, c \in A$ with $(a, b) \in R^*$ and $(b, c) \in R^*$. By definition of R^* we have $(a, b) \in R'$ and $(b, c) \in R'$ for all $R' \in R_0$. Since the elements of R_0 are all transitive, it follows that $(a, c) \in R'$ for all $R' \in R_0$ and hence $(a, c) \in R^*$. Consequently R^* is transitive.

(b) Let us first prove the following auxiliary claim. $\hat{R}$ is reflexive and transitive. Furthermore $R \subseteq \hat{R}$.

For arbitrary $a \in A$ we consider the single element sequence a_0 with $a_0 = a$. This gives $(a, a) \in \hat{R}$ and therefore $\hat{R}$ is reflexive. Now let $a, b, c \in A$ with $(a, b) \in \hat{R}$ and $(b, c) \in \hat{R}$. Then, by definition of $\hat{R}$, there are sequences $a_0, \ldots, a_n$ and $b_0, \ldots, b_m$ with $a_0 = a$, $a_n = b$, $(a_i, a_{i+1}) \in R$ for $0 \leq i < n$, $b_0 = b$, $b_m = c$ and $(b_j, b_{j+1}) \in R$ for $0 \leq j < m$. Consider the sequence $c_0, \ldots, c_{n+m}$ with $c_i = a_i$ for $0 \leq i \leq n$ and $c_i = b_{i-n}$ for $n + 1 \leq i \leq n + m$. Then $c_0 = a_0 = a$, $c_{n+m} = b_m = c$ and $c_n = a_n = b = b_0$. Therefore (c_i, c_{i+1}) in R for $0 \leq i < n + m$ and consequently $(a, c) \in \hat{R}$ by definition of $\hat{R}$. This proves transitivity of $\hat{R}$.

Finally, let $a, b \in A$ with $(a, b) \in R$. Considering the two element sequence a_0, a_1 with $a_0 = a$, $a_1 = b$ we note $(a, b) \in \hat{R}$. Hence $R \subseteq \hat{R}$.

The auxiliary claim yields $\hat{R} \in R_0$. From the definition of R^* it follows that $R^* \subseteq \hat{R}$. Finally, to prove $\hat{R} \subseteq R^*$, it is sufficient to show that $\hat{R} \subseteq R'$ for all $R' \in R_0$. Let $a, b \in A$ with $(a, b) \in \hat{R}$. By definition of $\hat{R}$, there is a sequence $a_0, \ldots, a_n$ with $a_0 = a$, $a_n = b$ and $(a_i, a_{i+1}) \in R$ for $0 \leq i < n$. For arbitrary $R' \in R_0$ we now show, by induction on i, that $(a_0, a_i) \in R'$ for all i, $0 \leq i \leq n$. For $i = 0$ (induction base) the property follows from the reflexivity of R'. The induction hypothesis $(a_0, a_i) \in R'$ together with $(a_i, a_{i+1}) \in R \subseteq R'$ and transitivity of R' implies $(a_0, a_{i+1}) \in R'$. Hence $(a_0, a_i) \in R'$ for all i. In particular, for $i = n$ we have $(a_0, a_n) \in R'$ i.e. $(a, b) \in R'$. This concludes the proof of Theorem 2.   ∎

Definition 3 and Theorem 2(b) provide two characterisations of the reflexive, transitive closure. Whereas Definition 3 is a "static" characterisation, "top down", i.e. in terms of intersection, Theorem 2(b) is a "constructive" characterisation "bottom up", i.e. based on the construction of R^* from R. Both characterisations have their own advantages. The constructive characterisation provides a means to actually obtain R^*. For this the top down characterisation is of little benefit. Using the top down characterisation, on the other hand, often leads to simpler and more elegant proofs. Both approaches will reoccur in Section 1.5.

Example (continued):   The reflexive, transitive closure
 – of "$<$" is "$\leq$";
 – of "$\leq$" is "$\leq$" itself;
 – of "is father of" is "is ancestor of".

Another important class of relations are orders.

Definition 4: Let $R \subseteq A \times A$ be a relation on a set A.

(a) R is called a **reflexive partial order** (or short **partial order**), if R is reflexive, antisymmetric and transitive.

(b) R is called a **linear order** if R is a partial order and for all $a, b \in A$ either $(a, b) \in R$ or $(b, a) \in R$.

(c) Let R be a partial order, $B \subseteq A$ and let $a \in A$. An element a is called **maximal** (**minimal**) in B if $a \in B$ and there is no $b \in B$ with $a \neq b$ and $(a, b) \in R$ (or $(b, a) \in R$). An element a is called **maximum** (**minimum**) in B if $(b, a) \in R$ $((a, b) \in R)$ for all $b \in B$.

(d) An **irreflexive partial order** is defined like a (reflexive) partial order except with "irreflexive" for "reflexive". Each (reflexive) partial order $R \subseteq A \times A$ corresponds in a natural way to an irreflexive partial order, namely $R - \{(a, a) \mid a \in A\}$ ∎

Example (continued):   "$<$" is an irreflexive partial order, "$\leq$" is a reflexive partial order. The order "$\leq$" on $\mathbb{N}$ is linear with minimum 0. There is no maximal element. "Divides" is a partial order on $\mathbb{N}$ with 1 as minimum.   ∎

We conclude this section with a remark concerning notation. If $R \subseteq A \times B$ is a relation then we frequently write aRb for $(a, b) \in R$, i.e. we use infix notation. Furthermore we use symbols $\leq, \preceq, \sqsubseteq$ for reflexive (partial and linear) orders, $<, \prec,$ $\sqsubset$ for the associated irreflexive orders and $\equiv$ for equivalence relations, respectively.

Exercises for 1.1

1) Let $A = \{1, 2, 3, 4\}$ and $R = \{(1,1), (2,2), (3,3), (4,4), (1,2)\}$ be a relation on A. Determine if R is reflexive, symmetric, antisymmetric, transitive, an equivalence relation, a partial order or a linear order?

2) Let R be a relation on a set A. Define the relations $R_0, R_1, \ldots$ as follows.
$R_0 = R \cup \{(a, a) \mid a \in A\}$
$R_{i+1} = R_i \cup \{(a, c) \mid \text{there exists } b \in A \text{ with } (a, b) \in R_i \text{ and } (b, c) \in R_i\}$, for all i.

Define $\hat{R} = \bigcup_{i \geq 0} R_i$. Show that $\hat{R} = R^*$.

3) Let R be a relation on a set A. Give a definition of the symmetric closure of R (similarly to Definition 3, but with "symmetric" instead of "reflexive and transitive"). State and prove a theorem similar to Theorem 2.

4) Repeat Exercise 3 for the reflexive, transitive and symmetric closure.

5) Let R be a transitive relation on a set A.

   a) Let the relation "$\equiv$" on A be defined by

$$a \equiv b \text{ if and only if } a = b \text{ or } aRb \text{ and } bRa.$$

   Show that "$\equiv$" is an equivalence relation on A.

   b) Let $A_{/\equiv}$ be the set of equivalence classes of "$\equiv$". Let relation "$\leq$" on $A_{/\equiv}$ be defined by

$$[a] \leq [b] \text{ if and only if } [a] = [b] \text{ or } aRb.$$

   Show that "$\leq$" is well defined and that "$\leq$" is a partial order on $A_{/\equiv}$.

1.2 Functions

Most of the following definitions should be familiar to the reader. Since we are mainly interested in partial functions, some differ from the usual definitions for total functions.

Definition 1: Let A and B be sets. A **(partial) function** F from A to B, symbolically $F : A \rightsquigarrow B$, is a relation $F \subseteq A \times B$ such that for each $a \in A$ there is at most one $b \in B$ with $(a,b) \in F$. A is called the **domain** and B the **range** of F. If A is a set of n-tuples, $n \geq 1$, then n is called the **arity** of the function.   ■

Notice that it is not required that for each $a \in A$ an element $b \in B$ with $(a,b) \in F$ exists. There may be elements $a \in A$ for which there is no $b \in B$ with $(a,b) \in F$. If such a b always exists then we call F a "total" function. Frequently functions will be defined by giving procedures (i.e. algorithms). The fact that such procedures (like programs) need not terminate for all inputs leads in a natural way to the concept of partial functions: $(a,b) \in F$ if and only if the procedure with input a yields b in finite time.

Definition 2: Let $F : A \rightsquigarrow B$ be a partial function.

(a) The set $Def(F) = \{a \in A \mid \exists b \in B : (a,b) \in F\}$ is called the **pre-image** of F.

(b) If $Def(F) = A$ then F is called a **total function**. We write $F : A \rightarrow B$.

    ■

Let $F : A \rightsquigarrow B$ be a partial function and let $(a,b) \in F$. Then b is called the **value** of F for a, denoted by $F(a)$. If $a \notin Def(F)$ then the expression $F(a)$ is meaningless. We say F is **undefined** for a and write $F(a) = $ undefined. The latter is a blatant misuse of notation but it is quite common. If $Def(F) = \emptyset$ then F is called the **totally undefined function**.

Example 1:
The relation $root = \{(n^2, n) \mid n \in \mathbb{N}\}$ is a function. More precisely, $root : \mathbb{N} \rightsquigarrow \mathbb{N}$ is a partial function. It is not a total function because the set for which $root$ is defined is just the set of squares.

$$Def(root) = \{n^2 \mid n \in \mathbb{N}\}$$

We have

$\qquad root(9) = 3;$

$\qquad root(8)$ is undefined.

We also write

$\qquad root(8) =$ undefined.

To specify the root function as subset of $\mathbb{N} \times \mathbb{N}$ is rather clumsy. In future we will use the following notation.

$\qquad root : \mathbb{N} \rightsquigarrow \mathbb{N}$ is the partial function defined by

$$root(x) = \begin{cases} n & \text{if } x = n^2 \text{ for some } n \in \mathbb{N} \\ \text{undefined} & \text{otherwise} \end{cases}$$

This notation highlights the pre-image of $root$ and the function value for elements in the pre-image. Some more concepts are needed.

Definition 3: Let $F, G : A \rightsquigarrow B$ and $H : B \rightsquigarrow C$ be partial functions.

(a) The **composition** $H \circ G : A \rightsquigarrow C$ of H and G is defined as
$H \circ G = \{(a, c) \mid a \in A, \; c \in C$ and there exists $b \in B$ with $(a, b) \in G$ and $(b, c) \in H\}$. Obviously $H \circ G$ is a function (and not only a relation).

(b) G is called an **extension** of F or G **extends** F, written $F \sqsubseteq G$, if $F \subseteq G$.

(c) Let $A' \subseteq A$. The **image** of A' under F is defined as
$\qquad F(A') = \{b \in B \mid \exists a \in A' : (a, b) \in F\}.$

(d) Let $A' \subseteq A$. The **restriction** of F to A' is $F|_{A'} = \{(a, b) \mid (a, b) \in F$ and $a \in A'\}.$

Again care must be taken. The composition of partial functions does not necessarily follow intuition. If, for instance, $H : B \rightsquigarrow C$ is a total function with constant value $c_0 \in C$, i.e. $H = \{(b, c_0) \mid b \in B\}$ then $(H \circ G)(a) = c_0$ for all $a \in Def(H \circ G)$, but $H \circ G$ need not be total. Obviously we have $Def(H \circ G) = Def(G)$.

Definition 4: Let $F : A \to B$ be a total function.

(a) F is **injective** if $F(x) = F(y)$ implies $x = y$.

(b) F is **surjective** if for each $b \in B$ there is an $a \in A$ with $F(a) = b$.

(c) F is **bijective** if F is injective and surjective. In this case

$$F^{-1} = \{(b, a) \mid (a, b) \in F\}$$

is a total function from B to A. It is called the **inverse function** of F.   ■

Finally, two notational conventions:

- $P(A, B) = \{F \mid F : A \rightsquigarrow B\}$ is the set of partial functions from A to B,
- $B^A = \{F \mid F : A \rightarrow B\}$ is the set of total functions from A to B.

Exercises for 1.2

1) Prove: The relation "$\sqsubseteq$" on $P(A, B)$ is a partial order.

2) Prove: Let A and B be finite sets and let $F : A \rightarrow B$ be a total function. Then F is injective if and only if F is bijective.

3) Given finite sets A and B with $n = |A|$ and $m = |B|$. How many functions are in $P(A, B)$ and B^A respectively?

4) Given $Square : \mathbb{N} \rightarrow \mathbb{N}$ with $Square(n) = n^2$ for all $n \in \mathbb{N}$. Characterise the functions $root \circ square$ and $square \circ root$.

1.3 Symbols and Strings

Symbols and strings or words are, besides numbers, the most important basic objects in computing. We are familiar with the mathematical properties of numbers, but less so with those of symbols and strings. We therefore introduce the most relevant concepts and properties.

Definition 1:

An **alphabet** is an arbitrary non-empty set, say Σ, whose elements are called **symbols**.

Symbols from Σ can be arranged to form strings. Formally, a **string** or **word** of length n over the alphabet Σ is a function

$$a : [1 \ldots n] \rightarrow \Sigma$$

where $n \in \mathbb{N}_0$ and $[1 \ldots n]$ is the set $\{1, 2, \ldots, n\}$.

A string $a : [1 \ldots n] \rightarrow \Sigma$ is uniquely given by the sequence of values

$$(a(1), a(2), \ldots, a(n)).$$

More often one writes

$$(a_1, a_2, \ldots, a_n)$$

or even

$$a_1 a_2 \ldots a_n$$

The last notation leads to ambiguity, since now there is no difference between a symbol in Σ and the string of length 1 over Σ consisting of exactly this symbol. More precisely, a symbol $b \in \Sigma$ and the string $a : [1] \to \Sigma$ with $a(1) = b$ are both represented by b. On the other hand, since there is a trivial correspondence between an alphabet Σ and the set of sequences of length 1 over Σ, this ambiguity normally does not raise problems.

Next, the set of strings of length n over an alphabet Σ, $n \in \mathbb{N}_0$, is

$$\Sigma^n = \{a \mid a : [1 \ldots n] \to \Sigma\}$$

Note that $\Sigma^0 = \{a \mid a : \emptyset \to \Sigma\}$ is a singleton set. The only element in this set is the **empty string** denoted by ϵ. Two further notations are

$$\Sigma^* = \bigcup_{n \geq 0} \Sigma^n$$

for the set of all strings over Σ and

$$\Sigma^+ = \bigcup_{n \geq 1} \Sigma^n$$

for the set of nonempty strings over Σ.

We now introduce some functions and relations on strings.

Definition 2:

(a) The function "concatenation" is defined as

$$Conc : \Sigma^* \times \Sigma^* \to \Sigma^* \text{ with}$$

$$Conc((a_1, \ldots, a_n), (b_1, \ldots, b_m)) = (a_1, \ldots, a_n, b_1, \ldots, b_m).$$

Function $Conc$ will be used frequently. Therefore we also use infix notation. Instead of $Conc(x, y)$ we write $x.y$ or even shorter xy.

(b) Function "length" is given by

$$|\quad| : \Sigma^* \to \mathbb{N}_0 \text{ with } |(a_1, \ldots, a_n)| = n$$

(c) Let $b \in \Sigma$. The function "number of occurrences of b" is given by

$$| \quad |_b : \Sigma^* \to \mathbb{N}_0 \text{ with}$$

$$|(a_1, \ldots, a_n)|_b = \text{number of elements } a_i,\ 1 \leq i \leq n, \text{ such that } a_i = b.$$

(d) The relation *prefix* $\subseteq \Sigma^* \times \Sigma^*$ is defined by

$$x \text{ } prefix \text{ } y \Leftrightarrow \text{ there exists } z \in \Sigma^* \text{ with } y = Conc(x, z)$$

The relation *suffix* $\subseteq \Sigma^* \times \Sigma^*$ is similarly defined by

$$x \text{ } suffix \text{ } y \Leftrightarrow \text{ there exists } z \in \Sigma^* \text{ with } y = Conc(z, x)$$

(e) Let $<$ be an irreflexive, linear order on Σ. The **lexicographic order** on Σ^*, symbolically $\leq_{lex}$, is defined by

$$x \leq_{lex} y \Leftrightarrow \text{ either } x \text{ } prefix \text{ } y$$
$$\text{or there are } w, x', y' \in \Sigma^*,\ a, b \in \Sigma$$
$$\text{with } x = wax',\ y = wby' \text{ and } a < b.$$

The lexicographic order on Σ^* is used in each lexicon.

With $\Sigma = \{A, B, \ldots, Z\}$ and the (irreflexive) order $A < B < \cdots < Z$, for instance, the following holds for $\leq_{lex}$ on Σ^*:

$$\text{LOECKX} \leq_{lex} \text{MEHL} \leq_{lex} \text{MEHLHORN} \leq_{lex} \text{WILHELM} \leq_{lex} \text{WILHELM}$$

Finally, we want to show that *prefix* **and the lexicographic order are in fact ordering relations.**

Lemma 1.

(a) *prefix is a partial order on* Σ^*.

(b) $\leq_{lex}$ *is a linear order on* Σ^*.

Proof:

(a) Because of $x = Conc(x, \epsilon)$ for all $x \in \Sigma^*$ (see Exercise 2) we have $x \text{ } prefix \text{ } x$. Thus *prefix* is reflexive.

From $x \text{ } prefix \text{ } y$ and $y \text{ } prefix \text{ } z$ follows, by definition of *prefix*, that there are $u, v \in \Sigma^*$ with $y = Conc(x, u)$ and $z = Conc(y, v)$. Since $Conc$ is associative (see Exercise 1) we have $z = Conc(Conc(x, u), v) = Conc(x, Conc(u, v))$, and therefore $x \text{ } prefix \text{ } z$. Thus *prefix* is transitive.

To show antisymmetry, let $x \text{ } prefix \text{ } y$ and $y \text{ } prefix \text{ } x$. Then there are $u, v \in \Sigma^*$ with $y = Conc(x, u)$ and $x = Conc(y, v)$, and therefore $x = Conc(x, Conc(u, v))$. This implies $Conc(u, v) = \epsilon$ and further $u = v = \epsilon$ (see Exercise 3). Thus $y = Conc(x, \epsilon) = x$ (because of Exercise 2).

(b) Reflexivity of $\leq_{lex}$ is obvious.

Transitivity can be shown as follows. Let $x, y, z \in \Sigma^*$ with $x \leq_{lex} y$ and $y \leq_{lex} z$. Let w be the longest common *prefix* of x, y and z, i.e. $x = wx', y = wy', z = wz'$ for strings $x', y', z' \in \Sigma^*$ where all three do not start with the same letter or where one of them is empty. If $x' = \epsilon$ then x *prefix* z and thus $x \leq_{lex} z$. Otherwise $x' = ax''$ with $a \in \Sigma$ and $x'' \in \Sigma^*$. Then $x \leq_{lex} y$ implies $y' = by'', b \in \Sigma$ and $y'' \in \Sigma^*$, with $a \leq b$. Furthermore $y \leq_{lex} z$ implies $z' = cz'', c \in \Sigma$ and $z'' \in \Sigma^*$, with $b \leq c$. The case $a = b = c$ is impossible by definition of w. Thus $a < c$ and therefore $x \leq_{lex} z$.

Antisymmetry of $\leq_{lex}$ is obvious. Together this proves that $\leq_{lex}$ is a partial order. We just have to show that $\leq_{lex}$ is a linear order. Let $x = (x_1, \ldots, x_n)$ and $y = (y_1, \ldots, y_m)$ be two arbitrary strings in Σ^*. We may assume w.l.o.g. that neither x is a prefix of y nor y is a prefix of x. Therefore there exists a $1 \leq j \leq min(n, m)$ such that $x_j \neq y_j$. Let

$$k = min\{j \mid x_j \neq y_j\}$$

Then $x = (x_1, \ldots, x_{k-1}, x_k, \ldots, x_n)$ and $y = (x_1, \ldots, x_{k-1}, y_k, \ldots, y_m)$ and by definition of $\leq_{lex}$ we have either $(x \leq_{lex} y)$ or $(y \leq_{lex} x)$. ∎

Exercises for 1.3

1) Prove: *Conc* is associative, i.e. for all $x, y, z \in \Sigma^*$:
$Conc(x, Conc(y, z)) = Conc(Conc(x, y), z)$.

2) Prove: ϵ is a unit with respect to *Conc*, i.e. for all $x \in \Sigma^*$:
$Conc(x, \epsilon) = Conc(\epsilon, x) = x$

3) Prove: For all $x, y, z, \in \Sigma^*$:
  a) $Conc(x, y) = Conc(x, z)$ implies $y = z$.
  b) $Conc(y, x) = Conc(z, x)$ implies $y = z$.

4) a) Given R on Σ^* as:
  $xRy \Leftrightarrow |x| < |y|$ or $(|x| = |y|$ and $x \leq_{lex} y)$

  Is R a linear order? Prove your answer.

  b) Given S on Σ^* as:
  $xSy \Leftrightarrow |x| < |y|$ or $x \leq_{lex} y$
  Is S a linear order?

1.4 Formal Languages and Context-free Grammars

The previous section introduced symbols and strings. In this section we will be concerned with sets of strings. Such sets are called "formal languages". Context-free grammars are a means to specify such languages.

Definition 1: Let T be a finite alphabet. A **formal language** over T is a set $L \subseteq T^*$. An element of a formal language is called a **sentence**.   ∎

We will now give an example of a formal language and, by way of that, introduce the concept of a context-free grammar.

Example 1:
Let L be the following set of four sentences over the alphabet
$T = \{$Jack, Jill, goes, runs$\}$:

$$\begin{array}{ll}
\text{Jack goes} & \text{Jack runs} \\
\text{Jill goes} & \text{Jill runs.}
\end{array}$$

The common structure of these sentences can be described by the following "rules".

> sentence → subject predicate
> subject → Jack
> subject → Jill
> predicate → goes
> predicate → runs

Informally, these rules state that a sentence consists of a subject and a predicate, "Jack" and "Jill" are subjects, and "goes" and "runs" are predicates. The sentence "Jill runs" can be derived as follows.

> sentence → subject predicate → Jill predicate → Jill runs

The structure of the sentence "Jill runs" can be illustrated by the following structure tree or derivation tree.

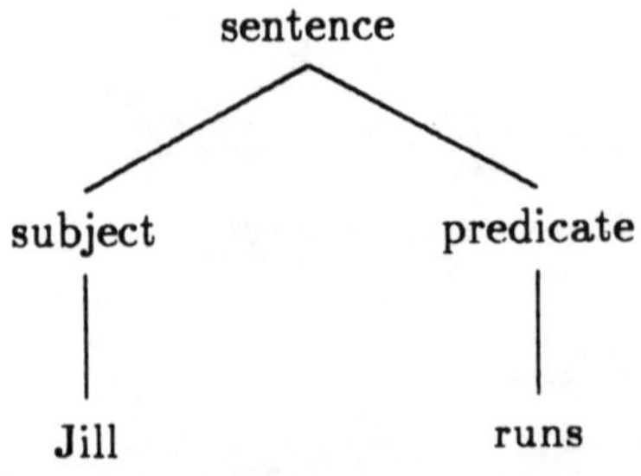

Fig. 1.

We shall now define the various concepts precisely.

Definition 2:

A **context-free grammar** is a quadruple $G = (N, T, P, S)$ where

(1) N and T are disjoint finite alphabets. The symbols of T are called **terminals**, those of N **nonterminals**. We call strings in T^* **terminal strings** and those in $(N \cup T)^*$ **sentential forms**.

(2) $P \subset N \times (N \cup T)^*$ is a finite set of pairs called **productions** (or **rules**).

(3) $S \in N$ is a nonterminal called **start symbol**.

Normally we will use the following notations.

$A, B, C, S, \ldots$ for nonterminals;
$a, b, c, \ldots$ for terminals;
$u, v, w, \ldots$ for terminal strings;
$\alpha, \beta, \gamma, \ldots$ for sentential forms;
$A \to \alpha$ for the production (A, α).

In Example 1 we have $N = \{$subject, predicate, sentence$\}$, the start symbol is sentence, and the productions are as above.

Next the concept of derivation is made precise.

Definition 3: Let $G = (N, T, P, S)$ be a context-free grammar. We define relations $\to, \to^*, \xrightarrow[can]{}, \xrightarrow[can]{}{}^*$ on the set of sentential forms $(N \cup T)^*$ by

(a) $\alpha \to \beta \Leftrightarrow$ there are $\alpha_1, \alpha_2, \alpha_3 \in (N \cup T)^*, A \in N$ and $A \to \alpha_3 \in P$,
    such that $\alpha = \alpha_1 A \alpha_2$ and $\beta = \alpha_1 \alpha_3 \alpha_2$;

(b) $\alpha \xrightarrow[can]{} \beta \Leftrightarrow \alpha \to \beta$ and $\alpha_1 \in T^*$ in the definition of $\to$ above;

(c) $\to^* \, (\xrightarrow[can]{}{}^*)$ is the reflexive, transitive closure of $\to \, (\xrightarrow[can]{})$;

(d) A sequence $\alpha_0, ..., \alpha_n$ with $\alpha_i \to \alpha_{i+1}$ for $0 \le i < n$ is called a **derivation** from α_0 to α_n and n is the **length** of the derivation. A **canonical derivation** is defined analogously with $\xrightarrow[can]{}$ instead of $\to$.
    A derivation step consists in replacing an occurrence of the lefthand side of a production by the righthand side of this production. In a canonical derivation the leftmost nonterminal is replaced. The derivation of the sentence "Jill runs" in Example 1 is canonical.

Definition 4:

(a) Let $G = (N, T, P, S)$ be a context-free grammar. For $A \in N$ the set of A-**constructs** is defined as

$$L_{G,A} = \{w \in T^* \mid A \to^* w\}.$$

The language **generated** by grammar G is the set of S-constructs. We write L_G instead of $L_{G,S}$.

(b) A context-free grammar G is called **unambiguous** if for each $A \in N$ and each A-construct $w \in L_{G,A}$ there is precisely one canonical derivation from A to w. Otherwise the grammar is called **ambiguous**.

(c) A formal language L is called **context-free** if there is a context-free grammar G with $L = L_G$.   ■

Example 2:

Let $G_2 = (\{A\}, \{a\}, \{A \to AA, A \to a\}, A)$.

G_2 obviously generates $L_2 = \{a^n \mid n \geq 1\}$.

For a^3 there are the following canonical derivations

$$A \xrightarrow[can]{} AA \xrightarrow[can]{} AAA \xrightarrow[can]{} aAA \xrightarrow[can]{} aaA \xrightarrow[can]{} aaa$$

and

$$A \xrightarrow[can]{} AA \xrightarrow[can]{} aA \xrightarrow[can]{} aAA \xrightarrow[can]{} aaA \xrightarrow[can]{} aaa$$

Thus G_2 is ambiguous. This ambiguity is illustrated by the two derivation trees (this concept will be made more precise after the examples) for the string aaa.

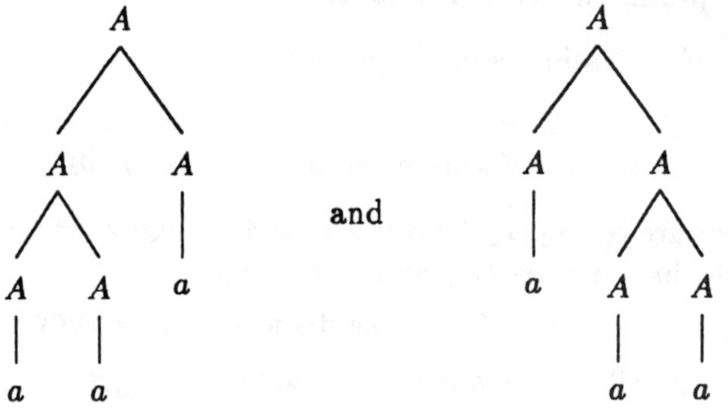

Fig. 2.

We do not prove the fact that G_2 generates language L_2. Such a proof will be presented in the next example.   ■

Example 3:

Let $G_3 = (\{S\}, \{a,b\}, \{S \to aSa,\ S \to bSb,\ S \to \epsilon\}, S)$ generate L_3. We have

$$\begin{aligned}
\epsilon \in L_3 \quad &\text{with derivation} \quad S \to \epsilon, \\
aa \in L_3 \quad &\text{with derivation} \quad S \to aSa \to aa, \\
abba \in L_3 \quad &\text{with derivation} \quad S \to aSa \to abSba \to abba
\end{aligned}$$

In general, L_3 contains precisely the strings of the form ww^R with $w \in \{a,b\}^*$ and w^R is the reverse of w. This we will now prove formally.

Lemma 1. *Let G_3 be defined as in Example 3.*

(a) Let $n \geq 1$ and let $a_1, \ldots, a_n \in \{a, b\}$. Then $a_1 \ldots a_n a_n \ldots a_1 \in L_3$

(b) Let $x \in L_3, x \neq \epsilon$. There exists $n \geq 1$ and $a_1, a_2, \ldots, a_n \in \{a, b\}$ with $x = a_1 \ldots a_n a_n \ldots a_1$.

(c) $L_3 = \{ww^R \mid w \in \{a, b\}^*\}$

Proof:

(c) We prove $S \to^* a_1 \ldots a_n S a_n \ldots a_1 \to a_1 \ldots a_n a_n \ldots a_1$ by induction on n. For $n = 1$ (induction base) $S \to a_1 S a_1 \to a_1 a_1$ is a derivation from S to $a_1 a_1$. Let now $n > 1$ (induction step). Then, by induction hypothesis, there exists a derivation from S to $a_1 a_2 \ldots a_{n-1} S a_{n-1} \ldots a_2 a_1$. Thus $S \to^* a_1 \ldots a_{n-1} S a_{n-1} \ldots a_1 \to a_1 \ldots a_n S a_n \ldots a_1 \to a_1 \ldots a_n a_n \ldots a_1$ and hence $a_1 \ldots a_n a_n \ldots a_1 \in L_3$.

(b) Let $\alpha_0, \alpha_1, \ldots, \alpha_m$ be a canonical derivation from S to x. Since $x \neq \epsilon$ we have $\alpha_0 = S$ and $\alpha_1 = a_1 S a_1$ for some $a_1 \in \{a, b\}$. Thus there is $y \in \{a, b\}^*$ such that $x = a_1 y a_1$ and $S \to^* y$. We now use induction on the length of y. The case $y = \epsilon$ (induction base) is obvious. If $y \neq \epsilon$ (induction step) then, by induction hypothesis, there exists some n and $a_2, \ldots, a_n \in \{a, b\}$ with $y = a_2 \ldots a_n a_n \ldots a_2$ which proves the claim.

(c) Follows immediately from (a) and (b). ∎

   Part (b) of the proof of the above lemma also shows that G_3 is unambiguous.

Example 4:

Let

$$G_4 = (\{A\}, \{[,], a, \#, \uparrow\}, P, A)$$

with

$$P = \{A \to [A \# A], A \to [A \uparrow A], A \to a\}.$$

This grammar generates the language L_4 which is the set of fully parenthesised expressions over the operand set $\{a\}$, the operator set $\{\#, \uparrow\}$ and the bracket symbols [and]. We intentionally chose the unusual operators $\#$ and $\uparrow$ so that the reader can follow the discussion without being influenced by what he knows about expressions.

Elements of the language L_4 are sentences like $a, [a \# a], [a \# [a \uparrow a]]$. The canonical derivation of string $[a \# [a \uparrow a]]$, for example, is

$$A \xrightarrow[can]{} [A \# A] \xrightarrow[can]{} [a \# A] \xrightarrow[can]{} [a \# [A \uparrow A]] \xrightarrow[can]{} [a \# [a \uparrow A]] \xrightarrow[can]{} [a \# [a \uparrow a]]$$

In addition there are other (non-canonical) derivations for this string, for example

$$A \to [A \# A] \to [A \# [A \uparrow A]] \to [a \# [A \uparrow A]] \to [a \# [A \uparrow a]] \to [a \# [a \uparrow a]]$$

Below we will show that G_4 is unambiguous. The derivation tree for the string $[a \# [a \uparrow a]]$ is shown in Figure 3.

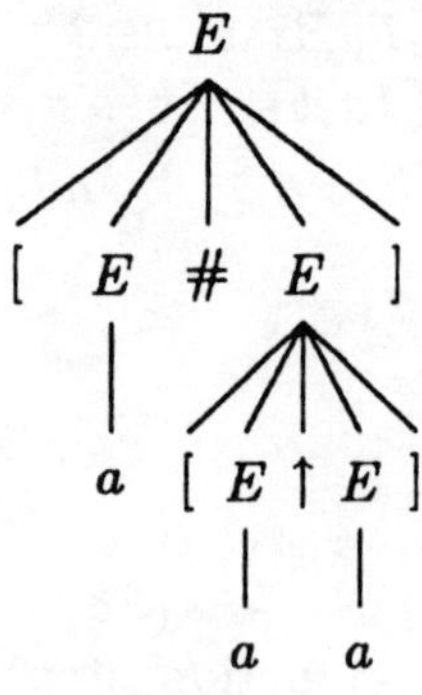

Fig. 3.

We shall now make the concept of a derivation tree precise. For that purpose we first introduce "tree domains" as templates and then define derivation trees as "labelled" tree domains. For example, the derivation tree of Example 4 is based on the template in Figure 4.

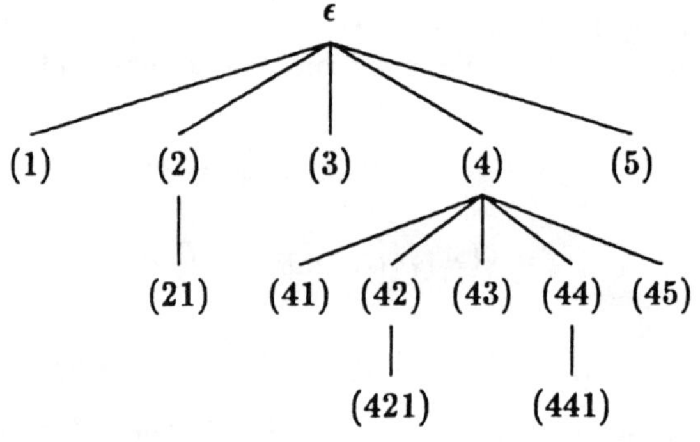

Fig. 4.

In such a template nodes have names which reflect their "descendency". These names are sequences of natural numbers, i.e. elements of $\mathbb{N}^*$. The root (i.e. the node of 0 th "generation") carries the name ϵ. The "children" of a node v have the names $v1, v2, v3,\ldots, vk$ for $k \in \mathbb{N}$. Node 4 in our example has the children 41, 42, 43, 44 and 45. The "labelling" of the tree domain $D = \{\epsilon, 1, 2, 3, 4, 5, 21, 41, 42, 43, 44, 45, 421, 441\}$ can now be specified by a function b with domain D:

$$b(\epsilon) = b(2) = b(4) = b(42) = b(44) = A,$$
$$b(1) = b(41) = [, \quad \text{etc.}$$

We now give an exact definition of tree domains and labelled trees.

Definition 5:

(a) The partial function $parent : \mathbb{N}^* \leadsto \mathbb{N}^*$ is given by

$$parent(w) = \begin{cases} v & \text{if } w = v.n \text{ with } v \in \mathbb{N}^* \text{ and } n \in \mathbb{N} \\ \text{undefined} & \text{if } w = \epsilon \end{cases}$$

The reflexive, transitive closure of *parent* is called *ancestor*. The relation *ancestor* coincides with relation *prefix*.

(b) **A tree domain** D is a finite subset of $\mathbb{N}^*$ which is closed under the function *parent*, i.e. $parent(D) \subseteq D$. The elements of a tree domain are called **nodes**.

(c) Let S be a set. An **S-tree** (or short **tree**) is a pair (D, b) where D is a tree domain and b a mapping $b : D \to S$. Mapping b is called the **labelling** of the tree and D its **domain**. $\mathbf{B}_S$ is the set of S-trees.

We will use the following terminology. The element $\epsilon \in \mathbb{N}^*$ is called **root**. If $v = parent(w)$ then w is a **child** of v, and if $v = ancestor(w)$ then w is a **descendent** of v. The number of children of a node is called the **degree** of the node. A node without children is a **leaf**. $B(D)$ denotes the set of leaves of a tree domain D.

We need some further concepts for trees which we will first explain by example.

Example (continued):   Consider the following three trees:

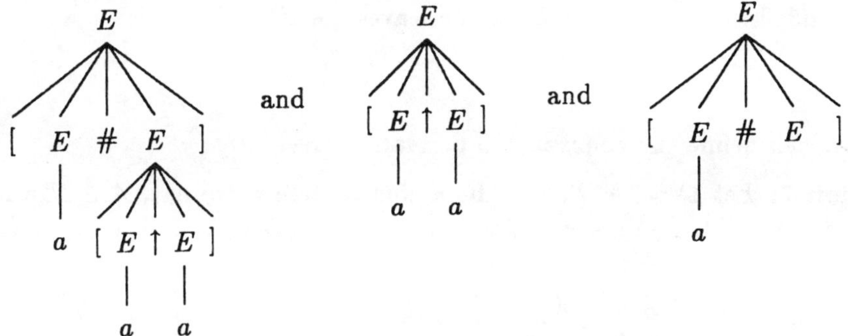

Fig. 5.

The first tree has "depth" 3, the maximal number of edges in a path from the root to a leaf. The second tree is a "subtree" of the first tree at node 4. "Substituting" the second tree at node 4 of the third tree yields the first tree. The "frontier" of the first tree is $[a\#[a \uparrow a]]$.

We shall now give the exact definitions of these concepts.

Definition 6:

(a) $depth : \mathbf{B}_S \leadsto \mathbb{N}_0$ is defined by

$$depth((D, b)) = \begin{cases} max\{|w| \mid w \in D\} & \text{if } D \neq \emptyset \\ \text{undefined} & \text{if } D = \emptyset \end{cases}$$

(b) *subtree* : $\mathbf{B}_S \times \mathbb{N}^* \to \mathbf{B}_S$ is defined by

$\quad$ *subtree*$((D,b),w) = (D',b')$ with
$\qquad D' = \{v \mid v \in N^* \text{ and } w.v \in D\},$
$\qquad b' : D' \to S$ with
$\qquad b'(v) = b(w.v)$ for all $v \in D'.$

(c) *subst* : $\mathbf{B}_S \times \mathbb{N}^* \times \mathbf{B}_S \rightsquigarrow \mathbf{B}_S$ is defined by

$$\textit{subst}((D,b),w,(D_1,b_1)) = \begin{cases} (D',b') & \text{if } w \in D \\ \text{undefined} & \text{if } w \notin D \end{cases}$$

$\quad$ **where**

$\qquad D' = \{v \in D \mid neg(w \text{ ancestor } v)\} \cup \{w.v \mid v \in D_1\}$
$\qquad b' : D' \to S$ with

$$b'(v) = \begin{cases} b(v) & \text{if } neg(w \text{ ancestor } v) \\ b_1(x) & \text{if } v = w.x \end{cases}$$

(d) *frontier* : $\mathbf{B}_S \rightsquigarrow S^*$ is defined by

$\quad$ *frontier*$((D,b)) =$

$$\begin{cases} b(v_1)b(v_2)\dots b(v_k) & \text{where } v_1, v_2, \dots, v_k \text{ are the leaves of } D,\ k \geq 1 \\ & \text{and } v_1 <_{lex} v_2 <_{lex} \dots <_{lex} v_k, \\ \text{undefined} & \text{if } D \text{ has no leaves, i.e. } D = \emptyset \end{cases}$$

$\hfill \blacksquare$

Finally we can define the concept of a derivation tree.

Definition 7: Let $G = (N,T,P,S)$ be a context-free grammar, $A \in N$ a nonterminal and $\alpha \in (N \cup T)^*$ a sentential form. A tree $(D,b) \in \mathbf{B}_{N \cup T \cup \{\epsilon\}}$ is called a **derivation tree** from A to α in G if

(1) the root is labelled A, i.e. $b(\epsilon) = A$;

(2) for each node w with children $w1, w2, \dots, wn$ and $n \geq 1$:

$\qquad$ either $b(w) \to b(w1)b(w2)\dots b(wn) \in P$ and $b(w1) \neq \epsilon, \dots, b(wn) \neq \epsilon$

$\qquad$ or $n = 1, b(w1) = \epsilon$ and $b(w) \to \epsilon \in P$;

(3) *frontier*$((D,b)) = \alpha.$ $\hfill \blacksquare$

Condition (2) of this definition guarantees that nodes together with their children always correspond to a production of the grammar.

If $A \to \alpha_1 \dots \alpha_m$ with $\alpha_i \in N \cup T$ for all i, $1 \leq i \leq m$, is the production used at node w then the labels of the tree are "locally" given by

We shall now show that a string belongs to a context-free language if and only if there is a derivation tree for it. Furthermore a grammar is unambiguous if and only if for each string there is exactly one derivation tree. We illustrate these properties by an example.

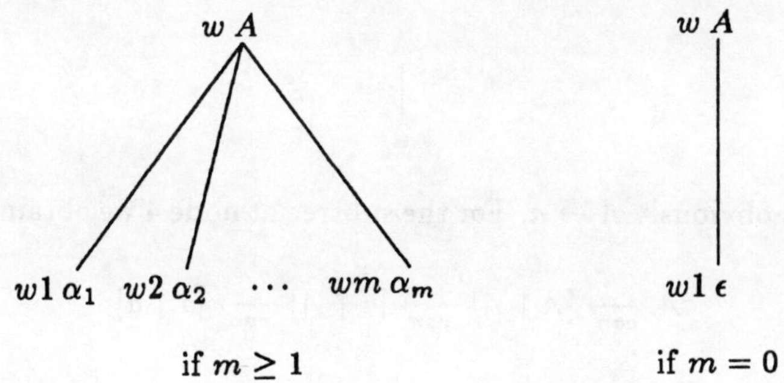

$$w1\,\alpha_1 \quad w2\,\alpha_2 \quad \cdots \quad wm\,\alpha_m$$

if $m \geq 1$ if $m = 0$

Fig. 6.

Example (continued):   The derivation of length 5

$$A \rightarrow [A\#A] \rightarrow [A\#[A \uparrow A]] \rightarrow [a\#[A \uparrow A]] \rightarrow [a\#[a \uparrow A]] \rightarrow [a\#[a \uparrow a]]$$

can in a simple way be associated with the following sequence of 6 derivation trees where the first only consists of the root (with $b(\epsilon) = A$) .

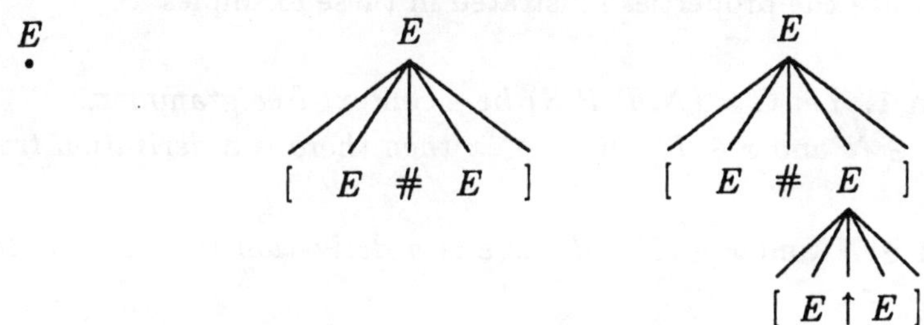

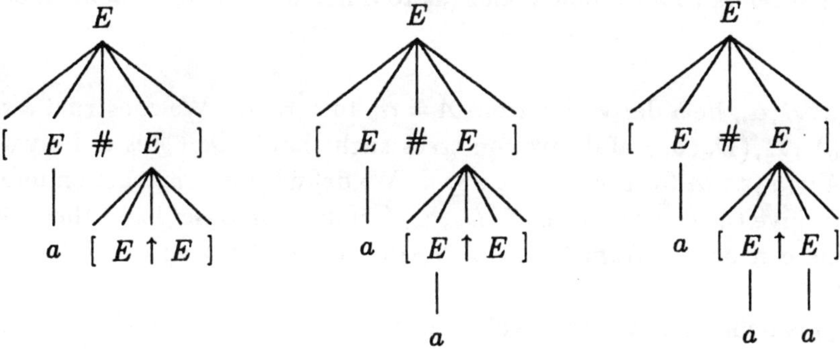

Fig. 7.

In this way one obtains from the above derivation from A to $[a\#[a \uparrow a]]$ a derivation tree from A to $[a\#[a \uparrow a]]$.

Conversely one can construct a canonical derivation from a derivation tree. For the subtree

the derivation is obviously $A \to a$. For the subtree at node 4 we obtain by "suffixing"

$$A \xrightarrow[can]{} [A \uparrow A] \xrightarrow[can]{} [a \uparrow A] \xrightarrow[can]{} [a \uparrow a]$$

and, finally, for the whole tree

$$A \xrightarrow[can]{} [A \# A] \xrightarrow[can]{} [a \# A] \xrightarrow[can]{} [a \# [A \uparrow A]] \xrightarrow[can]{} [a \# [a \uparrow A]] \xrightarrow[can]{} [a \# [a \uparrow a]]$$

In this way we associate with each derivation a derivation tree and with each derivation tree a canonical derivation. ∎

We now prove the properties illustrated in these examples.

Theorem 1. *Let $G = (N, T, P, S)$ be a context-free grammar.*
(a) Let $A \in N$ and $x \in T^*$. If $A \to^* x$ then there is a derivation tree from A to x in G.

(b) Let $A \in N$ and $x \in T^*$. If there is a derivation tree from A to x in G then $A \xrightarrow[can]{}^* x$.

(c) G is unambiguous if and only if there is exactly one derivation tree from A to x in G for all $A \in N$ and $x \in L_{G,A}$.

Note that (b) refers to a canonical and (a) to a not necessarily canonical derivation from A to x.

Proof:

(a) Let $\alpha_0, \ldots, \alpha_n$ be a derivation from $A = \alpha_0$ to $x = \alpha_n$. We construct a sequence $(D_0, b_0), \ldots, (D_n, b_n)$ of derivation trees such that (D_i, b_i) is a derivation tree from $A = \alpha_0$ to α_i for each i, $0 \leq i \leq n$. We define this construction inductively. First we give the construction of (D_0, b_0) ("induction base") and then we specify how one can obtain from (D_{i-1}, b_{i-1}) the derivation tree (D_i, b_i) ("induction step").

(D_0, b_0) is defined as the tree which consists of a node labelled A, i.e. $D_0 = \{\epsilon\}$ and $b_0(\epsilon) = A$. We have $frontier((D_0, b_0)) = A$.

For the induction step, let $1 \leq i \leq n$ and let (D_{i-1}, b_{i-1}) be constructed. Then

$$frontier((D_{i-1}, b_{i-1})) = \alpha_{i-1}.$$

Because $\alpha_{i-1} \to \alpha_i$ there are, by Definition 3(a), $\beta, \gamma \in (V \cup T)^*$ and $B \to \delta \in P$ such that $\alpha_{i-1} = \beta B \gamma$ and $\alpha_i = \beta \delta \gamma$. Now let $\delta = \delta_1 \delta_2 \ldots \delta_h$ with $h \geq 0$ and

$\delta_j \in N \cup T$ for all j, $1 \leq j \leq h$, and let (D', b') be a derivation tree for the production $B \to \delta$, i.e.

$$D' = \{\epsilon, 1, 2, \ldots, max\{1, h\}\}$$
$$b'(\epsilon) = B, \; b'(1) = \delta_1, \ldots, \; b'(h) = \delta_h, \qquad \text{if } h \geq 1$$
$$b'(\epsilon) = B, \; b'(1) = \epsilon, \qquad \text{if } h = 0.$$

Let $v_1 <_{lex} v_2 <_{lex} \cdots <_{lex} v_m$ be the leaves of D_{i-1}. Then there exists $k \geq 1$ with $\beta = b(v_1)\ldots b(v_{k-1})$, $B = b(v_k)$ and $\gamma = b(v_{k+1})\ldots b(v_m)$. The tree $(D_i, b_i) = subst((D_{i-1}, b_{i-1}), v_k, (D', b'))$ is a derivation tree from A to α_i as illustrated by Figure 8.

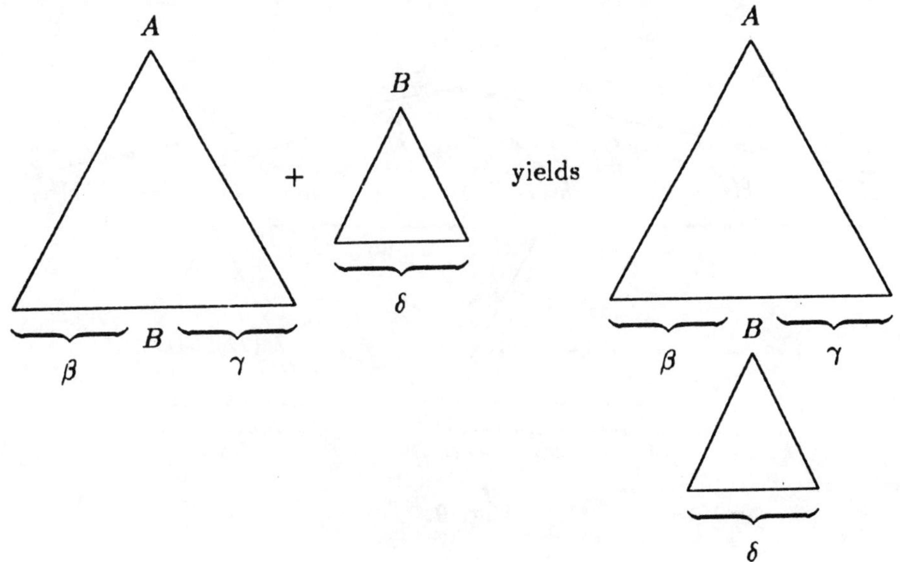

Fig. 8.

This proves part (a) of the theorem. For the proof of part (c) we keep the following relation between (D_i, b_i) and (D_{i-1}, b_{i-1}) in mind

$$D_{i-1} \subseteq D_i \text{ and } b_i|_{D_{i-1}} = b_{i-1} \text{ for all } i, \; 1 \leq i \leq n$$

or more general

$$D_i \subseteq D_j \text{ and } b_j|_{D_i} = b_i \text{ for all } i, j \text{ with } 1 \leq i < j \leq n.$$

(b) The proof is by induction on the depth h of the derivation tree (D, b) from A to x. The induction base corresponds to the case $h = 1$ since $h > 0$. Then $A \to x \in P$ and also $A \xrightarrow[can]{} x$. For the induction step, let $h > 1$ and let n be the degree of the root of (D, b). Then $b(\epsilon) = A$ and $b(\epsilon) \to b(1)\ldots b(n) \in P$.

Let $i_1,\ldots,i_m$ be those children of the root which are labelled with elements in N, $i_1 < \ldots < i_m$. From $h > 1$ follows $m \geq 1$. Consider l with $1 \leq l \leq m$. Then $(D_l, b_l) = subtree((D,b), i_l)$ is a derivation tree from $A_l = b(i_l)$ to $x_l = frontier((D_l, b_l))$ where $depth((D_l, b_l)) \leq h - 1$. Thus $A_l \xrightarrow[can]{} x_l$ by induction hypothesis. Now let

$$w_0 = b(1)\ldots b(i_1 - 1),$$
$$w_1 = b(i_1 + 1)\ldots b(i_2 - 1),$$
$$\vdots$$
$$w_m = b(i_m + 1)\ldots b(n).$$

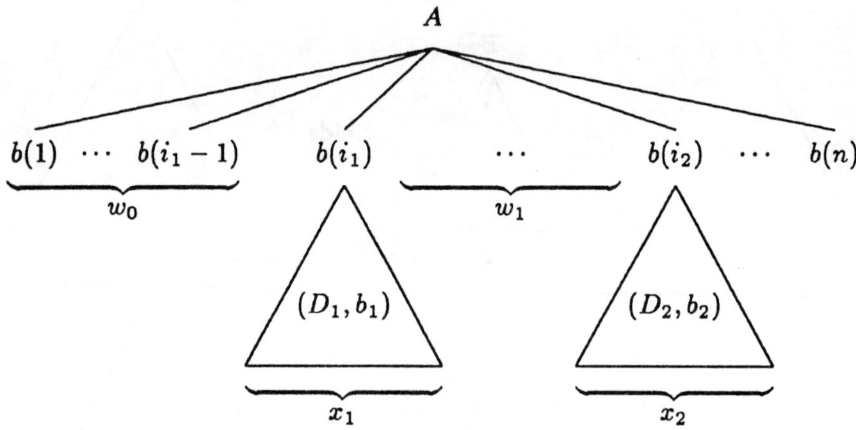

Fig. 9.

The derivation

$$A \xrightarrow[can]{} w_0 A_1 w_1 A_2 \ldots A_m w_m \xrightarrow[can]{*} w_0 x_1 w_1 A_2 \ldots A_m w_m$$
$$\xrightarrow[can]{*} w_0 x_1 w_2 x_2 w_3 A_3 \ldots A_m w_m \xrightarrow[can]{*} \cdots \xrightarrow[can]{*} w_0 x_1 w_2 x_2 \ldots x_m w_m = x$$

is a canonical derivation from A to x.

(c) It is sufficient to show that for all $A \in N, x \in L_{G,A}$:

there are at least two different derivation trees from A to x
$\Leftrightarrow$ there are at least two canonical derivations from A to x

"$\Leftarrow$": Let $A \in N$ and $x \in L_{G,A}$. Let $\alpha_0, \ldots, \alpha_n$ and $\beta_0, \ldots, \beta_m$ with $n, m \geq 1$ be two different canonical derivations from $A = \alpha_0 = \beta_0$ to $x = \alpha_n = \beta_m$. Then there exists $i \leq min(n,m)$ with $\alpha_i \neq \beta_i$. Otherwise $\alpha_k = \beta_k$ for each k, $0 \leq k \leq min(n,m)$. Since the derivations are different, we necessarily have $n \neq m$, for example $n < m$. But then $x = \alpha_n = \beta_n \xrightarrow[can]{} \beta_{n+1}$ in contradiction to $x \in T^*$. This shows the existence of $i \leq min(n,m)$ with $\alpha_i \neq \beta_i$.

Let now j be minimal where $\alpha_j \neq \beta_j$, i.e. $\alpha_0 = \beta_0, \ldots, \alpha_{j-1} = \beta_{j-1}$. Because of $\alpha_0 = \beta_0 = A$ we have $j > 0$. By Definition 3(b), $\alpha_{j-1} = \beta_{j-1} = yB\gamma$ for $y \in T^*, B \in N$ and $\gamma \in (N \cup T)^*$. Furthermore there are productions $B \to \delta_1$ and $B \to \delta_2$ in $P, \delta_1 \neq \delta_2$ with $\alpha_j = y\delta_1\gamma$ and $\beta_j = y\delta_2\gamma$.

Let now $(D_0, b_0), \ldots, (D_n, b_n)$ and $(D_0', b_0'), \ldots, (D_m', b_m')$ correspond to the respective canonical derivations $\alpha_0, \ldots, \alpha_n$ and $\beta_0, \ldots, \beta_m$ where the sequences of derivation trees are constructed according to the method of (a).

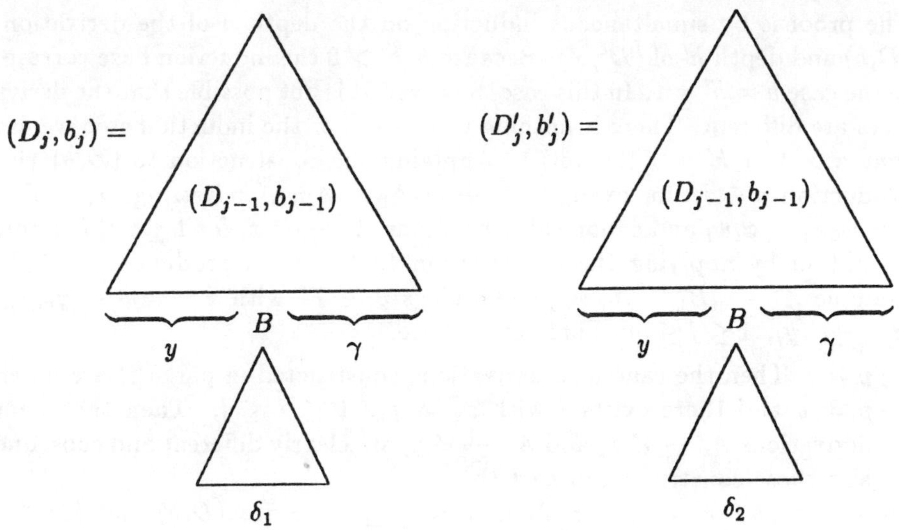

Fig. 10.

Then $(D_{j-1}, b_{j-1}) = (D_{j-1}', b_{j-1}')$ and

$$(D_j, b_j) = subst((D_{j-1}, b_{j-1}), v, (D', b')),$$
$$(D_j', b_j') = subst((D_{j-1}, b_{j-1}), v, (D'', b'')),$$

where v is the leaf of D_{j-1} with label B and (D', b'), (D'', b'') are derivation trees which correspond to the productions $B \to \delta_1$, $B \to \delta_2$, respectively. We now show that $(D_i, b_i) \neq (D_i', b_i')$. First observe that $\delta_1 \neq \delta_2$. We distinguish three cases.

- $|\delta_1| > |\delta_2| \geq 1$ or $|\delta_2| > |\delta_1| \geq 1$. In this case tree templates D' and D'' are different and therefore D_j and D_j' also. Formally, there is a child w of v with $w \in D_j - D_j'$ or $w \in D_j' - D_j$.

- $|\delta_1| = |\delta_2|$. In this case at least one label is different. Formally, there is a child w of v with $w \in D_j \cap D_j'$ and $b_j(w) \neq b_j'(w)$.

- $|\delta_1| = 0$ or $|\delta_2| = 0$. In this case the label of the first child is different.

Thus $(D_j, b_j) \neq (D_j', b_j')$.

Since no new children are added to node v in the course of the construction and the labels of constructed nodes remain unchanged it also follows that $(D_n, b_n) \neq (D'_m, b'_m)$.

"$\Rightarrow$": Let $A \in N$, $x \in L_{G,A}$ be arbitrary. Suppose there are two derivation trees (D, b) and (D', b') from A to x. The idea of the proof is to apply the construction of part (b) to both trees and to show that this construction leads to two different canonical derivations.

The proof is by simultaneous induction on the depth h of the derivation tree (D, b) and depth h' of (D', b'). Because $h, h' > 0$ the induction base corresponds to the case $h = h' = 1$. In this case, however, it is not possible that the derivation trees are different. There is nothing to prove. For the induction step we assume that $h > 1$ or $h' > 1$ (or both). Applying the construction to (D, b) yields a production $p \in P$, for example $A \to w_0 A_1 \ldots A_l w_l$, and strings $x_i \in T^*$ with $x = w_0 x_1 \ldots x_l w_l$ and canonical derivations $A_i \xrightarrow[can]{}{}^* x_i$ for $1 \leq i \leq l$. Similarly, we obtain by applying the construction to (D', b') a production $q \in P$, for example $A \to v_0 B_1 \ldots B_m v_m$, and strings $y_j \in T^*$ with $x = v_0 y_1 \ldots y_m v_m$ and $B_j \xrightarrow[can]{}{}^* y_j$, $1 \leq j \leq m$. Three cases arise.

- $p \neq q$. Then the canonical derivations constructed in part (b) are different.
- $p = q$ and there exists i with $x_i \neq y_i$, $1 \leq i \leq l$. Then the canonical derivations $A_i \xrightarrow[can]{}{}^* x_i$ and $A_i \xrightarrow[can]{}{}^* y_i$ are clearly different and consequently also those constructed in part (b).
- $p = q$ and $x_i = y_i$ for all i, $1 \leq i \leq l$. Since (D, b) and (D', b') are different, there must be i, $1 \leq i \leq l$, such that there are two different derivation trees from A_i to x_i. These derivation trees are subtrees of (D, b) and (D', b'), respectively. Since the depth of these subtrees is smaller than the depth of (D, b) or (D', b') the induction hypothesis applies, i.e. there are two different canonical derivations $A_i \xrightarrow[can]{}{}^* x_i$. Thus the canonical derivations constructed in part (b) are different. ∎

Theorem 1 establishes the equivalence of two interpretations of context-free grammars, the more constructive interpretation of derivations and the more static interpretation of derivation trees. Both approaches have their own advantages. This we demonstrate by proving that grammar G_4 for fully parenthesised expressions is unambiguous (see Example 4).

Lemma 2. *The context-free grammar G_4 of Example 4 is unambiguous.*

Proof: For the proof we use certain facts about the bracket structure of the generated strings.

Auxiliary claim 1: Let L_4 be the language generated by G_4.
For a string $w \in \{[,], a, \#, \uparrow\}^*$ let $Su(w) = |w|_[- |w|_]$ denote the "surplus" of opening brackets in w.

(a) For all $w \in L_4 : Su(w) = 0$

(b) For all $w \in L_4$: Let y be a prefix of w. Then $Su(y) \geq 0$. Furthermore $Su(y) = 0$ if and only if $y = \epsilon$ or $y = w$.

Proof: We first note that part (a) is a special case of part (b), namely the case $y = w$. Thus we only need to prove part (b). For that purpose we show the following stronger assertion.

> For all α with $A \xrightarrow[can]{*} \alpha$ and all prefixes β of α we have $Su(\beta) \geq 0$. Furthermore $Su(\beta) = 0$ if and only if $\beta = \epsilon$ or $\beta = \alpha$.

We prove the assertion by induction on the length of the shortest canonical derivation from A to α, i.e. by induction on

$$N(\alpha) = min\{n \mid \text{ there is a canonical derivation of length } n \text{ from } A \text{ to } \alpha\}.$$

The induction base is simple. From $N(\alpha) = 0$ follows $\alpha = A$ and the assertion is obviously correct. For the induction step consider an α with $N(\alpha) > 0$. Let $\alpha_0, \alpha_1, \ldots, \alpha_{n-1}, \alpha_n$ be a canonical derivation from $\alpha_0 = A$ to $\alpha_n = \alpha$ of length $n = N(\alpha)$. Then $N(\alpha_{n-1}) = n - 1$ and the assertion is true for string α_{n-1} by induction hypothesis. String α_n is obtained from α_{n-1} using a production, i.e. $\alpha_{n-1} = \gamma_1 A \gamma_2$ and $\alpha_n = \gamma_1 \gamma_3 \gamma_2$ where $\gamma_3 \in \{a, [A \# A], [A \uparrow A]\}$. In each of the three cases we have $Su(\alpha_n) = Su(\alpha_{n-1})$ and thus $Su(\alpha_n) = 0$ by induction hypothesis. Let now β be a prefix of α_n. Three cases arise.

Case 1: β is a prefix of γ_1. Then β is a prefix of α_{n-1} and thus $Su(\beta) \geq 0$. Furthermore $Su(\beta) = 0$ implies $\beta = \epsilon$.

Case 2: β is a prefix of $\gamma_1 \gamma_3$ but no prefix of γ_1. Then $Su(\beta) \geq Su(\gamma_1) > 0$ since $\gamma_1 \neq \epsilon$ and $\gamma_1 \neq \alpha_{n-1}$.

Case 3: β is no prefix of $\gamma_1 \gamma_3$. Then $\beta = \gamma_1 \gamma_3 \gamma_4$ for a prefix γ_4 of γ_2. Furthermore $Su(\beta) = Su(\gamma_1 \gamma_3 \gamma_4) = Su(\gamma_1 A \gamma_4) \geq 0$ since $\gamma_1 A \gamma_4$ is a prefix of α_{n-1}. Besides, $Su(\beta) = 0$ implies $Su(\gamma_1 A \gamma_4) = 0$ and hence $\gamma_1 A \gamma_4 = \alpha_{n-1}$ by induction hypothesis. Consequently $\beta = \alpha_n$.

This completes the induction step and the proof of Auxiliary claim 1. ∎

Auxiliary claim 2: Let $w \in L_4$, $|w| > 1$. Then there are uniquely determined strings $w_1, w_2 \in L_4$ and operator $op \in \{\#, \uparrow\}$ such that $w = [w_1 \; op \; w_2]$.

Proof: (by contradiction) Suppose w_1, w_2 and op are not uniquely determined. Then w can be written in two ways, $w = [w_1 \; op \; w_2]$ and $w = [w'_1 \; op' \; w'_2]$ with $op, op' \in \{\#, \uparrow\}$ and $w_1, w_2, w'_1, w'_2 \in L_4$. We may, without restricting generality, assume that $|w'_1| < |w_1|$. Then w'_1 is a prefix of w_1. Furthermore $w'_1 \neq w_1$ and $w'_1 \neq \epsilon$. Thus by Auxiliary claim (1), $Su(w'_1) > 0$. Since, on the other hand, $w'_1 \in L_4$ and thus $Su(w'_1) = 0$ we have a contradiction. Hence w_1 and consequently op and w_2 are uniquely determined. ∎

We can now prove Lemma 2. To this end we prove by induction on $|w|$ that for each $w \in L_4$ there is only one derivation tree from A to w. For $|w| = 1$ and therefore $w = a$ the claim is obvious. The tree

is the only derivation tree. Let $|w| > 1$ and let (D, b) be a derivation tree from A to w. At the root of (D, b) either production $A \to [A \# A]$ or production $A \to [A \uparrow A]$ is used. In both cases we consider the subtrees at node 2 and 4. Let $(D_1, b_1) = subtree((D, b), 2)$, $(D_2, b_2) = subtree((D, b), 4)$, and let $w_i = frontier((D_i, b_i))$ for $i = 1, 2$. Then (D_i, b_i) is a derivation tree from A to w_i and thus $w_i \in L_4, i = 1, 2$.

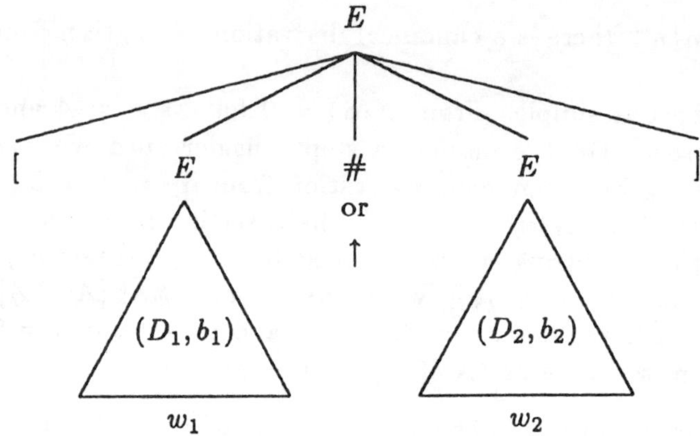

Fig. 11.

Furthermore $w = [w_1 \# w_2]$ or $w = [w_1 \uparrow w_2]$. Hence, by Auxiliary claim 2, w_1 and w_2 are uniquely determined, i.e. all derivation trees (D, b) from A to w yield the same w_1 and w_2. Strings w_1 and w_2 are shorter than w and thus, by induction hypothesis, the trees (D_1, b_1) and (D_2, b_2) are uniquely determined and therefore (D, b) also. This proves Lemma 2.   ∎

Context-free grammars which are unambiguous are particularly important in computer science because they permit a rather elegant definition of the semantics of the language. This can be seen throughout this book. The proof for a context-free grammar to be unambiguous is often difficult, see e.g. the Lemma above, Lemma 2 in Section 2.1.2 and Theorem 1 in Section 2.2. Within the theory of formal languages (cf. M.A. Harrison: Introduction to Formal Language Theory) methods were developed which permit automatic proofs of that property for many grammars. In particular, we want to mention the classes of LR- and LL-grammars. These classes have the following properties.

(a) All grammars in these classes are unambiguous.

(b) It can be checked mechanically whether a given grammar belongs to the class of LR(k) or LL(k) grammars for given k.

Furthermore these classes are quite large. For example, all grammars used in the sequel of this book are LR-grammars. Thus the theory of formal languages establishes that they are unambiguous. Nevertheless we will prove this in some cases explicitly — as it was done in Lemma 2.

We conclude this section with a notational simplification. If $A \rightarrow \alpha_1, A \rightarrow \alpha_2, \ldots, A \rightarrow \alpha_m$ are productions of a grammar, $m \geq 2$, then we shorten this to $A \rightarrow \alpha_1|\alpha_2|\ldots|\alpha_m$ (read: A goes to α_1 or α_2 or $\ldots$ or α_m). This abbreviation is well defined because in the grammars of this book the symbol "|" is never an element of $T \cup N$.

Exercises for 1.4

1) Give all derivations for $[[a\#a] \uparrow [a\#a]]$ with respect to grammar G_4 of Example 4. Determine the derivation tree. Using the method of Theorem 1, derive the canonical derivation from the derivation tree and vise versa.

2) Let $G = (\{S, A, B\}, \{a, b\}, P, S)$, with productions

$$S \rightarrow bA, \; S \rightarrow aB, \; A \rightarrow a, \quad B \rightarrow b,$$
$$A \rightarrow aS, \; B \rightarrow bS, \; A \rightarrow bAA, \; B \rightarrow aBB$$

   a) Give a derivation of the string $aabbab$.

   b) Is G unambiguous? Prove your answer.

   c) Prove that $L_G = \{w \in \{a,b\}^* \; | \; |w|_a = |w|_b\}$

3) Let $G = (\{S, A, B\}, \{a, b\}, P, S)$ with productions:

$$S \rightarrow aBS, \; S \rightarrow aB, \; S \rightarrow bAS, \quad S \rightarrow bA,$$
$$A \rightarrow bAA, \; A \rightarrow a, \quad B \rightarrow aBB, \; B \rightarrow b$$

   Do the same questions as in Exercise 2.

4) Let $G = (\{S\}, \{+, a\}, \{S \rightarrow a, \; S \rightarrow +SSS\}, S)$.

   a) Give the derivation tree for $+a + aaaa$.

   b) Describe L_G informally.

   c) Is G unambiguous? Prove your answer.

5) Prove by designing a context-free grammar that the following languages are context-free

   a) $\{a^n b^n \; | \; n \in \mathbb{N}\}$

   b) $\{ a^n \; | \; n \in \mathbb{N}$ and three divides $n\}$

   c) $\{w\$u \; | \; w, u \in \{a, b\}^*$ and $w \neq u\}$

6) Let L be a context-free language. Prove that there is a context-free grammar $G = (N, T, P, S)$ with $L_G = L$ such that for all productions $(A, \alpha) \in P : \alpha \in T$ or $\alpha = \epsilon$ or $\alpha \in N^2$. Can you show, in addition, that in the case of $\alpha = \epsilon$ only $A = S$ is necessary (Remark: A grammar G which satisfies these requirements is called a grammar in Chomsky normal form)?

7) Let $G = (N, T, P, S)$ be a context-free grammar with $n = |N|$, $m = max\{|\alpha| \mid (A, \alpha) \in P\}$ and $\alpha \neq \epsilon$ for all $(A, \alpha) \in P$.

a) Let (D, b) be a derivation tree with respect to G. Then

$$|frontier((D, b))| \leq m^{depth((D,b))}$$

b) Let $w \in L_G$ with $|w| \geq m^{n+1}$ and let (D, b) be a derivation tree for w. Using part a), show that $depth((D, b)) \geq n + 2$ and, furthermore, that there are nodes $u, v \in D$ with $u \neq v$, u *ancestor* v and $b(u) = b(v)$. Hint: Let $x \in D$ be a node with $|x| = depth((D, b))$ and let $x_i = parent^{(i)}(x)$, $i = 0, 1, 2, \ldots$. Show that there exists i and j with $i \neq j$ and $b(x_i) = b(x_j)$.

c) Let $w \in L_G$ with $|w| > m^{n+1}$. Show that w can be written as $w = w_1 w_2 w_3 w_4 w_5$ with $w_2 w_4 \neq \epsilon$ such that $w_1 w_2{}^q w_3 w_4{}^q w_5 \in L_G$ for all $q \in \mathbb{N}$. This assertion is often called the **pumping lemma** for context-free grammars.

Hint: Let (D, b) be a derivation tree for w and let $u, v \in D$ with $u \neq v$, u *ancestor* v and $b(u) = b(v)$. Let $(D_1, b_1) = subtree((D, b), u)$ and $(D_2, b_2) = subtree((D, b), v)$. Then $w_3 = frontier((D_2, b_2))$, $w_2 w_3 w_4 = frontier((D_1, b_1))$ and $w_1 w_2 w_3 w_4 w_5 = w = frontier((D, b))$. Now a derivation tree for $w_1 w_2{}^2 w_3 w_4{}^2 w_5$, for example, is given by

$$subst((D, b), v, (D_1, b_1))$$

d) Prove part c) without the assumption that $\alpha \neq \epsilon$ for all $(A, \alpha) \in P$.
Hint: Now it is not obvious that $w_2 w_4 \neq \epsilon$.

e) Using part d), show that $L = \{a^s b^s a^s \mid s \in \mathbb{N}\}$ is *not* context-free.
Hint: Prove by contradiction. Let G be a context-free grammar with $L = L_G$. Let $w \in L_G$ with $|w| > m^{n+1}$ where m and n are defined as above. Then one can write w as $w = w_1 w_2 w_3 w_4 w_5$ with $w_2 w_4 \neq \epsilon$ and $w_1 w_2{}^q w_3 w_4{}^q w_5 \in L_G$ for all $q \in \mathbb{N}$. Discuss the different possibilities for w_2 and w_4 and infer a contradiction.

1.5 Recursive Definition of Functions

In this section we discuss the method of **recursive definition** of functions. We will use this method frequently to define functions on formal languages. The main idea is the following. The sentences of a formal language generated by a context-free grammar bear a syntactic structure as illustrated by the derivation tree. This syntactic structure is used to define the value of a function for a sentence w in terms of the values of "simpler" sentences — namely substrings of w. This leads in a natural way to a recursive definition of functions.

Reconsider language L_4 of the previous section. It is generated by the unambiguous grammar

$$G_4 = (\{A\}, \{[,], a, \#, \uparrow\}, \{A \to a, A \to [A\#A], A \to [A \uparrow A]\}, A)$$

The elements of L_4 are fully parenthesised expressions over the operand set $\{a\}$ and the binary operator symbols $\#$ and $\uparrow$. Let us interpret symbol a as the natural number 1, symbol $\#$ as addition and symbol $\uparrow$ as multiplication for natural numbers. With this interpretation the value of $[[a\#a] \uparrow [a\#a]]$ is 4. How can we now define a function $S : L_4 \to \mathbb{N}$ which determines for each expression its corresponding value?

It seems obvious to define S recursively in terms of the structure of expressions in L_4. For the "simplest" expression a we set $S(a) = 1$. For "more complex" expressions, i.e. expressions of the form $[w_1\#w_2]$ and $[w_1 \uparrow w_2]$, S is defined in terms of simpler expressions, i.e. $S([w_1\#w_2]) = S(w_1) + S(w_2)$ and $S([w_1 \uparrow w_2]) = S(w_1) \cdot S(w_2)$. Altogether

$S : L_4 \to \mathbb{N}$ is defined as

$$\text{(I)} \qquad S(w) = \begin{cases} 1 & \text{if } w = a \\ S(w_1) + S(w_2) & \text{if } w = [w_1\#w_2] \text{ and } w_1, w_2 \in L_4 \\ S(w_1) \cdot S(w_2) & \text{if } w = [w_1 \uparrow w_2] \text{ and } w_1, w_2 \in L_4 \end{cases}$$

Note that according to Auxiliary claim 2 of Section 1.4 strings w_1 and w_2 in the second and third case are uniquely determined by w.

We must now give this definition an exact meaning. There are three possibilities, a constructive, a descriptive and an algorithmic definition. We shall examine these three possibilities one by one. The detailed treatment of this example serves to prepare for the formal definitions at the end of the section.

(1) The Constructive Interpretation

The above definition of S is based on the fact that the computation of the value for w can be reduced to that of the values for w_1 and w_2. Such a reduction, i.e. the decomposition of argument w into substrings w_1 and w_2, takes place until the case $w = a$ is reached. The constructive method consists in "composing" function S starting with the case $w = a$. We introduce a sequence of functions $S_0, S_1, S_2 \ldots$ such that

S_i computes the value of function S for each argument w which can be reduced to the case $w = a$ in at most i decomposition steps.

Formally,

$S_0 : L_4 \rightsquigarrow \mathbb{N}$ is defined as

$$S_0(w) = \begin{cases} 1 & \text{if } w = a \\ \text{undefined} & \text{otherwise} \end{cases}$$

and $S_i : L_4 \rightsquigarrow \mathbb{N}$, $i \geq 1$, is defined as

$$S_i(w) = \begin{cases} 1 & \text{if } w = a \\ S_{i-1}(w_1) + S_{i-1}(w_2) & \text{if } w = [w_1 \# w_2] \text{ and } w_1, w_2 \in L_4 \\ S_{i-1}(w_1) \cdot S_{i-1}(w_2) & \text{if } w = [w_1 \uparrow w_2] \text{ and } w_1, w_2 \in L_4 \end{cases}$$

Auxiliary claim 2, Section 1.4 ensures that functions S_i, $i \geq 0$ are well-defined. Note that it was essential in the proof that grammar G_4 be unambiguous.

Further note that functions S_i are all partial. For example $Def(S_0) = \{a\}$, $Def(S_1) = \{a, [a\#a], [a \uparrow a]\}, \ldots$. Obviously we can compute the value of more expressions by reducing $(i + 1)$-times than only i-times, i.e. function S_{i+1} is an extension of function S_i, symbolically $S_i \sqsubseteq S_{i+1}$. This property is so important that we want to give an exact proof.

Lemma 1. *For all* $i \geq 0 : S_i \sqsubseteq S_{i+1}$

Proof: The proof is by induction on i.

For $i = 0$ the claim follows from $Def(S_0) = \{a\}$ and $S_0(a) = 1 = S_1(a)$. For the induction step let $i \geq 1$ and $w \in Def(S_i)$. If $w = a$ then $S_i(w) = 1 = S_{i+1}(w)$. Otherwise $w = [w_1 \# w_2]$ or $w = [w_1 \uparrow w_2]$. In the first case (the second is analogous) we infer

$$\begin{aligned} S_i(w) &= S_{i-1}(w_1) + S_{i-1}(w_2) && \text{definition of } S_i \\ &= S_i(w_1) + S_i(w_2) && \text{since } S_{i-1} \sqsubseteq S_i \text{ by induction hypothesis} \\ & && \text{and } w_1, w_2 \in Def(S_{i-1}) \\ &= S_{i+1}(w) && \text{definition of } S_{i+1} \end{aligned}$$

Hence $S_i \sqsubseteq S_{i+1}$.   ∎

Because of $S_i \sqsubseteq S_{i+1}$ for all i we can "combine" the functions to a single function $W : L_4 \rightsquigarrow \mathbb{N}$ where $W = \bigcup_{i \geq 0} S_i$ (for didactic reasons we do not call the function S). We now prove what has been suggested, namely that W is a function.

Lemma 2. *W is a function from L_4 to* $\mathbb{N}$.

Proof: We have to show that for each $w \in L_4$ there is at most one $n \in \mathbb{N}$ with $(w, n) \in W$. Suppose this is not the case, i.e. $(w, n_1) \in W$ and $(w, n_2) \in W$ with $w \in L_4$, $n_1, n_2 \in \mathbb{N}$ and $n_1 \neq n_2$. Because of $W = \bigcup_{i \geq 0} S_i$ there exists m_1 with $(w, n_1) \in S_{m_1}$ and m_2 with $(w, n_2) \in S_{m_2}$. Let $m_1 \leq m_2$ without restricting generality. From $S_{m_1} \sqsubseteq S_{m_1+1} \sqsubseteq \ldots \sqsubseteq S_{m_2}$ follows $(w, n_1) \in S_{m_2}$ and thus $n_1 = n_2$ since S_{m_2} is a function. This is a contradiction.   ∎

The question is whether W is even a total function.

Lemma 3. *W is a total function from L_4 to* $\mathbb{N}$, *i.e.* $Def(W) = L_4$.

Proof: We prove by induction on i that if there is a derivation tree of depth i from A to $w \in L_4$ then $w \in Def(S_{i-1})$. For $i = 1$ and thus $w = a$ this is clear. Let now $i > 1$. Then $w = [w_1 \# w_2]$ or $w = [w_1 \uparrow w_2]$. Furthermore there are derivation trees of depth $i - 1$ or less for w_1 and w_2.
Thus $w_1 \in Def(S_{i-2})$ and $w_2 \in Def(S_{i-2})$, by induction hypothesis, and consequently $w \in Def(S_{i-1})$. This proves that W is total. ∎

Summarising we can say that equation (I), according to the constructive interpretation, defines a total function W with $W = \bigcup_{i \geq 0} S_i$ where functions S_i are defined in a "constructive" way.

(2) Descriptive Interpretation

The descriptive method consists in interpreting the definition of S as an equation. We define the set of functions

$$\mathcal{G} = \{F : L_4 \rightsquigarrow \mathbb{N}; \text{ function } F \text{ satisfies for all } w \in L_4 \text{ the equation}$$

$$F(w) = \begin{cases} 1 & \text{if } w = a \\ F(w_1) + F(w_2) & \text{if } w = [w_1 \# w_2] \text{ and } w_1, w_2 \in L_4 \\ F(w_1) \cdot F(w_2) & \text{if } w = [w_1 \uparrow w_2] \text{ and } w_1, w_2 \in L_4 \end{cases} \quad \}$$

We have to consider the following questions. Does the equation have a solution, i.e. is $\mathcal{G}$ not empty? Does it have several solutions and, if yes, how are they related? What is the relation of these solutions to the above introduced function W? These questions are answered by the following Lemma.

Lemma 4.
(a) $W \in \mathcal{G}$
(b) $W \sqsubseteq F$ for all $F \in \mathcal{G}$
(c) $W = \bigcap_{F \in \mathcal{G}} F$

Proof:
(a) We have to show that W satisfies the defining equation.
  Surely $W(a) = 1$. Let now $w \in L_4$, $w \neq a$. Then $w = [w_1 \# w_2]$ or $w = [w_1 \uparrow w_2]$. In the first case (the second holds analogously) we must show

$$W(w) = W(w_1) + W(w_2)$$

Let us assume that $W(w)$ is defined (Note that in this proof we do *not* use the fact that W is total). Then there exists a m with $w \in Def(S_m)$ and thus $w_1, w_2 \in Def(S_{m-1})$. Hence

$$\begin{aligned} W(w) &= S_m(w) \\ &= S_{m-1}(w_1) + S_{m-1}(w_2) \\ &= W(w_1) + W(w_2) \end{aligned}$$

Now suppose that $W(w_1)$ and $W(w_2)$ are defined. Then there exists a m with $w_1, w_2 \in Def(S_m)$ and thus $w \in Def(S_{m+1})$. Hence

$$
\begin{aligned}
W(w_1) + W(w_2) &= S_m(w_1) + S_m(w_2) \\
&= S_{m+1}(w) \\
&= W(w)
\end{aligned}
$$

This proves (a).

(b) Let $F \in \mathcal{G}$ be arbitrary. It suffices to show that $S_i \sqsubseteq F$ for all $i \geq 0$. We prove this by induction on i. For $i = 0$ we have $S_0 \sqsubseteq F$ because of $F(a) = 1$. For the induction step consider some $w \in Def(S_{i+1})$. Then for $w = [w_1 \# w_2], w_1, w_2 \in Def(S_i)$:

$$
\begin{aligned}
S_{i+1}(w) &= S_i(w_1) + S_i(w_2) \quad &\text{definition of } S_{i+1} \\
&= F(w_1) + F(w_2) \quad &\text{since } S_i \sqsubseteq F \text{ by induction hypothesis} \\
&= F(w) \quad &\text{since } F \in \mathcal{G}
\end{aligned}
$$

This completes the induction step.

(c) Since $W \sqsubseteq F$ for all $F \in \mathcal{G}$ we have $W \sqsubseteq \bigcap_{F \in \mathcal{G}} F$. Moreover $W \in \mathcal{G}$ implies $\bigcap_{F \in \mathcal{G}} F \sqsubseteq W$. Thus $W = \bigcap_{F \in \mathcal{G}} F$. ∎

Note again that in the proof of Lemma 4 totality of W was not used. It is needed though in the proof of the following Lemma.

Lemma 5. $\mathcal{G} = \{W\}$, i.e. W is the only solution of the system of equations.

Proof: Let $F \in \mathcal{G}$ be arbitrary. Then $W \sqsubseteq F$ by Lemma 4b. From W being total follows $W = F$. ∎

Summarising one can say that in the descriptive interpretation, definition (I) is viewed as an equation. This equation has a single solution, namely function W introduced in the constructive interpretation.

(3) Algorithmic Interpretation

We interpret definition (I) as a computation rule which serves to compute the value of function S for arbitrary arguments. For argument $[[a \uparrow a] \# [a \# a]]$, for example, one obtains

$$
\begin{aligned}
S([[a \uparrow a] \# [a \# a]]) &= S([a \uparrow a]) + S([a \# a]) \\
&= (S(a) \cdot S(a)) + (S(a) + S(a)) \\
&= (1 \cdot 1) + (1 + 1) \\
&= 1 + 2 \\
&= 3
\end{aligned}
$$

We return to the algorithmic interpretation in Chapters II and V. In particular, we will show in Chapter II that function W and the function defined by this computation rule are the same.

This concludes the discussion of function S, i.e. the interpretation of language L_4. Before we introduce the formal concepts, let us consider another example. Let $f : \mathbb{Z} \rightsquigarrow \mathbb{R}$ be defined recursively by

$$f(n) = \begin{cases} 1 & \text{if } n = 1 \\ n \cdot f(n-1) & \text{if } n \neq 1 \end{cases}$$

(the reason for using $f : \mathbb{Z} \rightsquigarrow \mathbb{R}$ instead of $f : \mathbb{Z} \rightarrow \mathbb{Z}$ will become apparent later)

Again we examine the constructive and descriptive interpretation. In the case of constructive interpretation we build the sequence of functions $f_0, f_1, f_2, \ldots$ with

$f_0 : \mathbb{Z} \rightsquigarrow \mathbb{R}$ defined as

$$f_0(n) = \begin{cases} 1 & \text{if } n = 1 \\ \text{undefined} & \text{otherwise} \end{cases}$$

$f_{i+1} : \mathbb{Z} \rightsquigarrow \mathbb{R}$, $i \geq 0$, is defined as

$$f_{i+1}(n) = \begin{cases} 1 & \text{if } n = 1 \\ n \cdot f_i(n-1) & \text{if } n \neq 1 \end{cases}$$

Now $Def(f_0) = \{1\}$, $Def(f_1) = \{1,2\}, \ldots$ and the following Lemma holds.

Lemma 6. $f_i \sqsubseteq f_{i+1}$ for all $i \geq 0$.

Proof: Similar to the proof of Lemma 1. The reader is strongly advised to attempt the proof. ∎

This example even permits an explicit definition of functions f_i, namely $f_i = g_i$ where

$$g_i(n) = \begin{cases} 1 & \text{if } n = 1 \\ n(n-1)\ldots 1 & \text{if } n \in \mathbb{N}, 1 \leq n \leq i+1 \\ \text{undefined} & \text{otherwise} \end{cases}$$

Lemma 7. $f_i = g_i$, for all $i \geq 0$.

Proof: The simple proof by induction is left to the reader. ∎

Let now $fac = \bigcup_{i \geq 0} f_i$ be the function obtained by the constructive interpretation. Then by Lemma 7

$$fac(n) = \begin{cases} 1 & \text{if } n = 1 \\ n(n-1)\ldots 1 & \text{if } n \in \mathbb{N} - \{1\} \\ \text{undefined} & \text{otherwise} \end{cases}$$

Consider now the descriptive interpretation. Let

$\mathcal{F} = \{f : \mathbb{Z} \rightsquigarrow \mathbb{R}; \ f$ satisfies the equation

$$f(n) = \begin{cases} 1 & \text{if } n = 1 \\ n \cdot f(n-1) & \text{otherwise} \end{cases} \qquad \}$$

We have the following Lemma.

Lemma 8.

(a) $fac \in \mathcal{F}$

(b) $fac \sqsubseteq f$ for all $f \in \mathcal{F}$

(c) $fac = \bigcap_{f \in \mathcal{F}}$

Proof: The proof is similar to that of Lemma 4. The reader is urged to try this proof.   ∎

Again we have the equivalence of constructive and of descriptive interpretation. This has been shown in the examples in the same way. The reader should note that the domain of W consists of all strings $w \in L_4$ which can be reduced in finitely many steps to the case $w = a$ where w is reduced to strings w_1 and w_2. These are all strings of L_4, hence W is total. The domain of fac consists of all numbers $n \in \mathbb{Z}$ which can be reduced in finitely many steps to the case $n = 1$ where number n is reduced to $n - 1$. These are just the natural numbers and therefore $Def(fac) = \mathbb{N} \neq \mathbb{Z}$.

For this reason Lemma 5 does not apply in the second example. Rather it is the case that for each $c \in \mathbb{R}$ function

$$f_c(x) = \begin{cases} fac(x) & \text{for } x \in \mathbb{N} \\ 0 & \text{for } x = 0 \\ c & \text{for } x = -1 \\ (-1)^{n-1}c/(n-1)! & \text{for } x = -n, \ n \in \mathbb{N} \end{cases}$$

is an element of $\mathcal{F}$.

The reader can find further examples of recursive definitions in the exercises and in later chapters. In all these examples one can show as in Lemmas 1, 2 and 4 that constructive interpretation and descriptive interpretation of the recursive definition specifies the same function. We will now show this connexion in general. Knowledge of the rest of Section 1.5 is not necessary for understanding the remainder of the book.

Definition 1: Let A and B be sets. A mapping $\phi : P(A, B) \rightarrow P(A, B)$ is called a **functional**. A functional is **monotonic** if for all $F, G \in P(A, B) : F \sqsubseteq G$ implies $\phi(F) \sqsubseteq \phi(G)$. A functional ϕ is **continuous** if for all increasing sequences of functions, i.e. sequences of the form $F_0, F_1, \ldots \in P(A, B)$ with $F_0 \sqsubseteq F_1 \sqsubseteq F_2 \sqsubseteq \ldots$, we have

$$\bigcup_{i \geq 0} \phi(F_i) = \phi\left(\bigcup_{i \geq 0} F_i\right)$$

Example: Let $A = L_4$ and let $B = \mathbb{N}$. Mapping $\phi : P(L_4, \mathbb{N}) \rightarrow P(L_4, \mathbb{N})$ with

$$\phi(F)(w) = \begin{cases} 1 & \text{if } w = a \\ F(w_1) + F(w_2) & \text{if } w = [w_1 \# w_2] \text{ with } w_1, w_2 \in L_4 \\ F(w_1) \cdot F(w_2) & \text{if } w = [w_1 \uparrow w_2] \text{ with } w_1, w_2 \in L_4 \end{cases}$$

is a monotonic, continuous functional as can be seen as follows.

Let $F, G \in P(L_4, \mathbb{N})$ with $F \sqsubseteq G$, and let $w \in Def(\phi(F))$. Then either $w = a$ and therefore $w \in Def(\phi(G))$ or $w = [w_1 \; op \; w_2]$ with $w_1, w_2 \in L_4$ and $op \in \{\uparrow, \#\}$. In the latter case $\phi(F)(w) = Op(F(w_1), F(w_2))$ with $w_1, w_2 \in Def(F)$ and $Op \in \{+, \cdot\}$. (For better legibility we write Op as prefix operator rather than infix operator) Because of $F \sqsubseteq G$ it follows that $w_1, w_2 \in Def(G)$ and thus $w \in Def(\phi(G))$. Hence ϕ is monotonic.

To show continuity let $F_0, F_1, F_2, \ldots \in P(L_4, \mathbb{N})$ with $F_0 \sqsubseteq F_1 \sqsubseteq \ldots$. Because of $F_i \sqsubseteq \bigcup_i F_i$ and monotonicity we have $\phi(F_i) \sqsubseteq \phi(\bigcup_i F_i)$ for all i and thus $\bigcup_i \phi(F_i) \sqsubseteq \phi(\bigcup_i F_i)$. To show the reverse inclusion, i.e. $\phi(\bigcup_i F_i) \sqsubseteq \bigcup_i \phi(F_i)$, let $w \in Def(\phi(\bigcup_i F_i))$. Then either $w = a$ and therefore $w \in Def(\phi(F_0)) \subseteq Def(\bigcup_i \phi(F_i))$ or $w = [w_1 \; op \; w_2]$ with $w_1, w_2 \in L_4$. In the latter case $\phi(\bigcup_i F_i)(w) = Op((\bigcup_i F_i(w_1)), (\bigcup_i F_i(w_2)))$ and hence $w_1, w_2 \in Def(\bigcup_i F_i)$. Thus there is an m with $w_1, w_2 \in Def(F_m)$ and consequently $\phi(F_m)(w) = \phi(\bigcup_i F_i)(w)$. This proves $\phi(\bigcup_i F_i) \sqsubseteq \bigcup_i \phi(F_i)$.   ∎

Using functionals one can express recursive definitions very concisely. Let A, B be sets and let $\phi : P(A, B) \to P(A, B)$ be a functional. Then

$$F(x) = \phi(F(x))$$

represents a recursive definition of function $F \in P(A, B)$. First we consider the constructive interpretation.

Lemma 9. *Let A, B be sets and let $\phi : P(A, B) \to P(A, B)$ be a monotonic functional. Let $G_{-1} = \emptyset$ be the undefined function and $G_i = \phi(G_{i-1})$ for $i \geq 0$.*

(a) $G_i \in P(A, B)$ *for each* i, $i \geq -1$.

(b) $G_{i-1} \sqsubseteq G_i$ *for each* i, $i \geq 0$.

(c) $G = \bigcup_{i \geq -1} G_i$ *is a function.*

(We say G is defined by the equation $F = \phi(F)$.)

Proof:
(a) We use induction on i. For $i = -1$ the assertion is true since $G_{-1} = \emptyset$. Let now $i \geq 0$. By induction hypothesis $G_{i-1} \in P(A, B)$ and consequently $G_i = \phi(G_{i-1}) \in P(A, B)$.

(b) We use induction on i. For $i = 0$ the property holds since $G_{-1} = \emptyset$ implies $G_{-1} \sqsubseteq G_0$. Let now $i > 0$. Then by induction hypothesis $G_{i-2} \sqsubseteq G_{i-1}$. Because of monotonicity of ϕ we also have $G_{i-1} = \phi(G_{i-2}) \sqsubseteq \phi(G_{i-1}) = G_i$.

(c) Let $(x, y_1) \in G$ and $(x, y_2) \in G$. We must show that $y_1 = y_2$. By definition of G there exists m_1 and m_2 with $(x, y_1) \in G_{m_1}$ and $(x, y_2) \in G_{m_2}$. Let $m_1 \leq m_2$ without restricting generality. Then part (a) implies $G_{m_1} \sqsubseteq G_{m_2}$ and thus $(x, y_1) \in G_{m_2}$. Hence $y_1 = y_2$ since G_{m_2} is a function.   ∎

Lemma 9 corresponds to Lemmas 1, 2 and 6. We now prove a theorem which corresponds to Lemmas 4 and 8.

Theorem 1. *Let A and B be sets, $\phi : P(A,B) \to P(A,B)$ a monotonic, continuous functional, $G \in P(A,B)$ the function defined by the equation $F = \phi(F)$ and let $\mathcal{F} = \{F \in P(A,B) \mid F = \phi(F)\}$ be the set of solutions of this equation. Then*

(a) $G \in \mathcal{F}$

(b) $G \sqsubseteq F$ for all $F \in \mathcal{F}$

(c) $G = \bigcap_{F \in \mathcal{F}} F$

Proof:

(a) By definition of G we have $G = \bigcup_{i \geq 0} G_i$ with $G_0 \sqsubseteq G_1 \sqsubseteq G_2 \sqsubseteq \ldots$. Since ϕ is a continuous functional it follows that

$$
\begin{aligned}
\phi(G) \;&=\; \phi(\textstyle\bigcup_{i \geq 0} G_i) \quad \text{definition of } G \\[2mm]
&=\; \textstyle\bigcup_{i \geq 0} \phi(G_i) \quad \text{since } \phi \text{ continuous} \\[2mm]
&=\; \textstyle\bigcup_{i \geq 0} G_{i+1} \quad \text{definition of } G_{i+1} \\[2mm]
&=\; G
\end{aligned}
$$

(b) Let $F \in \mathcal{F}$ be arbitrary. Since $G = \bigcup_{i \geq -1} G_i$ it suffices to show that $G_i \sqsubseteq F$ for all $i \geq -1$. We use induction on i. For $i = -1$ this is obvious since $G_{-1} = \phi$. For $i \geq 0$, by induction hypothesis, $G_{i-1} \sqsubseteq F$ and thus, by monotonicity of ϕ, we have $G_i = \phi(G_{i-1}) \sqsubseteq \phi(F) = F$.

(c) follows immediately from (a) and (b)   ∎

Note that in Theorem 1 monotonicity and continuity of the functional ϕ were used. Lemma 9 only uses monotonicity.

Exercises for 1.5

1) Let $m : \mathbb{N}_0^2 \rightsquigarrow \mathbb{N}_0$ be defined as

$$
m(x,y) = \begin{cases} 0 & \text{if } y = 0 \\ x + m(x, y-1) & \text{if } y \neq 0 \end{cases}
$$

a) Give the constructive interpretation. In particular, define the sequence of functions $m_0, m_1, m_2, \ldots$.

b) Show that function m is total.

c) Under which name is m known? Prove your answer.

2) a) Using functions $Succ : \mathbb{N} \to \mathbb{N}$, $Pred : \mathbb{N} \rightsquigarrow \mathbb{N}$ with

$$Succ(n) = n + 1$$

$$Pred(n) = \begin{cases} n - 1 & \text{if } n > 1 \\ \text{undefined} & \text{otherwise} \end{cases}$$

give a recursive definition of the addition operation.

b) Argue that your answer is correct.

3) Let $\phi : P(\mathbb{N},\mathbb{N}) \to P(\mathbb{N},\mathbb{N})$ be defined as

$$\phi(f)(x) = \begin{cases} 1 & \text{if } x = 1 \\ x \cdot f(x - 1) & \text{otherwise} \end{cases}$$

for all $f \in P(\mathbb{N},\mathbb{N})$. Show that ϕ is a monotonic, continuous functional.

4) Let $G = (\{A\}, \{a\}, \{A \to a|AA\}, A)$ be a context-free grammar.

a) Show that G is ambiguous.

b) Does the recursive definition

$$f(w) = \begin{cases} 2 & \text{if } w = a \\ f(w_1)^{f(w_2)} & \text{if } w = w_1 w_2 \text{ where } w_1, w_2 \in L_G \end{cases}$$

define a function $f \in P(L_G, \mathbb{N})$?

5) Let Σ be an alphabet and let $<$ be an ordering on Σ. Let $f : \Sigma^* \times \Sigma^* \to \{true, false\}$ be defined recursively as

$$f(x,y) = \begin{cases} true & \text{if } x = \epsilon, \text{ or } x \neq \epsilon, y \neq \epsilon \text{ and } x = ax', y = by' \\ & \quad \text{with } a, b \in \Sigma \text{ and } a < b \\ f(x',y') & \text{if } x \neq \epsilon, y \neq \epsilon \text{ and } x = ax' \text{ and } y = ay' \\ & \quad \text{where } a \in \Sigma \\ false & \text{otherwise} \end{cases}$$

a) Show that f is a total function.

b) Show that f coincides with the lexicographic order on Σ^*.

1.6 Attribute Grammars

In Section 1.4 we have shown that context-free grammars permit the description of the syntax (i.e. of the grammatical structure) of a formal language. We now introduce a mechanism which makes it possible to describe, in addition, the association of "meaning" with the sentences of the generated language: **attribute grammars.** These grammars can be viewed as an extension of context-free grammars. Attribute grammars go beyond the description mechanisms developed in Section 1.5. Whereas there we considered methods to label derivation trees which worked "bottom up " so to speak, "flow of information" in the case of attribute grammars is essentially more flexible. Attribute grammars will be used from Chapter III onwards.

Example 1:
Computing the value of a natural number from its binary representation with the help of an attribute grammar.

Binary representations of natural numbers are generated by the context-free grammar $G = (N, T, P, S)$ with $N = \{S, L, B\}$, $T = \{0, 1\}$, $P = \{S \rightarrow L, L \rightarrow LB, L \rightarrow B, B \rightarrow 0, B \rightarrow 1\}$. ($B$ for "bit" and L for "list of bits"). Figure 1 shows a derivation tree for the string $1101 \in L_G$.

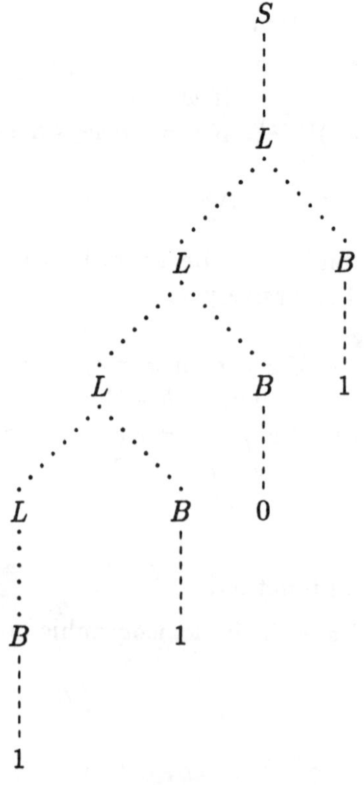

Fig. 1.

We now want to specify for each B-, L- and S-construct its "value". Observe that the "value" of a B-construct depends on the position of the bits in the terminal string. In string 1101, for example, the left "1" has the value $1 \cdot 2^3 = 8$ and the right has the value $1 \cdot 2^0 = 1$. We therefore associate with the nodes of the tree additional information in the form of two "attributes". Attribute *pos* indicates for each B-construct the position of the bits in the terminal string and for each L-construct the position of the rightmost bit of the construct (bits are counted from right to left). Attribute *value* indicates for each construct its value. The following diagram of the derivation tree for 1101 shows the respective attribute values for each node other than leaves. Attribute *pos* appears in a box to the left of a node and *value* to the right. Such a tree is called an "attributed" tree (see Figure 2).

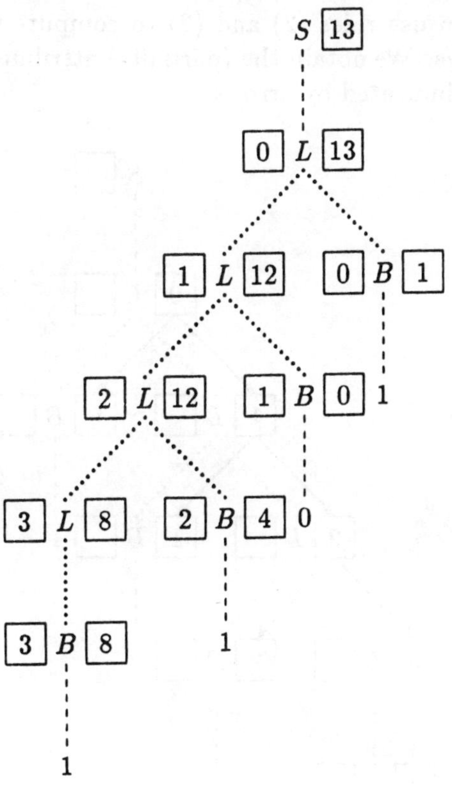

Fig. 2.

Obviously the contents of the boxes can be determined by the following quite simple rules.

(1) The *pos*-attribute of the child of the root is 0.

(2) If the *pos*-attribute of a node labelled L is n and production $L \rightarrow LB$ is used then the *pos*-attribute of the first child is $n + 1$ and the *pos*-attribute of the second child is n.

(3) If the *pos*-attribute of a node labelled L is n and production $L \to B$ is used then the *pos*-attribute of the single child of the node is also n.

(4) If the *pos*-attribute of a node labelled B is n and production $B \to a$ with $a \in \{0, 1\}$ is used then the *value*-attribute of the node is $a \cdot 2^n$.

(5) If the label of a node is L and production $L \to B$ is used then the *value*-attribute of the node is equal to the *value*-attribute of the child.

(6) If the label of a node is L and production $L \to LB$ is used, then the *value*-attribute of the node is the sum of the *value*-attributes of the children.

(7) The *value*-attribute of the root is equal to the *value*-attribute of its single child.

In our example we can determine the *pos*-attribute of the child of the root using rule (1). Then we can use rules (2) and (3) to compute the *pos*-attributes of all other nodes from above. We obtain the (partially) attributed tree of Figure 3. The "information flow" is indicated by arrows.

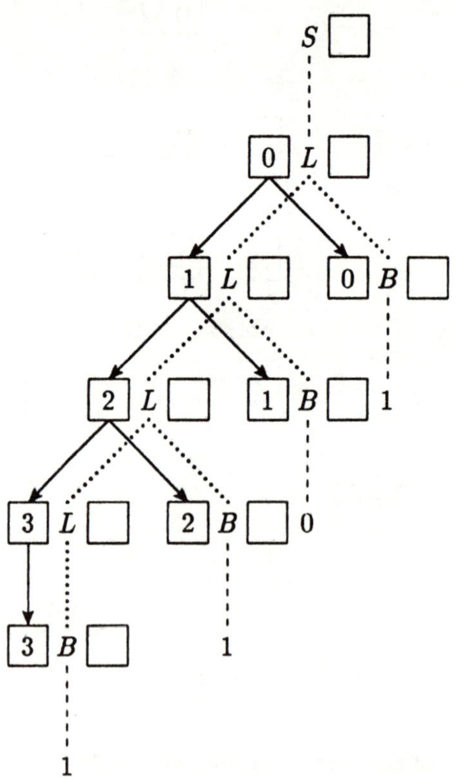

Fig. 3.

Next, using rule (4), the *value*-attributes of nodes labelled with B are determined. Flow of information is from left to right (see Figure 4). Finally, using rules (5), (6) and (7), the *value*-attributes of the other nodes are determined. This results in the

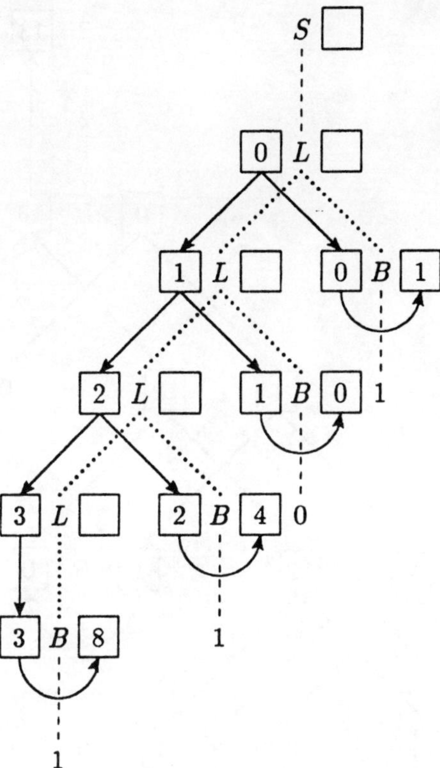

Fig. 4.

attributed tree of Figure 5 which also illustrates the information flow. The rules
to compute the attribute values relate the attribute values within one production.
It seems appropriate to specify these rules together with the grammar by adding
respective rules to each production of the grammar. We call these rules "semantic
rules" or "consistency conditions". Furthermore we express the rules more concisely
in the form of functions. For example we write rule (1) as $pos(L) == 0$. The double
equal symbol is to be read as "becomes". For our example we obtain the following
attribute grammar.

$$S \;\rightarrow\; L$$

$pos(L)$	$==$	0	rule (1)
$value(S)$	$==$	$value(L)$	rule (7)

$$L \;\rightarrow\; LB$$

$pos(L_2)$	$==$	$pos(L_1) + 1$	rule (2)
$pos(B)$	$==$	$pos(L_1)$	rule (2)
$value(L_1)$	$==$	$value(L_2) + value(B)$	rule (6)

$$L \;\rightarrow\; B$$

$pos(B)$	$==$	$pos(L)$	rule (3)
$value(L)$	$==$	$value(B)$	rule (5)

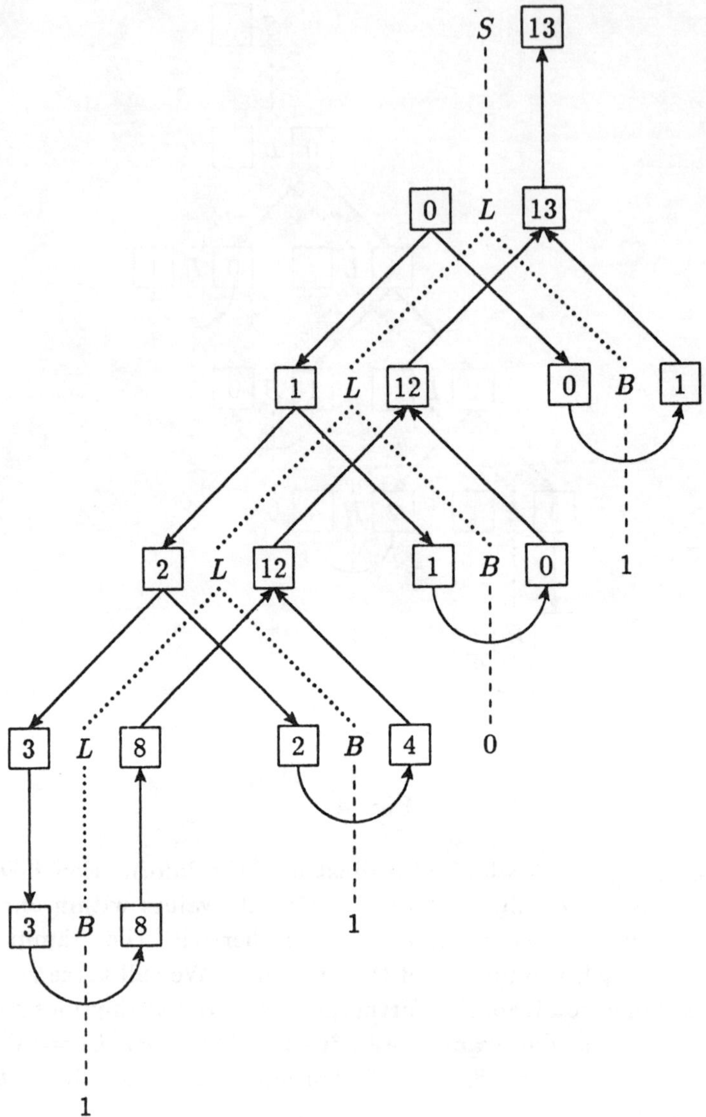

Fig. 5.

$$B \quad \rightarrow \quad 0$$
$$value(B) \quad == \quad 0 \cdot 2^{pos(B)} \qquad\qquad \text{rule (4)}$$

$$B \quad \rightarrow \quad 1$$
$$value(B) \quad == \quad 1 \cdot 2^{pos(B)} \qquad\qquad \text{rule (4)}$$

The semantic rules for production $L \rightarrow LB$ require more explanation. Since L occurs in $L \rightarrow LB$ twice we have numbered these occurrences from left to right. L_1 denotes the left occurrence and L_2 the right.

Leaving the example aside, we now abstract from the method sketched above. Let $G = (N, T, P, S)$ be a context-free grammar. Let Att be a set called the set of **attributes**. We associate with each attribute $a \in Att$ a set D_a called **domain** of attribute a, and with each $X \in N \cup T$ a set of attributes $Att(X) \subseteq Att$. Typical domains are the set $\{true, false\}$ of truth values, $\mathbb{N}^*, \Sigma^*, P(A, B)$. Furthermore we assume for each $X \in N \cup T$ a partitioning of $Att(X)$ into $S(X), I(X)$, i.e. $Att(X) = S(X) \cup I(X)$ and $S(X) \cap I(X) = \emptyset$. The attributes in $I(X)$ are called **inherited** attributes, the attributes in $S(X)$ are called **synthesised** or **derived** attributes of X. The names "inherited" and "derived" suggest how the attribute values for nodes are computed. Information flow for inherited attributes is top-down (from the ancestors to the descendants), information flow for derived attributes is bottom-up (from the descendants to the ancestors).

Example (continued):
We have $Att = \{pos, value\}$, $Att(L) = Att(B) = Att$, $Att(S) = \{value\}$, $Att(0) = Att(1) = \emptyset$. Furthermore $D_{pos} = D_{value} = \mathbb{N}_0$, $I(L) = I(B) = \{pos\}$, $S(L) = S(B) = S(S) = \{value\}$. ∎

Given a derivation tree (D, b) of a sentence of the language generated by G, an attribute annotation of this tree consists of an additional labelling, one for each attribute $a \in Att$. In other words, an **attribute annotation** consists of a family

$$val_a : D^{(a)} \to D_a, \ a \in Att$$

of labellings of the tree. Set

$$D^{(a)} = \{k \in D \mid a \in Att(b(k))\}$$

is the set of nodes which have an attribute a. For $k \in D^{(a)}$ we call $val_a(k)$ the **value of attribute** a at node k.

In our diagrams the values of attributes at node k are written in boxes. Boxes for inherited (derived) attributes are placed to the left (right) of the node.

Example (continued): In our example the attribute annotation comprises the functions val_{pos} and val_{value}. For a derivation tree (D, b) we have $D^{(value)} = D - \{k \in D \mid k$ is a leaf$\}$ and $D^{(pos)} = D^{(value)} - \{\epsilon\}$. The tables for the two functions are given by the boxes of the example derivation tree, e.g. $val_{pos}(111) = val_{pos}(1112) = 2$ and $val_{value}(1112) = 4$. ∎

An attribute annotation must satisfy the semantic rules specified in the attribute grammar. Semantic rules are specified for the smallest structural units of grammars, namely productions. They determine the relationships between the attribute values of different nodes of a derivation tree.

Example (continued): In our example we have for each "occurrence" of $L \to LB$ in a derivation tree, i.e. $b(k) = L$, $b(k1) = L$, $b(k2) = B$ for a node k:

$$val_{pos}(k1) = val_{pos}(k) + 1$$
$$val_{pos}(k2) = val_{pos}(k)$$
$$val_{value}(k) = val_{value}(k1) + val_{value}(k2)$$

or in form of a diagram:

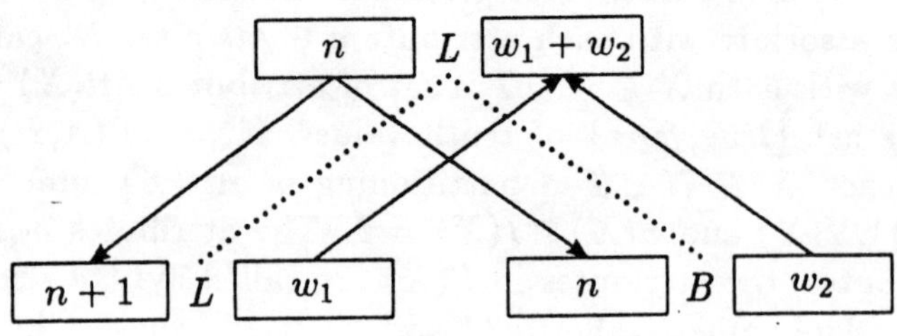

Fig. 6.

This diagram also shows the information flow within the rule.

These dependencies for production $L \to LB$ are specified by the following three semantic rules of the attribute grammar.

$$pos(L_2) == pos(L_1) + 1$$
$$pos(B) == pos(L_1)$$
$$value(L_1) == value(L_2) + value(B)$$

Rule $pos(L_2) == pos(L_1) + 1$, for example, states that $val_{pos}(k1)$ is given by $val_{pos}(k) + 1$ if production $L \to LB$ was applied in node k. Remember that L_2 (L_1) denotes the occurrence of L on the right (left) side of the production. Further note that there are semantic rules for each inherited attribute of a symbol on the right side $(pos(L_2)$ and $pos(B))$ and for each derived attribute on the left side $(value(L_1))$ of the production. This describes precisely the "information flow " within a rule (compare above diagram). In the case of inherited attributes information flow is top-down. For derived attributes the information flow is bottom-up.

Definition 1:
(a) Let $p = X_\epsilon \to X_1 X_2 \ldots X_n$ be a production of a context-free grammar (N, T, P, S) with $X_\epsilon \in N$, $X_1, \ldots, X_n \in N \cup T$, $n \geq 0$. Let furthermore Att be a set of attributes and $Att(X_j) \subseteq Att$ for $j \in \{\epsilon, 1, 2, \ldots, n\}$. A **semantic rule** for attribute a_{i_0} of X_{i_0} has the form

$$a_{i_0}(X_{i_0}) == f\left(a_{i_1}(X_{i_1}), \ldots, a_{i_m}(X_{i_m})\right)$$

where $m \geq 0$, $i_l \in \{\epsilon, 1, \ldots, n\}$, $a_{i_l} \in Att(X_{i_l})$, $0 \leq l \leq m$, and $f : D_{a_{i_1}} \times \ldots \times D_{a_{i_m}} \to D_{a_{i_0}}$ is a function. If $m = 0$ then f is an element in $D_{a_{i_0}}$.

Remark: In using the above general notation for productions $(X_\epsilon \to X_1 X_2 \ldots X_n)$, different occurrences of the same symbol of $N \cup T$ are distinguished by indices. In productions of an actual grammar (e.g. $L \to LB$) different occurrences are numbered from left to right.

(b) An **attribute grammar** AG consists of a context-free grammar $G = (N, T, P, S)$, a set Att of attributes, a domain D_a for each $a \in Att$, a partition $I(X), S(X)$ of $Att(X)$ for each $X \in N \cup T$ and a set of semantic rules for each production $p \in P$. More precisely, if $p = (X_\epsilon \to X_1 X_2 \ldots X_n)$ is a production then there is exactly one semantic rule for each derived attribute of X_ϵ and for each inherited attribute of $X_1, \ldots, X_n$.

(c) Let AG be an attribute grammar and (D, b) a derivation tree of a sentence with respect to the underlying context-free grammar. For $a \in Att$ let $D^{(a)} = \{k \in D \mid a \in Att(b(k))\}$. A family $val_a : D^{(a)} \to D_a$, $a \in Att$ of labellings of tree D is an **attribute annotation** with respect to AG if all semantic rules are satisfied, i.e. for each node $k \in D$ which is not a leaf the following holds. If $p = X_\epsilon \to X_1 X_2 \ldots X_n$ is the production used in node k and $a_{i_0}(X_{i_0}) == f(a_{i_1}(X_{i_1}), \ldots, a_{i_m}(X_{i_m}))$ is a semantic rule belonging to p, $m \geq 0$, $i_l \in \{\epsilon, 1, \ldots, n\}$, $a_{i_l} \in Att(X_{i_l})$ for $0 \leq l \leq m$, then $val_{a_{i_0}}(ki_0) = f(val_{a_{i_1}}(ki_1), \ldots, val_{a_{i_m}}(ki_m))$.   ∎

Example (continued):

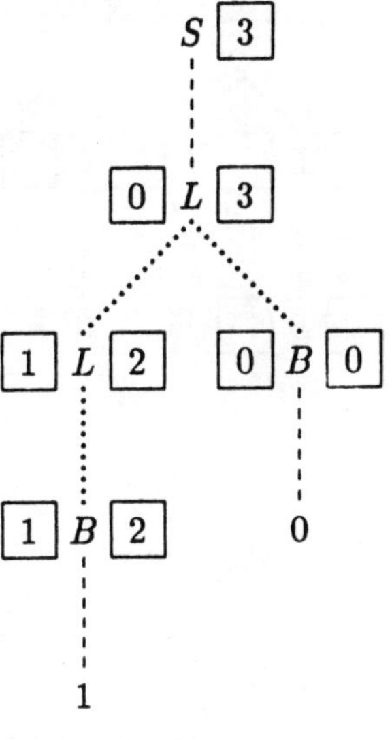

Fig. 7.

This is not an attribute annotation according to our attribute grammar since in node 1 the equality $val_{value}(1) = val_{value}(11) + val_{value}(12)$ does not hold, i.e. the semantic rule $value(L_1) == value(L_2) + value(B)$ is not satisfied in node 1.   ∎

We must now address the question of how to determine the attribute annotation of a derivation tree (D, b). To do that we will employ the methods from Section 1.5. Note that according to part (c) of Definition 1 an attribute annotation $val_a, a \in Att$ of a derivation tree (D, b) has to satisfy all semantic rules. These rules represent equations between attribute values at different nodes of the tree (D, b). An attribute annotation is thus a solution of this system of equations. The definition of attribute annotations follows closely the descriptive interpretation of a recursive definition.

A constructive interpretation is also possible. This is the reason why consistency conditions are also called attribute evaluation rules. Let (D, b) be a derivation tree. We start with totally undefined functions $val_a, a \in Att$. Informally, an empty box is established for each attribute $a \in Att$ and each node $k \in D^{(a)}$ Then the boxes are filled one by one.

Considering first semantic rules whose right side are constants we fill the respective boxes.

Example (continued): In our example it is the rule $pos(L) == 0$ for production $S \rightarrow L$. Accordingly after the first step we obtain a derivation tree from S to 10 (see Figure 8).

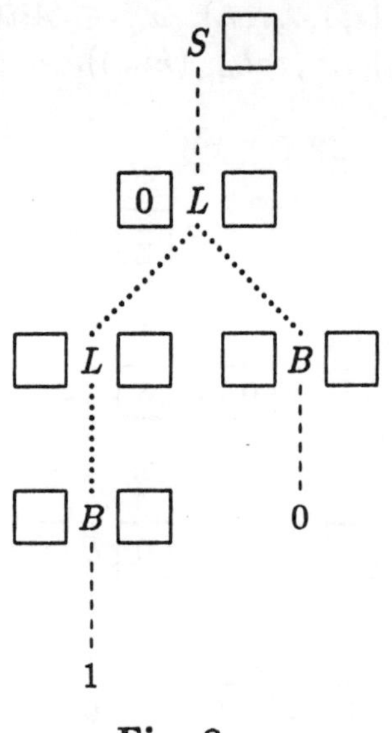

Fig. 8.

In the next step we consider the rules whose value on the left side can be computed and fill the respective boxes, etc.

Example (continued): The second step yields the partially annotated tree in Figure 9.

In this way we keep filling further boxes and thus determine an attribute annotation $val_a : D^{(a)} \rightarrow D_a, a \in Att$. We summarise this discussion in the following so-called **attribute evaluation algorithm.**

(1) Start with totally undefined functions $val_a : D^{(a)} \rightarrow D_a, a \in Att$

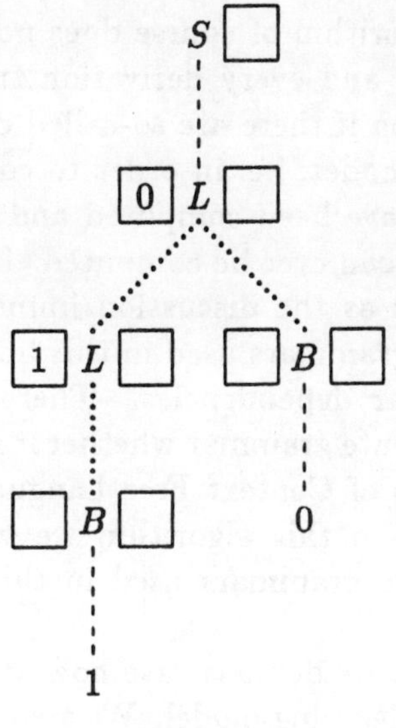

Fig. 9.

(2) Let $k \in D$ be a node and $p = (X_\epsilon \rightarrow X_1 \ldots X_n)$ the production used at node k. If $a_{i_0}(X_{i_0}) == f(a_{i_1}(X_{i_1}), \ldots, a_{i_m}(X_{i_m}))$ is a semantic rule for production p and values $val_{a_{i_1}}(ki_1), \ldots, val_{a_{i_m}}(ki_m)$ are defined, then $val_{a_{i_0}}(ki_0)$ is defined as $f(val_{a_{i_1}}(ki_1), \ldots, val_{a_{i_m}}(ki_m))$.

(3) Repeat step (2) until the attribute annotation does not change.

Section 1.5 ensures that the functions val_a, $a \in Att$ determined by the attribute evaluation algorithm satisfy all semantic rules. The name "attribute annotation" for functions val_a, $a \in Att$, is therefore justified. Furthermore it can be easily shown that there is precisely one attribute annotation of the tree (D, b) if the attribute evaluation algorithm leads to total functions val_a, $a \in Att$. In this case, therefore, the attribute annotation is unique. The following theorem summarises the discussion.

Theorem 1. *Let AG be an attribute grammar and (D, b) a derivation tree with respect to the underlying context-free grammar. If the attribute evaluation algorithm leads to total functions val_a, $a \in Att$ then there exists precisely one attribute annotation of the tree (D, b).*

Proof: Follows immediately from the discussion above.   ∎

Example (continued):   In the attribute grammar of the example functions val_{pos} and val_{value} are always total, since for each derivation tree we can first compute val_{pos} in a top down traversal of the tree and then in a second bottom up traversal val_{value}.   ∎

The attribute evaluation algorithm of course does not lead to total functions val_a for every attribute grammar and every derivation tree. In particular, it yields a non-total attribute annotation if there are so-called circular dependencies between attribute values at different nodes, i.e. in order to compute attribute a at node k, attribute b at node l must have been computed and vice versa. Obviously in this case none of those attributes can ever be computed. In our example grammar there are no circular dependencies as the discussion immediately following Theorem 1 indicates. For the attribute grammars used in this book a similar argument always shows the absence of circular dependencies. There even is an algorithm which decides for an arbitrary attribute grammar whether it is free of circular dependencies (see D. E. Knuth: Semantics of Context Free Languages, Math. system theory, 2, 27 (1986)). With reference to this algorithm we will claim absence of circular dependencies in the attribute grammars used in this book without proving it in each individual case.

To conclude this section, we demonstrate how attribute annotations can be illustrated by way of the so-called plug model. We associate with each nonterminal X two complementary plugs.

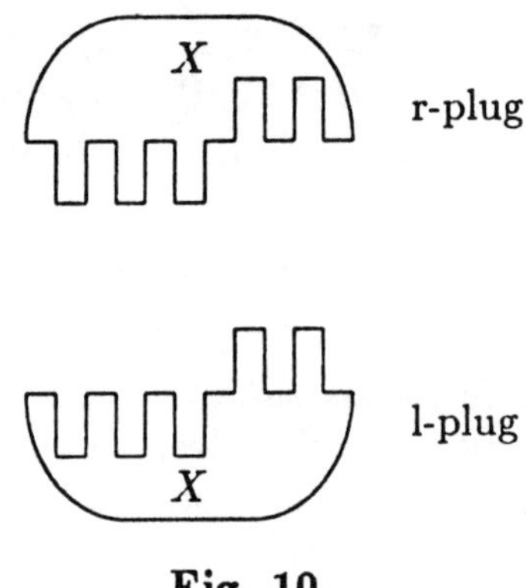

Fig. 10.

Inherited attributes occur as pins in an r-plug and as pin holes in an l-plug. For the derived attributes the reverse holds. Every occurrence of a nonterminal X on the right side of a production we draw as r-plug, each occurrence on the left side as l-plug.

Example (continued):
Furthermore the information flow through the production is illustrated by leads. Thus for example there are leads from $value(L_2)$, $value(B)$ to an adder $\oplus$ and from there to $value(L_1)$ (see Figure 11). Similarly, for production $B \rightarrow 1$ we obtain the diagram in Figure 12.
We can now "wire" a whole derivation tree (e.g. from S to 10) by plugging together the diagrams for the individual productions. Since l-plugs and r-plugs are complementary everything fits nicely.
This example shows how information, starting with the zero in attribute pos of the topmost L, spreads through the leads across the whole tree.   ∎

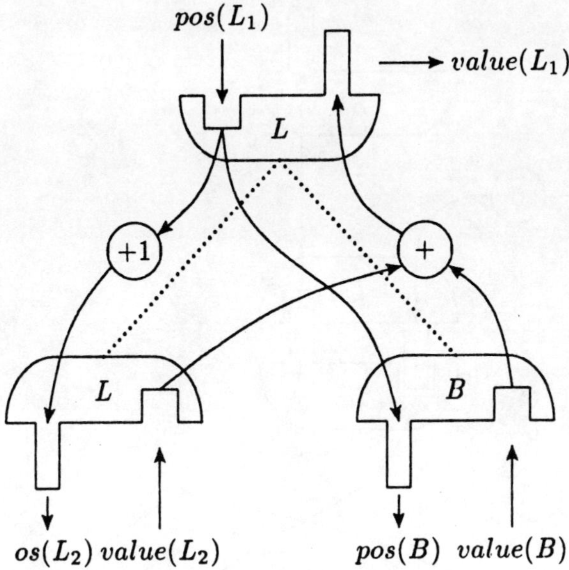

Fig. 11.

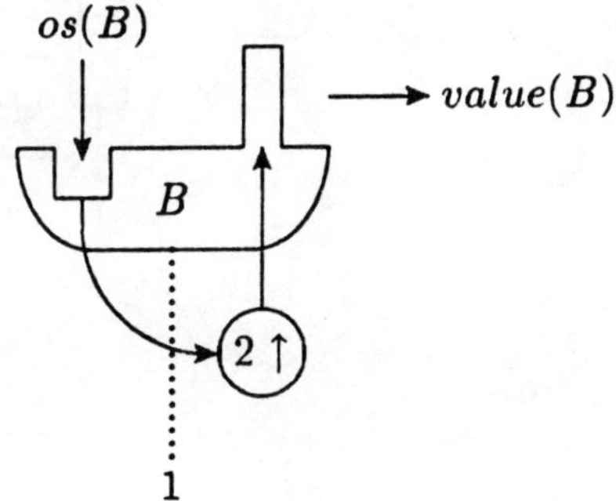

Fig. 12.

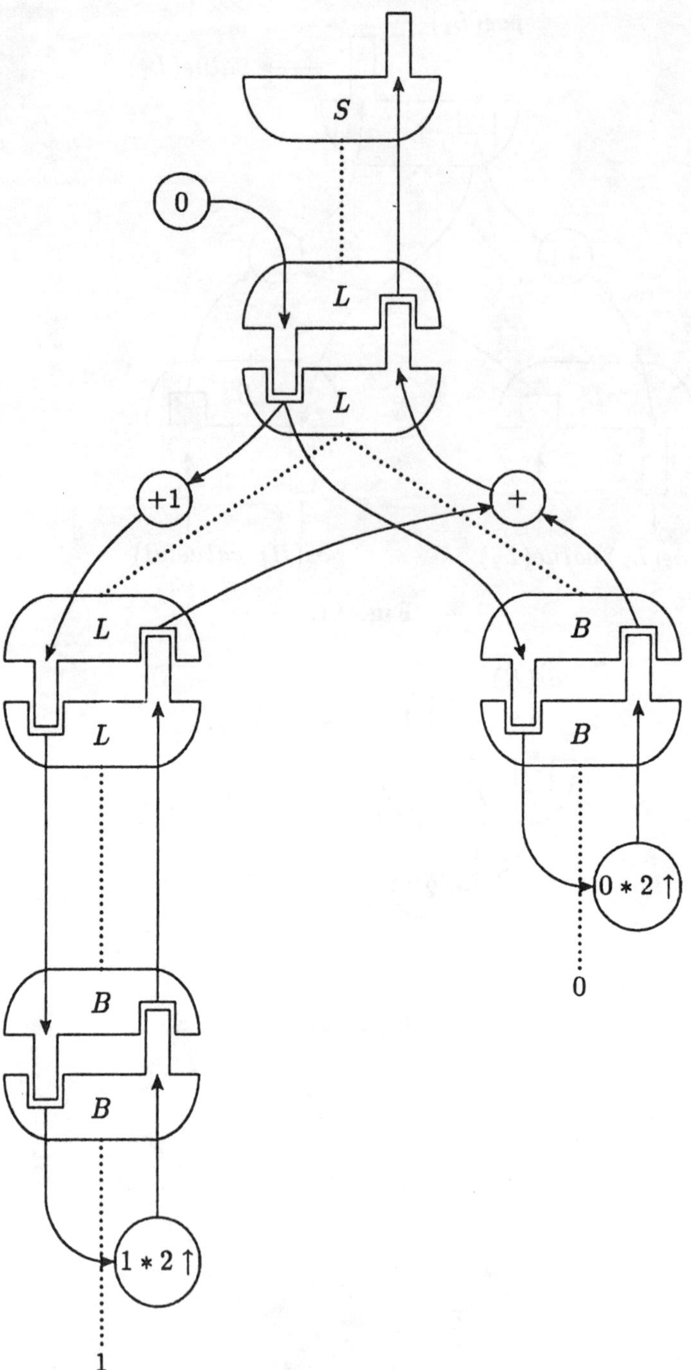

Fig. 13.

Exercises for 1.6

1) Consider the following context-free grammar with start symbol Z, productions

$$Z \rightarrow T.R$$
$$T \rightarrow TD|D$$
$$R \rightarrow RD|D$$
$$D \rightarrow 0|1|2|3|4|5|6|7|8|9$$

and terminals $0, 1, 2, 3, \ldots, 9$ as well as the dot symbol. The strings of the generated language correspond to the usual notation for real numbers. Specify an attribute grammar such that Z has an attribute *value* which is the real number denoted by the string derived from Z.

2) Let $L = \{a^i b^j c^k / i, j, k \geq 0\}$

    a) Give a context-free grammar G with $L = L_G$.

    b) Based on G, specify an attribute grammar such that for each $w \in L$ the root of the derivation tree for w has an attribute whose value is *true* if $i = j = k$ and *false* otherwise. Choose the range of attribute values and the operations on the attribute values yourself.

3) Specify for the example in this chapter an attribute grammar which only uses derived attributes. The semantic rule for $L \rightarrow LB$ could, for example, be of the form $value(L_1) == 2 \cdot value(L_2) + value(B)$.

1.7 Mathematical Machines

Mathematical machines are a fundamental concept in computer science and play a central role in the following chapters. Machines process inputs according to a program and produce outputs. Internally, a mathematical machine can assume a set of different states (we call these states the configurations of the machine) and operates as follows. The program together with the input determine the initial configuration. The machine now calculates in steps. In each step the machine moves, according to a transition function, into a new configuration. This takes place until no successor configuration exists. From the last configuration we then extract (if possible) the result of the computation. We will now give exact definitions and illustrate these by some examples. Since Section 1.7 should be read in parallel to Chapter II we will not elaborate on the examples. In Chapter II it will be indicated precisely which parts of this section must be known.

Definition 1: A (mathematical) machine M is an 8-tuple $M = (C, C^f, P, I, O, \delta, in, out)$ with

C	: set of **configurations**
P	: set of **programs**
I	: set of **inputs**
O	: set of **outputs**
$\delta : C \rightsquigarrow C$	: **transition function**
$C^f \subseteq C - Def(\delta)$	: set of **end configurations**
$in : P \times I \rightarrow C$	: **input function**
$out : C^f \rightarrow O$	: **output function**

A machine M is said to be **program-free** if $|P| = 1$. We then take as input function $in : I \rightarrow C$ and usually drop the program component P of the 8-tuple. ∎

How does such a machine operate? Mathematically, the behaviour of the machine is explained in terms of the sequence of configurations which it "traces". More precisely, for a program $p \in P$ and input $i \in I$ the machine starts in configuration $c_0 = in(p, i)$ called **start configuration**. It then operates according to the transition function δ, i.e. it goes through a sequence of configurations $c_0, c_1, c_2, \ldots$ with $c_{i+1} = \delta(c_i)$ for $i \geq 0$. We call this sequence a **computation** of program p for input i. Three cases may arise. Either the computation is infinitely long (it does not terminate), i.e. $c_i \in Def(\delta)$ for all $i \geq 0$, or it is of finite length (it terminates), i.e. there exists a t with $c_t \notin Def(\delta)$. In the second case either $c_t \notin C^f$ and the computation terminates with a run time error, or $c_t \in C^f$ and the computation terminates "successfully" (that is "normal" or "regular"). In the last case $out(c_t)$ is called the "result" of the computation and t the "computation time" (time-complexity, number of steps, length) of the computation. In the two other cases the computation produces no result and one says that its computation time is undefined. The precise definitions are as follows.

Definition 2:
Let $M = (C, C^f, P, I, O, \delta, in, out)$ be a mathematical machine.
(a) The function $comp_time_M : P \times I \rightsquigarrow \mathbb{N}_0$ is defined as

$$comp_time_M(p, i) = \begin{cases} t & \text{if } t \in \mathbb{N}_0 \text{ exists with } \delta^{(t)}(in(p, i)) \in C^f \\ \text{undefined} & \text{if no such } t \text{ exists} \end{cases}$$

Notation $\delta^{(t)}$ is defined by $\delta^{(0)}(c) = c$ and $\delta^{(i+1)}(c) = \delta^{(i)}(\delta(c))$ for all $i \in \mathbb{N}_0$ and all $c \in C$, i.e. $\delta^{(t)}$ denotes the t-fold application of δ. Notice that there is at most one t with $\delta^{(t)}(in(p, i)) \in C^f$ because C^f is a subset of $C - Def(\delta)$.

(b) For $p \in P$ the **input-output-behaviour** $I/O_M(p)$ — or I/O_M if $|P| = 1$ — of machine M with program p is a function

$$I/O_M(p) : I \rightsquigarrow O \text{ with } I/O_M(p)(i) =$$

$$\begin{cases} out\left(\delta^{(comp_time_M(p,i))}(in(p, i))\right) & \text{if } comp_time_M(p, i) \text{ is defined} \\ \text{undefined} & \text{otherwise.} \end{cases}$$

Informally speaking, the value $I/O_M(p)(i)$ is derived (using *out*) from the configuration which is obtained after $comp_time_M(p, i)$-fold application of δ to the start configuration $in(p, i)$. ∎

The input-output-behaviour $I/O_M(p)$ is the function computed by machine M under the control of program p mapping I into O. Program-free machines are special mechanisms to compute one single function. We will use program-free machines in Chapter II and general machines in the later chapters. Let us illustrate these definitions by two examples. The second is motivated by the last example in the introduction.

Example 1: We specify a machine which reads a pair of real numbers and then processes this pair according to a very simple program. A program for this machine is an arbitrary string in $\{T\}^*$. Each T in the program is executed, one by one. Executing an instruction T consists in dividing the first component of the pair by the second and then replacing the first by the result. If the second component is zero, the instruction can not be executed and the machine halts. Otherwise the next T is executed until all T's are processed. Then the first component of the pair is printed. The formal definition is as follows.

$$C = \{T\}^* \times \mathbb{R} \times \mathbb{R}$$

$$P = \{T\}^*$$

$$I = \mathbb{R} \times \mathbb{R}$$

$$O = \mathbb{R}$$

$\delta : C \rightsquigarrow C$ is defined as

$$\delta((p, x, y)) = \begin{cases} \text{undefined} & \text{if } p = \epsilon \text{ or } y = 0 \\ (p', x/y, y) & \text{if } p = Tp' \text{ and } y \neq 0 \end{cases}$$

$$\text{for all } (p, x, y) \in C$$

$$C^f = \{\epsilon\} \times \mathbb{R} \times \mathbb{R}$$

$$in(p, (x, y)) = (p, x, y) \qquad \text{for } p \in P \text{ and } (x, y) \in I$$

$$out(\epsilon, x, y) = x$$

For $x, y \in \mathbb{R}$ and $p = T^n \in P$ the computation according to program p for input $(x, y) \in I$ is the sequence (T^n, x, y), $(T^{n-1}, x/y, y)$, $(T^{n-2}, x/y^2, y)$, $\ldots$, $(T, x/y^{n-1}, y)$, $(\epsilon, x/y^n, y)$ if $y \neq 0$, and the sequence (T^n, x, y) if $y = 0$. Thus

$$comp_time_M(p, (x, y)) = \begin{cases} n & \text{if } p = T^n \text{ and } y \neq 0 \text{ or } n = 0 \\ \text{undefined} & \text{otherwise} \end{cases}$$

and therefore

$$I/O_M(T^n)((x, y)) = \begin{cases} x/y^n & \text{if } y \neq 0 \\ x & \text{if } y = 0 \text{ and } n = 0 \\ \text{undefined} & \text{if } y = 0 \text{ and } n > 0. \end{cases}$$

∎

Example 2:   Let the program-free machine $M_1 = (C, C^f, I, O, \delta_1, in, out)$ be given by

$$C = I = \mathbb{N} \times \mathbb{N}_0$$

$$C^f = \mathbb{N} \times \{0\}$$

$$\delta_1 : C \rightsquigarrow C \text{ with}$$

$$\delta_1((x,y)) = \begin{cases} (y, x \bmod y) & \text{if } y \neq 0 \\ \text{undefined} & \text{if } y = 0 \end{cases}$$

$$in : I \to C \text{ with } in((x,y)) = (x,y)$$

$$O = \mathbb{N}$$

$$out : C^f \to \mathbb{N} \text{ with } out((x,0)) = x$$

The computation for input $(18,4)$ is the sequence $(18,4)$, $(4,2)$, $(2,0)$. The output then is 2. We have shown in Claim 2 of the introduction that for all $(x,y) \in \mathbb{N} \times \mathbb{N}_0$:

$$comp_time_{M_1}((x,y)) \leq 2 + 2 \log y.$$

Furthermore $I/O_{M_1} : \mathbb{N} \times \mathbb{N}_0 \rightsquigarrow \mathbb{N}$ is the function $gcd : \mathbb{N} \times \mathbb{N}_0 \to \mathbb{N}$.   ∎

Very often we want to compare the capabilities of machines. The concept of simulation is important for this.

Definition 3: Let $M_i = (C_i, C_i{}^f, P_i, I, O, \delta_i, in_i, out_i)$, $i = 1, 2$, be two machines and $p_i \in P_i$ programs for M_i, $i = 1, 2$.

(a) A relation $R \subseteq C_1 \times C_2$ is called a **simulation** of machine M_1 with program p_1 on machine M_2 with program p_2 if:
   (1) $(in_1(p_1, i), in_2(p_2, i)) \in R$ for all $i \in I$;
   (2) for all $(c_1, c_2) \in R$ with $c_1 \in Def(\delta_1)$ there exists $i > 0$ and $j \geq 0$ such that $(\delta_1{}^{(i)}(c_1), \delta_2{}^{(j)}(c_2)) \in R$;
   (3) $(c_1, c_2) \in R$ and $c_1 \in C_1{}^f$ implies $c_2 \in C_2{}^f$ and $out_1(c_1) = out_2(c_2)$.

(b) Machine M_2 **can simulate** machine M_1 if for each program $p_1 \in P_1$ there is a program $p_2 \in P_2$ such that there is a simulation of M_1 with p_1 on M_2 with p_2.

(c) A simulation is k-**restricted**, $k \in \mathbb{N}$, if it is always possible to choose $j \leq k \cdot i$ in condition (2) of the simulation. It is called **restricted** if it is k-restricted for some $k \in \mathbb{N}$.

(d) A relation R is a **bisimulation** between M_1 with p_1 and M_2 with p_2 if R is a simulation of M_1 with p_1 on M_2 with p_2 and also a simulation of M_2 with p_2 on M_1 with p_1.   ∎

Definition (3a) is based on the following idea. Consider M_1 with p_1 and M_2 with p_2 for some input i. According to condition (1) the machines begin in start configurations which correspond to each other. After a certain number of steps (not necessarily the same number) they are, by condition (2), again in corresponding configuration. If M_1 reaches an end state then also M_2, and they produce the same output according to condition (3). Definition (3c) states the following. The simulation of M_1 (with p_1) by M_2 (with p_2) is k-restricted if M_2 is at most k times slower than M_1. These ideas will be made more precise in Theorem 1 below. Before that we give another example.

Example 2 (continued): Let $M_2 = (C, C^f, I, O, \delta_2, in, out)$ be a program-free machine where $\delta_2 : C \to C$ is defined as

$$\delta_2((x, y)) = \begin{cases} (x - y, y) & \text{if } x \geq y > 0 \\ (y, x) & \text{if } y > x \\ \text{undefined} & \text{if } y = 0 \end{cases}$$

The computation for input $(18, 4)$ is the sequence $(18, 4)$, $(14, 4)$, $(10, 4)$, $(6, 4)$, $(2, 4)$, $(4, 2)$, $(2, 2)$, $(0, 2)$, $(2, 0)$. Machine M_2 behaves similarly to machine M_1 except that it "simulates" integer division by repeated subtraction. We now give a simulation in the sense of Definition 3. Let R be the identity relation on C, i.e. $R = \{(k, k) \mid k \in C\}$. This relation surely satisfies conditions (1) and (3). We now prove condition (2). For that purpose let $(x, y) \in Def(\delta_1)$ and thus $y > 0$. We choose $i = 1$ and $j = \lfloor x/y \rfloor + 1$ and show $\delta_1((x, y)) = \delta_2^{(j)}((x, y))$. If $x < y$ and therefore $j = 1$ we have $\delta_2((x, y)) = (y, x) = (y, x \bmod y) = \delta_1((x, y))$. If $x \geq y$ and thus $j \geq 2$ then

$$\begin{aligned} \delta_2^{(j)}((x, y)) &= \delta_2^{(j-1)}((x - y, y)) \\ &= \delta_2^{(j-k)}((x - ky, y)) \qquad \text{for all } k \leq \lfloor x/y \rfloor \\ &= \delta_2^{(1)}((x \bmod y, y)) \\ &= (y, x \bmod y) \end{aligned}$$

This proves condition (2). One can show that R is not restricted and that it is a bisimulation. ∎

Theorem 1. *Let M_1 and M_2 be mathematical machines and let p_i be a program for M_i, $i = 1, 2$.*

(a) If there is a simulation of M_1 with p_1 on M_2 with p_2 then

$$I/O_{M_1}(p_1) \sqsubseteq I/O_{M_2}(p_2)$$

(b) If there is a k-restricted simulation of M_1 with p_1 on M_2 with p_2 then, in addition,

$$comp_time_{M_2}(p_2, e) \leq k \cdot comp_time_{M_1}(p_1, e)$$

for all inputs $i \in Def(I/O_{M_1}(p_1))$.

(c) If there is a bisimulation between M_1 with p_1 and M_2 with p_2 then

$$I/O_{M_1}(p_1) = I/O_{M_2}(p_2).$$

Proof:

(a) Let $e \in Def(I/O_{M_1}(p_1))$ be arbitrary, $c_0 = in_1(p_1, e)$ and $t = comp_time_{M_1}(p_1, e)$. Let furthermore $c_0, c_1, \ldots, c_t$ with $c_{i+1} = \delta_1(c_i)$ for $0 \leq i \leq t$ be the computation of M_1 with p_1 for input e. Let $c_0', c_1', \ldots$ with $c_0' = in_2(p_2, e)$ be the — possibly infinite — computation of M_2 with p_2 for input e. Finally, let R be a simulation of M_1 with p_1 on M_2 with p_2.

Lemma 1. *For all i, $0 \leq i \leq comp_time_{M_1}(p_1, e)$, there exist $h \geq i$ and l such that $(c_h, c_l') \in R$.*

Proof: (by induction on i). For $i = 0$ the lemma holds with $h = 0$ and $l = 0$ since $(c_0, c_0') = (in_1(p_1, e), in_2(p_2, e)) \in R$ by condition (1) of Definition (3a). Suppose for some i, $0 \leq i \leq comp_time_{M_1}(p_1, e)$, there are $h \geq i$ and l such that $(c_h, c_l') \in R$. We now prove that the lemma holds for $i + 1$. For $h \geq i + 1$ this is obvious. If $h = i$ then, by condition (2) of Definition (3a), there exist $i_1 > 0$ and $i_2 \geq 0$ such that $(\delta_1^{(i_1)}(c_h), \delta_2^{(i_2)}(c_l')) \in R$. Because of $\delta_1^{(i_1)}(c_h) = c_{h+i_1}$ and $\delta_2^{(i_2)}(c_l') = c_{l+i_2}'$ the induction step is complete. $\blacksquare$

We now use the lemma with $i = comp_time_{M_1}(p_1, e)$. Then there exist $h \geq i$ (i.e. $h = i$) and l with $(c_i, c_l') \in R$. Because of $c_i \in C_1^f$ it follows that $c_l' \in C_2^f$ and $out_1(c_i) = out_2(c_l')$ by condition (3) of Definition (3a). Thus $I/O_{M_1}(p_1)(e) = I/O_{M_2}(p_2)(e)$.

(b) Arguing as above, we strengthen Lemma 1 to Lemma 2.

Lemma 2. *For all i, $0 \leq i \leq comp_time_{M_1}(p_1, e)$, there exists $h \geq i$ and $l \leq c \cdot h$ such that $(c_h, c_l') \in R$.*

Proof: The proof is analogous to the one above. We observe in addition that in the induction step one can choose $i_2 \leq c \cdot i_1$. Thus $l + i_2 \leq c \cdot i + c \cdot i_1 = c(i + i_1)$ since, by induction hypothesis, $l \leq c \cdot i$. $\blacksquare$

Claim (b) of the theorem then follows immediately from Lemma 2.

(c) Let R be a bisimulation. Then R is a simulation of M_1 with p_1 on M_2 with p_2 and thus $I/O_{M_1}(p_1) \sqsubseteq I/O_{M_2}(p_2)$. Furthermore, R is a simulation of M_2 with p_2 on M_1 with p_1 and therefore $I/O_{M_2}(p_2) \sqsubseteq I/O_{M_1}(p_1)$. Together we conclude $I/O_{M_1}(p_1) = I/O_{M_2}(p_2)$. $\blacksquare$

Part (a) of Theorem 1 stated the following. If a machine M_2 with program p_2 simulates a machine M_1 with program p_1 then the I/O-behaviour of M_1 with p_1 is contained in the I/O-behaviour of M_2 with p_2. There may, of course, be inputs which can be processed by M_2 but not M_1. Part (b) states that if a simulation is k-restricted, the simulating machine is slower than the simulated machine by a factor k at most.

We now simplify the notation. For a machine $M = (\ldots, \delta, \ldots)$ we often write $c \underset{M}{\Rightarrow} c'$ instead of $\delta(c) = c'$, or even shorter $c \Rightarrow c'$. Then we can write a computations as

$$in(p, e) = c_0 \Rightarrow c_1 \Rightarrow c_2 \Rightarrow c_3 \Rightarrow \ldots$$

Here $\Rightarrow$ is a relation on the set of configurations. The transitive closure of $\Rightarrow$ is denoted as $\Rightarrow^*$.

The concept of simulation plays an important role in this book. We will use it frequently in the following situation. Let M_i, $i = 1, 2$, be mathematical machines and let $C : P_1 \to P_2$ be a mapping called translation or compilation. We now want to show that C preserves the semantics of programs, i.e.

$$I/O_{M_1}(p_1) = I/O_{M_2}(C(p_1))$$

for all $p_1 \in P_1$. To that end we only need to specify a bisimulation between M_1 with p_1 and M_2 with $C(p_1)$ for each $p_1 \in P_1$. In many applications we will have $M_1 = M_2$. In this case $C(p_1)$ will often be "simpler" in a certain sense than p_1.

Concluding the chapter we now introduce the **O-notation** to estimate the order of computation times. We saw in Example 2 that machine M_1 computed the greatest common divisor of two natural numbers n and m in time $2 + 2\log m$. The essential assertion is that the computation time is of logarithmic order in m. Whether it is $2 + 2\log m$ or $7 + 1.8\log m$ is of lesser interest for the moment. The mathematical short hand for "the computation time is of logarithmic order in m" is "the computation time is $O(\log m)$".

Definition 4: Let $f : \mathbb{N}_0 \to \mathbb{N}_0$ be a function. Then $O(f)$ denotes the following set of functions.

$$O(f) = \{g : \mathbb{N}_0 \to \mathbb{N}_0 \mid \exists\, c > 0 \; \exists\, n_0 : g(n) \leq cf(n) \text{ for all } n \geq n_0\}$$

It is customary to use the O-notation together with the equality symbol instead of membership relation $\in$ and containment relation $\subseteq$. Thus we write $n^2 + 5n = n^2 + O(n) = O(n^2)$ instead of $n^2 + 5n \in n^2 + O(n) \subseteq O(n^2)$. More precisely, if $\circ$ is an n-ary operation on functions, e.g. the binary operation $+$, and $A_1, \ldots, A_n$ are sets of functions then $\circ(A_1, \ldots, A_n)$ denotes the natural extension of the operation $\circ$, e.g. $A_1 + A_2 = \{a_1 + a_2 \mid a_1 \in A_1 \text{ and } a_2 \in A_2\}$. We identify singleton sets with their element. Expressions α and β containing O-notation then denote sets of functions. The notation $\alpha = \beta$ means $\alpha \subseteq \beta$. Equations which contain O-notation can therefore only be read *from left to right*. Hence, the members of a sequence $A_1 = A_2 = A_3 = \cdots = A_c$ stand for increasingly larger sets of functions. The imprecision of estimates grows from left to right.

Exercises for 1.7

1) Prove the following equations:

$$f(n) = O(f(n))$$
$$O(f(n)) + O(f(n)) = O(f(n))$$
$$c \cdot O(f(n)) = O(f(n))$$
$$O(f(n)) \cdot O(g(n)) = O(f(n) \cdot g(n))$$

2) Which of the following assertions are false?

$$2 + 2 \log n = O(\log n)$$
$$\log n = O(\ln n)$$
$$n^2 + O(n^{1.5}) = O(n^2)$$
$$2^n = O(3^n)$$
$$3^n = O(2^n)$$
$$2^n = O(n^7)$$

Chapter 2: **Expressions**

In this chapter we discuss arithmetic expressions such as $a_1 + a_2 \times a_3$. We will not only discuss classical notations known from elementary mathematics but also special forms — e.g. fully parenthesised expressions, bracket-free notation — especially suited to mechanical processing.

We begin with fully parenthesised expressions. The order of operations in these expressions is completely determined by brackets; a typical example is $(a_1 + (a_2 \times a_3))$. First of all we define their semantics, i.e. the value represented by expressions. This is done in two ways: algebraically and algorithmically. We have already met the algebraic method of definition in Section 1.5 in the context of the "descriptive interpretation". The algorithmic definition is given using a simple mathematical machine which evaluates expressions. This definition is related to the "algorithmic interpretation" in Section 1.5. The first central assertion of the chapter is the equivalence of both approaches. We also illustrate to what extent this machine recognises the syntactic structure of the expressions to be evaluated. We then introduce the concept of compilation or translation, i.e. the meaning preserving transformation of a formal language into another language. We show how fully parenthesised expressions can be transformed into unique bracket-free notation. Finally we compare different approaches to algorithmic definition and in this way illustrate the concept of simulation.

Fully parenthesised expressions are too restrictive to be of practical use. Partially parenthesised expressions with precedence — as for example $a_1 + a_2 \times a_3$ — are commonly used, for instance, in mathematics and in most programming languages. Therefore we repeat essential parts of the discussion for this important notation in Section 2.2.

2.1 Fully Parenthesised Expressions

In this section we consider expressions with **operands** in $M = \{a_1, a_2, \ldots, a_n\}$ and **operators** in $\{+, -, \times, /\}$. Here $n \geq 1$ is an arbitrary, but fixed, natural number.

To be more exact, *fully parenthesised expressions*, or *F-expressions* for short, are defined by the following context-free grammar.

$$G_f = (\{A\}, T_f, P_f, A) \text{ with}$$
$$T_f = M \cup \{+, -, \times, /, (,)\}$$
$$P_f = \{A \rightarrow a_1 \,|\, a_2 \,|\, \ldots \,|\, a_n \,|\, (A + A) \,|\, (A - A) \,|\, (A \times A) \,|\, (A/A)\}$$

Sentences of the generated language L_{G_f} —i.e. the expressions—are said to be fully parenthesised because the structure of subexpressions is completely "described" by brackets. A typical sentence of L_{G_f} is $((a_1 + a_2) \times (a_3 + a_1))$ with the derivation tree as in Figure 1.

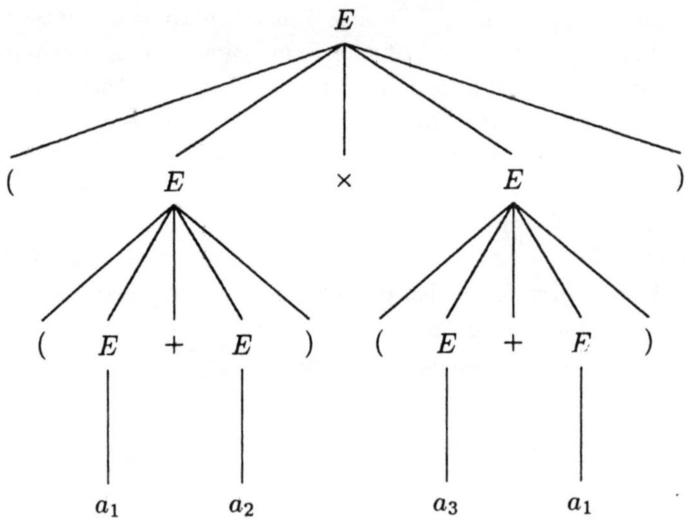

Fig. 1.

This example shows clearly that the brackets correspond to the form of the derivation tree. The grammar G_f is (for the most part) already familiar to us from Sections 1.4 and 1.5. (grammar G_4 of Example 4, Section 1.4). Again we have

Theorem 1. *The context-free grammar G_f is unambiguous.*

Proof: Similar to Lemma 3 in Section 1.4.   ∎

The F-expressions thus introduced are, for the moment, only strings without meaning. Yet we all connect some meaning with expressions. If the elements of the operand set M are replaced by numbers, then an expression yields a value. Our first task, therefore, is to capture this meaning of expressions precisely.

2.1.1 Algebraic and Algorithmic Semantics

First of all we give meaning to operators and operands.

For the operators $+, -, \times, /$ we choose their "standard interpretation".

$$
\begin{array}{lll}
+ & \text{stands for} & add : R \times R \to R \\
- & \text{stands for} & sub : R \times R \to R \\
\times & \text{stands for} & mul : R \times R \to R \\
/ & \text{stands for} & div : R \times R \to R
\end{array}
$$

R denotes the set of real numbers extended by the "error element" $error$, i.e. $R = \mathbb{R} \cup \{error\}$. Furthermore add, sub, mul, div are the usual operations of addition, subtraction, multiplication and division. The following holds: $div(x, 0) = error$ for all $x \in \mathbb{R}$ and $Op(error, x) = Op(x, error) = error$ for all $x \in R$ and all four operations $Op \in \{add, mul, sub, div\}$. It is very important in the sequel to differentiate between a symbol and the meaning of a symbol. Thus in expressions $+, -, \times, /$ are (operator) symbols. The meaning of these symbols are the 2-place functions add, sub, mul and div. If $op \in \{+, -, \times, /\}$ we write $Op \in \{add, mul, sub, div\}$ for the meaning of op. This explicit distinction between symbols and their meaning is often omitted in mathematics. In computer science, however, it is absolutely necessary because it must be possible to consider $+$ as a symbol (if, for example, we want to determine the number of operators in an expression) or as addition (if we want to evaluate the expression).

We define the meaning of operands by way of a function $b : M \to \mathbb{R}$ called **assignment**. b associates with each operand symbol $a \in M$ a real number $b(a)$.

Extending the meaning of operators and operands, we define the meaning of F-expressions as a function $I_f(b)$. This notation shows explicitly the dependence on the assignment of the operands.

Definition 1 (Algebraic Definition of Semantics): Let $b : M \to \mathbb{R}$ be an assignment. The **(algebraic) interpretation** $I_f(b) : L_{G_f} \to R$ of F-expressions is recursively defined as

$$
I_f(b)(w) = \begin{cases}
b(w) & \text{if } w \in M \\
Op(I_f(b)(w_1), I_f(b)(w_2)) & \text{if } w = (w_1 \; op \; w_2), \; w_1, w_2 \in L_{G_f} \\
& \qquad \text{and } op \in \{+, -, \times, /\}
\end{cases}
$$

$\blacksquare$

Note that the value of $I_f(b)$ is in $R = \mathbb{R} \cup \{error\}$ but the value of b in $\mathbb{R}$.

Theorem 2. *The recursive definition above specifies a total function $I_f(b)$ from L_{G_f} to R.*

Proof: The claim follows immediately using the methods developed in Section 1.5.

∎

Example 1:   Let $n = 3$ and $b(a_1) = 2$, $b(a_2) = 3$, $b(a_3) = 7$. Then

$$
\begin{aligned}
I_f(b)&(((a_1 + a_2) \times (a_3 + a_1))) \\
&= mul(I_f(b)((a_1 + a_2)), I_f(b)((a_3 + a_1))) \\
&= mul(add(I_f(b)(a_1), I_f(b)(a_2)), add(I_f(b)(a_3), I_f(b)(a_1))) \\
&= mul(add(2,3), add(7,2)) \\
&= mul(5,9) \\
&= 45
\end{aligned}
$$

∎

A note on notation. In the above sequence of equations we have used the symbols '(' and ')' in two ways. Firstly, '(' and ')' are terminals of the grammar G_f. Secondly, '(' and ')' are symbols of the "metalanguage"(i.e. English + mathematical notation) which we use to talk about expressions. For example:

$$
\begin{array}{l}
\text{symbols of the metalanguage} \\
\downarrow \downarrow\downarrow \qquad\qquad\qquad\quad \downarrow \\
I_f(b)(((a_1 + a_2)\times(a_3 + a_1))) \\
\quad \uparrow\uparrow \qquad \uparrow\ \uparrow \qquad\quad \uparrow\uparrow \\
\text{symbols of the grammar } G_f
\end{array}
$$

In our first discussion of expressions in Example 4, Section 1.4 we have made this difference typographically visible by using different letters (namely [and] for grammar terminals). However, it is usual not to make the difference explicit and we want the reader to become accustomed to this practice.

The algebraic definition of the semantics of expressions is very elegant and expressive. In practice, however, it is by no means trivial to recognise a long expression such as

$$((a_1 + (((a_1 + a_2) \times (a_1 + (a_3/a_1))) + ((a_1 + a_3) + (a_1 \times a_3)))) + a_4)$$

as an expression of the form $(w_1 + w_2)$. Algebraic definition thus presumes the evaluator to have non-trivial capabilities.

In the following algorithmic definition of the semantics of expressions lesser skills are required. For the most part only the ability to recognise terminals is necessary. The basic idea of algorithmic definition is as follows.

The expression is read, symbol by symbol, from left to right until the first closing bracket is encountered. Of necessity the last five symbols read are a string of the form $(x_1\ op\ x_2)$, where $op \in \{+, -, \times, /\}$. We can now replace this expression by its value and thus obtain a *smaller* expression. We apply the same procedure to this expression and thus obtain, finally, the value of the expression. When reading the expression it is not necessary to start at the beginning again. Rather one can continue at the point of replacement as there is no closing bracket to the left of it. The procedure is illustrated by the following example.

Example (continued): We read the expression $((a_1 + a_2) \times (a_3 + a_1))$ from left to right. Opening brackets are skipped. Encountered operands and operators are stored whilst replacing operands by their value according to the given assignment b. The store, called the **stack**, permits only very limited access. (One has to imagine the stack as a tube, closed at the bottom, and the elements to be stored as discs having the same diameter. Writing an element into the stack means inserting a disc corresponding to the element; deleting an element from the stack consists in removing the uppermost disc from the tube). When we read a closing bracket a subexpression is evaluated. Both operands and the operator are ready at the top of the stack. The result is stored in the stack. In the following illustrations the part of the expression not yet read is to the right of the stack. Symbol "$\Rightarrow$" indicates the reading of a symbol of the expression.

$((a_1 + a_2) \times (a_3 + a_1))$ $\Rightarrow$ $(a_1 + a_2) \times (a_3 + a_1)$ $\Rightarrow$ $a_1 + a_2) \times (a_3 + a_1)$

$\Rightarrow$ $+a_2) \times (a_3 + a_1)$ (stack: 2) $\Rightarrow$ $a_2) \times (a_3 + a_1)$ (stack: 2, +) $\Rightarrow$ $) \times (a_3 + a_1)$ (stack: 2, +, 3)

$\Rightarrow$ $\times (a_3 + a_1)$ (stack: 5) $\Rightarrow$ $(a_3 + a_1)$ (stack: 5, ×) $\Rightarrow$ $a_3 + a_1)$ (stack: 5, ×) $\Rightarrow$ $+a_1)$ (stack: 5, ×, 7)

$\Rightarrow$ $a_1)$ (stack: 5, ×, 7, +) $\Rightarrow$ $)$ (stack: 5, ×, 7, +, 2) $\Rightarrow$ (stack: 5, ×, 9) $\Rightarrow$ (stack: 45)

At the end of the computation the stack contains the value of the expression.

Formally, the algorithmic definition of the semantics of F-expressions is a mathematical machine called a **stack machine**. It specifies precisely the method indicated above. At this point the reader should study Section 1.7 up to Definition 3. The stack machine M_f is a program-free machine

$$M_f = (C, C^f, L_{G_f}, R, \delta, in, out)$$

with $C = (R \cup \{+, -, \times, /\})^* \times T_f^*$. A configuration thus consists of a pair (c^1, c^2). c^1 represents the stack contents and c^2 the rest of the expression. Given input $w \in L_{G_f}$ we start the machine in configuration (ϵ, w), i.e. $in(w) = (\epsilon, w)$. The transition function δ is given by the following table and corresponds to the case distinction according to the encountered input symbol as illustrated in the example above. c^1, c^2, h^1 and h^2 are defined by $\delta((c^1, c^2)) = (h^1, h^2)$. In addition, α stands for an arbitrary string in $(R \cup \{+, -, \times, /\})^*$ and x for an arbitrary string in T_f^*.

c^1	c^2	h^1	h^2	comment
α	$(x$	α	x	opening brackets are skipped
α	$a\ x$	$\alpha\ b(a)$	x	the values of operands are pushed onto stack
α	$op\ x$	$\alpha\ op$	x	operators are pushed onto stack
$\alpha\ m_1\ op\ m_2$	$)\ x$	$\alpha\ Op(m_1, m_2)$	x	closing brackets lead to evaluation of subexpressions

Note that the transition function δ is partial. On the one hand, each configuration $c = (c^1, c^2) \in C$ corresponds to at most one line of the table. Thus δ is well defined. On the other hand, δ is not defined for all configurations. In particular, if the rest-expression c^2 begins with symbol ")" then δ is well defined only if the three topmost stack symbols are two real numbers separated by an operation symbol. End configurations are characterised by an empty rest-expression and single element stacks, i.e. $C^f = R \times \{\epsilon\}$. Note that C^f and $Def(\delta)$ are disjoint — as required in Definition 1 of Section 1.7. Finally, $out((m, \epsilon)) = m$. The input-output behaviour of M depends of course on the assignment b. Hence we write $I/O_{M_f}(b)$ for the behaviour of M_f. $I/O_{M_f}(b)$ is by definition the **algorithmic interpretation** of F-expressions. We will show in Theorem 3 that this algorithmic interpretation is equivalent to the algebraic interpretation in Definition 1.

Example (continued): For input $w = ((a_1 + a_2) \times (a_3 + a_1))$ the start configuration is (ϵ, w). Given the assignment b as defined above and using the notation "$\Rightarrow$" introduced at the end of Section 1.7, the computation of M_f is as follows.

$$(\epsilon, ((a_1 + a_2) \times (a_3 + a_1))) \qquad \Rightarrow \quad (\epsilon, (a_1 + a_2) \times (a_3 + a_1)))$$
$$\Rightarrow \quad (\epsilon, a_1 + a_2) \times (a_3 + a_1))) \qquad \Rightarrow \quad (2, +a_2) \times (a_3 + a_1)))$$
$$\Rightarrow \qquad \ldots \qquad\qquad\qquad \Rightarrow \quad (45, \epsilon)$$

Thus $I/O_{M_f}(b)(x) = 45$. ∎

Theorem 3. *(Equivalence of algorithmic and algebraic interpretation of F-expressions)*
For all F-expressions $w \in L_{G_f}$ and all assignments $b \in \mathbb{R}^M$:

$$I_f(b)(w) \; = \; I/O_{M_f}(b)(w)$$

where I_f is the interpretation of Definition 1 and M_f is the stack machine introduced above.

Proof: Basically, the proof is by structural induction. First of all, however, we have to prove a more general assertion.

Lemma 1. Let $b \in \mathbb{R}^M$ be an assignment, $w \in L_{G_f}$, $y \in T_f^*$ and $\alpha \in (R \cup \{+,-,\times,/\})^*$. Then

$$(\alpha, \; wy) \Rightarrow^* (\alpha I_f(b)(w), \; y)$$

("$\Rightarrow^*$" is the notation introduced at the end of Section 1.7.)

Proof: The proof is by induction on the length of w.

If $|w| = 1$ then $w \in M$ and thus $(\alpha, \; wy) \Rightarrow (\alpha b(w), \; y)$, by definition of M_f. Because of $b(w) = I_f(b)(w)$ for $w \in M$ the claim holds.

If $|w| > 1$ then w can be uniquely written as $w = (w_1 \; op \; w_2)$ with $w_1, w_2 \in L_{G_f}$ and $op \in \{+,-,\times,/\}$. Furthermore the induction hypothesis states that for all $u \in L_{G_f}$, $|u| < |w|$, $z \in T_f^*$ and $\beta \in (R \cup \{+,-,\times,/\})^*$:

$$(\beta, uz) \Rightarrow^* (\beta I_f(b)(u), z)$$

Thus
$$(\alpha, \; (w_1 \; op \; w_2)y)$$

$\Rightarrow$	$(\alpha, \; w_1 \; op \; w_2)y)$	definition of δ
$\Rightarrow^*$	$(\alpha I_f(b)(w_1), \; op \; w_2)y)$	induction hypothesis
		with $\beta = \alpha, \; u = w_1, \; z = op \; w_2)y$
$\Rightarrow$	$(\alpha I_f(b)(w_1)op, \; w_2)y)$	definition of δ
$\Rightarrow^*$	$(\alpha I_f(b)(w_1) \; op \; I_f(b)(w_2), \;)y)$	induction hypothesis
		with $\beta = \alpha I_f(b)(w_1)op, \; u = w_2, \; z =)y$
$\Rightarrow$	$(\alpha Op(I_f(b)(w_1), \; I_f(b)(w_2)), \; y)$	definition of δ

Since $I_f(b)(w) = Op(I_f(b)(w_1), I_f(b)(w_2))$ the induction step is complete. ∎

The theorem now follows quite easily. The start configuration of M_f for input $w \in L_{G_f}$ is (ϵ, w). By Lemma 1 with $y = \epsilon$ and $\alpha = \epsilon$

$$(\epsilon, w) \Rightarrow^* (I_f(b)(w), \epsilon)$$

Since $(I_f(b)(w), \; \epsilon) \in C^f$ and $out((I_f(b)(w), \; \epsilon)) = I_f(b)(w)$ we have

$$I/O_{M_f}(b)(w) = I_f(b)(w)$$

∎

We add a simple assertion about the computation time of M_f.

Theorem 4. $comp_time_{M_f}(w) = |w|$ for all $w \in L_{G_f}$

Proof: The start configuration of M_f for input w is (ϵ, w). At every transition, i.e. at every application of the transition function δ, a symbol of w is read and at the end w is consumed completely. Thus the computation time is exactly $|w|$.   ∎

Theorems 3 and 4 state, firstly, that the algorithmic definition of the semantics is equivalent to the algebraic definition and, secondly, that the stack machine M_f computes the value of an expression in linear time i.e. the computation time is linear in the length of the expression. We now illustrate a connection to syntax analysis. Syntax analysis refers to methods to determine derivation trees.

Example (continued): The derivation tree for expression $w = ((a_1 + a_2) \times (a_3 + a_1))$ according to grammar G_f is shown in Figure 2.

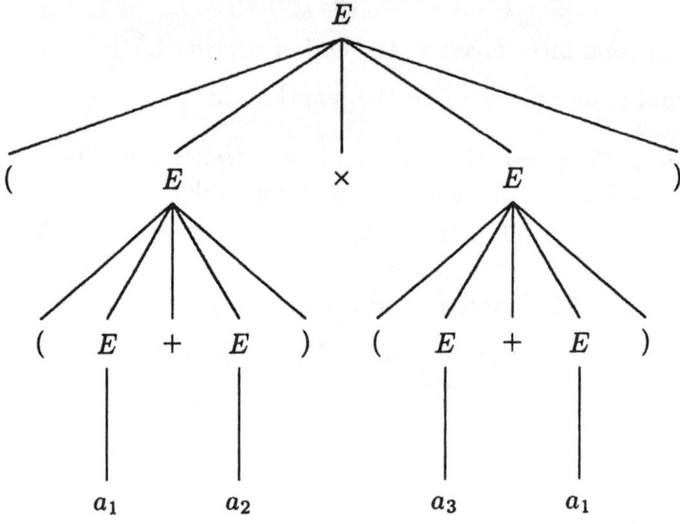

Fig. 2.

Now let us consider in which sense the stack machine M_f recognises the structure of this tree. M_f replaces operands $a_i \in M$, $1 \leq i \leq 3$ by their value $b(a_i)$. We can also say: it recognises the application of productions $A \to a_1 \mid a_2 \mid a_3$. We could even integrate this observation into the mode of operation of M_f by writing derivation trees instead of numbers into the stack. After reading the beginning of the expression $((a_1$ the tree

would be in the stack (instead of the number $b(a_1)$).
After reading $+$ and a_2 the three trees

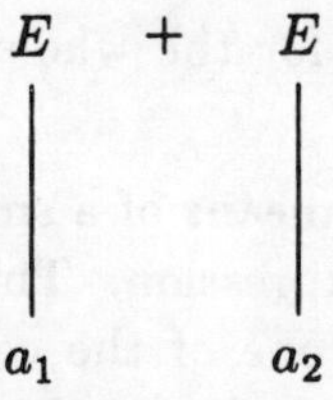

Fig. 3.

are in the stack. The left tree is at the bottom of the stack. On top of it is the central tree consisting only of a node labelled +. Finally, the right-hand tree is at the top of the stack. The machine now reads a closing bracket and in this way recognises a subexpression. It records this in the stack by taking the three topmost trees in the stack, "linking" them according to production $A \rightarrow (A + A)$. Now there is only one tree in the stack, namely

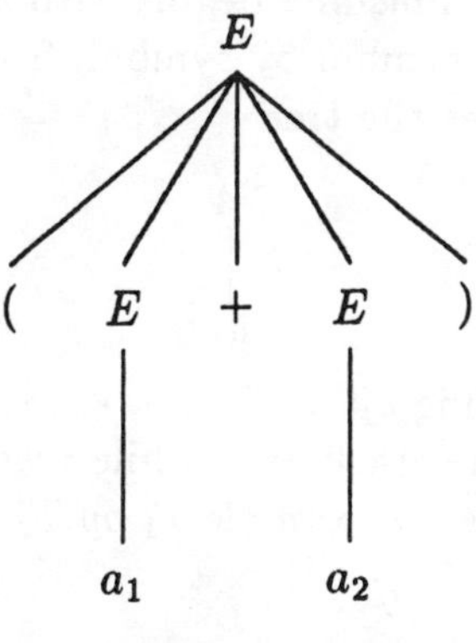

Fig. 4.

The machine continues to read the expression. Immediately after reading the second occurrence of a_1 there are five trees in the stack. Apart from the derivation tree from A to $(a_1 + a_2)$ these are the four trees

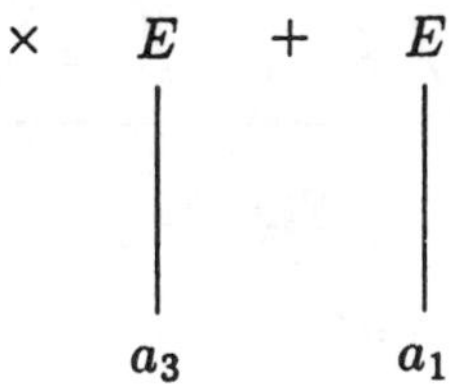

Fig. 5.

Reading the second last closing bracket prompts M_f to take the three topmost trees from the stack and to link them again according to production $A \rightarrow (A+A)$. Then there are only three trees in the stack, the top one of which is the derivation tree from A to $(a_3 + a_1)$. On reading the last closing bracket, M_f finally constructs in a similar way the derivation tree for the whole expression which is the only tree remaining in the stack.

This example shows that, by means of a small alteration, M_f is able to "compute" the derivation tree of an expression. This connection between context-free grammars and stack machines is one of the central topics in the area of syntax analysis and is dealt with thoroughly in future courses.   ∎

Exercises for 2.1.1

1) (Syntax analysis for F-expressions)
We have just considered a stack machine for syntax analysis with respect to G_f. It operates as follows. The machine begins with an empty stack and then reads the input string $w \in L_{G_f}$, symbol by symbol, from left to right. While reading $a_i \in M$, $1 \le i \le n$, it writes the tree

into the stack. While reading $op \in \{+, -, \times, /\}$, it writes the tree op (this tree has only one node) into the stack and, while reading a closing bracket, it takes the three topmost elements for example T_1 op T_2, constructs from them the tree

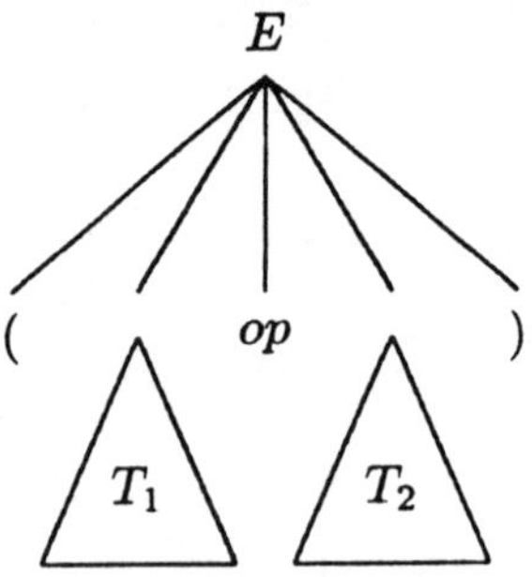

Fig. 6.

and writes this tree into the stack.

a) Determine the computation of this machine for inputs $((a_1 + a_2) + a_1)$ and $((a_1 + a_2) + (a_1 + ((a_3 + a_1) + a_1)))$.

b) Define the stack machine M_{sy} precisely. The configuration set C of this machine is, for example, $C = (\mathbf{B}_{\{A\} \cup T_f})^* \times T_f^*$, i.e. a configuration consists of a list of trees labelled with elements of $\{A\} \cup T_f$ and a rest expression. (Recall that $\mathbf{B}_{\{A\} \cup T_f}$ denotes the set of trees over $\{A\} \cup T_f$.)

c) Show that for all $w \in L_{G_f}$, $I/O_{M_{sy}}(w)$ is a derivation tree from A to w.

2.1.2 Translation into Polish Notation

Polish notation (after Lukasiewicz, a Polish logician) is a bracket-free notation for expressions. Polish notation is particularly suitable for mechanical evaluation (see Exercises 1 and 2 at the end of this section). It is worth while, therefore, to first transform F-expressions, which have to be evaluated frequently, into Polish notation. We will learn a method of doing this in this section.

Expressions in Polish notation are defined by the context-free grammar $G_p = (\{A\}, T_p, P_p, A)$ with

$$T_p = M \cup \{+, -, \times, /\}$$
$$P_p = \{A \rightarrow a_1 | a_2 | \ldots | a_n | AA + | AA - | AA \times | AA/\}.$$

Example (continued): $a_1 a_2 + a_3 a_1 + \times$ is an expression in Polish notation. The derivation tree for it is

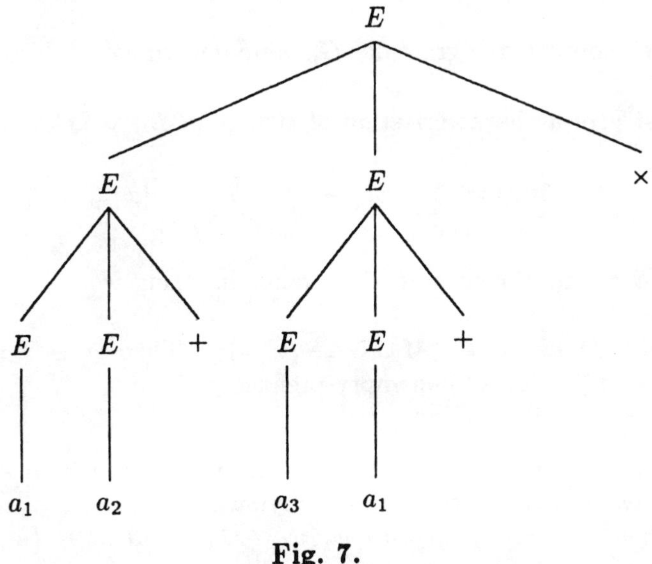

Fig. 7.

The derivation tree of an expression $w \in L_{G_p}$ can be constructed according to the following method. We read, from left to right, through the expression up to the first operation symbol. Then the two preceding symbols are necessarily in M. The expression consisting of these three symbols is replaced by its derivation tree and the procedure is repeated. Now, instead of operands, we may also have derivation trees. In the case of the above expression one obtains:

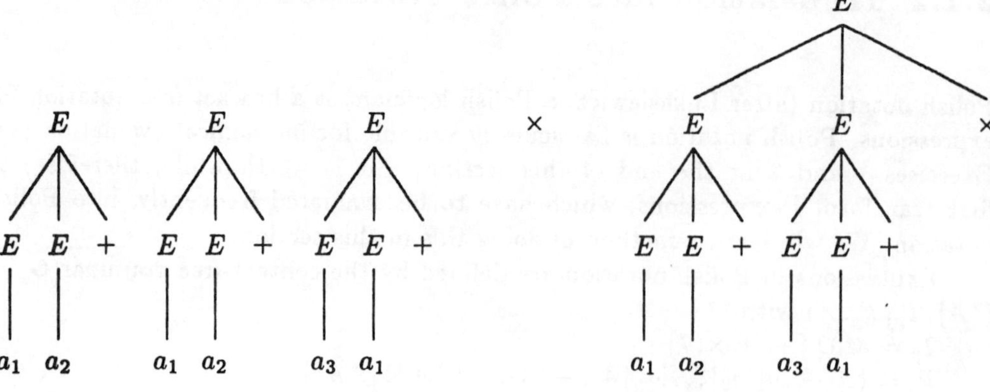

Fig. 8.

Lemma 2. *The context-free grammar G_p is unambiguous.*

Proof: We first give a characterisation of strings in L_{G_p}. Let $S : L_{G_p} \to \mathbb{N}_0$ be defined by

$$S(w) = \sum_{a \in M} |w|_a \; - \sum_{op \in \{+,-,/,\times\}} |w|_{op}$$

Thus function S counts the surplus of operands in string w.

Auxiliary claim 1: Let $w \in (M \cup \{+,-,\times,/\})^*$. Then $w \in L_{G_p}$ if and only if $S(w) = 1$ and $S(y) \geq 1$ for all nonempty prefixes y of w.

Proof:
"$\Rightarrow$":   We use induction on the depth h of a derivation tree from A to w.
For $h = 1$ we have $w = a$ and the claim is obvious.
Let $h > 1$. Then $w = w_1 w_2 \, op$ with $w_1, w_2 \in L_{G_p}$ and $op \in \{+,-,/,\times\}$. Furthermore w_1 and w_2 correspond to derivation trees of depth $< h$ and the induction hypothesis holds for w_1 and w_2. Thus $S(w) = S(w_1) + S(w_2) - 1 = 1 + 1 - 1 = 1$. Let now y be a nonempty proper prefix of w. Then y is either a prefix of w_1 and thus $S(y) \geq 1$ or $y = w_1 z$ where z is a nonempty prefix of w_2. Thus $S(y) = S(w_1) + S(z) \geq 1 + 1 \geq 1$. Hence in both cases $S(y) \geq 1$.

"$\Leftarrow$":   We use induction on the length of w. Because of $S(w) = 1$ we cannot have $|w| = 0$. Let now $|w| = 1$. Then $S(w) = 1$ implies $w \in M$ and thus $w \in L_{G_p}$. For the induction step we assume that $|w| > 1$. Since $S(w) = 1$ expression w can not consist of symbols of M (i.e. operands) only. Write $w = w_1 \, op \, w_2$ with $op \in \{+,-,/,\times\}$ and $w_1 \in M^*$. Because of $S(w_1 op) \geq 1$ it follows that $|w_1| \geq 2$. Thus $w_1 = z a_i a_j$ for some i and j with $a_i, a_j \in M$, and $z \in M^*$. Thus w is of the form $w = z a_i a_j \, op \, w_2$. Consider $w' = z a_1 w_2$ (instead of a_1 one could have used some other operand from M). Then $|w'| < |w|$, $S(w') = S(w) = 1$ and $S(y) \geq 1$

for each nonempty prefix y of w' (since $S(a_i a_j op) = S(a_1) = 1$). Thus $w' \in L_{G_p}$ by induction hypothesis and thus $w \in L_{G_p}$ also.   ∎

Auxiliary claim 2: Let $w \in L_{G_p}$, $w \neq a$. Then there are uniquely determined $w_1, w_2 \in L_{G_p}$ and $op \in \{+, -, /, \times\}$ such that $w = w_1 w_2 op$.

Proof: The existence of w_1 and w_2 is obvious. We only need to show the uniqueness of w_1 and w_2. Let $w = w_1 w_2 op = y_1 y_2 op$ with $w_1, w_2, y_1, y_2 \in L_{G_p}$ and $w_2 \neq y_2$. Let without loss of generality $|w_2| < |y_2|$. Then w_2 is a suffix of y_2, i.e. $y_2 = zw_2$ for some $z \neq \epsilon$. As z is a prefix of $y_2 \in L_{G_p}$, $S(z) \geq 1$. Furthermore $S(w_2) = 1$ and thus $S(y_2) \geq 2$ in contradiction to $S(y_2) = 1$. Thus the assumption $w_2 \neq y_2$ is refuted and the claim is shown.   ∎

Note that for the proof of the second claim only one direction of Auxiliary claim 1 was used. This observation is important for Exercises 2 and 3 at the end of this section.

With Auxiliary claim 2 it is now easy to show that G_p is unambiguous. We show by induction on $|w|$ that there is only one derivation tree from A to $w \in L_{G_p}$. For $|w| = 1$ and thus $w = a_i$ for some i, $1 \leq i \leq n$, this is obvious. Let now $|w| > 1$ and let (D, b) be a derivation tree from A to w. Then at the root production $A \to AA\ op$ must be used where op is the last symbol of w. Let now $(D_i, b_i) = subtree\ ((D, b), (i))$, $i = 1, 2$ and let $w_1, w_2 \in L_{G_p}$ be the uniquely defined strings according to Auxiliary claim 2 with $w = w_1 w_2 op$. Then (D_i, b_i) is a derivation tree from A to w_i, $i = 1, 2$. By induction hypothesis, however, (D_i, b_i), $i = 1, 2$, is uniquely defined and thus the tree (D, b) also.   ∎

Definition 2 (Algebraic Definition of Semantics): Let $b \in \mathbb{R}^M$ be an assignment. The **interpretation** $I_p(b) : L_{G_p} \to R$ of expressions in Polish notation is defined as

$$I_p(b)(w) = \begin{cases} b(w) & \text{if } w \in M \\ Op(I_p(b)(w_1), I_p(b)(w_2)) & \text{if } w = w_1 w_2\ op \text{ with } w_1, w_2 \in L_{G_p} \\ & \qquad \text{and } op \in \{+, -, \times, /\} \end{cases}$$

∎

Lemma 3. $I_p(b) : L_{G_p} \to R$ *is a total function*

Proof: Follows immediately from Section 1.5 and Lemma 2.   ∎

The semantics of expressions in Polish notation can also be defined algorithmically (Exercise 1).

We now come to the main issue of this section, the "translation " of F-expressions into Polish notation. Firstly we define the translation algebraically, as a function TR.

Definition 3 (Translation into Polish notation): The translation function $TR : L_{G_f} \to (M \cup \{+, \times, -, /\})^*$ is defined as

$$TR(w) = \begin{cases} w & \text{if } w \in M \\ TR(w_1)TR(w_2)op & \text{if } w = (w_1 \ op \ w_2), \text{ with } w_1, w_2 \in L_{G_f}, \\ & \qquad \text{and } op \in \{+, -, \times, /\} \end{cases}$$

∎

Example (continued):   We have

$$TR(((a_1 + a_2) \times (a_3 + a_1))) \ = \ TR((a_1 + a_2))TR((a_3 + a_1)) \times$$
$$= \ TR(a_1)TR(a_2) + TR(a_3)TR(a_1) + \times \ = \ a_1 a_2 + a_3 a_1 + \times \qquad ∎$$

The idea behind Definition 3 is quite simple. The productions of grammars G_f and G_p look similar; they differ only in the order of the symbols on the right side. We can simply transform derivation trees for G_f into derivation trees for G_p by suppressing brackets and altering the order of children $A \ op \ A$ into $A \ A \ op$. That is precisely what Definition 3 states.

Example (continued):   The derivation trees for

$((a_1 + a_2) \times (a_3 + a_1))$ with respect to G_f and $a_1 a_2 + a_3 a_1 + \times$ with respect to G_p are given in Figure 9.

∎

We must now show precisely that the translation function TR actually has the desired properties. Firstly, TR is a total function; secondly, the value of TR is always an expression in Polish notation; thirdly, argument and value of TR are "equivalent".

Theorem 5. (Correctness of the translation function TR)
Let TR be the translation function of Definition 3.
(a) TR is a total function.
(b) TR is a function from L_{G_f} to L_{G_p}.
(c) For all (fully parenthesised) expressions $w \in L_{G_f}$ and all assignments $b \in \mathbb{R}^M$:

$$I_f(b)(w) \ = \ I_p(b)(TR(w))$$

Proof:
(a) Follows immediately from Lemma 2 and Section 1.5.
(b) To prove that $TR(w) \in L_{G_p}$ for all $w \in L_{G_f}$ we use induction on the length $|w|$ of w.
   If $|w| = 1$, and thus $w \in M$, then the claim is obvious.
   If $|w| > 1$ then w can be written uniquely as $w = (w_1 \ op \ w_2)$ with $w_1, w_2 \in L_{G_f}$ and $op \in \{+, \times, -, /\}$. By induction hypothesis $TR(w_1), TR(w_2) \in L_{G_p}$. Thus $TR(w) = TR(w_1)TR(w_2)op \in L_{G_p}$.

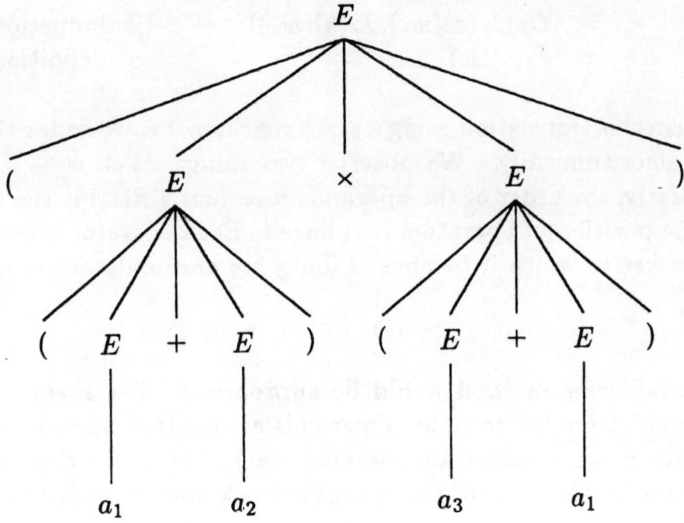

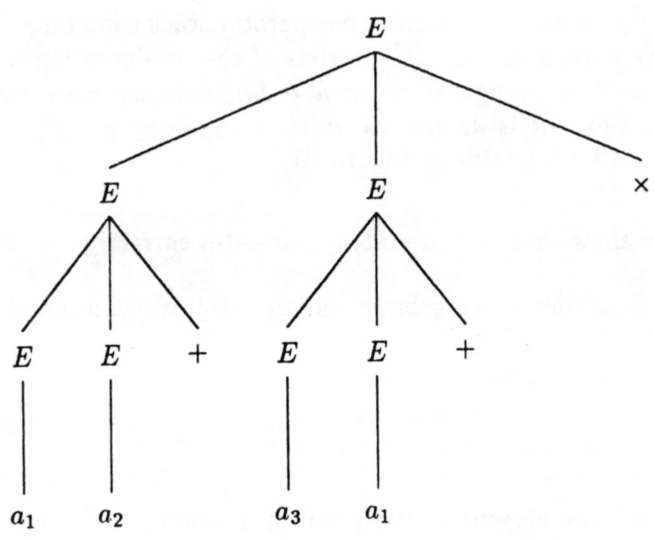

Fig. 9.

(c) **Again we use induction on the length** $|w|$ **of** w.

If $|w| = 1$, **and thus** $w \in M$, **then the claim is obvious as**

$$I_p(b)(TR(w)) = I_p(b)(w) = b(w) = I_f(b)(w).$$

If $|w| > 1$ **then** w **can be written uniquely as**

$w = (w_1\ op\ w_2)$ **with** $w_1, w_2 \in L_{G_f}$ **and** $op \in \{+, \times, -, /\}$. **By induction hypothesis** $I_p(b)(TR(w_i)) = I_f(b)(w_i)$ **for** $i = 1, 2$ **and thus**

$$
\begin{aligned}
I_p(b)(TR(w)) &= I_p(b)(TR(w_1)TR(w_2)op) && \text{definition of } TR \\
&= Op(I_p(b)(TR(w_1)), I_p(b)(TR(w_2))) && \text{definiton of } I_p(b)
\end{aligned}
$$

$$\begin{aligned} &= \quad Op(I_f(b)(w_1), I_f(b)(w_2)) & \text{induction hypothesis} \\ &= \quad I_f(b)(w) & \text{definition of } I_f(b) \end{aligned}$$

∎

Next we perform this translation using a stack machine, i.e. we define the translation function TR algorithmically. We observe two things. Let $w \in L_{G_f}$ be an F-expression. Firstly, the order of the operands in w and $TR(w)$ is the same. On the other hand, the position of operators is changed. Each operator must be shifted to the closing bracket to which it belongs. Finally we need only delete all brackets.

$$((a_1 + a_2) \times (a_3 + a_1))$$

Obviously the following method would be appropriate. The F-expression is read, symbol by symbol, from left to right. Operands are emitted immediately, operators are pushed onto a stack called an operator stack. At every closing bracket the topmost operator is taken out of the operator stack and appended to the output.

We now specify this method formally using a program-free machine $M_{TR} = (C, C^f, L_{G_f}, T_p^*, \delta, in, out)$ with $C = \{+, -, \times, /\}^* \times T_f^* \times T_p^*$. A configuration, therefore, is a triple (c^1, c^2, c^3) where c^1 represents the operator stack contents, c^2 the rest of the input and c^3 the partial output. C^f consists of the configuration (c^1, c^2, c^3) where $c^1 = c^2 = \epsilon$. The start configuration for $w \in L_{G_f}$ is (ϵ, w, ϵ), i.e. $in(w) = (\epsilon, w, \epsilon)$. The output function out is defined as $out((\epsilon, \epsilon, y)) = y$, $y \in T_p^*$. The transition function δ is given by the table in Figure 10.

We now have to show that machine M_{TR} translates correctly.

Theorem 6. *(Equivalence of algebraic and algorithmic definition of the translation function TR)*
For all F-expressions $w \in L_{G_f}$ we have

$$TR(w) = I/O_{M_{TR}}(w)$$

Proof: The proof is analogous to the proof of Theorem 3. First of all we show a general property.

Lemma 4. *Let $w \in L_{G_f}$, $x \in T_f^*$, $\beta \in \{+, -, \times, /\}^*$ and $y \in T_p^*$. Then the following holds for machine M_{TR} :*

$$(\beta, wx, y) \Rightarrow^* (\beta, x, y\, TR(w))$$

Proof: We use induction on the length of w.

If $|w| = 1$ and thus $w \in M$ then $(\beta, wx, y) \Rightarrow (\beta, x, yw)$. Because of $TR(w) = w$ the claim follows.

operator stack c^1	rest of input c^2	partial output c^3	operator stack h^1	rest of input h^2	partial output h^3	comment
β	$(x$	y	β	x	y	opening brackets are skipped
β	$a\,x$	y	β	x	$y\,a$	operands are emitted
β	$op\,x$	y	$\beta\,op$	x	y	operators are pushed onto stack
$\beta\,op$	$)x$	y	β	x	$y\,op$	closing brackets take topmost element out of stack and emit it

The table specifies the transition function of machine M_{TR}.

We have $\delta((c^1, c^2, c^3)) = (h^1, h^2, h^3)$, $\beta \in \{+, -, \times, /\}^*$, $op \in \{+, -, \times, /\}$, $x \in T_f^*$, $a \in M$, $y \in T_p^*$

Fig. 10

Let now $|w| > 1$. Then w can be written uniquely as $w = (w_1\ op\ w_2)$ with w_1, $w_2 \in L_{G_f}$, $op \in \{+, -, \times, /\}$. Thus

$$
\begin{array}{lll}
& (\beta,\ (w_1\ op\ w_2)x,\ y) & \\
\Rightarrow & (\beta,\ w_1\ op\ w_2)x,\ y) & \text{definition of } \delta \\
\Rightarrow^* & (\beta,\ op\,w_2)x,\ yTR(w_1)) & \text{induction hypothesis} \\
\Rightarrow & (\beta\,op,\ w_2)x,\ y\ TR(w_1)) & \text{definition of } \delta \\
\Rightarrow^* & (\beta\,op,\ )x,\ y\ TR(w_1)\ TR(w_2)) & \text{induction hypothesis} \\
\Rightarrow & (\beta,\ x,\ y\ TR(w_1)\tilde{(}w_2)op) & \text{definition of } \delta
\end{array}
$$

Because of $TR((w_1\ op\ w_2)) = TR(w_1)TR(w_2)op$ the induction step is complete. $\blacksquare$

The theorem now follows immediately from Lemma 4. For $w \in L_{G_f}$ we have $in(w) = (\epsilon, w, \epsilon)$. By Lemma 4 $(\epsilon, w, \epsilon) \Rightarrow^* (\epsilon, \epsilon, TR(w))$ and, by definition of machine M_{TR}, we have $out(\epsilon, \epsilon, TR(w)) = TR(w)$. Hence $I/O_{M_{TR}}(w) = TR(w)$. $\blacksquare$

Thus machine M_{TR} is a mechanical translator. It accepts F-expressions and transforms them into equivalent expressions in Polish notation.

Exercises for 2.1.2

1) Specify a machine which evaluates expressions in Polish notation.

2) Consider the context-free grammar $G = \{\{A\}, M \cup \{-_1, -_2\}, \{A \to a_1 | \ldots | a_n | A -_1 | AA-_2\}, A\}$.

    a) Prove that G is unambiguous. (Hint: Argue as in Lemma 2, but define $S(w) = |w|_{a_1} + \ldots + |w|_{a_n} - |w|_{-_2}$.)

    b) Define the algebraic semantics. The interpretation of $-_2$ is *Sub* and that of $-_1$ is *Minus* $: R \to R$ with $Minus(x) = -x$ respectively $Minus(error) = error$ ($-_2$ denotes subtraction, $-_1$ negation).

    c) Specify a machine which evaluates expressions in L_G and prove that it is equivalent to the algebraic semantics in b).

3) Let F be a set of symbols, called function symbols, and let $ar : F \to \mathbb{N}$ be a function, called arity. Consider the context-free grammar

$$G = (\{A\}, M \cup F, \{A \to a_1 | \ldots | a_n\} \cup \{A \to f \underbrace{AA \ldots A}_{ar(f)-\text{times}} ; f \in F\}, A).$$

Show that G is unambiguous. (Hint: Use function $S(w) = |w|_{a_1} + \ldots + |w|_{a_n} - \sum_{f \in F} |w|_f (ar(f) - 1)$.)

4) a) Specify the translation function which transforms expressions in Polish notation into F-expressions.

    b) Prove the correctness of the translation function similar to Theorem 5.

2.1.3 A Simulation

The stack machine in Section 2.1.1 uses a stack for operands and operators. In the formal description of machine M_f this stack corresponds to the first component of the configuration. It would seem reasonable (because of storage usage, uniformity of the types of stack contents) to replace machine M_f by a machine with two stacks. Then operands are written into an "operand stack" and operators into an "operator stack".

Formally speaking, this new machine is a program-free machine such as

$$\overline{M}_f = (\overline{C}, \overline{C}^f, L_{G_f}, R, \overline{\delta}, \overline{in}, \overline{out})$$

with $\overline{C} = R^* \times \{+, -, \times, /\}^* \times T_f^*$.

A configuration thus is a triple $\bar{c} = (\bar{c}^1, \bar{c}^2, \bar{c}^3)$ where $\bar{c}^1$ is the contents of the operand stack, $\bar{c}^2$ the contents of the operator stack and $\bar{c}^3$ the rest-expression. The end configurations in $\overline{C}^f$ are the configurations $(\bar{c}^1, \bar{c}^2, \bar{c}^3)$ with $\bar{c}^1 \in R$ (instead of R^*) and $\bar{c}^2 = \bar{c}^3 = \epsilon$. Given input $w \in L_{G_f}$, we start the machine in configuration (ϵ, ϵ, w), i.e. $\overline{in} : L_{G_f} \rightarrow \overline{C}$ with $\overline{in}(w) = (\epsilon, \epsilon, w)$. The output function $\overline{out}$ is defined by $\overline{out}((m, \epsilon, \epsilon)) = m$. The transition function $\bar{\delta}$ is given by the table in Figure 11.

operand stack $\bar{c}^1$	operator stack $\bar{c}^2$	rest expression $\bar{c}^3$	operand stack $\bar{h}^1$	operator stack $\bar{h}^2$	rest expression $\bar{h}^3$	comment
α	β	$(w$	α	β	w	opening brackets are skipped
α	β	aw	$\alpha\, b(a)$	β	w	values of operands are pushed onto operand stack
α	β	$op\ w$	α	$\beta\ op$	w	operators are written into the operator stack
$\alpha m_1 m_2$	$\beta\ op$	$)w$	$\alpha\ Op(m_1 m_2)$	β	w	when reading a closing bracket a sub-expression is evaluated

The table shows the transition function $\bar{\delta}$ of machine $\overline{M}_f$.

We have $\delta((\bar{c}^1, \bar{c}^2, \bar{c}^3)) = (\bar{h}^1, \bar{h}^2, \bar{h}^3)$, $\alpha \in R^*$, $m_1, m_2 \in R$, $\beta \in \{+, -, \times, /\}^*$, $op \in \{+, -, \times, /\}$, $w \in T_v^*$.

Fig. 11

Again the input-output-behaviour of $\overline{M}_f$ depends on the assignment b. Thus we write $I/O_{\overline{M}_f}(b)$ for this input-output-behaviour.

Example (continued): The mode of operation of $\overline{M}_f$ is now illustrated. We let machine M_f run in parallel and use diagrams as in the example of Section 2.1.1 which precedes the formal definition of the machine M_f.

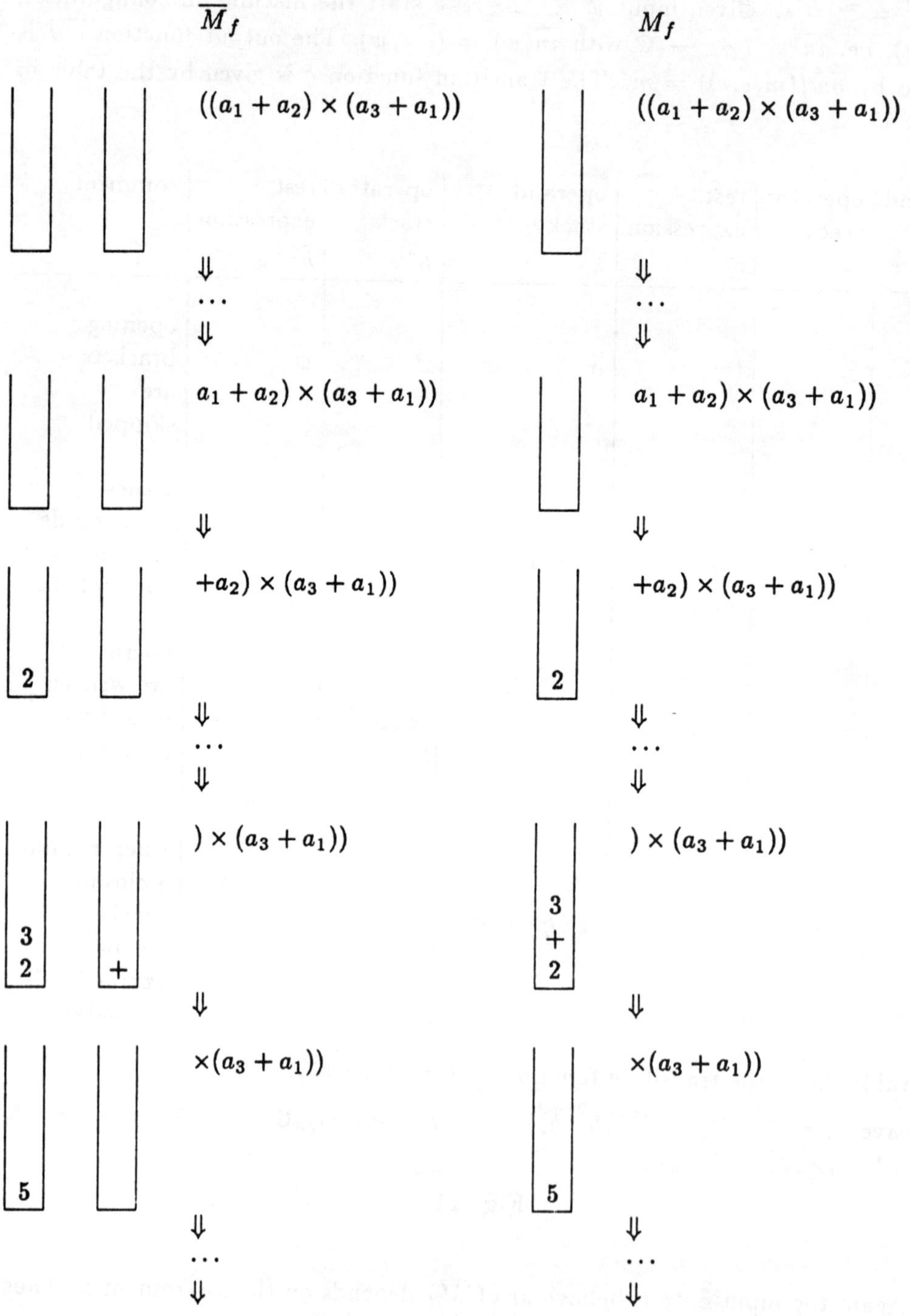

$$\overline{M}_f \qquad\qquad\qquad M_f$$

$$((a_1 + a_2) \times (a_3 + a_1)) \qquad\qquad ((a_1 + a_2) \times (a_3 + a_1))$$

$$\Downarrow \qquad\qquad\qquad \Downarrow$$
$$\cdots \qquad\qquad\qquad \cdots$$
$$\Downarrow \qquad\qquad\qquad \Downarrow$$

$$a_1 + a_2) \times (a_3 + a_1)) \qquad\qquad a_1 + a_2) \times (a_3 + a_1))$$

$$\Downarrow \qquad\qquad\qquad \Downarrow$$

$$+a_2) \times (a_3 + a_1)) \qquad\qquad +a_2) \times (a_3 + a_1))$$

(stack: 2) $\qquad\qquad$ (stack: 2)

$$\Downarrow \qquad\qquad\qquad \Downarrow$$
$$\cdots \qquad\qquad\qquad \cdots$$
$$\Downarrow \qquad\qquad\qquad \Downarrow$$

$$) \times (a_3 + a_1)) \qquad\qquad) \times (a_3 + a_1))$$

(stacks: 3 / 2 ; +) $\qquad\qquad$ (stack: 3 / + / 2)

$$\Downarrow \qquad\qquad\qquad \Downarrow$$

$$\times (a_3 + a_1)) \qquad\qquad \times (a_3 + a_1))$$

(stack: 5) $\qquad\qquad$ (stack: 5)

$$\Downarrow \qquad\qquad\qquad \Downarrow$$
$$\cdots \qquad\qquad\qquad \cdots$$
$$\Downarrow \qquad\qquad\qquad \Downarrow$$

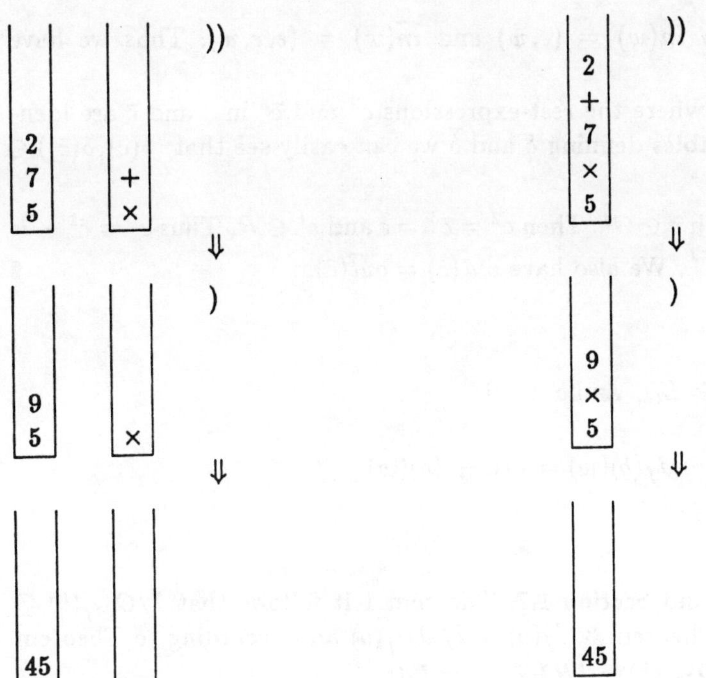

We see that the configurations of M_f and $\overline{M}_f$ are very similar. Essentially, only the content of the single stack of M_f is divided into two stacks of $\overline{M}_f$.

How can we convince ourselves of the correctness of $\overline{M}_f$, i.e. how do we show that $I_f(b)(w) = I/O_{\overline{M}_f}(b)(w)$ for all assignments b and expressions $w \in L_{G_f}$? There are different ways. We could, for example, modify the proof of Theorem 3 (Exercise 1). Alternatively, we show that $\overline{M}_f$ can simulate machine M_f. Then Theorem 1 of Section 1.7 can be applied. At this point the reader should once again read through the second part of Section 1.7 (from Definition 3 up to Theorem 1).

Theorem 7. *Machine* $\overline{M}_f$ *can simulate machine* M_f.

Proof: Let, as usual, $M_f = (C, C^f, L_{G_f}, R, \delta, in, out)$ and

$$\overline{M}_f = (\overline{C}, \overline{C}^f, L_{G_f}, R, \overline{\delta}, \overline{in}, \overline{out}).$$

We introduce a relation $Rel \subseteq C \times \overline{C}$ and verify that it is a simulation of machine M_f on machine $\overline{M}_f$. Let $c = (c^1, c^2) \in C$ and $\overline{c} = (\overline{c}^1, \overline{c}^2, \overline{c}^3) \in \overline{C}$. We define: $(c, \overline{c}) \in Rel$ if and only if

(a) $c^2 = \overline{c}^3$, i.e. the rest-expressions are identical

(b) $\overline{c}^1$ is obtained from c^1 by deleting all elements of $\{+, -, \times, /\}$

(c) $\overline{c}^2$ is derived from c^1 by deleting all elements of R.

One has to prove that Rel is a simulation, i.e. check if the three conditions from Section 1.7, Definition 3, are satisfied.

Let $w \in L_{G_f}$. Then $in(w) = (\epsilon, w)$ and $\overline{in}(w) = (\epsilon, \epsilon, w)$. Thus we have $(in(w), \overline{in}(w)) \in Rel$.

Now, let $(c, \bar{c}) \in Rel$ where the rest-expressions c^2 and $\bar{c}^3$ in c and $\bar{c}$ are identical. By inspecting the tables defining δ and $\bar{\delta}$ we can easily see that $(\delta(c), \delta(\bar{c})) \in Rel$.

Finally, let $(c, \bar{c}) \in Rel$ with $c \in C^f$. Then $c^2 = \bar{c}^3 = \epsilon$ and $c^1 \in R$. Thus $c^1 = \bar{c}^1 \in R$ and $\bar{c}^2 = \epsilon$ and thus $\bar{c} \in \overline{C}^f$. We also have $out(c) = \overline{out}(\bar{c})$. ∎

Theorem 8. *For all $w \in L_{G_f}$ and $b \in \mathbb{R}^M$:*

$$I_f(b)(w) = I/O_{\overline{M}_f}(b)(w)$$

Proof: From Theorem 7 and Section 1.7, Theorem 1 it follows that $I/O_{M_f}(b) \subseteq I/O_{\overline{M}_f}(b)$. According to Theorem 3, $I_f(b) = I/O_{M_f}(b)$ and according to Theorem 2, $I_f(b)$ is total. Thus $I/O_{M_f}(b) = I/O_{\overline{M}_f}(b) = I_f(b)$. ∎

The reader might point out, at this stage, that a proof similar to that of Theorem 3 would have been just as simple. On the other hand, the approach chosen here may be more obvious to the computer scientist as machines are being compared.

Exercises for 2.1.3

1) Prove, as in Theorem 3, that stack machine $\overline{M}_f$ works correctly.

2.2 Partially Parenthesised Expressions with Precedence

Fully parenthesised expressions discussed in Section 2.1 are in many ways inappropriate. Firstly, too many brackets must be used. Secondly, we have, for example, not permitted any unary operations.

Example 1:   We are all used to writing expressions of the form

$$a_1 + a_2 \cdot (a_3 + a_1) - - - a_2 + a_1 \cdot a_2/a_3 \cdot -a_1$$

or (with "$\times$" instead of "$\cdot$")

$$a_1 + a_2 \times (a_3 + a_1) - - - a_2 + a_1 \times a_2/a_3 \times -a_1$$

The rules "point computation has precedence over stroke computation", "unary Minus has precedence", "operations on the same level are executed from left to right" save many brackets. The fully parenthesised version of the above expressions thus is

$$(((a_1 + a_2 \times (a_3 + a_1)) - (-(-a_2))) + (((a_1 \times a_2)/a_3) \times (-a_1)))$$

We also use the symbol "$-$" safely in two ways. It stands for the binary operation "subtraction" and also for the unary operation "negation" which associates with each number its negative. ∎

Rules such as "point computation has precedence over stroke computation" and "unary Minus has preference" can be stated precisely by associating a **precedence** with operations. Operations of higher precedence are considered first. For example, in a term such as $a_1 + a_2 \times a_3$ multiplication must come before addition because "$\times$" is of higher precedence than "$+$".

Operator	Priorität
$+, -_2$	0
$\times, /$	1
$-_1$	2

In the precedence table it was necessary to differentiate syntactically between unary $(-_1)$ and binary $(-_2)$ minus.

How can we formally capture these different concepts? To this end we use a context-free grammar with a nonterminal for each precedence level. We use three nonterminals, say E, T and F. E (expression) will generate all expressions on precedence level 0, 1 and 2, T (term) all expressions on precedence level 1 and 2, and F (factor)

all expressions on precedence level 2. Furthermore we express implicit bracketing
on one precedence level by the form of the productions.

Formally, the context-free grammar $G_{pa} = (\{E,T,F\}, T_{pa}, P_{pa}, E)$ for partially
parenthesised expressions with precedence is:

$$
\begin{aligned}
T_{pa} &= M \cup \{+,-,\times,/,(,)\} \\
P_{pa} &= \{E \rightarrow T \mid E + T \mid E - T, \\
&\qquad T \rightarrow F \mid T \times F \mid T / F, \\
&\qquad F \rightarrow a_1 \mid a_2 \mid \ldots \mid a_n \mid - F \mid (E)\}
\end{aligned}
$$

The operand set M is defined as in Section 2.1.

Example (continued): The derivation tree for our example expression is shown
in Figure 1.

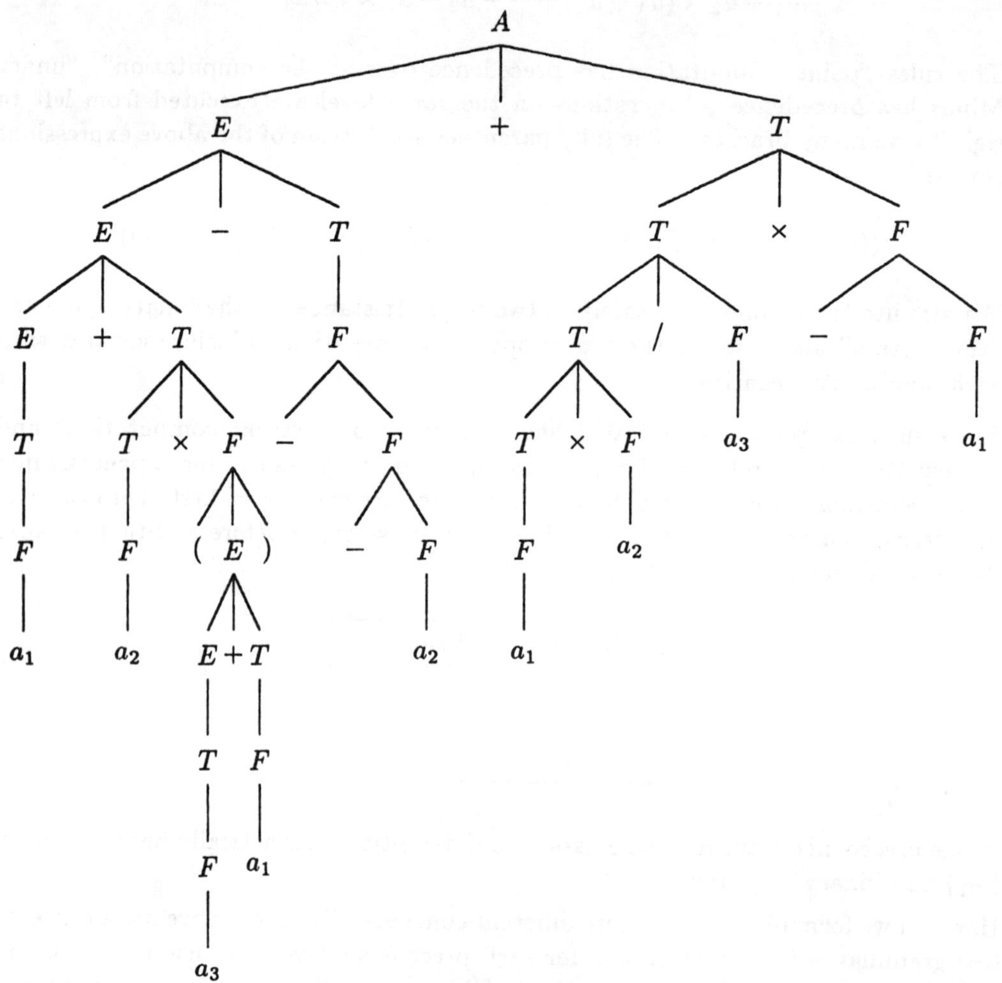

Fig. 1.

The structure of this tree exhibits implicit bracketing very clearly. The subtree in
Figure 2

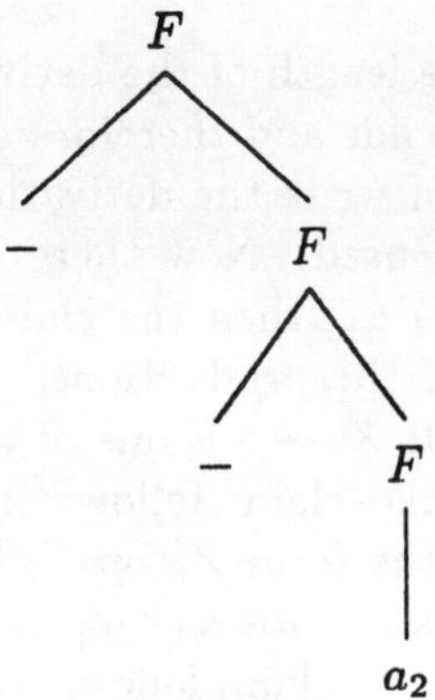

Fig. 2.

shows, for example, that $--a_2$ is to be read as $(-(-a_2))$. Similarly, the production
$E \to E+T$ shows that the brackets of an "expression" $T+T+T$ are like $((T+T)+T)$.
In general, the derivation tree of an expression with respect to grammar G_{pa} has
the same structure as the derivation tree of the corresponding F-expression with
respect to grammar G_f.

Theorem 1. *The context-free grammar G_{pa} is unambiguous.*

Proof 1: Using methods of the theory of syntax analysis, one can show automatically
that G_{pa} is an LR-grammar and therefore unambiguous (see concluding remarks to
Section 1.4).

Proof 2: We now prove this by elementary means. The proof uses several auxiliary
claims. We show first of all that the minus symbols can be classified unambiguously
as unary and binary. Lemmas 1, 2 and 3 stipulate that a minus symbol is binary
if and only if it follows an operand or a closing bracket. Then we show how the
implicit bracket structure can be recognised. Proceeding in steps, we firstly consider expressions without brackets which contain unary minus as a single operation
(Lemma 4), then we also permit the operations "×" and "/" (Lemma 5) and, finally, all the operations (Lemma 6). In conclusion we show unambiguity also for
expressions containing brackets.　　　　　　　　　　　　　　　　　　　　　　■

Lemma 1. *Let $X \in \{E, T, F\}$ be a nonterminal and $w \in L_{G_{pa}, X}$ an X-construct.
Then the last symbol in w is an operand or a closing bracket.*

Proof: Firstly, the form of the productions indicates that this is the case for $X = F$.
Then it also holds for $X = T$ and thus also for $X = E$.　　　　　　　　　　　■

Lemma 2. *Let $X \in \{E,T,F\}$ be a nonterminal. If $X \to^* \alpha_1 Y \alpha_2$ with $Y \in \{E,T,F\}$ and $\alpha_1, \alpha_2 \in (\{E,T,F\} \cup T_{pa})^*$ then α_1 is either empty or α_1 ends with a symbol in $\{(,+,-,\times,/\}$.*

Proof: We use induction on the length of the derivation from X to α.

If the length is 0 then $X = Y$ holds and therefore α_1 is empty.

If the length is > 0 then we can write the derivation as $X \to \beta \to^* \alpha_1 Y \alpha_2$ where $X \to \beta$ is the first production used. Now there are two cases. If the length of the derivation is 1, i.e. $\beta = \alpha_1 Y \alpha_2$, then the claim follows immediately from the form of the right-hand sides of the productions. If the length is > 1, again we distinguish between two cases. If $X \to \beta$ is one of the productions $E \to T, T \to F$, $F \to -F$ or $F \to (E)$ then the claim follows immediately from the induction hypothesis. Otherwise β is of the form $Z_1 \; op \; Z_2$ with $Z_1, Z_2 \in \{E,T,F\}$ and $op \in \{+,-,\times,/\}$. Then we can write $\alpha_1 Y \alpha_2$ as $\gamma_1 \; op \; \gamma_2$ with $Z_1 \to^* \gamma_1$ and $Z_2 \to^* \gamma_2$. If α_1 is a prefix of γ_1 the claim follows from the induction hypothesis for $Z_1 \to^* \gamma_1$. If α_1 is not a prefix of γ_1 then α_1 has the form $\gamma_1 \; op \; \alpha_3$ where α_3 is a prefix of γ_2. If $\alpha_3 = \epsilon$ then op is the symbol preceding Y and thus the claim holds. If $\alpha_3 \neq \epsilon$ then the claim follows from the induction hypothesis for $Z_2 \to^* \gamma_2$.   ■

Lemma 3. *Let $X \in \{E,T,F\}$ be a nonterminal, let $w \in L_{G_{pa},X}$ be an X-construct and let $w = w_1 - w_2$ with $w_1, w_2 \in T_{pa}^*$. Consider a derivation from X to w. If the minus symbol under consideration has been generated by the production $F \to -F$ then w_1 is either empty or ends in a symbol in $\{(,+,-,\times,/\}$. If the minus symbol under consideration has been generated by the production $E \to E - T$ then w_1 ends in a symbol in $M \cup \{)\}$.*

Proof: The first part of the claim follows immediately from Lemma 2. We can actually write the derivation from X to w as

$$X \to^* \beta_1 F \beta_2 \to \beta_1 - F \beta_2 \to^* w_1 - w_2$$

where $\beta_1 \to^* w_1$ and $F\beta_2 \to^* w_2$. According to Lemma 2 (with $Y = F$), β_1 is empty or ends with a symbol in $\{(,+,-,\times,/\}$. Thus w_1 is also empty or ends in such a symbol.

The second part of the claim follows from Lemma 1. If the minus symbol under consideration has been generated by the production $E \to E - T$ then we have a suffix w_3 of w_1 with $E \to^* w_3$. According to Lemma 1, w_3 ends with a symbol in $M \cup \{)\}$.   ■

Lemma 3 is important. It states that we can unambiguously classify minus symbols in an expression as unary (generated by $F \to -F$) or binary (generated by $E \to E - T$). The classification is determined by the preceding symbol. We assume, from now on, that all minus symbols in an expression w are classified in this way, and write $-_1$ or $-_2$. This is equivalent to the assumption that G_{pa}, instead of $F \to -F$ and $E \to E - T$, contains the productions $F \to -_1 F$ and $A \to A -_2 T$.

Example (continued):   In our example expression we obtain

$$a_1 + a_2 \times (a_3 + a_1) -_2 -_1 -_1 a_2 + a_1 \times a_2/a_3 \times -_1 a_1$$

Lemma 4. *Let* $w \in L_{G_{pa}} \cap (\{-_1\} \cup M)^*$. *Then there is exactly one derivation from* F *to* w.

Proof: By assumption w has only unary minus symbols as operators. Thus according to Lemma 3, w is of the form $-_1 -_1 \ldots -_1 w_1$ with $w_1 \in M^*$. From this form it even becomes clear that $w_1 \in M$. The only derivation from F to w thus is

$$F \;\to\; -_1 F \;\to\; -_1 -_1 F \;\to\; \cdots \;\to\; -_1 -_1 \cdots -_1 w_1$$

Lemma 5. *Let* $w \in L_{G_{pa}} \cap (\{-_1, \times, /\} \cup M)^*$. *Then there is exactly one canonical derivation from* T *to* w.

Proof: We prove this by induction on the number of occurrences of symbols from $\{\times, /\}$ in w.

If w contains no symbol of $\{\times, /\}$ then each derivation from T to w begins with the production $T \to F$. Furthermore $w \in L_{G_{pa}} \cap (\{-_1\} \cup M)^*$. Thus the statement of Lemma 4 follows.

If w now contains at least one symbol of $\{\times, /\}$ then each derivation from T to w has the form $T \to T \; op \; F \to^* w_1 \; op \; w_2$ with $op \in \{\times, /\}$, $w_1 \in L_{G_{pa},T}$, $w_2 \in L_{G_{pa},F}$. As each F-construct generated from F contains only unary minus symbols as operation symbols (since w contains no brackets production $F \to (E)$ can not be used) the following must hold: w_2 is the suffix of maximal length of w which contains no operation symbol of $\{\times, /\}$. Thus w_1 and w_2 are uniquely determined. Furthermore, according to the induction hypothesis, there is only one canonical derivation from T to w_1 and, according to Lemma 4, only one derivation from F to w_2. Thus there is only one canonical derivation from T to w.

Lemma 6. *Let* $w \in L_{G_{pa}} \cap (\{-_1, \times, /, -_2, +\} \cup M)^*$. *Then there is exactly one canonical derivation from* E *to* w.

Proof: Similarly to the proof of Lemma 5.

After this long sequence of lemmas we can now prove Theorem 1. We return to the original set of productions of grammar G_{pa} (without any difference between $-_1$ and $-_2$).

We use induction on the number of brackets in $w \in L_{G_{pa}}$.

If w contains no brackets the claim follows from Lemma 6.

If w contains brackets we consider the leftmost innermost pair of brackets in w, i.e. we write w as $w = w_1(w_2)w_3$ such that w_2 contains no brackets and w_1 no closing brackets. It follows from the form of the productions that $F \to (E) \to^* w_2$ must hold. According to Lemma 6, there is precisely one canonical derivation from F to (w_2). Furthermore $w' = w_1 a_1 w_3 \in L_{G_{pa}}$ (instead of a_1 an arbitrary operand from M could have been used). The expression w' contains less brackets than w. Thus, by the induction hypothesis, there is precisely one canonical derivation from E to w'. This, together with the unique canonical derivation from F to w_2, and the fact that each w_2 must be derived from F proves the claim. This concludes the proof of Theorem 1.   ∎

We have already seen that it was very difficult to prove G_{pa} to be unambiguous. This, on the one hand, indicates the importance of a general theory of syntax analysis. It also suggests the use as far as possible of bracketed structures. In programming languages we find many types of such bracketing: **begin** – **end**, **if** – **fi**, **proc** – **end**.

Theorem 1 paves the way to the algebraic definition of the semantics of partially parenthesised expressions with precedence. We introduce an interpretation for each nonterminal. Since grammar G_{pa} is unambiguous these functions, as usual, can be defined recursively.

Definition 1 (Algebraic Definition of Semantics): Let $b \in \mathbb{R}^M$ be an assignment. The **interpretations** $I_E(b) : L_{G_{pa},E} \to R$, $I_T(b) : L_{G_{pa},T} \to R$ and $I_F(b) : L_{G_{pa},F} \to R$ are defined as

$$I_F(b)(w) = \begin{cases} b(w) & \text{if } w \in M \\ \neg(I_F(b)(w_1)) & \text{if } w = -w_1 \text{ with } w_1 \in L_{G_{pa},F} \\ I_E(b)(w_1) & \text{if } w = (w_1) \text{ with } w_1 \in L_{G_{pa},E} \end{cases}$$

$$I_T(b)(w) = \begin{cases} I_F(b)(w) & \text{if } w \in L_{G_{pa},F} \\ Op(I_T(b)(w_1), I_F(b)(w_2)) & \text{if } w = w_1 \, op \, w_2 \text{ with} \\ & \quad w_1 \in L_{G_{pa},T}, \; w_2 \in L_{G_{pa},F} \\ & \quad \text{and } op \in \{\times, /\} \end{cases}$$

and

$$I_E(b)(w) = \begin{cases} I_T(b)(w) & \text{if } w \in L_{G_{pa},T} \\ Op(I_A(b)(w_1), I_T(b)(w_2)) & \text{if } w = w_1 \, op \, w_2 \text{ with} \\ & \quad w_1 \in L_{G_{pa},E}, \; w_2 \in L_{G_{pa},T} \\ & \quad \text{and } op \in \{+, -\} \end{cases}$$

The function $\neg : R \to R$ associates with each real number its negative and maps "error" to "error".

Theorem 2. *The interpretations $I_E(b)$, $I_F(b)$, $I_T(b)$ are well-defined for each assignment $b \in \mathbb{R}^M$. In particular they are total functions.*

Proof: If we consider $I_E(b)$, $I_F(b)$, $I_T(b)$ as partial functions well-definedness (as partial functions) is a consequence of the unamiguity of G_{pa}. Totality follows with the methods in Section 1.5.

Example: Let $b(a_1) = 2$, $b(a_2) = 3$. Then

$$
\begin{aligned}
I_E(b)(a_1 + -a_2 \times a_1) &= add(I_E(b)(a_1), I_T(b)(-a_2 \times a_1)) \\
&= add(I_T(b)(a_1), mul(I_T(b)(-a_2), I_F(b)(a_1))) \\
&= add(I_F(b)(a_1), mul(I_F(b)(-a_2), b(a_1))) \\
&= add(b(a_1), mul(neg(I_F(b)(a_2)), 2)) \\
&= add(2, mul(neg(b(a_2)), 2)) \\
&= add(2, mul(neg(3), 2)) \\
&= add(2, mul(-3, 2)) \\
&= add(2, -6) \\
&= -4
\end{aligned}
$$

The algebraic definition of the semantics of expressions is very elegant and expressive. However, it presumes considerable skills on the part of the "evaluator". We therefore present an algorithmic definition by way of a machine which, like the previous machines, uses a stack. The basic idea is not difficult. The machine reads the expression from left to right and stores operands and operators in the stack until it encounters the first (explicit or implicit) closing bracket. Then it evaluates a subexpression. To be more exact it proceeds as follows.

1) Operands are replaced immediately by their value.

2) Minus symbols are classified as unary and binary and are stored as such in the stack. In addition, the machine retains the information of whether the symbol of the expression read last (or, more precisely, processed last) is in class 1 $= \{\times, -, /, +, ($\} or class 2 $= M \cup \{$)\}. Class 1 symbols are succeeded by unary minus symbols, class 2 symbols by binary minus symbols (see Lemma 3). If no symbol has been read we proceed as in the first case (see Lemma 3).

3) Implicit closing brackets are recognised by the precedence of the operators. An implicit closing bracket is always present when an operator is succeeded by an operator of lesser or the same precedence.

Example 2: We now illustrate the machine (still to be exactly defined) using as example the expression $a_1 - - - a_2 + a_1 \times -a_2 + a_1$ with the assignment $b(a_1) = 2$, $b(a_2) = 3$. A configuration consists of three components: the stack content, the rest-expression and a number which specifies in which class the symbol read last is to be found. We obtain the following computation:

$a_1 - - - a_2 + a_1 \times -a_2 + a_1, 1$

$\Rightarrow$ (empty stack)

$- - a_2 + a_1 \times -a_2 + a_1, 1$

$\Rightarrow$ stack (bottom to top): $2, -_2$

$a_2 + a_1 \times -a_2 + a_1, 1$

$\Rightarrow$ stack (bottom to top): $2, -_2, -_1, -_1$

$+a_1 \times -a_2 + a_1, 2$

$\Rightarrow$ stack (bottom to top): $2, -_2, -_1, -_3$

Note: The topmost operator in the stack $(-_1)$ is of no lesser precedence than the next operator $(+)$; thus subexpression $-_1 3$ must be evaluated.

$+a_1 \times -a_2 + a_1, 2$

$\Rightarrow$ stack (bottom to top): $-_1$

Note: The topmost operator in the stack $(-_2)$ is of no lesser precedence than the next operator; thus subexpression $2 -_2 3$ must be evaluated.

$- - -a_2 + a_1 \times -a_2 + a_1, 2$

$\Rightarrow$ stack (bottom to top): 2

$-a_2 + a_1 \times -a_2 + a_1, 1$

$\Rightarrow$ stack (bottom to top): $2, -_2, -_1$

$+a_1 \times -a_2 + a_1, 2$

$\Rightarrow$ stack (bottom to top): $2, -_2, -_1, -_1, 3$

$+a_1 \times -a_2 + a_1, 2$

$\Rightarrow$ stack (bottom to top): $2, -_2, 3$

Note: The topmost operator in the stack $(-_1)$ is of no lesser precedence than the next operator $(+)$; thus subexpression $-_1(-3)$ must be evaluated.

$a_1 \times -a_2 + a_1, 1$

$\Rightarrow$ stack (bottom to top): $-_1, +$

$$\Rightarrow \quad \overset{\times - a_2 + a_1,\ 2}{\boxed{\begin{array}{c} \\ 2 \\ + \\ -1 \end{array}}} \qquad \Rightarrow \quad \overset{-a_2 + a_1,\ 1}{\boxed{\begin{array}{c} \times \\ 2 \\ + \\ -1 \end{array}}} \qquad \Rightarrow \quad \overset{a_2 + a_1,\ 1}{\boxed{\begin{array}{c} -_1 \\ \times \\ 2 \\ + \\ -1 \end{array}}}$$

$$\Rightarrow \quad \overset{+a_1,\ 2}{\boxed{\begin{array}{c} 3 \\ -_1 \\ \times \\ 2 \\ + \\ -1 \end{array}}} \quad \Rightarrow \quad \overset{+a_1,\ 2}{\boxed{\begin{array}{c} -3 \\ \times \\ 2 \\ + \\ -1 \end{array}}} \quad \Rightarrow \quad \overset{+a_1,\ 2}{\boxed{\begin{array}{c} \\ 6 \\ + \\ -1 \end{array}}} \quad \Rightarrow \quad \overset{+a_1,\ 2}{\boxed{\begin{array}{c} \\ -7 \end{array}}}$$

$$\Rightarrow \quad \overset{a_1,\ 1}{\boxed{\begin{array}{c} \\ + \\ -7 \end{array}}} \qquad \Rightarrow \quad \overset{\epsilon,\ 2}{\boxed{\begin{array}{c} 2 \\ + \\ -7 \end{array}}} \qquad \Rightarrow \quad \overset{\epsilon,\ 2}{\boxed{\begin{array}{c} \\ -5 \end{array}}}$$

The result of the computation is -5. ∎

For the formal definition of this machine we make two small changes which considerably reduce the size of the table for the transition function. Firstly, we do not start with an empty stack but with an additional "operation symbol" $\vdash$ having less precedence than all others (thus -1 in our case). Secondly, we append to the expression to be read an "operation symbol" $\dashv$ having likewise less precedence than all the others (here -1). The machine then is the program-free machine

$$M_{pa} = (C, C^f, L_G, R, \delta, in, out)$$

The set of the configuration is $C = (R \cup \{+, -_1, -_2, \times, /, \vdash, (,)\})^* \times (T_{pa} \cup \{\dashv\})^* \times \{1, 2\}$. In a configuration $c = (c^1, c^2, c^3)$, c^1 corresponds to the stack content, c^2 to the rest-expression and c^3 to the number of the class of the symbol read last. If therefore $c^3 = 1(2)$ then a following minus symbol is interpreted as a unary (binary) minus symbol, i.e. stored in the stack as $-_1(-_2)$. For an expression $w \in L_{G_{pa}}$ the start configuration is $(\vdash,\ w \dashv,\ 1)$, i.e. $in(w) = (\vdash,\ w \dashv,\ 1)$.

The machine M_{pa} stops with an "almost" empty stack and rest-expression, or, more precisely, $C^f = \{\vdash r;\ r \in R\} \times \{\dashv\} \times \{2\}$. For $(\vdash r,\ \dashv,\ 2) \in C^f$ we have $out((\vdash r,\ \dashv,\ 2)) = r$. The transition function δ is given by the table in Figure 3.

Z	c^1	c^2	c^3	h^1	h^2	h^3	condition	comment
1	α	$a\,w$	1	$\alpha\,b(a)$	w	2		values of operands are pushed onto stack
2	α	$(\,w$	1	$\alpha\,($	w	1		opening brackets are pushed onto stack
3	α	$-\,w$	1	$\alpha\,-_1$	w	1		unary (indicator $c^3 = 1$) minus symbol pushed onto stack
4	$\alpha\,-_1\,r$	$op_2\,w$	2	$\alpha\,neg(r)$	$op_2\,w$	2		unary minus is executed
5	$\alpha\,r\,op_1 s$	$op_2\,w$	2	$\alpha\,Op_1(r,s)$	$op_2\,w$	2	$p(op_1) \geq p(op_2)$	op_1 is executed
6	$\alpha\,op_1\,s$	$op_2\,w$	2	$\alpha\,op_1\,s\,\widetilde{op_2}$	w	1	$p(op_1) < p(op_2)$	op_2 pushed onto stack
7	$\alpha\,(\,r$	$)\,w$	2	$\alpha\,r$	w	2		closing bracket eliminates opening bracket

The table shows the transition function δ of M_{pa}.

$\delta((c^1, c^2, c^3)) = (h^1, h^2, h^3)$. Column Z are line numbers.

$\alpha \in (R \cup \{+, -_1, -_2, \times, /, \vdash, (,)\})^*,$ $op_1 \in \{+, -_2, \times, /,), \vdash\},$

$w \in (T_{pa} \cup \{\dashv\})^*,$ $op_2 \in \{+, -, \times, /,.), \dashv\}.$

$a \in M,\ b \in \mathbb{R}^M,\ r, s \in R,$

Furthermore the notation $\widetilde{op_2}$ is defined by $\widetilde{op_2} = -_2$ if $op_2 = -$ and $\widetilde{op_2} = op_2$ otherwise. Finally,

$$p(op) = \begin{cases} -1 & \text{for } op \in \{\vdash, \dashv, (,)\} \\ 0 & \text{for } op \in \{+, -, -_2\} \\ 1 & \text{for } op \in \{\times, /\} \\ 2 & \text{for } op \in \{-_1\} \end{cases}$$

Fig. 3

We must now verify that the table of Figure 3 actually defines a function. The cases of lines 1, 2 and 3 are disjoint from those of lines 4, 5, 6 and 7 as these lines differ in the indicator c^3. If the indicator $c^3 = 1$, the first symbol of the rest-expression determines uniquely the line to be applied. Let the indicator $c^3 = 2$. As $op_1 \in \{+, -_2, \times, /,), \vdash\}$, the second stack symbol from the top (from c^2) differentiates lines 5 and 6 from 4 and 7. Finally, the precedence $p(op_1)$ and $p(op_2)$ of the operators op_1 and op_2 distinguishes between lines 5 and 6. Thus we have shown that at most one line of the table applies for each configuration. Thus δ is a (partial) function.

$I/O_{M_{pa}}(b)$ is written as above in order to show explicitly the dependence of the I/O-behaviours on the assignment b.

We now show that the definition of M_{pa} is correct i.e. that the algorithmic definition of semantics given by machine M_{pa} is equivalent to the algebraic semantics in Definition 1.

Theorem 3. *(Equivalence of algorithmic and algebraic interpretation of expressions)* *For all assignments $b \in \mathbb{R}^M$ and all expressions $w \in L_{G_{pa}}$:*

$$I_E(b)(w) = I/O_{M_{pa}}(b)(w)$$

Proof: As in Theorems 3 and 5 of Section 2.1 we first of all show a stronger assertion.

Lemma 7. *Let $X \in \{E, T, F\}$, $w \in L_{G_{pa},X}$, $op' \in \{+, -_1, -_2, \times, /, (, \vdash\}$, $op'' \in \{+, -, \times, /,), \dashv\}$, $z \in (T_{pa} \cup \{\dashv\})^*$, $\alpha \in (R \cup \{+, -_1, -_2, \times, /, \vdash, (,)\})^*$. Let furthermore*

$$p(op') < \begin{cases} 0 & \text{if } X = E \\ 1 & \text{if } X = T \end{cases}$$

and

$$p(op'') \leq \begin{cases} 0 & \text{if } X = E \\ 1 & \text{if } X = T \end{cases}$$

where the notation $p(op)$ is that of Figure 3.
Then

$$(\alpha \; op', \; w \; op'' \; z, \; 1) \; \underset{M_{pa}}{\overset{*}{\Rightarrow}} \; (\alpha \; op' \; I_X(b)(w), \; op'' \; z, \; 2)$$

Proof: Induction on the length l of the canonical derivation from X to w.

If $l = 1$ then $X = F$ and $w \in M$. The claim then follows immediately from the definition of the transition function δ and the fact that $I_X(b)(w) = b(w)$.

Let $l > 1$. We distinguish various cases according to the first production used in the (canonical) derivation.

Case 1: The production is $F \to -F$.

Then $w = -w_1$ with $w_1 \in L_{G_{pa},F}$.
We have

$$
\begin{array}{lll}
 & (\alpha\ op',\ -w_1\ op''\ z,\ 1) & \\
\Rightarrow & (\alpha\ op'\ -_1,\ w_1\ op''\ z,\ 1) & \text{definition of } \delta, \text{ line 3} \\
\Rightarrow^* & (\alpha\ op'\ -_1\ I_F(b)(w_1),\ op''\ z,\ 2) & \text{induction hypothesis} \\
\Rightarrow & (\alpha\ op'\ neg(I_F(b)(w_1)),\ op''\ z,\ 2) & \text{definition of } \delta, \text{ line 4}
\end{array}
$$

(The reader should check carefully that the above application of the induction hypothesis is permitted and, in particular, that the configuration $(\alpha\ op'\ -_1,\ w_1\ op''\ z,\ 1)$ satisfies the conditions of the Lemma to be proved.)

Thus, because $I_F(b)(w) = neg(I_F(b)(w_1))$, the induction step is completed.

Case 2: The production is $F \to (E)$.

Then $w = (w_1)$ with $w_1 \in L_{G_{pa},E}$.
We have

$$
\begin{array}{lll}
 & (\alpha\ op',\ (w_1)\ op''\ z,\ 1) & \\
\Rightarrow & (\alpha\ op'\ (,\ w_1)\ op''\ z,\ 1) & \text{definition of } \delta, \text{ line 2} \\
\Rightarrow^* & (\alpha\ op'\ (I_E(b)(w_1),\ )\ op''\ z,\ 2) & \text{induction hypothesis} \\
\Rightarrow & (\alpha\ op'\ I_E(b)(w_1),\ op''\ z,\ 2) & \text{definition of } \delta, \text{ line 7}
\end{array}
$$

(As in Case 1 the reader should again check carefully the applicability of induction hypothesis.)

Thus, because of $I_F(b)(w) = I_E(b)(w_1)$, the induction step is completed.

Case 3: The production is $T \to F$.

Then $w \in L_{G_{pa},F}$ and the conclusion is trivial.

Case 4: The production is $T \to T\ op\ F$ with $op \in \{\times, /\}$.

Then $w = w_1\ op\ w_2$ with $w_1 \in L_{G_{pa},T}$ and $w_2 \in L_{G_{pa},F}$.
We have

$$
\begin{array}{lll}
 & (\alpha\ op',\ w_1\ op\ w_2\ op''\ z,\ 1) & \\
\Rightarrow^* & (\alpha\ op'\ I_T(b)(w_1),\ op\ w_2\ op''\ z,\ 2) & \text{induction hypothesis} \\
\Rightarrow & (\alpha\ op'\ I_T(b)(w_1)\ op,\ w_2\ op''\ z,\ 1) & \text{definition of } \delta, \text{ line 6} \\
\Rightarrow^* & (\alpha\ op'\ I_T(b)(w_1)\ op\ I_F(b)(w_2),\ op''\ z,\ 2) & \text{induction hypothesis} \\
\Rightarrow & (\alpha\ op'\ Op(I_T(b)(w_1),\ I_F(b)(w_2)),\ op''\ z,\ 2) & \text{definition of } \delta, \text{ line 5}
\end{array}
$$

Thus, because of $I_T(b)(w) = Op(I_T(b)(w_1),\ I_F(b)(w_2))$, the induction step is completed.

Case 5: The production is $E \to T$.

Similarly to Case 3.

Case 6: The production is $E \to E\ op\ T$ with $op \in \{+, -\}$.

Similarly to Case 4.

The theorem now follows immediately from Lemma 7 as $(\vdash, w \dashv, 1) = in(w)$. According to our Lemma

$$(\vdash, w \dashv, 1) \Rightarrow^* (\vdash I_E(b)(w), \dashv, 2)$$

which is an end configuration. Thus $I/O_{M_{pa}}(b)(w) = I_E(b)(w)$.   ∎

We conclude this chapter with an assertion about the computation time of machine M_{pa}. As M_{pa} does not process a symbol of the rest expression at each step the assertion is somewhat more complicated than in the case of machine M_f.

Theorem 4. *Let $w \in L_{G_{pa}}$ be an expression. Then*
$comp_time_{M_{pa}}(w) = |w| + $ *number of occurrences of operators in w.*
(This also means $comp_time_{M_{pa}}(w) < 2|w|$)

Proof 1: Prove by induction on the length of the derivation to w analogous to the proof of Theorem 3. The details are left to the reader (Exercise 5 at the end of this section).

Proof 2: Let $t_i(w)$, $1 \leq i \leq 7$, be the number of applications of line i of the table for the transition function δ in the computation of M_{pa} for input w. Then $t_1(w) + t_2(w) + t_3(w) + t_6(w) + t_7(w) = |w|$, as only lines 4 and 5 do not process a symbol of the rest-expression. Furthermore lines 3 and 6 indicate that each (processed) operator is pushed onto the stack. An application of lines 4 and 5 removes an operator from the stack. Thus $t_4(w) + t_5(w) = $ number of occurrences of operators in w. The claim follows from

$$comp_time_{M_{pa}}(w) = t_1(w) + t_2(w) + \ldots + t_7(w)$$

∎

In conclusion, note that an extension by additional operators (e.g. the unary function "root" or the binary function "modulo") would be straightforward.

Exercises for 2.2

1) Let G be the following context-free grammar
$G = (\{F, H\}, \{a, -, \uparrow\}, P, F)$ with $P = \{F \to H, F \to -F, F \to H \uparrow F, H \to a\}$.

   a) Determine the derivation trees for $-a \uparrow a$, $a \uparrow a \uparrow a$, and $a \uparrow -a \uparrow -a$.

   b) In which sense are the following rules reflected in this grammar?

        "$\uparrow$ binds stronger than $-$", i.e. $-a \uparrow a$ is equivalent to $-(a \uparrow a)$

        "$\uparrow$ associates to the right", i.e. $a \uparrow a \uparrow a$ is equivalent to

        $a \uparrow (a \uparrow a)$

   Write at least one page as justification.

2) Extend the context-free grammar for arithmetic expressions G_{pa} by an operator "$\uparrow$" for exponentiation where $\uparrow$ binds to the right i.e. $a \uparrow b \uparrow c$ is equivalent to $a \uparrow (b \uparrow c)$. In addition the following precedence apply:

   a) $-$ (unary) before $\uparrow$,

      $\uparrow$ before $*$ and $/$,

      $*$ and $/$ before $+$ and $-$ (binary).

   b) $\uparrow$ before $-$ (unary),

      $-$ (unary) before $*$ and $/$,

      $*$ and $/$ before $+$ and $-$ (binary).

There are languages in which a) holds and others in which b) holds. Determine, respectively, for a) and b) the derivation trees of the following expressions :

        $-a \uparrow b$, $\; - - a$, $\; a \uparrow -b$, $\; a \uparrow b \uparrow c$, $\; a - b \uparrow c$

3) a) Specify a machine which processes expressions extended by the operation symbol $\uparrow$ (see Exercise 2). Only the variant b) ($\uparrow$ before $-$ (unary)) is to be considered. Run the machine for expression $-a \uparrow -a \uparrow a \times a$ with $b(a) = 2$.

   b) Specify the algebraic semantics of the extended expressions (only variant (b) from Exercise 2). You can assume (without proof) that your grammar is unambiguous.

   c) Prove the equivalence of the algebraic and algorithmic definition.

4) Specify a machine which translates expressions into Polish notation. Demonstrate your machine using the example
$a + b \times -c - d \times e / f.$

5) Give a proof of Theorem 4 using induction on the length of a derivation of w.

Chapter 3 PROSA, a Simple Programming Language

In this chapter we start describing a programming language called PROSA (**Programming language Saarbrücken**), and, in doing so, will introduce the fundamental concepts of ALGOL-like higher programming languages. Furthermore we present several nontrivial examples to illustrate PROSA and hereby give the reader a first impression of algorithmic problem solving.

There are many different programming languages. Perhaps some hundred programming languages are in use. They are classified according to different criteria. We distinguish roughly between a class of machine and assembler languages and a class of problem-oriented programming languages.

Machine and Assembler Languages are associated with one specific computer. If a machine program is loaded into storage, the processor can interpret the instructions of the machine program. The external representation of a machine program, be it in binary, octal or hexadecimal form, is difficult for humans to read. Programming in machine language is thus very laborious and error-prone. Assembler languages are somewhat easier to use. Essentially there is a 1-1 correspondence between assembler and machine instructions. In assembler programs instructions are not represented as numbers, but symbolically. Likewise addresses of storage cells can have symbolic names. As each assembler language is also associated with one computer the same problem as with machine languages arises, namely that programs written in such a language can not run on another computer. We say that these programs are not **portable**. In Chapter V we will introduce a simple machine language to discuss the translation of higher programming languages into machine language.

Problem-oriented languages (also called **higher** programming languages) provide concepts to formulate procedures for solving certain kinds of problems. While largely abstracting from the structure of the computer, usual mathematical notations are adopted. The programming language ALGOL 60 was developed, for example, to formulate procedures of numerical mathematics. Therefore it features integers, real numbers, vectors and matrices (arrays). Thus we can largely disregard the computer representation of numbers. Coefficients of a polynomial can be represented by a vector (one-dimensional array), coefficients of a system of equations by a matrix (two-dimensional array). More or less based on ALGOL 60, a whole series of programming languages was later developed which are also suitable for nonnumerical data processing, e.g. ALGOL 68, Pascal, Ada and PL/I. The programming language PROSA introduced in this book is in this ALGOL-Pascal tradition.

This book is concerned with the concepts of (ALGOL-like) programming languages and with their formal definition. PROSA contains the most important of these concepts. A detailed study of PROSA as presented in the following chapters enables the reader to adopt other programming languages independently and quickly. An unambiguous definition of a programming language is important for several reasons. For the programmer, an exact definition determines uniquely the meaning of the program and it thus permits correctness proofs (compare Section 3.9) as well as an analysis of its computation time (compare Section 3.10). For the implementor of the language, that is the developer of the compiler, it specifies precisely which language the compiler must accept and what meaning the programs of the language have. For the computer scientist engaged in research it is important, because he can investigate the language on the basis of a formal description and probably even generate a compiler or an interpreter from the formal description with the help of a suitable system.

This chapter is structured as follows. In Section 3.1 we introduce the fundamental concepts: syntax, context conditions and semantics and fix some notations for the rest of the chapter. Programs manipulate objects (data). They are introduced in Section 3.2. In 3.3 a first example of a PROSA program is given and, using that, important aspects of algorithmic languages are discussed. In 3.4 we begin with the definition of the PROSA machine. The PROSA machine is a mathematical machine (see 1.7) which executes PROSA programs. In Sections 3.5 to 3.8 PROSA is formally defined: the declaration section in 3.5, the statement section in 3.7 and the program in 3.6. Section 3.8 is a short summary. In Sections 3.9 and 3.10 we discuss correctness proofs and analysis of computation time and harvest the results of the formal definition of PROSA. The meaning of PROSA programs is precisely defined and thus permits mathematical discussion.

Finally all concepts are elaborated on in 3.11 in further examples. We advise the reader to consult this section now and then.

3.1 Syntax, Context Conditions and Semantics

The formal description of PROSA can be divided into three parts: syntax, context conditions and semantics. The **syntax** of PROSA is given by a context-free grammar, the same way as in Chapter II for arithmetic expressions. This grammar defines the set of (syntactically correct) PROSA programs. Using the grammar, it is possible to decide if a given word over the PROSA alphabet is a (syntactically correct) PROSA program.

The set of syntactically correct PROSA programs contains, on the other hand, many undesirable programs. Among those there are such as can be found to be undesirable by checking the program text, i.e. without executing the program. These are, for example, programs in which names are declared twice or not declared at all, or operations are applied to operands of an unsuitable type. Such errors can not be excluded by a context-free grammar. For that purpose one specifies **context conditions** as conditions on attributes (see 1.6). Syntactically correct PROSA programs satisfying the context conditions are called **PROSA programs** from now on, and the set of PROSA programs is called **PROGRAM**.

The **semantics** is defined as operational semantics, i.e. the meaning of PROSA programs is described with the help of an abstract machine M_{PROSA}, that is of an interpreter. This abstract machine, applied to a PROSA program and an input, executes the program in steps, "consumes" the input sequence one element at a time and produces some output. It stops or continues indefinitely. If it stops, it stops either regularly, i.e. because the program is complete, or irregularly, i.e. the next instruction is not executable. The input/output behaviour of the PROSA machine defines the semantics of PROSA programs. It is a function

$$I/O_{M_{PROSA}} : \mathbf{PROGRAM} \times \mathbf{D}^* \rightsquigarrow \mathbf{D}^*,$$

where $\mathbf{D}$ is the set of elementary objects (compare 3.2). The PROSA machine therefore takes a program and an input sequence ($=$ sequence of elementary objects) and produces an output sequence from them.

As already mentioned, we will define the syntax of PROSA by means of a context-free grammar $G_{PROSA} = (N, T, P, \langle program \rangle)$. In the course of this chapter productions P and the nonterminal alphabet N will be defined. For better legibility we use as nonterminals arbitrary words including empty symbols, enclosed in angle brackets. Typical nonterminal symbols are $\langle program \rangle$, $\langle decls \rangle$, $\langle stats \rangle$, $\langle expr \rangle$, etc... The start symbol is $\langle program \rangle$.

Likewise the terminal alphabet will also be introduced in the course of the chapter. It comprises, in particular, the letters $a, b, c, \ldots, A, B, \ldots, Z$, the digits $0, 1, 2, \ldots, 9$, some special symbols such as $(,), +, -, \ldots$ and key words such as **begin, end, integer, ...**
Some rules of the PROSA grammar are:

$\langle ident \rangle \rightarrow A|B| \ldots |Z|a|b|c| \ldots |z$

$\langle ident \rangle \rightarrow \langle ident \rangle A| \ldots |\langle ident \rangle z|\langle ident \rangle 0| \ldots \langle ident \rangle 9,$

i.e. $\langle ident \rangle$ generates all sequences of letters and digits beginning with a letter. For brevity we introduce the following notation: if $\langle word \rangle \in N$ then $\langle word \rangle$ stands for $L_{G,\langle word \rangle}$. We write for example $I71 \in \langle ident \rangle$ and $result \in \langle ident \rangle$. It will always be obvious from the context if $\langle word \rangle$ indicates a nonterminal or the language generated from this nonterminal.

To formulate the context conditions precisely we use attribute grammars (from now on we assume Section 1.6 to be understood), i.e. we extend the context-free PROSA grammar by semantic rules. We use words composed of capitals as names for attributes, e.g. $CONTEXT$, $TYPE$. For the domains of attributes we use words composed of capital and small letters, starting with a capital, i.e. $Type$, $Context$. We then formulate the context conditions as conditions on occurrences of attributes in productions. We now illustrate this method by some examples. All these examples will be explained in detail in the course of the chapter. It is therefore not necessary that the reader understands them in full detail at this point. A general impression is sufficient.

Example 1:

$$\langle expr \rangle \rightarrow \langle expr \rangle + \langle term \rangle$$

Condition: $TYPE(\langle expr \rangle_2) = TYPE(\langle term \rangle)$ and $TYPE(\langle expr \rangle_2) \in \{int, real\}$

Then: $TYPE(\langle expr \rangle_1) == TYPE(\langle expr \rangle_2)$

This specifies type evaluation for expressions describing additions. The context condition requires that the two operands of an addition have the same type. That is, the strings derived from the two nonterminals $\langle expr \rangle$ and $\langle term \rangle$ on the right hand side are of the same type, namely of type *int* or *real*. The type of the sum, that is of the string derived from the nonterminal $\langle expr \rangle$ occurring on the left, is defined in this case as the type of the two operands. It is not defined if the context condition is not satisfied.

If for a given syntactically correct program p all attributes in its derivation tree can be evaluated and all conditions for those attributes are satisfied, we say "p satisfies the context conditions" and call p a PROSA program.

Example 2:

$$\langle decl\ seq \rangle \rightarrow \langle decl\ seq \rangle; \langle decl \rangle$$

Condition: $Def(MB(\langle decl\ seq \rangle_2)) \cap Def(MB(\langle decl \rangle)) = \emptyset$

Then: $MB(\langle decl\ seq \rangle_1) == MB(\langle decl\ seq \rangle_2) \cup MB(\langle decl \rangle)$

This context condition states that the mode binding function (the mode binding function MB associates with each declared name its kind (*const* or *var*) and its type (*int*, *real*, *bool*, *char* or *string*)) for a declaration sequence is defined if and only if no name in the declaration sequence has a multiple occurrence, i.e. when there is no double declaration. If this is the case for the whole declaration section, the complete mode binding information of all declarations of the program is available at the nonterminal $\langle decls \rangle$ as an attribute $CONTEXT$, compare Example 3. Thus the attribute $CONTEXT$ provides kind and type (together called mode) of each declared name.

Example 3:

$$\langle decls \rangle \rightarrow \langle decl\ seq \rangle$$

$$CONTEXT(\langle decls \rangle) == MB(\langle decl\ seq \rangle);$$

This context information is associated with nonterminal $\langle program \rangle$ and is then available in the whole statement section.

Example 4:

$\langle program \rangle \rightarrow$ **program** $\langle ident \rangle; \langle decls \rangle$ **begin** $\langle stats \rangle$ **end.**

$CONTEXT(\langle program \rangle) == CONTEXT(\langle decls \rangle)$

Examples 1 to 4 show how context information is collected in the declaration section and how it is fed into the statement section. Figure 1 shows the information flow within a derivation tree.

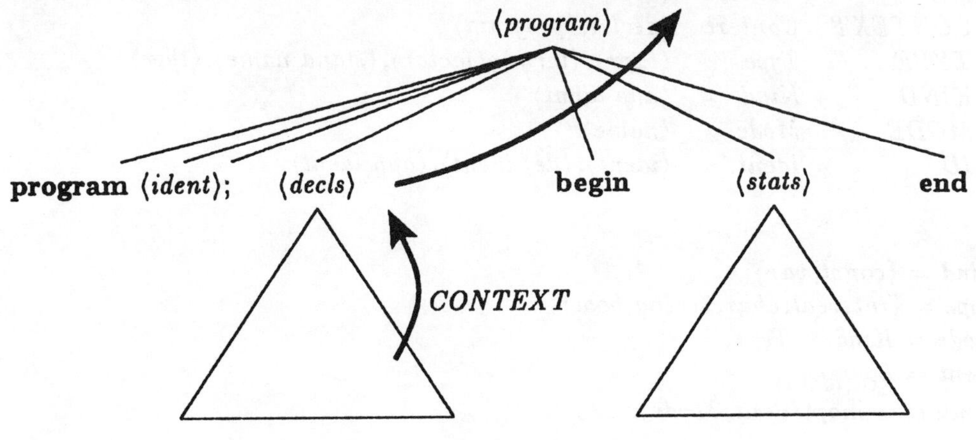

Fig. 1.

We now use attribute $CONTEXT(\langle program \rangle)$ in all places of the statement section where information about applied names is required.

Example 5:

$\langle name \rangle \rightarrow \langle app\ ident \rangle$

$MODE(\langle name \rangle) == CONTEXT(\langle program \rangle)(ID(\langle app\ ident \rangle))$

As mentioned above, one can retrieve the mode (= kind and type) of each name from attribute $CONTEXT$. $MODE(\langle name \rangle)$ is an element of $\{const,\ var\}$ $\times \{int,\ real,\ bool,\ char,\ string\}$. We use the mode of names to check, for example, the admissibility of assignments.

Example 6:

$\langle ass \rangle \rightarrow \langle name \rangle := \langle expr \rangle$

Condition: $MODE(\langle name \rangle) = (var, TYPE(\langle expr \rangle))$

An assignment has the form $n := E$ with $E \in \langle expr \rangle$ and $n \in \langle name \rangle$. The mode of n is retrieved from the context of the program (compare Example 5). The name must be a variable name and correspond in type to the expression. The type of the expression is computed as in Example 1.

Let us now collect all attributes, their domains and the nonterminals with which the attributes are associated in a table. This table is meant to be a reference for the rest of the chapter.

attribute	domain	nonterminal
MB	Context	$\langle decl \rangle$
CONTEXT	Context	$\langle decls \rangle, \langle program \rangle$
TYPE	Type	$\langle expr \rangle, \langle term \rangle, \langle factor \rangle, \langle stand\ name \rangle, \langle type \rangle$
KIND	Kind	$\langle app\ ident \rangle$
MODE	Mode	$\langle name \rangle$
ID	Ident	$\langle ident \rangle, \langle def\ ident \rangle, \langle app\ ident \rangle$

$$Kind = \{const, var\},$$
$$Type = \{int, real, char, string, bool\},$$
$$Mode = Kind \times Type,$$
$$Ident = L_{G, \langle ident \rangle},$$
$$Context = map(Ident, Mode).$$

3.2 Objects and Types

Programs manipulate **objects** (data) such as numbers, characters, truth values etc.. The set of objects, together with their properties and admissible operations, is in general adopted from a domain outside that of the programming language, mostly from mathematics. A set of objects with admissible operations is called a **data type**. In PROSA there are five **elementary data types**: integers (int), real numbers ($real$), characters ($char$), strings ($string$) and truth values ($bool$). The respective object sets are

$$\mathbf{D}_{int} \quad = \mathbb{Z}$$
$$\mathbf{D}_{real} \quad = \mathbb{R}$$
$$\mathbf{D}_{char} \quad = \{A, B, C, \ldots, Z, a, b, c, \ldots, z, 0, 1, \ldots, 9, \ , +, -, ., :, \ldots\}$$
$$\text{(finite, but not further specified here)}$$
$$\mathbf{D}_{string} = \mathbf{D}_{char}^{*}$$
$$\mathbf{D}_{bool} \quad = \{true, false\}$$

$\mathbf{D} = \mathbf{D}_{int} \cup \mathbf{D}_{real} \cup \mathbf{D}_{char} \cup \mathbf{D}_{string} \cup \mathbf{D}_{bool}$ is the set of all objects. PROSA includes the operations listed below. The meaning of most of these operations is well-known from the domain from which we have "borrowed" the objects. Arithmetic operations, in particular, will be known from mathematics. We use names such as *iplus* and *rplus* instead of the usual $+$ to differentiate between the operations on integers and real numbers and to distinguish the operation as such from the program notation for it.

Arithmetic operations:

$unaryminus : \mathbf{D}_{int} \to \mathbf{D}_{int}$

$div, mod : \mathbf{D}_{int} \times \mathbf{D}_{int} \rightsquigarrow \mathbf{D}_{int}$

$iplus, iminus, imul : \mathbf{D}_{int} \times \mathbf{D}_{int} \to \mathbf{D}_{int}$

$unaryrminus : \mathbf{D}_{real} \to \mathbf{D}_{real}$

$rplus, rminus, rmul : \mathbf{D}_{real} \times \mathbf{D}_{real} \to \mathbf{D}_{real}$

$rdiv : \mathbf{D}_{real} \times \mathbf{D}_{real} \rightsquigarrow \mathbf{D}_{real}$

For $x, y \in \mathbf{Z}$ we have $y = iplus(imul(x, div(y, x)), mod(y, x))$ and $0 \le mod(y, x) < x$ if $x > 0$, and $div(y, x)$ and $mod(y, x)$ undefined if $x \le 0$. The meaning of the remaining operations is obvious.

Logical Operations:

$non : \mathbf{D}_{bool} \to \mathbf{D}_{bool}$

$et, vel : \mathbf{D}_{bool} \times \mathbf{D}_{bool} \to \mathbf{D}_{bool}$

non is the negation, *et* is the boolean and-connective and *vel* is the boolean or-connective, i.e. $et(a, b) = true$ if and only if $a = b = true$, and $vel(a, b) = false$ if and only if $a = b = false$.

Relational operations:

$ilt, igt, ieq, ineq, ige, ile : \mathbf{D}_{int} \times \mathbf{D}_{int} \to \mathbf{D}_{bool}$

"*lt*" stands for "less then", "*gt*" for "greater then", etc.)

$rlt, rgt, req, rneq, rge, rle : \mathbf{D}_{real} \times \mathbf{D}_{real} \to \mathbf{D}_{bool}$

$clt, cgt, ceq, cneq, cge, cle : \mathbf{D}_{char} \times \mathbf{D}_{char} \to \mathbf{D}_{bool}$

We presume an ordering on $\mathbf{D}_{char}$.

String Operations:

$conc : \mathbf{D}_{string} \times \mathbf{D}_{string} \to \mathbf{D}_{string}$

$hd : \mathbf{D}_{string} \rightsquigarrow \mathbf{D}_{char}$

$tl : \mathbf{D}_{string} \rightsquigarrow \mathbf{D}_{string}$

$empty : \mathbf{D}_{string} \to \mathbf{D}_{bool}$

Operation *conc* is the concatenation, *hd* yields the first character of a nonempty string and $hd(\epsilon)$ is undefined. *tl* deletes the first character of a nonempty string and yields the rest of the string. $tl(\epsilon)$ is undefined.

Conversion operations:

$convcs : \mathbf{D}_{char} \rightarrow \mathbf{D}_{string}$

$convir : \mathbf{D}_{int} \rightarrow \mathbf{D}_{real}$

convcs produces a string of length one from a character and *convir* transforms an integer to a real number. For each nonempty string x the equation $x = conc(convcs(hd(x)), tl(x))$ holds.

Objects of $\mathbf{D}$ can be represented in PROSA programs by **standard names**. Standard names are chosen in such a way that they indicate the type of the represented object. In particular, characters and strings of length 1 have different representations. We give some examples for standard names.

$\mathbf{D}_{int}$: denary representation, e.g. 0 37 5

$\mathbf{D}_{real}$: decimal representation , e.g. 0.0 1.5 37.25

$\mathbf{D}_{char}$: character in quotes, e.g. 'A' 'b' ' '

$\mathbf{D}_{string}$: string in double quotes, e.g. "A" "PROSA" " "

$\mathbf{D}_{bool}$: **true   false**

The set of standard names is generated by the following grammar. For the context conditions we need attribute *TYPE* which yields the type for each standard name.

$\langle stand\ name \rangle \rightarrow \langle pos\ int\ stand\ name \rangle$

$TYPE(\langle stand\ name \rangle) == int$

$\langle stand\ name \rangle \rightarrow \langle pos\ real\ stand\ name \rangle$

$TYPE(\langle stand\ name \rangle) == real$

$\langle stand\ name \rangle \rightarrow \langle char\ stand\ name \rangle$

$TYPE(\langle stand\ name \rangle) == char$

$\langle stand\ name \rangle \rightarrow \langle string\ stand\ name \rangle$

$TYPE(\langle stand\ name \rangle) == string$

$\langle stand\ name \rangle \rightarrow \langle bool\ stand\ name \rangle$

$TYPE(\langle stand\ name \rangle) == bool$

$\langle pos\ int\ stand\ name \rangle \rightarrow \langle di \rangle | \langle pos\ int\ stand\ name \rangle \langle di \rangle$

$\langle pos\ real\ stand\ name \rangle \rightarrow \langle pos\ int\ stand\ name \rangle.\langle pos\ int\ stand\ name \rangle$

$\langle char\ stand\ name \rangle \rightarrow\ '\langle char \rangle'$

$\langle string\ stand\ name \rangle \rightarrow\ "\langle string \rangle"$

$\langle bool\ stand\ name \rangle \rightarrow$ **true**|**false**

$\langle di \rangle \rightarrow 0|\ldots|9$

$\langle char \rangle \rightarrow$ all representations of objects from $\mathbf{D}_{char}$

$\langle string \rangle \rightarrow$ all strings in $\langle char \rangle^*$ without "

A standard name denotes an object in $\mathbf{D}$. We make this connection explicit by a function $c : \langle stand\ name \rangle \rightarrow \mathbf{D}$ which associates with each standard name the object denoted by it. For example, $c(0) =$ integer *zero* in $\mathbf{D}_{int}$, $c(1.5) =$ real number *one point five* in $\mathbf{D}_{real}$.

When introducing elementary data types we implicitly assumed that the operations on the elementary types satisfy the usual laws. Unfortunately this does not match reality for the two arithmetic types, in particular for real numbers. Usually integers can be represented in a computer only in a certain range. For example, in many computers integers are represented by bitstrings of length 32 ; bitstring $a_{31}a_{30}\ldots a_0$ with $a_i \in \{0,1\}$ corresponds to the number $\sum_{i=0}^{30} a_i 2^i - a_{31} 2^{31}$. Thus just the numbers in the range of -2^{31} to $2^{31} - 1$ can be represented. If longer bitstrings are used we can, in principle, represent arbitrary integers.

With real numbers there is a genuine problem as they in general require an infinitely large representation. In computers we would usually represent real numbers as **floating point numbers** $m \times 2^e$; m is called the **mantissa** and e the **exponent**. If we use the above representation for mantissa and exponents and use 24 bits for the mantissa and 8 bits for the exponent then $-2^{23} \leq m < 2^{23}$ and $-2^7 \leq e < 2^7$. Of course only very "few" (finitely many!) real numbers can be represented in this way. Obviously arithmetic operations require rounding. An example for a calculation is

$$2^{23} \times 2^0 + 1 \times 2^{-1}$$

$\rightarrow\ 2^{23} \times 2^0 + 0.5 \times 2^0 \qquad$ make exponents equal

$\rightarrow\ (2^{23} + 0.5) \times 2^0 \qquad$ add mantissas

$\rightarrow\ 2^{23} \times 2^0 \qquad$ round mantissa to 24 bits

In this computation the equality symbol was left out intentionally. This example shows that real arithmetic on computers is subject to errors. Controlling rounding errors is studied intensively in numerical mathematics. In computer science there are attempts to replace floating point arithmetic by better methods. This lies outside the scope of this book. We exclude this problem in the following chapters by presuming that the integers and real numbers of mathematics together with their corresponding laws are available in PROSA.

3.3 A PROSA Program

By way of a simple example we now want to give a first idea of PROSA. Our program example evaluates a polynomial according to Horner's scheme. We assume that the input tape contains a sequence $n, x, a_n, \ldots, a_0$ with $n \in \mathbb{N}$ and $x, a_n, \ldots, a_0 \in \mathbb{R}$. Our task is to compute

$$\sum_{i=0}^{n} a_i x^i$$

An obvious method is to calculate in sequence the sums

$s_{n+1} = 0$
$s_n \quad = a_n$
$s_{n-1} = a_n x + a_{n-1} = s_n x + a_{n-1}$
$s_{n-2} = a_n x^2 + a_{n-1} x + a_{n-2} = s_{n-1} x + a_{n-2}$

$\qquad \cdot$
$\qquad \cdot$
$\qquad \cdot$

$s_0 \quad = a_n x^n + a_{n-1} x^{n-1} + \ldots + a_0 = s_1 x + a_0$

This method is known as **Horner's scheme**. Program 1 is a formulation of Horner's scheme in PROSA.

A PROSA program consists of the key word **program**, the name of the program (here *Horner_scheme*), the declaration section, the key word **begin**, the statement section and the key word **end** followed by a dot. The key words **begin** and **end** serve as brackets for the statement section and the dot indicates the end of the program. (In Chapter 6 we will permit nesting of programs by introducing procedures; **begin** ... **end** will then be of importance. In this chapter it is used only for uniformity). In a program one may insert comments at any place. A comment is an arbitrary text enclosed in brackets (* and *). They are intended for the reader of the program and should help him to understand the program. They have no bearing on the semantics of PROSA programs.

Variables and **constants** are introduced in the declaration section. A variable is declared by giving its name and its type. For example, an integer variable with the name N is introduced by **var** N : **integer**. Similarly, **var** X : **real** introduces a variable X which can assume real values. The declaration does not initialise a variable. It is not until the statement part that variables are assigned values. The value of a variable can change during the execution of the program.

```
program Horner_scheme;
(* the input tape holds a sequence n, x, aₙ, ..., a₀ with
```
$n \in \mathbb{N}, x \in \mathbb{R}, a_i \in \mathbb{R}$ for $0 \le i \le n$ *)
```
const  ZERO = 0.0;
var N : integer; var I : integer; var X : real; var A : real; var S : real;
begin  read N; read X; S := ZERO; I := N;
```
$\quad$ (* $N = n$, $X = x$, $I = n$, $S = \sum_{j=I+1}^{n} a_j x^{j-I-1}$,

$\quad\quad$ and input tape still holds $a_I, \ldots, a_0$ *)

$\quad$ **while** $I \ge 0$

$\quad$ **do** (* $N = n$, $X = x$, $S = \sum_{j=I+1}^{n} a_j x^{j-I-1}$

$\quad\quad\quad$ and input tape still holds $a_I, \ldots, a_0$ *)

```
    read A;
    S := S * X + A;
    I := I - 1
    od ;
```
$\quad$ (* $S = \sum_{j=0}^{n} a_j x^j$ *)
```
    print S
end.
```

_______________________ **Prog. 1** _______________________

A variable consists of three parts: a name, a storage location of a certain type and a value of this type. The value can be undefined. The PROSA machine has an infinite amount of storage locations of each of the five elementary types at its disposal.

$\mathbf{V}_{int} = \{v_1^{int}, v_2^{int}, \ldots\}$ is the name given to the set of storage locations of type *int*. Similarly we define $\mathbf{V}_{real}$, $\mathbf{V}_{bool}$, $\mathbf{V}_{char}$ and $\mathbf{V}_{string}$. The declaration **var** N : **integer** introduces the name N for a storage location in $\mathbf{V}_{int}$. We also say that the name N is bound to a storage location in $\mathbf{V}_{int}$, or that a storage location in $\mathbf{V}_{int}$ is bound to N. This storage location can then be used in the statement section to store integers. Thus, for example, **read** N has the effect of taking the first element of the input sequence (here n) and storing it in the storage location bound to N.

A constant name is introduced by giving its name and a standard name. In our example **const** $ZERO = 0.0$ introduces the identifier $ZERO$ as a name for the real number *zero*. After executing this declaration 0.0 and $ZERO$ are synonymous.

To summarise, in the declaration section we introduce names for variables and constants. In the case of variables we declare their type, for constants we specify the object for which the name should stand.

In our example the declaration section introduces six names, five variable names and a constant name. N and I are names for integer variables and X, A and S are names for real variables. Constant $ZERO$ stands for the real number *zero*.

The statement section specifies the computation proper. It consists of a sequence of statements which are executed one after the other. The simplest statements are the read statement (e.g. **read** N), the print statement (e.g. **print** S) and the assignment (e.g. $S := S * X + A$). The read statement takes the first element of the input sequence and stores it in the given variable. The print statement computes the value of an expression and appends it to the output sequence. Finally, in an assignment the value of the expression to the right of the assignment symbol $:=$ is assigned to the variable on the left. In the example, therefore, the expression $S * X + A$ is evaluated and the real number resulting is stored in the storage location called S.

Apart from simple statements there are compound statements. These are the conditional statement and the loop statement. In our example we have the loop statement

> **while** $I \geq 0$
>
> **do read** A; $S := S * X + A$; $I := I - 1$ **od**

The semantics of the loop statement is as follows. Firstly, the loop condition (here $I \geq 0$) is evaluated. If it yields *true* the body (here: **read** A; $S := S * X + A$; $I := I - 1$) and once again the loop statement is executed. (The key words **do** and **od** enclose the body of the loop.) If the loop condition yields *false* the execution of the loop statement terminates. In our example we enter the loop body with values $n, n - 1, \ldots, 0$ for I. If at entry I has the value i then numbers $a_i, \ldots, a_0$ are on the input tape and the value of variable S is s_{i+1}. We then read a_i and change the value of variable S to the value of the expression $S * X + A$. This value is $s_{i+1} \cdot x + a_i = s_i$. Finally we decrease I by 1. Thus we are in a situation similar to the situation before entering the loop body. Let i' $(= i - 1)$ be the new value of variable I. Then numbers $a_{i'}, \ldots, a_0$ are on the input tape and variable S has the value $s_{i'}$. The comment inserted in the loop body therefore remains correct. We also say that the comment is an invariant of the loop. Invariants are discussed in detail in Section 3.9.

3.4 The PROSA Machine

The **PROSA machine** M_{PROSA} executes PROSA programs. It has a processor
which executes the statements of the programs, a program store holding the programs to be executed, a data store in which intermediate results of computations
are stored, an input device which reads from the input tape and an output device
which writes onto the output tape. The data store of M (usually we write M
instead of M_{PROSA}) is divided into storage cells.

The PROSA machine is a mathematical machine in the sense of Section 1.7,
i.e.

$$M_{PROSA} = (\mathbf{C}, \mathbf{C}^f, \mathbf{PROGRAM}, \delta, \mathbf{I}, \mathbf{O}, in, out)$$

In this section we will define the configuration set $\mathbf{C}$, the end configurations $\mathbf{C}^f$,
the sets of inputs and outputs $\mathbf{I}$ and $\mathbf{O}$ and the functions in and out. The transition
function δ and the set **PROGRAM** of PROSA programs are introduced in Sections
3.5 to 3.8.

A configuration of the PROSA machine consists of the **program-rest** still to
be executed, of a **binding**, a **storage state**, an **input sequence** and an **output
sequence**, i.e.

$$\mathbf{C} = \mathbf{PR} \times \mathbf{B} \times \mathbf{S} \times \mathbf{D}^* \times \mathbf{D}^*$$

PR is the set of possible program-rests, **B** is the set of bindings and **S** the set of
storage states. The input and output sequences are sequences of elementary objects.

The storage of the PROSA machine is divided into five sections, one for each
of the five elementary types. Let $t \in Type$ be an elementary type. The t-storage $\mathbf{V}_t$
consists of infinitely many storage locations (also called storage cells) $v_1^t, v_2^t, v_3^t, \ldots,$
which can hold arbitrary objects of type t. $\mathbf{V} = \mathbf{V}_{int} \cup \mathbf{V}_{real} \cup \mathbf{V}_{string} \cup \mathbf{V}_{char} \cup \mathbf{V}_{bool}$
is the set of storage cells. The **storage state** is a function which associates with
each storage cell its contents. Clearly, storage cells in $\mathbf{V}_t$ can only hold objects from
$\mathbf{D}_t$. The set of storage states is

$$\mathbf{S} = \{s \mid s : \mathbf{V} \rightsquigarrow \mathbf{D} \text{ and } s(v) \in \mathbf{D}_t \text{ if } s(v) \text{ is defined and } v \in \mathbf{V}_t \text{ for some } t \in Type\}$$

The declarations of PROSA programs introduce names for storage locations
and objects. The PROSA machine records the meaning of the names introduced in
the program by means of binding b. The binding determines for each name either a
storage location (if the name denotes a storage location) or an object (if the name
denotes a constant), i.e.

$$\mathbf{B} = \{b \mid b : \langle ident \rangle \rightsquigarrow \mathbf{V} \cup \mathbf{D}\}$$

A program-rest is the part of a program not yet executed. It is a sequence of
statements possibly preceded by a sequence of declarations, thus

$$\mathbf{PR} = \{p; \mid p \in \langle stat\ seq \rangle \text{ or } p = d; q \text{ with } d \in \langle decl\ seq \rangle \text{ and } \\ q \in \langle stat\ seq \rangle\}$$

In an end configuration the program-rest and the input sequence are empty, i.e.

$$\mathbf{C}^f = \{(p,b,s,i,o) \in \mathbf{C} \mid p = \epsilon \text{ and } i = \epsilon\}$$

The set of outputs $\mathbf{O}$ is the set of sequences of elementary objects, i.e. $\mathbf{O} = \mathbf{D}^*$. Function *out* extracts the output sequence from each end state

$$out : \mathbf{C}^f \to \mathbf{D}^*$$
$$out((\epsilon,b,s,\epsilon,o)) = o$$

An input for the PROSA machine is an input sequence, i.e. $\mathbf{I} = \mathbf{D}^*$. Function $in : \mathbf{PROGRAM} \times \mathbf{I} \to \mathbf{C}$ yields the respective start configuration for each pair of PROSA program and input sequence. In start configuration binding and storage state are the empty functions, respectively, and the output sequence is the empty sequence of objects, i.e.

$in((p,i)) = (ds\ sts; , \emptyset, \emptyset, i, \epsilon)$
with $p = $ **program** $n;\ ds$ **begin** sts **end**.
$n \in \langle ident \rangle, ds \in \langle decls \rangle, sts \in \langle stats \rangle$ and $i \in \mathbf{D}^*$.

Thus the machine starts computation in a "virgin" state, i.e. all storage cells are still empty, no name has a meaning and the output tape is still empty.

We now illustrate these definitions using Program 1 of Section 3.3. As input sequence we take $i = (3, 1.0, 2.0, 4.7, 6.9, 3.2)$. The start configuration then is $(q; , \emptyset, \emptyset, i, \epsilon)$ where q is the program without key words **program**, **begin**, **end** and without program name *Horner_scheme*. The program name is semantically irrelevant. It can be used to refer to the program when necessary. After executing the declaration section (the definition of transition function δ is found in 3.5) we reach a configuration

$c_1 = (p_1, b_1, s_1, i, \epsilon)$ with

$p_1 = $ **read** $N;$ **read** $X;\ S := ZERO;\ I := N;$
      while $I \geq 0$
      do read $A;\ S := S * X + A;\ I := I - 1$ **od**;
      print $S;$

and $b_1 \in \mathbf{B}$ with

$$Def(b_1) = \{N, X, S, A, I, ZERO\}$$
$$b_1(N) = v_1^{int}, b_1(I) = v_2^{int}$$
$$b_1(X) = v_1^{real}, b_1(S) = v_2^{real}, b_1(A) = v_3^{real}, b_1(ZERO) = zero$$

We then read N and X and assign values to S and I. Next the loop is to be executed. The condition $I \geq 0$ yields *true* as I has value 3. Then A is read and a new value assigned to S. The configuration now reached is $c_2 = (p_2, b_1, s_2, i_2, \epsilon)$ where

$$p_2 = \begin{aligned}&I := I - 1;\\&\textbf{while } I \geq 0 \textbf{ do read } A;\ S := S * X + A;\ I := I - 1 \textbf{ od};\\&\textbf{print } S;\end{aligned}$$

$$s_2 \in S \ \text{ with}$$
$$Def(s_2) = \{v_1^{int}, v_2^{int}, v_1^{real}, v_2^{real}, v_3^{real}\}$$
$$s_2(v_1^{int}) = 3,\quad s_2(v_2^{int}) = 3,$$
$$s_2(v_1^{real}) = 1.0,\quad s_2(v_2^{real}) = 2.0,\quad s_2(v_3^{real}) = 2.0$$
$$i_2 = (4.7,\ 6.9,\ 3.2)$$

The above notation for binding and storage state is not very clear. Hence we mostly use a pictorial representation as illustrated by the "environment" (b_1, s_2) , compare Figure 1.

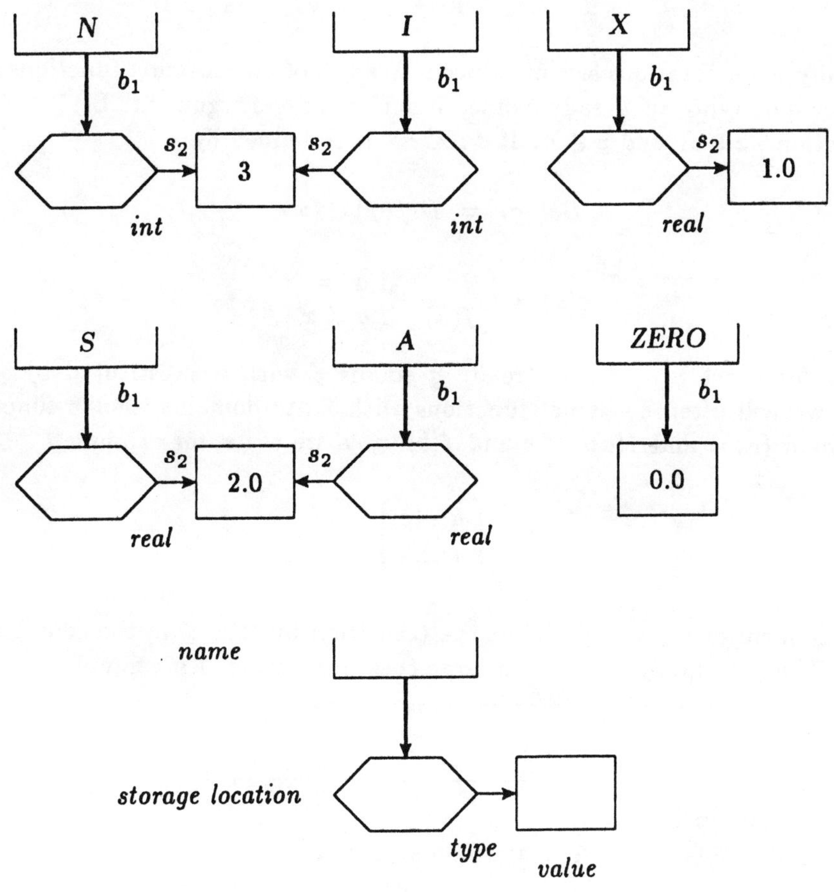

Fig. 1.

This diagram shows clearly the three components of a variable: name, storage location and value. We draw objects as boxes containing the standard name of the object, storage locations as boxes with "angle" corners and names as open

containers into which we write the names. Functions b and s are given by thick
or thin arrows, respectively. In the case of storage locations we usually indicate
their type. To simplify the illustrations we often draw several copies of an object,
compare Figure 2.

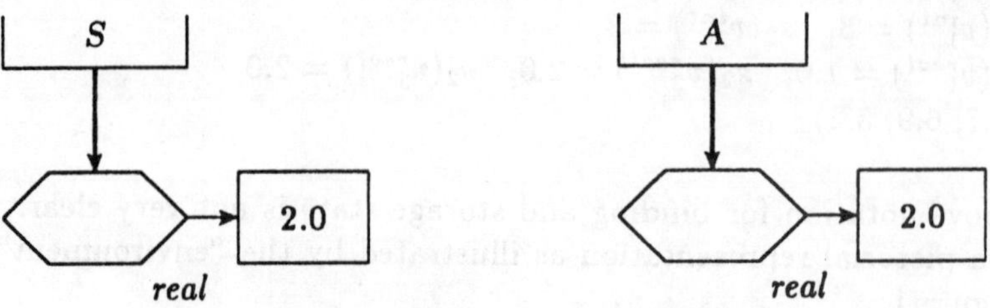

Fig. 2.

Finally some notations are introduced. We will often construct functions in this
chapter by modifying an already defined function for one argument. Let $f : X \rightsquigarrow Y$
be a function , $x \in X$ and $y \in Y$. If $g : X \rightsquigarrow Y$ is defined by

$$Def(g) \;=\; Def(f) \cup \{x\}$$

$$g(a) = \begin{cases} y & \text{if } a \;=\; x \\ f(a) & \text{if } a \neq x \end{cases},$$

We write for short $g \;=\; f[x \backslash y]$ (read: g equals f with x substituted by y). In
addition we will often construct functions with finite domains. For a function f
with domain $\{a,b\}$ and $f(a) \;=\; c$ and $f(b) \;=\; d$ we write, for example,

$$\left\{ \begin{array}{l} a \rightarrow c \\ b \rightarrow d \end{array} \right\}$$

As already mentioned, we will define the transition function δ in the course of this
chapter. This is done by means of a large case distinction. An example is

(CD)

---

p **has** the form **const** $n = t; p'$
        with $n \in \langle ident \rangle, t \in \langle stand\ name \rangle, p' \in \mathbf{PR}$.
Then
        $(p, b, s, i, o) \Rightarrow (p', b', s, i, o)$ with $b' = b[n \backslash c(t)]$

When defining the transition function, it is assumed that $c \;=\; (p, b, s, i, o)$ is the
current configuration. The case distinction in the definition of δ follows the syntactic
form of the program-rest. In our example the program-rest begins with a constant

declaration. In the successor configuration $\delta(c) = c' = (p', b', s, i, o)$ the program-rest and the binding are changed. All remaining components are unchanged. The new program-rest follows from the old by deleting the declaration. The new binding b' follows from the old binding b by setting the value for n to $c(t)$, i.e. in the new binding we record that n is the name of object $c(t)$. As a mnemonical abbreviation for this transition CD (Constant Declaration) is used.

Finally, two concepts are introduced, free storage locations and environment. A pair $(b, s) \in B \times S$ of binding and storage state is called **environment**. The set $\mathbf{FV}_{c,t}$ of **free storage locations** of type $t \in Type$ with respect to a configuration $c = (p, b, s, i, o)$ is given by

$$\mathbf{FV}_{c,t} = \mathbf{V}_t - image(b),$$

i.e. $\mathbf{FV}_{c,t}$ is the set of storage locations of type t not yet bound to any names.

3.5 The Declaration Section

The **declaration section** is at the beginning of a PROSA program. It is a (possibly empty) sequence of constant and variable declarations. In a **constant declaration** we introduce an identifier as a name for an object and in a **variable declaration** we introduce an identifier as a name for a storage location. The syntax of the declaration section is as follows.

$\langle decls \rangle \rightarrow \epsilon \,|\, \langle decl\ seq \rangle;$

$\langle decl\ seq \rangle \rightarrow \langle decl \rangle \,|\, \langle decl\ seq \rangle;\langle decl \rangle$

$\langle decl \rangle \rightarrow \langle const\ decl \rangle \,|\, \langle var\ decl \rangle$

$\langle const\ decl \rangle \rightarrow \mathbf{const}\ \langle def\ ident \rangle = \langle stand\ name \rangle$

$\langle var\ decl \rangle \rightarrow \mathbf{var}\ \langle def\ ident \rangle : \langle elem\ type \rangle$

$\langle elem\ type \rangle \rightarrow \mathbf{integer}\,|\,\mathbf{real}\,|\,\mathbf{char}\,|\,\mathbf{string}\,|\,\mathbf{boolean}$

$\langle def\ ident \rangle \rightarrow \langle ident \rangle$

Example 1:   Two examples for declaration sections are
(a) **var** a : **integer**; **const** $izero = 0$; **var** b : **real**; **const** $rzero = 0.0$;
(b) **var** a : **integer**; **var** c : **boolean**; **var** a : **real**;   ∎

The PROSA machine processes the declaration in a declaration section one by
one and successively constructs a binding. The transitions for the execution of a
constant (CD) or variable declaration (VD) are

(CD)

---

p **has** the form **const** $n = t; p'$
       with $n \in \langle ident \rangle, t \in \langle stand\ name \rangle, p' \in \mathbf{PR}$.
Then
$$(p, b, s, i, o) \Rightarrow (p', b', s, i, o) \text{ with } b' = b[n \backslash c(t)]$$

(VD)

---

p **has** the form **var** $n : t; p'$
       with $n \in \langle ident \rangle, t \in \langle elem\ type \rangle, p' \in \mathbf{PR}$
Then
$$(p, b, s, i, o) \Rightarrow (p', b', s, i, o) \text{ with } b' = b[n \backslash v].$$
$v \in \mathbf{FV}_{c,t}$ is arbitrary.

Explanation of VD: $\mathbf{FV}_{c,t}$ is the set of storage locations not yet bound to any
names. From this set we choose an arbitrary storage location and bind it to the
name n. In our examples we always choose $v = v_i^t$ where i is the smallest index for
which $v_i^t \epsilon \mathbf{FV}_{c,t}$.

Example (continued):   After processing the declaration section we obtain the
following binding b

(a) $Def(b) = \{a, izero, b, rzero\}$
    $b(a) = v_1^{int}$, $b(b) = v_1^{real}$, $b(izero) = c(0)$, $b(rzero) = c(0.0)$

(b) $Def(b) = \{a, c\}$
    $b(a) = v_1^{real}$, $b(c) = v_1^{bool}$ ∎

In Example 1b the name a is declared twice. Although the PROSA machine can
easily cope with multiple declarations (it always records only the last one), multiple
declarations are undesirable as they usually lead to misunderstandings on the part
of the reader of the program. We therefore forbid multiple declarations. Thus for
the nonterminals of the declaration grammar an attribute MB (**mode binding**)

is introduced in which declared names and their mode are recorded. The mode of a name consists of its sort (constant or variable name) and its type. We need the mode of declared names in order to check context conditions in the statement section (e.g. type correctness). A name occurring in the statement section is called **an applied** occurrence and names occurring in the declaration section are called **defining** occurrences. We require: each applied occurrence of a name corresponds to exactly one defining occurrence, i.e. names may only be declared once and each name must be declared. To be able to check this condition we have only to record the set of declared names. The additional information, mode and type of declared names, permits us to check the correct use of names in the statement section. Similar to Section 3.1 we introduce

$$Sort \;=\; \{const, var\}$$
$$Type \;=\; \{int, real, boolean, char, string\}$$
$$Mode \;=\; Sort \times Type$$
$$Context \;=\; map(\langle ident \rangle, Mode)$$

The evaluation of attributes of the declaration section takes place according to the following rules. First we deal with the productions for $\langle const\ decl \rangle$ and $\langle var\ decl \rangle$.

$$\langle const\ decl \rangle \rightarrow \textbf{const}\ \ \langle def\ ident \rangle = \langle stand\ name \rangle$$
$$MB(\langle const\ decl \rangle) == \{ ID(\langle def\ ident \rangle) \rightarrow (const, TYPE(\langle stand\ name \rangle)) \}$$

$$\langle var\ decl \rangle \rightarrow \textbf{var}\ \ \langle def\ ident \rangle : \langle elem\ type \rangle$$
$$MB(\langle var\ decl \rangle) == \{ ID(\langle def\ ident \rangle) \rightarrow (var, TYPE(\langle elem\ type \rangle)) \}$$

The attribute value for a nonterminal $\langle const\ decl \rangle$ or $\langle var\ decl \rangle$ is a mode binding function. This function has a singleton domain which consists of exactly the declared name. The function yields its mode, i.e. its sort (*const* or *var*) and its type. The declaration **var** a : **integer**, therefore, results in mode binding $\{a \rightarrow (var, int)\}$ and the declaration **const** *pi* = 3.14 in mode binding $\{pi \rightarrow (const, real)\}$. To make these examples completely understandable we need the evaluation of attributes of the productions for $\langle elem\ type \rangle$ and $\langle def\ ident \rangle$. In attribute *TYPE* of the nonterminal $\langle elem\ type \rangle$ we record the derived type. Attribute *ID* of a name and of a defined name records the derived word. Thus

$$\langle elem\ type \rangle \rightarrow \textbf{integer} \qquad\qquad \langle elem\ type \rangle \rightarrow \textbf{string}$$
$$TYPE(\langle elem\ type \rangle) == int \qquad\qquad TYPE(\langle elem\ type \rangle) == string$$

$$\langle elem\ type \rangle \rightarrow \textbf{real} \qquad\qquad \langle elem\ type \rangle \rightarrow \textbf{bool}$$
$$TYPE(\langle elem\ type \rangle) == real \qquad\qquad TYPE(\langle elem\ type \rangle) == bool$$

$$\langle elem\ type \rangle \rightarrow \textbf{char}$$
$$TYPE(\langle elem\ type \rangle) == char$$

$$\langle ident \rangle \rightarrow A \qquad\qquad\qquad \langle ident \rangle \rightarrow B$$
$$ID(\langle ident \rangle) == A \qquad\qquad\quad ID(\langle ident \rangle) == B$$

analogous for all other alternatives of the grammar for names (compare 3.1)

$$\langle ident \rangle \rightarrow \langle ident \rangle A$$
$$ID(\langle ident \rangle_1) == ID(\langle ident \rangle_2)A$$

analogous for all other alternatives of the grammar for names (compare 3.1)

$$\langle def\ ident \rangle \rightarrow \langle ident \rangle$$
$$ID(\langle def\ ident \rangle) == ID(\langle ident \rangle)$$

We obtain the mode binding of a sequence of declarations by collecting the mode bindings of individual declarations. We check each time for multiple declarations.

$$\langle decl \rangle \rightarrow \langle const\ decl \rangle$$
$$MB(\langle decl \rangle) == MB(\langle const\ decl \rangle)$$

$$\langle decl \rangle \rightarrow \langle var\ decl \rangle$$
$$MB(\langle decl \rangle) == MB(\langle var\ decl \rangle)$$

$$\langle decl\ seq \rangle \rightarrow \langle decl \rangle$$
$$MB(\langle decl\ seq \rangle) == MB(\langle decl \rangle)$$

$$\langle decl\ seq \rangle \rightarrow \langle decl\ seq \rangle; \langle decl \rangle$$

Condition: $Def(MB(\langle decl\ seq \rangle_2) \cap Def(MB(\langle decl \rangle)) = \emptyset$

Then: $\qquad MB(\langle decl\ seq \rangle_1) == MB(\langle decl\ seq \rangle_2) \cup MB(\langle decl \rangle)$

$$\langle decls \rangle \rightarrow \epsilon$$
$$CONTEXT(\langle decls \rangle) = \emptyset$$

$$\langle decls \rangle \rightarrow \langle decl\ seq \rangle;$$
$$CONTEXT(\langle decls \rangle) == MB(\langle decl\ seq \rangle)$$

The most interesting rule is the production $\langle decl\ seq\rangle \rightarrow \langle decl\ seq\rangle;\langle decl\rangle$. As context condition we state that the domains of the two mode binding functions must be disjoint, i.e. the name newly introduced in the declaration is not already declared in the preceding declaration sequence. Thus double declarations are excluded. The attribute evaluation for the left side of the rule succeeds only if this condition is satisfied.

Example (continued):

(a) The declaration section leads to the following context.
$$\{\ a\quad\ \rightarrow\quad (var, int),$$
$$\quad izero\ \rightarrow\quad (const, int),$$
$$\quad b\quad\ \rightarrow\quad (var, real),$$
$$\quad rzero\ \rightarrow\quad (const, real)\ \}$$

(b) In this example a context condition is violated. Figure 1 shows part of the derivation tree and the relevant attributes. The attribute values are given, respectively, in the box beside the nonterminal.

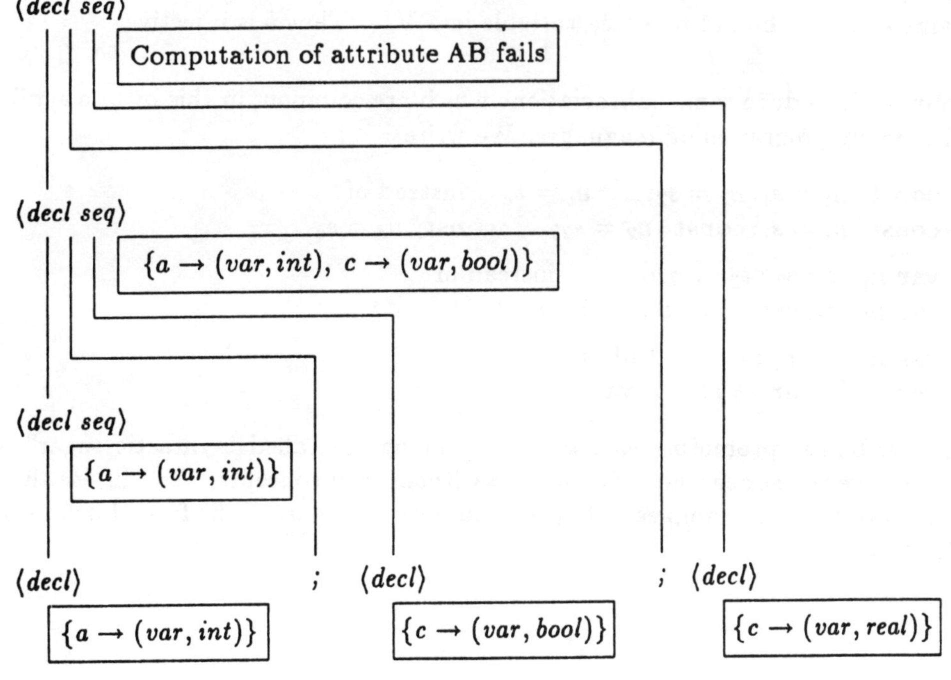

Fig. 1.

This concludes the definition of syntax, context conditions (with the help of attributes) and semantics (with the help of the PROSA machine) of the declaration section. The following theorem relates context conditions and semantics.

Theorem 1. *Let $ds \in \langle decls \rangle$ be a declaration section satisfying the context conditions, i.e. the attribute $CONTEXT$ at the root of the derivation tree from $\langle decls \rangle$ to ds can be successfully evaluated. Let $co \in Context$ be the value of this attribute at the root of the derivation tree. Let b be the binding obtained after execution of ds by the PROSA machine. We have*

(1) $Def(co) = Def(b)$

(2) *for all $n \in Def(b)$ and all $t \in Type$:*
$$b(n) \in \mathbf{D}_t \Leftrightarrow co(n) = (const, t)$$
$$b(n) \in \mathbf{V}_t \Leftrightarrow co(n) = (var, t)$$

(3) *for $n, m \in Def(b), n \neq m, b(n) \in \mathbf{V}, b(m) \in \mathbf{V} :\ b(n) \neq b(m)$*

Proof: These three properties are quite obvious. The first property follows from the fact that we collected information about individual declarations during attribute evaluation and during construction of the binding. For the second property we consider first of all an individual declaration. By comparing the semantic rules and the transitions of the PROSA machine we see that the second property is satisfied for an individual declaration. As the context conditions are satisfied and hence no name is multiply declared, it holds for the whole declaration section. The third property is, in conclusion, a direct consequence of the definition of transition VD. A name is always bound to a free variable in $\mathbf{FV}_{c,t}$. Thus b is injective.　　■

Finally, we introduce some abbreviations which are common, in this or in a similar way, in many programming languages. We write

(1) **const** $n_1 = s_1; n_2 = s_2; \ldots; n_c = s_c$　　instead of
$\quad$ **const** $n_1 = s_1;$ **const** $n_2 = s_2; \ldots;$ **const** $n_c = s_c$

(2) **var** $n_1 : t_1; n_2 : t_2; \ldots; n_c : t_c$　　instead of
$\quad$ **var** $n_1 : t_1;$ **var** $n_2 : t_2; \ldots;$ **var** $n_c : t_c$

(3) **var** $n_1, \ldots, n_c : t$　　instead of
$\quad$ **var** $n_1 : t;$ **var** $n_2 : t; \ldots;$ **var** $n_c : t$

Such possibilities promoting ease of programming are called "syntactic sugar" as they improve the appearance of programs without new concepts. We will use these abbreviations in our examples. They are, however, not part of the formal definition of PROSA.

3.6 The Program

A **PROSA program** consists of a declaration section introducing names and a statement section describing the algorithm. The statement section is enclosed in brackets **begin** ... **end** and is executed in the context given by the declaration section. The key word **program** and the program name precede the declaration section.

$\langle program \rangle \rightarrow$ **program** $\langle ident \rangle; \langle decls \rangle$ **begin** $\langle stats \rangle$ **end.**

$CONTEXT(\langle program \rangle) == CONTEXT(\langle decls \rangle)$

We have already seen a PROSA program in Section 3.3. Further examples are to be found in Section 3.11.

Let $p =$ **program** $n;$ ds **begin** sts **end.** be a PROSA program and let $i \in D^*$ be an input sequence. Then the start configuration of the PROSA machine for program p and input sequence i is $(ds\ sts; \emptyset,\ \emptyset,\ i,\ \epsilon)$ (compare 3.4). This defines, in particular, the semantics of program p.

3.7 The Statement Section

The **statement section** consists of a sequence of statements. A single statement is either an assignment, a conditional statement, an iteration statement, an input statement, an output statement or an error statement. Every statement is executed in the context given by the declaration section. The mode of each name in the statement section can be obtained from the attribute $CONTEXT(\langle program \rangle)$. The syntax of the statement section is as follows.

$\langle stats \rangle \rightarrow \langle stat\ seq \rangle$

$\langle stat\ seq \rangle \rightarrow \langle stat\ seq \rangle; \langle stat \rangle \,|\, \langle stat \rangle$

$\langle stat \rangle \rightarrow \langle ass \rangle \,|\, \langle cond \rangle \,|\, \langle iter \rangle \,|\, \langle input \rangle \,|\, \langle output \rangle \,|\, \langle error \rangle$

The statements of a statement sequence are executed in the textual order. In executing a statement (in the non-error case) M moves from configuration c to configuration c'. Two successive statements $Stat_1; Stat_2$ are executed by M in the following manner. M begins executing $Stat_1$ in configuration c and finishes it in configuration c'. Then M begins executing $Stat_2$ in configuration c'. We now discuss the various statements in Sections 3.7.1 to 3.7.7.

3.7.1 Assignments

An **assignment** consists of a name on the left side and an expression on the right
side of the assignment operator "$:=$". The name must be a variable name and its
type must coincide with the type of the expression.

By executing the assignment $n := E$ the storage state of machine M is changed.
The value for the argument $b(n)$, i.e. for the variable bound to n, is set to the value
of the expression E in the current environment.

We now give the formal definition of syntax, context conditions and semantics.

Syntax and Context conditions

$\langle ass \rangle \rightarrow \langle name \rangle := \langle expr \rangle$

Condition: $MODE(\langle name \rangle) = (var, TYPE(\langle expr \rangle))$

$\langle name \rangle \rightarrow \langle app\ ident \rangle$

$MODE(\langle name \rangle) == CONTEXT(\langle program \rangle)(ID(\langle app\ ident \rangle))$

$\langle app\ ident \rangle \rightarrow \langle ident \rangle$

$ID(\langle app\ ident \rangle == ID(\langle ident \rangle)$

These rules require explanation. Attribute $CONTEXT(\langle program \rangle)$ is a mode
binding, i.e. a function from *Ident* to *Mode*. It yields the mode for each declared
name. Thus we can apply function $CONTEXT(\langle program \rangle)$ to $ID(\langle app\ ident \rangle)$ and
obtain a mode:

$$\underbrace{\underbrace{CONTEXT(\langle program \rangle)}_{\in map(L_{G,\langle ident \rangle},\langle type \rangle)}\underbrace{(ID(\langle app\ ident \rangle))}_{\in L_{G,\langle ident \rangle}}}_{\in \langle type \rangle}$$

Note that the mode of a name is not defined if it has not been declared. In the
context condition of the assignment we demand that the name is a variable name
(the kind is *var*) and that its type coincides with that of the expression. Thus it is
guaranteed that the storage location bound to the name can hold the value of the
expression. The **semantics** of an assignment is as follows.

> **(AS)**
>
> ---
>
> p is of the form $n := E;\ p'$
> $\qquad$ with $n \in \langle name \rangle, E \in \langle expr \rangle, p' \in \mathbf{PR}$
> Then $(p, b, s, i, o) \Rightarrow (p', b, s[b(n)\backslash I(b, s, E)], i, o)$,
> $\qquad$ if $I(b, s, E)$ is defined.
> If $I(b, s, E)$ is undefined then the
> $\qquad$ successor configuration does not exist.

Thus expression E is evaluated in the current environment (b, s) (see 3.7.2). If its value is undefined the PROSA machine stops. If its value is defined it is stored in the storage location for n. The context conditions given above guarantee that n is a variable name and that the type of variable n coincides with the type of expression E, i.e. the storage location $b(n)$ can hold the value $I(b, s, E)$. Function I is defined precisely in Section 3.7.2.

Formally, due to the context conditions, we have
$CONTEXT(\langle program \rangle)(n) = (var, t)$ and $t = TYPE(\langle expr \rangle)$ for some $t \in Type$. According to Theorem 1 in Section 3.5, $b(n) \in \mathbf{V}_t$ and by Theorem 2 (see Section 3.7.2) $I(b, s, E) \in \mathbf{D}_t$ holds if $I(b, s, E)$ is defined. Thus storage state $s[b(n)\backslash I(b, s, E)]$ is permissible.

We illustrate the definition of this section using Example 1a of Section 3.5.

Example (continued): In the context of this declaration section the assignments

$\qquad$ a $:= izero + 5$ and $\quad$ b $:= rzero - 4.0$

are permissible. On the other hand the assignments

$\qquad$ a $:= rzero$ and $\quad izero := 4$

violate the context conditions. In the first case the types do not coincide and in the second case $izero$ is not a variable name. Executing the two permissible assignments leads to a storage state s with

$$s(v_1^{int}) = c(5) \quad \text{and} \quad s(v_1^{real}) = -c(4.0) \qquad \blacksquare$$

Remark: The distinction between names and applied names is still artificial at this point as all names are applied names. In Chapter IV we will extend the set of names considerably, e.g. names of the form $A[i]$ will also be permissible. However, an applied name always remains the occurrence of a name in the statement section. In anticipation of Chapter IV we have already distinguished between names and applied names here.

3.7.2 Expressions

We have dealt with expressions in detail in Chapter II. Because of the increased number of operators and operand types some elaboration is necessary. The increased number of operators does not need new concepts; those from Section 2.2 are sufficient. We assign precedences to the operators as follows.

		precedence
equality and relational operators	$=, \neq, <, \leq, >, \geq$	0
addition operators	$+, -, \mathbf{or}, \cdot$	1
multiplication operators	$*, /, \mathbf{and}$	2
unary operators	$-, \mathbf{not}, \mathbf{convir}, \mathbf{convcs}$	3
	$\mathbf{empty}, \mathbf{tl}, \mathbf{hd}$	

We use a specific nonterminal for each level. The nonterminals are

$\langle expr \rangle$ for level 0,
$\langle simp\ expr \rangle$ for level 1,
$\langle term \rangle$ for level 2 and
$\langle factor \rangle$ for level 3.

Type correctness of expressions is specified by attributes and context conditions. For each subexpression its result type is computed and retained in an attribute $TYPE$. One starts with the type of terminal operands. A terminal operand is either a standard name, and then the type is obvious from the syntax, or it is a name. Then the type is given by the context. For composite expressions the type is computed from the types of the subexpressions and the operator. We specify in a context condition that the types of the subexpressions are compatible to each other and to the operator.

Syntax and Context Conditions

$\langle eq\ op \rangle \quad \rightarrow\ =\ |\ \neq$
$\langle rel\ op \rangle \quad \rightarrow\ <\ |\ \leq\ |\ >\ |\ \geq$
$\langle add\ op \rangle \quad \rightarrow\ +\ |\ -$
$\langle mul\ op \rangle \quad \rightarrow\ *\ |\ /$

$\langle expr \rangle \rightarrow \langle simp\ expr \rangle \langle eq\ op \rangle \langle simp\ expr \rangle$

Condition: $TYPE(\langle simp\ expr \rangle_1) = TYPE(\langle simp\ expr \rangle_2)$ and
$\qquad\qquad TYPE(\langle simp\ expr \rangle_1) \neq string$

Then: $\qquad TYPE(\langle expr \rangle) == bool$

$\langle expr \rangle \rightarrow \langle simp\ expr \rangle \langle rel\ op \rangle \langle simp\ expr \rangle$

Condition: $TYPE(\langle simp\ expr \rangle_1) = TYPE(\langle simp\ expr \rangle_2)$ and
$\qquad\qquad TYPE(\langle simp\ expr \rangle_1) \in \{int, real, char\}$

Then: $\qquad TYPE(\langle expr \rangle) == bool$

$\langle expr \rangle \rightarrow \langle simp\ expr \rangle$
$TYPE(\langle expr \rangle) == TYPE(\langle simp\ expr \rangle)$

$\langle simp\ expr \rangle \rightarrow \langle simp\ expr \rangle \langle add\ op \rangle \langle term \rangle$
Condition: $TYPE(\langle simp\ expr \rangle_2) = TYPE(\langle term \rangle)$ and
$\qquad\qquad TYPE(\langle term \rangle) \in \{int, real\}$
Then: $\qquad TYPE(\langle simp\ expr \rangle_1) == TYPE(\langle term \rangle)$

$\langle simp\ expr \rangle \rightarrow \langle simp\ expr \rangle$ **or** $\langle term \rangle$
Condition: $TYPE(\langle simp\ expr \rangle_2) = TYPE(\langle term \rangle) = bool$
Then: $\qquad TYPE(\langle simp\ expr \rangle_1) == bool$

$\langle simp\ expr \rangle \rightarrow \langle simp\ expr \rangle \cdot \langle term \rangle$
Condition: $TYPE(\langle simp\ expr \rangle_2) = TYPE(\langle term \rangle) = string$
Then: $\qquad TYPE(\langle simp\ expr \rangle_1) == string$

$\langle simp\ expr \rangle \rightarrow \langle term \rangle$
$TYPE(\langle simp\ expr \rangle) == TYPE(\langle term \rangle)$

$\langle term \rangle \rightarrow \langle term \rangle \langle mul\ op \rangle \langle factor \rangle$
Condition: $TYPE(\langle term \rangle_2) = TYPE(\langle factor \rangle)$ and
$\qquad\qquad TYPE(\langle term \rangle_2) \in \{int, real\}$
Then: $\qquad TYPE(\langle term \rangle_1) == TYPE(\langle term \rangle_2)$

$\langle term \rangle \rightarrow \langle term \rangle$ **and** $\langle factor \rangle$
Condition: $TYPE(\langle term \rangle_2) = TYPE(\langle factor \rangle) = bool$
Then: $\qquad TYPE(\langle term \rangle_1) == bool$

$\langle term \rangle \rightarrow \langle factor \rangle$
$TYPE(\langle term \rangle) == TYPE(\langle factor \rangle)$

$\langle factor \rangle \rightarrow \langle stand\ name \rangle$
$TYPE(\langle factor \rangle) == TYPE(\langle stand\ name \rangle)$

$\langle factor \rangle \rightarrow \langle name \rangle$

Condition: $MODE(\langle name \rangle) = (const, t)$ or
$\qquad\qquad MODE(\langle name \rangle) = (var, t)$ for some $t \in Type$

Then: $\qquad TYPE(\langle factor \rangle) = t$

$\langle factor \rangle \rightarrow (\langle expr \rangle)$

$TYPE(\langle factor \rangle) == TYPE(\langle expr \rangle)$

$\langle factor \rangle \rightarrow -\langle factor \rangle$

Condition: $TYPE(\langle factor \rangle_2) \in \{int, real\}$

Then: $\qquad TYPE(\langle factor \rangle_1) == TYPE(\langle factor \rangle_2)$

$\langle factor \rangle \rightarrow \mathbf{hd}\ \langle factor \rangle$

Condition: $TYPE(\langle factor \rangle_2) = string$

Then: $\qquad TYPE(\langle factor \rangle_1) == char$

$\langle factor \rangle \rightarrow \mathbf{tl}\ \langle factor \rangle$

Condition: $TYPE(\langle factor \rangle_2) = string$

Then: $\qquad TYPE(\langle factor \rangle_1) == string$

$\langle factor \rangle \rightarrow \mathbf{empty}\ \langle factor \rangle$

Condition: $TYPE(\langle factor \rangle_2) = string$

Then: $\qquad TYPE(\langle factor \rangle_1) == bool$

$\langle factor \rangle \rightarrow \mathbf{not}\ \langle factor \rangle$

Condition: $TYPE(\langle factor \rangle_2) = bool$

Then: $\qquad TYPE(\langle factor \rangle_1) == bool$

$\langle factor \rangle \rightarrow \mathbf{convcs}\ \langle factor \rangle$

Condition: $TYPE(\langle factor \rangle_2) = char$

Then: $\qquad TYPE(\langle factor \rangle_1) == string$

$\langle factor \rangle \rightarrow$ **convir** $\langle factor \rangle$

Condition: $TYPE(\langle factor \rangle_2) = int$

Then: $TYPE((\langle factor \rangle_1) == real$

Lemma 1. *The above grammar for $\langle expr \rangle$ is unambiguous.*

Proof: The proof is analogous to the proof of Lemma 1 in Section 2.2 and is left to the reader. ∎

Semantics of Expressions. To define the semantics of expressions we use the algebraic method introduced in Chapter II. The value of an expression is defined inductively in terms of the values of its subexpressions. However, we must take into account that we now have operands of several types, and that the value of an expression is only defined relative to an environment (b, s). We take the latter into account by defining the interpretation as a function

$$I_N : \mathbf{B} \times \mathbf{S} \times L_{G,N} \rightsquigarrow \mathbf{D}$$

where N is an arbitrary nonterminal of the expression grammar. We cater for the former by using the types of (sub)expressions, computed for checking context conditions, in order to choose the correct operations for the operators.

Let N be a nonterminal of the expression grammar and let $x \in L_{G,N}$. We can evaluate the attributes for the derivation tree from N to x according to the semantic rules above and determine attribute $TYPE$ of the root. We write $TYPE(x)$ for the value of this attribute.

The function

$$I_{\langle simp\ expr \rangle} : \mathbf{B} \times \mathbf{S} \times L_{G,\langle simp\ expr \rangle} \rightsquigarrow \mathbf{D}$$

is defined as follows. Let

$$b \in \mathbf{B}, s \in \mathbf{S}, x \in L_{G,\langle simp\ expr \rangle}.$$

Then

$$I_{\langle simp\ expr\rangle}(b,s,x) =$$

$$\begin{cases}
\begin{aligned}
&iadd(I_{\langle simp\ expr\rangle}(b,s,x_1), I_{\langle term\rangle}(b,s,x_2))\\
&\qquad \text{if } x = x_1 + x_2 \text{ with}\\
&\qquad x_1 \in \langle simp\ expr\rangle,\ x_2 \in \langle term\rangle \text{ and}\\
&\qquad TYPE(x_1) \;=\; TYPE(x_2) \;=\; int
\end{aligned}\\[2ex]
\begin{aligned}
&radd(I_{\langle simp\ expr\rangle}(b,s,x_1), I_{\langle term\rangle}(b,s,x_2))\\
&\qquad \text{if } x = x_1 + x_2 \text{ with}\\
&\qquad x_1 \in \langle simp\ expr\rangle,\ x_2 \in \langle term\rangle \text{ and}\\
&\qquad TYPE(x_1) \;=\; TYPE(x_2) \;=\; real
\end{aligned}\\[2ex]
\begin{aligned}
&isub(I_{\langle simp\ expr\rangle}(b,s,x_1), I_{\langle term\rangle}(b,s,x_2))\\
&\qquad \text{if } x = x_1 - x_2 \text{ with}\\
&\qquad x_1 \in \langle simp\ expr\rangle,\ x_2 \in \langle term\rangle \text{ and}\\
&\qquad TYPE(x_1) \;=\; TYPE(x_2) \;=\; int
\end{aligned}\\[2ex]
\begin{aligned}
&rsub(I_{\langle simp\ expr\rangle}(b,s,x_1), I_{\langle term\rangle}(b,s,x_2))\\
&\qquad \text{if } x = x_1 - x_2 \text{ with}\\
&\qquad x_1 \in \langle simp\ expr\rangle,\ x_2 \in \langle term\rangle \text{ and}\\
&\qquad TYPE(x_1) \;=\; TYPE(x_2) \;=\; real
\end{aligned}\\[2ex]
\begin{aligned}
&vel(I_{\langle simp\ expr\rangle}(b,s,x_1), I_{\langle term\rangle}(b,s,x_2))\\
&\qquad \text{if } x = x_1 \textbf{ or } x_2 \text{ with}\\
&\qquad x_1 \in \langle simp\ expr\rangle,\ x_2 \in \langle term\rangle \text{ and}\\
&\qquad TYPE(x_1) \;=\; TYPE(x_2) \;=\; boolean
\end{aligned}\\[2ex]
\begin{aligned}
&conc(I_{\langle simp\ expr\rangle}(b,s,x_1), I_{\langle term\rangle}(b,s,x_2))\\
&\qquad \text{if } x = x_1 \cdot x_2 \text{ with}\\
&\qquad x_1 \in \langle simp\ expr\rangle,\ x_2 \in \langle term\rangle \text{ and}\\
&\qquad TYPE(x_1) \;=\; TYPE(x_2) \;=\; string
\end{aligned}
\end{cases}$$

The definition of functions

$$I_{\langle expression\rangle}, I_{\langle term\rangle}, I_{\langle factor\rangle}$$

is similar and is left to the reader.

Finally, for nonterminals $\langle stand\ name\rangle$ and $\langle name\rangle$ we have

$$I_{\langle stand\ name\rangle}(b,s,x) \;=\; c(x)$$

and

$$I_{\langle name\rangle}(b,s,x) \;=\;
\begin{cases}
b(x) & \text{if } MODE(x) = (const, t) \text{ for some } t \in Type\\
s(b(x)) & \text{if } MODE(x) = (var, t) \text{ for some } t \in Type
\end{cases}$$

We now want to establish the relation between context conditions and semantics.

Theorem 1. *Let co be the context of a program, b a binding and s a storage state. Furthermore let $Def(co) = Def(b)$ and for all $x \in Def(b)$ and all $t \in type$ we have $b(x) \in \mathbf{D}_t$ if and only if $co(x) = (const, t)$, and $b(x) \in \mathbf{V}_t$ if and only if $co(x) = (var, t)$. (According to Theorem 1 the premise is satisfied when co and b are constructed from the same declaration section.)*

Let E be an expression satisfying the context conditions. Then

(1) If $I_{\langle expr \rangle}(b, s, E)$ is defined then $I_{\langle expr \rangle}(b, s, E) \in \mathbf{D}_{TYPE(E)}$, i.e. attribute evaluation yields as type the actual result type.

(2) If $I_{\langle expr \rangle}(b, s, E)$ is not defined then one of the following cases must have occurred during evaluation :
division by 0, application of an operation hd, tl to the empty string or use of a non initialised variable, i.e. of a variable name n for which $s(b(n))$ is undefined.

Proof: Both properties are obvious by induction on the structure of expression E. This clearly applies when E is a standard name or a name. For composite expressions the first claim follows from the observation that computing the type during attribute evaluation and evaluating the expression are done in the same way. The second claim follows from observing that apart from division and *hd, tl* all operations are total. ∎

3.7.3 Conditional Statements

Conditional statements are of the form "**if** B **then** A_1 **else** A_2 **fi**" (two-sided version) and "**if** B **then** A_1 **fi**" (one-sided version). B is an expression with boolean result, A_1 and A_2 are sequences of statements. A two-sided conditional statement permits selective execution of A_1 or A_2 depending on the value of expression B. If B has the value *true* in the current environment then A_1 is executed, if B has the value *false* then A_2 is executed. In a one-sided conditional statement the statement sequence A_1 is executed if B has the value *true*, otherwise A_1 is "skipped" and execution continues with the statement following.

Syntax and Context Conditions
$\langle cond \rangle \rightarrow$ **if** $\langle expr \rangle$ **then** $\langle stat\ seq \rangle$ **else** $\langle stat\ seq \rangle$ **fi** $\mid$
$\qquad$ **if** $\langle expr \rangle$ **then** $\langle stat\ seq \rangle$ **fi**

Condition : $TYPE(\langle expr \rangle) = bool$

Semantics:

(IF1)

p is of the form **if** B **then** p_1 **fi**; p'
        with $B \in \langle expr \rangle$, $p_1 \in \langle stat\ seq \rangle$, $p' \in \mathbf{PR}$
Then $(p, b, s, i, o) \Rightarrow$
$$\begin{cases} (p_1; p', b, s, i, o) & \text{if } I(b, s, B) = true \\ (p', b, s, i, o) & \text{if } I(b, s, B) = false \end{cases}$$
If $I(b, s, B)$ is undefined then there is no
         successor configuration.

(IF2)

p is of the form **if** B **then** p_1 **else** p_2 **fi**; p'
        with $B \in \langle expr \rangle$, $p_1, p_2 \in \langle stat\ seq \rangle$, $p' \in \mathbf{PR}$.
Then $(p, b, s, i, o) \Rightarrow$
$$\begin{cases} (p_1; p', b, s, i, o) & \text{if } I(b, s, B) = true \\ (p_2; p', b, s, i, o) & \text{if } I(b, s, B) = false \end{cases}$$
If $I(b, s, B)$ is undefined then there is no
         successor configuration.

Observe how the transitions of the PROSA machine reflect the semantics of the conditional statements. Let **if** B **then** p_1 **else** p_2 **fi**; p' be the program-rest. If B has value *true* in the actual environment then the program still to be executed is $p_1; p'$. If B has value *false* we must still execute $p_2; p'$. If the value of B is undefined then the machine stops.

Example:

```
program absolute-value;
var sign: char; x, abs: real
begin  read  x;
        if x ≥ 0.0 then sign := '+'; abs := x
                else  sign := '-'; abs := -x
        fi
end.
```

Remark: Many programming languages (e.g. Pascal) do not have the closing symbol **fi** for conditional statements which was introduced in ALGOL 68. This leads to the following problem. Given

$$\text{if } B_1 \text{ then if } B_2 \text{ then } A_1 \text{ else } A_2$$

which **then** corresponds to **else** i.e. which of the two conditional statements is one-sided, which is two-sided? To remove ambiguity, the Pascal definition specifies, in

addition to the grammar, that each **else** is matched with the last "open" **then** ,
i.e. the Pascal statement above is equivalent to the PROSA statement

$$\textbf{if } B \textbf{ then if } B_2 \textbf{ then } A_1 \textbf{ else } A_2 \textbf{ fi fi}$$

We differ here, and in the following iterative statement, from the Pascal syntax
by using the brackets **if ... fi** and **do ... od**. This obviates the frequent use of
begin ... end brackets around sequences of statements in Pascal.   ∎

3.7.4 Iterative Statements

An iterative statement (loop) is of the form **while** B **do** A **od**. The boolean expression B is called the **loop condition**, the statement sequence A the **loop body**.
The effect of a loop statement is the repeated execution of the body. More precisely,
the statement sequence A is executed as long as the boolean expression B is *true*.

Syntax and Context Conditions:

$\langle iter \rangle \rightarrow$ **while** $\langle expr \rangle$ **do** $\langle stat\ seq \rangle$ **od**

Condition: $TYPE(\langle expr \rangle) = bool$

Semantics:

<table>
<tr><td>(IT)</td></tr>
<tr><td>

p is of the form   **while** B **do** p_1 **od**; p'
       with $B \in \langle expr \rangle,\ p_1 \in \langle stat\ seq \rangle,\ p' \in \textbf{PR}$
Then $(p, b, s, i, o) \Rightarrow$
$\begin{cases} (p_1; p, b, s, i, o) & \text{if } I(b, s, B) = true \\ (p', b, s, i, o) & \text{if } I(b, s, B) = false \end{cases}$
If $I(b, s, B)$ is undefined then there is no
      successor configuration

</td></tr>
</table>

Note that the program to be executed becomes longer when the loop condition
is *true*. In this case the body p_1 followed by the whole program p is executed.

Example: Consider the following program.

```
program example;
var  i,x,y : integer;
begin   i := 0, x := 11; y := 4;
        while x ≥ y do x := x − y; i := i + 1 od
end.
```

The **while**-loop is executed on the PROSA machine M as follows ($x \geq y$ is the condition B and $x := x - y$; $i := i + 1$ the loop body p_1).

program-rest	$s(b(i))$	$s(b(x))$	$s(b(y))$
while $x \geq y$ **do** $x := x - y$; $i := i + 1$ **od**;	0	11	4
$x := x - y$; $i := i + 1$; **while** $x \geq y$ **do** $x := x - y$; $i := i + 1$ **od**;	0	11	4
while $x \geq y$ **do** $x := x - y$; $i := i + 1$ **od**;	1	7	4
$x := x - y$; $i := i + 1$; **while** $x \geq y$ **do** $x := x - y$; $i := i + 1$ **od**;	1	7	4
while $x \geq y$ **do** $x := x - y$; $i := i + 1$ **od**;	2	3	4
ϵ	2	3	4

In general, the semantics of the **while**-loop is the following mapping from **S** to **S**. Let s be a storage state such that $s(b(x))$ and $s(b(y))$ are defined and $s(b(i)) = 0$. Then

$$(\textbf{while } x \geq y \textbf{ do } x := x - y; \ i := i + 1 \textbf{ od};, b, s, i, o) \ \Rightarrow^* \ (\epsilon, b, s', i, o) ,$$

where the following three cases have to be distinguished.

Case 1: $(s(b(x)) \geq s(b(y))) > 0$
Then
$$s'(b(x)) = s(b(x)) \quad mod \quad s(b(y))$$
$$s'(b(y)) = s(b(y))$$
$$s'(b(i)) = s(b(x)) \quad div \quad s(b(y))$$

Case 2: $s(b(x)) < s(b(y))$
Then $s' = s$

Case 3: $s(b(x)) \geq s(b(y))$ and $s(b(y)) < 0$
Then the program does not terminate, i.e. s' does not exist. We have a so-called "infinite loop".

At this point the reader should try to prove the relation between s and s' described above. This will be done in Section 3.9. ∎

Finally, we discuss some variants of the iteration statement. Besides the **while**-loop, Pascal has the **repeat statement** in the form **repeat** $\langle stat\ seq \rangle$ **until** $\langle expr \rangle$. "**repeat** A **until** B" is the same as "A; **while not** B **do** A **od**".

The **repeat** statement is very useful syntactic sugar as the statement sequence A may be very large. Without **repeat** statements one might have to write it twice. **while**- and **repeat**-statements can be illustrated by flow diagrams:

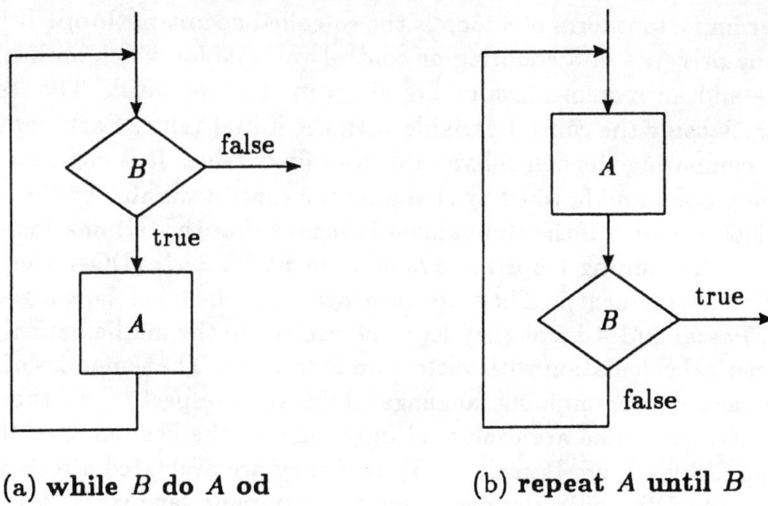

(a) **while** B **do** A **od**   (b) **repeat** A **until** B

Fig. 1.

The programming language Ada has an even more general loop concept. Loops are left by executing an **exit**-statement contained in them. Leaving the loop can take place under a condition described in the form **exit when** $\langle expr \rangle$. If loops are named (by a label) several nested loops can be left simultaneously by giving **exit** $\langle name \rangle$. A loop with several conditional exits may be illustrated by the flow diagram in Figure 2.

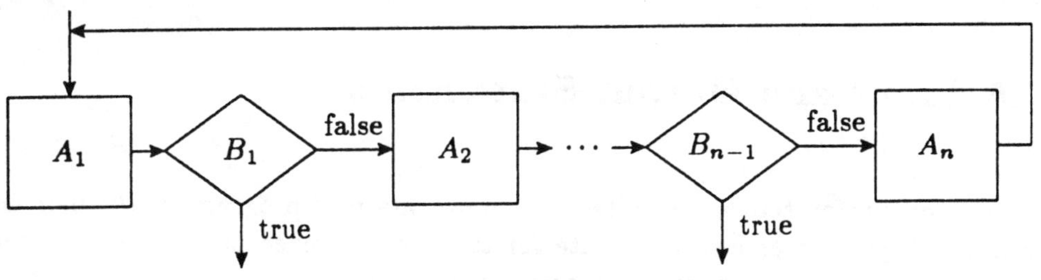

Fig. 2.

The Pascal statements **while** B_1 **do** A_1 and **repeat** A_2 **until** B_2 are written in

Ada as the two special cases

<table>
<tr><td>

loop
    exit when not B_1;
    A_1
end loop

</td><td>

loop
    A_2;
    exit when B_2
end loop

</td></tr>
</table>

Another important form of a loop is the so-called **counting loop**. It is characterised by the presence of a counting or control variable for which an initial value, a final value and an increment value are given in the loop head. The iteration is started by initialising the control variable with the initial value. Each iteration step is begun by comparing the control variable and final value. It is continued by executing the loop body and finished by changing the control variable by the increment value. The loop is exited if the comparsion indicates that the termination condition is satisfied. Such counting loops are available in FORTRAN (DO-statement) and ALGOL 60 (for-statement). They are also available in newer languages such as ALGOL 68, Pascal and Ada, as they lend themselves to the mathematical notation used for numerical calculation with vectors and matrices. The semantics of counting loops in the various programming languages differ with respect to whether the final value and increment value are evaluated only once at the beginning of the execution of a loop (ALGOL 68, Pascal, PL/I) or if they are evaluated afresh after each iteration step (ALGOL 60). Besides, some programming languages (Pascal, Ada) forbid explicit changes of the control variable in the loop body so as to make loops clearer and safer. Pascal and Ada restrict the step values to $+1$ and -1, or the successor and predecessor function of enumeration types. The two Pascal versions are

    for $\langle ident \rangle := \langle expr \rangle$ **to** $\langle expr \rangle$ **do** **begin** $\langle stat\ seq \rangle$ **end**

and

    for $\langle ident \rangle := \langle expr \rangle$ **downto** $\langle expr \rangle$ **do** **begin** $\langle stat\ seq \rangle$ **end**

3.7.5 Input and Output Statements

Input and output statements facilitate communication of programs with their environment. Input statements read data for the program execution from the input tape, output statements write the results on the output tape. The output tape of the PROSA machine has unlimited capacity. Therefore the only possible errors (during execution) are

- an input statement tries to read from an empty input tape;

- an input statement **read** n reads an object from an input tape which has not the type of n;
- an output statement attempts to write the value of an expression which is undefined in the current environment.

Syntax and Context Conditions

$\langle input \rangle \rightarrow$ **read** $\langle name \rangle$

Condition: $MODE(\langle name \rangle) = (var, t)$ for some $t \in Type$

$\langle output \rangle \rightarrow$ **print** $\langle expr \rangle$

Semantics

<table>
<tr><td>

(IN)

</td></tr>
<tr><td>

p is of the form **read** $n; p'$
       with $n \in \langle app\ ident \rangle$ and $p' \in$ **PR**.
Then $(p, b, s, i, o) \Rightarrow (p', b, s[b(n) \backslash head(i)], tail(i), o)$
       if $i \neq \epsilon$ and $head(i) \in \mathbf{D}_t$ where $MODE(n) = (var, t)$.
If this condition is not satisfied then the
       successor configuration does not exist.

</td></tr>
</table>

<table>
<tr><td>

(OUT)

</td></tr>
<tr><td>

p is of the form **print** $E; p'$
       with $E \in \langle expr \rangle$ and $p' \in$ **PR**.
Then $(p, b, s, i, o) \Rightarrow (p', b, s, i, conc(o, I(b, s, E))$
       if $I(b, s, E)$ defined.
If $I(b, s, E)$ is not defined then the
       successor configuration does not exist.

</td></tr>
</table>

The semantics of input and output statements are unusual because we permit reading and writing of arbitrary objects to be done in one step. In addition, we do not read and write representations of natural and real numbers but the numbers themselves, i.e. we write e.g. the natural number "seventeen" and not the string 17. Of course this differs considerably from reality, but it simplifies the presentation. Furthermore it is consistent with the fact that the PROSA machine calculates with integers and real numbers (compare Section 3.2), and the representation of these objects is disregarded in this book. However, to give the reader a better idea we give a program in Section 3.11 which computes for a natural number its binary representation. On actual computers this program precedes the print statement if the number is to be printed as a binary number. The number is then written digit by digit. Of course there is a similar program for decimal representation.

3.7.6 Error Statement

With the error statement one can stop the PROSA machine explicitly. It can
be used to interrupt computation if, for example, an input not permitted by the
program developer is read.

Syntax

$\langle error \rangle \rightarrow$ **error halt**

Semantics

(ERR)
p is of the form **error halt**$;p'$ with $p' \in$ **PR**   Then the successor configuration of (p, b, s, i, o) does not exist.

In the example program of Section 3.3 we could, for instance, insert the statement

$$\textbf{if } N < 0 \textbf{ then error halt}$$

before the iterative statement. The program would then test the condition $n \in \mathbb{N}_0$
and not rely on the input assertion.

3.7.7 Comments

A comment is an arbitrary string in which the brackets (* and *) do not occur.
It is enclosed in brackets (* and *). Comments may be inserted at any place in
a PROSA program and should improve legibility of programs. We use comments
intensively when we turn to correctness proofs of programs (compare Section 3.9).
Comments are not part of the PROSA program. They only appear in the text of
programs. The actual program is obtained by deleting the comments.

3.8 Summary

In previous sections syntax, context conditions and semantics of PROSA were defined. We now briefly summarise the semantics.

Let $p = $ **program** n; ds **begin** sts **end.** be a PROSA program satisfying the context conditions and let $i \in \mathbf{D}^*$ be an input sequence. Then

$$in((p,i)) = (ds\ sts; \emptyset, \emptyset, i, \epsilon)$$

is the start configuration of the PROSA machine for program p and input sequence i. M now computes according to the transition function of M defined above. The computation either leads to an end configuration $(\epsilon, b, s, \epsilon, o)$, and then o is the result of the computation, or it is infinitely long, or it ends in a configuration which is not an end configuration. In the last two cases the result of the computation and its computation time are undefined. Exact definitions of these concepts have already been given in Section 1.7. We will repeat them.

$$comp_time : \mathbf{PROGRAM} \times \mathbf{D}^* \rightsquigarrow \mathbb{N}_0$$

$$comp_time((p,i)) = \begin{cases} T & \text{if } \delta^{(T)}(in((p,i))) \in \mathbf{C}^f \\ undefined & \text{otherwise} \end{cases}$$

and

$$I/O_M : \mathbf{PROGRAM} \times \mathbf{D}^* \rightsquigarrow \mathbf{D}^*$$

$$I/O_M((p,i)) = out(\delta^{comp_time((p,i))}(in((p,i))))$$

In defining the transition function δ, we have discussed in detail when its value is not defined. The following run time errors are possible.

- division by zero
- application of hd, tl to an empty string
- attempted input from empty input tape
- input of an object of a wrong type
- use of a variable before the first assignment to the variable
- execution of the error statement.

Every PROSA program p defines a function f_p from $\mathbf{D}^*$ to $\mathbf{D}^*$, namely

$$f_p(i) = I \backslash O_M((p,i))$$

for all $i \in \mathbf{D}^*$. We call f_p the **function computed** by program p. A function $f : \mathbf{D}^* \rightsquigarrow \mathbf{D}^*$ is said to be **PROSA computable** if $f = f_p$ for some PROSA program p, i.e. if there is a PROSA program p that computes f. Two questions arise.

1) Are all functions $f : \mathbf{D}^* \rightsquigarrow \mathbf{D}^*$ PROSA computable?
2) If the answer to question 1) is no, can PROSA be extended so that the answer is yes?

These questions are discussed in detail in a course on "computability theory". We shall consider the answers briefly (the rest of the section is not essential for understanding this book). The answer to the first question is no. There are functions which are not PROSA computable. This assertion can be easily proved. Let $p_1, p_2, p_3, \ldots$ be an enumeration of the set **PROGRAM** in increasing lexicographic order and let $f_i = f_{p_i}$ be the function computed by program p_i. Then let $f : \mathbf{D}^* \rightsquigarrow \mathbf{D}^*$ be defined by

$$Def(f) = \mathbb{N}, \quad f(i) = \begin{cases} 0 & \text{if } f_i(i) \text{ undefined} \\ & \text{or } f_i(i) \notin \mathbb{N}_0 \\ f_i(i) + 1 & \text{if } f_i(i) \in \mathbb{N}_0 \end{cases}$$

Then $f \neq f_i$ for all i, because $f(i) \neq f_i(i)$. Thus f is not PROSA computable. If f were PROSA computable then necessarily $f = f_i$ for all i.

Can we extend PROSA in such a way that all functions are PROSA computable? This question is of a different quality than the first. As we have not defined the concept of extension, it is — contrary to the first question — not a question in the mathematical sense, but an informal question. Therefore only an informal answer can be given, i.e. the correctness of the answer can only be made plausible but not proved. What is the answer? The answer is no for the following reason. If we assume that one writes down the programs of PROSA extended with a finite alphabet (how else!) then we can carry out the above construction of a non computable function for the extension. In an extension, therefore, not all functions are computable although more than with PROSA. Even that is not to be expected. In the past many different precise definitions of the concept "computable" have been proposed, just as we propose the definition PROSA computable here. All have proved to be equivalent. In this book we will also meet the concept RESA computable and in Chapters V and VII we will show that a function is RESA computable if it is PROSA computable.

Exercises for 3.1–3.8

1) Consider the grammar for standard names. Define attributes for the grammar in such a way that the axiom ⟨*stand name*⟩ has an attribute *OBJECT* whose value is the object denoted by the standard name.

2) Check the following PROSA program for errors deriving from violations of the context conditions. Proceed as follows.

   a) Construct a syntax tree according to the PROSA grammar.

   b) Compute the attributes necessary for checking the context conditions at each node of the tree. Compute all attributes in the subtree with root ⟨*decls*⟩.

Correct the errors found so that a correct attribute *CONTEXT* from the declaration section can be used to compute the attributes in the statement section.

```
program false;
var a: integer; var b: integer;
var c: string; var d: string; var a: string;
begin
  read (c); read (d); read (char);
  if hd c = char then a := tl c
                 else  h := d
  fi;
  c := a + b
end.
```

3) Write a PROSA program which reads two integers into variables named *ONE* and *TWO*. If $ONE > TWO$ then 1 should be printed, otherwise the values of *ONE* and *TWO* should be swapped and 0 printed.

Specify for each program step how b and s change if the input tape holds 5 and 10.

4) Extend the formal description of PROSA so that a variable can be initialised in the declaration. The initialisation (example: **var** x: **integer**:=5) value can be given by a standard name of the same type or by a name. For this name the context condition are

a) it must be a constant name of the same type or

b) it must be a constant name of the same type or a name of an initialised variable of the same type.

Specify attributes for the declaration section which check the new context conditions in addition to the original ones. Specify the modified transition function of the PROSA machine.

5) Write a PROSA program which inputs a number n and prints all prime numbers smaller than n.

6) Let two boolean variables a and b be given. Determine for all combinations of values for a and b the value of variable c after executing the following program section.

```
if not b then d := not a
         else  d := true
fi;
if d then if not a then c := not b
                    else  c := true
          fi
     else  c := false
fi
```

7) Prove Lemma 1 of 3.7.2.

8) Write a PROSA program which computes the factorial function $n!$ for any $n > 0$. Describe the program execution for input value 2 by means of a table containing for each configuration $c = (p, b, s, i, o)$

- program p
- domain of b
- value $s(b(x))$ for each $x \in Def_b$
- o and i.

3.9 Correctness Proofs

We write PROSA programs to solve problems algorithmically. Naturally, we must always convince ourselves that the programs we developed actually solve the problems. We did that in the example of Section 3.3 by giving detailed comments and thus explained the mode of operation of the program. In this section a method to prove the correctness of programs is introduced.

Let us presume we want to solve the following problem. Two natural numbers n and m are given; n may be zero, but not m. We are now to write a program which reads numbers n and m from the input tape and then computes and prints natural numbers c and d with the property $n = c \cdot m + d$ and $0 \le d < m$. (It is easy to see that numbers c and d are uniquely determined. $c = n \ div \ m$ and $d = n \ mod \ m$). At this point the reader should try to write a PROSA program and then attempt to convince another person that this program actually solves the given problem.

The authors suggest the PROSA program in Figure 1 for solving the problem. In this program we have specified the problem precisely by way of two comments (called input assertion and output assertion).

```
program division_with_rest;
(* we expect on the input tape numbers n and m
    with n ∈ N₀ and m ∈ N, i.e. i = (n, m) *)
var i, x, y: integer;
begin  read x; read y; i := 0;
        while x ≥ y do x := x − y;  i := i + 1 od;
        print i; print x
        (* on the output tape are numbers c, d with
            n = c · m + d, 0 ≤ d < m and c, d ∈ N₀ *)
end.
```

Fig. 1.   A PROSA program to compute functions *div* and *mod*.

In the input assertion we determine which input sequences are permissible for our program. Names for the elements of input sequences are introduced so as to be able to refer to them in the output assertion. Thus in our example we expect that the input sequence i has the form n, m with $n \in \mathbb{N}_0$ and $m \in \mathbb{N}$. In the output assertion we require that the program yields two numbers c and d having the properties $n = c \cdot m + d$, $0 \le d < m$ and $c, d \in \mathbb{N}_0$. The input and output assertions together determine the intended I/O-behaviour of the program: a program is to compute from a pair (n, m) with $n \in \mathbb{N}_0$, $m \in \mathbb{N}$ the pair $(n\ div\ m,\ n\ mod\ m)$. The actual I/O-behaviour of the program is, however, fixed by the program text and the semantics of PROSA. We now want to convince ourselves that the actual I/O-behaviour coincides with the intended I/O-behaviour, i.e. the program produces for *all* inputs (n, m) with $n \in \mathbb{N}_0$, $m \in \mathbb{N}$ the output $(n\ div\ m,\ n\ mod\ m)$. This is easily checked for a concrete pair of numbers, for example $(13, 5)$. We need only execute the PROSA program and see if the generated output has the required property. The output for input $(13, 5)$ is $(2, 3)$ and in fact $13 = 2 \cdot 5 + 3$. Of course this does not mean that the program works correctly for *all* inputs. This is precisely what we would like to be sure of.

We further annotate the program with (intermediate) assertions which provide information about the configuration of the PROSA machine during computation. Figure 2 shows the above program with such additional assertions. Contrary to Figure 1, we only assert in the input assertion that $m \in \mathbb{Z}$. This will enable us to later illustrate the difference between total and partial correctness.

The assertion after **do** in the **while**-loop states that at any time when the loop body is started

$$s(b(y)) = m, \quad n = s(b(i)) \cdot s(b(y)) + s(b(x)), \quad s(b(x)) \in \mathbb{N}_0 \text{ and } s(b(x)) \ge s(b(y)),$$

i.e. the value of variable y is m, the values $s(b(i))$, $s(b(y))$, $s(b(x))$ of variables i, y and x satisfy $n = s(b(i)) \cdot s(b(y)) + s(b(x))$, the value of x is a natural number and is not smaller than the value of y.

How can we show the validity of this assertion? When we enter the loop body for the first time $s(b(x)) = n$, $s(b(y)) = m$ and $s(b(i)) = 0$, because we have assigned these values to the variables in the first lines of the statement section. Therefore $n = s(b(x)) + s(b(y)) \cdot s(b(i))$. Furthermore $s(b(x)) \ge s(b(y))$ as this condition is checked before entering the body. Now $x := x - y$; $i := i + 1$ are executed. Of course $n = s(b(x)) + s(b(y)) \cdot s(b(i))$ still holds, since the value of x is decreased by $m \ (= s(b(y)))$ and the value of i is increased by one. Also the value of x is now not negative. Note that the assertion at the end of the body is identical to the assertion at the beginning of the body. At the beginning we also have the loop condition $s(b(x)) \ge s(b(y))$. Thus we know that the assertion also holds on entering body the second time. The same argument shows that the assertion also holds at the third, fourth, ... entering of the body. Since the assertion holds each time the body is entered this is called the **loop invariant**. At some stage the loop condition is no longer satisfied, at least when $m \ge 0$. (this assertion must of course be proved

```
program division_with_rest;
(* we expect on the input tape numbers n and m;
    n ∈ ℕ₀, m ∈ ℤ *);
var i, x, y: integer;
begin read x; read y; i := 0;
        (* s(b(x)) = n ≥ 0, s(b(y)) = m, s(b(i)) = 0
            and n = s(b(i)) · s(b(y)) + s(b(x)) *)
        while x ≥ y
        do (* s(b(y)) = m, n = s(b(i)) · s(b(y)) + s(b(x)),
                s(b(x)) ≥ s(b(y)) and s(b(x)) ∈ ℕ₀ *)


            x := x − y; i := i + 1


            (* s(b(y)) = m, n = s(b(i)) · s(b(y)) + s(b(x))
                and s(b(x)) ∈ ℕ₀ *)
        od;


        (* s(b(y)) = m, n = s(b(i)) · s(b(y)) + s(b(x)),
            s(b(x)) ∈ ℕ₀ and s(b(x)) < s(b(y)) *)
        print i; print x
        (* the output tape contains numbers c, d with c, d ∈ ℕ₀,
            n = c · m + d and 0 ≤ d < m *)
end.
```

Fig. 2.   Program of Fig. 1 with assertions

and this will be done in Section 3.10. If $m \leq 0$ then the loop does not terminate).
At this point the loop invariant holds and in addition $s(b(x)) < s(b(y))$. Note
that the assertion after the **while** loop is precisely the loop invariant together with
$s(b(x)) < s(b(y))$. Now the values of i and x are printed. These values satisfy the
final assertion and thus the correctness of our program (apart from termination) is
shown. Note that in our argumentation we have never reasoned about the whole
program but only about small sections between the assertions. We will now give a
general description of the proof method used in this example. Firstly the concept
assertion is defined precisely.

Definition 1:

(a) **An assertion** Z is a function $Z : \mathbf{B} \times \mathbf{S} \times \mathbf{D}^* \times \mathbf{D}^* \to \mathbf{D}_{bool}$.

(b) **An input assertion** Z is a function $Z : \mathbf{D}^* \to \mathbf{D}_{bool}$. In it we also introduce
     names for the elements of the input tape.   ∎

An input assertion Z determines for each input sequence $i \in \mathbf{D}^*$ if it is permissible
($Z(i) = true$) or if it is not permissible as input for the program ($Z(i) = false$). In
our example the input assertion for an input sequence $i = (i_1, i_2, \ldots, e_k)$ is true if
and only if $k = 2$, $i_1 \in \mathbb{N}_0$ and $i_2 \in \mathbb{Z}$. The input assertion further determines that
the two elements of the input sequence are called n and m. The remaining asser-

tions Z have 4-tuples (b, s, i, o) as arguments. They comprise the current binding $b \in \mathbf{B}$, the storage state $s \in \mathbf{S}$, the input sequence $i \in \mathbf{D}^*$ and the output sequence $o \in \mathbf{D}^*$. The meaning of the truth value $Z(b, s, i, o)$ is explained after Definition 2. Assertions are formulated as it is common in mathematics, i.e. English text combined with usual mathematical symbolisation. Of course in formulating assertions the names introduced in the input assertion may be used.

Definition 2:

(a) Let P and Q be assertions and p a statement sequence.
   Then $\{P\}\, p\, \{Q\}$ is called a **Hoare triple** (after the English computer scientist C.A.R. Hoare).

(b) Let $\{P\}\, p\, \{Q\}$ be a Hoare triple. The statement sequence p is said to be **partially correct** with respect to assertions P and Q, or the triple $\{P\}\, p\, \{Q\}$ is said to be partially correct, if for all $b \in \mathbf{B}$, $s \in \mathbf{S}$, $i \in \mathbf{D}^*$, $o \in \mathbf{D}^*$ with $P(b, s, i, o) = true$ the following holds: A computation starting in configuration (p, b, s, i, o) is either infinitely long or it ends in a configuration $(\epsilon, b', s', i', o')$ where $Q(b', s', i', o') = true$.

(c) Let $\{P\}\, p\, \{Q\}$ be a Hoare triple. The statement sequence p is said to be **totally correct** with respect to assertions P and Q, or the triple is said to be totally correct, if for all $b \in \mathbf{B}$, $s \in \mathbf{S}$, $i \in \mathbf{D}^*$, $o \in \mathbf{D}^*$ with $P(b, s, i, o) = true$ the following holds: A computation starting in configuration (p, b, s, i, o) is finite and ends in a configuration $(\epsilon, b', s', i', o')$ with $Q(b', s', i', o') = true$.   ∎

These definitions require further explanation. In this section we include assertions in curly brackets $\{$ and $\}$. This is usual in the theory of program verification. In our example programs comment brackets continue to be used. Let $b \in \mathbf{B}$, $s \in \mathbf{S}$, $i \in \mathbf{D}^*$, $o \in \mathbf{D}^*$ with $P(b, s, i, o) = true$. Partial correctness of $\{P\}\, p\, \{Q\}$ then says that a computation from state (p, b, s, i, o) does not lead to any error. Furthermore, the end configuration $(\epsilon, b', s', i', o')$ satisfies assertion Q, i.e. $Q(b', s', i', o') = true$ if the computation is finite. In the case of total correctness we claim, in addition, that the computation is finite. Partial correctness thus follows from total correctness. If the triple $\{P\}\, p\, \{Q\}$ is totally correct for a program p, an input assertion P and a final assertion Q, then the intended and the actual I/O-behaviour coincides. In this section it will be shown how to prove the partial correctness of a program. Total correctness is discussed in the next section. In particular, we will show that the program in Figure 6 is partially correct with respect to the given assertions. This has already been done informally before Definition 1. It is not totally correct as, for example, the computation for input $5, -7$ is infinitely long. Note that we permit $m \leq 0$ in Figure 6. The program in Figure 5 is totally correct.

Some further examples.

Example 1:

(a) The triple
   $\{$the first element of the input sequence is 5 and $b(i) \in \mathbf{V}_{int}\}$ **read** i $\{s(b(i)) = 5\}$

is totally correct.

(b) The triple

$\{b(i) \in \mathbf{V}_{int}$ and $s(b(i)) \in \mathbb{N}\}$ **while** $i \neq 0$ **do** $i := i - 1$ **od** $\{s(b(i)) = 0\}$

is totally correct.

(c) The triple

$\{b(i) \in \mathbf{V}_{int}$ and $s(b(i)) \in \mathbb{Z}\}$ **while** $i \neq 0$ **do** $i := i - 1$ **od** $\{s(b(i)) = 0\}$

is partially correct, but not totally correct.

Note the difference between (b) and (c). In both cases we are sure that the computation runs error-free and that i has the value 0 after the loop is left. Yet only in case (b) can we be sure that the loop terminates. Hence the triple in (b) is totally correct, while the triple in (c) is only partially correct. ∎

Next we specify the rules for deriving partially correct or totally correct Hoare triples. First we specify rules for a single simple statement (assignment, read statement or print statement) and then discuss compound statements. The rules enable us to prove the correctness of our example programs by induction on the structure of the program text.

Lemma 1.

Let E be an expression, $x \in \langle ident \rangle$ a name and P and Q assertions.

(a) The triple $\{P\}$ $x := E$ $\{Q\}$ is totally correct if for all $b \in \mathbf{B}$, $s \in \mathbf{S}$, $i \in \mathbf{D}^*$, $o \in \mathbf{D}^*$:

From $P(b, s, i, o) = true$ follows:

$\qquad I(b, s, E)$ is defined,

$\qquad b(x) \in \mathbf{V}_t$ and $I(b, s, E) \in \mathbf{D}_t$ for some $t \in Type$ and

$\qquad Q(b, s[b(x)\backslash I(b, s, E)], i, o) = true.$

(b) The triple $\{P\}$ **read** x $\{Q\}$ is totally correct if for all $b \in \mathbf{B}$, $s \in \mathbf{S}$, $i \in \mathbf{D}^*$, $o \in \mathbf{D}^*$:

From $P(b, s, i, o) = true$ follows:

$\qquad i \neq \epsilon,$

$\qquad head(i) \in \mathbf{D}_t$ and $b(x) \in \mathbf{V}_t$ for some $t \in Type$ and

$\qquad Q(b, s[b(x)\backslash head(i)], tail(i), o) = true.$

(c) The triple $\{P\}$ **print** E $\{Q\}$ is totally correct if for all $b \in \mathbf{B}$, $s \in \mathbf{S}$, $i \in \mathbf{D}^*$, $o \in \mathbf{D}^*$:

From $P(b, s, i, o) = true$ follows:

$\qquad I(b, s, E)$ is defined and

$\qquad Q(b, s, i, conc(o, I(b, s, E))) = true.$

Proof: In all three cases the proof is very simple. Therefore we only prove part (a). Let $b \in \mathbf{B}$, $s \in \mathbf{S}$, $i \in \mathbf{D}^*$, $o \in \mathbf{D}^*$ with $P(b, s, i, o) = true$. From the premises follows that $I(b, s, E)$ is defined, that x is a variable name and that the types of x and E coincide. Computation from start configuration $(x := E; , b, s, i, o)$ does not lead to an error. It rather ends in configuration $(\epsilon, b, s[b(x)\backslash I(b, s, E)], i, o)$. By assumption then $Q(b, s[b(x)\backslash I(b, s, E)], i, o) = true.$ ∎

We will use Lemma (1a) only for assignments in PROSA programs. The conditions $b(x) \in \mathbf{V}_t$ and $I(b, s, E) \in \mathbf{D}_t$ for some $t \in \textit{Type}$ then are automatically fulfilled because of the context conditions. Therefore we usually omit such conditions in examples.

Example 2:

(a) Example (1a) is an application of Lemma (1b).

(b) Lemma (1a) implies the total correctness of

$$\{s(b(y)) = m, \, n = s(b(i)) \cdot s(b(y)) + s(b(x)), \, s(b(x)) \in \mathbb{N}_0, \, s(b(x)) \geq s(b(y))\}$$
$$x := x - y$$
$$\{s(b(y)) = m, \, n = (s(b(i)) + 1) \cdot s(b(y)) + s(b(x)), \, s(b(x)) \in \mathbb{N}_0\}$$

(c) Lemma (1a) implies the total correctness of

$$\{s(b(y)) = m, \, n = (s(b(i)) + 1) \cdot s(b(y)) + s(b(x)), \, s(b(x)) \in \mathbb{N}_0\}$$
$$i := i + 1$$
$$\{s(b(y)) = m, \, n = s(b(i)) \cdot s(b(y)) + s(b(x)), \, s(b(x)) \in \mathbb{N}_0\} \qquad \blacksquare$$

Lemma 1 allows the construction of correct triples for simple statements. The following Lemma specifies how one can construct correct triples for compound programs from correct triples for the parts. We do this for sequential statements (part (a)), conditional statements (part (c)) and iteration statements (part (e)). The iteration statement is the most interesting case. Part (e) says that the partial correctness of a triple $\{P\}$ **while** B **do** p **od** $\{P \wedge \neg B\}$ follows in essence from the partial correctness of the triple $\{P \wedge B\}$ p $\{P\}$. This is relatively easy to understand (compare the discussion preceding Definition 1). A computation of program **while** B **do** p **od** has the form of Figure 3.

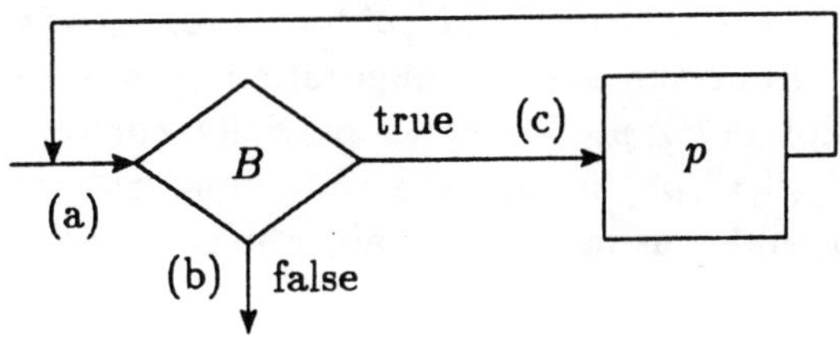

Fig. 3.   A computation of the program **while** B **do** p **od**

Suppose we start in a configuration (arc (a)) satisfying P. If B is satisfied then the configuration even satisfies $P \wedge B$ and we reach arc (c). We begin the execution of p in a configuration satisfying $P \wedge B$ and finish it, by assumption, in a configuration satisfying P. We now subject this configuration to test $B, \ldots$. Repeating this argument shows that we always reach condition B in a configuration satisfying P. Thus after leaving the loop P and $\neg B$ hold. Having discussed this informally we now give the details.

Lemma 2.   Let P, Q, R, T be assertions, p, q statement sequences and B a boolean expression.

(a) If $\{P\}\ p\ \{Q\}$ and $\{Q\}\ q\ \{R\}$ are partially correct then $\{P\}\ p;\ q\ \{R\}$ is also partially correct.

(b) If $\{Q\}\ p\ \{R\}$ is partially correct, P *implies* Q and R *implies* T then $\{P\}\ p\ \{T\}$ is partially correct.

(c) If $\{P \wedge B\}\ p\ \{Q\}$ and $\{P \wedge \neg B\}\ q\ \{Q\}$ are partially correct and if $P(b, s, i, o)$ $= true$ implies $I(b, s, B)$ is defined for all $b \in \mathbf{B}$, $s \in \mathbf{S}$, $i \in \mathbf{D}^*$, $o \in \mathbf{D}^*$ then $\{P\}$ **if** B **then** p **else** q **fi** $\{Q\}$ is partially correct. $P \wedge B$ *(analogously $P \wedge \neg B$)* is defined as $(P \wedge B)(b, s, i, o) = true$ if and only if $P(b, s, i, o) = true$ and $I(b, s, B) = true$.

(d) The assertions (a), (b) and (c) are also valid when "partially correct" is replaced by "totally correct".

(e) If $\{P \wedge B\}\ p\ \{P\}$ is partially correct and if $P(b, s, i, o) = true$ implies $I(b, s, B)$ is defined for all $b \in \mathbf{B}$, $s \in \mathbf{S}$, $e \in \mathbf{D}^*$, $a \in \mathbf{D}^*$ then
$\{P\}$ **while** B **do** p **od** $\{P \wedge \neg B\}$ is partially correct.

Proof: For this proof we call a quadruple (b, s, i, o) with $b \in \mathbf{B}$, $s \in \mathbf{S}$, $i \in \mathbf{D}^*$, $o \in \mathbf{D}^*$ an environment.

(a) Let (b, s, i, o) be an environment with $P(b, s, i, o) = true$. As the triple $\{P\}\ p\ \{Q\}$ is partially correct, the computation from start configuration (p, b, s, i, o) is either infinitely long or it ends in a configuration $(\epsilon, b', s', i', o')$ with $Q(b', s', i', o') = true$. In the first case the computation from start configuration $(p; q, b, s, i, o)$ is infinitely long and thus the triple $\{P\}\ p;\ q\{Q\}$ is partially correct. In the second case we consider the computation from the start configuration (q, b', s', i', o'). As the triple $\{Q\}\ q\ \{R\}$ is partially correct this computation is either infinitely long or it ends in a configuration $(\epsilon, b'', s'', i'', o'')$ with $R(b'', s'', i'', o'') = true$. In the first of these cases the computation from the start configuration (p, b, s, i, o) is infinitely long and thus the triple $\{P\}\ p;\ q\ \{R\}$ is partially correct. In the second of these cases $(\epsilon, b'', s'', i'', o'')$ is also the end configuration for start configuration $(p; q, b, s, i, o)$ and thus in this case also the triple $\{P\}\ p;\ q\ \{R\}$ is partially correct.

(b) Let (b, s, i, o) be an environment with $P(b, s, i, o) = true$. From "P implies Q" follows $Q(b, s, i, o) = true$. As the triple $\{Q\}\ p\ \{R\}$ is partially correct the computation from start configuration (p, b, s, i, o) is either infinitely long or it terminates in a configuration $(\epsilon, b', s', i', o')$ with $R(b', s', i', o') = true$ and thus $T(b', s', i', o') = true$. In each of the two cases we have proved partial correctness of $\{P\}\ p\ \{T\}$.

(c) Let (b, s, i, o) be an environment with $P(b, s, i, o) = true$. By assumption $I(b, s, B)$ is then defined.

Case 1: $I(b, s, B) = true$. Then $\delta(\textbf{if } B \textbf{ then } p \textbf{ else } q \textbf{ fi}, b, s, i, o) = (p, b, s, i, o)$ and $P(b, s, i, o) \wedge I(b, s, B) = true$. As the triple $\{P \wedge B\}\ p\ \{Q\}$ is partially correct the computation from start configuration (p, b, s, i, o) is either infinitely long or it ends in a state $(\epsilon, b', s', i', o')$ with $Q(b', s', i', o') = true$. In each of the two cases partial correctness of $\{P\}$ **if** B **then** p **else** q **fi** $\{Q\}$ is shown.

Case 2: $I(b, s, B) = false$. This case is analogous to Case 1 and is left to the reader.

(d) For total correctness we need only shorten the proofs of cases (a), (b) and (c) by deleting, respectively, the possibility that a computation could be infinitely long.

(e) Let (b, s, i, o) be an environment with $P(b, s, i, o) = true$.
Let $c_0, c_1, c_2, \ldots, c_k = (p_k, b, s_k, i_k, o_k)$, be the computation from start state $c_0 = ($**while** B **do** p **od**; $, b, s, i, o)$. We must show that the computation is either infinitely long or ends in a state c_m with $(P \wedge \neg B)(b, s_m, i_m, o_m) = true$ and $p_m = \epsilon$. We therefore assume that the computation is finite and has length m and show the following auxiliary claim.

Claim: *For all* k, $0 \leq k \leq m$, *there exists* j, $k \leq j \leq m$, *with* $P(b, s_j, i_j, o_j) = true$ *and furthermore* $p_j = $ **while** B **do** p **od** *or* $p_j = \epsilon$ *and* $I(b, s_j, B) = false$.

Remark: For $k < m$, c_j is the next configuration in which the loop condition is tested. For $k = m$ the auxiliary claim is precisely the assertion of the Lemma.

Proof: For $k = 0$ the claim with $j = 0$ holds. Let $m > k \geq 0$ and the claim hold for k. We now want to show the claim for $k + 1$. Let $j \geq k$ be chosen such that j satisfies the claim for k. If $j > k$ then j also satisfies the claim for $k + 1$. We have only to discuss the case $j = k$. Then, in particular, $P(b, s_k, i_k, o_k) = true$ and $p_k = \epsilon$ or $p_k = $ **while** B **do** p **od**; . Because $k < m$ the case $p_k = \epsilon$ can not arise. Thus $p_k = $ **while** B **do** p **od**. By assumption, $P(b, s_k, i_k, o_k) = true$ implies $I(b, s_k, B)$ is defined. We distinguish between two cases.

Case 1: $I(b, s_k, B) = true$. Then $c_{k+1} = (p;$ **while** B **do** p **od**; $, b, s_k, i_k, o_k)$. According to premise the triple $\{P \wedge B\}$ p $\{P\}$ is partially correct. Thus a computation from the start state $c' = (p;, b, s_k, i_k, o_k)$ is either infinitely long or it ends in a state $(\epsilon, b, s', i', o')$ with $P(b, s', i', o') = true$. In the first case the computation from the start state c_{k+1}, and thus for the initial state c_0, would be infinitely long. This, by assumption, is not the case. Thus we have the second case. Now there exists $j \geq k + 1$ with $c_j = ($**while** B **do** p **od**; $, b, s', i', o')$ and $P(b, s', i', o') = true$ and the induction step is accomplished.

Case 2: $I(b, s_k, B) = false$. Then $c_{k+1} = (\epsilon, b, s_k, i_k, o_k)$ and $k + 1 = m$. The claim holds with $j = m$.
We now use the claim with $k = m$. Then $j = m$ and, as c_m is the last configuration of the computation, $p_m = \epsilon$, $I(b, s_m, B) = false$ and $P(b, s_m, i_m, o_m) = true$. Now part (e) has been proved. ∎

Example 3:   From Example (2b) and Lemma 2a the partial correctness of

$$\{s(b(y)) = m, \; n = s(b(i)) \cdot s(b(y)) + s(b(x)), \; s(b(x)) \in \mathbb{N}_0, \; s(b(x)) \geq s(b(y))\}$$

$$x := x - y; \; i := i + 1$$

$$\{s(b(y)) = m, \; n = s(b(i)) \cdot s(b(y)) + s(b(x)), \; s(b(x)) \in \mathbb{N}_0\} \text{ follows.}$$

Furthermore, Lemma 2e with $B = (x \geq y)$ and
$P = (s(b(y)) = m$ and $n = s(b(i)) \cdot s(b(y)) + s(b(x))$ and $s(b(x)) \in \mathbb{N}_0)$ implies the
partial correctness of

$\{P\}$ **while** $x \geq y$ **do** $x := x - y; \; i := i + 1$ **od** $\{P \wedge s(b(x)) < s(b(y))\}$.
Let now $Q = $ (input tape contains numbers n and m, $n \in \mathbb{N}_0$, $m \in \mathbb{Z}$),
$\qquad R = (s(b(x)) = n \geq 0, \; s(b(y)) = m$ and $s(b(i)) = 0)$
and $T = (s(b(x)) = n \bmod m$ and $s(b(i)) = n \operatorname{div} m)$
$\qquad$ Then the triple
$\{Q\}$**read** x; **read** y; $i := 0\{R\}$
is partially correct. Furthermore R *implies* P and $(P \wedge s(b(x)) < s(b(y)))$ *implies* T.
Thus Lemma 2a and Lemma 2b imply partial correctness of

> $\{$input tape contains numbers n and m; $n \in \mathbb{N}_0$, $m \in \mathbb{Z}\}$
>
> **read** x; **read** y; $i := 0$;
>
> **while** $x \geq y$ **do** $x := x - y$; $i := i + 1$ **od**;
>
> $\{s(b(x)) = n \bmod m$ and $s(b(i)) = n \operatorname{div} m\}$

Thus our program computes $n \bmod m$ and $n \operatorname{div} m$ (at least when it terminates).
Note, however, that we have not proved that the program terminates for all inputs.
In fact the program does not terminate, for instance, for input $0,0$. We will refer
to this problem again in the next section.

At this point the reader should try to prove partial correctness of the program
in Section 3.3 using the given assertions. In these assertions we have used the
following simplified notation which we will use from now on. If x is a variable
name we write x instead of $s(b(x))$. In this section we wrote $s(b(x))$ to clarify the
difference between variable names x, y and i and the names n and m. With a little
accuracy, this difference in the simplified notation is also clear. Program 2 presents
our example in simplified notation.

This section concludes with a further example, a program to compute the
integer factor of the root of a natural number, i.e. for input $m \in \mathbb{N}$ it computes a
number $k \in \mathbb{N}$ with $k^2 \leq m < (k+1)^2$. For didactical reasons we aim for a program
without multiplications. As opposed to our first example, we will not specify a
program and prove it to be correct *afterwards*, but we will develop the correctness
proof simultaneously with the program. A rough solution of the problem is easily
found. We compute in sequence the square numbers until we have found the desired
k. This leads to the basic structure shown in Program 3 .

---

program *division_with_rest*;
(∗ we expect numbers n, m with
   $n \in \mathbb{N}_0$ and $m \in \mathbb{Z}$ on the input tape ∗)
var i, x, y: **integer**;
begin read x; **read** y; $i := 0$;

      (∗ $x = n \geq 0$, $y = m$, $i = 0$, $n = i \cdot y + x$, $x \in \mathbb{N}_0$ ∗)
      while $x \geq y$
      do (∗ $y = m$, $n = i \cdot y + x$, $x \in N_0$ and $x \geq y$ ∗)
         $x := x - y$; $i := i + 1$
         (∗ $y = m$, $n = i \cdot y + x$, $x \in \mathbb{N}_0$ ∗)
      od

      (∗ $y = m$, $n = i \cdot y + x$; $x \in \mathbb{N}_0$, $x < y$ ∗)
      print i; **print** x
      (∗ output tape contains n *div* m and n *mod* m ∗)
end.

—————————————————— **Prog. 2** ——————————————————

```
(0)      program extract_the_root;
(1)      (∗ we expect m ∈ N on input tape ∗)
(2)      var n, z: integer;
(3)      begin read n; z := 1;
(4)          while the square following z ≤ n
(5)          do (∗ z = k² and (k + 1)² ≤ n for some k ∈ N and n = m ∗)
(6)              z := the next square number
(7)              (∗ z = (k + 1)² ≤ n for some k ∈ N and n = m ∗)
(8)          od
(9)          (∗ z = k² ≤ n < (k + 1)² for some k ∈ N and n = m ∗)
(10)         output k
(11)     end.
```

—————————————————— **Prog. 3** ——————————————————

The partial correctness of this program is immediately obvious from the assertions.
We can now concentrate on the two statements which are not PROSA statements.
In order to print k we declare a variable y in line 2, initialise it with 1 in line 3,
insert $y := y + 1$ in line 6 and substitute line 10 by **print** y. In the assertion we
can now substitute y for k. Of course we no longer need to speak of the existence
of a number k. We already know the number. It is the value of variable y. We
obtain Program 4.

```
(0)    program extract_the_root;
(1)    (* we expect: input tape contains m ∈ ℕ *)
(2)    var n, z, y: integer;
(3)    begin  read  n; z := 1; y := 1;
(4)           while the square following z ≤ n
(5)           do (* z = y² and (y + 1)² ≤ n and n = m *)
(6)              z := the next square number; y := y + 1
(7)                (* z = y² ≤ n and n = m *)
(8)           od
(9)           (* z = y² ≤ n < (y + 1)² and n = m *)
(10)          print  y
(11)   end.
```

—————————————————— **Prog. 4** ——————————————————— —

How can we compute the square number which follows z? On entering the
body of the loop we have $z = k^2$. We would like to achieve $z = (k + 1)^2$ when
leaving the body. Because $(k + 1)^2 = k^2 + 2k + 1$ we need only increase z by $2k + 1$.
We now introduce a variable x always having the value $2y + 1$ by appending to
line 3 the assignment $x := 3$ and to line 6 the assignment $x := x + 2$. Finally, we
can substitute the assignment to z in line 6 by $z := z + x$ and the test in line 4 by
$z + x \leq n$. We thus obtain the *partially correct* PROSA program 5.

```
(0)    program extract_the_root;
(1)    (* we expect: input tape contains m ∈ ℕ *)
(2)    var n, z, y, x: integer;
(3)    begin  read  n; z := 1; y := 1; x := 3;
(4)           while z + x ≤ n
(5)           do (* z = y², (y + 1)² ≤ n, x = 2y + 1 and n = m *)
(6)              z := z + x; y := y + 1; x := x + 2
(7)                (* z = y² ≤ n, x = 2y + 1 and n = m *)
(8)           od
(10)          print  y
(11)   end.
```

—————————————————— **Prog. 5** ——————————————————

3.10 Computation Time and Termination

We can now already prove partial correctness of programs. However this is not sufficient. We would also like to know that our programs always yield an answer and terminate, and furthermore, we are interested in the computation time of our programs. This is discussed in this section.

Firstly we consider the program in Figure 5, Section 3.9. It is quite easy to see that this program terminates for each input $n \in \mathbb{N}_0$ and $m \in \mathbb{N}$. The value of variable x is always a natural number and is reduced at each iteration of the loop (namely by $m > 0$). The values of variable x at the different iterations form a decreasing sequence of natural numbers. As such a sequence can not be longer than its first element, the loop must terminate and thus, naturally, the whole program. Thus the program in Figure 5, Section 3.9 is totally correct with respect to the given input and output assertions.

What about the program in Figure 6? As opposed to Figure 5 we have only changed the input assertion. m may now be an arbitrary integer. The sequence of values x is no longer necessarily decreasing (if $m < 0$ it even increases) and thus the loop does not terminate in each case. The program therefore is only partially correct for the input and output assertions in Figure 6.

For $n \in \mathbb{N}_0$, $m \in \mathbb{N}$ the program always stops. What is the computation time for input n and m? We observe that variable i counts the number of iterations of the loop. The final value of i is $n \ div \ m$ and thus the body of the loop is executed precisely $n \ div \ m$ times. Hence the computation time of our program for input n and m is $3 \cdot (n \ div \ m) + 9$ time units, namely $3 \cdot (n \ div \ m)$ time units for the $n \ div \ m$ executions of the loop body (one time unit for the evaluation of the condition and two time units for the body itself) and 9 time units for the remaining statements (three time units for processing the declarations, three time units for the read statements and the initialisation of i, one time unit for the last evaluation of the condition which leads to the loop exit and two time units for the print statements). Using O-notation we can say that the computation time of our program for input n and m is $O(n \ div \ m)$.

Proceeding to the second example in Section 3.9, we show its termination and analyse the computation time. For termination we observe that the difference between z and n becomes smaller at each iteration, i.e. the value of the expressions $n - z$ diminishes at each execution of the body. This value is always non-negative and thus the body can only be executed a finite number of times. The iteration statement terminates and thus the whole program. As we have already proved partial correctness in Section 3.9 the program is totally correct with respect to the given input and output assertions.

The computation time for input n is also easily determined. Variable y counts the number of iterations of the loop. At termination $y^2 \leq n$ and thus the loop is executed $\sqrt{n}$-times at most. Computation time is therefore $O(\sqrt{n})$.

Abstracting from these two examples, we now discuss termination of an iteration statement **while** B **do** p **od** in general.

Theorem 1. *Let P be an assertion, B a boolean expression and p a statement sequence. Furthermore let $\{P \wedge B\}\, p\, \{P\}$ be totally correct and let $t : \mathbf{B} \times \mathbf{S} \times \mathbf{D}^* \times \mathbf{D}^* \to \mathbb{N}_0$ be a function with the following property:*

> *for all environments (b, s, i, o) with $P \wedge B(b, s, i, o) = true$:*
> *Each start configuration (p, b, s, i, o) leads to a configuration $(\epsilon, b', s', i', o')$ with $t(b', s', i', o') < t(b, s, i, o)$, i.e. each iteration of the loop decrements the value of t.*
> *Then $\{P\}$ **while** B **do** p **od** $\{P \wedge \neg B\}$ is totally correct.*

Proof: We already know that $\{P\}$ **while** B **do** p **od** $\{P \wedge \neg B\}$ is partially correct (see Lemma 2e in Section 3.9). We must exclude that the computation is infinitely long.

As $\{P \wedge B\}\, p\, \{P\}$ is totally correct, the case of an infinite computation would imply that for the start configuration $c_0 = ($**while** B **do** p **od**$;\ ,b_0, s_0, i_0, o_0)$ an infinite sequence of configurations $c_k = ($**while** B **do** p **od**$;\ ,b_k, s_k, i_k, o_k)$, $k \geq 0$, with $I(b_k, s_k, B) = true$ and $(p;\ ,b_k, s_k, i_k, o_k) \Rightarrow^* (\epsilon, b_{k+1}, s_{k+1}, i_{k+1}, o_{k+1})$ would exist. The latter assertion states that the environment $(b_{k+1}, s_{k+1}, i_{k+1}, o_{k+1})$ follows from the environment (b_k, s_k, i_k, o_k) by a single execution of the body. Let $n_k = t(b_k, s_k, i_k, o_k)$. Then $n_k \in \mathbb{N}_0$ and $n_{k+1} < n_k$. Since there are no infinite decreasing sequences of natural numbers, we have a contradiction .∎

In the above examples we have implicitly used the functions $t(b, s, i, o) = s(b(x))$ and $t(b, s, i, o) = n - s(b(x))$.

To estimate the computation time we count the number of executions of the individual statements. Of course the loops are the main problem. We must try to relate the number of iterations of the loop body to the inputs and thus estimate the computation time. It is not possible to give a general scheme. The reader will find many examples in this book and can thus develop his skill in analysing the computation time of programs.

Exercises for 3.9. and 3.10

1) Write a PROSA program which inputs a sequence of positive real numbers (ending with 0) and prints the largest number.
Prove that your program is correct.

2) Write a PROSA program which prints the binary representation of the numbers from 0 to 15 , i.e. $0000, 0001, \ldots 1111$ should appear on the output tape. Use a **while**-loop in whose body the binary representation for the iteration variable is computed and printed.
Prove the program correct.

3) The following PROSA program is given:

```
program compute;
var i,j,n: integer;
begin i := 0;
      j := 1;
      read  n;
      while i < n
      do i := i + 1;
         j := j + i
      od;
      print  j
end.
```

a) Determine the computations for inputs 3, 2 and 1.

b) What is the relation between the inputs and outputs of the given program?

c) Find a suitable loop invariant and prove the correctness of the program with respect to the specification found in b).

d) Determine the computation time and justify your claim.

3.11 Further Examples

In this section we give four more examples. In each example we prove the given solution correct by specifying assertions and we analyse the computation time of the programs. The reader should try to find a solution of his own for each one, show its correctness and analyse its computation time.

Example 1: Given a natural number $n > 0$. We want to compute the **binary representation** of n, i.e. the sequence of digits $a_k, \ldots, a_0$ with $a_i \in \{0, 1\}$ for $0 \leq i \leq k$ and $a_k = 1$ such that

$$n = \sum_{i=0}^{k} a_i 2^i$$

The digit sequence should be printed as a string $a_k \ldots a_0 \in \{0, 1\}^*$. The rough structure of our solution is:

1) read n;
2) compute k;
3) compute $a_k, \ldots, a_0$ in this order;
4) print the string $a_k \ldots a_0$.

To obtain k we compute in succession 2^0, 2^1, $\ldots$ until a power of 2 is reached which exceeds n. The last power below n yields the desired k. This leads to Program 6 (we presuppose the declarations **var** N, K, POT: **integer** and assume that N has the value n):

$K := 0;\ POT := 1;$
$(*\ POT = 2^K,\ POT \leq N$ and $N = n\ *)$

while $POT + POT \leq N$
do $(*\ POT = 2^K,\ 2 \cdot POT \leq N$ and $N = n\ *)$
   $K := K + 1;\ POT := POT + POT$
   $(*\ POT = 2^K,\ POT \leq N$ and $N = n\ *)$
od;

$(*\ POT = 2^K,\ POT \leq N < 2 \cdot POT$ and $N = n$ i.e. $K = k\ *)$
—————————————— **Prog. 6** ——————————————

We now have $k(= K)$ and $2^k(= POT)$. Since we increase K by 1 at each iteration, K initially is 0 and has the final value $k = \lfloor \log n \rfloor$, the computation time of this program section is $O(\log n)$. The sequence $a_k, \ldots, a_0$ can now be determined step by step. Of course $a_k = 1$. We subtract $a_k \cdot 2^k$ from n and compute 2^{k-1}. Testing $n - a_k 2^k \geq 2^{k-1}$ determines the value of a_{k-1}. We then subtract $a_{k-1} 2^{k-1}$, compute $a_{k-2}, \ldots$. This leads to Program 7 (with the additional declaration **var** RES : **string**).

$(*\ POT = 2^K,\ POT \leq n < 2 \cdot POT$ and $N = n\ *)$
$RES := \ ""$;
$(*\ POT = 2^K,\ K = k,\ RES = a_k \ldots a_{K+1}$ and $N = \sum_{i=0}^{K} a_i 2^i\ *)$

while $K \geq 0$
do $(*\ POT = 2^K,\ k \geq K \geq 0,\ RES = a_k \ldots a_{K+1}$ and $N = \sum_{i=0}^{K} a_i 2^i\ *)$

   if $N \geq POT$ **then** $(*\ a_K = 1\ *)$
                    $RES := RES \cdot "1";$
                    $N := N - POT$
        else $(*\ a_K = 0\ *)$
                    $RES := RES \cdot "0";$
  fi;
$K := K - 1;\ POT := POT/2$
$(*\ k \geq K \geq -1,\ RES = a_k \ldots a_{K+1}$ and $N = \sum_{i=0}^{K} a_i 2^i;$
   furthermore $POT = 2^K$ if $K \geq 0\ *)$
od

$(*\ RES = a_k \ldots a_{K+1}$ and $K = -1$, i.e. $RES = a_k \ldots a_0\ *)$
—————————————— **Prog. 7** ——————————————

The computation time of this program is obviously $O(k) = O(\log\ n)$. Altogether we obtain Program 8.

---

program *Binary_representation*;
(∗ input tape contains a natural number $n > 0$.
   Let $k \in \mathbb{N}_0$, $a_k, \ldots, a_0 \in \{0, 1\}$ be defined as
   $a_k = 1$ and $n = \sum_{i=0}^{k} a_i 2^i$. The following program
   computes the string $a_k \ldots a_0$ in time $O(k) = O(\log\ n)$ ∗)
var N, K, POT: **integer**; **var** RES: **string**;
begin

        read N;
        $K := 0$; $POT := 1$;

        while $POT + POT \leq N$
        do (∗ $POT = 2^K$, $2 \cdot POT \leq N$ and $N = n$ ∗)
           $K := K + 1$; $POT := POT + POT$
        od;

        (∗ $POT = 2^K$, $K = k$, $N = n$ ∗)
        $RES := ""$;

        while $K \geq 0$
        do (∗ es $POT = 2^K$, $RES = a_k \ldots a_{K+1}$, $k \geq K \geq 0$
              and $N = \sum_{i=0}^{K} a_i 2^i$ ∗)

           if $N \geq POT$ **then** $RES := RES \cdot "1"$;
                          $N := N - POT$
                else $RES := RES \cdot "0"$;
          fi;
        $K := K - 1$; $POT := POT/2$
        od

        (∗ $RES = a_k \ldots a_0$ ∗)
        print RES
end.

—————— **Prog. 8** ——————

Example 2: Given a string $s = s_k \ldots s_0$ with $s_i \in \{0, 1\}$ on the input tape. Compute and print the string $rev(s) = s_0 \ldots s_k$. This problem has a very simple solution. We need only shorten s step-by-step by deleting the first symbol repeatedly and simultaneously construct the result. Program 9 is the corresponding PROSA program.

---

program *Reversing_a_string*;
(* input tape contains a string $s = s_k \ldots s_0$.
   The string $s_0 \ldots s_k$ is produced in time $O(k + 1)$ *)
var *S, RES*: **string**;
begin

      read *S*; *RES* := "";

      while not empty *S*
      do (* there exists $i \geq 0$ with $S = s_i \ldots s_0$ and $RES = s_{i+1} \ldots s_k$ *)
          RES := (**convcs hd** *S*) · *RES*; *S* := **tl** *S*
      od;

      (* $S = \epsilon$ and $RES = rev(s)$ *)
      print *RES*
end.

———————————— **Prog. 9** ————————————

Computation time of this program is obviously $O(k + 1)$ because a symbol of s is deleted at each iteration.

Example 3: Given an input tape with two natural numbers n and m, $n > 0$, $m > 0$. Compute the product $n \cdot m$ without using the multiplication operator. Let $a_k \ldots a_0$ be the binary representation of n with $a_k = 1$, $a_i \in \{0, 1\}$, $n = \sum_{i=0}^{k} a_i 2^i$.

According to Example 1 we can compute the string $a_k \ldots a_0$ in time $O(k)$.

$$m \cdot n = m \cdot \sum_{i=0}^{k} a_i 2^i = \sum_{i=0}^{k} a_i m 2^i$$

The latter sum can now be easily computed using the Horner scheme of Section 3.3. Altogether this leads to Program 10.

---

program *Multiplication*;
(* input tape contains natural numbers n and m. Let $a_k \ldots a_0$
   with $a_i \in \{0, 1\}$, $a_k = 1$, and $n = \sum_{i=0}^{k} a_i 2^i$ be the binary representation of n.
   We compute $n \cdot m$ in time $O(\log\ n)$*. *)
var *N, M, POT, K, ERG*: **integer**; **var** *RES*: **string**;
begin

      read *N*; **read** *M*;
      (* use the program of Example 1 to compute $RES = a_k \ldots a_0$.
          Imagine a copy of this program here.
          Furthermore $M = m$ *)
      ERG := 0;

```
      while not empty RES
      do  (* we have i ≥ 0 with RES = a_i ... a_0 and
              ERG = m · ∑_{j=i+1}^{k} a_j 2^{j-(i+1)} *)

          if hd RES = '1'
          then  ERG := ERG + ERG + M
          else  ERG := ERG + ERG
          fi;
          RES := tl RES
      od
      (* ERG = n · m *)

      print ERG
end.
```

──────────────────── **Prog. 10** ────────────────────

The computation time of the program of Example 1 was $O(k)$. The same estimate applies for the added part because one symbol of RES is deleted at each iteration. Thus, together, the computation time is $O(k) = O(\log n)$.

Example 4:

The context-free grammar $G = (\{S\}, \{[,],(,)\}, \{S \to \epsilon \,|\, [S] \,|\, (S) \,|\, SS\}, S)$ generates well-formed expressions over round and square brackets. We want to write a program which decides for a string $w \in \{(,),[,]\}^*$ if $w \in L_G$ or not. We proceed as in Chapter II and implement a push down automaton which recognises the language. This automaton reads the string from left to right. Opening brackets are written into the stack (**var** ST : **string**). In the case of a closing bracket we compare it with the topmost bracket in the stack. If they are of the same kind (round or square) we continue, otherwise we reject the string. These considerations lead to Program 11.

The given invariants require some explanation. It is obvious that the string ST always consists of opening brackets only and that on entering the loop $W \neq \epsilon$ and $RES = true$. When entering the first time then $w \in L_G$ if and only if $rev(ST).W \in L_G$, since $W = w$ and $ST = \epsilon$. We now show that the postcondition of the loop body holds if the precondition holds. If C is an opening bracket this is obvious. For the case of a closing bracket we have the following Lemma.

Lemma 3. Let $st \in \{(,[\}^*, c \in \{),]\}, v \in \{(,[,),]\}^*$. Then $rev(st)cv \in L_G$ if and only if the following three conditions hold:

1) $st \neq \epsilon$
2) $c = ')'$ and $hd(st) = '('$ or
   $c = ']'$ and $hd(st) = '['$
3) $rev(tl(st))v \in L_G$

---

program *Brackets*;
(* The input tape contains a string $w \in \{(,),[,]\}^*$.
   We decide $w \in L_G$ in time $O(|w|)$. In
   the invariants we use function *rev* of example 2 *)
var W, ST : **string**; **var** C : **char**; **var** RES : **bool**;
begin

       read W; $ST :=$ ""; $RES :=$ **true**

       while not empty W **and** RES
       do (* $w \in L_G$ if and only if $rev(ST).W \in L_G$,
           $W \neq \epsilon$, $rev(ST) \in \{(,[\}^*$ and $RES = true$ *)

          $C :=$ **hd** W; $W :=$ **tl** W;
          if $C =$ '(' **or** $C =$ '['
          then $ST :=$ **convcs** $C \cdot ST$
          else **if not empty** ST
              then if ($C =$ ')' **and hd** $ST =$ '(')
                  or ($C =$ ']' **and hd** $ST =$ '[')
              then $ST :=$ **tl** ST
              else $RES :=$ **false**
              fi
            else $RES :=$ **false**
            fi
        fi
        (* $w \in L_G$ if and only if $rev(ST).W \in L_G$ and $RES = true$;
         furthermore $rev(ST) \in \{(,[\}^*$ *)
       od;
       (* $w \in L_G$ if and only if $ST = \epsilon$ and $RES = true$ *)

       print RES **and empty** ST
end.

_______________________ **Prog. 11** _______________________

Proof: Let $rev(st)cv \in L_G$. Then 1) holds as no string in L_G starts with a closing
bracket, 2) holds because the symbol combination ( ] and [ ) does not occur in a
string of L_G, and 3) holds because by deleting the first pair of brackets from a
string in L_G we obtain again a string in L_G (The reader should try to elaborate
this brief argument).
If, conversely, conditions 1), 2) and 3) hold then $rev(st)cv \in L_G$, as we may insert
a pair of brackets in a string in L_G at an arbitrary place and obtain again a string
in L_G.   ■

From the Lemma and the preceding remark it follows that the postcondition of the body holds if the precondition holds. The postcondition and the test

not empty W **and** RES imply the precondition. Thus the loop invariant is verified. On leaving the loop:

1) $w \in L_G$ if and only if $rev(ST).W \in L_G$ and $RES = true$
2) $rev(ST) \in \{(,[\}^*$
3) $W = \epsilon$ or $RES = false$

Thus $w \in L_G$ if and only if $ST = \epsilon$ and $RES = true$ which can be seen as follows.

Let $w \in L_G$. Then $RES = true$ according to 1) and hence $W = \epsilon$ according to 3) and hence $rev(ST) \in L_G$ according to 1). Because of $rev(ST) \in \{(,[\}^*$ it follows that $ST = \epsilon$. Conversely, let $ST = \epsilon$ and $RES = true$. Then $W = \epsilon$ follows from 3) and hence $rev(ST).W = \epsilon \in L_G$. Thus $w \in L_G$ according to 1) and the correctness of the program is proved.

Computation time is obviously $O(|w|)$ as in each iteration a symbol of W has been removed.

Chapter 4   Data Structures

The five types (*int, real, bool, char, string*) introduced in PROSA so far were called "elementary". In this chapter we introduce complex data types, namely arrays, records and pointer variables. An array (row) is a collection of several variables of the same type, a record (structure) is a collection of several variables of arbitrary type. The pointers are a new set of variables. A pointer variable can assume a record as a value. These new language constructs increase the power of PROSA considerably. A mathematician would scarcely write a program to solve a system of equations $A \cdot x = b$ in a language which would not offer him the data type array. Only with the aid of this type can he declare and use the matrix A of coefficients and the vectors x and b. Records, together with pointers, permit the construction of large plexi. An example is the suitable storing of larger data sets in "ordered" trees for efficient searching. Besides, a program can create new record objects as required, e.g. depending on the length of the input. In PROSA up to now the number of variables with which a program can operate is given by the declaration section and thus fixed.

This chapter is structured as follows. In the first section we introduce arrays and explain them using some examples. In the second section we do the same for records and pointers. Finally, in the third section, we formally describe the new concepts and specify precisely the extended syntax and semantics of PROSA.

4.1 Arrays

An array is a collection of several variables of the same type. The variables can be arranged in one or several dimensions. An array of dimension one is a vector, an array of dimension 2 is a matrix, etc Figure 1 shows a one-dimensional and a two-dimensional array. The one-dimensional array comprises three variables of type *int* which are selected by the indices 1, 2 and 3. The two-dimensional array comprises four variables of type *int* selected by index pairs (4,2), (4,3), (5,2) and (5,3).

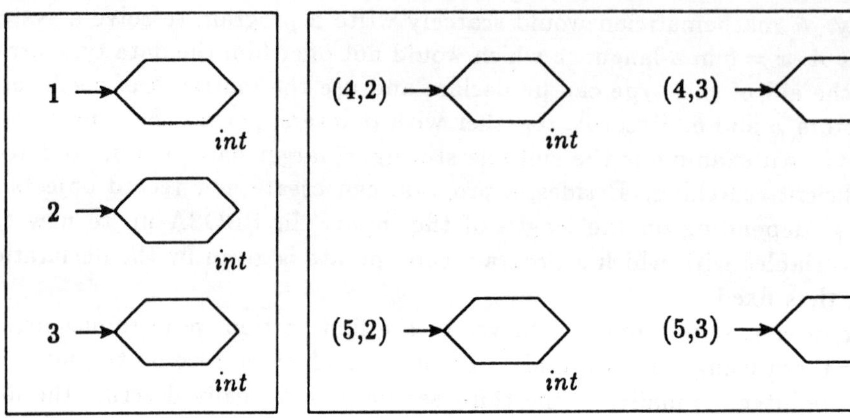

Fig. 1.

An array object is created by a declaration in which it is also bound to a name. The **array declarations**

    var *v*: **array** [1..3] **of integer**;

    var *m*: **array** [4..5, 2..3] **of integer**;

establish the environment of Figure 2.

In a declaration of an array we describe the type of an individual array component (in our example *int*) and specify its dimension. For each of the dimensions we specify the index range (in our example 1..3 (read: 1 to 3) or 4..5 and 2..3). Execution of such a declaration generates the respective array and binds it to the specified name. Note that names *v* and *m* in the above declarations are bound to array objects and not to variables. However, an array is an aggregate of several variables and this explains historically the use of the key word **var** in an array declaration. The authors prefer to read **var** as a combination of the letters v (for variable), a (for array) and r (for record). Then variable declarations (e.g. **var** *x*: **integer**), array declarations (e.g. **var** *m*: **array**[4..5,2..3] **of integer**) and record declarations (e.g. **var** *y*: **record** *age*: **integer**; *name*: **string end**) are all introduced by the same key word **var** and only the key word behind the colon distinguishes between the three cases.

How do we select a component of an array? We specify a list of integer expressions, one for each dimension of the array. This index list is placed behind the

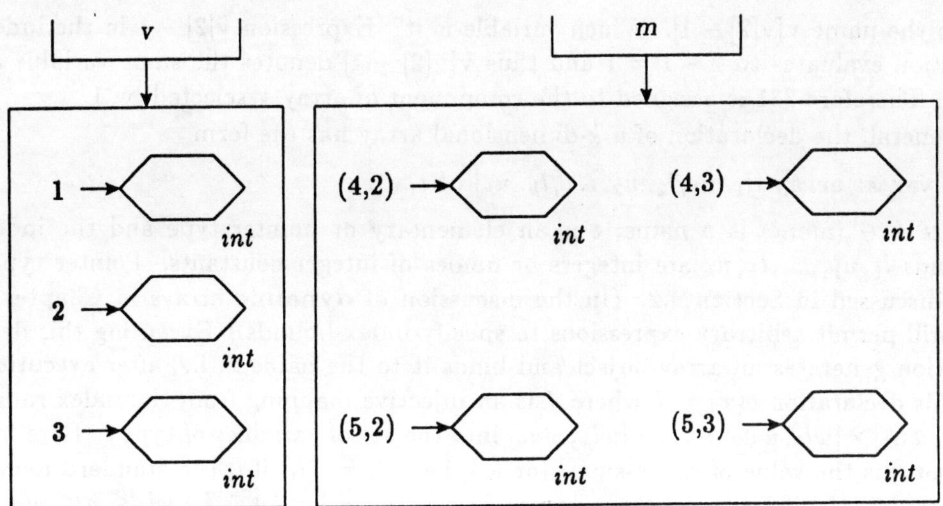

Fig. 2.

array name in square brackets. In our example $v[2]$, $v[3*5-12]$ and $m[5,2]$ select components of a   ya v and m. $v[3]$ and $v[3*5-12]$ select the same component. The names for array components constructed in this way can now be used like the names of simple variables in expressions and assignments. Executing the following assignments

$$v[2] := 2;\ v[3] := 17;$$
$$m[4,2] := 4;\ m[4,3] := 19;\ m[5,2] := 33,\ m[5,3] := 0;$$
$$v[v[2]-1] := m[4,2]*v[2] + m[4,3]*v[3];$$

yields the environment of Figure 3.

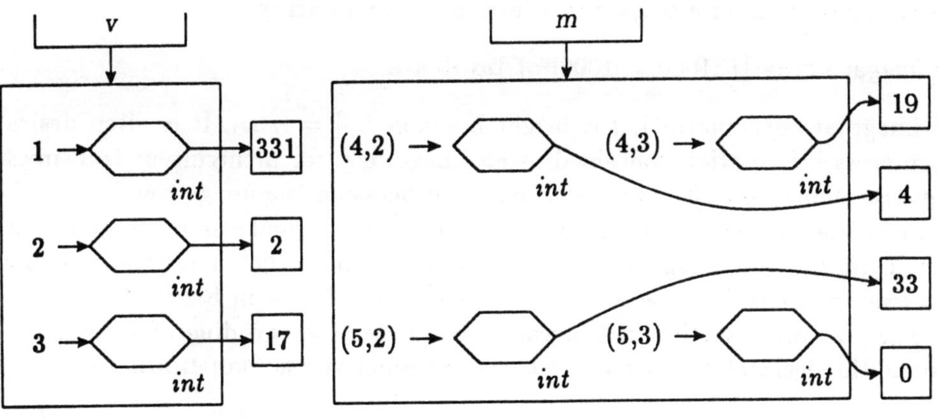

Fig. 3.

Let us have a closer look at the last of these assignments. Expression $m[4,2]*v[2] + m[4,3]*v[3]$ has the value $4\cdot 2 + 19\cdot 17 = 331$. This value is assigned to the variable with the name $v[v[2] - 1]$. Which variable is it? Expression $v[2] - 1$ in the index position evaluates to $2 - 1 = 1$ and thus $v[v[2] - 1]$ denotes the same variable as $v[1]$. Therefore 331 is assigned to the component of array v selected by 1.

In general, the declaration of a k-dimensional array has the form

$$\textbf{var } x\text{: } \textbf{array } [l_1..u_1, l_2..u_2, \ldots, l_k..u_k] \textbf{ of } t,$$

where $x \in \langle ident \rangle$ is a name, t is an elementary or pointer type and the index bounds $l_1, u_1, \ldots, l_k, u_k$ are integers or names of integer constants. Pointer types are discussed in Section 4.2. (In the discussion of **dynamic** arrays in Chapter 5 we will permit arbitrary expressions to specify index bounds.) Executing this declaration generates an array object and binds it to the name x, i.e. after execution of this declaration $b(x) = f$ where f is an injective mapping from the index range $[wl_1, wu_1] \times [wl_2, wu_2] \times \ldots \times [wl_k, wu_k]$ into the set of variables of type t. Here wl_i (or wu_i) is the value of expression l_i(or u_i), i.e. $wl_i = c(l_i)$ if l_i is a standard name, and $wl_i = b(l_i)$ if l_i is a constant name. Also $[wl_i, wu_i] = \{n \in \mathbb{Z} \mid wl_i \leq n \leq wu_i\}$. If x is the name of a k-dimensional array of type t and $e_1, \ldots, e_k$ are expressions of type int then $x[e_1, \ldots, e_k]$ is the name of a variable of type t. In the environment (b, s), $x[e_1, \ldots, e_k]$ denotes the variable $b(x)(I(b, s, e_1), \ldots, I(b, s, e_k))$, i.e. the expressions $e_1, \ldots, e_k$ are evaluated in the environment (b, s) and the resulting values select a certain component of the array $b(x)$.

Now we discuss a few examples.

Example 1 (Scalar Product of two Vectors): The input tape contains 20 real numbers. The first ten are the components of a vector A and the last ten are the components of a vector B. We compute the scalar product of the two vectors.

Example 2 (Image Compression): In graphical data processing two-dimensional arrays are often used to represent images. For example, we can store a 1000 by 1000 raster scan of a black and white image in an array

var *image*: **array** $[1..1000, 1..1000]$ **of boolean.**

The image at coordinates i, j is bright if $image[i,j] = true$. It is often desirable to compress information contained in an image, e.g. for archiving or transmission purposes. A method often used consists in processing the image row by row from top to bottom recording the length of sequences of equal value. Together with $image[1,1]$, this encoding describes the image completely. The following image ($w = true$, b $= false$) of size 5 by 5 is therefore encoded as in Figure 4.

The statement section in Program 2 computes the encoding of an image. We presume the declarations **var** $i, j, length$: **integer**; **var** *actual*: **boolean**.

Example 3 (Searching in a Sorted Array): For the following examples we assume the declarations

    var A: **array** $[1..10000]$ **of real**; **var** x: **real**;

    var $bottom, top, i, next$: **integer**;

```
program scalar_product;
var i: integer; var s: real;
var A: array [1..10] of real; var B: array [1..10] of real;
begin i := 1; while i ≤ 10 do read A[i]; i := i + 1 od;
      i := 1; while i ≤ 10 do read B[i]; i := i + 1 od;
```

(* both vectors are read

and now $\sum_{j=1}^{i-1} A[j] \cdot B[j]$ for $i = 1, \ldots, 11$ is computed; *)

$i := 1;\ s := 0.0;$

$(*\ :\ s = \sum_{j=1}^{i-1} A[j] \cdot B[j]$ and $i \leq 11;\ *)$

while $i \leq 10$

do $(*\ s = \sum_{j=1}^{i-1} A[j] \cdot B[j]$ and $i \leq 10;\ *)$

$\quad s := s + A[i] * B[i];$

$\quad i := i + 1$

$\quad (*\ s = \sum_{j=1}^{i-1} A[j] \cdot B[j]$ and $i \leq 11\ *)$

od;

$(*\ s = \sum_{j=1}^{i-1} A[j] \cdot B[j]$ and $i \leq 11$ and $i > 10$, i.e. $i = 11$,

and thus

$s = \sum_{j=1}^{10} A[j] \cdot B[j];\ *)$

print s

end.

—————————————————— Prog. 1 ——————————————————

$$
\begin{array}{ccccc}
b & b & b & b & b \\
w & w & w & w & w \\
b & b & w & b & b \\
b & b & w & b & b \\
b & b & w & b & b \\
\end{array}
\quad \overset{encoding}{\longrightarrow} \quad
false, 5, 5, 2, 1, 4, 1, 4, 1, 2
$$

stands for b's in positions
$image[3, 4], image[3, 5], image[4, 1], image[4, 2]$

Fig. 4

Given an initialised array A with $A[1] \leq A[2] \leq \ldots \leq A[10000]$ and a real number in x, we want to search for x in array A. That is, at termination of the program either an index i is found with $A[i] = x$ or $A[j] \neq x$ for all j, $1 \leq j \leq 10000$. The simplest method is to inspect array A linearly, i.e. to compare x successively with $A[1], A[2], \ldots$. Let us presume that we have already compared x with $A[1], \ldots, A[i-1]$ and not yet found x. This means that x can only be one of the elements $A[i], \ldots, A[10000]$. If $i = 10000$ or $x \leq A[i]$ then x must be equal to $A[i]$ if it is in the array at all. A simple comparison thus concludes searching. Otherwise, i.e. if $i < 10000$ and $x > A[i]$, we increase i by 1 and are again in the above situation.

```
(* array image contains the image to be compressed. *)
print image[1, 1];
actual := image[1, 1]; i := 1; length := 0;
while i ≤ 1000
do (* we now process the i-th row. *)
    j := 1;
    while j ≤ 1000
    do (* the last length image points including image[i, j − 1]
        (or image[i − 1, 1000], if j = 1) have the value actual *)
        if image[i, j] = actual
        then (* image[i, j] has the same value as the previous image points *)
                length := length + 1
        else  (* the value changes and we must end a sequence *)
                print length; length := 1; actual := image[i, j]
        fi;
        j := j + 1
    od;
i := i + 1
od
```

$$\text{____________________ \textbf{Prog. 2} ____________________}$$

These considerations lead to the following statement section. In the assertions we use S for the set $\{A[1], \ldots, A[10000]\}$.

```
i := 1;
(* i ≤ 10000 and if x ∈ S then x ∈ {A[i], ..., A[10000]} *)
while x > A[i] and i < 10000
do (* i < 10000 and if x ∈ S then x ∈ {A[i + 1], ..., A[10000]} *)
    i := i + 1
    (* i ≤ 10000 and if x ∈ S then x ∈ {A[i], ..., A[10000]} *)
od;
(* i ≤ 10000 and if x ∈ S then x ∈ {A[i], ..., A[10000]} and
(x ≤ A[i] or i ≥ 10000); in other words, if x ∈ S then x = A[i] *)
if  x = A[i]
    then (* x ∈ S *)
            print i
    else  (* x ∉ S *)
            print "not found"
fi
```

$$\text{____________________ \textbf{Prog. 3} ____________________}$$

The search in Program 3 requires up to 10000 iterations to decide if x occures in array A. In each iteration assignment $i := i + 1$ is executed and the expression $x > A[i]$ and $i < 10000$ is evaluated. Computation time of the program on the PROSA machine therefore is at most $20000 + c$ where c is a small constant which takes the transitions outside the loop into account. However, evaluation of the loop condition is more costly than the assignment (compare Chapter V).

The loop condition can be simplified. Omitting the conjunct $i < 10000$ only leads to an error if $x > A[j]$ for all j, $1 \leq j \leq 10000$. If we add an array element $A[10001]$ and store a number in it not smaller than x, for example x itself, then we no longer need the test $i < 10000$ and obtain the following modified statement section (see Program 4).

```
i := 1; A[10001] := x;
(* i ≤ 10001, A[10001] = x and if x ∈ S then x ∈ {A[i],...,A[10000]} *)
while x > A[i]
do (* i ≤ 10001, A[10001] = x, if x ∈ S then x ∈ {A[i],...,A[10000]}
    and x > A[i];
    i ≤ 10000, A[10001] = x, if x ∈ S then x ∈ {A[i + 1],...,A[10000]} *)
  i := i + 1
    (* i ≤ 10001, A[10001] = x, if x ∈ S then x ∈ {A[i],...,A[10000]} *)
od;
(* i ≤ 10001, A[10001] = x, if x ∈ S then x ∈ {A[i],...,A[10000]}
and x ≤ A[i] *)
if x = A[i] and i ≠ 10001
  then (* x ∈ S *)
       print i
  else (* x ∉ S *)
       print "not found"
fi
end
```

--- **Prog. 4** ---

Computation time of the modified program is at most $20000+c+1$ ($+1$ accounts for statement $A[10001] := x$), thus slightly higher than that of the initial program. In practice, however, the modified program runs faster as the simpler condition can be evaluated more quickly (compare Chapter V, exercises).

The above modification did not alter the strategy of linear searching. We have only implemented it more efficiently. In linear searching, the search space is reduced by one element in each iteration and thus requires up to 10000 iterations to solve the search problem. We can proceed more skilfully and halve the size of the search space in each step (called **binary search**). Suppose we have indices $bottom$, top with $bottom \leq top$, and we know that $x \in \{A[bottom],...,A[top]\}$ if $x \in S$. Now if $top < bottom$ then $x \notin S$. If $bottom \leq top$ we choose an index next with $bottom \leq next \leq top$, for example $next := \lfloor (bottom + top)/2 \rfloor$ (binary search!), and compare x with $A[next]$. If $x = A[next]$ we can finish the search (in the program we note this in a boolean variable). If $x < A[next]$ then we can narrow the search to the set $\{A[bottom], \ldots, A[next - 1]\}$ (we do that in the program by executing $top := next - 1$), and if $x > A[next]$ then we can narrow the search to the set $\{A[next + 1], \ldots, A[top]\}$ ($bottom := next + 1$). These considerations lead to Program 5 in which the reader can ignore lines (3), (6), (16) and (19) for the moment.

```
(1)   bottom := 1; top := 10000; found := false;
(2)   (*if x ∈ S then x ∈ {A[bottom],...,A[top]} *)
(3)   (* k := 0; top − bottom + 1 ≤ 10000/2^k *)
(4)   while ¬found and bottom ≤ top
(5)   do (* bottom ≤ top and if x ∈ S then x ∈ {A[bottom],...,A[top]};
(6)        top − bottom + 1 ≤ 10000/2^k *)

(7)        next := ⌊(bottom + top)/2⌋;
(8)        (* bottom ≤ next ≤ top *)
(9)        if x = A[next]
(10)          then found := true
(11)          else (* x ≠ A[next] *)
(12)               if x < A[next]
(13)                  then top := next − 1
(14)                  else bottom := next + 1
(15)               fi
(16)               (* k := k + 1 *)
(17)        fi

(18)        (* if found = true then x = A[next] and
                if found = false then x ∈ S even implies
                x ∈ {A[bottom],...,A[top]};
(19)             top − bottom + 1 ≤ 10000/2^k *)
(20)  od;
(21)  (* if found = true then x = A[next] and
          if found = false then top < bottom and x ∉ S *)
```

──────────────────────── **Prog. 5** ────────────────────────

In line (7) the integer part of division $bottom + top$ by 2 is assigned to $next$. This operation is available in almost all programming languages. Thus we also use it in PROSA, although it was not introduced in Section 3.7.2.

(Partial) correctness of this program follows immediately from the assertions. Before we show termination and estimate the computation time, we will illustrate the program by an example. Let $A[i] = i$, $1 \leq i \leq 10000$ and $x = 4053$. Then we have the following values after the $k+1$-st iteration at line (7).

k	$bottom$	top	$next$	$top - bottom + 1$
0	1	10000	5000	10000
1	1	4999	2500	4999
3	2501	4999	3750	2499
4	3751	4999	4375	1249
5	3751	4374	4062	624
6	3751	4061	3906	311
7	3907	4061	3984	155
8	3985	4061	4023	77
9	4024	4061	4042	38
10	4043	4061	4052	19
11	4053	4061	4057	9
12	4053	4056	4054	4
13	4053	4053	4053	1

After only 14 iterations of the loop, element x is found. We see furthermore that the value of expression $top - bottom + 1$ is halved at each iteration. We want to show this in general. Let us consider a variable k which counts the iterations. As we do not actually introduce k in the program, we put the assignments for k in comments. The claim regarding the value of expression $top - bottom + 1$ can now be formulated as the assertion $top - bottom + 1 \leq 10000/2^k$. We must convince ourselves as to the correctness of this. First we observe that k is increased by one if and only if the value of $top - bottom + 1$ changes. In this case $x \neq A[next]$ and the new value of the expression is either $next - 1 - bottom + 1$ or $top - (next + 1) + 1$. In each case the new value of the expressions is bound by

$$
\begin{aligned}
&\max(next - bottom, top - next) \\
&\leq \max(\lfloor (bottom + top)/2 \rfloor - bottom, top - \lfloor (bottom + top)/2 \rfloor) \\
&\leq \max((bottom + top)/2 - bottom, top - (bottom + top)/2 + 1/2) \\
&\leq \max((top - bottom)/2, (top - bottom + 1)/2) \\
&\leq (top - bottom + 1)/2,
\end{aligned}
$$

where the second inequation follows from the fact that $(bottom+top)/2$ is a multiple of $1/2$. We have thus shown that the assertion $top - bottom + 1 \leq 10000/2^k$ is an invariant of the loop.

It is now easy to derive an upper bound for the number of iterations. When we reach line (6) we have $bottom \leq top$ and thus $1 \leq top - bottom + 1 \leq 10000/2^k$. It follows that $2^k \leq 10000$ or $k \leq \log 10000 = 13.\ldots$. As k is increased by 1 during each execution of the body, apart from the last, it follows that the body is executed 14 times at most, namely for $k = 0, 1, \ldots, 13$. (For a specific x it is quite possible that we may need less than 14 iterations. As a single iteration requires at most 4 PROSA steps, we conclude that the total computation time is bound by $4 \log 10000 + c$. c is a small constant representing the number of steps outside of the loop. In general, the computation time for an array A: **array**$[1..n]$ is bound by $c + 4(1 + \log n) = O(\log n)$. Binary search therefore is much faster than linear search. For example, when searching for elements in an array with $2^{20} \approx 10^6$, linear search requires up to 2^{20} iterations, while binary search always takes at most $1 + \log 2^{20} = 21$ iterations.

Binary search is a program where the analysis of correctness and computation time is not trivial. To check that this is understood, the reader should consider the following variants, proving respectively correctness and termination (if possible).

(1) Line (7) is changed to *next* := *bottom*;

(2) Line (7) is changed to *next* := $\lceil(bottom + top)/2\rceil$;

(3) Lines (13) and (14) are changed to *top* := *next* and *bottom* := *next*

Example 4:   We implement the pushdown automaton for evaluating fully parenthesised expressions as it was specified in Section 2.1.3. This pushdown automaton uses two stacks, an operand stack and an operator stack. We implement both stacks by an array and a variable for each.

> **var** *operands*: **array**[1..100] **of real; var** *top1*: **integer;**
> **var** *operators*: **array**[1..100] **of char; var** *top2*: **integer;**

For each of the two arrays we store the length of the used part in a variable *top1* or *top2*, i.e. if, for example, the operator stack is empty then $top2 = 0$ and if the operator stack contains $op_1, op_2, \ldots, op_k$ with $op_i \in \{+, -, *, /\}$ then $top2 = k$ and $operators[i] = op_i$ for $1 \leq i \leq k$.

Initialisation of the push down automaton is now very simple.

$$top1 := 0; \quad top2 := 0;$$

ensures that both stacks are empty at the beginning.

We assume the expression to be evaluated is on the input tape as a string over the alphabet $\{(,), +, -, *, /, 1, \dashv\}$. For the sake of simplicity, we presume for our program that as an operand only the number 1 is used and as an operator only $+$ is used. The general case is left as an exercise. Furthermore we assume that the input string is terminated by the symbol $\dashv$. The set of inputs is therefore generated by the following grammar with start symbol S:

$$S \rightarrow A \dashv$$
$$A \rightarrow (A + A)|1$$

In the following statement section (Program 6) we also use — apart from the variables introduced above — the variable **var** *symbol*: **char** into which we always read the next input symbol and a variable **var** *ok*: **boolean.**

As this program is a realisation of the push down automaton of Section 2.1.3 in PROSA, correctness follows from Section 2.1.3.

```
read symbol; ok := true;
while symbol ≠ '⊣' and ok
do (* the subexpression read up to now was processed according to the table in
        Section 2.1.3, symbol contains the first symbol of the rest expression *)
    if symbol = '('
    then (* no action required *) symbol := symbol
    else if symbol = '1'
            then (* we must store 1 in the operand stack *)
                    top1 := top1 + 1;
                    operands[top1] := 1.0
            else if symbol = '+'
                    then top2 := top2 + 1;
                            operators[top2] := symbol
                    else if symbol = ')'
                            then (* we must now evaluate a subexpression. This of course
                                    is only possible if the operator stack contains at least
                                    one symbol and the operand stack at least two
                                    operands *)
                                    if top1 < 2 or top2 < 1
                                    then (* input is not permissible *)
                                            ok := false
                                    else (* evaluation *)
                                            operands[top1 − 1] := operands[top1 − 1]]
                                                                +operands[top1];
                                            top1 := top1 − 1; top2 := top2 − 1
                                    fi
                            else (* non-permissible symbol *) ok := false
                            fi
                    fi
            fi
    fi;
    read symbol
od;
if ok and symbol = '⊣' and top1 = 1 and top2 = 0
then (* pushdown automaton is in an end state *)
        print operands[1]
else print "non-permissible input"
fi
```

_______________________ **Prog. 6** _______________________

Exercises for 4.1

1) Given two 10×10 matrices A, B (to be read row by row from the input tape). Write a PROSA program which computes the product C of these matrices. (Use 2-dimensional arrays).

2) Given two arrays p, q: **array**$[1..100]$ **of integer**. Array p contains a permutation of the numbers 1 to 100, i.e. $p[i] \in \{1, 2, \ldots, 100\}$ and $p[i] \neq p[j]$ for $i \neq j$. Write a program which rearranges q according to p , i.e.

$$q_{after}[p[i]] = q_{before}[i] \qquad \text{for } 1 \leq i \leq 100.$$

Here q_{before} (q_{after}) denote the contents of array q before or after executing the program. Argue that your program is correct. What is the computation time of your program?

3) Discuss the three variants of binary search given at the end of Example 3. Give an example for one of the three variants for which the program does *not* terminate. Prove the correctness of the other two variants and analyse the computation time.

4) Assume in the binary search program (Example 3) that the array is extended to the left and the right by one component. Add new lines $(1')(1'')$ after line (1) with

$$(1') \quad A[bottom - 1] := \min(A[bottom], x) - 1.0;$$

$$(1'') \quad A[top + 1] := \max(A[top], x) + 1.0;$$

Next replace line (7) by

$$(7) \quad next := bottom + \lfloor (x - A[bottom - 1])/(A[top + 1]$$
$$- (A[bottom - 1]) \times (top - bottom + 1) \rfloor;$$

Why is this search method called search by interpolation? Prove correctness and termination

5) Extend the program in Example 4 so that it

a) copes with operators $-$, $*$ and $/$ and

b) arbitrary integer operands.

4.2 Records and Pointers

A record is a collection of several variables of arbitrary type. In order to access the different variables in a record we use names (selectors). The following figure shows a record in which three variables which are selected by the identifiers *firstname*, *residence* and *postcode* are combined. This record is of type *dataform*. The new data type *dataform* is introduced by a type declaration.

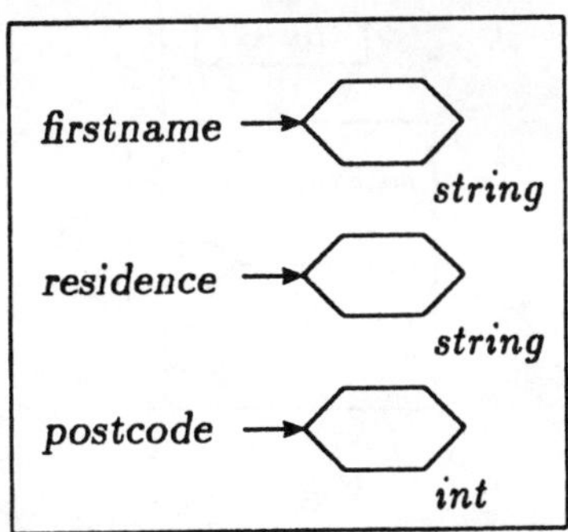

Fig. 1.   A record

$$\textbf{type } \textit{dataform} = \textbf{record } \textit{firstname}: \textbf{ string};$$
$$\textit{residence}: \textbf{ string};$$
$$\textit{postcode}: \textbf{ integer}$$
$$\textbf{end}$$

Objects of type *dataform* consist of two variables of type *string* and of one variable of type *int*. These variables are selected by the identifiers *firstname*, *residence* or *postcode*. In mathematical notation an object of type *dataform* is an injective function
$$f : \{firstname, residence, postcode\} \to V$$
with $f(firstname) \in \mathbf{V}_{string}$, $f(residence) \in \mathbf{V}_{string}$, $f(postcode) \in \mathbf{V}_{int}$. We draw records as in Figure 1, i.e. we include the graphical representation of a function in an object box. The set **REC** of all records is therefore the set of injective functions from a finite set of identifiers (selectors) to the set of variables.

Objects of elementary type, e.g. integer five, can be directly bound to a name in PROSA (by a constant declaration) and they can be assigned as a value to variables of corresponding type (assignment). In complete analogy, records can be bound directly to identifiers (by a record declaration) or can be assigned as a value to variables (by an assignment). For that purpose we introduce the set $\mathbf{V}_{pointer}$ of pointer variables. A pointer variable $v \in \mathbf{V}_{pointer}$ takes a record as a value, just as a variable in $\mathbf{V}_{int}$ takes an integer as a value. One often says: variable v points to the record $s(v)$.

Consider the following declarations and assignments.

const $n = 1$; **const** $m = 2$;

var *Mehlhorn: dataform*; **var** *Loeckx: dataform*; **var** *Wilhelm: dataform*;

var *x*: **integer**; **var** *author*: ↑*dataform*; $x := n$; *author* := *Loeckx*

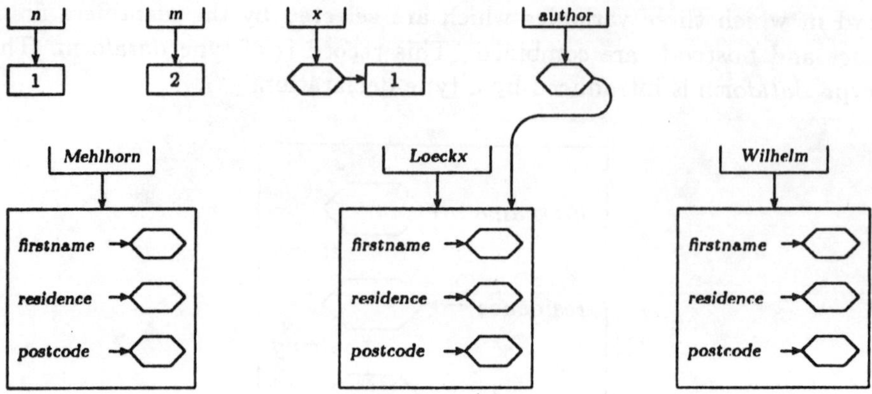

Fig. 2.

They produce the environment of Figure 2. The constant declaration **const** $n = 1$
binds the object "integer 1" to n, the **variable** declaration **var** x: **integer** binds an
integer variable to x, and finally in $x := n$ we assign the object "integer 1" as a
value to the variable named x. In complete analogy, the three record declarations
var *Loeckx: dataform*, **var** *Mehlhorn: dataform* and **var** *Wilhelm: dataform* create three objects of type *dataform* and bind them to the three identifiers. By means
of the variable declaration **var** *author*: ↑*dataform* we bind *author* to a pointer variable (indicated by the symbol ↑; this symbol also represents the syntactic difference
to a record declaration). The pointer variable can take as values objects of type
dataform (can point to objects of type *dataform*). In *author* := *Loeckx* we assign
the data form bound to *Loeckx* as a value to the variable bound to *author* ↑.

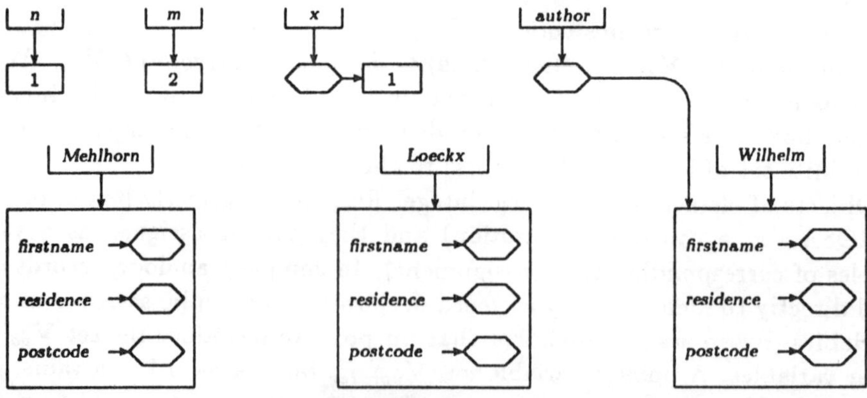

Fig. 3.

With the environment of Figure 2 assignments $x := m$ and $author := Wilhelm$ are possible. They lead to the environment of Figure 3. Assignments $n := m$ and $Mehlhorn := Wilhelm$, on the other hand, are nonsensical as n and $Mehlhorn$ do not denote variables but an integer object and a record, respectively.

Having justified why the assignment $Mehlhorn := Wilhelm$ is nonsensical, we can now explain why it is permissible in Pascal and what it means there. It is just an abbreviation for

$$Mehlhorn.firstname := Wilhelm.firstname;$$
$$Mehlhorn.residence := Wilhelm.residence;$$
$$Mehlhorn.postcode := Wilhelm.postcode.$$

So much for the analogy to elementary objects. We would not have introduced records if they were not something new. Records are collections of variables. (This explains historically the use of symbol **var** for a record declaration. We prefer the interpretation of Section 4.1; **var** consists of the initial letters of variable, array and record). Values can be assigned to these variables just as to all other variables. Assignments

$$Loeckx.firstname := "Jacques";$$
$$Mehlhorn.firstname := "Kurt";$$
$$Wilhelm.firstname := "Reinhard";$$
$$author \uparrow .residence := "Scheidt";$$
$$Mehlhorn.residence := Loeckx.residence$$

change the environment in Figure 2 to the environment in Figure 4. The name $Loeckx$ denotes a record. By means of *.firstname* we select one of the variables from this object. $Loeckx.firstname :="Jacques"$ is an assignment to this variable. The meaning of the next two assignments is similarly explained. Let us now have a look at the applied name $author\uparrow.residence$. $author$ denotes a pointer variable. The arrow $\uparrow$ indicates that we do not mean the variable itself but its value. This value is a record. By *.residence* we select the second component from it.

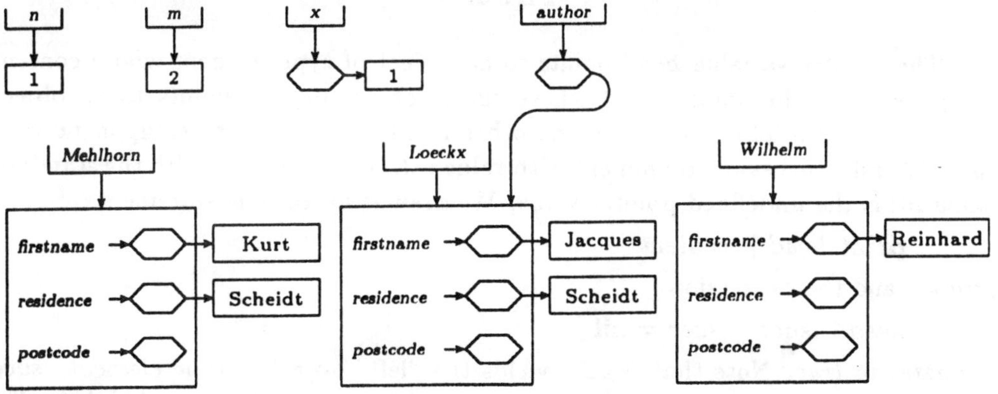

Fig. 4.

Note that the applied names $author\!\uparrow\!.residence$ and $Loeckx.residence$ denote the same variable in the actual environment. We could therefore replace the fourth assignment by $Loeckx.residence :=$"Scheidt" and write $Mehlhorn.residence :=$ $author \uparrow .residence$ in the fifth assignment.

As already mentioned, $V_{pointer}$ denotes the set $\{v_1^{pointer}, v_2^{pointer}, \ldots\}$ of the pointer variables. Thus from now on the set of variables is

$$V = V_{int} \cup V_{real} \cup V_{char} \cup V_{string} \cup V_{bool} \cup V_{pointer}.$$

Pointer variables can take arbitrary records as values. However, by context conditions we will restrict this freedom and make sure that only records of type t are assigned to pointer variables declared as **var** x: $\uparrow t$.

Pointer variables can also occur as components of records and in arrays. This allows us to construct recursive data types and plexi of records as we shall now demonstrate. The type declaration

> **type** *element* = **record** *content*: **integer**;
> $\qquad\qquad\qquad\qquad$ *succ*: $\uparrow$*element*
> $\qquad$ **end**

introduces the record type *element*. An object of this type is a pair comprising an integer variable and a pointer variable which can point to objects of type *element*. Figure 5 shows a plexus of two objects of type *element*.

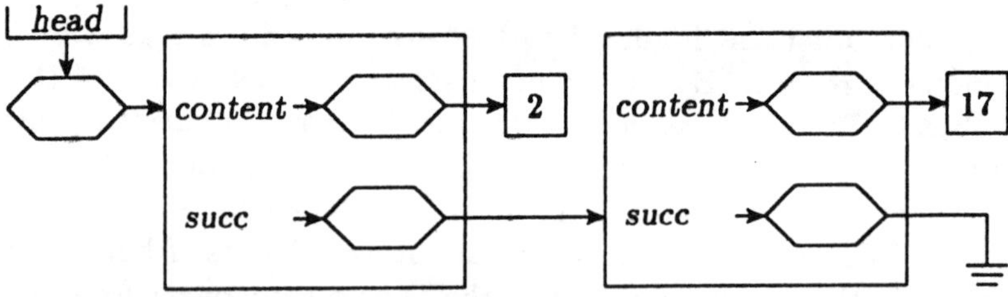

Fig. 5.

The pointer variable *head* points to an object of type *element* whose content component has the value 2 and whose successor component points to an object of type *element*. This object, on the other hand, has a content component with value 17 and a successor component with value *nil*. The object *nil* with the standard name **nil** is the undefined pointer value. We draw it as $\doteq$. The statement

> **print** *head* $\uparrow$ *.content*

prints 2 and the expression

> $head \uparrow .succ \uparrow .succ = $ **nil**

evaluates to *true*. Note that $head \uparrow$ yields the "left" object of type *element*, *.succ* selects the successor component from it, $\uparrow$ then yields the "right" record and, finally, *.succ* chooses the successor component from it. The value of this component is *nil*.

We frequently use *nil* to terminate the traversal of plexi. Thus, for example, the following program section prints the contents of the objects accessable from *head*. *p* is declared as **var** *p*: ↑*element*.

```
p := head;
while p ≠ nil
do print p ↑ .content;
     p := p ↑ .succ
od
```

By **print** *p* ↑ *.content* we print the content of the element to which *p* currently points and by *p* := *p* ↑ *.succ* we shift the pointer *p* one position further. We do this as long as *p* points to a defined element.

In the above plexus both records are **anonymous**, i.e. they are not denoted by any of the names introduced in the declaration section, but are only reachable through the variable *head* via pointers. Anonymous objects can be generated dynamically during program execution using the **new**-statement.

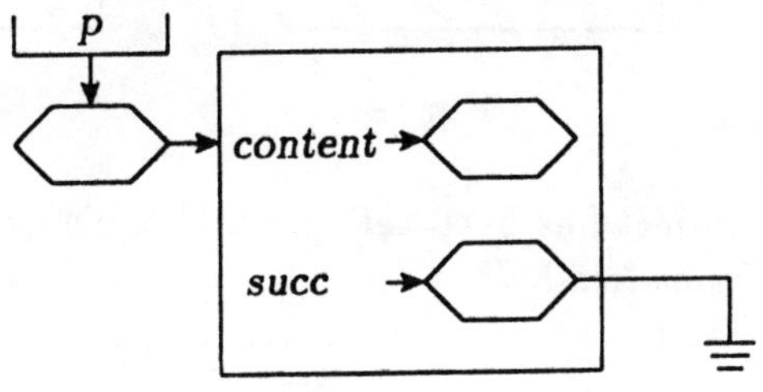

Fig. 6.

For example

$$p := \textbf{new}\ element$$

generates a new object of type *element* and assignes it to the pointer variable *p*. We obtain the environment of Figure 6. (where *p*↑*.succ* is *nil*).

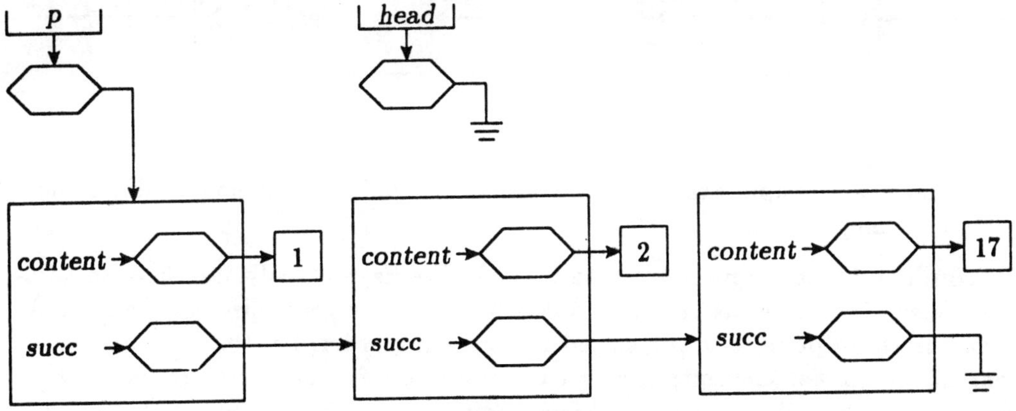

Fig. 7.

By

$$p \uparrow .content := 1;$$
$$p \uparrow .succ := head$$

we achieve the situation in Figure 7.

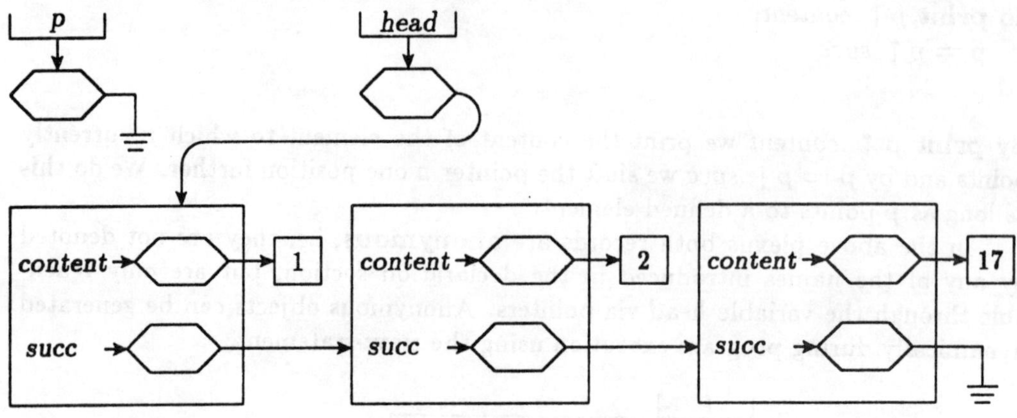

Fig. 8.

The content of the new object has been set to 1 and the successor component now points to the same object as *head*. **By**

$$head := p$$
$$p := \mathbf{nil}$$

we achieve, finally, the situation in Figure 8.

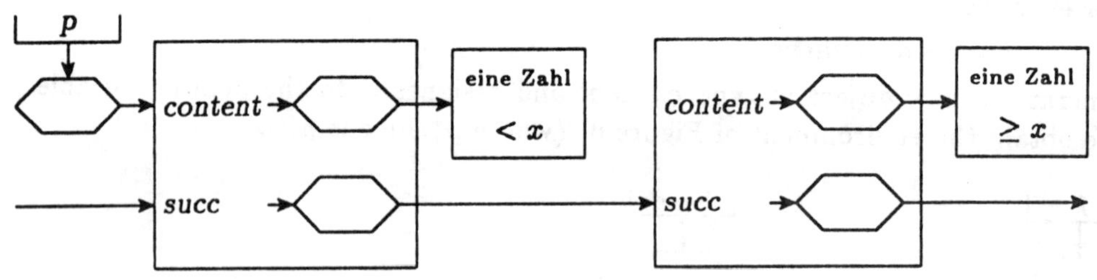

Fig. 9.

After these simple examples for records and pointers we now consider more complex examples.

Example 1 (Insertion in a Sorted List): We have already seen how an additional element can be inserted into a list. We will now generalize the method. As above, let *head* point to a list sorted in increasing order, i.e. the sequence of the contents of the list elements form an increasing series. Furthermore let x be an integer variable. For simplicity sake, we assume that the content of the first list element is smaller than x and the content of the last list element is greater than x.

We now want to insert x in the correct place in the list. First of all we determine an element of the list, and let p point to it, such that

$$p \uparrow .content < x \leq p \uparrow .succ \uparrow .content$$

Then we link a new element with content x into the list after the object $p \uparrow$. Note that our assumption regarding the first and last element guarantees that there is an object $p \uparrow$ with the desired property. How do we find the object $p \uparrow$? We use linear search. We need only set p to point to the first list element (then $p \uparrow .content < x$ already holds) and then advance until $x \leq p \uparrow .succ \uparrow .content$ also applies. This yields the following program section whose effect is illustrated in Figure 9.

```
p := head;
(* x > p ↑ .content *);
while x > p ↑ .succ ↑ .content
do (* x > p ↑ .succ ↑ .content *);
    p := p ↑ .succ;
    (* x > p ↑ .content *)
od;
(* p ↑ .content < x ≤ p ↑ .succ ↑ .content. *)
```

———————————————— **Prog. 7** ————————————————

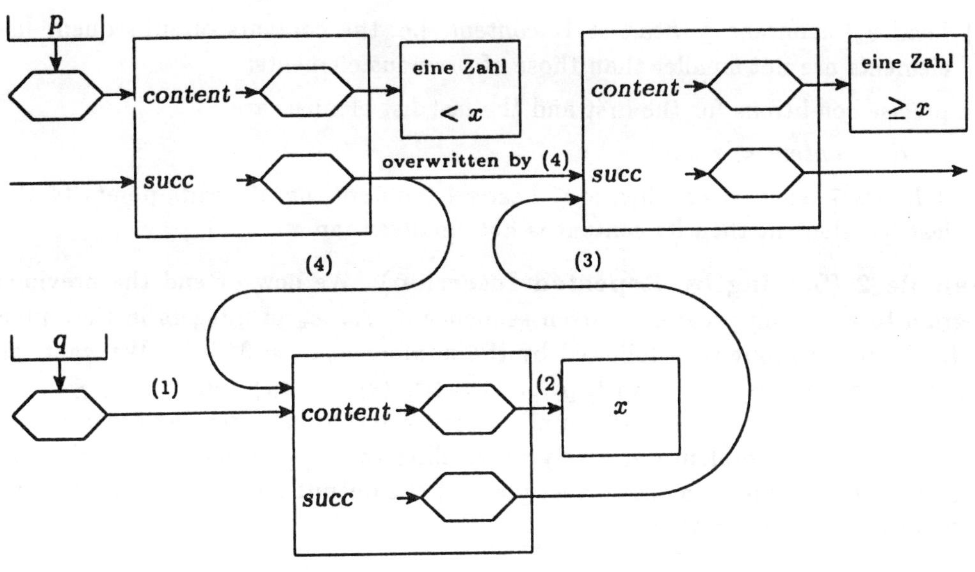

Fig. 10.

We now insert a new element after object $p \uparrow$ and store x there. Let q be another pointer variable of type *element*.

$$q := \textbf{new } element; \qquad\qquad (* \ (1) \ *)$$
$$q \uparrow .content := x; \qquad\qquad (* \ (2) \ *)$$
$$q \uparrow .succ := p \uparrow .succ \qquad\qquad (* \ (3) \ *)$$
$$p \uparrow .succ := q \qquad\qquad (* \ (4) \ *)$$

These four statements establish the situation in Figure 10. In this figure the newly constructed pointers are labelled with the number of the respective statement. The reader should also draw the situation after the j-th assignment, $1 \leq j \leq 3$.

Obviously the loop in this program will be executed at most i-times if we insert x in a list of i elements. Thus the computation time of this program is $O(i)$.

While writing this program and the assertions, we assumed that the reader intuitively understands the concept of "list sorted in increasing order". We shall now give a formal definition. Variable *head* points to a linear list sorted in increasing order if

(1) no list element points to its predecessor and

(2) the content of each list element is not greater than that of the subsequent list element.

We can write this in a more formal way. An arbitrary list element is reached from *head* by following the pointers. For $s \in \{\uparrow .succ\}^*$, say $s = \uparrow .succ \uparrow .succ$, *head s* is the name of a list element. Thus we can express (1) and (2) as follows. For all $s, t \in \{\uparrow .succ\}^*$ with $t \neq \epsilon$:

(1) *head s* $\neq$ *head st*, i.e. the names *head s* and *head st* denote different list elements,

(2) *head s* $\uparrow$ *.content* $\leq$ *head st* $\uparrow$ *.content*, i.e. the contents of subsequent list elements are not smaller than those of previous elements.

The precise conditions for the first and the last list element are

(3) *head* $\uparrow$ *.content* $< x$, and

(4) if *heads* $\uparrow$ *.succ* = **nil** then $x \leq$ *heads* $\uparrow$ *.content*, i.e. if *heads* points to the last list element then its content is not smaller than x.

Example 2 (Sorting by Repeated Insertion): We now extend the previous program to a sorting program. Given sequence $e_1, \ldots, e_n$ of integers in the range $[-M, M]$ on the input tape followed by the number $e_{n+1} = M + 1$. We want, as output, a sequence $a_1, \ldots, a_n$ with $\{a_1, \ldots, a_n\} = \{e_1, \ldots, e_n\}$ and $a_1 \leq a_2 \leq \ldots \leq a_n$, i.e. the output sequence is the input sequence sorted in increasing order.

We solve this problem iteratively by reading the input sequence, number by number, and inserting it in the correct place of the output sequence. That leads to the following program outline.

```
        program sort;
        var x: integer;
(I)     begin Initialize the data structure;
```

```
           read x; (* i := 0; x = e_{i+1} *);
           while x ≠ M + 1
           do (* we have already read and sorted e_1, e_2, ... e_i ,
               x = e_{i+1} *);
(R)            insert x at the correct place of the sorted sequence ;
               read x;
               (* i := i + 1, we have already read and sorted e_1, ..., e_i
               x = e_{i+1} *)
           od
           (* the whole sequence is read and sorted *)
     end.
```

$$\text{—————————— Prog. 8 ——————————}$$

We can use the solution from Example 1 to represent the sorted sequence and to insert x at the correct place. We need only replace line (R) by the program in Example 1. There we assumed that the sorted sequence is enclosed by an element smaller than x and an element greater than x. To make sure of this assumption we construct at place (I) the structure in Figure 11. Altogether we obtain

```
program sort;
type element = record content: integer;
                        succ: ↑ element
             end;
var x: integer;
var head, p, q: ↑ element;

begin (* we initialize the data structure *);
      head := new element; p := new element;
      head ↑ .content := −M − 1; p ↑ .content := M + 1;
      head ↑ .succ := p;

      read x;
      while x ≠ M + 1
      do (* program section from Example 1 *);
         p := head;
         while x > p ↑ .succ ↑ .content
         do p := p ↑ .succ
         od;
         q := new element;
         q ↑ .content := x;
         q ↑ .succ := p ↑ .succ;
         p ↑ .succ := q;
```

```
        read x
    od
    (* the sorted sequence is printed.
    The two additional numbers −M − 1 and
    M + 1 are omitted.*);
    p := head ↑ .succ;
    while p ↑ .content ≠ M + 1
    do print p ↑ .content;
        p := p ↑ .succ
    od
end.
```

—————————————————————— **Prog. 9** ——————————————————————

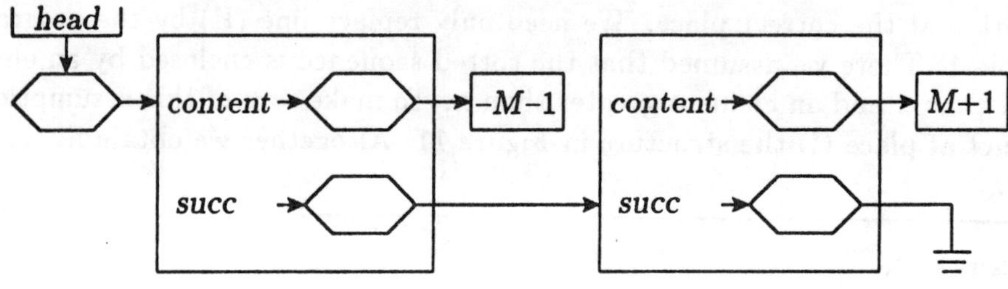

Fig. 11.

Finally, we analyse the computation time of the program. We saw above that $O(i)$ steps were necessary to insert e_i, i.e. at most $c \cdot i$ steps for some constant c. Altogether at most

$$\sum_{i=1}^{n} c \cdot i = c \cdot \sum_{i=1}^{n} i = cn(n+1)/2 = O(n^2)$$

steps are necessary to sort a sequence of n numbers. There are also methods of the order $O(n \log n)$.   ∎

Example 3 (General Plexi): In this example we introduce general plexi in which each node has several pointers. We use type

```
type person = record name: string;
                mother: ↑person;
                spouse: ↑person;
                youngestchild: ↑person;
                sibling: ↑person
            end
```

and assume that there is an object of this type for every person who ever lived. Each object records his name and there are pointers to other records, namely to the mother, the spouse, the youngest child and the next oldest sibling. The second author of this book has 3 children at the moment and thus, as part of this plexus, we have the structure in Figure 12.

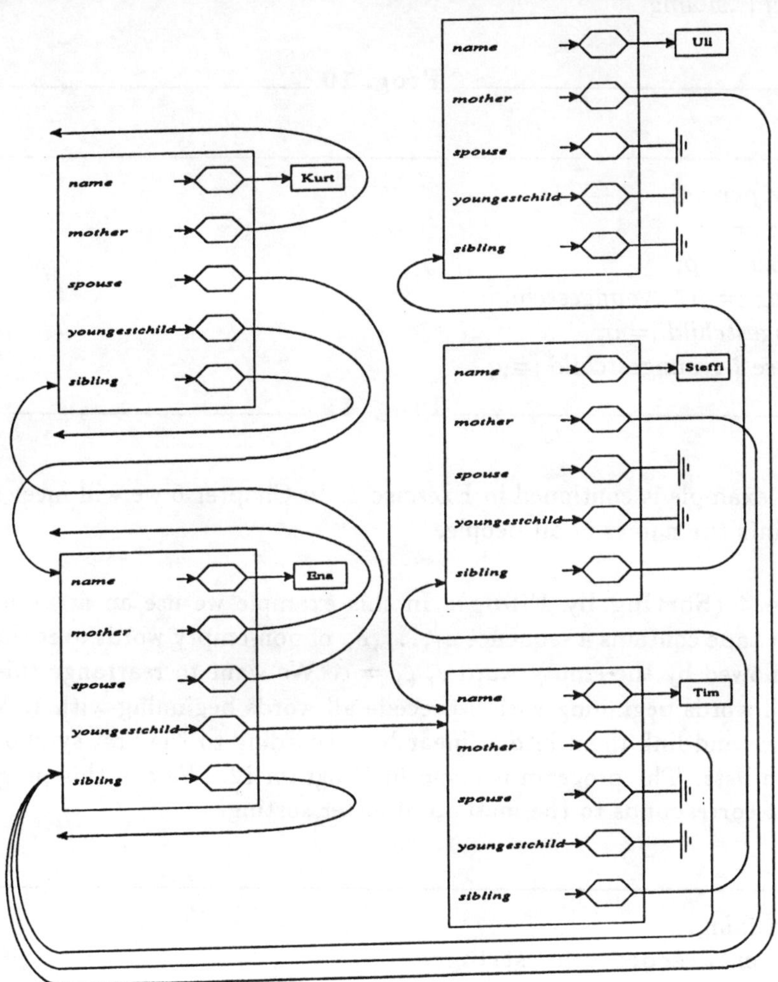

Fig. 12

For the following program sections we presume the declarations **var** *Adam*, *p*, *q*, *r*: ↑*person*. Variable *Adam* points to the object which describes the first person.

The following program section prints the names of all siblings of a person given by the pointer *p* (including himself).

The next program section registers a newly born child with the name *x* (*x* is a variable of type *string*). The mother is given by the pointer *p*.

```
(* p points to a person *);
q := p ↑ .mother; q := q ↑ .youngestchild;
(* q now points to the youngest sibling of p *);
while q ≠ nil
do print q ↑ .name;
     q := q ↑ .sibling
od
```

-- **Prog. 10** --

```
q := new person;
q ↑ .name := x;
q ↑ .mother := p;
q ↑ .sibling := p ↑ .youngestchild;
p ↑ .youngestchild := q;
p ↑ .spouse ↑ .youngestchild := q
```

-- **Prog. 11** --

This example is continued in Exercise 3. In Chapter 6 we will meet a program which prints the names of all people. ∎

Example 4 (Sorting by Filing): In this example we use an array of pointers. The input tape contains a sequence $e_1, \ldots, e_n$ of non-empty words over the alphabet $\{0, 1\}$, followed by the empty word $e_{n+1} = \epsilon$. We want to rearrange this sequence so that all words beginning with 0 precede all words beginning with 1. We read e_i in sequence and link them into a linear list according to the first symbol and then print both lists. The program is given in Program 12. We call this program filing because it corresponds to the method of letter sorting.

```
program filing;
type element=record cont: string;
                      succ:↑ element
            end;
var p: ↑ element;
var head: array[0..1] of ↑ element;
var i: integer;

begin p :=new element;
      read p↑.cont;
      while not empty p↑.cont
      do (* all words beginning with 0 are in the list with head head[0]
```

```
            and all words beginning with 1 are in the list with head head[1] *)
            if hd p ↑ .cont ='0'
            then p ↑ .succ := head[0];
                    head[0] := p
            else p ↑ .succ := head[1];
                    head[1] := p
            fi;
            p :=new element;
            read p↑.cont
        od;
        i := 0;
        while i ≤ 1
        do p := head[i];
            while p ≠ nil
            do print p ↑ .cont;
                p := p ↑ .succ
            od;
            i := i + 1
        od
end.
```

───────────────────────── **Prog. 12** ───────────────────────

∎

In this section we introduced an additional set of variables, the pointer variables. Pointer variables can have arbitrary records as a value. How does this tie in with the idea that variables correspond to storage locations in real computers and thus can only accomodate objects of restricted size? The solution is quite simple. A record is realized on an actual computer by several successive storage locations; a "pointer storage cell" pointing to a record contains the number of the first of these storage cells. We describe the realization of records and pointers on actual computers in detail in Section 5.6.

Exercises for 4.2

1) Change the program in Example 1 so that it also works if the element to be inserted is smaller than the first or greater than the last in the sorted list.

2) Write a PROSA program with the following property. The program maintains a list of natural numbers which is empty at the beginning. Now numbers are read from the input tape. If the number is positive it is appended to the list. If it is negative, that is of the form $-n$ with $n \in \mathbb{N}_0$, the first n numbers of the sequence are removed and printed followed by a star. Input $2, 3, -1, 2, 2, 2, -3, 2, -1, -1, \ldots$ leads to output $2, *, 3, 2, 2, *, 2, *, 2, *$. Use the following type to maintain the list.

> **type** *list*=**record** *cont*: **integer**;
>   *next*: $\uparrow$*list*
>   **end**

3) This exercise is a continuation of Example 3.

   a) Write a program which prints the names of all sisters-in-law and brothers-in-law of a given person.

   b) Write a program section which keeps relationships and their representation consistent when two persons given by pointers p and q get married.

   c) Write a program which prints the maternal chain of ancestors of a given person, i.e. the mother, then her mother etc..

   d) Write a program which prints for two given persons the first common element of the maternal chain of ancestors.

   e) Write a program which prints all descendants of a given person. (very difficult)

4) A word is a sequence of letters. Use a data type

> **type** *letters* = **record** *cont*: **char**;
>   *succ*: $\uparrow$*letters*
>   **end**

to represent words. Write programs for operations *head* and *tail* corresponding to the operations **hd** and **tl** on strings.

5) The input tape contains a sequence of words over the alphabet $\{0, 1\}$. Write a program which sorts this sequence in increasing lexicographic order.

   a) Extend the solution in Example 2 by developing a program which computes $\leq_{lex}$. Use this program to evaluate the required relational operations.

   b) Extend the program in Example 3. Note that this program already differentiates according to the first symbol. Proceed similarly for the second symbol, etc.

4.3 Extended Syntax and Semantics of PROSA

In this chapter we shall describe exactly the newly introduced concepts and extend the syntax and semantics of PROSA accordingly. Methods introduced in Chapter III will be used. We firstly discuss the declaration section and then the statement section.

4.3.1 The Declaration Section

The declaration section features two innovations. We now have additional types, namely arrays and records, and we can introduce names for types in type declarations. While the second change brings only minor alterations to our grammar, the first leads to a substantial extension of the subgrammar for types.

A declaration section now consists of three parts, one each for constants, types and variables, arrays and records. The declarations are introduced by the key words **const** (for constants), **type** (for types) and **var** (for variables, arrays and records). As usual the types of declared names are recorded in attribute $CONTEXT$ of the declaration section. The mode comprises the sort and type. The sort indicates whether a name denotes a constant, a variable , a type, a record or an array. Thus

$$Sort = \{const, var, record, array, type\}.$$

Depending on the sort, the type then provides more precise information about the names. Constants can be of elementary type. Thus

$$Elementarytype = \{int, real, bool, char, string\}.$$

Variables are either of elementary type or of pointer type. A pointer type is given by a freely chosen name (which must be introduced in a type declaration). Thus

$$Pointertype = L_{G, \langle ident \rangle}$$

We collect elementary types and pointer types and call them small types. Thus

$$Smalltype = Elementarytype \cup Pointertype.$$

For records we record the set of selectors and for each selector the mode of the selected component. We describe this relation by a mode binding which associates with each selector the mode of the component. Record components can be arbitrary variables. Thus

$$Recordtype = map(L_{G,\langle ident \rangle}, \{var\} \times Smalltype).$$

For an array we record the dimension and the mode of the components. Again components can be arbitrary variables, thus

$$Arraytype = \mathbb{N} \times (\{var\} \times Smalltype).$$

For a type name we record the mode of the record which it denotes.
In this way we can define the set *Mode* as

$$Mode = Constmode \cup Varmode \cup Recordmode \cup Arraymode \cup Typemode$$

with
$$Constmode = \{const\} \times Elementarytype$$
$$Varmode = \{var\} \times Smalltype$$
$$Recordmode = \{record\} \times Recordtype$$
$$Arraymode = \{array\} \times Arraytype$$
$$Typemode = \{type\} \times Recordmode$$

Having defined the set *Mode* we now specify syntax and context conditions of the declaration section. We proceed exactly as in Chapter III, i.e. for each individual declaration we compute an attribute *MB* in which the declared name is bound to its mode. We collect the mode bindings of all declarations in the attribute *CONTEXT* of the program. As the productions for the declaration section are highly recursive the reader should read the next pages superficially at first and then study them thoroughly.

$\langle decls \rangle \rightarrow \langle const\ decls \rangle \langle type\ decls \rangle \langle var\ decls \rangle$

Condition: Each name may be defined only once in the declaration section.

Then: $\quad CONTEXT(\langle program \rangle)$ is a function in $map(Ident, Mode)$ where
$\quad\quad\quad CONTEXT(\langle program \rangle)(x) = (s,t)$ if there is a declaration for x in the
$\quad\quad\quad$ declaration section with mode binding $\{x \rightarrow (s,t)\}$.

$\langle const\ decls \rangle \rightarrow \langle const\ decl\ seq \rangle; | \ \epsilon$

$\langle const\ decl\ seq \rangle \rightarrow \langle const\ decl\ seq \rangle; \langle const\ decl \rangle \ | \ \langle const\ decl \rangle$

$\langle const\ decl \rangle \rightarrow \textbf{const}\ \langle def\ ident \rangle = \langle stand\ name \rangle$
$MB(\langle const\ decl \rangle) == \{ID(\langle def\ ident \rangle) \rightarrow (const, TYPE(\langle stand\ name \rangle))\}$

Explanation: Nothing has changed for constants.

$\langle type\ decls\rangle \rightarrow \langle type\ decl\ seq\rangle;\,|\ \epsilon$

$\langle type\ decl\ seq\rangle \rightarrow \langle type\ decl\ seq\rangle; \langle type\ decl\rangle\ |\ \langle type\ decl\rangle$

$\langle type\ decl\rangle \rightarrow \mathbf{type}\ \langle def\ ident\rangle = \langle record\ type\rangle$
$MB(\langle type\ decl\rangle) == \{ID(\langle def\ ident\rangle) \rightarrow (type,(record, TYPE(\langle record\ type\rangle))))\}$

Explanation: The mode binding MB records the sort (namely *type*) of the declared name and the mode of the record. A declaration

type *element*=**record** *cont:* **integer;**
$\qquad\qquad\qquad\qquad succ:\ \uparrow element$
$\qquad\qquad$ **end**

leads to the mode binding

$$\{element \rightarrow (type,(record, \begin{cases} cont \rightarrow (var, int) \\ succ \rightarrow (var, element) \end{cases}})))\}$$

$\langle var\ decls\rangle \rightarrow \langle var\ decl\ seq\rangle;\,|\ \epsilon$

$\langle var\ decl\ seq\rangle \rightarrow \langle var\ decl\ seq\rangle; \langle var\ decl\rangle\ |\ \langle var\ decl\rangle$

$\langle var\ decl\rangle \rightarrow \langle variable\ decl\rangle\ |\ \langle record\ decl\rangle\ |\ \langle array\ decl\rangle$

Explanation: A var-declaration is either a variable declaration, a record declaration or an array declaration.

$\langle variable\ decl\rangle \rightarrow \mathbf{var}\ \langle def\ ident\rangle :\ \langle small\ type\rangle$
$MB(\langle variable\ decl\rangle) == \{ID(\langle def\ ident\rangle) \rightarrow (var, TYPE(\langle small\ type\rangle))\}$

$\langle record\ decl\rangle \rightarrow \mathbf{var}\ \langle def\ ident\rangle :\ \langle record\ type\rangle$
$MB(\langle record\ decl\rangle) == \{ID(\langle def\ ident\rangle) \rightarrow (record, TYPE(\langle record\ type\rangle))\}$

$\langle record\ decl\rangle \rightarrow \mathbf{var}\ \langle def\ ident\rangle :\ \langle app\ ident\rangle$
Condition: $CONTEXT(\langle program\rangle)(ID(\langle app\ ident\rangle)) = (type, a)$
$\qquad\qquad$ for some $a \in Recordmode$

Then: $\qquad MB(\langle record\ decl\rangle) == \{ID(\langle def\ ident\rangle) \rightarrow a\}$

$\langle array\ decl\rangle \rightarrow \mathbf{var}\ \langle def\ ident\rangle :\ \langle array\ type\rangle$
$MB(\langle array\ decl\rangle) == \{ID(\langle def\ ident\rangle) \rightarrow (array, TYPE(\langle array\ type\rangle))\}$

Explanation: In each of the three cases we record sort and type in attribute MB. In the case of record declarations two forms are possible. Either one specifies the record type explicitly or one refers to a type name introduced by a type declaration. Declarations

var x: ↑*element*;   (* a variable declaration *)
var y: *element*;   (* a record declaration *)
var z: **record** *age*: **integer**; *Pcode*: **integer end**; (* a record declaration *)
var A: **array**[1..2] **of** ↑*element*   (* an array declaration *)

yield the mode binding

$$x \rightarrow (var, element)$$

$$y \rightarrow \left(record, \left\{ \begin{array}{l} cont \rightarrow (var, int) \\ succ \rightarrow (var, element) \end{array} \right\} \right)$$

$$z \rightarrow \left(record, \left\{ \begin{array}{l} age \rightarrow (var, int) \\ Pcode \rightarrow (var, int) \end{array} \right\} \right)$$

$$A \rightarrow (array, (1, (var, element)))$$

We must now specify the subgrammars for $\langle small\ type \rangle$, $\langle record\ type \rangle$ and $\langle array\ type \rangle$.

$\langle small\ type \rangle \rightarrow \langle elem\ type \rangle$
$TYPE(\langle small\ type \rangle) == TYPE(\langle elem\ type \rangle)$

$\langle small\ type \rangle \rightarrow \langle pointer\ type \rangle$
$TYPE(\langle small\ type \rangle) == TYPE(\langle pointer\ type \rangle)$

$\langle elem\ type \rangle \rightarrow$ **integer** $\langle elem\ type \rangle \rightarrow$ **real**
$TYPE(\langle elem\ type \rangle == int$ $TYPE(\langle elem\ type \rangle) == real$

$\langle elem\ type \rangle \rightarrow$ **string** $\langle elem\ type \rangle \rightarrow$ **boolean**
$TYPE(\langle elem\ type \rangle == string$ $TYPE(\langle elem\ type \rangle) == bool$

$\langle elem\ type \rangle \rightarrow$ **char**
$TYPE(\langle elem\ type \rangle) == char$

$\langle pointer\ type \rangle \rightarrow \uparrow \langle app\ ident \rangle$
Condition: $CONTEXT(\langle program \rangle)(ID(\langle app\ ident \rangle)) == (type, a)$ for some $a \in$
            $Recordmode$.
Then: $TYPE(\langle pointer\ type \rangle) == ID(\langle app\ ident \rangle)$

Explanation: The elementary types are defined as in Chapter III. A **pointer type** is specified by a type name with preceding $\uparrow$. The condition in the rule for $\langle pointer\ type \rangle$ tests if the name is a type name. The TYPE of a $\langle pointer\ type \rangle$ is the derived name. The type of $\uparrow element$, therefore, is *element*.

A **record type** is given by the list of its components. For each component we specify the **selector** which must be unique, and the mode of the component. The relation between selectors and modes of components is represented by a mode binding.

$\langle record\ type \rangle \rightarrow$ **record** $\langle comp\ seq \rangle$ **end**

Condition: Names of components are unique.

Then: $MB(\langle comp\ seq \rangle)$ is a mapping in $map(Ident, Mode)$, namely
              $MB(\langle comp\ seq \rangle)(x) = a$ if there is a component with mode binding
              $\{x \rightarrow a\}$ in this record declaration.
              $TYPE(\langle record\ type \rangle) == MB(\langle comp\ seq \rangle)$

$\langle comp\ seq \rangle \rightarrow \langle comp\ seq \rangle; \langle comp \rangle | \langle comp \rangle$

$\langle comp \rangle \rightarrow \langle ident \rangle : \langle small\ type \rangle$
$MB(\langle comp \rangle) == \{ID(\langle ident \rangle) \rightarrow (var, TYPE(\langle small\ type \rangle))\}$

The $TYPE$ of

$$\textbf{record } cont: \textbf{ integer}; succ: \uparrow element \textbf{ end}$$

is

$$\left\{ \begin{array}{l} cont \rightarrow (var, int) \\ succ \rightarrow (var, element) \end{array} \right\}$$

An **array type** is described by specifying the component type and the ranges for the various dimensions. A range is defined by its lower and upper bound given as integer constants or as a constant name which denotes an integer. Attribute $TYPE$ records the dimension and the component mode.

$\langle array\ type \rangle \rightarrow$ **array**$[\langle ran\ seq \rangle]$ **of** $\langle small\ type \rangle$
$TYPE(\langle array\ type \rangle) == (LENGTH(\langle ran\ seq \rangle), (var, TYPE(\langle small\ type \rangle)))$

$\langle ran\ seq \rangle \rightarrow \langle range \rangle$
$LENGTH(\langle ran\ seq \rangle) == 1$

$\langle ran\ seq \rangle \rightarrow \langle ran\ seq \rangle, \langle range \rangle$
$LENGTH(\langle ran\ seq \rangle_1) == LENGTH(\langle ran\ seq \rangle_2) + 1$

$\langle range \rangle \rightarrow \langle bound \rangle .. \langle bound \rangle$

$\langle bound \rangle \rightarrow \langle expr \rangle$

Condition: $TYPE(\langle expr \rangle) = int$ and $\langle expr \rangle$ only contains integers or constant names for integers.

Example: The type of

$$\textbf{array}[1..n] \textbf{ of } \uparrow element$$

is

$$(1, (var, element))$$

This concludes the syntax of the declaration section. We give a summarising example. The declaration section

> **const** $n = 10$;
> **type** $element = $ **record** $cont$: **integer**; $succ$: $\uparrow$ $element$ **end**;
> **var** a: **array**$[1..n, 1..n]$ **of** $\uparrow$ $element$;
> **var** e : $element$;
> **var** p : $\uparrow element$

leads to the following $CONTEXT$

$$n \rightarrow (const, int)$$

$$element \rightarrow \left(type, \left(record, \left\{ \begin{array}{l} cont \rightarrow (var, int) \\ succ \rightarrow (var, element) \end{array} \right\} \right)\right)$$

$$a \rightarrow (array, (2, (var, element)))$$

$$e \rightarrow \left(record, \left\{ \begin{array}{l} cont \rightarrow (var, int) \\ succ \rightarrow (var, element) \end{array} \right\} \right)$$

$$p \rightarrow (var, element)$$

At last we come to the semantics of the declaration section. The set $\mathbf{V}_{pointer}$ is added as a new set of variables. Thus from now on

$$\mathbf{V} = \mathbf{V}_{int} \cup \mathbf{V}_{real} \cup \mathbf{V}_{char} \cup \mathbf{V}_{string} \cup \mathbf{V}_{bool} \cup \mathbf{V}_{pointer}.$$

Pointer variables take records as values or the trivial value nil. Thus the set $\mathbf{S}$ of storage states now is

$$\mathbf{S} = map(\mathbf{V}, \mathbf{D} \cup \mathbf{REC} \cup \{nil\}),$$

where $\mathbf{D}$ is defined as in Chapter III and

$$\mathbf{REC} = \{ f \in map(\langle ident \rangle, \mathbf{V}) \mid f \text{ injective and } ef(f) \text{ finite} \}$$

In a declaration a name can be bound to a constant, a type, a variable, a record or an array. Thus from now on the set of bindings is $\mathbf{B} = map(\langle ident \rangle, \mathbf{D} \cup \mathbf{V} \cup \langle record\ type \rangle \cup \mathbf{REC} \cup \mathbf{ARR})$ where

$$\mathbf{ARR} = \{f\,|\,f : [l_1, u_1] \times \ldots \times [l_k, u_k] \to \mathbf{V}_t \text{ for some } k,$$
$$l_i, u_i \in \mathbf{Z},\ l_i \leq u_i,\ t \in Elementarytype \cup \{pointer\}.$$
$$\text{and } f \text{ injective}\}$$

A configuration of the PROSA machine is, as it has been up to now, a 5-tuple $c = (p, b, s, i, o)$. Before specifying the semantics we must reconsider the notion of **free variables**. A variable v can be specified in PROSA in several ways. It can either be bound directly to a name ($v \in image(b)$)in a variable declaration, or it can, by way of a record or array declaration, be part of a record or of an array ($v \in image(f)$ with $f \in image(b) \cap (\mathbf{REC} \cup \mathbf{ARR})$). Finally, it can be a component of a record created by the **new**-statement. In this case there must be a variable pointing to that record and thus $v \in image(f)$ for some $f \in image(s) \cap \mathbf{REC}$. Altogether we define the set of free variables of type $t \in Elementarytype \cup \{pointer\}$ in configuration c as

$$FV_{c,t} = V_t - image(b) - \bigcup_{f \in image(b) \cap (\mathbf{REC} \cup \mathbf{ARR})} image(f) - \bigcup_{f \in image(s) \cap \mathbf{REC}} image(f).$$

And now for the declaration section. The PROSA machine processes the declaration sections, one declaration after the other. Let $c = (p, b, s, i, o)$ be a configuration in which the program-rest p begins with a declaration and $c' = \delta(c) = (p', b', s', i', o')$. We distinguish seven cases.

Case 1 (**Constant declaration**):
p has the form **const** $n = m;\ p'$ with $n \in \langle ident \rangle$ and $m \in \langle stand\ name \rangle$.
Then
$$c' = \delta(c) = (p', b[n \backslash c(m)], s, i, o)$$

Explanation: The name is bound to the object denoted by the standard name

Case 2 (**Variable declaration of elementary type**):
p has the form **var** $n: t;\ p'$ with $n \in \langle ident \rangle$ and $t \in \langle elem\ type \rangle$.
Then
$$c' = \delta(c) = (p', b[n \backslash v], s[v \backslash \text{undefined}], i, o).$$

$v \in \mathbf{FV}_{c,u}$ arbitrary, $u = TYPE(t)$.

Explanation: The declared name is bound to a free variable of corresponding type. The value of these variables is undefined.

Case 3 (**Variable declaration of pointer type**):
p has the form **var** $n: \uparrow m;\ p'$ with $n, m \in \langle ident \rangle$.
Then
$$c' = \delta(c) = (p', b[n \backslash v], s[v \backslash nil], i, o)$$

$v \in \mathbf{FV}_{c, pointer}$ is arbitrary.

Explanation: The declared name is bound to a free variable in $\mathbf{V}_{pointer}$. The variable is set to the value nil.

Case 4 (Type declaration):
p has the form **type** $n = t;\ p'$ with $n \in \langle ident \rangle$ and $t \in \langle record\ type \rangle$.
Then
$$c' = \delta(c) = (p', b[n\backslash t], s, i, o).$$

Explanation: The declared name is bound to text t which describes the type. This text is used, for example, in Case 6. The declaration

> **type** $element = $ **record** $cont$: **integer**; $succ$:$\uparrow$ $element$ **end**

leads to the binding

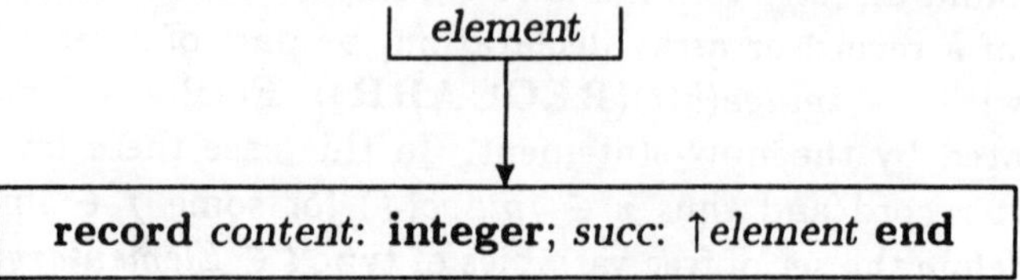

Case 5 (Record declaration with explicit type):
p has the form

var n: **record** sel_1: t_1; sel_2: t_2; $\ldots$; sel_m: t_m **end**; p'

with $n, sel_1, \ldots, sel_m \in \langle ident \rangle$ and $t_1, \ldots, t_m \in \langle small\ type \rangle$.
Then
$$c' = \delta(c) = (p', b[n\backslash f], s', i, o)$$

with $f \in \mathbf{REC}$, $ef(f) = \{sel_1, \ldots, sel_m\}$, $f(sel_i) \in \mathbf{FV}_{c,t'_i}$ where $t'_i = TYPE(t_i)$ if $t_i \in \langle elem\ type \rangle$ and $t'_i = pointer$ if $t_i \in \langle pointer\ type \rangle$, $1 \le i \le m$. Furthermore

$$s'(w) = \begin{cases} \text{undefined}, & \text{if } w = f(sel_i) \text{ for some } i \text{ and } t_i \in \langle elem\ type \rangle; \\ nil, & \text{if } w = f(sel_i) \text{ for some } i \text{ and } t_i \in \langle pointer\ type \rangle; \\ s(w), & \text{otherwise.} \end{cases}$$

Explanation: When executing a record declaration a record object f is created. This object associates free variables of the corresponding type with the component names. The variables get the undefined value or the value nil. The declaration

> **var** e : **record** $cont$: **integer**; $succ$:$\uparrow$ $element$ **end**

leads to the environment

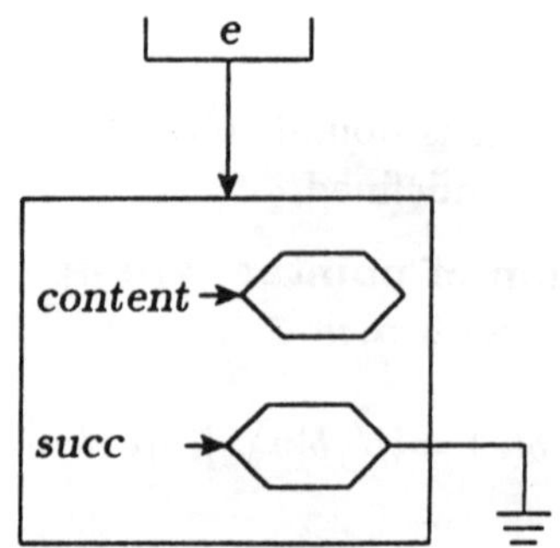

Case 6 (Record declaration with type names):
p has the form **var** n: m; p' with $n, m \in \langle ident \rangle$.
Then

$$c' = (\textbf{var } n:\ b(m); p', b, s, i, o)$$

Explanation: Type name m already introduced in a type declaration (see Case 4) is replaced by the corresponding record type $b(m)$. We then have a record declaration with explicit type and we proceed in the next transition as in Case 5. The declaration

var e : *element*

is processed in two steps. In the first step we modify the program text and replace *element* by $b(element) =$**record** *cont*: **integer**; *succ*: ↑*element* **end**. In the second step we proceed as in the previous example.

Case 7 (Array declaration):
p has the form var n: $\textbf{array}[l_1..u_1, \ldots, l_m..u_m]$ **of** t; p' with $n \in \langle ident \rangle$, $l_1, u_1, \ldots,$ $l_m, u_m \in \langle expr \rangle$ and $t \in \langle small\ type \rangle$.
Then

$$c' = \delta(c) = (p', b[n \backslash f], s', i, o)$$

with $f \in \textbf{ARR}$, $ef(f) = \times_{i=1}^{m}[I(b, s, l_i), I(b, s, u_i)]$, $image(f) \subseteq \textbf{FV}_{c,t'}$ where $t' = TYPE(t)$ if $t \in \langle elem\ type \rangle$, and $t' = pointer$ if $t \in \langle pointer\ type \rangle$. Furthermore

$$s'(w) = \begin{cases} undefined, & \text{if } w \in image(f) \text{ and } t \in \langle elem\ type \rangle; \\ nil, & \text{if } w \in image(f) \text{ and } t \in \langle pointer\ type \rangle; \\ s(w), & \text{otherwise.} \end{cases}$$

Explanation: An array object f is created and bound to the name of the array. f associates a free variable of the corresponding type with each permissible sequence of indices. The variables get the undefined value or nil.

This concludes the semantics of the declaration section. We illustrate the definitions using the same example as in the syntax section. After processing this declaration section we obtain environment (b, s) with

$$ef(b) = \{a, n, element, p, e\}$$

$$b(n) =\ \text{number } 10$$

$$b(a) = f \text{ with } ef(f) = \{(i, j) \in \mathbb{N} \mid 1 \le i, j \le 10\}$$
$$\text{and } f(i, j) = v_{10(i-1)+j}^{pointer}$$

$$b(element) = \textbf{record } cont: \textbf{integer}; succ: ↑element \textbf{ end}$$
$$b(p) = v_{101}^{pointer}$$

$$b(e) = g \text{ with } ef(g) = \{cont, succ\} \text{ and}$$
$$g(cont) = v_1^{int}, \ g(succ) = v_{102}^{pointer}$$

and

$$ef(s) = \{v_i^{pointer} \mid 1 \le i \le 102\} \cup \{v_1^{int}\}$$

with

$$s(v_1^{pointer}) = \ldots = s(v_{102}^{pointer}) = nil$$

and

$$s(w) = \text{undefined for all other variables } w.$$

We now discuss the connection between syntax and semantics. Let $ds \in \langle decls \rangle$ be a declaration section satisfying the context conditions. Let furthermore co be the value of attribute $CONTEXT$ for this declaration section. We consider the computation of the PROSA machine with start state $(ds, \emptyset, \emptyset, i, \epsilon)$.

This computation terminates in a normal way, i.e. it leads to a configuration $(\epsilon, b, s, i, \epsilon)$. This is seen as follows. Firstly, the PROSA grammar only permits the seven cases discussed above. In each of the seven cases the context conditions ensure that the transition of the PROSA machine is well-defined. In Case 6, particularly, the name m is in fact the name of a type, in Case 7 l_i and u_i are integer expressions, and in Case 4 the string t is actually a record type.

We can also make the relation between attribute co and binding b more precise. First of all it is obvious that $ef(co) = ef(b)$. Let $n \in ef(co)$. Then $co(n) = (so, t)$ for some sort $so \in \{const, type, var, record, array\}$ and some type t. We now consider the value $b(n)$.

Case 1: $so = const$.
Then t is an elementary type and $b(n) \in D_t$

Case 2: $so = type$.
Then $b(n) \in \langle record\ type \rangle$ and $t = (record, TYPE(b(n)))$, i.e. if we evaluate the attributes of the derivation tree for $b(n)$ then t is essentially the same as the $TYPE$-attribute of the root.

Case 3: $so = var$.
Then t is either an elementary type or a pointer type. We distinguish between these two cases.

Case 3.1: $t \in Elementarytype$
Then $b(n) \in \mathbf{V}_t$.

Case 3.2: $t \in pointer\ type$.
Then $b(n) \in \mathbf{V}_{pointer}$.

Case 4: $so = record$.
Then $t \in Recordtype$ is a mode binding and $b(n) \in \mathbf{REC}$ with $ef(b(n)) = ef(t)$. For all $x \in ef(t) : b(n)(x) \in \mathbf{V}_{t(x)}$ if $t(x) \in Elementarytype$ and $b(n)(x) \in \mathbf{V}_{pointer}$ otherwise.

Case 5: $so = array$.

Then $t = (d, (var, t'))$ for some $t' \in Smalltype$. Furthermore $b(n) = f \in \mathbf{ARR}$ where $ef(f)$ is a d-fold cartesian product and $image(f) \subseteq \mathbf{V}_{t'}$ if $t' \in Elementarytype$ and $image(f) \subseteq \mathbf{V}_{pointer}$ otherwise.

The type construction facilities in PROSA are restricted by comparison to Pascal. To discuss the complete type variety of Pascal — to which part of the success of PASCAL is due — would extend the size of the description unduly without introducing anything new. However, we would like to mention briefly the additional possibilities in Pascal.

To begin with, it has some additional elementary types. The user can define an enumeration type as an ordered set of values given by identifiers. He can define subtypes of existing types, for example intervals of integer. He can work with subsets of existing elementary types. Furthermore, as an additional structured type, sequential *files* are available. In addition, contrary to PROSA, Pascal permits (almost) all types as component types of records and arrays. In particular, records and arrays as components of records and arrays can occur.

4.3.2 The Statement Section

The statement section also needs to be extended.

- Besides simple names such as n, there are also composite names like $a[3,4]\uparrow$ $.succ\uparrow.cont$.
- **nil** is a new standard name and we can test pointer values for equality.
- We now have assignments to pointer variables.
- We have the **new-statement**.

As in the declaration section all the productions, context conditions and transitions of the PROSA machine given in Chapter III remain the same. Only the four extensions have to be discussed.

Up to now only identifiers were possible as names. Introducing records, arrays and pointers result in a large variety of names. We now specify the extended syntax and afterwards the semantics explaining all definitions using the example above.

$\langle name \rangle \rightarrow \langle app\ ident \rangle$

$MODE(\langle name \rangle) == CONTEXT(\langle program \rangle)(ID(\langle app\ ident \rangle))$

Explanation: The mode of a name is obtained by consulting the context of the program. In our example the mode of n is $(const, int)$ and the mode of a equals $(array, (2, (var, element)))$.

$\langle name \rangle \rightarrow \langle name \rangle.\langle ident \rangle$

Condition: $MODE(\langle name \rangle_2) = (record, f)$ for a $f \in record\ type$ and $ID(\langle ident \rangle) \in ef(f)$

Then: $MODE(\langle name \rangle_1) == f(ID(\langle ident \rangle))$

Explanation: A name of the form $n_1.n_2$ is admissible only if n_1 denotes a record and n_2 belongs to the permitted selectors. Then the mode of $n_1.n_2$ is given by the mode of the selected component. In our example $e.cont$ is of the mode (var, int), $p\uparrow.succ$ is of the mode $(var, element)$ and $a[2,3]\uparrow.cont$ is of the mode (var, int). On the other hand, the name $p.cont$ is not admissible since the mode of p is $(var, element)$.

$\langle name \rangle \rightarrow \langle name \rangle\uparrow$

Condition: $MODE(\langle name \rangle_2) = (var, m)$ and $CONTEXT(\langle program \rangle)(m) = (type, (record, f))$ for some $m \in Pointertype$ and some $f \in Recordtype$

Then: $MODE(\langle name \rangle_1) == (record, f)$

Explanation: A name of the form $n\uparrow$ is admissible only if n denotes a pointer variable. If m is the type of this pointer variable and m has been bound to a record mode by a type declaration then this record mode is the mode of the name $n\uparrow$. In our example $p\uparrow$ and $a[2,3]\uparrow$ have the mode

$$\left(record,\left\{\begin{array}{l} cont \rightarrow (var, int) \\ succ \rightarrow (var, element) \end{array}\right\}\right).$$

On the other hand, the name $e\uparrow$ is not admissible as e does not denote a pointer.

$\langle name \rangle \rightarrow \langle name \rangle[\langle index\ seq \rangle]$

Condition: $MODE(\langle name \rangle_2) = (array, (d, t))$ for some $d \in \mathbb{N}$ and some $t \in Var$ mode and $LENGTH\langle index\ seq \rangle) = d$

Then: $MODE(\langle name \rangle_1) == t$

$\langle index\ seq \rangle \rightarrow \langle expr \rangle$

Condition: $TYPE(\langle expr \rangle) = int$

Then: $LENGTH(\langle index\ seq \rangle) == 1$

$\langle index\ seq \rangle \rightarrow \langle expr \rangle, \langle index\ seq \rangle$

Condition: $TYPE(\langle expr \rangle) = int$

Then: $LENGTH(\langle index\ seq \rangle_1) == LENGTH(\langle index\ seq \rangle_2) + 1$

Explanation: A name of the form $n[E_1, E_2, \ldots, E_d]$ is admissible if n is the name of an array of dimension d and $E_1, \ldots, E_d$ are integer expressions. The mode of the name is the mode of the components of the array. In our example $a[2, 3]$ is of the mode $(var, element)$. On the other hand, the name $p[2]$ is not admissible.

We now come to the **semantics of names**. We define a function

$$L : \langle name \rangle \times \mathbf{B} \times \mathbf{S} \rightsquigarrow \mathbf{V} \cup \mathbf{ARR} \cup \mathbf{REC} \cup \{nil\}.$$

$L(x, b, s)$ yields the object or variable denoted by x in the environment (b, s) for some $x \in \langle name \rangle$. Function L is defined as follows.

$$
L(x,b,s) = \begin{cases}
b(x), & \text{if } x \in \langle ident \rangle; \\[1.5ex]
L(y,b,s)(z), & \text{if } x = y.z \text{ with } y \in \langle name \rangle, \\
& z \in \langle ident \rangle \\
& \text{and } L(y,b,s) \in REC; \\[1.5ex]
\text{undefined}, & \text{if } x = y.z \text{ with } y \in \langle name \rangle, \\
& z \in \langle ident \rangle \\
& \text{and } L(y,b,s) = nil; \\[1.5ex]
s(L(y,b,s)), & \text{if } x = y\uparrow \text{ with } y \in \langle name \rangle \\
& \text{and } L(y,b,s) \in V_{pointer}; \\[1.5ex]
L(y,b,s)(I(E_1,b,s),\ldots,I(E_d,b,s)), & \text{if } x = y[E_1,\ldots,E_d].
\end{cases}
$$

Explanation: If x is an identifier then x of course denotes the object $b(x)$. Otherwise x is either of the form $y.z$ (record selection), of the form $y\uparrow$ (taking the value of a pointer variable (also called dereferencing)) or of the form $y[E_1,\ldots,E_d]$ (array selection). In each of the three cases we first obtain the object $L(y,b,s)$ denoted by y. In the first case this is a record object (case 1a) or nil (case 1b), in the second case it is a pointer variable and in the third case it is an array object. In case 1a and in the third case we select the corresponding component (of course in an array selection we must evaluate the expressions on index position), in the second case we turn to the value of the pointer variables and in case 1b L is undefined, as one cannot select the undefined record object.

In our example, for instance, (with the additional assumption $s(v_{13}^{pointer}) = g$)

$$
\begin{aligned}
L(\mathrm{a}[2,3]\uparrow.cont,b,s) &= L(\mathrm{a}[2,3]\uparrow,b,s)(cont) \\
&= s(L(\mathrm{a}[2,3],b,s))(cont) \\
&= s(L(\mathrm{a},b,s)(I(2,b,s),I(3,b,s)))(cont) \\
&= s(f(2,3))(cont) \\
&= s(v_{13}^{pointer})(cont) \\
&= g(cont) \\
&= v_1^{int}
\end{aligned}
$$

Thus the syntax and semantics of names is specified. We clarify briefly the relation between syntax and semantics. Let x be a name in a PROSA program p and let (b,s) be an environment occurring during the execution of p. Furthermore let $L(x,b,s)$ be defined. Then

$$
\begin{aligned}
MODE(x) = (array,\ldots) &\Leftrightarrow L(x,b,s) \in ARR \\
MODE(x) = (record,\ldots) &\Leftrightarrow L(x,b,s) \in REC \cup \{nil\} \\
MODE(x) = (var,\ldots) &\Leftrightarrow L(x,b,s) \in V \\
MODE(x) = (const,\ldots) &\Leftrightarrow L(x,b,s) \in D \\
MODE(x) = (type,\ldots) &\Leftrightarrow L(x,b,s) \in \langle record\ type \rangle.
\end{aligned}
$$

In which circumstances can $L(x, b, s)$ be undefined? Let y be the smallest prefix of x with $L(y, b, s)$ undefined. Then there are two possibilities. Either $y = z_1.z_2$ with $L(z_1, b, s) = nil$, or $y = z[E_1, \ldots, E_k]$ and one of the expressions is undefined or its value lies outside of the admissible index range, (note that the other two possibilities of undefinedness, namely $y = x$ and $b(x)$ undefined or $y = z_1.z_2$ and z_2 is not an admissible selector in the record object $L(z_1, b, s)$ are excluded by the context conditions.)

As for expressions, the syntax hardly changes. We only need two additional rules which permit comparison of pointers with *nil* and with each other. If two pointers are tested for equality they must have the same type.

$\langle expr \rangle \rightarrow \langle name \rangle = \mathbf{nil}$

Condition: $MODE(\langle name \rangle) = (var, m)$ for some $m \in Pointertype$

Then: $\qquad TYPE(\langle expr \rangle) == bool$

$\langle expr \rangle \rightarrow \langle name \rangle = \langle name \rangle$

Condition: $MODE(\langle name \rangle_1) = (var, m) = MODE(\langle name \rangle_2)$ for some $m \in Pointertype$

Then: $\qquad TYPE(\langle expr \rangle) == bool$

In our example, therefore, $(n = 10)$ **and** $(a[2, 3] = p)$ is admissible, whereas $p = n$ is not admissible.

The semantics of expressions changes only slightly. The two new rules are easily dealt with and we leave them to the reader. A second change affects the interpretation of names. We define

$$I_{\langle name \rangle}(x, b, s) = \begin{cases} b(x), & \text{if } MODE(x) = (const, \ldots); \\ s(L(x, b, s)), & \text{if } MODE(x) = (var, \ldots); \end{cases}$$

and thus cope with the larger set of names.

Next we discuss the assignment. Up to now we had

$\langle ass \rangle \rightarrow \langle name \rangle := \langle expr \rangle$

Condition: $MODE(\langle name \rangle) = (var, TYPE(\langle expr \rangle))$

This covers assignments of the form

$$a[2, 3]\uparrow.cont := 10$$
$$p\uparrow.cont := e.cont$$
$$a[2, 3] := p$$

Note that the last assignment refers to a pointer variable, i.e. the production from Chapter III already covers pointers. Note also that in the case of pointer variables we check that types match, i.e. we make sure that only objects of type t are assigned to a name of mode (var, t) with $t \in Pointertype$. This context condition makes sure that pointers in PROSA are in effect also typed, although we use the same set of variables for all pointer types. Only the assignment of *nil* must be considered separately, as we use the same standard name **nil** for all types.

$\langle ass \rangle \rightarrow \langle name \rangle := $ **nil**

Condition: $MODE(\langle name \rangle) = (var, m)$ for some $m \in Pointertype$

This concludes the syntax of assignments. The semantics of assignments is the same as in Chapter III.

Finally, let us consider the **new**-statement. It is an additional statement. Thus

$\langle stat \rangle \rightarrow \langle new\ stat \rangle$

A **new**-statement is in essence an assignment. Using it we create a new object of a record type and assign it to a pointer variable. Of course the type of the record object and that of the pointer variable must coincide. This is ensured by a context condition.

$\langle new\ stat \rangle \rightarrow \langle name \rangle := $ **new** $\ \langle app\ ident \rangle$

Condition: $MODE(\langle name \rangle) = (var, ID(\langle app\ ident \rangle))$

Explanation: The name on the left side of the assignment must denote some pointer variable, i.e. its mode must be (var, m) for some $m \in Pointertype$. The pointer type m must coincide with the type specified by the type name on the right side. In our example, therefore, the following two **new**-statements are admissible,

$$p := \textbf{new}\ element$$
$$a[2, 3]\!\uparrow.succ := \textbf{new}\ element$$

On the other hand

$$e := \textbf{new}\ element$$

is not admissible as e does not denote a pointer variable and

$$p := \textbf{new}\ node$$

is not admissible since the mode of p is not $(var, node)$ but $(var, element)$.

We now come to the semantics of the **new**-statement. Executing a **new**-statement creates an anonymous object of the given record type and assigns it to a pointer variable of this type. Type equivalence is already guaranteed by the context conditions and no longer needs checking.

Let $c = (p, b, s, i, o)$ be a configuration of the PROSA machine where p has the form $n := \mathbf{new}\ \ m;\ p',\ n \in \langle name \rangle$, $m \in \langle app\ ident \rangle$ and $b(m) = \mathbf{record}\ sel_1:\ t_1;\ sel_2:\ t_2;\ \ldots;\ sel_h:\ t_h\ \mathbf{end}$. Then $\delta(c) = c' = (p', b, s', i, o)$ with

$$s'(w) = \begin{cases} f, & \text{if } w = L(n, b, s); \\ \text{undefined}, & \text{if } w = f(sel_i) \text{ and } t_i \in \langle elem\ type \rangle \text{ for some } i; \\ nil, & \text{if } w = f(sel_i) \text{ and } t_i \in \langle pointer\ type \rangle \text{ for some } i; \\ s(w), & \text{otherwise}; \end{cases}$$

Here $f \in \mathbf{REC}$ with

$$ef(f) = \{sel_1, sel_2, \ldots, sel_h\} \text{ and } f(sel_i) \in \mathbf{FV}_{c,t_i'}$$

with $t_i' = TYPE(t_i)$ if $t_i \in \langle elem\ type \rangle$ and $t_i' = pointer$ if $t_i \in \langle pointer\ type \rangle$.

Explanation: n is the name of a pointer variables of type m. The type name m was bound during execution of its type declaration to an element in $\langle record\ type \rangle$. We use the information contained in this text to create a new record object. As usual the variables contained in f are initialised with nil or the undefined value depending on the type. Object f is assigned to variable $L(n, b, s)$ denoted by n. In our example after executing

$$p := \mathbf{new}\ \ element$$

we obtain the storage state s' with

$$s'(v_{101}^{pointer}) = h \text{ with } ef(h) = \{cont, succ\}$$
$$\text{and } h(cont) = v_2^{int},\ h(succ) = v_{103}^{pointer}$$
$$s'(v_{103}^{pointer}) = nil$$
$$s'(w) = s(w) \text{ for } w \neq v_{101}^{pointer},\ w \neq v_{103}^{pointer}$$

Exercises for 4.3

1) Given the declaration section

    $\mathbf{const}\ n = 10$;

    $\mathbf{type}\ node = \mathbf{record}\ cont:\ \mathbf{integer};$

                     $left:\ \uparrow node$;

                     $right:\ \uparrow node$

              $\mathbf{end}$;

    $\mathbf{var}\ a:\ \uparrow node$;

    $\mathbf{var}\ c:\ \mathbf{array}[1..10]\ \mathbf{of}\ \uparrow node$

Determine the value of attribute $CONTEXT$.

2) Which of the following names are permissible according to the declaration section
in Exercise 1?

$$c[n]\uparrow.links\uparrow.cont$$
$$c[n].cont$$
$$a[3]$$
$$a\uparrow.left\uparrow.right$$

Which context condition is violated in the case of non-admissible names.

Chapter 5   Translating PROSA into RESA, Part 1

Higher programming languages such as Pascal and PROSA are programming tools. Programs in higher programming languages are therefore easily readable (or at least should be!). They can, however, not be executed directly on a computer. One could even conveniently define the "height" of a programming language as the "distance" of the language from the machine language of a typical computer. Programs in higher programming languages must, therefore, be translated into the machine language of the computer before it can execute them. This chapter introduces a simple computer called RESA (**RE**chner **SA**arbrücken) and its machine language. We also show how one can translate PROSA programs into RESA programs.

RESA is a mathematical abstraction of simple computers. Its structure corresponds to that of some older micro processors and main frames. Its instruction set is restricted to a necessary minimum. RESA, together with its machine language, will be introduced in Section 5.1. Neither its internal construction nor its technical realisation will be discussed. This is left to a "computer architecture" course.

This chapter has two objectives. The first is to derive the following theorem.

Theorem 1. *For each simple PROSA program p_1 there is an equivalent RESA program p_2. Program p_2 can effectively be constructed from program p_1. Furthermore, there exist constants c and d depending on p_1 but not on i, such that for all input sequences $i \in \mathbf{Z}^* : comp_time(p_2, i) \leq c + d \cdot comp_time(p_1, i)$.*

                                                           ■

A few notions in this theorem have to be explained.

Definition 1: Simple PROSA is the programming language introduced in Chapters III and IV with two restrictions.
(a) The only elementary data types are *int* and *bool*.

(b) As input and output sequences only sequences of integers are permitted.   ■

These are not grave restrictions. The methods introduced in this chapter would cope with the compilation problem without these restrictions. However, the chapter would then be more extensive.

The concept of program equivalence was introduced in Chapter I. We repeat the definition. Let p_k be a program for machine M_k, $k = 1, 2$. Then p_1 and p_2 are **equivalent** if for all input sequences $i : I/O_{M_1}(p_1, i) = I/O_{M_2}(p_2, i)$.

Theorem 1 contains three propositions. First, for each PROSA program p_1 there is an equivalent RESA program p_2. This means, in particular, that each function computed by a PROSA program can also be computed by a RESA program. Furthermore the theorem states that the RESA program p_2 can effectively be constructed from the PROSA program p_1. This means that p_2 can be obtained from p_1 algorithmically. We will specify this algorithm in this chapter informally. It could, in principle, be also formulated as a RESA program (or as PROSA program). This will be done for one part of the algorithm. Let us assume we have a RESA program C (for compiler) which translates PROSA programs into equivalent RESA programs. Let p_1 be an arbitrary PROSA program and i an input sequence. We first run program C with input p_1 on the RESA machine and obtain a RESA program p_2. Then we run p_2 with input i on the RESA machine. From the outside the RESA machine then behaves like a PROSA machine, i.e. with help of the compiler program C it can also process PROSA programs.

The third proposition states that the computation time of the RESA program p_2 for an input i is at most $c + d \cdot comp_time(p_1, i)$ steps. Constant d is essentially the maximal number of RESA instructions generated for a PROSA statement. Constant c is the number of RESA instructions needed for the initialisation of administrative entities. From the estimate of the computation time of the generated RESA program it follows that estimates for PROSA programs have an immediate practical meaning. If we have determined an upper bound for the computation time of PROSA program p_1 for input i, we have also achieved an estimate for that of the derived RESA program p_2 for input i. We are mainly interested in the latter since only the RESA machine — and not the PROSA machine — can be technically realised. Obviously an everyday computer is not a RESA machine. On the other hand, the similarity is so great that after studying this chapter the reader should have no difficulties to prove a theorem analogous to Theorem 1 for his computer. The computation time of a PROSA program on the abstract PROSA machine is therefore a direct measure for the computation time on real computers.

The translation of PROSA to RESA takes place in two large steps. First we translate so-called primitive PROSA to RESA. Then it will be shown how simple PROSA can be translated into primitive PROSA.

Definition 2: A PROSA program p is said to be **primitive** if

(1) p contains only integer variables.

(2) There are no type declarations in p and neither pointers, records nor constant names are used.

(3) All arrays used in p are one-dimensional and have an index range which starts at 0. Furthermore array selection only occurs in assignments of the form $x :=$ $a[i]$ and $a[i] := x$ where i and x are simple variables and the value of i is in the index range of a.

(4) Print and read statements refer only to simple variables.

(5) Boolean expressions occur only in tests of conditional statements and iterative statements. They are of the form $x = 0$ or $x > 0$ with simple variable x.

(6) Expressions contain at most one operation symbol. If an expression contains an operation symbol then both operands are variable names.

(7) There is at most one array $H :$ **array** $[0 .. \infty]$ **of integer** of infinite length in p which is the last declaration in the declaration section.   ∎

Definition 2 and in particular point (7) needs explanation. PROSA has been extended implicitly by now permitting the declaration of an infinite array H. Executing the declaration of such an array creates no difficulties. We need only bind H to a function h with $Def(h) = \mathbb{N}_0$ and $image(h) \subseteq \mathbf{FV}_{c,int}$ (c is the actual configuration). As the set of variables of type *int* is infinite there is no problem. We need array H (usually called **heap**) to simulate pointers and records (see Section 5.4). In essence, we pack all record objects created by a new-statement during program execution into array H. During each concrete finite program run, obviously only a finite part of array H will be used. Yet it is not clear before the end of the program run how big this part is. In this sense, therefore, array H is only potentially infinite.

Primitive PROSA is quite similar to the programming language of RESA and the translation of primitive PROSA to RESA (Section 5.3.) is rather simple. The translation of simple PROSA to primitive PROSA will be done in several steps. Every step transforms the program and makes it "more primitive". In 5.4 constants and record names (part of property 2) are eliminated, in 5.5 the data type *bool* is reduced to the data type *int* (properties 1 and 5), in 5.6 we simulate pointers and records by arrays (property 2), in 5.7 we reduce multi-dimensional arrays to one-dimensional arrays (property 3), and finally, in 5.8 we break up complex expressions into primitive expressions (property 4 and 6).

For each step we present an algorithm which realises it. These algorithms process the program text from left to right (called a **pass** through the program) and modify it, as already mentioned, in such a way that the resulting program is "more primitive" than the original program. The correctness of these algorithms, i.e. the fact that the program generated by the algorithm is equivalent to the original program, is obvious for steps 5.4 and 5.5. For the other steps we prove correctness in detail using the concept of bisimulation which was introduced in Section 1.7.

Decomposing the translation in the indicated way has above all the advantage of making the individual steps understandable and provable. When constructing actual compilers, on the other hand, efficiency demands slightly different algorithms and, in addition, a combination of several single steps to more complex compilation steps. Most compilers for simple programming languages like Pascal or PROSA even translate into machine language in one pass, thus performing one iteration through the program.

This brings us to the second objective of the chapter, the informal description of actual compilers. In parallel to the discussion of the compilation process following the indicated decomposition we sketch how actual compilers transform PROSA programs directly into RESA programs. In essence, this consists of a description of the combined effect of several steps and of a less abstract description of the steps. The central data structure for that, the **symbol table**, will be introduced in Section 5.2 as an extension of the attribute $CONTEXT$. The following sections then consist of a more theoretical first part and a more practical second part which will be introduced by the title "Actual Compiler".

5.1 The RESA Computer

We introduce a simple computer, called RESA (**RE**chner **SA**arbrücken), and its machine language. RESA consists of a program storage, a data storage, an input tape, an output tape and a central processing unit (CPU). The CPU has three registers: the accumulator, the instruction counter and the index register (see Figure 1).

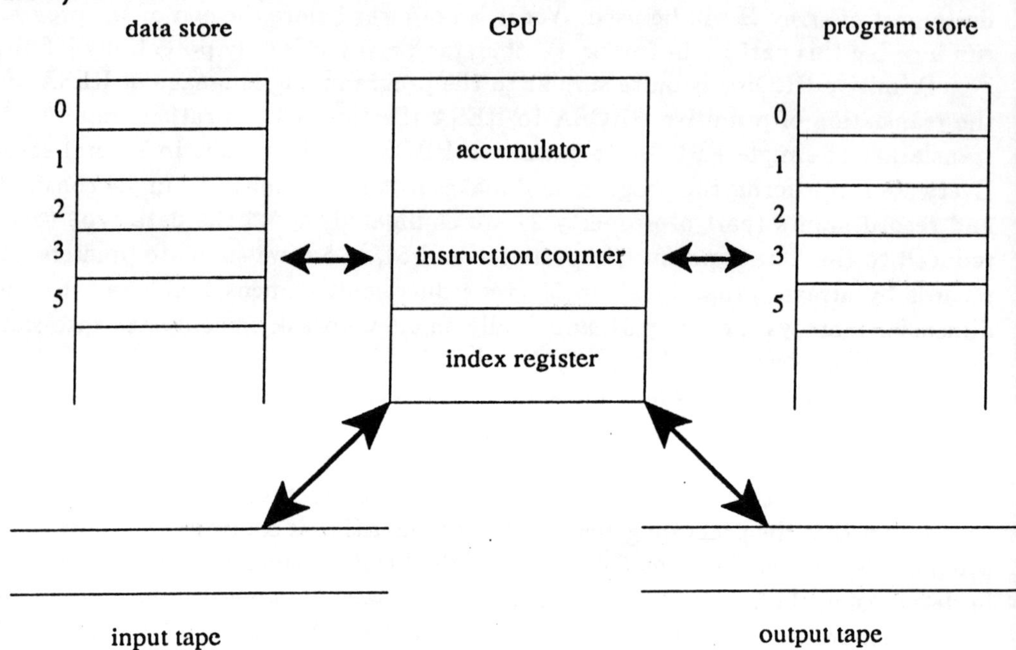

Fig. 1

Formally, the RESA machine is a mathematical machine in the sense of Section 1.7, that is

$$M_{RESA} = (\mathbf{C}, \mathbf{C^f}, \mathbf{P}, \delta, \mathbf{I}, \mathbf{O}, in, out).$$

A **RESA program** is a sequence of **RESA instructions**. Thus $\mathbf{P} = \mathbf{INST^*}$. The set **INST** of RESA instructions is defined as

$$\mathbf{INST} = \{\text{READ, PRINT, ERROR HALT, HALT, STORE IR, LOAD IR}\}$$
$$\cup \{\text{LOAD, STORE, ADD, SUB, MUL, JUMPFORW,}$$
$$\text{JUMPBACKW, JUMPFORW=, JUMPFORW>,}$$
$$\text{LOADIR, STOREIR, LOADNUM}\} \times \mathbb{N}_0.$$

The set of configurations is given by

$$\mathbf{C} = \mathbf{PS} \times \mathbf{Z} \times \mathbf{Z} \times \mathbf{DS} \times \mathbf{Z} \times \mathbf{Z^*} \times \mathbf{Z^*}$$

where

$$\mathbf{DS} = \{ds \mid ds : \mathbb{N}_0 \rightsquigarrow \mathbf{Z}\}$$

is the set of **data storage states** and

$$\mathbf{PS} = \{ps \mid ps : \mathbb{N}_0 \rightsquigarrow \mathbf{INST}\}$$

is the set of **program storage states**. We shall now explain the individual components of a configuration, say $(ps, ac, ir, ds, ic, i, o) \in \mathbf{C}$.

- $ps \in \mathbf{PS}$ is the program storage and contains the program to be executed.
- $ac \in \mathbf{Z}$ is the content of a register, called **accumulator**, in which the operations are carried out.
- $ir \in \mathbf{Z}$ is the content of another register, called **index register**.
- $ds \in \mathbf{DS}$ is the data storage containing the data for the computation.
- $ic \in \mathbf{Z}$ is called the **instruction counter**; it determines which instruction in the program storage must be executed next.
- $i \in \mathbf{Z}^*$ and $o \in \mathbf{Z}^*$ are as usual the rest of the input and the output sequence.

A RESA program $p = (inst_0, \ldots, inst_m)$ is started with some input $i \in \mathbf{Z}^*$ (i.e. $\mathbf{I} = \mathbf{Z}^*$) by loading program p into the program storage and placing input i onto the input tape. The accumulator, the instruction counter and the index register are set to 0, all data storage cells are undefined and the output tape is empty. Thus

$$in(p, i) = (ps, 0, 0, \emptyset, 0, i, \epsilon)$$

where

$$ps(j) = \begin{cases} inst_j & \text{if } 0 \le j \le m \\ \text{undefined} & \text{if } j > m \end{cases}$$

The RESA machine is defined by the transition function $\delta : \mathbf{C} \rightsquigarrow \mathbf{C}$. Let $c = (ps, ac, ir, ds, ic, i, o)$ be a configuration. The RESA machine executes instruction $ps(ic)$ by changing the contents of some registers (the instruction counter also) and some data storage cells. After that a new instruction is executed. This is done until a configuration is reached which has no successor configuration. The details are as follows. If $ps(ic)$ is undefined then $\delta(c)$ is undefined. If $ps(ic) = inst \in \mathbf{INST}$ then the successor configuration is $c' = \delta(c) = (ps, ac', ir', ds', ic', i', o')$ as defined in Table 1.

In this table the successor configuration c' is given by cases according to instruction $ps(ic)$. For each instruction $ps(ic)$ the column "condition" may further differentiate. Empty entries in this table indicate that those components do not change. Empty lines indicate an undefined successor state. Thus in the case of $ps(ic) =$ READ, for example, we have $ac' = head(i)$, $ir' = ir$, $ds' = ds$, $ic' = ic + 1$, $i' = tail(i)$, $o' = o$, if $i \ne \epsilon$, and c' is undefined if $i = \epsilon$. All instructions reading from storage are executable only if the content of the accessed storage cell is defined. Otherwise there is no successor configuration. The set of final states is

$$\mathbf{C}^f = \{(ps, ac, ir, ds, ic, i, o) \mid ps(ic) = \text{HALT and } i = \epsilon\}.$$

Function $out : \mathbf{C}^f \rightsquigarrow \mathbf{Z}^*$ (i.e. $\mathbf{O} = \mathbf{Z}^*$) extracts the output sequence, i.e. $out\,((ps, ac, ir, ds, ic, i, o)) = o$. This completes the definition of the RESA machine. We explain the definitions by way of an example.

ps(ic)		ac'	ir'	ds'	ic'	i'	o'	condition
READ		$head(i)$			$ic+1$	$tail(i)$		$i \neq \epsilon$
PRINT					$ic+1$		$o \cdot ac$	
STORE	IR		ac		$ic+1$			
LOAD	IR	ir			$ic+1$			
LOAD	a	$ds(a)$			$ic+1$			$ds(a)$ defined
STORE	a			$ds[a \backslash ac]$	$ic+1$			
ADD	a	$ac+ds(a)$			$ic+1$			$ds(a)$ defined
SUB	a	$ac-ds(a)$			$ic+1$			$ds(a)$ defined
MUL	a	$ac \cdot ds(a)$			$ic+1$			$ds(a)$ defined
JUMPFORW	a				$ic+a$			
JUMPBACKW	a				$ic-a$			
JUMPFORW=	a				$ic+a$			$ac=0$
					$ic+1$			$ac \neq 0$
JUMPFORW>	a				$ic+a$			$ac>0$
					$ic+1$			$ac \leq 0$
LOADIR	a	$ds(a+ir)$			$ic+1$			$ds(a+ir)$ def
STOREIR	a			$ds[a+ir \backslash ac]$	$ic+1$			$a+ir \geq 0$
LOADNUM	a	a			$ic+1$			
HALT								
ERROR HALT								

Table 1: The transition function δ of the RESA machine.

Example 1: Let the input tape contain numbers $n \in \mathbb{N}$, $x \in \mathbb{Z}, a_n, ..., a_0 \in \mathbb{Z}$. We want to compute $\sum_{i=0}^{n} a_i x^i$. The PROSA program of Section 3.3 solves this problem. Note, however, that instead of real coefficients a_i and argument x we now presume integer values.

```
program Horner_scheme;
  const Zero = 0;
  var N, X, A, S, I: integer;
  begin
    read N; read X;
    S := Zero ; I := N;
    while I ≥ 0
    do read A;
```

$$S := S*X+ A;$$
$$I := I- 1$$
  od;
  print S
end.

We now give an equivalent RESA program. The data storage cells of RESA are used to implement PROSA variables. In particular, cell 0 (1, 2, 3, 4) plays the role of variable N (X, A, S, I). Constant name *Zero* is eliminated by changing assignment $S := Zero$ to $S := 0$. We obtain the following RESA program where instructions are grouped according to PROSA statements.

```
READ
STORE        0        } read  N

READ
STORE        1        } read  X

LOADNUM      0        } S := Zero
STORE        3

LOAD         0        } I := N
STORE        4

LOADNUM      0        } if 0 − I > 0,
SUB          4        } then jump to the end of the loop
JUMFORW      13

READ                  } read  A
STORE        2

LOAD         3
MUL          1        } S := S * X + A
ADD          2
STORE        3

LOADNUM      1
STORE        5
LOAD         4        } I := I − 1
SUB          5
STORE        4

JUMPBACKW    14       } jump to test 0 − I > 0

LOAD         3        } print S
PRINT

HALT                  }
```

Given the comments, this RESA program should be almost self-explanatory. The iteration statement was translated as follows:

> (1) check if $I < 0$
> (2) if yes then jump to (5)
> (3) translation of the body
> (4) jump to test at (1)
> (5)

Since RESA only allows very restricted tests we simulate the test $I < 0$ by $0 - I > 0$.

∎

    The instruction set of RESA is very small, while actual computers often have an instruction set of over 100 instructions. It is, on the other hand, sufficient to translate PROSA to RESA. In Chapter VII (Translation of PROSA with procedures) we use a slightly extended instruction set. Instead of the single index register IR, four index registers IR, IR1, BFS and BAP will be used. For the additional index registers the same instructions as for index register IR are available. Furthermore we introduce for $OP \in \{ADD, SUB, MUL\}$ the instructions OPIR a with the meaning $ac' := ac \ op \ ds(a + ir)$. Finally we need a jump instruction with computed target. JUMPAC sets ic' to the value ac of the accumulator. A garbage collection instruction, CLEARBFS, removes the contents of all storage cells whose address is greater or equal to the content of BFS, i.e. after the instruction we have $ds(i) = $ undefined for $i \geq bfs$ where bfs is the content of BFS.

    When writing RESA programs two conventions are used. Either we write one instruction per line and use no separator, or we write several instructions on a line and then use the a semicolon as separator. In defining RESA we abstract from existing computers. Obviously real computers only have a finite (data and program) storage. We deviated from reality in a further point. When starting a real machine, all storage cells are given a defined value (in many cases it is the value 0) and not the undefined value as with RESA. While, in the case of RESA, reading from a storage cell which has not yet been written to leads to an error, this is not so with real machines. Rather the value is read which was stored in the cell when the machine was switched on. We will return to this difference in Section 5.3.

Exercises for 5.1

1) Given $2n^2 + 1$ numbers $n, a_{11}, a_{12}, \cdots, a_{1n}, a_{21}, \cdots, a_{nn}, b_{11}, \cdots, b_{nn}$ on the input tape of the RESA machine. Write a RESA program which prints numbers $c_{11}, \cdots, c_{nn}$ where

$$c_{ik} = \sum_{j=1}^{n} a_{ij} b_{jk}$$

First write the program in primitive PROSA (as defined in the introduction to this chapter). Provide useful comments in the RESA program.

2) Suppose RESA had no index register, but instead the (so-called indirect) instructions OPIND, OP$\in$ {LOAD, STORE, ADD, MUL, ...} are available. Their meaning is given in the following table.

ps(ic)	ac$'$	ds$'$	ic$'$	condition
LOADIND a	$ds(ds(a))$		$ic + 1$	$ds(a)$ defined; $ds(a) \in \mathbb{N}_0$ and $ds(ds(a))$ defined
STOREIND a		$ds[ds(a)\backslash ac]$	$ic + 1$	$ds(a)$ defined; $ds(a) \in \mathbb{N}_0$
ADDIND a	$ac + ds(ds(a))$		$ic + 1$	$ds(a)$ defined; $ds(a) \in \mathbb{N}_0$ and $ds(ds(a))$ defined
$\vdots$	$\vdots$	$\vdots$	$\vdots$	$\vdots$

a) Write the program of Exercise 1 using this computer!

b) For each IR-instruction give a sequence of statements with indirect instructions which simulates it. Organise the data storage suitably. In particular, take care of possible error cases.

c) Write the program of Exercise 1 anew, simulating the IR-instruction according to b).

d) Determine and compare the computation times of the programs of a) and c).

Remark: Actual computers usually feature indirect instructions as well as several index registers.

3) Discuss limitations of the RESA computer if it has neither index registers nor indirect instructions.

Hint: Can the number of data storage cells used by a program depend on the input?

4) Show that for each RESA program p_1 an equivalent primitive PROSA program p_2 can be constructed. Hint: The program starts with the declarations **var** AC, IR, IC : **integer**; **var** DS : **array**$[0..\infty]$**of integer**. If p_1 comprises the instructions $inst_0, \cdots, inst_m$ then the statement section of p_2 has the form

$IC := 0;\ AC := 0;\ IR := 0;$
while $IC \leq m$
do translation of $inst_0$;
    translation of $inst_1$;

   $\vdots$

od

The j-th instruction $inst_j$ is translated as follows. Let, for example, $inst_j$ be LOAD a. Then one writes

$$\text{if } IC = j \text{ then } AC := DS[a];\ IC := IC + 1 \text{ fi}$$

If $inst_j$ is JUMPFORW> a then one writes

```
if  IC = j
then
    if  AC > 0
    then  IC  :=  IC + a
    else  IC  :=  IC + 1
    fi
fi
```

Give the translation for the other instructions!

5.2 The Symbol Table in Compilers

In preceding chapters we have introduced the attribute $CONTEXT$ in order to check context conditions. It keeps track of the mode binding of all declared names in a PROSA program. The mode of a name, on the other hand, is not only important for checking context conditions, but it also contains information which is important for the translation into machine language. If, for example, name x occurs in an expression then, depending on the sort of x, one of the RESA instructions LOADNUM, LOAD, or LOADIR would be used to load the value of x into the accumulator.

Suppose the sort of x is *const*. Then $CONTEXT$ would indicate that a LOADNUM-instruction must be generated. On the other hand, $CONTEXT$ provides no information about the operands of the LOADNUM-instruction. The value of the constant to which x is bound is not available in $CONTEXT$.

Compilers therefore use an extension of the attribute $CONTEXT$, the **symbol table**, to record all the information contained in the declaration section of a program. This is mainly done for efficiency reasons. Although the text of the declaration section contains the same information, it does not permit fast retrieval of information about names whose applied occurrence is processed. Using methods as might be discussed in a course on "data structures", the symbol table can be organised in such a way that all the necessary operations, particularly searching, are realised efficiently. Besides, the symbol table contains information about names which has to be computed from the declaration section. An example is the correspondence of addresses and names after storage allocation. These computations can be carried out once and the results then entered in the symbol table. If one were to compute the same information from the declaration section in each case anew, the effort would be unacceptable. We therefore note: every practical compiler uses a data structure (an attribute), called symbol table, where all relevant information for the translation from the declaration section is stored.

We shall now extend the attribute $CONTEXT$ for simple PROSA to an attribute ST. In ST the extended mode binding for different sorts has the following form (an explanatory example follows each definition).

Constant names:

$Ident \rightarrow \{const\} \times ((\{int\} \times \mathbb{Z}) \cup (\{bool\} \times \{true, false\}))$

Constant names thus are also bound to the constants denoted by them.

Variable names:

$Ident \rightarrow \{var\} \times \{int, bool\} \times Adr$ with $Adr = \mathbb{N}$.

Names of simple variables are in addition bound to the address of a RESA data storage cell. How such addresses are chosen, i.e. how storage allocation is done, will be discussed in detail in the following sections.

Array names:

$Ident \rightarrow \{array\} \times Type \times Dim \times Bounds \times Adr \times Size$ with

$\qquad Bounds = Pairof Bounds^*$

$\qquad Pairof Bounds = Lbound \times Ubound$

$\qquad Size = \mathbb{N}$

$\qquad Lbound = Ubound = \mathbb{Z}$.

In addition to the dimension Dim and the component type $Type$, both already contained in CONTEXT, other relevant information about array names now consists of the values of lower and upper bounds and again a data storage address, the initial address of the array. The size component specifies the storage requirement for the array.

Record names:

$Ident \rightarrow \{record\} \times CompDesc^* \times Adr \times Size$ with

$\qquad CompDesc = Ident \rightarrow Sort \times Type \times Adr$.

If a name of type record is declared one can, consecutive placement of components in storage presumed, allocate an initial address to it and likewise to each of its components. A possible way of allocating addresses to record components will be introduced in Section 5.4. The size determines the storage requirement for record objects of this type.

Pointers:

$Ident \rightarrow \{var\} \times Ident \times Adr$.

Pointer names are also given a fixed address in the RESA data storage.

Let us summarise. Declared names for variables, arrays, records and pointers, together with their declaration information and in addition a RESA data storage address, are entered in the symbol table. These addresses are used to determine operands of LOAD and STORE instructions while translating an access to these objects.

Type names:

$$Ident \rightarrow \{Type\} \times CompDesc^* \times Size$$

A declared type name, in essence, is associated with the description of the record. The computed size of objects of this type can, for example, be used when translating *new*-statements to direct storage allocation on the heap (see Section 5.6).

Example 1:
The declaration section

```
const  zero   = 0 ; tt = true;
type  v       = record
                      comp1 : integer;
                      comp2 : ↑ v
                end;
var  rec : v ;
     b : boolean ;
     a : array [zero.. 5] of integer;
     x : integer;
```

would (according to a storage allocation strategy described later) lead to the following symbol table.

$$
\begin{aligned}
zero &\rightarrow & (const, int, 0)\\
tt &\rightarrow & (const, bool, true)\\
v &\rightarrow & (type, (comp1 \rightarrow (var, int, 0)\\
& & \quad comp2 \rightarrow (var,\ \ v, 1)), 2)\\
rec &\rightarrow & (record, (comp1 \rightarrow (var, int, 0)\\
& & \quad\quad comp2 \rightarrow (var,\ \ v, 1)),\\
& & \quad 0, 2)\\
b &\rightarrow & (var, bool, 2)\\
a &\rightarrow & (array, int, 1, (0, 5), 3, 6)\\
x &\rightarrow & (var, int, 9)
\end{aligned}
$$

This symbol table allocates addresses as follows: 0 for *rec*, 2 for *b*, 3 for *a* and 9 for *x*. Note that the values of the size components are just 2 (for *rec*), 1 (for *b*) and 6 (for *a*). Figure 1 shows the the RESA storage allocation.

Note also that the data storage cell allocated for *rec.comp2*, for example, has number 0 (= the address allocated for *rec*) + 1 (= the address allocated for *comp2* relative to the initial address of the record) and that the data storage cell allocated to a[4], for example, has number 3 (= the initial address allocated for with a) + 4 (= index). We discuss this allocation in detail in the next sections. ∎

<table>
<tr><td>0</td><td></td><td>rec.comp1</td></tr>
<tr><td>1</td><td></td><td>rec.comp2</td></tr>
<tr><td>2</td><td></td><td>b</td></tr>
<tr><td>3</td><td></td><td>a[0]</td></tr>
<tr><td>4</td><td></td><td>a[1]</td></tr>
<tr><td>5</td><td></td><td>a[2]</td></tr>
<tr><td>6</td><td></td><td>a[3]</td></tr>
<tr><td>7</td><td></td><td>a[4]</td></tr>
<tr><td>8</td><td></td><td>a[5]</td></tr>
<tr><td>9</td><td></td><td>x</td></tr>
</table>

Fig. 1.   Storage Allocation

5.3 Translating primitive PROSA to RESA

In this section programs in primitive PROSA are translated to RESA. To achieve that the following two differences have to be dealt with.

1) In PROSA storage cells are referred to by name while in RESA integers (addresses) are used. Furthermore PROSA features arrays.

2) PROSA has control structures (conditional statement and iteration statement) while in RESA control is determined by jumps.

We now resolve both these differences. Let **program** n ; ds **begin** sts **end.** be a primitive PROSA program with declaration section ds and statement section sts. The declaration section ds consists of a sequence d_1; d_2; ...; d_k; of declarations. We may assume that d_k is the declaration of the infinite array **var** H : **array** $[0 .. \infty]$ **of integer.** Let b denote the binding obtained after executing the declaration section ds. Then $Def(b) = \{n_1, \ldots, n_k\}$ where n_i is the name declared in d_i. Consider

$$rad : Def(b) \; \rightarrow \; \mathbb{N}_0 \quad \text{with}$$

$$rad(n_i) \; = \; \sum_{j=0}^{i-1} si(n_j)$$

where

$$si(n_i) = \begin{cases} 1 & \text{if } d_i = \textbf{var } n_i : \textbf{integer} \\ l_i + 1 & \text{if } d_i = \textbf{var } n_i : \textbf{array } [0 .. l_i] \textbf{ of integer} \end{cases}$$

Thus $si(n_i)$ is the number of storage locations occupied by declaration d_i. The relative address $rad(n_i)$ indicates which storage locations of the RESA machine play the role of PROSA machine storage locations determined by the declaration d_i. We use the following principle.

If $d_i = $ **var** n_i : **integer** then storage location $rad(n_i)$ of the RESA machine plays the role of storage location $b(n_i)$ of the PROSA machine. If $d_i = $ **var** n_i : **array**$[0 .. l_i]$ **of integer** then storage location $rad(n_i) + k$ of the RESA machine, $0 \leq k \leq l_i$, plays the role of storage location $b(n_i)(k)$ of the PROSA machine.

Obviously each storage location of the RESA machine corresponds to at most one storage location of the PROSA machine. Thus

Lemma 1. *Let* $V_1 = \mathbf{V} \cap (image(b) \cup \bigcup\{image(f) \mid f \in \mathbf{ARR} \cap image(b)\})$ *be the set of allocated storage locations determined by the binding* b. *Then the mapping* $\alpha : V_1 \to \mathbb{N}_0$ *with*

$$\alpha(v) = \begin{cases} rad(n) & \text{if } v = b(n) \\ rad(n) + h & \text{if } f = b(n) \in \mathbf{ARR} \text{ and } v = f(h) \end{cases}$$

is injective.

Proof: Follows immediately from the definition of mapping rad. ∎

Example 1:   For the following declaration section
    var i : **integer**;
    var a : **array** $[0.. 3]$ **of integer**;
    var b : **integer**; **var** c : **integer**;
    var H : **array** $[0.. \infty]$ **of integer**;
we have $rad(i) = 0$, $rad(a) = 1$, $rad(b) = 5$, $rad(c) = 6$ and $rad(H) = 7$.

The role of storage location a[2] is played by the RESA storage location $3 = rad(a) + 2$. Mapping α of Lemma 1 is shown in the following table.

PROSA name	i	a[0]	a[1]	a[2]	a[3]	b	c	H[0]
address of corresponding RESA storage location	0	1	2	3	4	5	6	7

∎

We must now transform the statement section *sts*. We define a function *translate* which translates PROSA statement sequences into RESA instruction sequences. A translated PROSA program then is

    translate(*sts*) ; HALT

i.e. the translated statement sequence *sts* followed by the HALT-instruction. The value of function *translate* for a statement sequence p is defined by cases as follows.

Case 1: $p = p_1; p_2$ where p_1 is a statement and p_2 a statement sequence. Then
$$translate(p) = translate(p_1); translate(p_2)$$

Case 2: p is a read statement **read** x with name x. Then
$$translate(p) = \text{READ}$$
$$\text{STORE} \quad rad(x)$$

Case 3: p is a print statement **print** x with name x. Then
$$translate(p) = \text{LOAD} \quad rad(x)$$
$$\text{PRINT}$$

Case 4: p is an assignment. Then

$$translate(p) = \begin{cases}
\begin{array}{lll}
\text{LOAD} & rad(y) & \text{if } p = x := y \\
\text{STORE} & rad(x) & \text{with } x, y \text{ identifiers} \\
\\
\text{LOAD} & rad(i) & \text{if } p = a[i] := x \\
\text{STORE} & \text{IR} & \text{with } i, x, a \text{ identifiers} \\
\text{LOAD} & rad(x) & \\
\text{STOREIR} & rad(a) & \\
\\
\text{LOAD} & rad(i) & \text{if } p = x := a[i] \\
\text{STORE} & \text{IR} & \text{with } i, x, a \text{ identifiers} \\
\text{LOADIR} & rad(a) & \\
\text{STORE} & rad(x) & \\
\\
\text{LOAD} & rad(y) & \text{if } p = x := y \text{ } op \text{ } z \\
\text{OP} & rad(z) & \text{with } x, y, z \text{ identifiers} \\
\text{STORE} & rad(x) & \\
\\
\text{LOADNUM} & c(n) & \text{if } p = x := n \text{ with } x \text{ name} \\
\text{STORE} & rad(x) & \text{and } n \text{ standard name}
\end{array}
\end{cases}$$

Case 5: p is a conditional statement **if** x op 0 **then** p_1 **else** p_2 **fi** with name x, $op \in \{>, =\}$ and p_1, p_2 statement sequences. Then
$$translate(p) = \begin{array}{ll}
\text{LOAD} & rad(x) \\
\text{JUMPFORWop} & L_2 + 2 \\
translate(p_2) & \\
\text{JUMPFORW} & L_1 + 1 \\
translate(p_1) &
\end{array}$$

where L_i is the length of the instruction sequence $translate(p_i)$, $i = 1, 2$. Note that we first load the value of x. If x op 0 is true then we jump behind the result of the translation of p_2 to the first line of the translation of p_1. If x op 0 is false we execute the translation of p_2 and then jump across the translation of p_1.

Case 6: p is a conditional statement **if** x op 0 **then** p_1 **fi** with name x, $op \in \{>, =\}$ and p_1 statement sequence. Then

$$
\begin{aligned}
translate(p) = \; &\text{LOAD} && rad(x) \\
&\text{JUMPFORW}op && 2 \\
&\text{JUMPFORW} && L_1 + 1 \\
&translate(p_1)
\end{aligned}
$$

where L_1 is the length of the instruction sequence $translate(p_1)$.

Case 7: p is an iteration statement **while** x op 0 **do** p_1 **od** with name x, $op \in \{>, =\}$ and p_1 statement sequence. Then

$$
\begin{aligned}
translate(p) = \; &\text{LOAD} && rad(x) \\
&\text{JUMPFORW}op && 2 \\
&\text{JUMPFORW} && L_1 + 2 \\
&translate(p_1) \\
&\text{JUMPBACKW} && L_1 + 3
\end{aligned}
$$

where L_1 is the length of the instruction sequence $translate(p_1)$.

Case 8: p is the error statement **error halt**. Then

$$
translate(p) = \text{ERROR HALT}.
$$

Example 1 (continued):   The statement section

$$
\begin{aligned}
&i := 3; \\
&b := 0; \\
&c := b - i; \\
&\textbf{if}\, c > 0 \ \textbf{then error halt fi}; \\
&b := 3; \\
&c := i - b; \\
&\textbf{if}\, c > 0 \ \textbf{then error halt fi}\ ; \\
&a[i] := i;
\end{aligned}
$$

is translated into (we use mapping rad of above):

$$
\begin{array}{lll}
\text{LOADNUM} & 3 & \left.\begin{array}{l} \\ \end{array}\right\} i := 3 \\
\text{STORE} & 0 & \\
\text{LOADNUM} & 0 & \left.\begin{array}{l} \\ \end{array}\right\} b := 0 \\
\text{STORE} & 5 &
\end{array}
$$

LOAD	5	
SUB	0	$c := b - i$
STORE	6	
LOAD	6	
JUMPFORW>	2	
JUMPFORW	2	**if** $c > 0$ **then error halt fi**
ERROR HALT		
LOADNUM	3	
STORE	5	$b := 3$
LOAD	0	
SUB	5	$c := i - b$
STORE	6	
LOAD	6	
JUMPFORW>	2	
JUMPFORW	2	**if** $c > 0$ **then error halt fi**
ERROR HALT		
LOAD	0	
STORE	IR	
LOAD	0	$a[i] := i$
STOREIR	1	

We now must show that the given translation is correct. Probably the reader is already convinced of that since the translation is quite simple and obvious. We therefore point out two traps into which we fell ourselves while writing this chapter.

In a former version of this book the RESA machine began computation with zero in all storage cells. Then a PROSA assignment can lead to an error if the expression on the right side is not defined. On the other hand, the translated statement does not lead to an error. We had also omitted in the previous definition of primitive PROSA that in array selections, e.g. $a[i]$, the value of variable i was definitely in the index range of array a. If in our example i has value 4 the PROSA statement

$$a[i] := i$$

leads to an error, the RESA statement sequence

LOAD	0
STORE	IR
LOAD	0
STOREIR	1

on the other hand, stores number 4 into storage cell 5.

These examples show that the correctness of the translation is not completely obvious. In particular, it is not clear whether statements in PROSA lead to errors precisely when this is the case for the corresponding RESA instruction sequences. We will now show

Lemma 2. *Let $c = (pr, b, s, i, o)$ be a state of the PROSA machine such that the program-rest pr is primitive. Let mapping α be defined as in Lemma 1. Let $\overline{c} = (qr, ac, ir, t, 0, i, o)$ be a state of the RESA machine with $qr = translate(pr)$; HALT and $t(\alpha(v)) = s(v)$ for all variables v.*

1) If the computation on the PROSA machine from start state c is infinite then the computation on the RESA machine with start state $\overline{c}$ is infinite.

2) If the computation on the PROSA machine from start state c is finite and ends in a normal state $(\epsilon, b, s', i', o')$ then the computation on the RESA machine from start state $\overline{c}$ ends in a state $\overline{c'} = (qr, ac', ir', t', |qr|, i', o')$ with $s'(v) = t'(\alpha(v))$ for all variables $v \in V_1$. If the PROSA machine ends in an error state so does the RESA machine.

3) If the computation on the PROSA machine takes T steps then the computation on the RESA machine takes at most $4\,T$ steps.

Explanation: As was said above, the RESA storage location $\alpha(v)$ plays the role of PROSA variable v. Condition $s(v) = t(\alpha(v))$ states this precisely. Thus if we start the PROSA and RESA machines in corresponding configurations c and $\overline{c}$, the computations are either both infinite or both finite. In the second case they end either both in an error state or in corresponding states. In particular $s'(v) = t'(\alpha(v))$ for all variables v.

Proof: The proof is by induction on the structure of the program-rest pr. For the induction base we must consider the cases of assignment, the read and print statement and the error statement. Sequential, conditional and iteration statements are considered in the induction step.

Let therefore pr be an assignment, say $a[i] := x$ with a, i and x identifiers. The other cases of the induction base are similar and are left to the reader. Then

$$
\begin{array}{lll}
translate(pr) = & \text{LOAD} & rad(i) \\
& \text{STORE} & \text{IR} \\
& \text{LOAD} & rad(x) \\
& \text{STOREIR} & rad(a)
\end{array}
$$

Clearly, the computations on the two machines are finite and claim 3 holds. Part (3) of the definition of primitive PROSA ensures that the value of i is in the index range of a and therefore assignment $a[i] := x$ leads to an error if and only if $s(b(x))$ is undefined. Because of $s(v) = t(\alpha(v))$ for all variables v and because of the definition of α

$$
s(b(i)) = t(rad(i)) \qquad \text{and}
$$

$$
s(b(x)) = t(rad(x))
$$

Therefore $t(rad(i))$ is defined and greater equal to zero since $s(b(i))$ lies in the index range of a. Thus statements LOAD $rad(i)$, STORE IR and STOREIR $rad(a)$ are each executable and LOAD $rad(x)$ leads to an error if and only if $s(b(x))$ is undefined. Thus the computations on the two machines either lead to an error or both end normally. Let now $s(b(x))$ be defined. Then

$$
s' = s[b(a)(s(b(i)))\backslash s(b(x))] \qquad \text{and}
$$

$$
t' = t[rad(a) + t(rad(i))\backslash t(rad(x))].
$$

Recall that $b(a) \in \mathbf{ARR}$ and thus $b(a)(s(b(i)))$ denotes variable $a[i]$.

The definition of α (see Lemma 1) with $n = a$ and $k = s(b(i))$ implies

$$\alpha(b(a)(s(b(i)))) = rad(a) + s(b(i))$$
$$= rad(a) + t(rad(i))$$

Since α is injective it follows that $s'(v) = t'(\alpha(v))$ for all variables $v \in V_1$.

For the induction step we treat the case of the conditional statement **if** $x = 0$ **then** p_1 **fi**. All other cases are similar and are left to the reader. We have

$$\begin{aligned}
translate(pr) \; &= \text{LOAD} && rad(x) \\
&\text{JUMPFORW} = && 2 \\
&\text{JUMPFORW} && L_1 + 1 \\
&translate(p_1)
\end{aligned}$$

where L_1 is the length of the instruction sequence $translate(p_1)$. If $s(b(x))$ is undefined then $t(rad(x)) = s(b(x))$ is undefined and both computations lead to an error. Let now $s(b(x))$ be defined. If $s(b(x)) \neq 0$ and thus $t(rad(x)) \neq 0$ then $s' = s$, $t' = t$, $i' = i$ and $o' = o$. Now suppose $s(b(x)) = 0$ and therefore $t(rad(x)) = 0$. Then

$$\delta_{PROSA}(c) = (p_1, b, s, i, o) \qquad \text{and}$$
$$\delta^{(2)}_{RESA}(c) = (qr, s(b(x)), ir, t, 3, i, o)$$

Applying the induction hypothesis to p_1 and observing that the computation on the RESA machine with the start configurations

$$\begin{aligned}
(translate(p_1), \; &ac, \; ir, \; t, \; 0, \; i, \; o) \qquad \text{and} \\
(qr \qquad\qquad , \; &ac, \; ir, \; t, \; 3, \; i, \; o)
\end{aligned}$$

only differ with respect to the instruction counter (in the second computation it is always increased by three) and the program (in the second computation there are three additional instructions in the program store), proves the induction step.   ∎

Lemma 2 now implies

Theorem 1. *For each primitive PROSA program p there is an equivalent RESA program q. Program q can be effectively constructed from p and $comp_time(q, i)$ $\leq 4 \cdot comp_time(p, i)$ for all $i \in \mathbb{Z}^*$.*

Proof: Let $p = \mathbf{program}\; n; ds\; \mathbf{begin}\; sts\; \mathbf{end}.$ and let $q = translate(sts); \text{HALT}$. After executing the declaration section of p the PROSA machine is in state $(sts; , b, \emptyset, i, \epsilon)$, where i is an input sequence. Let now α be defined as in Lemma 1. RESA state $\overline{c} = (translate(sts); \text{HALT}, 0, 0, \emptyset, 0, i, \epsilon)$ then satisfies the premises of Lemma 2 which implies the equivalence of p and q as well as the claim concerning the computation time.   ∎

As explained immediately before Lemma 2, for the correctness of the translation of PROSA into RESA it is essential that the values of all RESA storage cells are undefined at the beginning of the computation. We already mentioned in Section 5.1 that this assumption is unrealistic. We shall now specify translations which do not require this assumption. Let us first assume that all storage cells get the initial value 0, and later that nothing is known about the initial values.

Thus suppose that at the beginning of a computation of the RESA machine all storage cells have value 0. We then associate with each PROSA variable two storage cells. One of them contains the value 1 or 0, depending on whether the variable has already been assigned to (value 1) or not (value 0). The other storage cell contains the actual value of the variable if it exists and 0 otherwise. Note that the initial storage state of the RESA machine (all storage cells have value 0) then correctly represents the situation where no PROSA variable has yet been assigned to. If we now want to read the value of a PROSA variable we first have to check with the help of the additional storage cell whether this value exists. If we want to write to a PROSA variable then the additional storage cell is set to 1. An assignment $x := y$, with x, y identifiers, will then be translated to the following instruction sequence (assuming that x is allocated storage cells $2 \cdot rad(x)$ and $1 + 2 \cdot rad(x)$):

LOAD	$2 \cdot rad(y)$
JUMPFORW>	2
ERROR HALT	
LOAD	$1 + 2 \cdot rad(y)$
STORE	$1 + 2 \cdot rad(x)$
LOADNUM	1
STORE	$2 \cdot rad(x)$

The other cases of assignments are treated analogously.

We now come to the more complicated case where nothing is known about the initial storage state of the RESA machine. This case arises in the following situation. After termination of a program p_1 a program p_2 is started. Then, for some machines, the initial storage state for p_2 is the final storage state of p_1. How can one cope with this case? In Exercise 2 we describe a possible solution which, however, because of the expense in computation time and storage will rarely be used. An attractive alternative is to change the PROSA semantics and "define away" the initialisation problem. For each elementary data type a default value is defined which is stored automatically whenever a variable of the corresponding type is declared. We will later choose this solution for pointer variables. As the definition of such a default value for some data types (e.g. *char* or *bool*) is unnatural we cannot use this method in general.

Primitive PROSA is restricted to such an extent that storage allocation raises no big problems. All programs written in primitive PROSA only contain declarations of objects for which a compiler can allocate fixed RESA data storage addresses. To this extent, storage allocation and address association according to function *rad* is realistic. An actual compiler would compute the addresses of declared names and enter them in the symbol table in a similar way. Function *translate* is equally a realistic possibility to generate RESA instruction sequences for PROSA statements. Here the evaluation of function *rad* for a name x corresponds to consulting the address component of x in the symbol table.

Exercises for 5.3

1) Suppose the initial value of all RESA storage cells is 0. Give correct translations for assignments $a[i] := x$ and $x := a[i]$.

2) Under the assumption that RESA storage cells have arbitrary initial values, allocate for each PROSA variable two RESA storage cells. Add at the beginning of the generated RESA program assignments setting those storage cells to 0. Based on this idea, develop a correct translation of primitive PROSA to RESA. Only translation of primitive PROSA programs which do not use the infinite array H is required.
Remark: The general case is treated in Section 5.6, Exercise 5.

3) Supposing RESA provides a conditional jump for each of the operators $op \in \{=, \neq, >, \geq, \leq, <\}$, can the translation schemes for conditional statements and iteration statements be simplified? Is it still necessary to swap the **then** and **else** part of conditional statements? Can the evaluation of boolean expressions (see Section 5.5) be simplified? Give examples!

4) Translate the example programs of chapter IV into RESA.

5) How does the compiler on hand deal with the initialisation problem?

5.4 Eliminating Constant and Record Names

Constant names denote objects of elementary type. They are introduced in constant declarations of the form **const** $n = m$ where n is an identifier and m a standard name. We can eliminate such constant declarations by replacing each applied occurrence of n by m. Then, naturally, the constant declaration will no longer be needed and it can be deleted from the declaration section. In this way one obtains a program without constant declarations.

Example 1:

$$\vdots$$

$$\textbf{const} \quad zero = 0.0;$$

$$\vdots$$

$$x := zero;$$

$$\vdots$$

becomes

$$\vdots$$

$$x := 0.0;$$

$$\vdots$$

Record names denote record objects. They are introduced by declarations of the form **var** $n : XYZ$ where n is an identifier and XYZ is either the name of a record type or of the form **record** $s_1 : t_1; \ldots; s_k : t_k$ **end** with $s_i \in \langle ident \rangle$ and $t_i \in \langle small\ type \rangle$. We can reduce the second alternative to the first by adding a type declaration

$$\textbf{type} \quad \overline{XYZ} = XYZ$$

at the beginning of the declaration section (here $\overline{XYZ}$ is a new name) and replacing declaration **var** $n : XYZ$ by **var** $n : \overline{XYZ}$. This obviously does not change the meaning.

Example 2:

$$\vdots$$

$$\textbf{var} \quad e : \textbf{record} \ a : \textbf{integer}; \ b : \uparrow t \ \textbf{end};$$

$$\vdots$$

becomes

$$\textbf{type } ty = \textbf{record } a : \textbf{integer} ; \; b : \uparrow t \textbf{ end};$$

$$\vdots$$

$$\textbf{var } e : ty;$$

$$\vdots$$

We can therefore assume that each declaration of a record name is of the form
var n: XYZ where XYZ is the name of a record type. We now do three things.

1) Replace declaration **var** $n : XYZ$ by the declaration of a pointer variable
   var $n : \uparrow XYZ$.
2) Insert the **new**-statement
   $n := \textbf{new } XYZ$ immediately after the declaration section.
3) Replace each occurrence of $n.$ (the period is the selection symbol) by $n \uparrow.$ in
   the statement section.

We claim that programs modified in this way are equivalent to the original programs. This can be seen easily. Executing declaration **var** $n : XYZ$ and declaration
var $n : \uparrow XYZ$ together with statement $n := \textbf{new } XYZ$ yields respectively

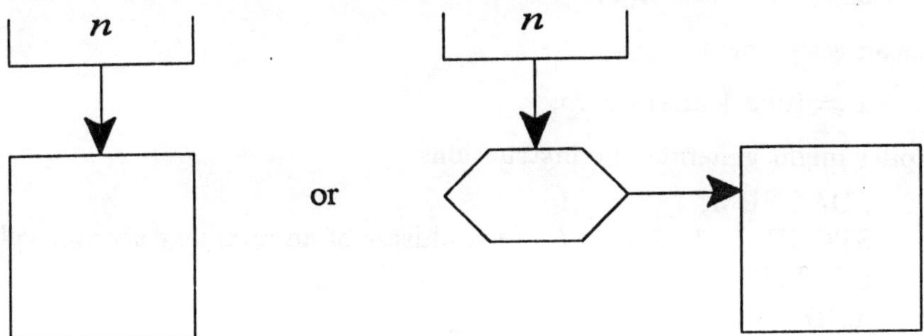

Fig. 1

where the box in each case represents a record of type XYZ. In the statement
section, obviously, $n.sel$ in the old program (sel is a selector) selects the same
component as $n\uparrow.sel$ in new program.

In summary:

Definition 1: A simple PROSA program is called **1–simple** if it does not contain
declarations for constant names and record names.

Theorem 1. *For each simple PROSA program p there is an equivalent 1-simple
PROSA program q. Program q can effectively be constructed from p and*

$$comp_time(q,i) \leq 2 \cdot comp_time(p,i)$$

for all inputs $i \in \mathbf{Z}^*$.

Proof: Follows immediately from the discussion above. The computation time can at most increase by a factor 2 since for each of the additional new-statements the corresponding declaration is also processed. ∎

In actual compilers a transformation step which eliminates constant declarations by inserting corresponding standard names for the applied occurrence of the constant names is too expensive. It would require processing the whole program and using expensive string operations.

Actual compilers enter the information as to which constant a constant name is bound in the symbol table. This does not take place in a special pass over the declaration section but together with the processing of the other declarations. Afterwards, when statements are translated, the values of constant names are retrieved from the symbol table.

Example 3: For constant declarations

$$\textbf{const} \quad zero = 0; \quad one = 1;$$

the symbol table would have entries

$$zero \rightarrow (const, int, 0)$$
$$one \rightarrow (const, int, 1)$$

and for an assignment

$$x := (one + one) * zero;$$

a compiler might generate the instructions

LOADNUM	1	
STORE	t	(* t address of an auxiliary storage cell *)
LOADNUM	1	
ADD	t	
STORE	t	
LOADNUM	0	
MUL	t	
STORE	$rad(x)$	

A more sophisticated compiler, however, would detect that the two instructions

LOADNUM	0
STORE	$rad(x)$

suffice.

In actual compilers the method of reducing record names to dynamically created anonymous record objects is not used. A record requires a fixed number of storage cells, one each for every component of the object. According to the scheme described in Section 5.3 one can therefore allocate RESA addresses to them. These addresses, one for the record as a whole and one for each component, are entered in the symbol table.

Example 4:   Consider declarations
type t = **record** $b1$: **integer** ; $b2$: $\uparrow t$ **end**;
var r : t;
var s : t;
     and assume that for records r and s cell 17 and following are allocated. We get the following symbol table (see Section 5.2):

$$
\begin{aligned}
t \to \quad & (type \ , \ (b1 \to \quad (var \ , \ int \ , \ 0) \\
& \qquad\qquad b2 \to (var \ , \ t \ , \ 1)) \ , \ 2) \\
r \to \quad & (record \ , \ (b1 \to \quad (var \ , \ int \ , \ 0) \\
& \qquad\qquad b2 \to (var \ , \ t \ , \ 1)) \ , \ 17 \ , \ 2) \\
s \to \quad & (record \ , \ (b1 \to \quad (var \ , \ int \ , \ 0) \\
& \qquad\qquad b2 \to (var \ , \ t \ , \ 1)) \ , \ 19 \ , \ 2).
\end{aligned}
$$

Record s thus is placed in cells 19 and 20 where component $s.b1$ occupies cell $19 = 19 + 0$ and component $s.b2$ cell $20 = 19 + 1$; the symbol table, therefore, contains the addresses of components of a record relative to the initial address of the record. The initial address of the "translated" record is kept in a RESA storage cell which corresponds to a pointer variable (see Section 5.6). Assignment $r.b1 := 0$ is translated into

$$
\begin{aligned}
&\text{LOADNUM} \quad 0 \\
&\text{STORE} \qquad\ \ 17
\end{aligned}
$$

assignment $r.b2 := s.b2$ is translated into

$$
\begin{aligned}
&\text{LOAD} \quad 20 \\
&\text{STORE} \ \ 18
\end{aligned}
$$

and assignment $r.b2 \uparrow .b2 := s.b2$ is translated into

$$
\begin{aligned}
&\text{LOAD} \qquad 18 \\
&\text{STORE} \qquad \text{IR} \\
&\text{LOAD} \qquad 20 \\
&\text{STOREIR} \quad 1
\end{aligned}
$$

     Note the difference between the last two assignments. While the address of component $b2$ in record r can be computed directly, namely $18 = 17 + 1$, this is not possible for component $b2$ of record $r.b2 \uparrow$ since the content of component $b2$ of r needs to be known. This component, or more precisely its corresponding RESA storage cell, contains the initial address of $r.b2 \uparrow$. To compute the initial address of this record a few RESA instructions are required. Note that LOAD 18 loads the initial address of $r.b2 \uparrow$ into the accumulator. STORE IR then places this address into the index register and STOREIR 1 stores into cell 1 relative to this address, i.e. into $r.b2 \uparrow .b2$. ∎

This example introduced an important principle in compilation, namely the distinction between **compile-time**, that is the time when a PROSA program is translated into a RESA program, and **run-time**, that is the time of execution of the generated RESA program. Information about a PROSA program and its execution already known at compile-time is called **compile-time information** (also **static**). Information known only at run-time is called **run-time information** (or **dynamic**). Component addresses of declared records are known at compile-time and are therefore static information. Having to add the initial address and relative address to determine that of the component involves two static values and therefore the result is also static. If, however, as in the case above, a record is accessed via a pointer variable then the initial address of the record is only known in the course of executing the RESA program. The address of a component of this record is equally the result of adding the relative address to the initial address. Here, on the other hand, one factor of the sum, the initial address, is dynamic and the other, the relative address, is static. The addition can therefore no longer be done by the compiler but must be realised by RESA instructions (in this case by an index register instruction).

Exercises for 5.4

1) Consider the example programs of Chapter IV and eliminate constant and record names.

5.5 Reducing Data Type bool to int

In this section the data type *bool* will be reduced to the data type *int*. This is also possible for *string* and *char*. This will be sketched briefly at the end of the section. Step 5.5 serves as preparation for step 5.6. There we will reduce records to arrays by "packing" all records created in a program into an integer array H. But then, to avoid type conflicts, there can only be one data type. In actual compilers step 5.5 is unnecessary since storage locations of actual computers can accommodate integer as well as boolean values. They also provide the basic operations for these values as machine instructions. This section therefore pays tribute to the simplicity of the RESA machine and the choice of describing the compilation process as far as possible as transformations of PROSA programs.

In order to keep this section transparent we proceed in several steps. In the first step we show that of the operators $=, \neq, >, \geq, <, \leq$ only $=$ and $>$ are really needed and that comparisons with 0 are sufficient. The second step separates the evaluation of expressions, by inserting auxiliary variables, into an arithmetic and a boolean part and in the third step we finally eliminate boolean variable and the boolean operators **AND, OR** and **NOT**. We shall now discuss the various steps in more detail.

Let E_1 and E_2 be integer expressions and $op \in \{=, \neq, >, \geq, <, \leq\}$. Because $(E_1 \; op \; E_2) = ((E_1 - E_2) \; op \; 0)$ we can confine ourselves to comparisons with 0 and may thus assume that all comparisons are of the form $E \; op \; 0$ where E is an integer expression. Because of $E \geq 0 = \textbf{not} \; (E < 0)$ and $E \leq 0 = \textbf{not} \; (E > 0)$ we may assume that only the relational operators $>$ and $<$ are used and, since $(E < 0) = (\textbf{not} \; ((E > 0) \; \textbf{or} \; (E = 0)))$, we even make do with the relational operator $>$. Finally, because of $(E \neq 0) = (\textbf{not} \; (E = 0))$ we can also assume that only the equality operator $=$ is used. Therefore all comparisons are of the form $E \; op \; 0$ where E is an integer expression and $op \in \{=, >\}$. This completes the first step.

Example 1:   According to these rules, expression $x < y$ will first be transformed into $x - y < 0$ and then into $\textbf{not} \; (((x - y) > 0) \; \textbf{or} \; ((x - y) = 0))$ ∎

In the second step we first restrict the occurrence of composed boolean expressions and then separate all expressions by introducing new variables into a boolean and an arithmetic part. We first want to achieve that conditional and iteration statements only test simple boolean variables. For each such statement we therefore introduce a new boolean variable, say b, and then transform the statement according to the following schema.

> **if** E **then** S_1 **else** S_2 **fi**

becomes

> $b := E$;
>
> **if** b **then** S_1 **else** S_2 **fi**

and

$$\textbf{while } E \textbf{ do } S \textbf{ od}$$

becomes

$$b := E;$$
$$\textbf{while } b \textbf{ do } S;\ b := E \textbf{ od}$$

Obviously this alteration leaves the meaning of the program unchanged.

Example 2:

$$\textbf{var } x, y : \textbf{integer};$$
$$x := 5;\ y := 2;$$
$$\textbf{while } (x - y > 0 \textbf{ and } y > 0) \textbf{ do } x := x - y \textbf{ od}$$

is therefore transformed into

$$\textbf{var } x, y : \textbf{integer}; \textbf{var } b : \textbf{boolean};$$
$$x := 5; y := 2;$$
$$b := x - y > 0 \textbf{ and } y > 0;$$
$$\textbf{while } b \textbf{ do } x := x - y; b := (x - y > 0 \textbf{ and } y > 0) \textbf{ od}$$

∎

Next we separate expressions into an arithmetic and a boolean part. Let E be an integer expression, $op \in \{=, >\}$ and let $E\ op\ 0$ be a subexpression of a boolean expression F. Finally, let F be the right-hand side of an assignment $x := F$. We introduce two new variables, say i and b (**var** i : **integer**; **var** b : **boolean**), and replace the assignment $x := F$ by

$$i := E;$$
$$\textbf{if } i\ op\ 0 \textbf{ then } b := \textbf{true}\ \textbf{ else } b := \textbf{false fi};$$
$$x := F'$$

Here F' is obtained from F by replacing $E\ op\ 0$ by b. Obviously this step also leaves the meaning unchanged. We apply the second step to all subexpressions $E\ op\ 0$ occurring in a program. The result is that all tests are of the form $i\ op\ 0$ with integer variable i and $op \in \{=, >\}$ or of the form b where b is a boolean variable. Besides that, all composed boolean expressions now only contain boolean variables, constants *true* and *false* and the operators **AND, OR, NOT**.

Example 2 (continued): The program is further transformed into

var x, y : **integer**; **var** b, b_1, b_2, b_3, b_4 : **boolean**; **var** i_1, i_2, i_3, i_4 : **integer**;
$x := 5, y := 2;$
$i_1 := x - y;$
$i_2 := y;$
if $i_1 > 0$ **then** $b_1 := $ **true** **else** $b_1 := $ **false fi**;
if $i_2 > 0$ **then** $b_2 := $ **true** **else** $b_2 := $ **false fi**;
$b := b_1$ **and** b_2;
while b
do $x := x - y;$
      $i_3 := x - y;$

$$i_4 := y;$$
if $i_3 > 0$ **then** $b_3 :=$ **true** **else** $b_3 :=$ **false fi**;
if $i_4 > 0$ **then** $b_4 :=$ **true** **else** $b_4 :=$ **false fi**;
$$b := b_3 \text{ and } b_4$$
od

In the third step we now replace all boolean variables by integer variables. We simulate *true* by 1 and *false* by 0. We proceed as follows.

(a) Replace each declaration of a boolean variable by the corresponding declaration of an integer variable, i.e. replace **var** b : **boolean** by **var** b : **integer** for all names b.

(b) Replace each boolean expression E on the right-hand side of an assignment by $conv(E)$ where function $conv$ is defined on boolean expressions as follows:

$$conv(E) = \begin{cases} E & E \text{ is a variable-name} \\ 1 & E = \text{true} \\ 0 & E = \text{false} \\ conv(E_1) * conv(E_2) & E = E_1 \text{ and } E_2 \\ (1 - (1 - conv(E_1)) * (1 - conv(E_2))) & E = E_1 \text{ or } E_2 \\ (1 - conv(E_1)) & E = \text{not } E_1 \\ conv(E_1) & E = (E_1) \end{cases}$$

(c) Replace each test b where b is a boolean variable by the comparison $b > 0$.

Example 3:   The boolean expression
$$b_1 \text{ or } (b_2 \text{ and } b_3)$$
is transformed into
$$(1 - (1 - b_1) * (1 - (b_2 * b_3))).$$

Example 2 (continued):   The program is further transformed into

var $x, y, b, b_1, b_2, b_3, b_4, i_1, i_2, i_3, i_4$: **integer**;
$$x := 5; y := 2;$$
$$i_1 := x - y;$$
$$i_2 := y;$$
if $i_1 > 0$ **then** $b_1 := 1$ **else** $b_1 := 0$ **fi**;
if $i_2 > 0$ **then** $b_1 := 1$ **else** $b_2 := 0$ **fi**;
$$b := (b_1 * b_2);$$
while $b > 0$
do $x := x - y;$
$\quad i_3 := x - y;$
$\quad i_4 := y;$

> **if** $i_3 > 0$ **then** $b_3 := 1$ **else** $b_3 := 0$ **fi**;
> **if** $i_4 > 0$ **then** $b_4 := 1$ **else** $b_4 := 0$ **fi**;
> $b := b_3 * b_4$
od

The correctness of the third step is not obvious. It follows, though, from a simple consideration. Let $i : \{true, false\} \to \mathbf{Z}$ with $i(true) = 1$ and $i(false) = 0$ be the embedding of truth values in the integers used in our simulation. Then for all $x, y \in \{true, false\}$:

$$i(x \text{ **and** } y) = i(x) \cdot i(y)$$
$$i(x \text{ **or** } y) = 1 - (1 - i(x)) * (1 - i(y))$$
$$i(\text{**not** } x) = 1 - i(x)$$

The reader can easily check these equations by trying different values for x and y. For example,

$$i(true \text{ **or** } false) = i(true) = 1$$

and

$$1 - (1 - i(true)) \cdot (1 - i(false)) = 1 - (1 - 1) \cdot (1 - 0) = 1$$

The definition of *conv* just uses the above identities. This proves the correctness of the third step. Let us summarise the discussion of this section.

Definition 1: A PROSA program is called **2-simple** if it is 1-simple, only integer variables are used and all boolean expressions are of the form $h \; op \; 0$ where $op \in \{=, >\}$ and h is an integer variable. Furthermore, boolean expressions only occur in tests of conditional statements and iteration statements.

Theorem 1. *For each simple PROSA program p there is an equivalent 2-simple PROSA program q. Program q can effectively be constructed and $comp_time(q, i) \le c + d \cdot comp_time(p, i)$ for all inputs $i \in \mathbf{Z}^*$. Here c and d are constants which depend on p but not on i.*

Proof: The first part of the theorem follows immediately from the above discussion. The assertion about *comp_time* can be seen as follows. We obtain program q from p in four steps. Let $q_i, 1 \le i \le 4$, be the program after the i-th step, and let $i \in \mathbf{Z}^*$ be arbitrary. The first step only changes the shape of the expressions and thus $comp_time(q_1, i) \le comp_time(p, i)$. The second step adds for each condition an assignment and thus $comp_time(q_2, i) \le 2 \cdot comp_time(q_1, i)$. In the third step we separate boolean expressions into an arithmetic and a boolean part. Let F be a boolean expression which has $b(F)$ subexpressions of the form $E \; op \; 0$. Then we introduce $2b(F)$ additional declarations, $b(F)$ assignments and $b(F)$ conditional statements (which take 2 steps). Altogether we add $c = \sum 2b(F)$ declarations (summation is over all boolean expressions occurring in q_2) and replace assignment

$x := F$ by a sequence of statements with computation time $3b(F) + 1$. Thus $comp_time(q_3, i) \leq c + d \cdot comp_time(q_2, i)$, where $d = max\{1 + 3b(F)\}$. The fourth step, finally, does not change the computation time, i.e. $comp_time(q_4, i) = comp_time(q_3, i)$. Together $comp_time(q, i) \leq c + 2d \cdot comp_time(q_2, i)$ ∎

Concluding we will briefly sketch the treatment of types *char* and *string*. Data type *char* is rather simple to deal with. Numbering the symbols of the alphabet like

$$a \leftrightarrow 0 \quad b \leftrightarrow 1 \quad c \leftrightarrow 2 \quad \ldots$$

leaves us with integers only. Since the only operations on symbols are comparisons we just have to be careful that the numbering reflects the alphabetical order of the symbols. The data type *string* is more difficult to treat. Usually strings are realised as linear lists of symbols. We will return to that in Section 6.2.

Exercises for 5.5

1) Determine $conv((b_1 \text{ and } (b_2 \text{ or not } (b_3 \text{ and } b_4))) \text{ or } b_5)$.

2) In the proof of Theorem 1 constants c and d were defined, for example $c = \sum b(F)$, where summation is over all boolean expressions F in program q_2. How must the definition of c be altered if the summation is over all boolean expressions in program p?

3) Apply the compilation step of this section to the example programs of Chapter IV.

5.6 Representing Records and Pointers by Arrays

We now show how records and pointers are represented by arrays. The method
is first introduced by example and then, by abstraction, the general method is
presented.

The following PROSA program reads a sequence of non-negative numbers,
builds from them a linear list and prints the second last element of the sequence.

```
program list;
  (* the input tape contains e_1,...,e_n,e_{n+1} with e_i ∈ N_0 for 1 ≤ i ≤ n and e_{n+1} ∈
  Z, e_{n+1} < 0 *)

  type element = record cont : integer; succ : ↑ element end;
  var i : integer; var p, q :↑ element ;

  (* we use p as list head and q as auxiliary variable *)

  begin
      read i ;
      while i ≥ 0
      do (* We have already constructed a list from e_1,...,e_{j-1}.
          The list head is p
          and i contains e_j for some j ≤ n.
          We now create a new list element,
          store e_j in it and append it at the front
          of the already existing list. *)
          q := new element;
          q↑. cont := i ;
          q↑. succ := p ;
          p := q ;
          read i
      od;

      (* next e_{n-2} is printed *)

      print p↑.succ↑.succ↑.cont
  end.
```

We shall now specify an equivalent program using only arrays. For that purpose
we employ two one-dimensional arrays *content* and *successor* and represent an object
of type *element* by a line, i.e. two variables of the two arrays with the same index.
The list head is replaced by an integer variable. The list of Figure 1 can then be
represented as shown in Figure 2.

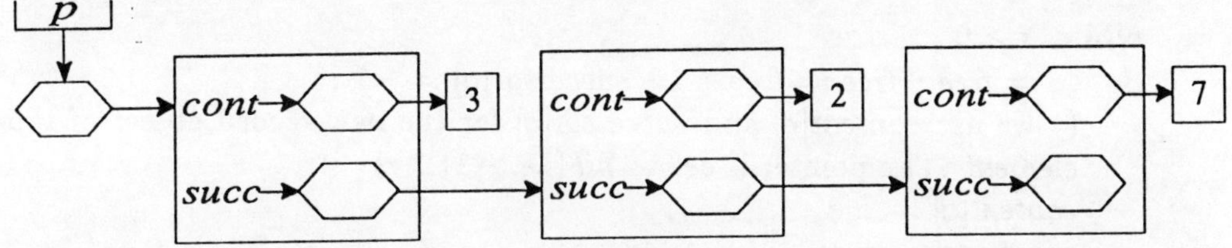

Fig. 1

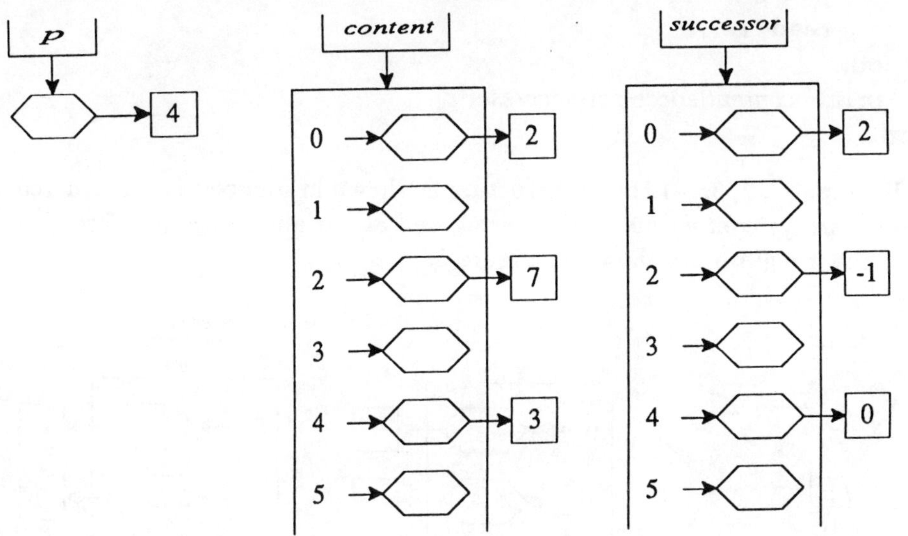

Fig. 2

In this example the first list element is stored in line 4 of the two arrays, thus p is 4. The second list element is in line 0 of the two arrays. thus $successor[4]$ has value 0. Finally, the last list element is in line 2, thus $successor[0] = 2$. The pointer of the last list element is *nil* which is represented by -1. Note that record objects are placed at arbitrary lines of the arrays.

With arrays our example program can now be written as follows.

```
program list1;
    var content , successor array[0 .. ∞]  of integer;
    var free : integer;
    var i: integer; var  p, q: integer;
    begin
        free := 0; p := -1; q := -1;
        (* nil is represented by -1 and thus p and q must be initialised with -1.
        In variable free we record which array elements are already used for record
        objects. Array elements with index 0,..., free-1 are already occupied and array
        elements free, free+1, ... are still available *)
        read  i ;
```

> **while** $i \geq 0$
> **do** $q := \textit{free}$; $\textit{free} := \textit{free} + 1$; $\textit{successor}[q] := -1$;
>   (* we use $\textit{content}[q]$ and $\textit{successor}[q]$ for the new record object of type
>   element. The pointer is set to $\textit{nil}$ (i.e. -1) . *)
> $\textit{content}[q] := i$;
> $\textit{successor}[q] := p$;
>   (* this sets the two components of the new element *)
> $p := q$;
>   **read** i
> **od**;
> **print** $\textit{content}[\textit{successor}[\textit{successor}[p]]]$
end.

For input 7, 2, 3, -1 the list structure as shown in Figure 1 is constructed. The values in arrays *content* and *successor* as well as variables p, q and *free* generated by the new program are shown in Figure 3.

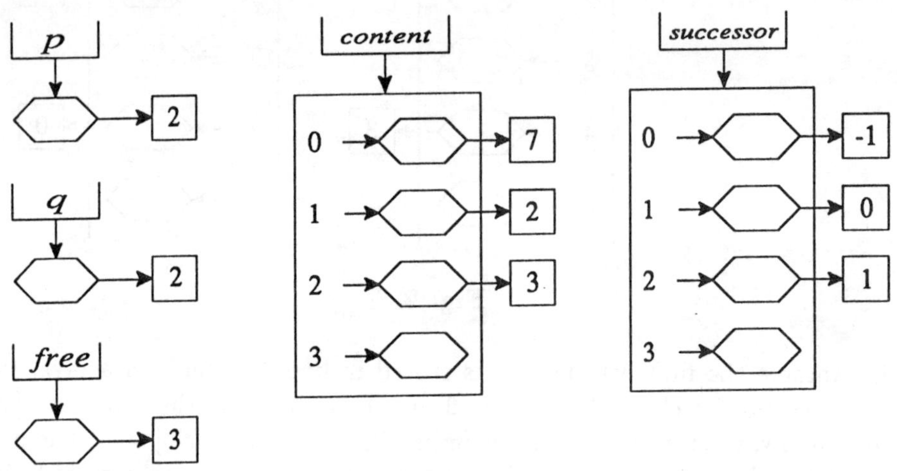

Fig. 3

In both programs the **print**-statement outputs number 7.

Before describing the method in general we will modify it slightly. With the above method, a potential infinite array is needed for each component of a record type. It is, however, difficult in RESA to accomplish several (potentially) infinite arrays efficiently. This is only feasible for one array (see Section 5.3). We therefore replace the two arrays *content* and *successor* by only one array H (H is usually called **heap**) and realise an object of type *element* by two successive array elements. This leads to the following program.

program *list2*;
   var H :**array**$[0\ ..\infty]$ **of integer**;
   var *free*: **integer**;

```
var i: integer; var p, q: integer;
begin
    free := 0; p := -2; q := -2;
    (* array elements H[free], H[free+1], ... are still available;
    -2 corresponds to nil *)
    read i;
    while i ≥ 0
    do  q := free; free := free+2; H[q+1] := -2;
        (* array elements H[q], H[q+1] realise the new object
        of type element;
        H[q] corresponds to the content component and
        H[q+1] to the successor component *)
        H[q] := i; H[q+1] := p;
        (* the components of the new object are set *)
        p := q ;
        read i
    od;
    print H[H[H[p+1]+1]]
end.
```

Input 7,2,3,−1 leads to an array H and variables *free*, q and p as shown in Figure 4.

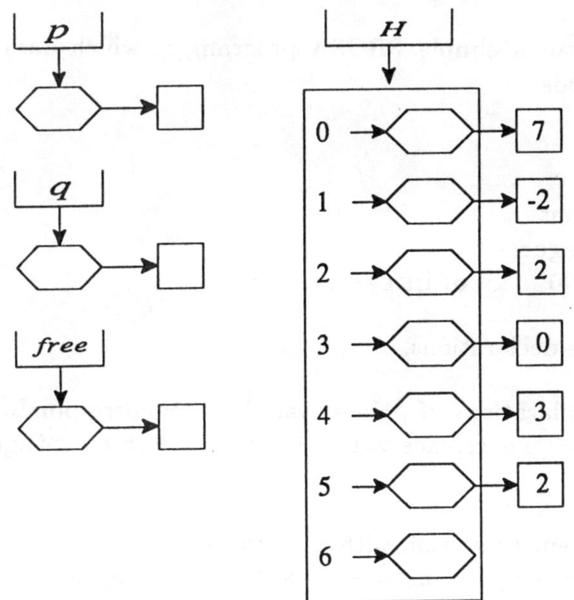

Fig. 4

Here $H[0]$ and $H[1]$ constitute the third list element, $H[2]$ and $H[3]$ the second and $H[4]$ and $H[5]$ the first list element. A pointer to a list element which is represented by cells $H[j]$ and $H[j+1]$ is realised by the number j. If, therefore, p is a pointer then

$H[p]$ corresponds to the component $p\uparrow.cont$ and $H[p+1]$ to the component $p\uparrow.succ$ of the object to which p refers. In particular, $H[H[H[p+1]+1]]$ corresponds to the component $p\uparrow.succ\uparrow.succ\uparrow.cont$. Furthermore replacing nil by -2 guarantees that, with $z = nil$ and therefore $z\uparrow.cont$ and $z\uparrow.succ$ undefined, $H[-2+0]$ and $H[-2+1]$ are also undefined.

After this introductory example we now give a general method for transforming a simple PROSA program into a program without records.

Algorithm for translating a simple PROSA program into a simple PROSA program without pointers and records

Input : A simple PROSA program p_1 without declarations for names H and *free*.

Output : An equivalent simple PROSA program p_2 which does not use pointers and records.

Method :

1) Add declarations
   var *free* : **integer**;
   var H : **array**$[0 .. \infty]$ **of integer**.

2) Delete all type declarations.

3) Replace all declarations of pointer variables by corresponding declarations of integer variables, i.e. replace **var** n: $\uparrow XYZ$ by **var** n: **integer** where XYZ is a type name.

4) Prefix the statement section with assignments
   free := 0; n_1 := $-c$; $\cdots$; n_k := $-c$; where $n_1,\ldots,n_k$ are the pointer variables declared in program p_1 and c is the maximal number of components of a record type.

5) Replace each name x in assignments, expressions and read statements by *subst*(x). Function *subst* :$\langle name \rangle \rightarrow \langle name \rangle$ is defined as follows (see the grammar for names in Section 4.3.2).

$$
subst(x) = \begin{cases}
x & \text{if } x \in \langle ident \rangle \\[2ex]
\begin{aligned}
&y[E_1', \ldots, E_k'] \\
&\quad \text{where } E_i' \text{ is } E_i \text{ with} \\
&\quad \text{names} \\
&\quad z \text{ replaced by } subst(z)
\end{aligned}
& \begin{aligned}
&\text{if } x = y[E_1, \ldots, E_k] \text{ with} \\
&\quad y \in \langle ident \rangle \text{ and} \\
&\quad E_1, \ldots, E_k \in \langle Expr \rangle
\end{aligned} \\[4ex]
H[subst(y) + k - 1]
& \begin{aligned}
&\text{if } x = y \uparrow .sel \\
&\quad \text{with } y \in \langle name \rangle \text{ and} \\
&\quad Type(y) = (var, XYZ) \\
&\quad \text{and } sel \text{ is the } k\text{-th se-} \\
&\quad \text{lector in record type} \\
&\quad XYZ
\end{aligned}
\end{cases}
$$

Explanation: Function *subst* replaces each selection via pointers by a selection of array H. If y is a pointer, then cells $H[subst(y)], \ldots$ represent the components of the record $y \uparrow$. In particular, $H[subst(y) + b - 1]$ corresponds to the b-th component of $y \uparrow$.

6) Replace each new-statement $x :=$ **new** XYZ where XYZ is a type name by the assignments

   $subst(x) :=$ free;
   free := free $+ k$;
   $H[subst(x) + i_1 - 1] := -c$;

   $\vdots$

   $H[subst(x) + i_l - 1] := -c$;

Here k is the number of components of the record type XYZ and components $i_1, \ldots, i_l$ of this record type are pointers.

Explanation : We allocate k cells on the heap for the record object. All components which are pointers are initialised by *nil*.

7) Replace **nil** by $-c$ ∎

We now illustrate this algorithm using our example. According to rules 1), 2) and 3) the declaration section becomes

$$\textbf{var } i : \textbf{integer} \; ; \; \textbf{var } p, q : \textbf{integer} \; ;$$
$$\textbf{var } \textit{free} : \textbf{integer} \; ;$$
$$\textbf{var } H : \textbf{array}[0 \, .. \, \infty] \textbf{ of integer};$$

In rule 4) the statement section is prefixed by the assignments

$$\textit{free} := \; 0 \; ; \; p := -2 \; ; \; q := -2 \; ;$$

Note that in our example $c = 2$. Rule 6) determines that

$$q := \textbf{new } \textit{element}$$

is replaced by

$$q := \textit{free} \; ; \; \textit{free} := \textit{free} + 2 \; ; H[q + 1] := -2;$$

Note that $\textit{subst}(q) = q$. Assignment $q \uparrow .\textit{cont} := i$ is replaced by $H[q + 1 - 1] := i$ and assignment $q \uparrow .\textit{succ} := p$ by $H[q + 2 - 1] := p$. Finally, the name in the print statement is changed to

$$\begin{aligned}
\textit{subst}&(p \uparrow .\textit{succ} \uparrow .\textit{succ} \uparrow .\textit{cont}) \\
&= H[\textit{subst}(p \uparrow .\textit{succ} \uparrow .\textit{succ}) + 1 - 1] \\
&= H[H[\textit{subst}(p \uparrow .\textit{succ}) + 2 - 1] + 1 - 1] \\
&= H[H[H[\textit{subst}(p) + 2 - 1] + 2 - 1] + 1 - 1] \\
&= H[H[H[p + 1] + 1]]
\end{aligned}$$

Taken together, the algorithm yields, at least in this example, the desired result. This has to be proved in general.

Definition 1: A PROSA program is called **3-simple** if it is 2-simple and, in addition, no pointers and records are used. The program may use an infinite array $H : \textbf{array}[0 .. \infty]$ **of integer**.

Theorem 1. *Let p_1 be a 2-simple PROSA program where names H and free are not used and let p_2 be obtained from p_1 according to the above algorithm. Then p_2 is 3-simple and p_1 and p_2 are equivalent, i.e. for all $i \in \mathbf{Z}^*$:*
$$I/O_M(p_1, \, i) = I/O_M(p_2, \, i).$$
Furthermore for all $i \in \mathbf{Z}^*$:
$$\textit{comp_time}(p_2, \, i) \; \le \; c_1 \; + \; c_2 \cdot \textit{comp_time}(p_1, \, i).$$
Here c_1 and c_2 are constants which depend on p_1 but not on i.

Remark: The proof of this theorem is large and consists in specifying a bisimulation R, see Section 1.7. R describes the relation between corresponding configurations of the original program p_1 and program p_2 obtained from it. We will first define R, then this definition will be explained in general and then using our example. The reader should study the following proof at least up to and including the explanations. The general explanations should be read in parallel to the definitions. In the rest of the proof we verify that R is a bisimulation. The verification is extensive and rather technical. It is done by an exhaustive discussion of possible PROSA statements. Although the verification carries a lot of technical detail it is, in principle, simple since it only requires mechanical application of the PROSA transition function and of the translation algorithm. The intellectual effort therefore lies mainly in specifying the translation algorithm and the bisimulation R.

Proof: First we define the bisimulation R. Let $c_k = (pr_k, \, b_k, \, s_k, \, i_k, \, o_k)$, $k = 1, \, 2$, be configurations of the PROSA machine. Then $(c_1, \, c_2) \in R$ if either $c_1 = in(p_1, i)$ and $c_2 = in(p_2, \, i)$ for some $i \in \mathbf{Z}^*$, or if the following four conditions are satisfied.

(1) pr_1 is a statement sequence and pr_2 is obtained from pr_1 using rules 5, 6 and 7 of the algorithm ;

(2) $i_1 = i_2$ and $o_1 = o_2$;

(3) $Def(b_2) = Def(b_1) \cup \{H, free\} - \{XYZ; XYZ$ is a type name in $p_1\}$,
$b_2(H) = h \in \mathbf{ARR}$, $Def(h) = \mathbb{N}_0$, $image(h) \subseteq \mathbf{V}_{int}$ and $b_2(free) \in \mathbf{V}_{int}$;

(4) Let $V_i = \mathbf{V} - \mathbf{FV}_{c_i}$, $i = 1, 2$, be the set of allocated variables in c_i. Then there is an injective mapping
$$\alpha : V_1 \to V_2 - \{b_2(H)(i); \ i \geq s_2(b_2(free))\} - \{b_2(free)\}$$
with the following properties:

  (a) for all $x \in Def(b_1)$ with $b_1(x) \in V_1 : \alpha(b_1(x)) = b_2(x)$;

  (b) for all $x \in Def(b_1)$ with $b_1(x) \in \mathbf{ARR} : Def(b_1(x)) = Def(b_2(x))$ and
    $\alpha(b_1(x)(i)) = b_2(x)(i)$ for all $i \in Def(b_1)$;

  (c) for all $v \in V_1 \cap \mathbf{V}_{int} : s_1(v) = s_2(\alpha(v))$;

  (d) for all $v \in V_1 \cap \mathbf{V}_{pointer}$:
    if $s_1(v) = nil$ then $s_2(\alpha(v)) = -c$
    and $s_1(v) = f \in \mathbf{REC}$ implies $\alpha(f(sel)) = b_2(H)(s_2(\alpha(v)) + i - 1)$
    for the i-th selector sel in the record type of f .

Explanation: The start configurations $c_1 = in(p_1, i)$ and $c_2 = in(p_2, i)$ obviously correspond to each other. Suppose now that c_1 is not a start configuration. We only consider the case that the declaration section of p_1 is already completely processed. We then require the program-rests in c_1 and c_2 to correspond, i.e. the program-rest in c_2 results from the translation algorithm applied to the program-rest in c_1 (property (1)). Input sequences and the output sequences should, of course, be equal (property (2)). The relation (property (3)) between bindings b_1 and b_2 is also obvious. Names H and $free$ are added to b_2 and all type names are dropped. Property (4) is most important. We require that for each allocated variable v in c_1 a corresponding variable $\alpha(v)$ in c_2 exists. Clearly, $\alpha(v)$ must be in the section of H which is already in use, i.e. before index $free$. Besides, variable $b_2(free)$ does not correspond to any variable in c_1. Mapping α must have properties (a) to (d). Property (a) states that variables with identifiers as names correspond to each other according to α, i.e. if name x denotes variable $b_1(x)$ in c_1 then it denotes variable $b_2(x) = \alpha(b_1(x))$ in c_2. Property (b) is a similar property for variables of arrays. If, for example, x is an array name, i.e. $b_1(x) \in \mathbf{ARR}$, then it is also an array name in c_2, an array of exactly the same size. Thus $b_2(x) \in \mathbf{ARR}$ and $Def(b_1(x)) = Def(b_2(x))$. Let now $i \in Def(b_1)$ be a permissible array index (if x is the name of a d-dimensional array then i is a d-tuple of integers). Then $b_1(x)(i)$ and $b_2(x)(i)$ are variables which must correspond to each other according to α, i.e. $\alpha(b_1(x)(i)) = b_2(x)(i)$. In (c) we require that corresponding integer variables have the same value. In (d) the analogous property for pointer variables is expressed. If v is nil then $\alpha(v)$ is $-c$. If the value of v is a record object f of type XYZ then the (say k) variables of f correspond to k successive variables in array H. More precisely, the relation is as follows. If $s_1(v) = f \in \mathbf{REC}$ then $s_2(\alpha(v))$ is an integer such that the variables with indices $s_2(\alpha(v)), \ldots, s_2(\alpha(v)) + k - 1$ in array H correspond to the k variables of the record f. For the i-th selector *sel* of f, in particular, we have the equation : $\alpha(f(sel)) = b_2(H)(s_2(\alpha(v)) + i - 1)$.

We now explain the bisimulation R using our example. Consider configurations with empty program rest. In Figure 5 the function α is indicated by dotted arrows. Note that $c = 2$.

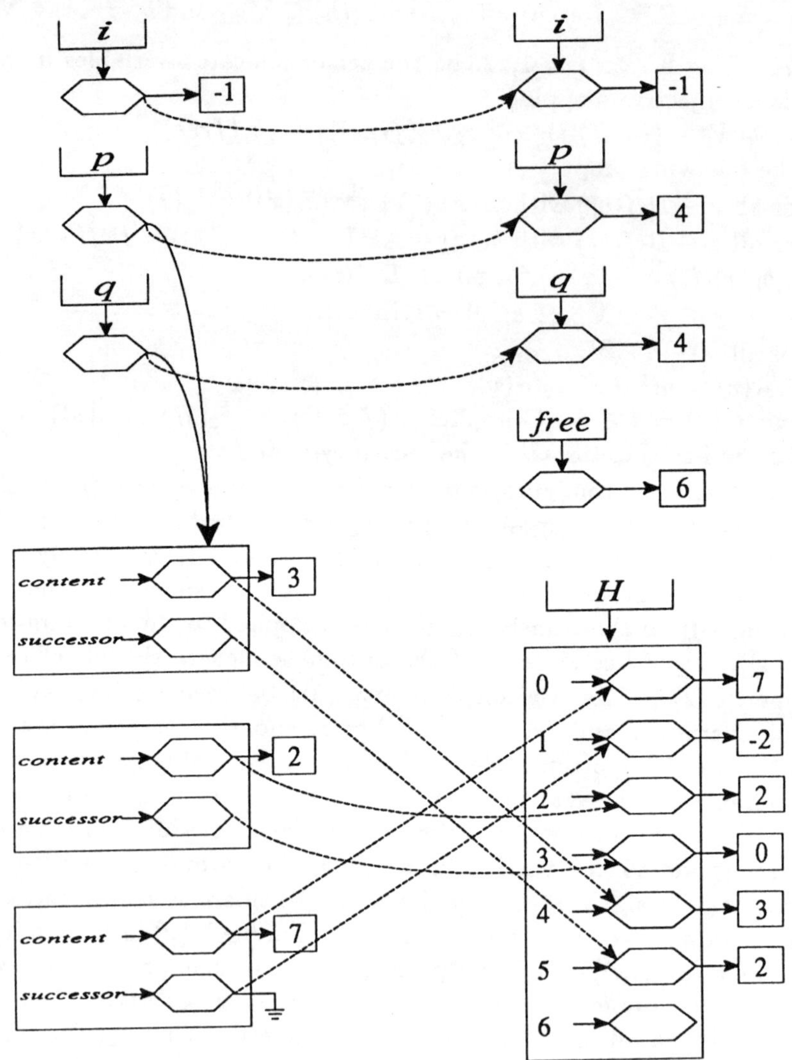

Fig. 5

For pointer variable v in the first list element, for example, $s_1(v)$ is the second list element. In this element *succ* selects variable w. We have $\alpha(w) = b_2(H)(3)$. Equation $s_2(\alpha(v)) = 2$ implies $3 = s_2(\alpha(v)) + 2 - 1$, i.e. property (4d) is satisfied.

We now commence with the proof of the theorem. Of the defining properties of a bisimulation the conditions concerning start states $((in(p_1, i), in(p_2, i)) \in R)$ and final states (for all c_1, c_2 : $(c_1, c_2) \in R$ implies $c_1 \in \mathbf{C}^f$ if and only if

$c_2 \in \mathbf{C}^f$) are obviously satisfied. We must therefore verify the condition for the transition function, i.e. for all c_1, c_2 with $(c_1, c_2) \in R$ there exists $i > 0, j > 0$ with $(\delta^{(i)}(c_1), \delta^{(j)}(c_2)) \in R$. We distinguish two cases.

Case 1: $c_1 = in(p_1, i)$, $c_2 = in(p_2, i)$ for some $i \in \mathbb{Z}^*$. We show $(c_1', c_2') \in R$, where c_1' results from c_1 by executing the declaration section of p_1 and c_2' is obtained from c_2 by executing the declaration section of p_2 plus the assignments generated by rule 4. Properties (1), (2) and (3) are obviously satisfied. For property (4) we must first define function α. For $v \in V_1$ and $v = b_1(n)$ for some name n define $\alpha(v) = b_2(n)$. For $v \in V_1$ and $v = b_1(n)(i)$ for some name n and an array index i (v is part of an array) define $\alpha(v) = b_2(n)(i)$. Then properties (4a) to (4d) are also satisfied. Thus $(c_1', c_2') \in R$.

Case 2 (not Case 1): The program-rest pr_1 starts in this case with a statement. We argue by case distinction according to this statement. Before that we prove a Lemma concerning the semantics of names and expressions.

Lemma 1. *Let $(c_1, c_2) \in R$, let x be a variable name which occurs in p_1 and let E be an expression occurring in p_1. Then*
a) *$\alpha(L(x, b_1, s_1)) = L(subst(x), b_2, s_2)$, i.e. x and $subst(x)$ denote corresponding variables.*
b) *$I(b_1, s_1, E)$ is defined if and only if $I(b_2, s_2, E')$ is defined. Furthermore from $I(b_1, s_1, E) \in \mathbb{Z}$ follows $I(b_1, s_1, E) = I(b_2, s_2, E')$. Expression E' in this case is obtained from E by replacing all variable names x by $subst(x)$.*

Proof: We prove the two parts jointly by structural induction.

Induction base: For part a) let $x \in \langle ident \rangle$. Then

$$
\begin{aligned}
\alpha(L(x, b_1, s_1)) &= \alpha(b_1(x)), && \text{def. of } L \\
&= b_2(x) && \text{by property (4a)} \\
&= L(x, b_2, s_2) && \text{def. of } L \\
&= L(subst(x), b_2, s_2) && \text{def. of } subst
\end{aligned}
$$

In part b) we must consider three cases, E is a standard name, E is a constant name or E is variable name. The first two cases are obvious. In the third case we distinguish between the subcases $L(E, b_1, s_1) \in \mathbf{V}_{int}$ and $L(E, b_1, s_1) \in \mathbf{V}_{pointer}$. If $L(E, b_1, s_1) \in \mathbf{V}_{int}$ then

$$
\begin{aligned}
I(b_1, s_1, E) &= s_1(L(E, b_1, s_1)) && \text{def. of } I \\
&= s_2(\alpha(L(E, b_1, s_1))) && \text{property (4c)} \\
&= s_2(L(subst(E), b_2, s_2)) && \text{by part a)} \\
&= I(b_2, s_2, subst(E)) && \text{def. of } I
\end{aligned}
$$

If $L(E, b_1, s_1) \in \mathbf{V}_{pointer}$ then $I(b_1, s_1, E) = s_1(L(E, b_1, s_1))$ is defined in each case (the value can be *nil*).
Thus by property (4d),

$$s_2(\alpha(L(E, b_1, s_1))) = s_2(L(subst(E), b_2, s_2)) = I(b_2, s_2, subst(E))$$

is also defined in each case.

Induction step: We first consider part a). The name x is either of the form $y[E_1, \ldots, E_k]$ or of the form $y \uparrow .n$.

Let $x = y[E_1, \ldots, E_k]$ where y is an array name and $E_1, \ldots, E_k$ are integer expressions. Then $subst(x) = y[E_1', \ldots, E_k']$ where E_i' results from E_i by replacing variable names z by $subst(z)$. By induction hypothesis $I(s_1, b_1, E_i) = I(s_2, b_2, E_i')$ for $1 \leq i \leq k$. Furthermore

$$\begin{aligned}
\alpha(L(x, b_1, s_1)) &= \alpha(b_1(y)(I(s_1, b_1, E_1), \ldots, I(s_1, b_1, E_k))) & \text{def. of } L \\
&= \alpha(b_1(y)(I(s_2, b_2, E_1'), \ldots, I(s_2, b_2, E_k'))) & \text{ind. hyp.} \\
&= b_2(y)(I(s_2, b_2, E_1'), \ldots, I(s_2, b_2, E_k')) & \text{property (4b)} \\
&= L(y[E_1', \ldots, E_k'], b_2, s_2) & \text{def. of } L \\
&= L(subst(x), b_2, s_2) & \text{def. of } subst
\end{aligned}$$

This completes the induction step in this case.

Let now $x = y \uparrow .n$ where y denotes a pointer variable of type XYZ and n the i-th selector in record type XYZ. By induction hypothesis $\alpha(L(y, b_1, s_1)) = L(subst(y), b_2, s_2)$. Furthermore $subst(x) = H[subst(y) + i - 1]$. We now distinguish between three cases.

Case 1: $L(y, b_1, s_1)$ is undefined. With $\alpha(L(y, b_1, s_1)) = L(subst(y), b_2, s_2)$ the term $L(subst(y), b_2, s_2)$ is also undefined and thus $s_1(L(y, b_1, s_1)) = s_2(L(subst(y), b_2, s_2))$ is undefined.

Case 2: $L(y, b_1, s)$ is defined and $s_1(L(y, b_1, s_1)) = nil$. Then $L(x, b_1, s_1)$ is undefined. Furthermore, by induction hypothesis, $\alpha(L(y, b_1, s_1)) = L(subst(y), b_2, s_2)$ and thus, by property (4d), $s_2(L(subst(y), b_2, s_2)) = -c$. Hence $s_2(L(subst(y), b_2, s_2)) + i - 1 < 0$ and consequently $L(subst(x), b_2, s_2) = L(H[subst(y) + i - 1], b_2, s_2)$ undefined. If, therefore, $s_1(L(y, b_1, s_1)) = nil$ then $L(x, b_1, s_1)$ as well as $L(subst(x), b_2, s_2)$ undefined.

Case 3: $L(y, b_1, s_1)$ is defined and $s_1(L(y, b_1, s_1)) \neq nil$. Then $s_1(L(y, b_1, s_1)) = f \in \mathbf{REC}$ and

$$\begin{aligned}
\alpha(L(x, b_1, s_1)) &= \alpha(s_1(L(y, b_1, s_1))(n)) & \text{def. of } L \\
&= b_2(H)(s_2(\alpha(L(y, b_1, s_1)) + i - 1) & \text{property (4d)} \\
&= b_2(H)(s_2(L(subst(y), b_2, s_2)) + i - 1) & \text{induction hypothesis} \\
&= b_2(H)(I(b_2, s_2, subst(y) + i - 1)) & \text{def. of } I \\
&= L(H[subst(y) + i - 1], b_2, s_2) & \text{def. of } L \\
&= L(subst(x), b_2, s_2) & \text{def. of } subst
\end{aligned}$$

This proves the induction step in the second case and thus altogether part a).

The induction step for part b) is trivial. Surely, the claim for a composite expression is correct if it holds for the subexpressions.

Returning to the proof of the theorem, we check, using Lemma 1, the transition conditions of a bisimulation. We proceed by case distinction on the first statement of the program-rest pr_1.

Case 1: The program-rest pr_1 starts with an assignment, i.e.
$pr_1 = x := E; pr_1'$ with $x \in \langle name \rangle$ and $E \in \langle expr \rangle$.
Then, by property (1) of relation R, the program-rest pr_2 is of the form $pr_2 = subst(x) := E'; pr_2'$ where E' results from E by applying $subst$ to all variable names in E and pr_2' is obtained from pr_1' by applying rules 5, 6 and 7 of the translation algorithm. We now distinguish between two cases depending on whether x denotes an integer variable or a pointer variable.

Case 1.1: x denotes an integer variable. By Lemma 1 we have $I(b_1, s_1, E) = I(b_2, s_2, E')$ and $\alpha(L(x, b_1, s_1)) = L(subst(x), b_2, s_2)$. Hence for the successor configurations $c_1' = \delta(c_1)$ and $c_2' = \delta(c_2)$ we have: if either $I(b_1, s_1, E)$ or $L(x, b_1, s_1)$ are undefined then so are $I(b_2, s_2, E')$ or $L(subst(x), b_2, s_2)$, respectively. In both cases there exists no successor state. Let now all four be defined. Then $c_1' = (pr_1', b_1, s_1', i_1, o_1)$ and $c_2' = (pr_1', b_2, s_2', i_1, o_1)$ with

$$s_1' = s_1[L(x, b_1, s_1) \backslash I(b_1, s_1, E)] \text{ and}$$
$$s_2' = s_2[L(subst(x), b_2, s_2) \backslash I(b_2, s_2, E')]$$

Thus surely properties (1), (2), (3), (4a), (4b) and (4d) for the pair (c_1', c_2') are satisfied. We must still prove (4c). Let $v \in V_1 \cap \mathbf{V}_{int}$ be arbitrary. If $v = L(x, b_1, s_1)$ then

$$\begin{aligned}
s_1'(v) &= I(b_1, s_1, E) && \text{def. of } s_1' \\
&= I(b_2, s_2, E') && \text{Lemma 1} \\
&= s_2'(L(subst(x), b_2, s_2)) && \text{def. of } s_2' \\
&= s_2'(\alpha(L(x, b_1, s_1))) && \text{Lemma 1} \\
&= s_2'(\alpha(v)) && \text{def. of } v
\end{aligned}$$

and (4c) is shown. If $v \neq L(x, b_1, s_1)$ then $s_1'(v) = s_1(v)$. Furthermore, because α is injective, we also have $\alpha(v) \neq \alpha(L(x, b_1, s_1)) = L(subst(x), b_2, s_2)$ and thus $s_2'(\alpha(v)) = s_2(\alpha(v))$. This proves property (4c) in this case because $s_1(v) = s_2(\alpha(v))$.

Case 1.2: x denotes a pointer variable. Then E is also the name of a pointer variable. Let $c_1' = \delta(c_1)$ and $c_2' = \delta(c_2)$. As in case 1.1 one can see that either both transitions do not exist or both transitions exist. In the first case there is nothing to be shown. In the second case we have $c_1' = (pr_1', b_1, s_1', i_1, o_1)$ and $c_2' = (pr_2', b_2, s_2', i_1, o_1)$ with

$$s_1' = s_1[L(x, b_1, s_1) \backslash I(b_1, s_1, E)] \text{ and}$$
$$s_2' = s_2[L(subst(x), b_2, s_2) \backslash I(b_2, s_2, E')]$$

Thus properties (1), (2), (3), (4a), (4b), (4c) for the pair (c_1', c_2') are clearly satisfied. We must now prove property (4d). Since E is the name of a pointer variable, by definition of I,

$$I(b_1, s_1, E) \;=\; s_1(L(E, b_1, s_1))$$

and

$$
\begin{aligned}
I(b_2, s_2, E') &= s_2(L(E', b_2, s_2)) && \text{def. of } I \\
&= s_2(L(subst(E), b_2, s_2)) && \text{since } E' = subst(E) \\
&= s_2(\alpha(L(E, b_1, s_1))) && \text{Lemma 1}
\end{aligned}
$$

With $v = L(x, b_1, s_1)$ and $w = L(E, b_1, s_1)$ we can also write

$$
\begin{aligned}
s_1' &= s_1[v \backslash s_1(w)] \quad \text{and} \\
s_2' &= s_2[\alpha(v) \backslash s_2(\alpha(w))]
\end{aligned}
$$

If now $s_1(w) = nil$ then, by (4d), $s_2(\alpha(w)) = -c$ and one can see as in case 1.1 that property (4d) holds for s_1' and s_2'. Let now $s_1(w) \neq nil$. Then $s_1(w) = f$ for some $f \in \mathbf{REC}$ and hence $s_1'(v) = f$. Let sel be the i-th selector in the record type of f. Then

$$
\begin{aligned}
\alpha(f(sel)) &= b_2(H)(s_2(\alpha(w)) + i - 1), && \text{since (4d) holds for } c_1, \ c_2 \\
&= b_2(H)(s_2'(\alpha(v)) + i - 1) \ , && \text{by def. of } \alpha'
\end{aligned}
$$

and consequently (4d) is also satisfied for s_1' and s_2'. This concludes case 1.2 and the discussion of the assignment.

Case 2: The program-rest pr_1 starts with a new-statement, i.e. $pr_1 = x \; :=$ **new** XYZ; pr_1' with $x \in \langle name \rangle$ and $XYZ \in \langle ident \rangle$. x denotes a pointer variable of type XYZ and XYZ denotes a record type. Let $n_1, \ldots, n_k$ be the selectors of this record type and let t_i be the type of the i-th component. t_i is either an elementary type and then equal to *int* or a pointer type. Let $i_1, \ i_2, \ldots, i_l$ be the components which are pointers. Then pr_2 has the form

$$
\begin{aligned}
&subst(x) := free; \\
&free := free + k; \\
&H[subst(x) + i_1 - 1] := -c; \\
&\qquad\qquad \vdots \\
&H[subst(x) + i_l - 1] := -c; \ pr_2'
\end{aligned}
$$

where pr_2' results from pr_1' by applying rules 5, 6 and 7 of the translation algorithm. If $L(x, b_1, s_1)$ is undefined then, by Lemma 1, $L(subst(x), b_2, s_2)$ is also undefined and in both cases the successor configurations do not exist. Let now $L(x, b_1, s_1)$ be defined. Then $L(subst(x), b_2, s_2)$ is also defined.
For $c_1' = \delta(c_1) = (pr_1', b_1, s_1', i_1, o_1)$ and $c_2' = \delta^{(2+l)}(c_2) = (pr_2', b_2, s_2', i_1, o_1)$, Figure 6 shows how s_1' changes into s_1 and s_2' changes into s_2. Here $m = s_2(b_2(free))$.

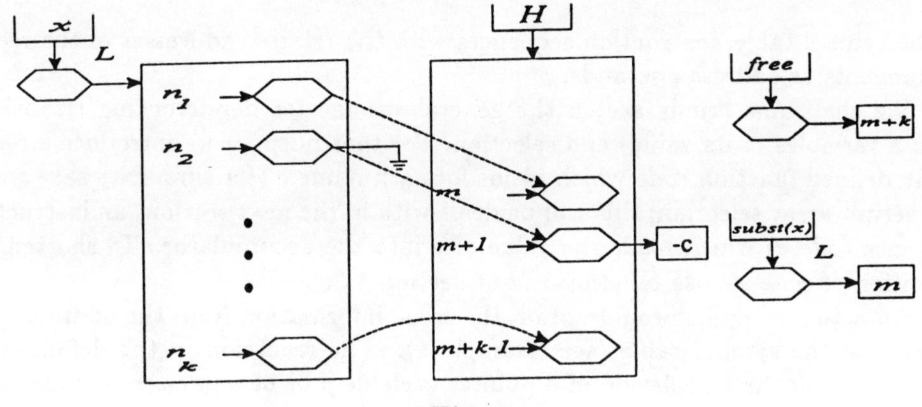

Fig. 6

In the diagram we further assumed that n_2 selects a pointer variable. We now only need to extend mapping α to a mapping α' as given by the dotted arrows. Then the pair (c_1', c_2') together with α' obviously satisfies conditions (1) to (4). Thus $(c_1', c_2') \in R$. This completes the discussion of the new-statement.

The remaining cases are the read and print statement, the conditional statement and the iteration statement. They are all simpler than the treated cases and thus are left to the reader.

Finally, we must show the claim concerning computation time. We first observe that by rules (5), (6) and (7) a statement of p_1 gives rise to at most $c+2$ statements of p_2. c is the maximal number of components in a record type. Furthermore rules (1), (2) and (3) extend the declaration section by at most 2 declarations and rule (4) appends at most $d+1$ statements. Here d is the number of declarations in p_1. Together therefore

$$comp_time(p_2, e) \leq (c+2) \cdot comp_time(p_1, e) + d + 3,$$

and the claim is established. ∎

We now have taken the most difficult step on the way from simple to primitive PROSA. In the next two sections we will reduce multi-dimensional arrays to one-dimensional arrays and simplify the syntax of expressions. Before we come to that, though, some considerations concerning actual compilers are necessary.

An actual compiler discards record declarations and record selections not by a translation from PROSA to PROSA, but directly generates RESA instruction sequences for the record selections (in the multi-stepped approach chosen here these instruction sequences are also generated. However, the relation between PROSA statement and generated RESA instruction sequence is no longer obvious.) In order to enable the generation of instructions an actual compiler enters all information about a record declaration in the symbol table. In this case it is the binding of component names to their type and their address relative to the beginning of the record. Besides, the storage requirement for all objects of a record type is the same. It can be determined at compile time and can equally be entered into the symbol table. If the compiler encounters a name it generates for it, with the help of the symbol table, instruction sequences with the relative addresses of the record components as address operands.

We shall now briefly sketch the general scheme for dereferencing (transition from a variables to its value) and selection. For that purpose we introduce a recursively defined function *code* which yields for each name e (for simplicity sake we do not permit array selection; this will be dealt with in the next section) an instruction sequence $code(e)$ which loads the value of e into the accumulator. To shorten the definition of *code* we use function *rad* of Section 5.3.

An actual compiler would obtain the same information from the address components of the symbol table (see Example 1). The recursion in the definition of *code* ends with the translation of a pointer variable p or of a pointer component of a record v.

$$
\begin{aligned}
code(p) &= \text{LOAD} & rad(p) \\
code(v.x) &= \text{LOADNUM} & rad(v) \\
&= \text{STORE} & \text{IR} \\
&= \text{LOADIR} & rad(x)
\end{aligned}
$$

In general

$$
\begin{aligned}
code(e \uparrow .x) &= code(e) \\
&= \text{STORE} & \text{IR} \\
&= \text{test for } nil \\
&= \text{LOADIR} & rad(x)
\end{aligned}
$$

Here "test for nil" stands for an instruction sequence which leads to an error halt if e points to nil. Next we extend function *code* to assignments. Let y be a simple variable. When generating the instruction sequences we must take into account whether the value of a selected component or its address is required. We have

$$
\begin{aligned}
code(e \uparrow .x := y) &= code(e) \\
&= \text{STORE} & \text{IR} \\
&= \text{test for } nil \\
&= \text{LOAD} & rad(y) \\
&= \text{STOREIR} & rad(x) \\
code(y := e \uparrow .x) &= code(e \uparrow .x) \\
&= \text{STORE} & rad(y)
\end{aligned}
$$

Because of the shortage of registers in RESA we must consider the following case especially.

$$
\begin{aligned}
code(e_1 \uparrow .x_1 := e_2 \uparrow .x_2) = &= code(e_1) \\
&= \text{STORE} & t_1 \\
&= \text{test for } nil \\
&= code(e_2 \uparrow .x_2) \\
&= \text{STORE} & t_2 \\
&= \text{LOAD} & t_1 \\
&= \text{STORE} & \text{IR} \\
&= \text{LOAD} & t_2 \\
&= \text{STOREIR} & rad(x_1)
\end{aligned}
$$

Thus in this case the address of the record referred to by e_1 and the value of
component x_2 in the record referred to by e_2 must be stored in auxiliary storage
cells t_1 and t_2. A general mechanism which guarantees that these auxiliary storage
cells can be chosen without side effect on the rest of the storage state can be found
in Section 5.8.

Example 1:   Consider the declaration section
type *person* = **record**

$$\begin{array}{lll} pn & : & \textbf{integer}; \\ spouse & : & \uparrow person\,; \\ age & : & \textbf{integer} \end{array}$$

       end;

var p: $\uparrow$ *person*; **var** q: **integer**.

This leads to symbol table entries

$$\begin{aligned} person \rightarrow\ & (type, \\ & \quad (pn \rightarrow (var,\ int,\ 0) \\ & \quad\ spouse \rightarrow (var,person,\ 1) \\ & \quad\ age \rightarrow (var,\ int,\ 2)),\ 3) \\ p \quad\ & \rightarrow (var,\ person,\ 37) \\ q \quad\ & \rightarrow (var,\ int,\ 38). \end{aligned}$$

The assignment

$$q := p \uparrow .spouse \uparrow .spouse \uparrow .age$$

is translated into

```
LOAD        37
STORE       IR
test for nil
LOADIR       1
STORE       IR
test for nil
LOADIR       1
STORE       IR
test for nil
LOADIR       2
STORE       38
```

For the representation of *nil* we choose value -1 since it is no valid RESA
data storage address. Every test for *nil* above will therefore be translated into a
test for -1. Note the difference to the treatment of *nil* at the beginning of the
section. There we did not explicitly test for *nil*, but intended that a selection for
a *nil*-object leads to a non-permissible index in array H. The two ways of treating
nil are equivalent.

Exercises for 5.6

1) Apply step 5.6 to the example programs of Chapter IV.

2) Fill in the missing parts in the proof of Theorem 1, i.e. complete the proof for the read and print statement, the conditional statement and the iteration statement.

3) Compute constants c_1 and c_2 for the example program used in this section.

4) Translate the example programs to RESA.

5) (Exercise 2 of Section 5.3 continued) Modify the translation in such a way that it also works if all RESA storage cells have value 0 at the beginning of the computation. Hint: Allocate for a record with b elements $2b$ elements of array H and use k of them to record which components have a defined value.

5.7 Multi-dimensional Arrays

In this section multi-dimensional arrays are reduced to one-dimensional arrays.

Example 1: Let a be a two-dimensional array with index ranges 3 .. 5 and 2 .. 3. We write the array elements as a matrix and number the matrix line by line starting with 0

$$
\begin{array}{cc}
a[3,2] & a[3,3] \\
0 & 1 \\
a[4,2] & a[4,3] \\
2 & 3 \\
a[5,2] & a[5,3] \\
4 & 5
\end{array}
$$

The number of the array element $a[i,j]$ can easily be computed using the formula $(i-3)\cdot(3-2+1)+j-2$. Here $3-2+1$ is the number of elements per line. Instead of array a we can thus declare an array $\tilde{a}$ with index range $[0 .. 5]$ and replace each occurrence of $a[i,j]$ by $\tilde{a}[(i-3)*2+(j-2)]$.   ∎

In general this method is based on the following Lemma.

Lemma 1. *Let $l_1, u_1, l_2, u_2, \ldots, l_k, u_k$ be integers with $l_i \leq u_i$ for $1 \leq i \leq k$. Let $D = [l_1 \ .. \ u_1] \times [l_2 \ .. \ u_2] \times \ldots \times [l_k \ .. \ u_k]$, and let $\tilde{D} = [0 \ .. \ \prod_{i=1}^{k}(u_i - l_i + 1) - 1]$. Then the mapping*

$$\alpha : D \to \tilde{D}$$

with

$$\alpha(i_1, \ldots, i_k) = \sum_{j=1}^{k}\{(i_j - l_j) \cdot \prod_{n=j+1}^{k}(u_n - l_n + 1)\}$$

is a bijection.

Proof: Note first that $|D| = |\tilde{D}|$ and $\alpha(D) \subseteq \tilde{D}$. We must therefore only show that α is injective. With $(i_1, \ldots, i_k), (i'_1, \ldots, i'_k)$ two different elements of D and m the smallest index for which $i_m \neq i'_m$, for example $i_m < i'_m$, we have

$$\alpha(i'_1, \ldots, i'_k) - \alpha(i_1, \ldots, i_k)$$

$$\geq \alpha(i'_1, \ldots, i'_m, l_{m+1}, \ldots, l_k) - \alpha(i_1, \ldots, i_m, u_{m+1}, \ldots, u_k)$$

$$= (i'_m - i_m) \prod_{n=m+1}^{k}(u_n - l_n + 1) - \sum_{j=m+1}^{k}\{(u_j - l_j) \prod_{n=j+1}^{k}(u_n - l_n + 1)\}$$

since $i'_n = i_n$ for $1 \leq l < m$

$$\geq \prod_{n=m+1}^{k}(u_n - l_n + 1) - \sum_{j=m+1}^{k}\{(u_j - l_j) \prod_{n=j+1}^{k}(u_n - l_n + 1)\}$$

since $i'_m \geq i_m + 1$

$$= (u_{m+1} - l_{m+1} + 1) \prod_{n=m+2}^{k}(u_n - l_n + 1) - (u_{m+1} - l_{m+1}) \prod_{n=m+2}^{k}(u_n - l_n + 1)$$

$$- \sum_{j=m+2}^{k}\{(u_j - l_j) \prod_{n=j+1}^{k}(u_n - l_n + 1)\},$$

by extracting the first term of the product and separating a term from the sum,

$$= \prod_{n=m+2}^{k}(u_n - l_n + 1) - \sum_{j=m+2}^{k}\{(u_j - l_j) \prod_{n=j+1}^{k}(u_n - l_n + 1)\}$$

by subtracting the first two terms. Note that the formula now has the same form as in line four except that $m+1$ is replaced by $m+2$. We can thus continue in the same way.

$$= \cdots$$

$$= (u_k - l_k + 1) - (u_k - l_k) = 1.$$

∎

Lemma 1 suggests simulating a k-dimensional array $a[l_1 \mathbin{..} u_1, \ldots, l_k \mathbin{..} u_k]$ by a one-dimensional array $\tilde{a}[0 \mathbin{..} \prod_{i=1}^{k}(u_i - l_i + 1) - 1]$. We then only need to replace each selection $a[i_1, \ldots, i_k]$ by a selection $\tilde{a}[\alpha(i_1, \ldots, i_k)]$. This has to be done carefully.

Example 1 (continued): We have $\alpha(i,j) = (i-3) \times 2 + j - 2$. The selection $a[3,4]$ leads to an error, but selection $\tilde{a}[(3-3) \times 2 + 4 - 2]$ is permitted. ∎

The example shows that mapping α of Lemma 1 can also map elements from outside D onto elements within $\tilde{D}$. It is therefore not sufficient just to replace a k-tuple $(i_1, \ldots, i_k)$ by $\alpha(i_1, \ldots, i_k)$. We rather must test if all indices i_n are permissible, i.e. we must test $l_n \leq i_n \leq u_n$ for all $n, 1 \leq n \leq k$. This leads to the following method which we first illustrate by an example.

Example 2: Consider the following PROSA program section

```
var  a : array[3..5, 2..3] of integer;
var  j: integer;
begin
    a[3,2] := 5;
    j := 4;
    a[a[3, j − 2], j − 2] := 6
end.
```

We first replace the declaration of array a by **var** $\tilde{a}$: **array**$[0 \mathbin{..} 5]$ **of integer**. In the statement section we then must replace selections of a by selections of $\tilde{a}$ and the necessary checks of the indices. We treat the different selections of a one by one. In the case of nested selections we proceed inside out. In the example we first deal with selections $a[3,2]$ and $a[3,j-2]$. We introduce for each of the two selections two new variables (here i_1, x_1 and i_2, x_2) and compute in one the index and in the other the value of the array element.

```
var  ã : array[0 .. 5] of integer;
var  j : integer; var  i₁, i₂, x₁, x₂ : integer;
begin
    if  (3 < 3) or (3 > 5) or (2 < 2) or (2 > 3)
    then error halt
    fi;
    i₁ := (3 − 3) * (3 − 2 + 1) + (2 − 2);
    x₁ := 5;
    a[i₁] := x₁;
    j := 4;
```

if $(3 < 3)$**or** $(3 > 5)$**or** $(j - 2 < 2)$**or** $(j - 2 > 3)$
then error halt
fi;
$i_2 := (3 - 3) * (3 - 2 + 1) + j - 2 - 2;$
$x_2 := \tilde{a}[i_2];$
$a[x_2, j - 2] := 6$
end
Next we deal with $a[x_2, j - 2]$ in the same way and replace it by

if $(x_2 < 3)$**or** $(x_2 > 5)$**or** $(j - 2 < 2)$**or** $(j - 2 > 3)$
then error halt fi;
$i_3 := (x_2 - 3) * (3 - 2 + 1) + j - 2 - 2;$
$x_3 := 6;$
$\tilde{a}[i_3] := x_3$

We now have a program which only uses one-dimensional arrays. Furthermore there are only simple variables in index position now, and no array selections occurs in composite expressions. Unfortunately the program now is no longer 2-simple . We thus apply the algorithm of Section 5.3 once again to restore 2-simplicity.   ∎

In general we proceed according to the following algorithm.
(1) Replace each array declaration
    var a : **array**$[l_1 .. u_1, l_2 .. u_2, \ldots, l_k .. u_k]$ **of integer**
in the declaration section by
    var $\tilde{a}$: **array**$[0 .. \prod_{j=1}^{k}(u_j - l_j + 1) - 1]$ **of integer**

(2) Process the statement section as follows:
  (a) mark all occurrences of array names as non-processed;
  (b) **while** there is a non-processed occurrence of an array name
    do Let $a[E_1, \ldots, E_k]$ be a non-processed occurrence where expressions E_1, $\ldots, E_k$ do not contain array names

    (∗ note that array names only can occur in assignments and print statements ∗);

    immediately before the statement which contains the non-processed array selection $a[E_1, \ldots, E_k]$ insert the statement sequence
      if $(E_1 < l_1)$ **or** $(E_1 > u_1)$ **or** $\ldots$ **or** $(E_k < l_k)$ **or** $(E_k > u_k)$
      then error halt fi;
      $i := \sum_{j=1}^{k}(E_j - l_j) \prod_{n=j+1}^{k}(u_n - l_n + 1);$
    where i is a new integer variable ;
    if $a[E_1, \ldots, E_k]$ is on the left-hand side of an assignment
    $a[E_1, \ldots, E_k] := E$ then replace this assignment by

        $x := E;$
        $\tilde{a}[i] := x$

    if $a[E_1, \ldots, E_k]$ occurs in a read statement **read** $a[E_1, \ldots, E_k]$
    then replace this statement by

$$\textbf{read } x; \quad \tilde{a}[i] := x$$

if $a[E_1, \ldots, E_k]$ is part of an expressions E then add statement

$$x := \tilde{a}[i];$$

and replace $a[E_1, \ldots, E_k]$ in E by x;

x is in each case a new integer variable.

(3) Make the program obtained by (1) and (2) 2-simple (see Section 5.3). ∎

The reader should check again that we proceeded in our example above exactly as specified in the algorithm. We now summarise the discussion.

Definition 1: A PROSA program is called **4-simple** if it is 3-simple and, in addition, satisfies the following properties. All used arrays are one-dimensional and the index range always starts at 0. Only simple variables occur in index positions of array selections. Furthermore array selections only occur in assignments of the form $x := a[i]$ and $a[i] := x$ where i and x are simple variables.

Theorem 1. *For each 3-simple PROSA program p_1 there is an equivalent 4-simple PROSA program p_2. Program p_2 can be generated using the algorithm above. Furthermore for all $e \in \mathbf{Z}^* : comp_time(p_2, e) \le c_1 + c_2 comp_time \cdot (p_1, e)$. Here c_1 and c_2 are constants which depend on p_1 but not on e.*

Proof: Let p_1 be a 3-simple PROSA program and let p_2 be the result of applying the above algorithm to p_1. We first show that p_2 is 4-simple. Obviously p_2 only contains one-dimensional arrays whose index range starts at 0. Furthermore all newly generated array selections occur in assignments of the form $\tilde{a}[i] := x$ and $x := \tilde{a}[i]$ with i and x simple variables. All array selections in p_2 are of the desired form since each array selection in p_1 is processed by the algorithm. Insertion of conditional statements for index checks destroys 2-simplicity. This is restored in step three. Thus p_2 is 4-simple.

It remains to show that p_2 and p_1 are equivalent. The inserted conditional statements check if the indices are in the permissible range. For permissible indices function α of Lemma 1 is bijective. Hence there is a one-one correspondence between the elements of the arrays in program p_1 and the arrays in p_2. Thus p_1 and p_2 are equivalent. Processing array selections generates a certain number of declarations and statements. Thus for all $i \in \mathbf{Z}^* : comp_time(p_2, i) \le c_1 + c_2 \cdot comp_time(p_1, i)$ for suitable constants c_1 and c_2 which depend on p_1 but not on e. ∎

Actual compilers directly generate RESA instruction sequences for array selection. The symbol table entry for an array was already described in Section 5.2. It contains, besides type and dimension, a description of the array bounds and the initial address of the array. For the two-dimensional array a in Example 1 the description of bounds is $(3,5)$, $(2,3)$.

Considering the bijective mapping $\alpha \; : \; D \to \tilde{D}$ of Lemma 1 indicates the form of a RESA instruction sequence which selects element $a[i_1,\ldots,i_k]$ of array $a[l_1 \,..\, u_1, l_2 \,..\, u_2, \ldots, l_k \,..\, u_k]$. Given a placement of the array at the RESA address $c = rad(a)$, an array component $a[i_1,\ldots,i_k]$ has the address $c + \alpha(i_1,\ldots,i_k)$. Component $a[l_1,\ldots,l_k]$ therefore has address c, $a[l_1,l_2,\ldots,l_k+1]$ is located at address $c+1$ and $a[l_1+1,l_2,\ldots,l_k]$ at $c + \prod_{n=2}^{k}(u_n - l_n + 1)$.

Let us consider the static and the dynamic parts of the expression for $\alpha(i_1,\ldots,i_k)$. Since the array bounds l_n and u_n are taken from the declaration, i.e. they are static, we can compute the size of the n-th dimension $d_n = u_n - l_n + 1$ statically. If the compiler is to be efficient one enters this value in the symbol table. The expression for $\alpha(i_1,\ldots,i_k)$ then is

$$\sum_{j=1}^{k}(i_j - l_j) \times \prod_{n=j+1}^{k} d_n.$$

Such expressions can be evaluated by Horner's scheme, i.e.

$$\alpha(i_1,\ldots,i_k) \; = \; (\ldots((i_1 - l_1) \times d_1 + i_2 - l_2) \times d_2 + \ldots i_k - l_k) \times d_k$$

This can be written easily as a PROSA program:

```
l := 1;  t := 0;
while  l ≤ k do
t := (t + iₙ - lₙ) × dₙ;
l := l + 1
od
```

For the translation of the while-loop into RESA see Section 5.3. The translation of expressions will be discussed in Section 5.8. Once again note the different sorts of names in the PROSA program for the selection of an array component: k, $l_1,\ldots.l_k, d_1,\ldots,d_k$ denote static quantities and are therefore constants when the compiler generates RESA instructions; $i_1,\ldots, i_k$ are index expressions in the PROSA program to be translated. They are, in general, not static. For their evaluation RESA instruction sequences must be generated. l and t are additional names which correspond to additional storage cells in the RESA data storage.

Exercises for 5.7

1) Translate the example program of this section into RESA.

2) Compute constants c_1 and c_2 for the example program of this section. Give a general definition of c_1 and c_2.

3) Apply step 5.7 to the example programs of Chapter IV.

4) The elements of a multi-dimensional array were numbered in this section line by line. Number them column-wise and rewrite this section accordingly.

5.8 Translating Expressions into primitive Expressions

The previous sections brought quite an achievement. For each simple PROSA program an equivalent 4-simple PROSA program was constructed. In this section we will take the last step in the translation to primitive PROSA. 4-simple PROSA programs already satisfy properties (1), (2), (3), (5) and (7) of Definition 2 in Section 5.1. Furthermore read statements are already of the form **read** x where x is the name of a simple variable.

We now transform print statements to the desired form. For that purpose we introduce a new integer variable, say **var** n : **integer**, and replace each print statement, for example

       print E

by

       $n := E$; **print** n.

Thus condition (4) for primitive PROSA is also satisfied.

We must now take care of property (6) which demands that expressions contain at most one operation symbol. We first replace each unary minus symbol by a subtraction, i.e. $-E$ is replaced by $0 - E$. Let now op be a binary operation symbol and $E = E_1 \; op \; E_2$ an expression in which two or more operation symbols occur. Expression E is the right-hand side of an assignment, e.g. $x := E$. We introduce two new integer variables, say **var** h_1, h_2 : **integer**, and replace assignment

       $x := E$

by

       $h_1 := E_1$;
       $h_2 := E_2$;
       $x := h_1 \; op \; h_2$

If E_1 or E_2 contain more than one operation symbol we repeat the process. Clearly in this way property (6) is established and a primitive PROSA program is generated.

Theorem 1. *For each simple PROSA program p there is an equivalent primitive PROSA program q. Program q can effectively be constructed from program p. Furthermore for all $i \in \mathbb{Z}^* : comp_time(q,i) \leq c_1 + c_2 \cdot comp_time(p,i)$ where c_1 and c_2 are constants which depend on p but not on i.*

Proof: Follows immediately from the discussion above.   ∎

This concludes the translation into primitive PROSA. In particular, the key theorem of this chapter is now proved. For each of the translation steps we gave an algorithm which accomplishes the step. In principle, we could also have formulated these algorithms in PROSA. This we now want to do, at least for the last step.

Chapter II introduced stack machines for the evaluation and syntax analysis of expressions. We shall now modify this stack machine such that it produces a sequence of assignments whose execution evaluates the expression.

Example 1:   Expression $(((a+b)*c)/(e-f))$ could, for example, be transformed into the following program section where h_1, h_2, h_3 are additional variables (usually called auxiliary variables).

$$h_1 := a;$$
$$h_2 := b;$$
$$h_1 := h_1 + h_2;$$
$$h_2 := c;$$
$$h_1 := h_1 * h_2;$$
$$h_2 := e;$$
$$h_3 := f;$$
$$h_2 := h_2 - h_3;$$
$$h_1 := h_1 / h_2;$$

Execution of this program section terminates with the value of the expression in h_1. Notice the close relationship between the program and the mode of operation of the push down automaton of Chapter II. The auxiliary variables h_1, h_2, h_3 precisely correspond to the operand stack. The pushdown automaton first stacks the values of a ($h_1 := a$) and b ($h_2 := b$). After reading the first closing bracket it replaces the two values by their sum $h_1 := h_1 + h_2$. The above program section therefore just reflects the arithmetic actions of the push down automaton.   ∎

We shall now formalise this method by modifying the push down automaton of Chapter II such that, instead of evaluating the expression, it rather prints an equivalent sequence of simple assignments. (These simple assignments are usually called **three address instructions** since three variables occur in them.) For simplicity sake we restrict the input to fully parenthesised expressions without unary minus symbol. The push down automaton has to be changed as follows.

input symbol	before	now
(	no action	no action
identifier a	push value of a onto operand stack	print instruction $h_i := a$;
$+, -, *, /$)	push onto operator stack the top element of the operator stack is applied to the two top elements of the operand stack and they are replaced by the result	push onto operator stack print instruction $h_i := h_j \; op \; h_k$; where op is the top element of the operator stack

One problem remains. Which indices must be given to the auxilliary variables h? For that purpose we introduce a counter $toph$ whose value always is the index of the last auxiliary variable used. In the case of reading an identifier a, for example, and $toph$ having value 5, $toph$ is increased to 6 and instruction $h_6 := a$ printed. We now describe this push down automaton as PROSA program.

program *Translation_of_Expressions;*

(* Input : A fully parenthesised expression E without unary minus symbol. For simplicity sake we assume that all identifiers consist of exactly one letter. We further assume that expression E is followed by symbol $\dashv$ on the input tape.

Output : A sequence of simple assignments (three address instructions) whose execution evaluates the expression.

Remark : The program uses an array $k :$ **array** $[1 .. \infty]$ **of char** and two integer variables $topk, toph$. The sequence $k[1], \dots, k[topk]$ corresponds to the operator stack of Chapter II. Variable $toph$ always contains the length of the operand stack.*)

```
var toph, topk : integer; x : char;
var k : array [1.. ∞] of char;
begin
    toph := 0; topk := 0;
    read x;
    while  x ≠ ' ⊣'
    do if  x = '('
        then x := x  (* an instruction which has no effect *)
        else if  x = 'a' or x = 'b' or ... or x = 'z'
            then (* read identifier *)
                    toph := toph + 1;
                    print 'h'; print  toph; print  ":=";
                    print  x; print  ';'
            else  (* read operator symbol *)
                    if  x = '+' or x = '−' or x = '*' or x = /
```

$$\textbf{then} \;\; topk := topk + 1;$$
$$k[topk] := x$$
$$\textbf{else} \;\; (* \; x = \text{')'} \; *)$$
$$\textbf{print} \;\; 'h'; \; \textbf{print} \;\; toph - 1; \; \textbf{print} \;\; \text{" := } h\text{"};$$
$$\textbf{print} \;\; toph - 1; \; \textbf{print} \;\; k[topk]; \; \textbf{print} \;\; 'h';$$
$$\textbf{print} \;\; toph; \; \textbf{print} \;\; ';';$$
$$toph := toph - 1; \;\; topk := topk - 1$$
$$\textbf{fi}$$
$$\textbf{fi}$$
$$\textbf{fi};$$
$$\textbf{read} \; x$$
$$\textbf{od}$$
end.

The reader should run this program for several examples so as to become familiar with the confusing change between symbols and values of variables. Let, for example, 5 be the value of variable $toph$ immediately after the comment $(* x = ')' *)$ and let $op \in \{+, -, *, /\}$ be the value of $k[toph]$. Then the assignment

$$h4 := h4 \; op \; h5;$$

is printed.

Example 1 (continued):   Input $((a + b) * c / (e - f)) \dashv$ produces the sequence of assignments given in the example.   ∎

Lemma 1. *Let E be a fully parenthesised integer expression of length n without minus symbol. Then the computation time of the above program with input $E \dashv$ is linear in n.*

Proof: The body of the while-loop is executed n-times and each execution comprises a constant number of statements.   ∎

Lemma 2. *Let E be a fully parenthesised integer expression without unary minus symbol, let b be a binding, s a storage state and let p be the statement sequence generated from E by the above program when started with value $i \in \mathbb{N}$ (instead of 0) for toph. Furthermore let $\tilde{b}$ be a binding which is b extended by auxiliary variables $h1$, $h2$, $h3, \ldots$ and let $c_{end} = (\epsilon, \; \tilde{b}, \; s_{end}, \ldots)$. be the end configuration of the PROSA machine for start configuration $(p, \; \tilde{b}, \; s, \ldots)$. Then*

$$I(b, \; s, \; E) = s_{end}(\tilde{b}(h(i + 1))),$$

i.e. the value of expression E in environment (b, s) is equal to the value of variable $h(i + 1)$ after executing p.

Proof: The proof is by induction on the length of E. If E has length 1, i.e. it is only a single identifier a, then only assignment $h(i + 1) := a$ is generated; the claim is therefore correct. If E is longer then $E = (E_1 \ op \ E_2)$. First program p_1 is generated from E_1 then program p_2 from E_2 and finally, while reading ')', the assignment $h(i+1) := h(i+1) \ op \ h(i+2)$. Note that expression E_2 is executed with the initial value $i+1$ for $toph$. Together, therefore, the program $p_1; \ p_2; \ h(i+1) := h(i+1) \ op \ h(i+2)$ will be generated. Let s_1 be the storage state which ensues after executing p_1. Then, by induction hypothesis, $I(b, \ s, \ E_1) = s_1(\tilde{b}(h(i+1)))$. Furthermore all simple variables have the same value relative to s and s_1. Let now s_2 be the storage state after execution of p_2 beginning in $(p_2, \ \tilde{b}, \ s_1 , \ldots)$ and let s_2' be the storage state after execution of $p_1; \ p_2$ starting in $(p_1; \ p_2, \tilde{b}, \ s, \ \ldots)$. By induction hypothesis $I(b, \ s, \ E_2) = I(b, \ s_1, \ E_2) = s_2(\tilde{b}(h(i+2))) = s_2'(\tilde{b}(h(i+2)))$. Furthermore program p_2 does not change the value of $h(i+1)$. Thus for s_2' we have $I(b, \ s, \ E_1) = s_2'(\tilde{b}(h(i+1)))$. Hence assignment $h(i+1) := h(i+1) \ op \ h(i+2)$ finally computes the value $I(b, \ s, \ E)$. ∎

For $i = 0$, Lemma 2 just proves the above program correct. We are now at the end of a long journey in which we transformed simple PROSA step-by-step into primitive PROSA. For all steps the translation was specified as an algorithm which realised it. For the last step this algorithm was even formulated in PROSA.

To conclude the chapter we describe how **actual compilers** directly generate RESA instructions for the evaluation of expressions. For that we just have to explain which RESA storage cells are used instead of the additional variables $h1, h2, \ldots$. Note that the explicit declaration of auxiliary variables $h1, h2, \ldots$ precludes a translation in one pass since the number of necessary auxiliary variables – it corresponds to the maximal number of operators in an expression – is known only after a complete pass through the program text. This number, on the other hand, has to be known in order to determine an initial address for the infinite array H. Actual compilers solve this problem by allocating storage for the heap H in a way other than described by us. Every computer clearly has a finite storage, for example with the addresses 0 to $maxad - 1$. One allocates storage for the declared variables at the beginning of the data storage, i.e. as described in Section 5.3, starting with cell 0. The heap H is placed at the upper end of the storage, i.e. starting with address $maxad - 1$. Note that the size of the lower part is fixed by the program text and does not depend on a particular computation of the program. Thus we can use the cells following this fixed section as auxiliary storage cells for the evaluation of expressions. If, therefore, c is the address of the first free cell after the statically allocated storage section, the evaluation of expressions will use the cells with addresses $c, c+1, \ldots, c+k$ to deposit intermediate results. k is also statically fixed.

Example 2:   Expression $(((a+b)*c)/(e-f))$ might be translated into the following

RESA program section where the first free storage cell has address 100.

```
LOAD    rad(a)
ADD     rad(b)
MUL     rad(c)
STORE   100
LOAD    rad(e)
SUB     rad(f)
STORE   101
LOAD    100
DIV     101
```

The following pushdown automaton translates arithmetic expressions (fully parenthesised and without unary minus symbol) into RESA programs. The columns have the following meaning. *Op_and* shows the relevant (right) end of the operand stack before and after a transition. *Op_or*, correspondingly, shows the relevant content of the operator stack. *In_sym* is the current input symbol. Counter h records the actual address of the top of the stack. Column *Code* contains the instruction sequence to be printed. Note that incrementing and decrementing h takes place **before** generating the RESA instructions. In the last line $op = +$, OP = ADD, or $op = -$, OP = SUB etc. has to be inserted.

Op_and	Op_or	Input_sym	Op_and	Op_or	h	Code
		(		(		
		identifier a	h		$h+1$	LOAD $rad(a)$
						STORE h
		$op \in \{+,-,*,/\}$		op		
m,n	(op	)			$h-1$	LOAD n
						OP m
						STORE h

Exercises for 5.8

1) Write a PROSA program which realises the push down automaton at the end of 5.8, i.e. it takes as input a fully parenthesised expression and produces the corresponding RESA instruction sequence as output. Function 'rad' is available.

2) Specify a push down automaton (a PROSA program) which translates ordinary expressions into sequences of three address instructions (into RESA instruction sequences).

3) Like Exercise 1), but operands of the form $a[i]$ are also permitted.

Chapter 6   **Procedures**

Writing a program for a non-trivial application and of realistic size (one or two hundred pages) with the language concepts of PROSA introduced so far would be hardly possible. As we can assume that several programmers would participate in such a program, a reasonable distribution of the problem and of the program must be found. Just as seven tool makers working simultaneously on a workpiece cannot construct a useful product, seven programmers working together on a loop program cannot achieve the desired effect. Reasonable structuring of a program into manageable parts, however, is scarcely possible in PROSA so far. In particular, all declared names are accessible everywhere in the statement section. Hence variables are readable and alterable everywhere.

In this chapter the new concept of "procedures" is introduced. It solves the above problems at least to some extent. It offers the possibility of programming individual "closed" program sections separately and of "hiding" details irrelevant for the remaining program. The advantages of procedures are

- modularity, i.e. a program can be organised in manageable closed sections which co-operate with their environment in a controlled way,

- abstraction, i.e. after a procedure is written and verified, only what it does is of interest (e.g. solving a system of equations), but not how it is done (e.g. by elimination or iteration),

- extendibility of the language, i.e. the programming language can be extended by "higher" operations in providing a list of procedures,

- expressive power, i.e. recursive procedures often permit very efficient and short programs,

- hiding principle, i.e. implementation details can be hidden from the environment.

We proceed as follows. In Section 6.1 essential new concepts are introduced informally by way of an example. As we are introducing a large number of new concepts heavily dependent on each other, it is difficult to read Section 6.1 sequentially. We therefore recommend that this section be read frequently and with increasing accuracy. In Section 6.2 we discuss the new concepts in detail using more examples. These examples illustrate the advantages of procedures as listed above. In addition, correctness proofs and analysis of computation time of programs with procedures will be considered. In Section 6.3 we formally define the syntax and in Section 6.4 the semantics.

6.1 Introduction

A procedure is characterised by
 - its name,
 - its body,
 - its formal parameter list,
 - its result type (only in function procedures),
 - the binding at the place of declaration.

Procedures are introduced by procedure declarations. A procedure declaration explicitly specifies name, body, formal parameters and, in the case of function procedures, the result type. The binding at the place of declaration is implicitly given by the place of the declaration. The body of a procedure, like a program, consists of a declaration section and a statement section enclosed in the brackets **begin** and **end**. Procedures are invoked by procedure calls. They are of the form 'name of a procedure followed by a list of actual parameters', see Figure 1. For example, the program *LawsofGravity* (see next page) declares procedures *WeightonEarth*, *DistanceofFalling*, *square* and *WeightonMoon*.

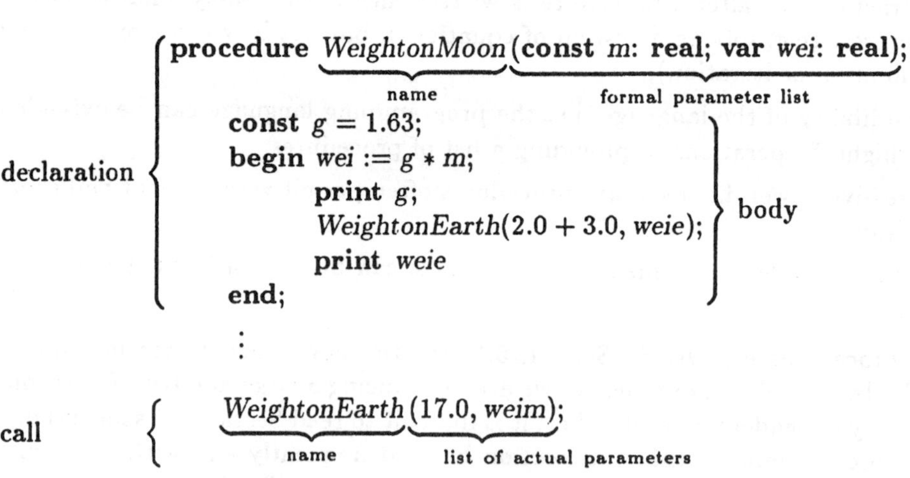

Fig. 1.   A procedure declaration and a procedure call

A procedure communicates with the place where it is called via parameters and global names. We have two versions of parameter lists, namely lists of formal parameters (in procedure declarations) and lists of actual parameters (in procedure calls). Formal parameters are place holders for actual parameters. We know this concept from function definitions in mathematics. For instance, we write $f(x) = x^2$ and mean that function f maps each number to its square. Here the formal parameter x (in mathematics one usually speaks of variables, but we have already used this term) stands for an arbitrary number. For each number, i.e. for each actual parameter, we can compute the value of f by replacing the formal parameter by the actual parameter. For example $f(3) = 3^2$. Parameter passing for procedure calls works similarly. Formal parameters of the procedure body are substituted by the actual parameters and then the modified procedure body is executed. The details, however, are slightly more complicated. If, for instance, an actual parameter x is a variable, should we replace the formal parameter by the string x or by the variable denoted by x or by the value of this variable or should we proceed differently? Various possibilities make sense and are used in higher programming languages. In this section we discuss what is called var and const parameter passing in more detail; name-passing, a historic relict from the sixties, and value-passing, used for example in Pascal, are discussed in Section 6.2. Alternatives are chosen by respective key words (**var, const**, etc.) in front of the formal parameter.

Example:

program *LawsofGravity*;
    (* Some of the **print**-statements may not appear very sensible; they are used to explain the control flow of the program *)
    (* the two earth-procedures use earth acceleration; for this we introduce a constant *)
    const $g = 9.81$;
    var *weie, weim*: **real**; (* weight on earth and on moon *)

    procedure *WeightonEarth* (**const** *m*: **real**; **var** *wei*: **real**);
        (* computes the weight of mass m on the earth and assigns it to the formal parameter *wei* *)
        begin
            wei := $g * m$;
            print g (* prints 9.81 *)
        end:

    procedure *DistanceofFalling* (**const** *t*: **real**; **var** *s*: **real**);
        (* computes the distance of falling in t seconds *)
        var *h*: **real**;
        procedure *square* (**const** *x*: **real**; **var** *q*: **real**);
            begin $q := x * x$ **end**;
        begin
            square(t, h);
            $s := (g/2.0) * h$
        end;

    procedure *WeightonMoon*(**const** *m*: **real**; **var** *wei*: **real**);
        (* computes the weight on the moon *)
        const $g = 1.63$;
            (* the name g is introduced for moon acceleration *)
        begin

```
            wei := g * m;
            print g ; (* prints 1.63 *)
            WeightonEarth(2.0 + 3.0, weie);
            print weie
        end;
begin
    print g; (* prints 9.81 *)
    WeightonEarth(2.0 + 3.0, weie); print weie;
    WeightonEarth(17.0, weie); print weie;
    WeightonMoon(17.0, weim); print weim
end.
```

The syntax of formal parameter lists is similar to declaration sequences. In fact, with regard to the body, formal parameters behave, syntactically, like declared constants or variables. A formal parameter specified with **const** may therefore be used in the procedure body exactly as a constant name, and a formal parameter specified with **var** may be used exactly as a variable name. Thus within *WeightonEarth*, m is a constant and *wei* is a variable name. For const-parameters the corresponding actual parameter must be an expression. In the case of procedure *WeightonEarth*, the first actual parameter is therefore always an expression. When calling the procedure this expression is evaluated and its value bound to the formal parameter, see Figure 2.

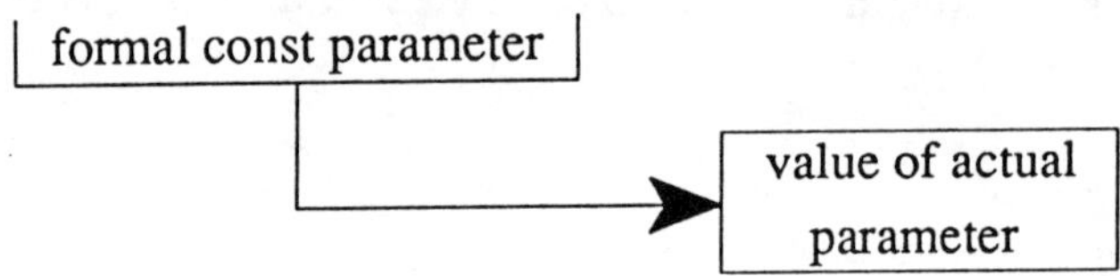

Fig. 2. Parameter passing for a const-parameter. The value of the actual parameter is bound to the formal parameter.

When *WeightonEarth* is first called in the main program, m is bound to the number 5.0 and during the second call to number 17.0. The effect of the call is the same as preceding the procedure body with a constant declaration **const** $m = 5.0$ or **const** $m = 17.0$. In the procedure body which corresponds to the first call, m denotes 5.0 and the constant 17.0 in the second. The major difference to a normal constant declaration is that the value on the right side of the constant declaration is determined as the value of the actual parameter only when the procedure is called.

We now discuss var-parameters. For var-parameters the corresponding actual parameter must always be a variable name. In procedure *WeightonEarth*, therefore, the second actual parameter is always the name of a real variable. During parameter passing the variable denoted by the actual parameter is bound to the formal parameter, see Figure 3.

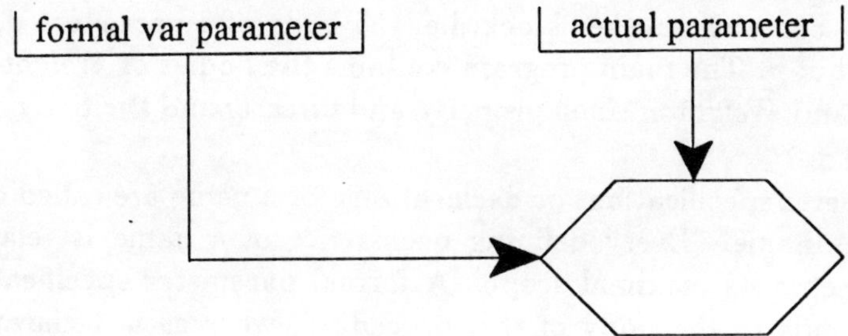

Fig. 3.   Parameter passing for a var-parameter. The variable bound to the actual parameter is also bound to the formal parameter.

During execution of the body, the formal parameter denotes the same variable as the actual parameter. In particular, an assignment to the formal parameter causes an assignment to the actual parameter ("aliasing"). In a call $WeightonEarth(17.0, weie)$, therefore, $wei := g * m$ causes $17.0 * 9.81 = 166.77$ to be assigned to variable $weie$. This value is printed after the call.

In summary, in a call a formal const-parameter is bound to the value of the actual parameter and a formal var-parameter is bound to the variable denoted by the actual parameter. When the body is executed the formal parameter then denotes this value or this variable. This binding is forgotten after the call (return from the procedure). The formal parameters can be bound to other objects and variables during the next call.

The possibility of declaring a name several times forces us to introduce further concepts. The name g is used in procedures $WeightonEarth$ and $DistanceofFalling$, but it is neither declared in them nor specified as a formal parameter. These occurrences of g refer to the constant declaration **const** $g = 9.81$ in the main program and not, for example, to the declaration **const** $g = 1.63$ local to procedure $WeightonMoon$. Only the two applied occurrences of g within the procedure $WeightonMoon$ refer to the latter.

Every programming language permitting more than one declaration of a name in a program has **scope rules** that determine which applied occurrences refer to which declaration. That part of a program in which all applied occurrences of a name refer to the same declaration is called its **scope**.

To specify the scope rules for PROSA (and Pascal) we must widen the context. Scopes are defined in terms of the nesting of procedures. A procedure body, just as the relevant part of a program, is a **block**, that is a sequence of declarations and statements enclosed in brackets **begin** and **end**. The declaration section of a block can again contain procedure declarations which give rise to nested procedures and blocks. We say that a block B **contains** block B' if the text of B' is part of B. B **properly contains** B' if B contains B' and $B \neq B'$. B **directly contains** B' if B contains B' and there is no block B'' which properly contains B' and is properly contained in B. Since PROSA (and Pascal) permit nesting of blocks only via nested procedure declarations, a block, i.e. the body of a procedure p or the main program, contains another block, i.e. the body of a procedure q, directly if q is declared within p. The main program contains the bodies of *WeightonEarth*, *DistanceofFalling* and *WeightonMoon* properly and directly and the body of *square* properly.

Formal parameter specifications or declarations for a name are called **defining** occurrences of this name. Every defining occurrence of a name is related to a block which represents its maximal scope. A formal parameter specification of a procedure corresponds to the body of this procedure, whereas a declaration of a name corresponds to the block in whose declaration section it occurs.

In our example we have the following association of blocks with defining occurrences of names.

const $g = 9.81$	main program
const $g = 1.63$	body of *WeightonMoon*
var *wei*: **real** in *WeightonEarth*	body of *WeightonEarth*
var *wei*: **real** in *WeightonMoon*	body of *WeightonMoon*

If a defining occurrence of a name x is associated with a block B then x is said to be **local** to B. If x is not local to B, but local to a block containing B, then x is said to be **global** to B, see Figure 4.

body of	local names	global names
WeightonEarth	m, *wei*	g, *weie*, *weim*, *WeightonEarth*, *DistanceofFalling*, *WeightonMoon*
DistanceofFalling	t, s, h, *square*	g, *weie*, *weim*, *WeightonEarth*, *DistanceofFalling*, *WeightonMoon*
WeightonMoon	m, *wei*, g	*weie*, *weim*, *WeightonEarth*, *DistanceofFalling*, *WeightonMoon*

Fig. 4. Procedures and their local and global names in the program *LawsofGravity*.

Before defining the scope rules for PROSA precisely, we shall illustrate them using our example program. The two procedures *WeightonEarth* and *DistanceofFalling* both use earth acceleration which we have named g in the main program. Procedure *WeightonMoon* uses moon acceleration which we—somewhat unsymmetrically—have also named g in this procedure. Within procedure *WeightonMoon* one could say moon conditions prevail. Outside the procedure we have terrestrial conditions. The call of *WeightonEarth* in procedure *WeightonMoon* should demonstrate that in computing a "terrestrial weight" on the moon the moon conditions, that is the constant declaration **const** $g = 1.63$, do not influence the result. We will explain presently how that is achieved. The procedure calls *WeightonEarth*(17.0, *weie*) and *WeightonMoon*(17.0, *weim*) compute the weight of a mass of 17 (kg) on the earth and on the moon, respectively. The program prints the sequence 9.81, 9.81, 49.05, 9.81, 166.77, 1.63, 9.81, 49.05, 27.71 .

We now specify the scope rules of PROSA precisely. The **scope** of a defining occurrence of a name x is defined as the block B associated with this name, excluding all blocks properly contained in B which are also associated with a defining occurrence of x, see Figure 5.

def. occurrence	scope
const $g = 9.81$	the whole program apart from the body of *WeightonMoon*
const $g = 1.63$	body of *WeightonMoon*

Fig. 5.   The scope of the two defining occurrences of g in program *LawsofGravity*.

We now know what the scope of a defining occurrence is. The opposite question is also interesting. How does one find a corresponding defining occurrence for a given applied occurrence of a name x? For that purpose we have a simple rule following immediately from the definition of scopes. Let B be the smallest block containing the given applied occurrence, and let B' be the smallest block containing B with which a defining occurrence of x is associated. Then this defining occurrence corresponds to the given applied occurrence. If there is no such block B' the program is erroneous. In a more algorithmic way this rule can be formulated as follows. First search for a defining occurrence associated with B. If there is none, repeat the procedure for the block directly containing B and so on. If this algorithm continues unsuccessfully to the outermost block, i.e. as far as the main program, we have a program error. The context conditions are later fixed so that they are violated in this case. Figure 6 specifies the corresponding defining occurrence to each applied occurrence of a name in program *LawsofGravity*.

The above scope rule naturally fixes the meaning of global names in procedure bodies. The occurrence of g in *WeightonEarth* and *DistanceofFalling* refer to the declaration of g in the main program, i.e. g denotes the constant 9.81. The applied occurrence of g in *WeightonMoon* refers to the local declaration in *WeightonMoon*, i.e. here g denotes the constant 1.63. Thus the print statement in *WeightonEarth* prints 9.81 in both calls and the print statement in the body of *WeightonMoon* prints 1.63. Note that the call of *WeightonEarth* within *WeightonMoon* also prints 9.82 for g, although g has the value 1.63 at the point of call. Our definition of scopes specifies that the meaning of a global name in a procedure is determined by the place where the procedure is declared and not where it is called.

This scope rule is often called the **"principle of static binding"**. By this we mean that the binding of an applied occurrence of a name is given by its defining occurrence in the program text, i.e. it is determined **statically**. The alternative to the principle of static binding is the **principle of dynamic binding**. The binding of an applied occurrence of a name is determined by the declaration of the name processed last during program execution. With dynamic binding, the print statement in our example would print 1.63 in the call of *WeightonEarth* in *WeightonMoon*. The dynamic binding violates the principle of local context and

app. occurrence			respective def. occurrence
wei, *m*	in	*WeightonEarth*	form. parameter of *WeightonEarth*
g	in	*WeightonEarth*	const. decl. in main program
q, x	in	*square*	form. parameter of *square*
t, s	in	*DistanceofFalling*	form. parameter in *DistanceofFalling*
h	in	*DistanceofFalling*	variable-decl. in *DistanceofFalling*
square	in	*DistanceofFalling*	procedure decl. in *DistanceofFalling*
g	in	*DistanceofFalling*	const. decl. in main program
wei, *m*	in	*WeightonMoon*	form. parameter in *WeightonMoon*
g	in	*WeightonMoon*	const. decl. in *WeightonMoon*
WeightonEarth	in	*WeightonMoon*	procedure decl. in main program
weie	in	*WeightonMoon*	variable-decl. in main program
g	in	main program	const. decl. in main program
WeightonEarth	in	main program	procedure decl. in main program
WeightonMoon	in	main program	procedure decl. in main program
weie, weim	in	main program	variable-decl. in main program

Fig. 6. Correspondence of applied and defining occurrences of names in program *LawsofGravity*.

makes it almost impossible to keep track of the binding of global names. In particular, the binding of global names and thus the meaning of the procedure depends on where the procedure is called. Therefore, in general, it is impossible to verify a procedure independent of the calling point. This is a grave disadvantage and therefore almost all modern programming languages (with the exception of LISP) follow the principle of static binding. In our program *LawsofGravity*, procedure *WeightonEarth* could not be characterised by the sentence "compute the weight of mass m on earth and pass it through formal parameter *wei*", since the value of the global name *g* would be determined by the place where the procedure is called.

We have now introduced a multiplicity of new concepts. In the rest of this section we illustrate how the PROSA machine processes programs with procedures. The reader will be surprised to find how simple it is, and how little we have to modify the PROSA machine in order to deal with the new concepts.

Let us consider the configuration of the modified PROSA machine after the main program has called the procedure *WeightonMoon*, but before entering the procedure body. This configuration is

$$c_1 = (pr_1, bs_1, s_1, \epsilon, o_1);$$

The program-rest pr_1, the binding stack $bs_1 = ((b_1, 0), (b_2, 1))$ and the storage state are shown in Figure 7. The output up to now is $o_1 = 9.81, 9.81, 49.05, 9.81, 166.77$.

We must explain this configuration in more detail. The program-rest is, as usual, the part of the program still to be executed. The binding stack is new. **A binding stack** bs is a sequence

$$((b_1, sv_1), \ldots, (b_m, sv_m))$$

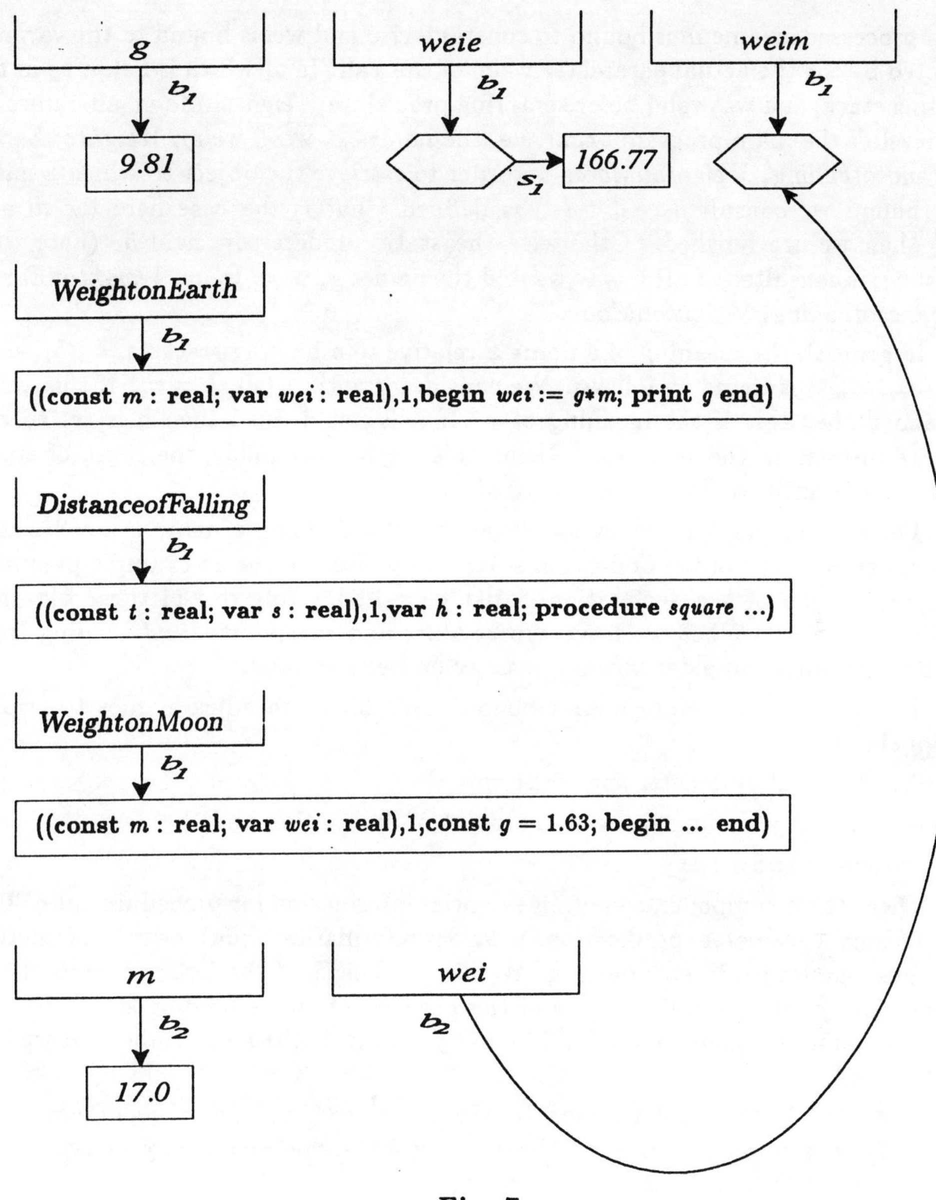

Fig. 7

of pairs (b_i, sv_i) with $1 \leq i \leq m$. Here b_i is a binding in the usual sense and $sv_i \in \mathbb{N}_0$, with $sv_i < i$, is the index of the **static predecessor** of b_i. sv_i is called the **static link** of binding b_i. The binding stack contains a (local) binding for each procedure which was entered but has not yet been left. Such a binding records the meaning of formal parameters and local names of this procedure. That of global names is found via the static links which will be explained soon.

In our example only names m and wei occur in the actual binding b_2 (b_m is called **actual binding**) since the declaration of g in $WeightonMoon$ has not yet been processed. Name m is bound to constant 17.0 and *wei* is bound to the variable denoted by the the actual parameter *weim* of this call. In b_1 which is below b_2 in the binding stack, and was valid before entering procedure *WeightonMoon*, all names on the level of the main program occur, i.e. the names g, *weie*, *weim*, *WeightonEarth*, *DistanceofFalling*, *WeightonMoon*. In order to retrieve the object to which a name x is bound we consult b_2. If $b_2(x)$ is defined (that is the case here for m and *wei*) then we are finished. Otherwise the static predecessor, here b_1 (note that $sv_2 = 1$), is consulted. In this way we find the names g, *weie*, *weim*, *WeightonEarth*, *DistanceofFalling*, *WeightonMoon*.

In general, the meaning of a name x relative to a binding stack $bs = ((b_1, sv_1), \ldots, (b_m, sv_m))$ is found as follows. We consider x with $b_h(x)$, $h = m$. If this value is defined then this is the meaning of x. If it is not defined then h is set to sv_h and we proceed in the same way. Using this method we follow the chain of static predecessors until we find the meaning of x.

The binding stack provides an elegant way of defining a name x locally, as x may of course occur in the domain of several b_i's. We will see an example presently in the execution of the declaration **const** $g = 1.63$. Only one of these bindings applies at a time. When we leave a procedure and remove its local binding from the binding stack, an older meaning can again become valid.

To what are procedure names bound? We bind procedure names to triples comprising the

- list of formal parameter specifications, the
- length of the binding stack at the point of declaration and the
- procedure body.

These three components contain essential information for procedure calls. The list of formal parameter specifications provides information about formal parameters and thus enables parameter passing. We use the length of the binding stack at the declaration to set the static link sv of the pair (b, sv) in the binding stack. In this way one can access global entities. The body, finally, is the block to be executed in a call.

Number 1 in the triples bound to *WeightonEarth* and *DistanceofFalling* (see Figure 7), therefore, means that the binding stack contained only b_1 when the declarations of these procedures were processed.

The other components of a configuration, namely storage state, input and output sequence are defined as hitherto.

We now return to our example with configuration c_1 and binding stack $bs_1 = ((b_1, 0), (b_2, 1))$. The next configuration to be considered more closely is the one reached before the call *WeightonEarth*$(2.0 + 3.0, weie)$ in *WeightonMoon*. The PROSA machine has executed the constant declaration **const** $g = 1.63$ and extended b_2 to b_2' by binding g to 1.63. In addition, it has executed the assignment to *wei* and thus changed the storage state. Note that assigning to the formal parameter *wei* gave a value to the actual parameter *weim* since both names denote the same variable. Executing the **print** statement has extended the output sequence by 1.63. The new configuration is

$$c_2 = (pr_2, bs_2, s_2, \epsilon, o_2).$$

Here $pr_2 = WeightonEarth(2.0 + 3.0, weie);$ **print** *weie;* **end; print** *weim;* **end;**. and $bs_2 = ((b_1, 0), (b'_2, 1))$. Bindings b_1, b'_2 and storage state s_2 are shown in Figure 8. Note that g is in the domain of b_1 as well as in that of b'_2. $b_1(g) = 9.81$ and $b'_2(g) = 1.63$. The actual value of g is thus given by the declaration of g in *WeightonMoon*. This agrees exactly with our scope rule. On leaving *WeightonMoon*, on the other hand, the declaration of g in the main program is valid again because $(b'_2, 1)$ is removed from the binding stack.

The next transition executes the call $WeightonEarth(2.0 + 3.0, weie)$. Let us recall what we expect during a procedure call. Firstly, parameters are passed and then the body of the procedure is executed. This is achieved by replacing the call by the procedure body preceded by the lists of formal parameter specifications and actual parameters. Hence the new program rest is $pr_3 = ($**const** m: **real; var** *wei*: **real**$) (2.0+3.0, weie)$ *wei* $:= g * m$; **print** g; **end; print** *weie;* **end; print** *weim;* **end;**. Parameters are passed later when the two lists, i.e. the formal and the actual parameter list, are processed. For the procedure we establish a new local binding (b_3, sv_3) in which we record the meaning of local names. As long as no parameter has been passed there are no local names and thus $b_3 = \emptyset$ is the empty function. The meaning of global names is given by the binding stack relative to the point of declaration. When the called procedure was declared the binding stack consisted only of binding b_1 and thus $sv_3 = 1$. Configuration c_3 is

$$c_3 = (pr_3, ((b_1, 0), (b'_2, 1), (\emptyset, 1)), s_2, \epsilon, o_2).$$

Note that $b_1(WeightonEarth)$ contains all information needed for this transition. From it we take the list of formal parameter specifications, the length of the binding stack at the point of declaration and the body. The second component enables setting the static link sv_3 to 1, and the other two components were incorporated in the program-rest. The list of actual parameters is taken from the call. Note further that g is earth acceleration again. In the actual binding which is still empty, g has no meaning. Therefore we consider binding b_1 ($sv_3 = 1$!) and find $b_1(g) = 9.81$. This example shows very nicely how the PROSA machine realises the principle of static binding in using pointers to the static predecessor. A small technical remark is necessary at this point. When copying the procedure body to the program-rest we omit the key word **begin** and insert a semicolon before **end** . Thus we have a semicolon after each statement (also after the last of a body) and we can dispense with unnecessary case distinctions when describing the transition function of the PROSA machine.

Now parameter passing takes place. We bind m to 5.0 and *wei* to variable $b_1(weie)$ denoted by the actual parameter. The necessary transitions of the PROSA machine process the list of formal parameter specifications and the lists of actual

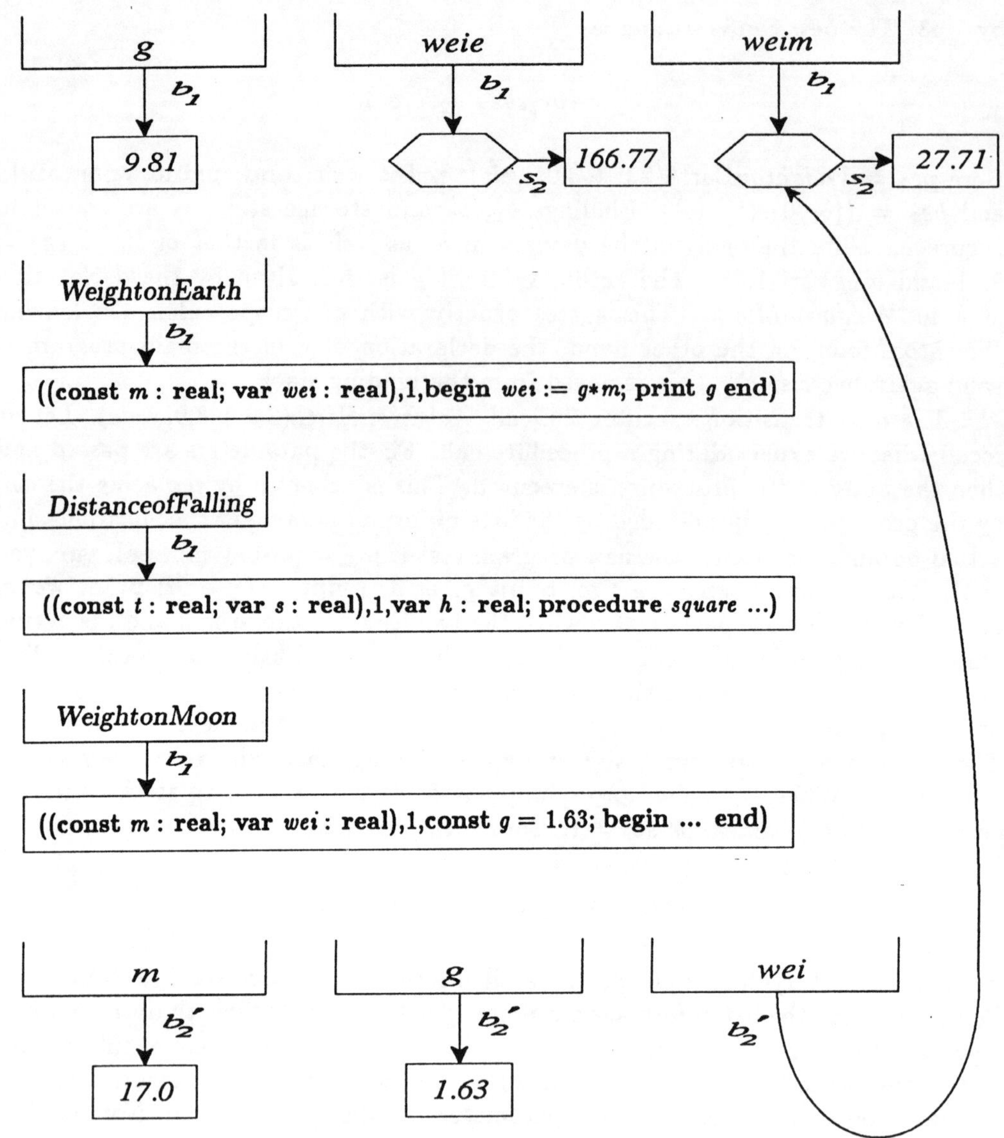

Fig. 8

parameters one by one, extending the actual binding accordingly. Details can be found in Section 6.4. We obtain configuration

$$c_4 = (pr_4, ((b_1, 0), (b_2', 1), (b_3, 1)), s_2, \epsilon, o_2)$$

with $pr_4 = $ **wei** $:= g * m;$ **print** $g;$ **end**; **print** *weie*; **end**; **print** *weim*; **end**;. Bindings b_1, b_2' and b_3 and storage state s_2 can be seen in Figure 9.

Executing the next two statements alter storage state and output tape. First consider assignment *wei* $:= g * m$. The actual binding b_3 yields the meaning of

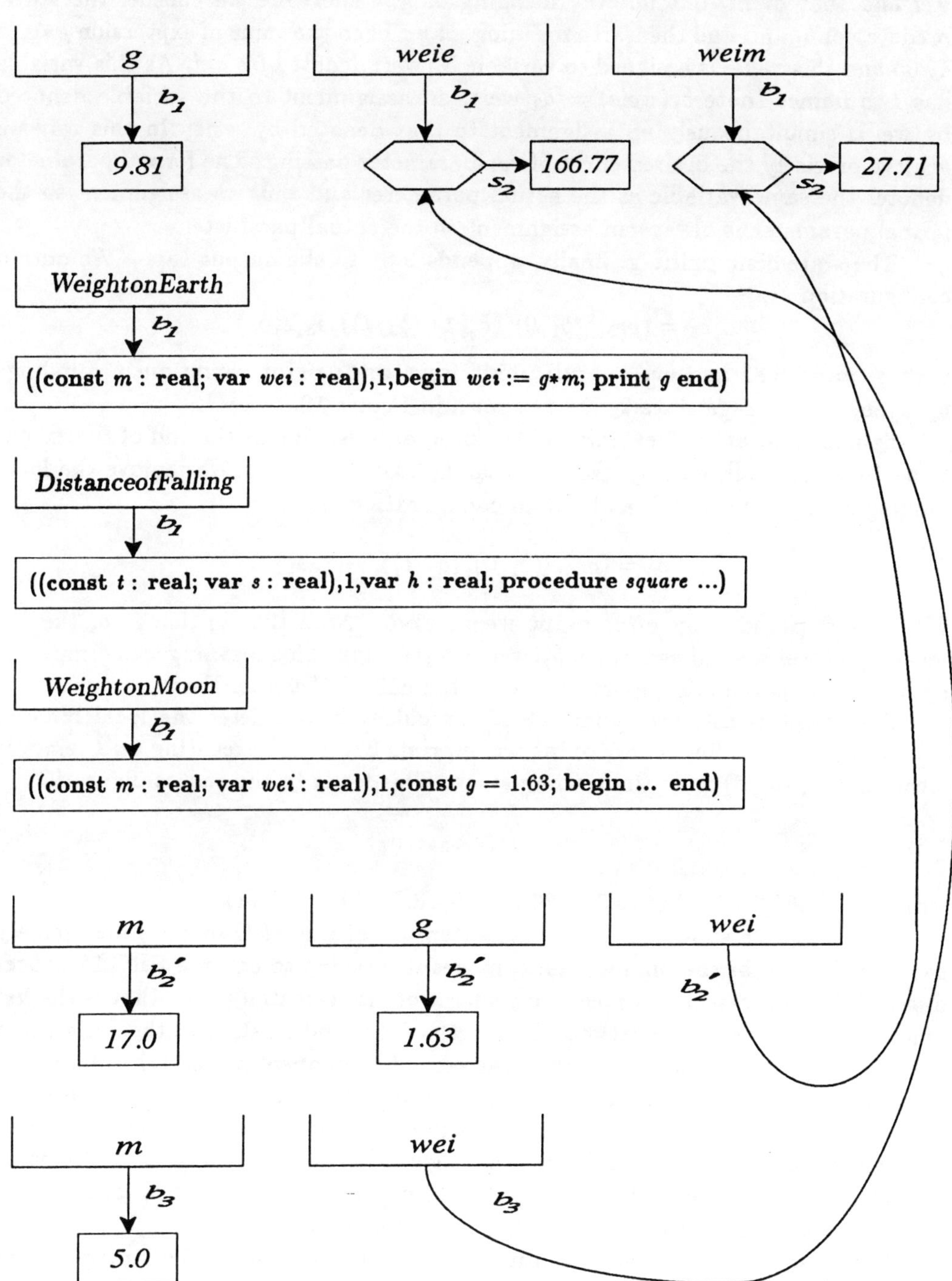

g
weie
weim
b_1
b_1
b_1
9.81
s_2
166.77
s_2
27.71
WeightonEarth
b_1
((const m : real; var wei : real),1,begin $wei := g*m$; print g end)
DistanceofFalling
b_1
((const t : real; var s : real),1,var h : real; procedure $square$ ...)
WeightonMoon
b_1
((const m : real; var wei : real),1,const $g = 1.63$; begin ... end)
m
g
wei
b_2'
b_2'
b_2'
17.0
1.63
m
wei
b_3
b_3
5.0

Fig. 9

wei and that of m, but not the meaning of g. Therefore we consult the static predecessor b_1 and find the 'earth meaning' of g. Then the value of expression $g*m$ is 49.05 and this value is assigned to variable $b_3(wei)$ denoted by *wei*. As this variable has *two* names (note $b_1(weie) = b_3(wei)$) an assignment to the variable denoted by *wei* is simultaneously an assignment to that denoted by *weie*. In this way we achieve precisely the desired effect of var-parameter passing. The formal parameter denotes the same variable as the actual parameter and thus an assignment to the formal parameter is always an assignment to the actual parameter.

The statement **print** g, finally, appends 9.81 to the output tape. We obtain configuration

$$c_5 = (pr_5, ((b_1, 0), (b_2', 1), (b_3, 1)), s_3, \epsilon, o_5)$$

with $o_5 = o_2 . 9.81$ and $pr_5 = $ **end**; **print** *weie*; **end**; **print** *weim*; **end**;. Bindings b_1, b_2', b_3 and storage state s_3 are as shown in Figure 10.

Symbol **end** at the beginning of the program-rest signals the end of the execution of the last call, namely $WeightonEarth(2.0 + 3.0, weie)$. We remove the local binding set up for this call and obtain configuration

$$c_6 = (pr_6, ((b_1, 0), (b_2', 1)), s_3, \epsilon, o_5)$$

with $pr_6 = $ **print** *weie*; **end**; **print** *weim*; **end**;. Note that in doing so, the old meaning of *wei* is valid again, i.e. $b_2'(wei) = b_1(weim)$. This meaning was temporarily hidden by parameter passing to *wei* in the call of *WeightonEarth*.

Statement **print** *weie* prints 49.05, executing **end** deletes the local binding $(b_2', 1)$ from the binding stack, **print** *weim* prints 27.71 and executing **end** removes local binding $(b_1, 0)$ from the binding stack. This leads to the end configuration

$$c_7 = (\epsilon, \epsilon, s_3, \epsilon, o_7)$$

with $o_7 = (9.81, 9.81, 49.05, 9.81, 166.77, 1.63, 9.81, 49.05, 27.71)$.

This example showed that a small extension of the PROSA machine, namely the introduction of the binding stack, makes it possible to execute PROSA procedures. When processing a procedure declaration, its essential parts, that is the list of formal parameter specifications, the length of the binding stack at the declaration and the body are bound to its name. The second component permits the binding at the point of declaration to be restored during a call and thus the correct meaning to be given to the global names. In our example, when *WeightonEarth* is called, we set the static link sv to 1. Thus g has again the same meaning as at the point of declaration of the procedure. The list of formal parameter specifications enables parameter passing. Subsequently the body is executed.

In this section we introduced a multiplicity of new concepts illustrating them by a continuing example. The reader should study this section repeatedly until he has a good intuitive understanding of the new concepts. In the next section this understanding is deepened and rounded off by way of examples. We will also discuss those concepts which we omitted here, e.g. function procedures, non elementary data types and procedures as parameters.

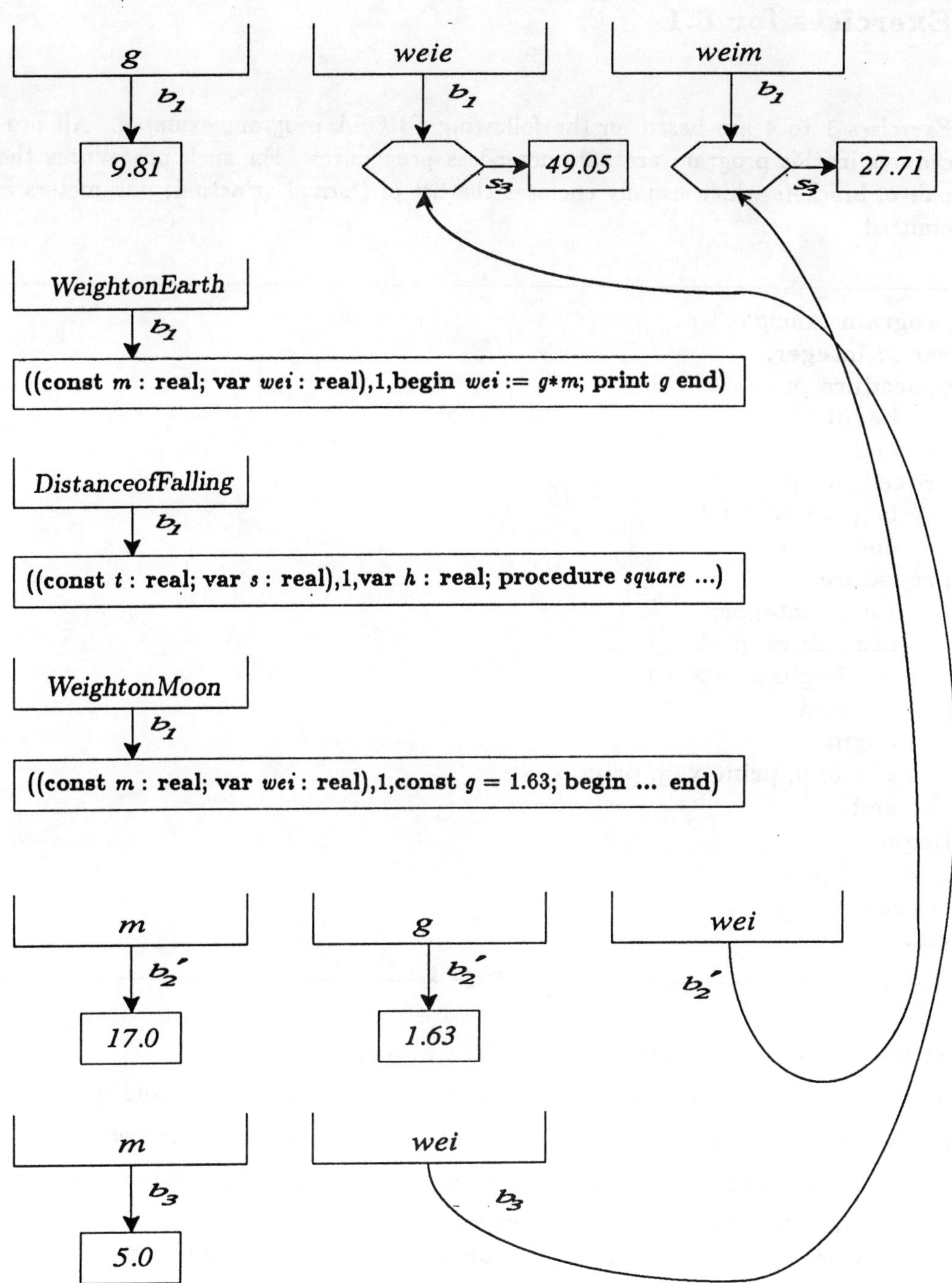

g
weie
weim
b_1
b_1
b_1
9.81
49.05
27.71
s_3
s_3
WeightonEarth
b_1
((const m : real; var wei : real),1,begin $wei := g*m$; print g end)
DistanceofFalling
b_1
((const t : real; var s : real),1,var h : real; procedure $square$ ...)
WeightonMoon
b_1
((const m : real; var wei : real),1,const $g = 1.63$; begin ... end)
m
g
wei
b_2'
b_2'
b_2'
17.0
1.63
m
wei
b_3
b_3
5.0

Fig. 10

Exercises for 6.1

Exercises 1 to 4 are based on the following PROSA program *example*. All procedures in this program are parameter-less procedures. For such procedures the pair of brackets which usually encloses the list of (formal or actual) parameters is omitted.

```
program example;
var x: integer;
procedure p;
    begin q
    end;
procedure q;
    begin x := x + 1
    end;
procedure r
    var x: integer;
    procedure q;
        begin x := x - 1
        end;
    begin
    x := 0; p; print x; q; print x
    end;
begin
x := 0; p; print x;
r; print x;
end.
```

———————————————————— Prog. 1 ————————————————————

1) Determine local and global names of the various procedures.

2) Determine the respective scope for the defining occurrences of x and q.

3) Determine for each applied occurrence of a name its defining occurrence.

4) Document a run of the program by giving the sequence of configurations.

5) Consider the PROSA program *exercise*.
  a) Which sequence of numbers appears on the output tape after executing the program?
  b) Specify for each number on the output tape the configuration of the PROSA machine immediately before the corresponding **print**-statement.

```
program exercise;
var i: integer;
procedure printi;
    begin print i;
        i := i + 1
    end;
procedure q;
    var i: integer;
    begin i := 10;
        printi;
        print i;
    end;
begin
    i := 0;
    q;
    print i
end.
```

————————————— **Prog. 2** —————————————

6.2 Elaboration and Further Examples

We now discuss the new concepts in more detail. A formal treatment follows in the next section. To be more specific about syntax, we give some of the context-free productions for procedure declarations.

Procedure declarations are an additional part of the declaration section. From now on we have

$\langle decls \rangle \rightarrow \langle const\ decls \rangle \langle type\ decls \rangle \langle var\ decls \rangle \langle proc\ decls \rangle$

The procedure declaration section is a sequence of procedure declarations.

$\langle proc\ decls \rangle \rightarrow \langle proc\ decl\ seq \rangle; \mid \epsilon$

$\langle proc\ decl\ seq \rangle \rightarrow \langle proc\ decl\ seq \rangle; \langle proc\ decl \rangle \mid \langle proc\ decl \rangle$

The declaration of a proper procedure, i.e. a procedure with no result, consists of the key word **procedure**, the name of the procedure, the parameter list and the body. In function procedures, i.e. procedures with result, the declaration begins with the key word **function**. The result type is also specified.

$\langle proc\ decl \rangle \rightarrow$ **procedure** $\langle def\ ident \rangle(\langle par\ spec\ seq \rangle); \langle block \rangle$

$\langle proc\ decl \rangle \rightarrow$ **function** $\langle def\ ident \rangle(\langle par\ spec\ seq \rangle) : \langle small\ type \rangle; \langle block \rangle$

$\langle block \rangle \rightarrow \langle decls \rangle$ **begin** $\langle stats \rangle$ **end**

A parameter specification sequence is a sequence of parameter specifications.

$\langle par\ spec\ seq \rangle \rightarrow \langle par\ spec \rangle \mid \langle par\ spec\ seq \rangle; \langle par\ spec \rangle$

A parameter specification consists of one of the key words **const** or **var**, a name and of a type name. The context-free grammar will be extended later.

Example 1: The following function procedure takes two strings as parameters and computes the relation $\leq_{lex}$.

function *lexlessequal* (**const** *x*: **string**; **const** *y*: **string**): **boolean**;
 (∗ computes $x \leq_{lex} y$ ∗)
 var *xh*, *yh*: **string**; **var** *res*, *finished*: **boolean**;
 begin
   xh := *x*; *yh* := *y*; *finished* := **false**;
   while not *finished*
   do (∗ *xh* $\leq_{lex}$ *yh* if and only if $x \leq_{lex} y$ ∗)
    if empty *xh*
    then *res* := **true**; *finished* := **true**
    else
     if empty *yh*
     then *res* := **false**; *finished* := **true**
     else
      if hd *xh* $\neq$ **hd** *yh*
      then
       if hd *xh* $<$ **hd** *yh*
       then *res* := **true**; *finished* := **true**
       else *res* := **false**; *finished* := **true**
       fi
      else *xh* := **tl** *xh*; *yh* := **tl** *yh*
      fi
     fi
    fi
   od;
   lexlessequal := *res*
 end;

Let us once more consider the individual parts of a procedure declaration using this example. The name is *lexlessequal*. Specifications **const** *x*: **string** and **const** *y*: **string** constitute the formal parameter list. This means that *x* and *y* behave like constant names in the body. The result type is *bool*. The body consists of the declarations for local variables *xh*, *yh*, *res* and *finished* and a statement section. The name *lexlessequal* of the function procedure is used in the body like a boolean variable. The result of the procedure call is the value of this variable at the end of the execution of the body. As the call of a function procedure yields a value, such calls can be used in expressions. Examples of calls are (we assume declarations **var** *a*: **boolean** and **var** *s*, *t*: **string**)

 print *lexlessequal*("Hannah", "Eva");
 a := *lexlessequal*(s, t);
 if *lexlessequal*("Barbara", s) **then** ...   ∎

Example 1 illustrates some advantages of procedures. Function procedure *lexlessequal* extends PROSA by one operation. Correctness of the implementation of this operation is obvious from the loop invariant. Any user of this procedure is interested only in "what" the procedure does, i.e. the procedure evaluates the relation $\leq_{lex}$. "How" this is achieved, e.g. by a while-loop, is irrelevant.

Example 2:   In this example we use var-parameters.

procedure *swap*(**var** *x*: **integer**; **var** *y*: **integer**);
  (∗ a call *swap*(*a*, *b*) exchanges the values of variables *a* and *b* ∗)
  var *z*: **integer**;
  begin
     z := *x*; *x* := *y*; *y* := *z*
  end;

Procedure *swap* has two var-parameters, *x* and *y*. In the procedure body *x* and *y* are names for integer variables. However, *x* and *y* are not bound to variables in declarations. Rather this takes place during parameter passing. Consider the following program.

program *trivial*;
var *A*: **array**[1..2] **of integer**;
procedure *swap*(**var** *x*: **integer**; **var** *y*: **integer**);
  var *z*: **integer**;
  begin
     z := *x*; *x* := *y*; *y* := *z*
  end;
begin
  A[1] := 1; *A*[2] := 2;
  swap(*A*[1], *A*[2]);
  print *A*[1]
end.

Immediately before the call *swap*($A[1], A[2]$), the PROSA machine is in configuration $(pr_1, ((b_1, 0)), s_1, \epsilon, \epsilon)$ with $pr_1 = swap(A[1], A[2])$; **print** $A[1]$; **end**;. Figure 1 shows binding b_1 and storage state s_1.

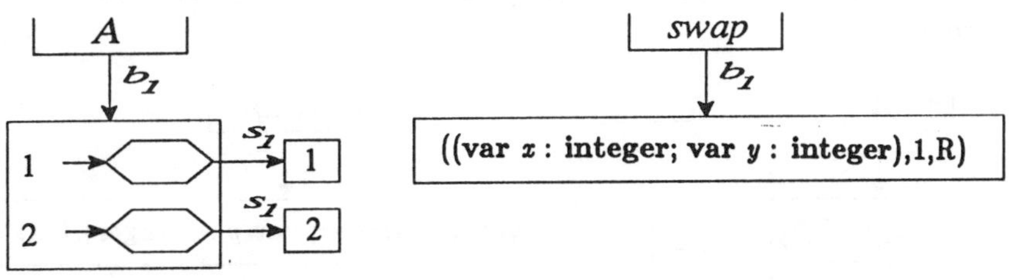

Fig. 1.   Environment before the call *swap*($A[1], A[2]$). *R* is an abbreviation for the body **var** *z*: **integer**; **begin** *z* := *x*; *x* := *y*; *y* := *z* **end** of *swap*.

We now call $swap(A[1], A[2])$. Parameter passing introduces the formal parameters x and y as variable names. They denote *the same* variables as the actual parameters $A[1]$ and $A[2]$. We obtain the configuration $(pr_2, ((b_1, 0), (b_2, 1)), s_1, \epsilon, \epsilon)$. Figure 2 shows bindings b_1 and b_2 and storage state s_1.

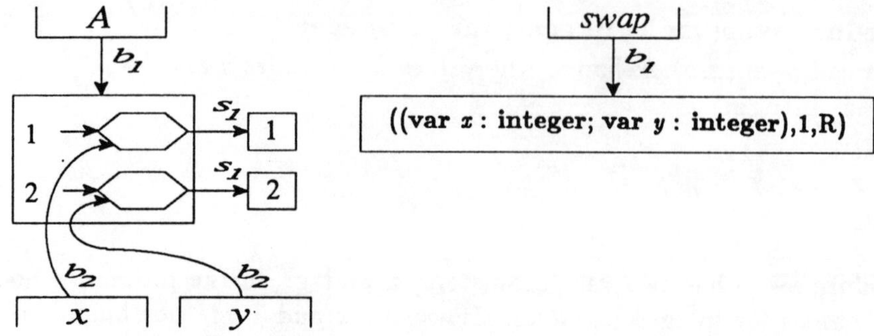

Fig. 2.   Bindings b_1, b_2 and storage state s_1

Proceeding from this configuration the procedure body is now executed. The declaration extends b_2 to b_2' and the assignments swap the values of the variables bound to x and y. We obtain the environment of Figure 3. Returning from the call eliminates the pair $(b_2', 1)$ from the binding stack and we obtain Figure 4.

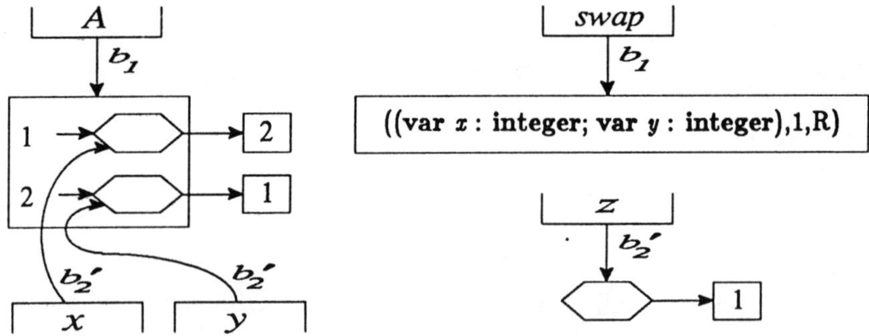

Fig. 3.   Environment after executing the body, but before returning from the procedure call.

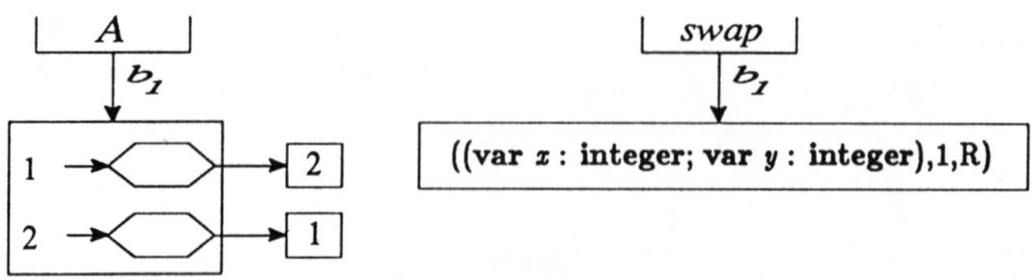

Fig. 4.   After returning from call $swap(A[1], A[2])$

A call $swap(A[1], 1)$ is, of course, nonsensical since 1 is not a variable name. It leads to an error.   ∎

Example 3:   *Bubblesort* takes an array of reals as argument and sorts it in increasing order.

```
procedure bubblesort (var A: array[l..u] of real);
   (* precondition: none; we use S for the set {A[l],...,A[u]}.
      postcondition: S = {A[l],...,A[u]} and A[l] ≤ A[l+1] ≤ ... ≤ A[u].
      computation time: O(n²) where n = u - l + 1. *)
var i, j: integer;
var a: real;
begin
   (* A is sorted by sorting increasingly larger front sections *)
   i := l + 1;
   while i ≤ u

   do (* A[l] ≤ A[l+1] ≤ ... ≤ A[i - 1] and S = {A[l], A[l+1],...,A[u]} *)
      a := A[i];
      (* we now insert A[i] at the correct place by comparing a with A[i -
      1], A[i - 2],... and shifting all elements larger than a one position to the
      right *)
      j := i - 1;
      while j ≥ l and a < A[j]

      do (* S = {a, A[l],...,A[j], A[j+2],...,A[u]},
         A[l] ≤ A[l+1] ≤ ... ≤ A[j] ≤ A[j+2] ≤ ... ≤ A[u] and a < A[j] *)
         A[j+1] := A[j]; j := j - 1;
      od;
      A[j+1] := a
   od
end;
```

With declarations

```
var B: array[1..7] of real
var C: array[4..10] of real
```

calls

```
bubblesort(B);
bubblesort(C);
```

are possible. Parameter passing for $bubblesort(B)$ has the following effect. Names A, l and u are introduced anew, A is an array name and l , u are names for integer constants. A denotes the same array as the actual parameter B, l denotes constant 1, i.e. the lower bound of B, and u constant 7, i.e. the upper bound of B. Figure 5 shows the environment after parameter passing.

With this environment the procedure body is now executed. As already indicated in the comments of the procedure declaration, we sort array A and thus

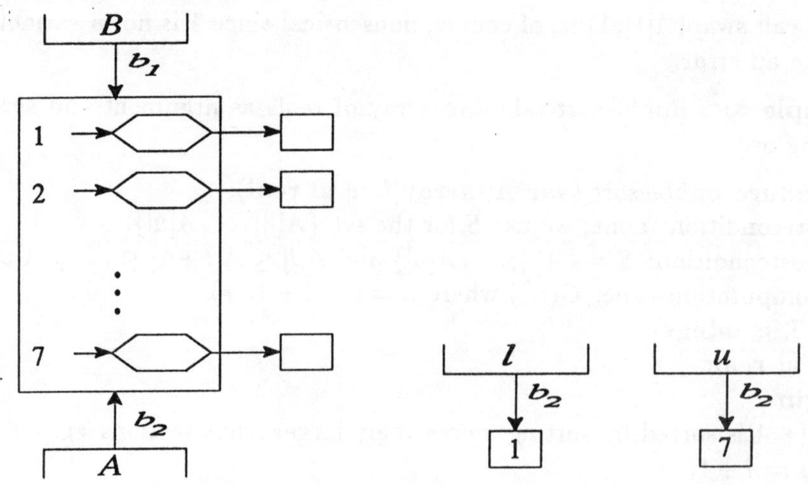

Fig. 5.   Binding stack after a call of *bubblesort*

array B by sorting increasingly larger front sections. In order to add $A[i]$, we need only insert it at the correct place in the section already sorted.

The comment at the beginning of the procedure declaration describes the effect of the procedure in terms of of a pre and a postcondition. It also specifies the computation time. The precondition states the conditions which the actual parameters must satisfy (in our example there are none), and introduces names for the initial values of variables. Thus we introduce S as a name for the set $\{A[l],\ldots,A[u]\}$, i.e. for the set of values stored in the array. We can refer to this name in the postcondition and in the intermediate assertions used to verify the body. The postcondition asserts relationships which hold after executing the body. In our example, therefore, we state that array A still contains the set S, that is the same set as before, and that the elements of A are now arranged in increasing order. Furthermore we claim that the computation time is $O(n^2)$ where $n = u - l + 1$. This can be seen as follows. The outer loop is executed for $i = l + 1, l + 2, \ldots, u$. For fixed i the inner loop is executed at most for $j = i - 1, i - 2, \ldots, l$. Thus the total number of operations is in the order of

$$\sum_{k=1}^{n} k = n(n+1)/2 = O(n^2)$$

For the user (i.e. "caller") of the procedure only the procedure heading, i.e. the name, the parameter list, the pre and postconditions and the computation time is important, whereas the body is totally irrelevant. The name and the parameter list determine the syntax of calls, pre and postcondition specify the semantics and the computation time specification provides information about the time complexity of a call. The user does not need to know any more. We could even replace the body by another which guarantees the same conditions without hampering the user.

The syntax of array parameter specifications is

$\langle par\ spec\rangle \rightarrow \textbf{var}\ \langle def\ ident\rangle : \langle array\ par\ type\rangle$

$\langle array\ par\ type\rangle \rightarrow \textbf{array}[\langle def\ bound\ seq\rangle]\ \textbf{of}\ \langle small\ type\rangle$

$\langle def\ bound\ seq\rangle \rightarrow \langle def\ ident\rangle..\langle def\ ident\rangle|$
$\qquad\qquad\qquad \langle def\ ident\rangle..\langle def\ ident\rangle, \langle def\ bound\ seq\rangle$

An array parameter introduces a name for the array as well as constant names for
the bounds. In Example 3 these are l and u. For an array parameter specified by
var a: array$[l1..u1,\ldots,lk..uk]$ **of** t any k-dimensional array of type t may be used
as an actual parameter. In the body a is the name of a k-dimensional array and
$l1, u1, \ldots, lk, uk$ are constant names. Parameter passing binds a to the array given
by the actual parameter and $l1, u1, \ldots, lk, uk$ are bound to the corresponding array
bounds.

Next we will have a closer look at procedure calls. A procedure call is a
procedure name followed by a sequence of actual parameters. It is a statement.

$\langle stat\rangle \rightarrow \langle proc\ call\rangle$

$\langle proc\ call\rangle \rightarrow \langle app\ ident\rangle((\langle act\ par\ seq\rangle))$

$\langle act\ par\ seq\rangle \rightarrow \langle act\ par\rangle|\langle act\ par\ seq\rangle, \langle act\ par\rangle$

$\langle act\ par\rangle \rightarrow \langle expr\rangle|\langle app\ ident\rangle$

The sequence of actual parameters is a sequence of expressions or names. The length
of this sequence must coincide with the length of the corresponding list of formal
parameters. Let L be this length. Then the i-th actual parameter, $1 \leq i \leq L$, must
have the same type as the i-th formal parameter. If the i-th formal parameter is
specified as const then the actual parameter is an expression. If it is specified as
var or proc (proc-parameters are explained below) then the actual parameter must
be an applied name, see. Figure 6.

What happens exactly during a procedure call? As already mentioned, the
PROSA machine has a binding stack instead of the previous binding. A binding
stack is a sequence of pairs (b_i, sv_i). b_i is a binding in the usual sense and $sv_i \in \mathbb{N}_0$,
$sv_i < i$. The number sv_i is the static link of binding b_i. If we call the set of binding
stacks **BS** then

$$\textbf{BS} = (\textbf{B} \times \mathbb{N}_0)^*$$

and the set of configurations

$$\textbf{C} = \textbf{PR} \times \textbf{BS} \times \textbf{S} \times \textbf{I} \times \textbf{O}.$$

We use $bs, bs_1, \ldots$ as names for binding stacks.

A procedure call is processed as follows. Let $n(apl);\ p'$ be a call of procedure n with the actual parameter sequence apl followed by the program-rest p'. Let
furthermore $bs = ((b_1, sv_1), \ldots, (b_m, sv_m))$ be the binding stack.

1) Retrieve from bs the object to which name n is bound. We find $bs(n)$, as
already mentioned, by the following algorithm:

formal parameter specification	act. parameter	explanation
const n: t	E	$t \in \langle elem\ type \rangle$, E is an expression of type t.
var n: t	y	$t \in \langle small\ type \rangle$, y is an applied name denoting a variable of type t.
var n: t	y	$t \in \langle array\ par\ type \rangle$, y is an applied array name. The dimension of y must match the dimension specification in t.
proc $n(psl)$	y	$psl \in \langle mode\ seq \rangle$, y is an applied procedure name whose type coincides with the mode sequence psl.

Fig. 6.   Relation between formal parameter specification and actual parameter. $n \in \langle ident \rangle$.

Set h to m. If $b_h(n)$ is defined then $bs(n) = b_h(n)$. Otherwise set h to sv_h and repeat.

Let $bs(n) = ((psl), i, ds\ \textbf{begin}\ sts\ \textbf{end})$ where psl is the sequence of parameter specifications, i is the length of the binding stack at declaration and $ds\ \textbf{begin}\ sts\ \textbf{end}$ is the body. We change the binding stack to $bs' = ((b_1, sv_1), \ldots, (b_m, sv_m), (b_{m+1}, i))$ in preparation for the execution of the body. Here $b_{m+1} = \emptyset$. Setting $sv_{m+1} = i$ means that the meaning of global names is determined with the same binding stack as is used at the declaration. Thus global names are treated correctly.

2) Now we turn to parameter passing. Let $n_1, \ldots, n_k$ be the names of formal parameters. We take $\{n_1, \ldots, n_k\}$ as domain of b'_{m+1} and define (e_i is the i-th actual parameter) for $1 \le i \le k$

$$b'_{m+1}(n_i) = \begin{cases} I(bs, s, e_i), & \text{if } n_i \text{ is a const-parameter;} \\ L(bs, s, e_i), & \text{if } n_i \text{ is a var-parameter;} \\ bs(e_i), & \text{if } n_i \text{ is a proc-parameter.} \end{cases}$$

s is the actual storage state. After parameter passing the actual binding "knows" the meaning of the formal parameters. A const-parameter is treated like a constant name. Its value is given by the value of the actual parameter at the call. Note that actual parameters are evaluated in the environment (bs, s), i.e. in the environment of the call. A var-parameter is treated like a variable name. It is bound to the variable denoted by the actual parameter. Similarly, a proc-parameter is treated as a procedure name. It is bound to the procedure denoted by the actual parameter.

3) We now execute the body with actual environment (bs', s). We place ds sts; **end**; in front of the the program-rest and then process the declarations and

statements. The latter will in general alter the binding bs' and the storage state s. Let s' be the new storage state.

4) When finished we return from the procedure by executing **end**. This deletes the last member of the binding stack. Then we continue with the rest of the program p' in environment (bs, s').

To round off the discussion let us consider how the PROSA machine processes a procedure declaration. Consider a declaration $n(psl); D$ with a parameter specification sequence psl and a body D. Let $bs = ((b_1, sv_1), \ldots, (b_m, sv_m))$ be the actual binding stack. Executing the declaration changes b_m into $b_m{'}$ with

$$b_m{'} = b_m[n \backslash (psl, m, D)],$$

i.e. triple (psl, m, D) is bound to the procedure name n. Component m indicates that $((b_1, sv_1), \ldots, (b_m, sv_m))$ was the actual binding stack at declaration. Setting the static link appropriately ensures that this binding stack is referred to when procedure n is called (compare step 1 above). Thus the meaning of global names in the body is determined relative to the place of the procedure declaration.

Example 4: *GCD* computes the greatest common divisor of two integers recursively.

```
program greatest_common_divisor;
var a, b, c: integer;
procedure GCD(const x: integer; const y: integer; var z: integer);
   (* precondition: x ≥ 0 and y ≥ 0;
      postcondition : z = gcd(x, y);
      computation time: O(log max(x, y)) *)
   begin
      if y = 0
      then z := x
      else GCD(y, x mod y, z)
      fi;
      print x
   end;
begin (* main program *)
   a := 8; b := 6;
   GCD(a, b, c);
   print c
end.
```

Immediately before the call of *GCD*, the PROSA machine is in configuration

$$(GCD(a, b, c); \ \textbf{print } c; \ \textbf{end};, ((b_1, 0)), s, \epsilon, \epsilon),$$

where b_1 and s are specified in Figure 7.

The call and parameter passing establishes configuration

$$(sts; \ \textbf{end}; \ \textbf{print } c; \ \textbf{end};, ((b_1, 0), (b_2, 1)), s, \epsilon, \epsilon),$$

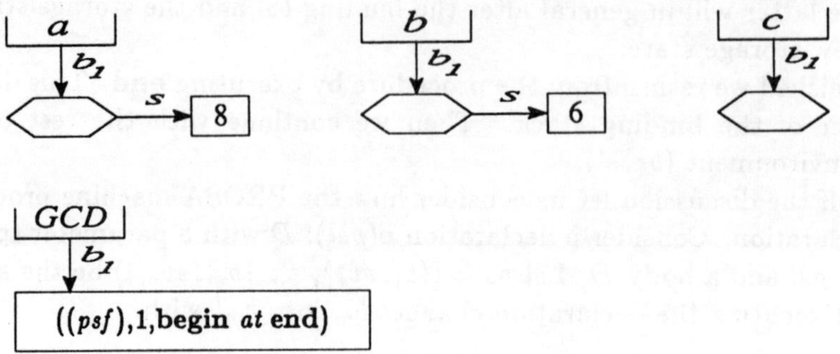

Fig. 7.   Situation before the first call.

$sts = $ **if** $y = 0$ **then** $z := x$ **else** $GCD(y, x$ **mod** $y, z)$ **fi**; **print** x and
$psl = $ **const** x: **integer**; **const** y: **integer**; **var** z: **integer**.

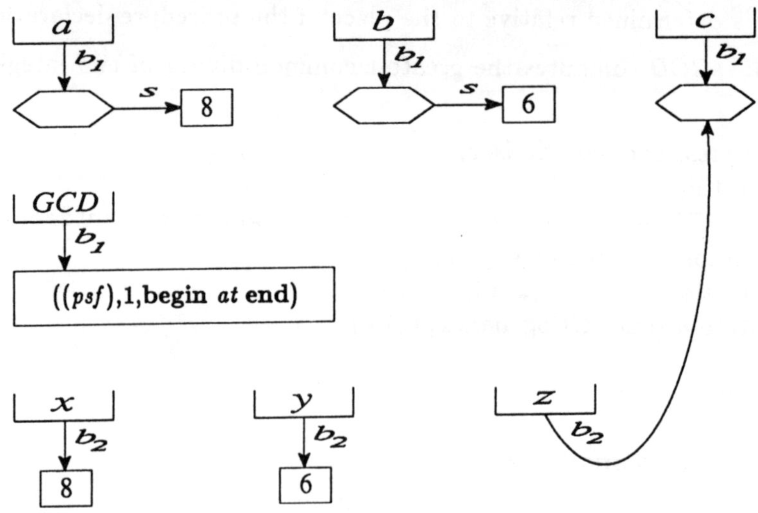

Fig. 8.   Situation after the first call.

where b_1, b_2 and s are specified in Figure 8.

In the program-rest we have substituted the call by sts; **end** . **end** marks the point where the call is finished. In b_2 name x is bound to 8, y to 6 and z to the variable $b_1(c)$.

The next configuration is

$$(GCD(y, x \textbf{ mod } y, z); \textbf{ print } x; \textbf{ end}; \textbf{ print } c; \textbf{ end};, ((b_1, 0), (b_2, 1)), s, \epsilon, \epsilon).$$

Call and parameter passing achieves

$$(sts; \textbf{ end}; \textbf{ print } x; \textbf{ end}; \textbf{ print } c; \textbf{ end};, ((b_1, 0), (b_2, 1), (b_3, 1)), s, \epsilon, \epsilon),$$

where b_1, b_2, b_3 and s are shown in Figure 9. In b_3 name x is bound to 6, i.e.
the value of expression y at the point of call, y to 2, i.e. the value of expression
x mod y at the point of call and z to the variable $b_2(z) = b_1(c)$.

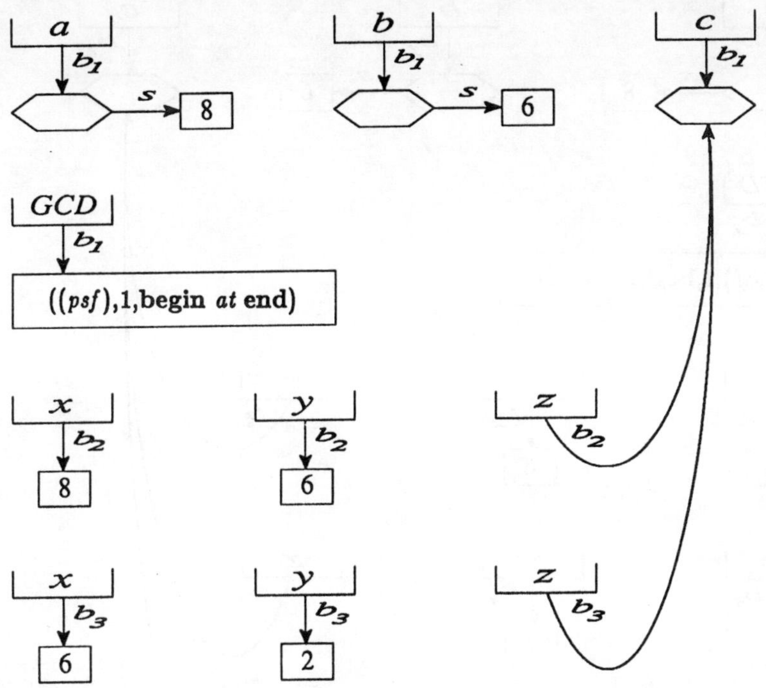

Fig. 9.   Situation after the second call.

The next configuration is

$(GCD(y, x \bmod y, z);$ **print** $x;$ **end; print** $x;$ **end; print** $c;$ **end**$;, bs, s, \epsilon, \epsilon)$

with $bs = ((b_1, 0), (b_2, 1), (b_3, 1))$. Call and parameter passing establish the configuration

$(sts;$ **end; print** $x;$ **end; print** $x;$ **end; print** $c;$ **end**$;, bs, s, \epsilon, \epsilon)$

with $bs = ((b_1, 0), (b_2, 1), (b_3, 1), (b_4, 1))$. In b_4 name x is bound to 2, y to 0 and z
to the variable $b_3(z) = b_2(z) = b_1(z)$. We now assign the value of expression x in
the actual environment (bs, s), i.e. 2, to the variable denoted by z and print this
value. We obtain

$($**end; print** $x;$ **end; print** $x;$ **end; print** $c;$ **end**$;, bs, s', \epsilon, (2)),$

where b_1, b_2, b_3, b_4 and s' are shown in Figure 10.

end at the beginning of the rest-program indicates completion of the last call.
We delete $(b_4, 1)$ from the stack and obtain

$($**print** $x;$ **end; print** $x;$ **end; print** $c;$ **end**$;, bs, s', \epsilon, (2))$

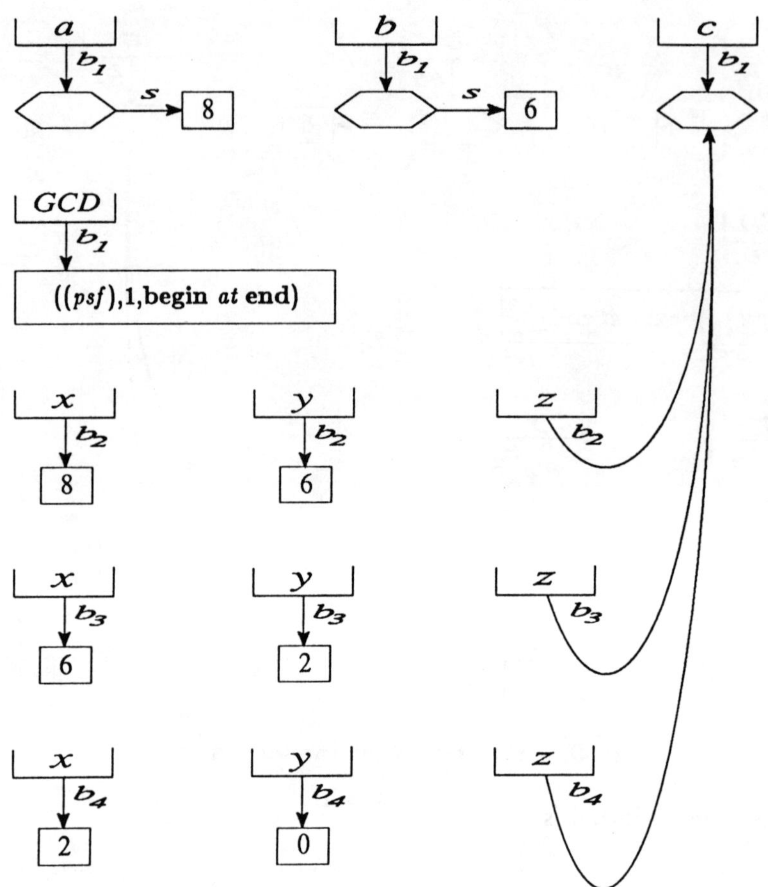

Fig. 10.   Situation after the third call and execution of the body.

with $bs = ((b_1, 0), (b_2, 1), (b_3, 1))$. We now print $I(((b_1, 0), (b_2, 1), (b_3, 1)), s', x) = s'(b_3(x)) = 6$ and move to

$$(\textbf{end; print } x; \textbf{ end; print } c; \textbf{ end};, ((b_1, 0), (b_2, 1), (b_3, 1)), s', \epsilon, (2, 6)).$$

The next configurations are

$$(\textbf{print } x; \textbf{ end; print } c; \textbf{ end};, ((b_1, 0), (b_2, 1)), s', \epsilon, (2, 6)),$$

then

$$(\textbf{end; print } c; \textbf{ end};, ((b_1, 0), (b_2, 1)), s', \epsilon, (2, 6, 8)),$$

then

$$(\textbf{print } c; \textbf{ end};, ((b_1, 0)), s', \epsilon, (2, 6, 8)),$$

then

$$(\textbf{end};, ((b_1, 0)), s', \epsilon, (2, 6, 8, 2)),$$

and finally

$$(\epsilon, \epsilon, s', \epsilon, (2, 6, 8, 2)).$$

The computation now ends with sequence $2, 6, 8, 2$ as result.

Procedure GCD is the PROSA formulation of the corresponding recursive procedure in the introduction. As in the introduction, we show correctness and computation time specification by induction on y. We demonstrate this once again for correctness. If y is equal to 0 then $x = gcd(x, 0) = gcd(x, y)$ is assigned to z. In this case, therefore, the procedure operates correctly. Let $y > 0$. Then GCD is called recursively with the parameters y, $x \textbf{ mod } y$ and z. The induction hypothesis states that the recursive call assigns $gcd(y, x \textbf{ mod } y) = gcd(x, y)$ to the variable denoted by z. Since $x \textbf{ mod } y < y$ we can use the induction hypothesis and thus show that the procedure operates correctly in this case.   ∎

Example 4 illustrates very nicely how the binding stack keeps different meanings of a name apart. Name x, for instance, obtains a new meaning with each call. The old meaning thus becomes temporarily invisible. However it is not lost. On returning from a call the old meaning is visible again. We achieve this effect by means of the stack principle. A call of a procedure pushes a new binding onto the stack and when returning it is popped again. In this way names can be given a new meaning for the duration of a call either by parameter passing or by a local declaration. The old meaning is available again on return.

The meaning of global names is found with the help of the chain of static links. In our example $sv_i = 1$ for $i = 2, 3, 4$. This corresponds to our view that the global objects, i.e. a, b, c and GCD, are declared in the main program and their meaning therefore is given by b_1.

The semantics of function procedures is similar to that of proper procedures. The call of a function procedure is a factor, thus

$$\langle factor \rangle \rightarrow \langle proc\ call \rangle$$

When called the body of the procedure is executed as usual. Assignments to the names of function procedures are permitted and necessary, see Example 1. The result of the call, and thus the value of the factor, is the final value of the variable denoted by the name of the function procedure.

Example 5:   A function procedure to compute the greatest common divisor.

```
function GCDF (const x: integer; const y: integer): integer;
   (* precondition: x ≥ 0, y ≥ 0;
      postcondition : result is gcd(x,y) ,
      computation time: O(log max(x,y) *)
   begin
```

```
      if y = 0
      then GCDF := x
      else GCDF := GCDF(y, x mod y)
      fi
   end;
begin
   if GCDF(18, 8) = 2
   then print 4 + GCDF(17, 9)
   fi
end;
```

GCDF computes the greatest common divisor of its arguments. Calls of *GCDF* can be used as factors in integer expressions. Thus using function procedures is more elegant than using proper procedures (Example 4).

Let us consider some further examples.

Example 6:   A function procedure to compute the factorial function.

```
procedure fac(const n: integer): integer;
   (* precondition: none;
      postconditions: yields n! if n ≥ 0 and 1 otherwise;
      computation time: O(n), if n ≥ 0 and O(1) otherwise *)
   begin
      if n ≤ 0
      then fac := 1
      else fac := n * fac(n − 1)
      fi
   end;
```

Example 7:   A function procedure to search in an ordered array. *Binary_search* implements the method of Chapter IV, Example 3.

```
function binary_search(var: array A[l..u] of string, const x: string): integer;
   (* precondition: A[l] ≤_lex A[l + 1] ≤_lex ... ≤_lex A[u];
      postcondition: result is i with A[i] = x if
                        i exists and
                        0 otherwise;
      computation time: O(log n) with n = u − l + 1 *)
   function iter(const upper, lower: integer): integer;
      (* precondition: lower ≤ upper and if there exists i with A[i] = x
                        then lower ≤ i ≤ upper;
         postcondition: as for binary_search;
         computation time: O(log(upper − lower + 1)) *)
      var res, centre: integer;
      begin
          centre := (lower + upper)/2;
          if A[centre] = x
```

```
          then res := centre
          else if lower = upper
                  then res := 0
                  else (* A[centre] ≠ x and lower < upper *)
                     if lexlessequal(x, A[centre])
                        (* A call of the procedure from Example 1 *)
                        then res := iter(lower, centre − 1)
                        else res := iter(centre + 1, top)
                     fi
               fi
        fi;
        iter := res
     end;
  begin
     binary_search := iter(l, u)
  end;
```

A call $binary_search(A, x)$ determines the position of x in array A. The actual work is done in function $iter$ declared locally to $binary_search$. Other than in Chapter IV, we formulate the iteration as a recursive procedure and not as a **while-loop**. The mode of operation of $binary_search$ thus becomes more obvious. The phrase "compare x with the element in the middle and in the case of inequality continue with the left or right half respectively" is reflected almost directly in the program text.   ∎

Example 8:   Let $G = (N, T, P, S)$ be a context-free grammar and let $x \in T^*$ be a string. In this example we will specify a procedure which decides whether $x \in L_G$. For simplicity sake we assume that grammar G is in Chomsky normal form, i.e. for all productions $(A, \alpha) \in P$:

1) $|\alpha| = 1$ or $|\alpha| = 2$;
2) if $|\alpha| = 1$ then $\alpha \in T$;
3) if $|\alpha| = 2$ then $\alpha \in N^2$.

Note that for each $A \in N$ and $x \in T^*$ the fact $A \rightarrow^* x$ implies $x \neq \epsilon$. Grammar $G = (\{A, B, S\}, \{a, b\}, P, S)$ with $P = \{S \rightarrow AB, A \rightarrow BA, B \rightarrow AB, A \rightarrow a, B \rightarrow b\}$ is an example of a grammar in Chomsky normal form. Let $x \in T^* - \{\epsilon\}$. How can we decide whether $x \in L_G$ or, in general, $X \rightarrow^* x$ for some $X \in N$? Two simple observations:

1) if $|x| = 1$ then $X \rightarrow^* x$ if and only if $(X, x) \in P$.
2) if $|x| > 1$ then $X \rightarrow^* x$ if and only if there are strings $y, z \in T^*$ and a production $(X, YZ) \in P$ with $Y \rightarrow^* y$ and $Z \rightarrow^* z$.

These two observations suggest the following method (often called **backtrack** parsing). If $|x| = 1$ then check whether (X, x) is a production of the grammar. If $|x| > 1$ then check for all decompositions $x = yz$ of x into strings $y, z \in T^* - \{\epsilon\}$ and all productions $(X, YZ) \in P$ whether $Y \rightarrow^* y$ and $Z \rightarrow^* z$. To check the latter two apply the same method as for x. Note that $y, z \in T^* - \{\epsilon\}$ implies $|y| < |x|$ and $|z| < |x|$ and thus the recursive application of the method terminates.

Before we can formulate this method in PROSA, we must fix a representation for grammar G and string x. For x we suggest an array **var** W: **array**$[1..n]$ **of char** and for the productions of G two arrays **var** $P1$: **array**$[1..m, 1..2]$ **of char** and **var** $P2$: **array**$[1..k, 1..3]$ **of char**. For $1 \le i \le m$,

$$P1[i, 1] \rightarrow P1[i, 2]$$

is a production of G and for $1 \le i \le k$,

$$P2[i, 1] \rightarrow P2[i, 2]P2[i, 3]$$

is a production of G. Array W contains string x as a sequence of letters, i.e. $x = W[1] \ldots W[n]$. How do we represent a substring of x? The simplest way is to use two indices l and u in array W. The substring then is $W[l] \ldots W[u]$. We now specify the function procedure *decompose* such that a call $decompose(1, n, X)$ decides for $x \in T^* - \{\epsilon\}$ and $X \in N$ whether $X \rightarrow^* x$.

```
function decompose(const l, u: integer; X: char): boolean;
   (* precondition: 1 ≤ l ≤ u ≤ n;
      postcondition : result is true if and only if X →* W[l] ... W[u];
      computation time: see remark after Lemma 2 *)
   var derivable: boolean;
   var i, j, h: integer;
   begin
      derivable := false;
      if l = u
      then (* the string to be derived has length 1; we check if X → W[l] occurs
      in table P1 *)
         i := 1;
         while not derivable and i ≤ m
         do if P1[i, 1] = X and P1[i, 2] = W[l]
            then derivable := true
            else (* try next production *)
               i := i + 1
            fi
         od
      else (* the string to be derived has length > 1; we now go through all pro-
      ductions in P2 (iteration variable h) and all decompositions
         W[l] ... W[u] = W[l] ... W[j]W[j + 1] ... W[u]
      and check if
      P2[h, 1] = X and P2[h, 2] →* W[l] ... W[j] and P2[h, 3] →* W[j+1] ... W[u]
      *)
```

```
      h := 1;
      while not derivable and  h ≤ k
      do (* try all possible j *)
          j := l;
          while not derivable and  j < u
          do derivable := ((P2[h, 1] = X) and
                      decompose(l, j, P2[h, 2]) and decompose(j + 1, u, P2[h, 3]);
              j := j + 1
          od;
          h := h + 1
      od;
   fi;
   decompose := derivable
end;
```

The correctness of this program should be evident from the preliminary remarks
and the comments. However, we have still to determine its computation time. Let
$L(s)$ denote the maximal computation time for a call $decompose(l, u, X)$ with $s \in \mathbb{N}$
and $s = u - l + 1$. That is we measure the computation time of the program relative
to the length of the string to be derived. For $s = 1$ we just check the productions
of table $P1$ and thus

$$L(1) \leq c_1 m$$

for a suitable constant c_1. For $s > 1$ we go through the productions in table $P2$.
For each production we try all possible values of j, i.e. $j = l, l + 1, \ldots, u - 1$, and
call $decompose(l, j, P2[h, 2])$ and $decompose(j + 1, u, P2[h, 3])$ recursively. With
$s_1 = j - i + 1$ and $s_2 = u - (j + 1) + 1$ the time required by these calls is bound by
$L(s_1)$ and $L(s_2)$. Furthermore $s_1 + s_2 = s$ and $1 \leq s_1 < s$. Thus for $s \geq 2$

$$L(s) \leq c_2 + k \sum_{s_1=1}^{s-1} (c_2 + L(s_1) + L(s - s_1))$$

for a suitable constant c_2. Constant c_2 accounts for the actions outside the recursive calls. With these estimates for $L(s)$ we can now easily determine bounds for
$L(1), L(2), L(3), \ldots$.

$$L(2) \leq c_2 + k(c_2 + L(1) + L(1))$$
$$\leq (k + 1)c_2 + 2c_1 km.$$

$$L(3) \leq c_2 + k \sum_{s_1=1}^{2} (c_2 + L(s_1) + L(s - s_1))$$

$$\leq c_2 + k((c_2) + L(1) + L(2)) + (c_2 + L(2) + L(1))$$
$$\leq (2k + 1)c_2 + 2k(k + 1)c_2 + 2k(2k + 1)c_1 m.$$

We could of course derive a bound for $L(100)$ in the same laborious way. Clearly
we would rather have an explicit bound which we can evaluate directly. We will

now derive such a bound. (The rest of this example is not essential in the sequel,
but it gives the reader an idea how complex algorithms can be analysed). Firstly,
we define a function $S(s)$ replacing $\leq$ by $=$ in the above inequalities, thus

$$S(1) = c_1 m$$

$$S(s) = c_2 + k \sum_{i=1}^{s-1} (c_2 + S(i) + S(s-i)), \quad \text{for } s \geq 2.$$

Function $S(s)$ is indeed an upper bound for $L(s)$.

Lemma 1. *For all* $s \in \mathbb{N} : L(s) \leq S(s)$.

Proof: By induction on s. For $s = 1$ we have

$$L(1) \leq c_1 m = S(1),$$

and for $s \geq 1$

$$L(s) \leq c_2 + k \sum_{i=1}^{s-1} (c_2 + L(i) + L(s-i))$$

$$\leq c_2 + k \sum_{i=1}^{s-1} (c_2 + S(i) + S(s-i)), \quad \text{by ind. hyp.}$$

$$= S(s).$$

$\blacksquare$

We must now find an explicit description of $S(s)$. To do this we simplify the second
equation.

$$S(s) = c_2 + k \sum_{i=1}^{s-1} (c_2 + S(i) + S(s-i))$$

$$= c_2 + c_2(s-1)k + k \sum_{i=1}^{s-1} S(i) + k \sum_{i=1}^{s-1} S(s-i)$$

$$= c_2(1 + (s-1)k) + k \sum_{i=1}^{s-1} S(i) + k \sum_{i=1}^{s-1} S(i)$$

$$= c_2(1 + (s-1)k) + 2k \sum_{i=1}^{s-1} S(i)$$

Thus

$$S(s) = c_2(1 + (s-1)k) + 2k \sum_{i=1}^{s-1} S(i)$$

for $s \geq 2$. For $s \geq 3$ we now subtract from this equation the same equation for $s - 1$, thus

$$S(s) - S(s-1) = c_2(1 + (s-1)k) + 2k\sum_{i=1}^{s-1} S(i) - (c_2(1 + (s-2)k) + 2k\sum_{i=1}^{s-2} S(i))$$

$$= c_2 \cdot k + 2k \cdot S(s-1)$$

and hence

$$S(s) = c_2 k + (2k+1) \cdot S(s-1)$$

for all $s \geq 3$. We still have a recursion equation for function S, but it is of a much simpler form. Several substitutions yield

$$S(s) = c_2 \cdot k + (2k+1) \cdot S(s-1)$$
$$= c_2 \cdot k + (2k+1)(c_2 \cdot k + (2k+1) \cdot S(s-2))$$
$$= c_2 \cdot k + (2k+1)(c_2 \cdot k + (2k+1)^2(c_2 \cdot k + (2k+1) \cdot S(s-3))$$
$$\vdots$$
$$= c_2 \cdot k \cdot \sum_{i=0}^{s-3}(2k+1)^i + (2k+1)^{s-2} \cdot S(2)$$

The "dots" in this derivation are less harmless than they appear. We verify the result by induction.

Lemma 2. For $s \geq 2 : S(s) = c_2 \cdot k \cdot \sum_{i=0}^{s-3}(2k+1)^i + (2k+1)^{s-2} \cdot S(2)$.

Proof: For $s = 2$ the claim is obvious. Let $s \geq 3$. Then

$$S(s) = c_2 \cdot k + (2k+1) \cdot S(s-1) \qquad \text{recursion equation}$$

$$= c_2 \cdot k + (2k+1)\left[c_2 \cdot k \cdot \sum_{i=o}^{s-1-3}(2k+1)^i + (2k+1)^{s-1-2}) \cdot S(2)\right] \quad \text{by ind. hyp.}$$

$$= c_2 \cdot k(2k+1)^0 + c_2 \cdot k \cdot \sum_{i=1}^{s-3}(2k+1)^i + (2k+1)^{s-2} \cdot S(2)$$

$$= c_2 \cdot k\sum_{i=0}^{s-3}(2k+1)^i + (2k+1)^{s-2} \cdot S(2)$$

$\blacksquare$

Because $S(2) = (k+1)c_2 + 2c_1 km$ we have

$$S(s) = \begin{cases} c_1 m & \text{for } s = 1; \\ c_2 \cdot \frac{(2k+1)^{s-2}-1}{2k} + (2k+1)^{s-2}[(k+1)c_2 + 2c_1 km] & \text{for } s \geq 2. \end{cases}$$

We have used

$$\sum_{i=0}^{s-3} x^i = \frac{x^{s-2} - 1}{x - 1}$$

for the geometric series. Thus the desired explicit description of the bound $S(s)$ is achieved. With our example grammar we have $m = 2$, $k = 3$ and thus

$$S(s) = c_2 \cdot (7^{s-2} - 1)/2 + 7^{s-2}(4c_2 + 12c_1) = O(7^s)$$

Even for small s, e.g. $s = 100$, $S(s)$ is very large. The reader may well suggest that our estimate is extremely pessimistic, since we do not have to try out all possibilities at every call until we find a derivation. This objection is not very strong. Let us take, for instance, an input string $x = c^s$. Then all calls result in *false* and in fact we do try out all possibilities.

From these considerations it becomes clear that the above procedure *decompose* is only useful for short strings x. For long strings the method would be too inefficient. We shall now briefly describe an improvement (often called **syntax analysis** by **dynamic programming**) which reduces computation time to $O(s^3)$. The inefficiency of the above method is due to the fact that *decompose* may be called frequently with identical parameters. We can avoid this if we record the results of *decompose* in a table. We use an array **var** Z: **array**$[1..n, 1..n, 1..K]$ **of integer** with $K = |N|$. Furthermore we presume a function

function *num* (**const** X: **char**): **integer**;
   ($*$ precondition: X is a nonterminal
     postcondition : $num(X) \in [1..|N|]$ and *num* is injective. $*$)

which we do not explain further. The effect of function *num* is to number the nonterminals from 1 to $|N|$. Entries $Z[i,j,h]$, $i \leq j$, have the following meaning. Let $X \in N$ with $num(X) = h$.

if $Z[i,j,h] = 0$ then $neg(X \rightarrow^* W[i] \ldots W[j])$;

if $Z[i,j,h] = 1$ then $X \rightarrow^* W[i] \ldots W[j]$;

if $Z[i,j,h] = 2$ then it is not known whether X derives $W[i] \ldots W[j]$, i.e. either $X \rightarrow^* W[i] \ldots W[j]$ or $neg(X \rightarrow^* W[i] \ldots W[j])$.

We modify our program as follows. Outside of *decompose* we set $Z[i,j,h]$ to 2 for all $1 \leq i,j \leq n$, $1 \leq h \leq K$. In the body of *decompose* we insert immediately before the assignment *decompose* := *derivable* the statement

    if *derivable*
    then $Z[l, u, num(X)] := 1$
    else $Z[l, u, num(X)] := 0$
    fi;

Finally we replace the line

$derivable := ((P2[h,1] = X)$ **and** $decompose\ (l,\ j,\ P2[h,2])$ **and** $decompose\ (j{+}1,u,\ P2[h,3]))$

by

> **if** $Z[l,j,num(P2[h,2])] \neq 2$
> > **then** $derivable1 := (Z[l,j,num(P2[h,2])] = 1)$
> > **else** $derivable1 := decompose(l,j,P2[h,2])$
>
> **fi**;
> **if** $Z[j+1,u,num(P2[h,3])] \neq 2$
> > **then** $derivable2 := (Z[j+1,u,num(P2[h,3])] = 1)$
> > **else** $derivable2 := decompose(j+1,u,P2[h,3])$
>
> **fi**;
> $derivable := (P2[h,1] = X)$ **and** $derivable1$ **and** $derivable2$;

$derivable1$ and $derivable2$ are additional variables. Thus before each call of *decompose* we check if we have already called *decompose* with this parameter list by inspecting table Z. If this is the case we take the result from table Z. This small change has a big effect. We consider a call $decompose(1,n,X)$ and make the following observations.

1) For all i, j, h with $1 \leq i \leq j \leq n$, $1 \leq h \leq K$ there is at most *one* call $decompose(i,j,X)$ where $h = num(X)$. This holds because the first call already sets $Z[i,j,h]$ to 0 or 1 and thus all further calls are replaced by consulting the array Z.

2) Let i, j, h with $1 \leq i \leq j \leq n$ and $1 \leq h \leq K$ be arbitrary. Let furthermore $h = num(X)$. Then for a call $decompose(i,j,X)$ we have: if $j = i$ then executing the body requires $c_1 m$ time units for some constant c_1. If $j < i$ then executing the body *without* the time spent in recursive calls takes $c_2 k(j - i + 1)$ time units for a suitable constant c_2. Considering that for each i, j, h there is no more than one call, the total computation time is at most

$$\sum_{i=1}^{n}\sum_{h=1}^{K} c_1 m + \sum_{1 \leq i < j \leq n}\sum_{h=1}^{K} c_2 k(j - i + 1)$$

$$\leq c_1 m K n + \sum_{i=1}^{n}\sum_{j=1}^{n}\sum_{h=1}^{K} c_2 k n$$

$$\leq c_1 m K n + c_2 k K n^3$$

In our example $m = 2$, $k = 3$ and $K = 3$. Thus the modified procedure *decompose* requires at most $c_1 \cdot 6n + c_2 \cdot 9n^3 = O(n^3)$ time units for an input string x of length n. For medium size n, say $n \leq 1000$, this is certainly acceptable. For very large n, as it occurs in practice, the method just introduced is still too inefficient. One has to use methods tailored to the particular grammar on hand. Such methods are discussed in courses on "syntax analysis".

■

Example 9:   In this example we implement the data type "string" as linear lists and answer the question left open in Chapter V as to the realisation of this data type in RESA. Note that the following procedures can be translated into RESA using the methods of Chapters V and VII.

To represent strings we use

type *string* = **record** *symbol*: **char**;

                  rest: $\uparrow$*string*

       end

A pointer variable v, declared as **var** v: $\uparrow$*string*, then represents the string $rep(v)$ with

$$rep(v) = \begin{cases} \epsilon, & \text{if } v = nil; \\ conc(v \uparrow .symbol, rep(v \uparrow .rest)), & \text{if } v \neq nil. \end{cases}$$

Functions *Empty* (which corresponds to *empty*) and *Firstsymbol* (for *head*) are easy.

function *Empty*(**var** w: $\uparrow$*string*): **boolean**;

    (∗ precondition: none;

       postcondition : computes $rep(w) = \epsilon$;

       computation time: $O(1)$ ∗)

    begin if $w = $ **nil**

          then *Empty* := **true**;

          else   *Empty* := **false**

          fi

    end;

function *Firstsymbol*(**var** w: $\uparrow$*string*): **char**;

    (∗ precondition: none;

       postcondition : computes $head(rep(w))$;

       computation time: $O(1)$ ∗)

    begin if $w = $ **nil**

          then error halt

          else   *Firstsymbol* := $w \uparrow .symbol$

          fi

    end;

For functions *Reststring* (corresponding to *tail*) and *Conc* (for *conc*) we need a function *Copy* which produces a copy of a string.

function *Copy*(**var** w: $\uparrow$*string*): $\uparrow$*string*;

    (∗ precondition: none;

       postcondition : result is a record representing $rep(w)$;

       computation time: $O(|rep(w)|)$ ∗)

    begin if $w = $ **nil**

          then *Copy* := **nil**

          else   *Copy* := **new** *string*;

$$Copy \uparrow .symbol := Firstsymbol(w);$$
$$Copy \uparrow .rest := Copy(w \uparrow .rest)$$
fi
end;

function *Reststring*(**var** *w*: $\uparrow string$): $\uparrow string$;
    (* precondition: none;
        postcondition : result is a record representing $tail(rep(w))$;
        computation time: $O(|rep(w)|)$ *)
    begin if $w =$ **nil**
        then error halt
        else *Reststring* := $Copy(w \uparrow .rest)$
        fi
    end;

function *Conc*(**var** *v, w*: $\uparrow string$): $\uparrow string$;
    (* precondition: none;
        postcondition : result is a record representing $conc(rep(v), rep(w))$;
        computation time: $O(|rep(v)| + |rep(w)|)$ *)
    var *s*: $\uparrow string$;
    begin if $v =$ **nil**
        then *Conc* := $Copy(w)$
        else *Conc* := $Copy(v)$;
            $s := Conc$;
            while $s \uparrow .rest \neq$ **nil do** $s := s \uparrow .rest$ **od**;
            $s \uparrow .rest := Copy(w)$
        fi
    end;

Function *Copy* in *Reststring* and *Conc* is absolutely necessary. The reader should consider the two procedures without the use of Copy but with the following assignments.

$$a := Conc(b, c);$$
$$d := Conc(b, b).$$

Do they serve the purpose?

    The computation times of functions *Reststring* and *Conc* are linear (in the length of arguments) and not constant as in the case of the corresponding PROSA operations. The claim in the key theorem of Chapter V regarding computation time of a PROSA program and the RESA program constructed from it is therefore no longer correct if we are to include data type "string".

    Example 9 illustrates how a language can be extended using the procedure concept. In a language without the data type "string" this can be made available in the form of a "package" consisting for the most part of a type declaration and some procedure declarations. However there is a difference. We cannot hide the chosen implementation (here linear lists) of our "string manipulation package" from the user and, therefore, cannot prevent a user making use of properties of this realisation. He could e.g. write a procedure yielding the symbols of a string one by one, by traversing the linear list and not by repeatedly calling the procedures *Reststring* and *Firstsymbol*. It would be more efficient, but it would destroy modularity, since we can no longer swap our package for an equivalent package based on another implementation without possibly invalidating the program. In Chapter VIII we will introduced modules as a language concept which permits strict encapsulation and "hides" the implementation of the packages.   ∎

Example 10:   In Chapter I we introduced tree domains and trees. In this example we examine an important application of trees, namely **search trees**. First some definitions. A tree domain $D \subseteq \mathbb{N}^*$ is called a **binary tree domain** if $D \subseteq \{1,2\}^*$, i.e. every node of D has at most two children. Let D be a binary tree domain and $b : D \to \mathbb{N}$ an injective labelling. Then the tree (D,b) is said to be a **binary search tree** for the set $b(D)$ if for all $x, y, z \in \{1,2\}^*$ with x, $x1y$, $x2z \in D$:

$$b(x1y) < b(x) < b(x2z) ,$$

i.e. the labels of all nodes in the subtree for node $x1$ (usually called **left child**) are smaller than the labels of all nodes in the subtree for node $x2$ (called **right child**). Figure 11 shows a binary search tree for the set $\{2, 7, 14, 23, 37, 46\}$ and its realisation in PROSA. In PROSA we can realise binary search trees with the help of

```
type node = record cont : integer;
                    lchild : ↑ node;
                    rchild : ↑ node
            end
```

For each node v we use a record of type *node* whose *cont*-component has the value $b(v)$ and whose pointers point to the records for the children or to *nil*, see Figure 11. The following procedure prints the contents of all nodes in increasing order.

```
procedure List(var v:↑node);
    (* precondition: none;
        postcondition : prints the contents of nodes in
            the subtree for v in increasing order ;
        computation time: O(number of nodes in the subtree for v) *)
    begin if v ≠ nil
            then List(v↑.lchild);
                 print v↑.cont;
                 List(v↑.rchild)
          fi
    end
```

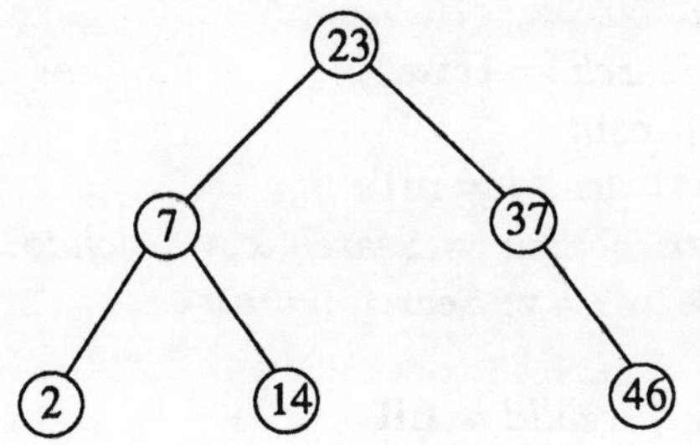

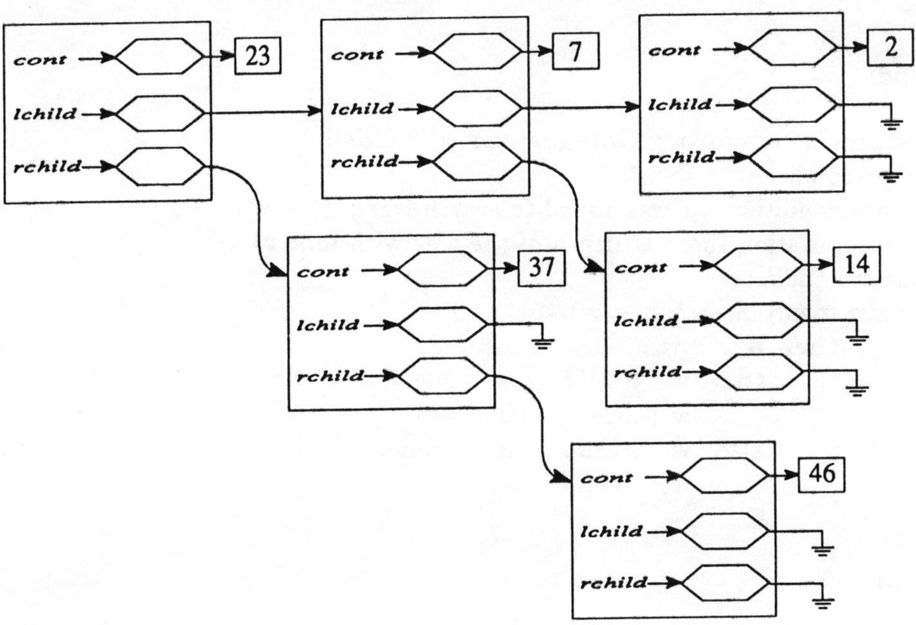

Fig. 11.   A binary search tree and its realisation in PROSA

The computation time follows immediately from the observation that procedure *List* is called once and only once for each node of the tree.

   In search trees one can search for an element using a method similar to binary search. The following function procedure searches for a value *x* in the set represented by the search tree and yields *true* or *false* depending on whether the search was successful or not. In addition, when the search succeeds, the variable *w* points to the node with content *x*. Otherwise *w* points to a node which could have *x* as child. The insertion action is provided by procedure *Insert*.

function *Search*(**const** *x*: **integer**; **var** *v, w*: ↑*node*): **boolean**;
    (* precondition: $v \neq nil$;
       postcondition : see above;
       computation time: O(depth of the tree with root *v*) *)

```
      begin if v ↑ .cont = x
            then w := v; Search := true
            else  if x < v ↑ .cont
                  then if v ↑ .lchild ≠ nil
                       then Search := Search(x, v ↑ .lchild, w)
                       else w := v; Search := false
                       fi
                  else  if v ↑ .rchild ≠ nil
                        then Search := Search(x, v ↑ .rchild, w)
                        else w := v; Search := false
                  fi
            fi
      end;
```

```
procedure Insert(const x: integer; var v: ↑node);
   (* precondition: v ≠ nil;
      postcondition : x was added to search tree ;
      computation time: O(depth of the tree with root v) *)
   var w: ↑node;
   begin if not Search(x, v, w)
         then if x < w ↑ .cont
              then w ↑ .lchild := new node;
                   w ↑ .lchild ↑ .cont := x
              else  w ↑ .rchild := new node;
                    w ↑ .rchild ↑ .cont := x
              fi
         fi
   end;
```

This example will be further elaborated in Exercise 2. In particular, it will be examined how a set of numbers can be sorted in increasing order by repeated insertion.

Suppose an ordering other than the usual < is to be used in the definition of binary search trees. Then we could of course rewrite the above procedures for the new order relation by suitably replacing all occurrences of <. It is simpler to pass the order to procedures *Search* and *Insert* as an additional parameter in the form of a function procedure. This leads to

```
function Search(const x: integer; var v, w: ↑node;
                function less(const : integer; const : integer): boolean):
                boolean;
      begin if v ↑ .cont = x
            then w := v; Search := true
            else  if less(x, v ↑ .cont)
                  then if v ↑ .lchild ≠ nil
                       then Search := Search(x, v ↑ .lchild, w)
```

$$\text{else } w := v; \text{ Search} := \textbf{false}$$
$$\textbf{fi}$$
$$\textbf{else } \textbf{if } v \uparrow .rchild \neq \textbf{nil}$$
$$\textbf{then } Search := Search(x, v \uparrow .rchild, w)$$
$$\textbf{else } w := v; \text{ Search} := \textbf{false}$$
$$\textbf{fi}$$
$$\textbf{fi}$$

end;

The fourth parameter of *Search* is a function procedure with two const-parameters of type *int* and a boolean result. In the body of *Search* we call *less* to determine the relation between x and $v\uparrow.cont$. In the context of declarations

function *less_usual*(**const** x, y: **integer**): **boolean**;
  begin *less_usual* := $(x < y)$ **end**;

function *less_unusual*(**const** x, y: **integer**): **boolean**;
  begin *less_unusual* := $(x * x < y * y)$ **or**
$$((x * x \geq y * y) \textbf{ and } x < 0 \textbf{ and } 0 < y)$$

  end

we can search with

$$search(\ \dots \ , less_usual)$$

in search trees ordered in the usual way and with

$$search(\ \dots \ , less_unusual)$$

in search trees ordered in an unusual way.   ∎

Example 11 (Continuation of Example 3 in Section 4.2): We specify a procedure *all* listing the names of all(!) the people who have ever lived. We presuppose

type *person* = **record** *name*: **string**;
                    visited: **boolean**;
                    mother: ↑*person*;
                    spouse: ↑*person*;
                    youngestchild: ↑*person*;
                    sibling: ↑*person*
        end

and assume that, when procedure *all* is called, the *visited*-component of all objects of type *person* is *false* .

procedure *all*(**var** v: ↑*person*)
    (∗ precondition: none;
        postcondition : prints the names of all people;
        computation time: O(number of descendants of $v \uparrow .name$) ∗)
    begin if not $v \uparrow .visited$

$$\textbf{then } v \uparrow .\textit{visited} := \textbf{true};$$
$$\textbf{print } v \uparrow .\textit{name};$$
$$\textbf{if } v \uparrow .\textit{spouse} \neq \textbf{nil then } \textit{all}(v \uparrow .\textit{spouse}) \textbf{ fi};$$
$$\textbf{if } v \uparrow .\textit{youngestchild} \neq \textbf{nil then } \textit{all}(v \uparrow .\textit{youngestchild}) \textbf{ fi};$$
$$\textbf{if } v \uparrow .\textit{sibling} \neq \textbf{nil then } \textit{all}(v \uparrow .\textit{sibling}) \textbf{ fi}$$
$$\textbf{fi}$$
$$\textbf{end};$$

A call $\textit{all}(v)$ with $v \uparrow .\textit{name} =$ "Adam" or $v \uparrow .\textit{name} =$ "Eve" prints the names of
all people. Obviously every person is reachable by *spouse*, *youngestchild* and *sibling*
pointers from *Adam*. Thus $\textit{all}(v)$ is called for each person v. As the first call $\textit{all}(v)$
sets the variable $v \uparrow .\textit{visited}$ to *true*, v initiates further calls only once. Thus each
pointer in our plexus of people leads to only one call and thus the computation time
of the above call is proportional to the number of people.   ∎

Example 12 (Dynamic Arrays): Consider the following program

```
program arrays;
var n: integer;
procedure Dynarray(const n: integer);
            var a: array[1..n] of integer; var i: integer;
            begin i := 1;
                    while i ≤ n do read a[i]; i := i + 1 od
            end;
begin       read n;
            Dynarray(n)
end.
```

This program reads a natural number n and then calls *Dynarray*. Within *Dynarray*
an array a is declared whose size depends on the parameter n. Arrays whose size
depends on the input are called **dynamic arrays**, in the other case they are called
static arrays. Some programming languages, e.g. Pascal, do not permit dynamic
arrays since their implementation on computers like RESA is more complex than
that of static arrays; see Chapter VII. Dynamic arrays are very useful if one has to
solve the same problem for changing problem sizes, see Exercises 6 and 7. Without dynamic arrays one must provide a static array for such problems which is
"sufficiently" large to cope with all inputs.   ∎

To conclude this section we examine two further kinds of parameter passing,
name-parameters and value-parameters.

Let XYZ n: t with $XYZ \in \{\textbf{name}, \textbf{value}\}$, $n \in \langle \textit{ident} \rangle$ and $t \in \langle \textit{small type} \rangle$
specify a name or value parameter of a procedure. In the procedure body n is in
both cases the name of a variable of type t. This is the same as in the case of
var-parameters. Parameter passing, on the other hand, is different. When passed
by value, the actual parameter (which must be an expression of type t) is evaluated
and then this value is assigned to variable n. The effect is thus similar to passing
a const-parameter. However, n is not a constant name. Hence assignments to n

are permitted. Such assignments have, on the other hand, no effect on the actual parameter. In name-passing all occurrences of the formal parameter within p are textually substituted by the actual parameter (which must be an expression of type t). Then the body is executed.

Example 13 (different kinds of parameter passing): For PROSA program

```
program passing;
var i: integer;
var B: array[1..2] of integer;
procedure q (spec x: integer);
    begin i := 1; x := x + 2; print x; B[i] := 10;
          i := 2; x := x + 2; print x
    end;
begin
    B[1] := 1; B[2] := 1; i := 1;
    q(B[i]); print B[1]; print B[2]
end.
```

we consider the four possibilities, namely **const, var, value** and **name** for **spec**. In the case of const-passing, the assignments $x := x + 2$ violate context conditions. In the other three cases we have a legal PROSA program. The following table specifies the output sequences for the three possible specifications.

specification	output sequence
var	3, 12, 12, 1
value	3, 5, 10, 1
name	3, 3, 10, 3

How are the different output sequences to be explained? In var-passing we execute the body in the environment of Figure 12.

First we increase $B[1]$ from 1 to 3, then print this value, set $B[1]$ to 10 and later to 12. Then 12 is printed and the final values of $B[1]$ and $B[2]$ are 12 and 1. In value-passing we execute the body in the environment of Figure 13, i.e. x is the name of a new variable. This variable is initialised with the value of the actual parameter.

We increase x (not $B[1]$!) to 3, then print 3, set $B[1]$ to 10, increase x to 5 and print 5. The final values of $B[1]$ and $B[2]$ are 10 and 1. In name-passing, finally, we execute the modified body (x is replaced by $B[i]$)

$$i := 1; \ B[i] := B[i] + 2; \ \textbf{print } B[i]; \ B[i] := 10;$$
$$i := 2; \ B[i] := B[i] + 2; \ \textbf{print } B[i]$$

in the environment of the main program. Thus the output sequence is 3, 3, 10, 3. ∎

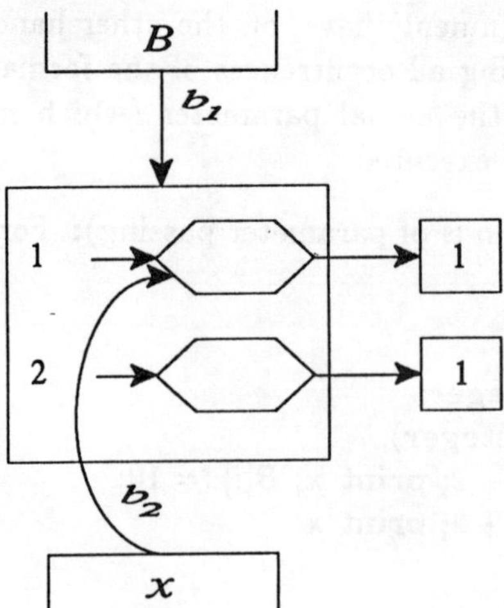

Fig. 12.   var-passing

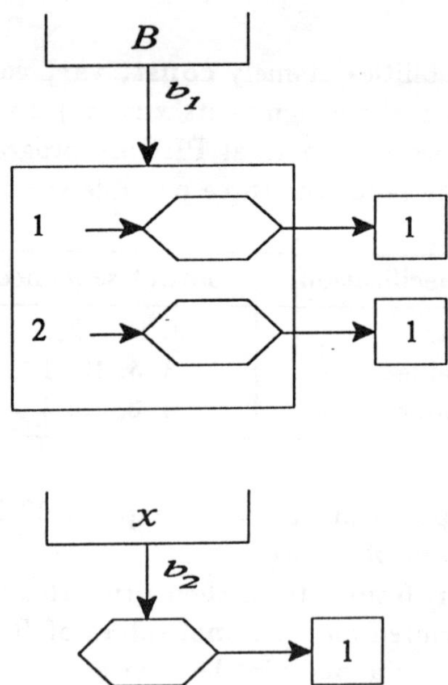

Fig. 13.   value-passing

Algol 60 features name-parameters, but they are no longer used in modern languages since their effects are obscure and they are difficult to implement in RESA. Almost all modern languages (e.g. Pascal, Algol 68, Ada) use var-parameters instead. Language designers did not show any preference as regards const or value parameters. Thus we have const-parameters in Algol 68 and value-parameters in Pascal (the key word **value** need not be specified in Pascal).

Exercises for 6.2

1) Write a recursive function procedure for the predicate $\leq_{lex}$.

2) Use the procedures of Example 10 to sort a set of numbers. Hint: Read the set one element at a time (compare Example 6 in Section 4.2) and construct a search tree using procedure *Insert*. Then print the set in sorted order with the help of procedure *List*. Which tree is constructed for input sequence 1, 17, 10, 13, 8, 16, 4, 7 and which tree for input sequence 1, 2, 3, 4, 5, 6?

Specify the computation time of the sorting method as a function of the length of the input sequence. How does the computation time compare with that of the method in Example 6, Section 4.2? Which method is better for a "random" input sequence? An answer to the last question firstly requires a precise definition of the concept "random".

Introduce a procedure parameter for the order relation in procedure *Insert*.

3) In Example 10 we met a PROSA implementation for binary tree domains. Write procedures which realise the tree functions defined in Section 1.4 (e.g. *depth*, *subtree*, *frontier*,...) for binary tree domains.

How could arbitrary tree domains be implemented in PROSA? Hint: Descendancy trees as in Example 11 are arbitrary tree domains. Extend your solutions to arbitrary tree domains.

4) (Merge sort): Given a sequence (in PROSA: a linear list) of n numbers, divide the sequence into two subsequences of length $\lfloor n/2 \rfloor$ and $\lceil n/2 \rceil$ and sort these two subsequences using the same method recursively. The two sorted subsequences are then merged to form one sorted sequence.

   a) Write a function procedure *merge*(**var** a, b: ↑ *element*): ↑ *element* which merges two sorted linear lists a and b to form one sorted list. What is the computation time?

   b) Write a function procedure *mergesort*(**var** a: ↑ *element*; **const** n: **integer**): ↑ *element* which takes a linear list a of length n and yields this list as a sorted list. What is the computation time?

5) (Continuation of Example 8) Let $G = (N, T, P, S)$ be a context-free grammar and let $w \in L_G$ be a string. Write a procedure which computes and prints a canonical derivation of w. To be more exact, let $S \xrightarrow[can]{} \alpha_1 \xrightarrow[can]{} \alpha_2 \xrightarrow[can]{} \cdots \xrightarrow[can]{} w$ be a canonical derivation of w and let $p_i \in P$ be the production used in the transition from α_i to α_{i+1}. Then the procedure should print the sequence $p_0, p_1, \ldots$. Hint: Modify procedure *decompose* such that a derivation is produced (as a linear list).

6) Given a number $n \in \mathbb{N}$ followed by n numbers $a_1, \ldots, a_n \in \mathbb{N}$ on the input tape, write a program which reads these n numbers into an array and then prints them in the order $a_n, \ldots, a_1$. Hint: Extend procedure *Dynarray* of Example 12.

Is there a solution which manages with static arrays and copes with arbitrary $n \in \mathbb{N}$?

7) Let G be a context-free grammar in Chomsky normal form (compare Example 8). Write a program which reads a string w, determines whether $w \in L_G$ and prints the result. Hint: Write a suitable framework for the procedure *decompose* of Example 8.

8) As in Example 2, write a procedure which swaps the values of two integer variables. Specify the formal parameter as name-parameter this time. What happens for calls of the form $swap(i, A[i])$ or $swap(A[i], i)$?

9) Consider the following program.

```
program unusual;
var i: integer;
var a: array[1..10] of integer;
procedure b(spec x: integer);
          begin i := 1;
                while i ≤ 10 do x := i; i := i + 1 od
          end;
begin i := 7;
      b(a[i]);
      print a[10]
end.
```

What is the output for **spec** $\in \{\textbf{name}, \textbf{value}, \textbf{var}\}$?

10) Write a function procedure *trapezoid* which approximates the integral

$$\int_a^b \delta(x)dx$$

by $(b - a)(\delta(x) + \delta(y))/2$. *trapezoid* should have two const-parameters and a proc-parameter of mode **function (const : real): real** .

6.3 Syntax of PROSA with Procedures

In this section we specify the syntax (context-free grammar and context conditions) of PROSA with procedures. Section 6.4 is dedicated to semantics. Large parts of Section 6.4 can be read without detailed knowledge of 6.3. To formulate the context conditions we proceed as usual. First we show how to construct attribute *CONTEXT* from the declaration sections and then how this is used in the statement section for type checking.

Every block of a PROSA program has its own declaration section. It is by no means prohibited and in fact reasonable to declare the same names in different blocks. Naturally, in view of the semantics, we must keep the different declarations of a name apart. Each applied occurrence of a name (this is indicated by the use of production $\langle app\ ident\rangle \rightarrow \langle ident\rangle$) must be associated with the respective defining occurrence according to the "scope rules" of the programming language. This problem is called the "identification of names". The PROSA machine keeps all valid bindings of names in a stack and implements the scope rules of PROSA in the way it searches for names in this stack. Context conditions are written in the style of Chapters III and IV. First the names of a program are made unique by consistent renaming. Consistent renaming always involves a defining occurrence of a name and all related applied occurrences. Identification of names must therefore take place before renaming. Names are made unique by adding to them a unique identification of the procedure which contains their respective defining occurrence. This renaming process is described in Section 6.3.1. In PROSA programs with unique names we can construct attribute *CONTEXT* as usual by going through all declarations of a program. In Section 6.3.2 we specify which information for procedure and function names is stored in attribute *CONTEXT*. Essentially it is the list of the formal parameter modes. The statement section is treated in Section 6.3.3. There we show how to utilise context information to guarantee type correctness of PROSA programs.

In preparation for the next two sections we briefly summarise the final version of the context-free grammar for the declaration section. PROSA programs (like Pascal-programs) are named blocks. A block consists of a declaration section and a statement section enclosed in **begin** – **end**. The declaration section contains a (possibly empty) sequence of constant declarations followed by one for types, one for variables and one for procedures.

$\langle program\rangle \rightarrow$ **program** $\langle ident\rangle$; $\langle block\rangle$.

$\langle block\rangle \rightarrow \langle decls\rangle$ **begin** $\langle stats\rangle$ **end**

$\langle decls\rangle \rightarrow \langle const\ decls\rangle\langle type\ decls\rangle\langle var\ decls\rangle\langle proc\ decls\rangle$

The declaration sections for constants, types, variables, arrays and records were discussed in Chapters III and IV. We use them with one alteration. In array declarations we now permit arbitrary integer expressions on bound position, but demand that all variables occurring in them are global and that no function procedures are called. The context condition for production $\langle bound \rangle \rightarrow \langle expr \rangle$ is therefore altered accordingly. The first restriction disallows local variables because they have as yet no value when the array declaration is executed. The second restriction is rather artificial. ALGOL 60 and ALGOL 68 do not have it. It is a consequence of our way of defining the semantics of function procedures (see Section 6.4). There function procedures are considered as "syntactic sugar" and reduced to proper procedures. Calls of proper procedures are, however, not permitted in declarations. The declaration section for procedures is a (possibly empty) sequence of procedure declarations separated by a semicolon.

$\langle proc\ decls \rangle \rightarrow \langle proc\ decl\ seq \rangle; \mid \epsilon$

$\langle proc\ decl\ seq \rangle \rightarrow \langle proc\ decl\ seq \rangle; \langle proc\ decl \rangle \mid \langle proc\ decl \rangle$

A procedure declaration consists of the key word **procedure** or **function**, the name of the procedure, the list of formal parameter specifications and the procedure body. In function procedures the result type is also specified. A procedure body is a block. The extended body consists of the parameter specification list and the procedure body.

$\langle proc\ decl \rangle \rightarrow$ **procedure** $\langle def\ ident \rangle\ \langle ext\ proc\ body \rangle \mid$
$\qquad\qquad$ **function** $\langle def\ ident \rangle\ \langle ext\ funct\ body \rangle$

$\langle ext\ proc\ body \rangle \rightarrow \langle par\ spec\ list \rangle; \langle block \rangle$

$\langle ext\ funct\ body \rangle \rightarrow \langle par\ spec\ list \rangle : \langle small\ type \rangle; \langle block \rangle$

$\langle par\ spec\ list \rangle \rightarrow \epsilon \mid (\langle par\ spec\ seq \rangle)$

$\langle par\ spec\ seq \rangle \rightarrow \langle par\ spec \rangle \mid \langle par\ spec\ seq \rangle; \langle par\ spec \rangle$

A parameter specification consists of the key word **const**, **var**, **procedure** or **function**, an identifier and a type. For procedure parameters the type is given as a sequence of parameter modes and probably a result type.

$\langle par\ spec \rangle \rightarrow$ **const** $\langle def\ ident \rangle : \langle elem\ type \rangle \mid$
$\qquad\qquad$ **var** $\langle def\ ident \rangle : \langle small\ type \rangle \mid$
$\qquad\qquad$ **var** $\langle def\ ident \rangle : \langle array\ par\ type \rangle \mid$
$\qquad\qquad$ **procedure** $\langle def\ ident \rangle(\langle mode\ seq \rangle) \mid$
$\qquad\qquad$ **function** $\langle def\ ident \rangle(\langle mode\ seq \rangle) : \langle small\ type \rangle$

For specifying formal array parameters, the syntax of array declarations needs to be changed. Array declarations permit expressions on bound positions. Their evaluation yields the array bounds. When specifying an array parameter we only permit defining occurrences of names on bound positions; in a procedure call these names "inherit" their values from the corresponding bounds of the actual parameter. Hence the productions for $\langle array\ par\ type \rangle$ are

$\langle array\ par\ type \rangle \rightarrow$ **array**$[\langle def\ bound\ seq \rangle]$ **of** $\langle small\ type \rangle$

⟨*def bound seq*⟩ → ⟨*def ident*⟩..⟨*def ident*⟩ |
            ⟨*def ident*⟩..⟨*def ident*⟩, ⟨*def bound seq*⟩

6.3.1 PROSA Programs with Unique Names

The same name may be defined in a PROSA program several times, however, no more than once in each procedure. If a name is defined more than once we have a **name collision**. In the example of Figure 1 there are collisions for names *element* and *x*.

```
program example1;
type element = record cont: integer;
                      succ: ↑element
              end;
var y; ↑element; var x: integer;
procedure p(var a: ↑element);
var element: real;
begin
    a↑.succ↑.cont := 5; element := 1.0
end;
procedure q;
var x: integer;
begin
    x := 6;
    p(y)
end;
begin
    x := 5;
    p(y);
    q
end.
```

Fig. 1.   A program with three blocks B_1, B_2 and B_3

In this section we show how to resolve name collisions by consistent renaming of defining and corresponding applied occurrences. Thus we can transform each PROSA program into one with unique names. In practice this transformation takes place during compilation and is not noticed by the programmer. We make use of renaming only to check context conditions. The PROSA machine itself processes the original program. For didactical reasons we discuss renaming in two steps. In the first step we derive an algorithm for renaming, and in the second step we sketch how collision resolving can be done with the help of an attribute grammar.

PROSA programs may have **defining occurrences** of names in two syntactic positions.

1) In the declaration section of the main program or of a procedure P. These defining occurrences are generated by productions of the form

$$\langle \ldots \; decl \rangle \rightarrow XYZ \; \langle def\,ident \rangle \ldots$$

with $XYZ \in \{\textbf{const}, \textbf{var}, \textbf{type}, \textbf{procedure}, \textbf{function}\}$. We associate them with the main program or the body of P.

2) In the formal parameter list of a procedure. These defining occurrences are generated by productions

$$\langle par \; spec \rangle \rightarrow XYZ \; \langle def\,ident \rangle \ldots$$

with $XYZ \in \{\textbf{const}, \textbf{var}, \textbf{procedure}, \textbf{function}\}$. They are also associated with the procedure body.

If we want to distinguish between defining occurrences according to their syntactic position we use the term **declaring occurrence** in case 1) and **specifying occurrence** in case 2). In our example of Figure 1 there are defining occurrences of *element* for blocks B_1 and B_2, of y for block B_1, of x for blocks B_1 and B_3, of p and q for block B_1 and of a for block B_2. Note that in the case of procedure declarations the defining occurrence of the procedure name belongs to the block in which it occurs, and that of the formal parameter to the procedure body, see Figure 2.

A PROSA program is said to have **unique names** if there is at most one defining occurrence for each name $x \in \langle ident \rangle$. If the names in a PROSA program are not unique we must resolve collisions by renaming. Firstly we clarify the concept of applied occurrence of a name. **Applied occurrences** of a name are all those occurrences of the name which are not defining occurrences. In our example of Figure 1 the name *element* has four applied occurrences, namely

```
type element = record cont: integer;
                      succ: ↑element
             end;
var y: ↑element;
procedure p(var a: ↑element);
element := 1.0;
```

The first three refer to the defining occurrence of *element* in block B_1 (after **type**), since B_1 is the smallest block which textually contains a defining occurrence of *element* and an applied occurrence. Correspondingly, the fourth applied occurrence refers to the defining occurrence in block B_2 (after **var**). We define this relationship between defining and applied occurrences in general (as repetition of Section 6.1) and introduce an additional notation.

```
                 program example1;
                 type element = record cont: integer;
                                       succ: ↑element
                            end;
                 var y; ↑element; var x: integer;
                 procedure p(var a: ↑element);
                 var element: real;
                 begin
                     a↑.succ↑.cont := 5; element := 1.0
                 end;
                 procedure q;
                 var x: integer;
                 begin
                     x := 6;
                     p(y)
                 end;
                 begin
                     x := 5;
                     p(y);
                     q
                 end.
```

Fig. 2. Defining occurrences in the dotted area are associated with block B_2 (compare Figure 1).

Definition:

a) Let *ao* be an applied occurrence of a name x and let B be the smallest block which textually contains *ao* and a defining occurrence *do* of x. Then *do* is the defining occurrence which belongs to *ao*.

b) Let *do* be a defining occurrence of a name. Then

$$Ao(do) = \{ao \,|\, do \text{ is the defining occurrence which belongs to the applied}$$
$$\text{occurrence } ao\}.$$

In the example of Figure 1 the set *Ao* (defining occurrence of *element* in block B_1) consists of three applied occurrences, namely *succ*: ↑*element*, *y*: ↑*element* and *a*: ↑*element*.

We want to point out a consequence of this definition for procedure declarations. Consider, for instance, a declaration **procedure** $p(fpl)$; ... **begin** ... **end** in a block B. The occurrence of p is a defining occurrence in block B. The defining occurrences of names in the parameter specifications *fpl* are defining occurrences in the procedure body and, therefore, not visible in B outside the procedure declaration. This reflects precisely the principle of modularity. The meaning of applied (type) names in the parameter specifications is fixed by declarations in block B and surrounding blocks. Thus in the example of Figure 1 the applied occurrence of *element* in **var** a: $\uparrow$*element* refers to the defining occurrence in block B_1.

We can now formulate an **algorithm to establish unique names**.

Let p be a PROSA program with $do_1, do_2, \ldots, do_k$ defining occurrences of names in p. Choose an injective mapping

$$subst : \{do_1, \ldots, do_k\} \to \langle ident \rangle$$

and construct PROSA program p' from p as follows. For all i, $1 \le i \le k$, do: Replace all occurrences in $\{do_i\} \cup Ao(do_i)$ by $subst(do_i)$.

```
program example1;
type element = record cont: integer;
                      succ: ↑element
            end;
var y; ↑element; var x: integer;
procedure p(var a1: ↑element);
var element1: real;
begin
    a1↑.succ↑.cont := 5; element1 := 1.0
end;
procedure q;
var x2: integer;
begin
    x2 := 6;
    p(y)
end;
begin
    x := 5;
    p(y);
    q
end.
```

Fig. 3. The program of Figure 1 with unique names

In our example we obtain the program of Figure 3. We have chosen mapping *subst* in the same way as it would be done in actual compilers. Figure 4 reflects the nesting of procedures in our example. Nesting of procedures and of the main program is tree-like and thus we can assign to each procedure its position in this tree. To be more precise, this position, called **procedure identification**, is a node i.e. an element of $\mathbb{N}^*$ and is defined as follows. The main program has procedure identification $PI(\langle program \rangle) = \epsilon$. If P is the main program or a procedure with identification p and if $P_1, \ldots, P_n$ are all procedures directly contained in P (in this order) then P_i has procedure identification $PI(p) = p.(i)$ with $1 \leq i \leq n$. In our example we therefore have $PI(\text{main program}) = \epsilon$, $PI(p) = (1)$, $PI(q) = (2)$. We choose function *subst* as follows. If *do* is a defining occurrence of name n in the main program or procedure P then $subst(n) = nPI(P)$. In our example we have omitted the sequence brackets for the sake of simplicity, i.e. we write, for example, $x1$ instead of $x(1)$.

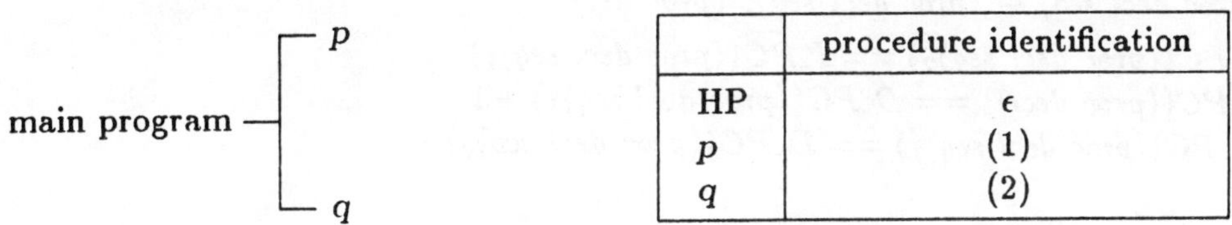

Fig. 4.   Procedure nesting in the program of Figure 1

In the rest of this section we sketch how resolving of name collisions can be defined formally by means of an attribute grammar. Figure 4 shows the procedure identifications in our example. We now specify the attributes to compute procedure identifications and for resolving name collisions. First we assign an attribute, called procedure identification PI, to nonterminals $\langle ext\ proc\ body\rangle$, $\langle ext\ funct\ body\rangle$ and $\langle block\rangle$. The value of this attribute will be precisely the procedure identification just introduced. It is computed in the following way. We number the procedure declarations in the declaration section using two attributes I_PC and D_PC (see below). The number thus computed is appended to the procedure identification of the enclosing procedure in order to determine the identification of the procedure in question. Note that in our informal description we relied on the identification of the containing procedure. This will be reflected in the formal description.

First we introduce some notations to simplify the formulation of semantic rules. Let A be an attribute name, $N_1, \ldots, N_k$ nonterminals and $X \to \alpha$ a production. By $A(encl\ N_1, \ldots, N_k)$ in a semantic rule of this production we mean the value of attribute A at the youngest ancestor of node X which is labelled by one of the nonterminals $N_1, \ldots, N_k$. In other words, we traverse the derivation tree from the node labelled X upwards until we meet a node N_1 or N_2 or $\ldots$ or N_k. The value of attribute A at this node is called $A(encl N_1, \ldots, N_k)$. The word *encl* is explained by the fact that traversing upwards in the derivation tree corresponds to textual enclosure.

The following productions describe how PI is computed in PROSA programs. Blocks directly contained in a block are counted using attributes I_PC and D_PC. I_PC is an inherited attribute, D_PC is a derived attribute. In a procedure declaration sequence I_PC is the number of the first declaration of this sequence and D_PC is the number of the last declaration.

$\langle program \rangle \rightarrow$ **program** $\langle ident \rangle; \langle block \rangle.$

$PI(\langle block \rangle) == \epsilon$

$\langle proc\ decls \rangle \rightarrow \langle proc\ decl\ seq \rangle; \mid \epsilon$

$I_PC(\langle proc\ decl\ seq \rangle) == 1$

$\langle proc\ decl\ seq \rangle \rightarrow \langle proc\ decl\ seq \rangle; \langle proc\ decl \rangle$

$I_PC(\langle proc\ decl\ seq \rangle_2) == I_PC(\langle proc\ decl\ seq \rangle_1)$

$I_PC(\langle proc\ decl \rangle) == D_PC(\langle proc\ decl\ seq \rangle_1) + 1$

$D_PC(\langle proc\ decl\ seq \rangle_1) == D_PC(\langle proc\ decl\ seq \rangle_2) + 1$

$\langle proc\ decl\ seq \rangle \rightarrow \langle proc\ decl \rangle$

$I_PC(\langle proc\ decl \rangle) == I_PC(\langle proc\ decl\ seq \rangle)$

$D_PC(\langle proc\ decl\ seq \rangle) == I_PC(\langle proc\ decl\ seq \rangle)$

$\langle proc\ decl \rangle \rightarrow$ **procedure** $\langle def\ ident \rangle \langle ext\ proc\ body \rangle$

$PI(\langle ext\ proc\ body \rangle) == PI(encl\ \langle block \rangle).I_PC(\langle proc\ decl \rangle)$

$\langle proc\ decl \rangle \rightarrow$ **function** $\langle def\ ident \rangle \langle ext\ funct\ body \rangle$

$PI(\langle ext\ funct\ body \rangle) == PI(encl\ \langle block \rangle).I_PC(\langle proc\ decl \rangle)$

$\langle ext\ proc\ body \rangle \rightarrow \langle par\ spec\ list \rangle; \langle block \rangle$

$PI(\langle block \rangle) == PI(\langle ext\ proc\ body \rangle)$

$\langle ext\ funct\ body \rangle \rightarrow \langle par\ spec\ list \rangle : \langle small\ type \rangle; \langle block \rangle$

$PI(\langle block \rangle) == PI(\langle ext\ funct\ body \rangle)$

We now use these attributes to assign to each defining occurrence of a name the procedure identification of its associated block. Figure 5 shows sections of syntax trees indicating where the right instance of attribute *PI* is to be found.

A name declared in the main program obtains its procedure identification from the block of the main program. Specifying occurrences in parameter lists get their identification from the parent node $\langle ext\ proc\ body \rangle$ or $\langle ext\ funct\ body \rangle$ and declaring occurrences in a procedure from $\langle block \rangle$. Thus formal parameters and local names of a procedure obtain the same identification. The name of the procedure, on

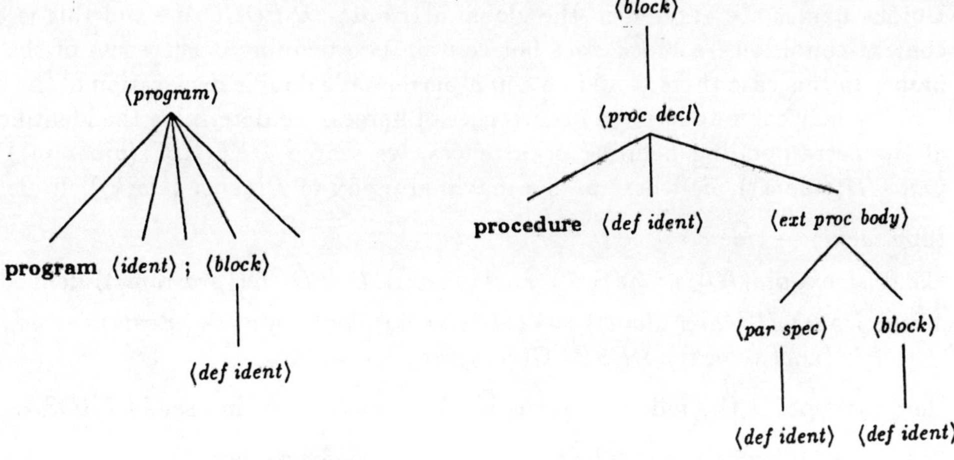

Fig. 5. Relevant sections of trees to determine $PI(\langle def\ ident\rangle)$

the other hand, obtains that of the block in which it is contained. $PI(encl\ \langle block\rangle,$ $\langle ext\ proc\ body\rangle, \langle ext\ funct\ body\rangle)$ thus yields the correct procedure identification for each defining occurrence. First this identification is combined at each defining, later at each applied occurrence with the names to form a **unique name**. This we store in attribute $UNIQ_ID$. We keep a record of all unique names in a global attribute $DEFOCC$. The new attributes and their domains are

attribute	attribute domain	at nonterminals
PI	Pi	$\langle block\rangle, \langle proc\ decl\rangle, \langle ext\ proc\ body\rangle,$ $\langle ext\ funct\ body\rangle$
$UNIQ_ID$	$Uniq_Id$	$\langle def\ ident\rangle, \langle app\ ident\rangle$
$DEFOCC$	$Defocc$	$\langle program\rangle$

where

$$Pi = \mathbb{N}^*$$
$$Uniq_Id = \langle ident\rangle \times Pi$$
$$Defocc = \mathcal{P}(Uniq_Id)$$

The following production describes the computation of procedure identifications at defining occurrences.

$\langle def\ ident\rangle \rightarrow \langle ident\rangle$

Cond.: $(ID(\langle ident\rangle), PI(encl\ \langle ext\ proc\ body\rangle, \langle ext\ funct\ body\rangle, \langle block\rangle))$
$$\notin DEFOCC(\langle program\rangle)$$

Then: $UNIQ_ID(\langle def\ ident\rangle) == (ID(\langle ident\rangle)), PI(encl\ \langle ext\ proc\ body\rangle,$
$\langle ext\ funct\ body\rangle, \langle block\rangle))$
$DEFOCC(\langle program\rangle) == DEFOCC(\langle program\rangle)$
$\cup\{UNIQ_ID(\langle def\ ident\rangle)\}$

Unique names are entered in the global attribute *DEFOCC* if—and this is a new context condition—a block does not contain two defining occurrences of the same name. In this case there would be a non-permissible double declaration of the name.

We now come to applied occurrences of names. To determine the identification of the corresponding defining occurrences, we search $DEFOCC(\langle program \rangle)$ for a pair $(ID(\langle ident \rangle), pi)$ where pi is a maximal prefix of $PI(encl\ \langle block \rangle)$. In detail

$\langle app\ ident \rangle \rightarrow \langle ident \rangle$

Cond.: $lookuppi(ID(\langle name \rangle), PI(encl\ \langle block \rangle), DEFOCC(\langle program \rangle))$ defined

Then: $UNIQ_ID(\langle app\ ident \rangle) == (ID(\langle ident \rangle), lookuppi(ID(\langle ident \rangle),$
$\qquad PI(encl\ \langle block \rangle), DEFOCC(\langle program \rangle))))$

Here *lookuppi* is the following recursive function written in pseudo-PROSA.

```
function lookuppi(const ident: Ident, pi: Pi, defocc: Defocc): Pi;
    if (ident, pi) ∈ defocc
    then lookuppi := pi
    else  if pi ≠ ε
          then lookuppi := lookuppi(ident, parent(pi), defocc)
          fi
    fi
end
```

Function *lookuppi* thus searches the procedures of the program from the inside outwards, beginning with the block containing the applied occurrence of *ident*. It yields the procedure identification of the smallest block which textually contains a defining occurrence and the applied occurrence.

Defining and applied names now have the attribute *UNIQ_ID*, whereas up to now (Chapter III and IV) they had attribute *ID*. We therefore replace in the productions of Chapters III and IV all occurrences of $ID(\langle app\ ident \rangle)$ and $ID(\langle def\ ident \rangle)$ by $UNIQ_ID(\langle app\ ident \rangle)$ or by $UNIQ_ID(\langle def\ ident \rangle)$. Then we can use attribute *CONTEXT* of Chapter IV. Instances of this attribute are now, of course, functions in

$$Context = map(Uniq_Id, Mode).$$

We replace names by unique names in the set of modes as well. Furthermore the set of procedure modes is now added. Details can be found in the next section.

6.3.2 The Attribute CONTEXT

Attribute *CONTEXT* records, as before, the kind and type of all declared names. Until now, names could be of the kind *const*, *var*, *record*, *array* and *type*. For each of these there was a corresponding set of types (see Section 4.3.1). As before, we call a pair of kind and type a mode. We now have a new kind *proc* for procedure names, i.e. from now on

$$Kind = \{const, var, record, array, type, proc\}$$

and

$$Mode = Constmode \cup Varmode \cup Recordmode \cup Arraymode \cup Typemode \cup Procmode$$

with

$$Procmode = \{proc\} \times Proctype.$$

The sets *Constmode*, *Varmode*, *Recordmode*, *Arraymode* and *Typemode* were defined in Section 4.3.1. We take them unchanged, but we replace the definition of Pointertype (used in *small type* and thus in *Varmode*, *Arraymode*, *Recordmode* and *Typemode*) by

$$Pointertype = \langle ident \rangle \times \mathbb{N}^*.$$

This reflects the fact that names are made unique by way of procedure identifications.

The main task of this section is to define the set *Proctype*, i.e. to define the type of a procedure. We proceed in complete analogy to Chapters III and IV. The mode of a name recorded in attribute *CONTEXT* should permit checking the correct use of the name in the statement section. Procedure names are applied in procedure calls. A procedure call is syntactically correct if the number of actual parameters in the call is the same as the number of formal parameters in the declaration, and if the actual parameters have the form required by kind and type of the formal parameters. If, for example, the formal parameter is specified as var-parameter of type *int* then the actual parameter must be a name of an integer variable. In the case of function procedures we also have a respective condition for the result type.

Example 1:   The declaration

procedure $f(\textbf{const } x: \textbf{integer}; \textbf{var } y: \textbf{integer})$;

specifies the following mode for f

$$(proc, (\underbrace{((const, int), (var, int))}_{\text{listof parameter modes}}, \underbrace{void}_{\text{resulttype}})).$$
$$\underbrace{}_{\text{type of procedure}}$$

The first parameter of f has the mode $(const, int)$ and the second has mode (var, int). Thus the list of parameter modes is $((const, int), (var, int))$. As f is a proper procedure there is no result type. For that we use the symbol *void*. Note that the type of f gives us precise information as to how the procedure might be called. Firstly, f is a proper procedure (result type *void*). Furthermore f requires two actual parameters, the first parameter must be an integer expression and the second parameter the name of an integer variable.   ∎

Example 2:   With declaration

function g(**procedure** h(**const** : **integer**; **var** : **integer**)): *element*;

g is of the mode

$$(proc, (((proc, (((const, int), (var, int)), void))), element)).$$

Procedure g has one parameter. This parameter is of the mode $(proc, (t, void))$ where $t = ((const, int), (var, int))$. Thus g has the mode $(proc, (((proc, (t, void))), element))$ as specified above. A call $g(f)$, where f is the procedure of Example 1, is permissible, since the mode of f is exactly the mode of the parameter of g.　■

Example 3:   With declaration

procedure G(**var** X: **array**[$l1..u1, l2..u2$] **of** ↑*element*);

G is of the mode

$$(proc, ((((array, (2, (var, element))))), void))$$

since the parameter is of mode $(array, (2, (var, element)))$. In the context of a declaration

var Z: **array**[$1..5, 1..5$] **of** ↑*element*

a call $G(Z)$ would be permissible.　■

Example 4:   Declaration

function a(**var** b: **array**[$l..u$] **of** ↑*element*,
　　　　procedure g(**var** : **array**[,] **of** ↑*element*)): ↑*element*;

determines for a the mode

$$(proc, (f, element))$$

where $f = (a_1, a_2)$ and a_i is the mode of the i-th formal parameter, $i = 1, 2$. The first parameter is a one-dimensional array whose components are of type *element*. Thus

$$a_1 = (array, (1, (var, element))).$$

The second parameter is a proper procedure. Consequently

$$a_2 = (proc, (f_1, void))$$

where f_1 is the list of modes of the formal parameters. The formal parameter of g is a two-dimensional array whose components are variables of type *element*. Thus

$$f_1 = ((array, (2, (var, element)))).$$

After substitution, we obtain the mode of a as the following expression

$$(proc, (((array, (1, (var, element)))), (proc, ((((array, (2, (var, element)))))),$$
$$void))), element)).$$

This is hardly readable in linear form. Note, however, that this expression has a simple structure, (compare Figure 6) and is thus quite suitable for mechanical processing.

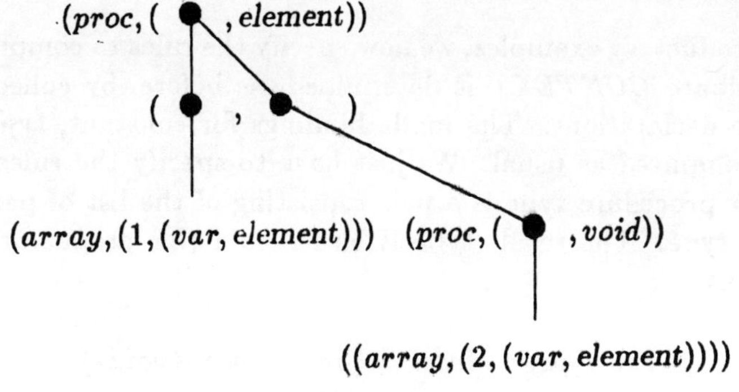

Fig. 6

Let us examine the two array parameters in more detail. The specifications of bounds l and u in the parameter list represent defining occurrences of names of integer constants. We will record this in $CONTEXT$ and can thus check the correct use of these names in the body of a. For calls of a it is only important that the first parameter is a one-dimensional array. The names of the bounds are irrelevant. Thus l and u do not appear in the mode of a. The list after identifier g describes the type of the formal procedure parameter g. Here it is only of interest that g expects a two-dimensional array (dimension specification [,]) as a parameter. Of course we do not need names for the bounds.

In the context of declaration

var B: **array**[1..10] **of** ↑*element*

the call $a(B, G)$ might occur. Note that a_2 is precisely the mode of procedure G in Example 3. ∎

Example 5:   We now list attribute $CONTEXT$ for the program of Figure 1 in Section 6.3.1.

$$(element, \epsilon) \rightarrow \left(record, \left\{ \begin{array}{l} cont \rightarrow (var, int) \\ succ \rightarrow (var, (element, \epsilon)) \end{array} \right\} \right)$$

$$(y, \epsilon) \rightarrow (var, (element, \epsilon))$$

$$(x, \epsilon) \rightarrow (var, int)$$

$$(p, \epsilon) \rightarrow (proc, (((var, (element, \epsilon))), void))$$

$$(a, 1) \rightarrow (var, (element, \epsilon))$$

$$(element, 1) \rightarrow (var, real)$$

$$(x, 2) \rightarrow (var, int)$$

It can be seen very nicely how the different defining occurrences are kept apart by
the procedure identifications. It can also be seen that the applied occurrences of
the type names *element* all refer to the declaration in the main program. Using
the information collected in *CONTEXT* the context conditions in the statement
sections can now easily be checked. This will be discussed in Section 6.3.3.   ∎

After these introductory examples, we now specify the rules to compute *CONTEXT*
precisely. Attribute *CONTEXT* is determined, as before, by collecting the mode
bindings of the declarations. The mode bindings for constant, type and var declarations are computed as usual. We just have to specify the rules for procedure
declarations. A procedure type is a pair consisting of the list of parameter modes
and the result type. The result type is either *void* (for proper procedures) or a
small type. Thus

$$Proctype = Mode^* \times (Smalltype \cup \{void\})$$

Using the new attributes *PARSPEC* and *PARSPECSEQ*, we now consider the
productions of the procedure declaration section. In attribute *PARSPEC*, with
domain *Mode*, we store the mode of a formal parameter and in *PARSPECSEQ*,
with domain *Mode**, we store the list of modes of the formal parameters.

   To understand the following it is useful to reconsider the previous examples.

$\langle proc\ decl \rangle \rightarrow$ **procedure** $\langle def\ ident \rangle \langle ext\ proc\ body \rangle$

$MB(\langle proc\ decl \rangle) == \{ UNIQ_ID(\langle def\ ident \rangle) \rightarrow (proc, TYPE(\langle ext\ proc\ body \rangle)) \}$

$\langle ext\ proc\ body \rangle \rightarrow \langle par\ spec\ list \rangle; \langle block \rangle$

$TYPE(\langle ext\ proc\ body \rangle) == (PARSPECSEQ(\langle par\ spec\ list \rangle), void)$

Explanation: The type of a proper procedure is a pair $(psl, void)$ with $psl \in Mode^*$.
The list of formal parameter modes psl is computed from the list of parameter
specifications.

$\langle proc\ decl \rangle \rightarrow$ **function** $\langle def\ ident \rangle \langle ext\ funct\ body \rangle$

$MB(\langle proc\ decl \rangle) == \{ UNIQ_ID(\langle def\ ident \rangle) \rightarrow (proc, TYPE(\langle ext\ funct\ body \rangle)) \}$

$\langle ext\ funct\ body \rangle \rightarrow \langle par\ spec\ list \rangle : \langle small\ type \rangle; \langle block \rangle$

$$TYPE(\langle ext\ funct\ body \rangle) == (PARSPECSEQ(\langle par\ spec\ list \rangle),$$
$$TYPE(\langle small\ type \rangle))$$

Explanation: The type of a function procedure is a pair $(psl, t) \in Mode^* \times Smalltype$.
List psl is computed from the list of parameter specification and type t is derived
from the given result type.

   The next rules tell us how to collect the information of the individual specifications in a parameter specification list.

$\langle par\ spec\ list \rangle \to \epsilon$
$PARSPECSEQ(\langle par\ spec\ list \rangle) == \epsilon$

$\langle par\ spec\ list \rangle \to (\langle par\ spec\ seq \rangle)$
$PARSPECSEQ(\langle par\ spec\ list \rangle) == PARSPECSEQ(\langle par\ spec\ seq \rangle)$

$\langle par\ spec\ seq \rangle \to \langle par\ spec \rangle$
$PARSPECSEQ(\langle par\ spec\ seq \rangle) == PARSPEC(\langle par\ spec \rangle)$

$\langle par\ spec\ seq \rangle \to \langle par\ spec\ seq \rangle; \langle par\ spec \rangle$
$PARSPECSEQ(\langle par\ spec\ seq \rangle_1) ==$
$\qquad PARSPECSEQ(\langle par\ spec\ seq \rangle_2).PARSPEC(\langle par\ spec \rangle)$

As for the individual parameter specifications, let us start with const-parameters.

$\langle par\ spec \rangle \to \textbf{const}\ \langle def\ ident \rangle : \langle elem\ type \rangle$
$PARSPEC(\langle par\ spec \rangle) == (const, TYPE(\langle elem\ type \rangle))$
$MB(\langle par\ spec \rangle) == \{ UNIQ_ID(\langle def\ ident \rangle) \to PARSPEC(\langle par\ spec \rangle) \}$

Explanation: A const-parameter of type t is of mode $(const, t)$. We record this pair in attribute $PARSPEC$. For the procedure body the parameter specification is equivalent to a constant declaration. Hence we add

$$UNIQ_ID(\langle def\ ident \rangle) \to PARSPEC(\langle par\ spec \rangle)$$

to $CONTEXT$ of the program. Remember that in $CONTEXT$ we collect the mode binding of all declarations and specifications.

Next we discuss var-parameters. In the procedure body the specification of a var-parameter is equivalent to a corresponding declaration. Thus we compute the mode of the specification in the same way as for a var-declaration.

$\langle par\ spec \rangle \to \textbf{var}\ \langle def\ ident \rangle : \langle small\ type \rangle$
$PARSPEC(\langle par\ spec \rangle) == (var, TYPE(\langle small\ type \rangle))$
$MB(\langle par\ spec \rangle) == \{ UNIQ_ID(\langle def\ ident \rangle) \to PARSPEC(\langle par\ spec \rangle) \}$

$\langle par\ spec \rangle \to \textbf{var}\ \langle def\ ident \rangle : \langle array\ par\ type \rangle$
Let $l_1, \dots, l_k, u_1, \dots, u_k,\ k \geq 1$, be the names defined on bound positions in $\langle array\ par\ type \rangle$. Then

$$PARSPEC(\langle par\ spec \rangle) == (array, TYPE(\langle array\ par\ type \rangle))$$

$$MB(\langle par\ spec \rangle) == \left\{ \begin{array}{l} UNIQ_ID(\langle def\ ident \rangle) \to PARSPEC(\langle par\ spec \rangle), \\ UNIQ_ID(l_1) \to (const, int), \\ \vdots \\ UNIQ_ID(u_k) \to (const, int) \end{array} \right\}.$$

Explanation: In array parameters the specifications of bounds must all be identifiers. These identifiers are constant names for the procedure body and thus $UNIQ_ID(l_1) \rightarrow (const, int), \ldots, UNIQ_ID(u_k) \rightarrow (const, int)$ are added to the mode binding and hence to CONTEXT. The parameter itself is of *array* kind and has the type given by the array type.

Finally, we must discuss procedure parameters with and without parameters.

$\langle par\ spec \rangle \rightarrow$ **procedure** $\langle def\ ident \rangle(\langle mode\ seq \rangle)$

$PARSPEC(\langle par\ spec \rangle) == (proc, (PARSPECSEQ(\langle mode\ seq \rangle), void))$
$MB(\langle par\ spec \rangle) == \{ UNIQ_ID(\langle def\ ident \rangle) \rightarrow PARSPEC(\langle par\ spec \rangle)\}$

$\langle par\ spec \rangle \rightarrow$ **procedure** $\langle def\ ident \rangle$

$PARSPEC(\langle par\ spec \rangle) == (proc, (\epsilon, void))$
$MB(\langle par\ spec \rangle) == \{ UNIQ_ID(\langle def\ ident \rangle) \rightarrow PARSPEC(\langle par\ spec \rangle)\}$

Explanation: The type of a procedure is given by the list of parameter modes and the result type (here *void*).

In the case of function procedures as parameters the attribute specification is the same.

$\langle par\ spec \rangle \rightarrow$ **function** $\langle def\ ident \rangle(\langle mode\ seq \rangle) : \langle small\ type \rangle$

$PARSPEC(\langle par\ spec \rangle) ==$
$$(proc, (PARSPECSEQ(\langle mode\ seq \rangle), TYPE(\langle small\ type \rangle)))$$
$MB(\langle par\ spec \rangle) == \{ UNIQ_ID(\langle def\ ident \rangle) \rightarrow PARSPEC(\langle par\ spec \rangle)\}$

$\langle par\ spec \rangle \rightarrow$ **function** $\langle def\ ident \rangle : \langle small\ type \rangle$

$PARSPEC(\langle par\ spec \rangle) == (proc, (\epsilon, TYPE(\langle small\ type \rangle)))$
$MB(\langle par\ spec \rangle) == \{ UNIQ_ID(\langle def\ ident \rangle) \rightarrow PARSPEC(\langle par\ spec \rangle)\}$

The subgrammar for $\langle mode\ seq \rangle$ is analogous to the subgrammar for $\langle par\ spec\ seq \rangle$ except that formal parameters do not get names. The same applies for bound specifications in array parameters, i.e. the dimension specification is only a sequence of commas (compare Example 4). In addition, we disallow procedures as parameters of formal procedures. Thus

$\langle mode\ seq \rangle \rightarrow \langle mode \rangle \mid \langle mode\ seq \rangle; \langle mode \rangle$

$\langle mode \rangle \rightarrow$ **const** $: \langle elem\ type \rangle \mid$
   var $: \langle small\ type \rangle \mid$
   var $: \langle red\ array\ type \rangle$

$\langle red\ array\ type \rangle \rightarrow [\langle dimensions \rangle]$ **of** $\langle small\ type \rangle$

$\langle dimensions \rangle \rightarrow \epsilon \mid \langle dimensions \rangle,$

Attributes are specified in a similar way. Here we only need *PARSPEC*. Attribute *MB* is superfluous as no new names are introduced. We give the attribute specification for production $\langle mode \rangle \to$ **const** : $\langle elem\ type \rangle$ and leave the remaining productions to the reader.

$\langle mode \rangle \to$ **const** : $\langle elem\ type \rangle$

$PARSPEC(\langle mode \rangle) == (const, TYPE(\langle elem\ type \rangle)).$

6.3.3 The Statement Section

After preparatory work in Sections 6.3.1 and 6.3.2, we now reap the benefit and show how to check syntactic correctness of procedure and function calls. Hardly anything changes for the other statements and we proceed exactly as described in Chapters III and IV.

A call of a procedure consists of an applied occurrence of the procedure name followed by a list of actual parameters. The list must have the same length as the list of parameter specifications. The actual and formal parameters correspond to each other according to their position in the respective list. Actual parameters, i.e. expressions or var-names, determine the arguments of the procedure for this call and where results have to be deposited. The call of a proper procedure is a statement.

$\langle stat \rangle \to \langle app\ ident \rangle \langle act\ par\ list \rangle$

Cond.: $CONTEXT(\langle program \rangle)(UNIQ_ID(\langle app\ ident \rangle) = (proc,(pars, void))$

Then: $FORMPARSSEQ(\langle act\ par\ list \rangle) == pars$

$\langle act\ par\ list \rangle \to \epsilon$

Cond.: $FORMPARSSEQ(\langle act\ par\ list \rangle) = \epsilon$

$\langle act\ par\ list \rangle \to (\langle act\ par\ seq \rangle)$

Cond.: $FORMPARS2(\langle act\ par\ seq \rangle) = \epsilon$

Then: $FORMPARS1(\langle act\ par\ seq \rangle) == FORMPARSSEQ(\langle act\ par\ list \rangle)$

$\langle act\ par\ seq \rangle \to \langle act\ par \rangle$

$FORMPAR(\langle act\ par \rangle) == head(FORMPARS1(\langle act\ par\ seq \rangle))$
$FORMPARS2(\langle act\ par\ seq \rangle) == tail(FORMPARS1(\langle act\ par\ seq \rangle))$

$$\langle act\ par\ seq \rangle \rightarrow \langle act\ par\ seq \rangle, \langle act\ par \rangle$$
$$FORMPARS1(\langle act\ par\ seq \rangle_2) == FORMPARS1(\langle act\ par\ seq \rangle_1)$$
$$FORMPAR(\langle act\ par \rangle) == head(FORMPARS2(\langle act\ par\ seq \rangle_2))$$
$$FORMPARS2(\langle act\ par\ seq \rangle) == tail(FORMPARS2(\langle act\ par\ seq \rangle_2))$$

These semantic rules distribute the formal parameter specifications to the corresponding actual parameters depending on the position in the call list. This is achieved quite simply. If $\langle act\ par\ seq \rangle$ generates a sequence of k actual parameters then the value of $FORMPARS2$ is that of $FORMPARS1$ without the first k elements of the list. The k list elements cut off, are available in the $FORMPAR$ attributes of the k actual parameters. If the formal parameter list is shorter than that of the actual parameters then a context condition is violated. In this case *head* is applied to an empty sequence leading to an undefined attribute value. If the list of formal parameters exceeds that of the actual parameters then the context condition $FORMPARS2(\langle act\ par\ seq \rangle) = \epsilon$ at production $\langle act\ par\ list \rangle \rightarrow \langle act\ par\ seq \rangle$ is violated.

The next two productions describe the various cases for individual parameters.

$$\langle act\ par \rangle \rightarrow \langle expr \rangle$$

Cond.: $FORMPAR(\langle act\ par \rangle) = (const, TYPE(\langle expr \rangle))$

Explanation: For const-parameters we allow arbitrary expressions of suitable type as actual parameters.

$$\langle act\ par \rangle \rightarrow \langle name \rangle$$

Cond.: $FORMPAR(\langle act\ par \rangle) = MODE(\langle name \rangle)$

Explanation: In the case of var-parameters only names are permitted as actual parameters. The mode of the formal and actual parameters must coincide.

The call of a function procedure is a factor. The type of the factor is the result type of the function procedure. Thus

$$\langle factor \rangle \rightarrow \langle app\ ident \rangle \langle act\ par\ list \rangle$$

Cond.: $CONTEXT(\langle program \rangle)(UNIQ_ID(\langle app\ ident \rangle)) = (proc, (pars, t))$
        with $t \neq void$

Then: $TYPE(\langle factor \rangle) == t$
        $FORMPARSSEQ(\langle act\ par\ list \rangle) == pars$

Finally, we must describe how the call of a function procedure yields a result. This is achieved by assignments to the name of the function procedure. The production for assignments must now permit the name of a function procedure on the left.

$$\langle ass \rangle \rightarrow \langle name \rangle := \langle expr \rangle$$

Cond.: $MODE(\langle name \rangle) = (var, TYPE(\langle expr \rangle))$
      or
      $MODE(\langle name \rangle) = (proc, (pars, TYPE(\langle expr \rangle)))$

This concludes the statement section. We explain these definitions using the examples of Section 6.3.2.

Example 6 (Continuation of Example 5 in 6.3.2): The call $p(y)$ is syntactically correct since

$$CONTEXT(\langle program \rangle)((p, \epsilon)) = (proc, (pars, void))$$

with $pars = ((var, (element, \epsilon)))$ and

$$CONTEXT(\langle program \rangle)((y, \epsilon)) = (var, (element, \epsilon)).$$

Thus the formal and actual parameter have the same mode. Calls such as $p(x)$ or $p(y, y)$ are incorrect and violate context conditions. For completeness sake we discuss some other statements of Figure 1, Section 6.3.2. Assignment *element* := 1.0 is admissible as this applied occurrence of *element* is of mode $(var, real)$. Consider

$$a \uparrow .succ \uparrow .cont := 5$$

Figure 7 shows the modes of the various "parts" of the left side and therefore this assignment is correct.

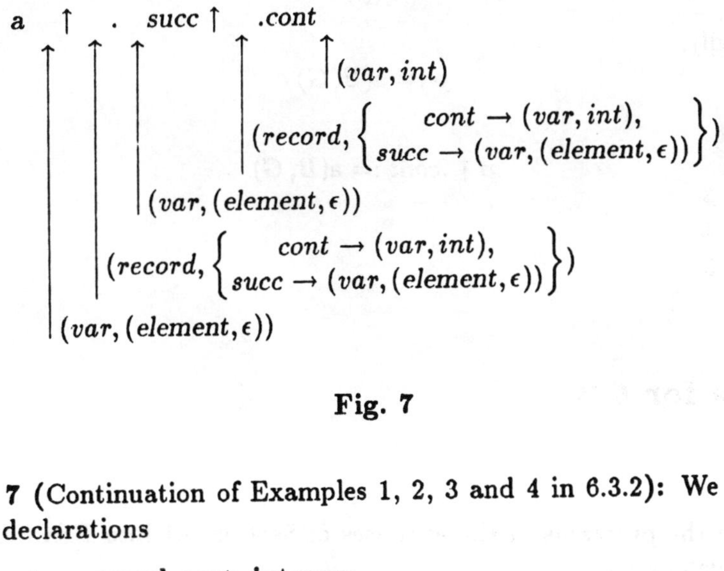

$$
\begin{array}{llll}
a & \uparrow & . \quad succ \uparrow & .cont
\end{array}
$$

$$(var, int)$$

$$\left(record, \left\{ \begin{array}{l} cont \rightarrow (var, int), \\ succ \rightarrow (var, (element, \epsilon)) \end{array} \right\}\right)$$

$$(var, (element, \epsilon))$$

$$\left(record, \left\{ \begin{array}{l} cont \rightarrow (var, int), \\ succ \rightarrow (var, (element, \epsilon)) \end{array} \right\}\right)$$

$$(var, (element, \epsilon))$$

Fig. 7

Example 7 (Continuation of Examples 1, 2, 3 and 4 in 6.3.2): We presume the additional declarations

type *element* = **record** *cont*: **integer**;
                succ: $\uparrow$*element*
      end;
var p, q: $\uparrow$*element*;
var r: **integer**;
var B: **array**[1..10] **of** $\uparrow$*element*;
var Z: **array**[1..2, 5..9] **of** $\uparrow$*element*.

Then the calls

$$f(7 + r, r)$$
$$f(p \uparrow .cont + r, q \uparrow .cont).$$

are admissible, but not the calls

$$f(7.0, r)$$
$$f(r, 7)$$

In the first case the type of expression 7.0 is incorrect and in the second case expression 7 is not allowed as an actual var-parameter. Furthermore

$$p := g(f)$$
$$p \uparrow .succ := g(f)$$

are admissible and

$$p := g(g)$$

not. The call

$$G(Z)$$

is allowed but

$$G(B)$$
$$G(p)$$

are not. Finally,

$$p := a(B, G)$$

is correct but

$$p \uparrow .cont := a(B, G)$$

is wrong.

Exercises for 6.3

1) Transform the programs in the exercises of Section 6.1 into PROSA programs with unique names.

2) Determine attribute *CONTEXT* for these programs.

3) Extend PROSA by const-parameters of record type. Change syntax and context conditions accordingly.

4) Change syntax and context conditions to cope with value and name parameters.

6.4 Semantics of PROSA with Procedures

A configuration of the PROSA machine consists of a program-rest, a binding stack, a storage state, an input sequence and an output sequence. The binding stack replaces the binding used hitherto, as already explained in Section 6.1. Thus

$$\mathbf{C} = \mathbf{PR} \times \mathbf{BS} \times \mathbf{S} \times \mathbf{D}^* \times \mathbf{D}^*$$

While $\mathbf{S}$ and $\mathbf{D}$ are the same as in Chapter III and IV, $\mathbf{PR}$ is a superset of the corresponding set in Chapter IV. This will become clear when procedure calls are discussed. The set $\mathbf{BS}$ of binding stacks is defined as follows.

Definition 1 (binding stack):
$$\mathbf{BS} = \{((b_1, sv_1), \ldots, (b_m, sv_m)) \mid m \geq 0, b_i \in \mathbf{B} \text{ and } sv_i \in \mathbb{N}_0, sv_i < i \text{ for } 1 \leq i \leq m\} \qquad \blacksquare$$

Thus a binding stack bs is a sequence of pairs (b_i, sv_i) where b_i are bindings in the usual sense and sv_i are integers with $sv_i < i$. The number sv_i, as already indicated in Section 6.1, is called the index of the static predecessor of binding b_i or the static link. The binding stack holds a pair (b_i, sv_i) for each procedure entered but not left. When a procedure is called a pair is pushed onto the binding stack and the topmost pair removed when a procedure is left. In every (local) binding we record the meaning of local names and parameters.

We determine the meaning of global names using the static link as explained in Section 6.1. Let, for example, $bs = ((b_1, sv_1), \ldots, (b_m, sv_m))$ be a binding stack and $x \in \langle ident \rangle$. Set h to m. If $x \in Def(b_h)$ then the meaning of x is $b_h(x)$. If $x \notin Def(b_h)$ then set h to sv_h and repeat. In this way we follow the chain of static links and find the meaning of x.

Definition 2 (Finding a name in a binding stack):
Let $x \in \langle ident \rangle$ and let $bs = ((b_1, sv_1), \ldots, (b_m, sv_m))$ be a binding stack. Then $find(bs, x)$ is defined by

$$find(bs, x) = \begin{cases} b_{sv^{(l)}(m)}(x), & \text{if } l = \min\{t \mid x \in Def(b_{sv^{(t)}(m)})\} \\ \text{undefined}, & \text{if } x \notin Def(b_{sv^{(t)}(m)}) \text{ for all } t. \end{cases}$$

Here $sv^{(0)}(m) = m$ and $sv^{(t+1)}(m) = sv_{sv^{(t)}(m)}$. $\qquad \blacksquare$

Remark: Instead of $find(bs, x)$ we will write $bs(x)$.

Example 1: Let $bs = ((b_1, 0), (b_2, 1), (b_3, 1))$ and let b_1, b_2, b_3 be given as in Figure 4 (see below). Then $bs(A) = b_1(A)$ because $l = 1$ in Definition 2. $\qquad \blacksquare$

Since we have replaced bindings by binding stacks in the configuration of the
PROSA machine, we must explain how the transitions of the machine in Chap-
ters III and IV change. This is quite simple. We replace all occurrences of b by bs.
Take assignments for example. Let $c = (n := E; p', bs, s, i, o)$ with $n \in \langle name \rangle$ and
$E \in \langle expr \rangle$. Then

$$c' = (p', bs, s[L(n, bs, s) \backslash I(bs, s, E)], i, o),$$

i.e. the value of the variable (denoted by n) $L(n, bs, s)$ is changed to $I(bs, s, E)$.
Functions L (see Section 4.3.2) and I (see Section 3.7.2) are defined as hitherto;
however, we replace b by bs everywhere.

Example 1 (continued):   The value of expression $x + y$ is

$$\begin{aligned}
I(bs, s_3, x + y) &= iplus(I(bs, s_3, x), I(bs, s_3, y)) \\
&= iplus(s_3(b_3(x)), s_3(b_3(y))) \\
&= iplus(2, 2) = 4
\end{aligned}$$

            ∎

When processing a declaration we change the topmost binding and thus the binding
stack. We use the same notation as before.

Definition: Let $bs = ((b_1, sv_1), \ldots, (b_m, sv_m))$ be a nonempty binding stack, let x
be an identifier and y an object. Then we write $bs[x \backslash y]$ where

$$bs[x \backslash y] = ((b_1, sv_1), \ldots, (b_m[x \backslash y], sv_m)).$$

        ∎

Now we specify the semantics of procedures. First we discuss proper procedures
and then reduce function procedures to proper procedures.

(DP)   Declaration of a proper procedure

Let $c = (\textbf{procedure } n \ psl; R; p', bs, s, i, o)$
with $n \in \langle ident \rangle$, $psl \in \langle par \ spec \ list \rangle$ and $R \in \langle block \rangle$.
Then
$c' = (p', bs[n \backslash (psl, |bs|, R)], s, i, o);$
  where $|bs|$ is the length of the sequence bs.

Explanation: We bind the procedure name to a triple consisting of the list of
parameter specifications, the length of the binding stack and the body. The second
component provides the binding stack at the point of declaration and thus the
meaning of global names. This is needed when dealing with procedure calls.

Example 2:   We use the program in Figure 1 as a continuing example.

$$
\begin{array}{l}
\textbf{program } complicated; \\
\textbf{var } x\text{: integer};
\end{array}
$$

```
program complicated;
var x: integer;

    procedure D(var y: integer);
        begin
            print x;
            print y;          ] sts_D
            y := y + 1
        end;
    procedure A(procedure C(var : integer));
        var x: integer;
        procedure B(var y: integer);
            begin
                print x;
                print y;      ] sts_B      ] ds_A
                y := y + 1
            end;
        begin
            x := 2;
            C(x);             ] sts_A
            A(B)
        end;
    begin
        x := 1;
        A(D)
    end.
```

Fig. 1.   This program does not terminate. It prints the sequence 1, 2, 3, 2, 3, 2, ...

This example is complex and confusing (and thus bad style). Without a formal definition of the PROSA semantics it is hardly intelligible. In the main program we declare variable x and two procedures D and A. Then we set x to 1 and call $A(D)$. Procedure A is recursive, i.e. it calls itself. It has a procedure parameter C, a local variable x and a local procedure B. Naturally, at each call of A new instances of x and B are created. The respective instance (also called incarnation) of B has the respective instance of x as a global object. In the statement section of A we first set x to 2, then call the formal procedure C with parameter x and then call $A(B)$. At this point we would request the reader to study the program and to determine the output sequence.

The declarations in the main program and assignment $x := 1$ lead to configuration $c_1 = (A(D); \textbf{end}; , bs_1, s_1, \epsilon, \epsilon)$. $bs_1 = ((b_1, 0))$. Binding b_1 and storage state s_1 are shown in Figure 2. Here ds_X denotes the declaration section and sts_X the statement section of X, $X \in \{A, B, D\}$.

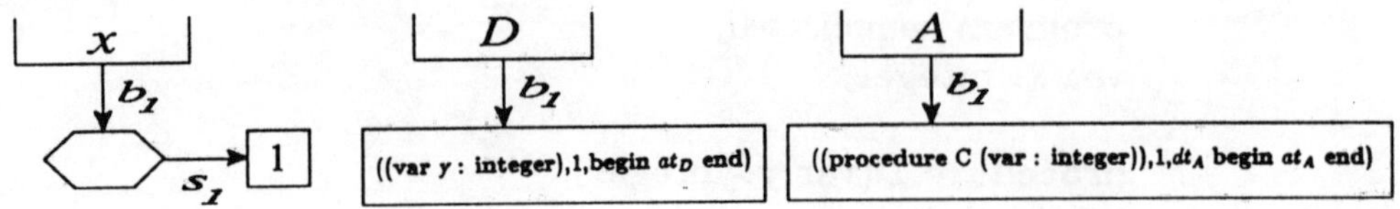

Fig. 2.   Binding stack $(b_1, 0)$ and storage state s_1

(PC)   Procedure call

Let $c = (n\ apl; p', bs, s, i, o)$
with $n \in \langle ident \rangle$ and $apl \in \langle act\ par\ list \rangle$.
Let $bs(n) = (psl, i, ds\ \textbf{begin}\ sts\ \textbf{end})$.
Then
$c' = (psl\ apl\ ds\ sts;\ \textbf{end};\ p', bs(\emptyset, i), s, i, o)$

Explanation: We place $ds\ sts\ \textbf{end}$; before the program-rest and thus execute the body. **end** indicates the end of execution of the call. This is preceded by parameter passing. Transitions for processing lists psl and apl follow later. For the execution of the body a new local binding is established. This is empty at first. The meaning of global names is given by the binding stack at declaration which consists of the first i elements of bs. Thus the index of the static predecessor is i. Note that in the case of a parameter-less procedure $n\ psl = \epsilon$. Context conditions ensure that $apl = \epsilon$. No parameters have to be passed and we continue with the execution of the body ds; $sts\ \textbf{end}$;.

Example 2 (continued):   In our example call $A(D)$ leads to configuration

$((\textbf{procedure}\ C(\textbf{var} : \textbf{integer}))(D)\ ds_A\ sts_A;\ \textbf{end};\ \textbf{end};, ((b_1, 0), (\emptyset, 1)), s_1, \epsilon, \epsilon)$

(PP)   Parameter passing

Let $c = ((psl)(apl)q, bs, s, i, o)$
with $psl \in \langle par\ spec\ seq \rangle$ and $apl \in \langle act\ par\ seq \rangle$.
Then $c' = (p', bs', s, i, o)$ where p' and bs' are defined as follows.

---

1) Definition of p'.

If $tail(psl) = \epsilon$ and thus, because of context conditions, $tail(apl) = \epsilon$ then $p' = q$, i.e. parameter passing is finished. If $tail(psl) \neq \epsilon$ then $p' = (tail(psl))(tail(apl))q$, i.e. the rests of the two lists have still to be processed.

2) Definition of bs'.

We define bs' by case distinction according to sort and type of the formal parameter. In each of the cases we use the notation $\overline{bs}$ to indicate bs without its last member, i.e. if $bs = ((b_1, sv_1), \ldots, (b_m, sv_m))$, $m \geq 1$ then $\overline{bs} = ((b_1, sv_1), \ldots, (b_{m-1}, sv_{m-1}))$. $\overline{bs}$ is therefore the binding stack at calling point.

const-parameter: Let $head(psl) = $ **const** $n : t$ with $n \in \langle ident \rangle$ and $t \in \langle elem\ type \rangle$ and $head(apl) = E$ with $E \in \langle expr \rangle$. Then

$$bs' = bs[n \backslash I(\overline{bs}, s, E)].$$

Explanation: The actual parameter is evaluated in the environment of the calling point and the resulting value is bound to n.

var-parameter (small type): Let $head(psl) = $ **var** $n : t$ with $n \in \langle ident \rangle$ and $t \in \langle small\ type \rangle$ and $head(apl) = y \in \langle ident \rangle$. Then

$$bs' = bs[n \backslash L(bs, s, y)].$$

Explanation: The meaning of the actual parameter in the environment of the calling point is bound to n.

var-parameter (array type): Let $head(psl) = $ **var** n: **array**$[l1..u1, \ldots, lk..uk]$ **of** t with $n, l1, u1, \ldots, lk, uk \in \langle ident \rangle$ and $t \in \langle small\ type \rangle$ and $head(apl) = y \in \langle ident \rangle$ with $\overline{bs}(y) = f \in ARR$, $Def(f) = [c1..d1] \times \ldots \times [ck..dk]$ with $ci, di \in \mathbf{Z}$ for $1 \leq i \leq k$. Then

$$bs' = bs[n \backslash f][l1 \backslash c1][u1 \backslash d1] \ldots [lk \backslash ck][uk \backslash dk].$$

Explanation: We obtain the meaning of array name y and bind it to n. Furthermore we bind the array bounds to names $l1, u1, \ldots, lk, uk$ introduced in the parameter specification. These names behave just like names of constants.

procedure-parameter: Let $head(psl) = $ **procedure** $n(psl1)$ or $head(psl) = $ **procedure** n with $n \in \langle ident \rangle$ and $psl1 \in \langle mode\ seq \rangle$ and let $head(apl) = y \in \langle ident \rangle$. Then

$$bs' = bs[n \backslash \overline{bs}(y)].$$

Explanation: The meaning of procedure name y in the environment of the calling point is bound to n.

Example 2 (continued): The next configuration is

$$(ds_A\ sts_A; \ \mathbf{end;}\ \mathbf{end;}, ((b_1, 0), (b_2', 1)), s_1, \epsilon, \epsilon),$$

where $Def(b_2') = \{C\}$ and $b_2'(C) = b_1(D)$. After the declaration section of A and assignment $x := 2$ we obtain configuration

$$c_2 = (C(x);\ A(B); \ \mathbf{end}\ ; \mathbf{end;}, bs_2, s_2, \epsilon, \epsilon).$$

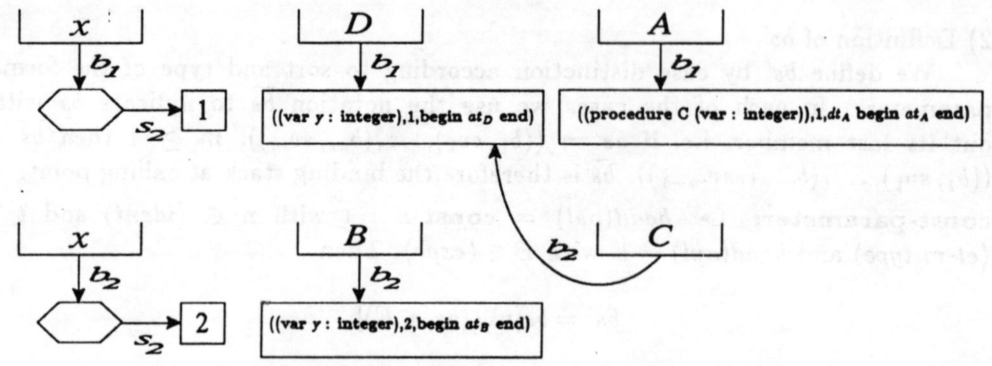

Fig. 3. Binding stack $((b_1, 0), (b_2, 1))$ and storage state s_2

$bs_2 = ((b_1, 0), (b_2, 1))$. Bindings b_1, b_2 and storage state s_2 are shown in Figure 3. Now $C(x)$ is called. We first add $(\emptyset, 1)$ to the binding stack. Parameter passing has the effect that y is bound to $bs_2(x) = b_2(x)$. We obtain configuration c_3 with

$$c_3 = (\text{print } x; \text{ print } y; \; y := y + 1; \text{ end}; \; A(B); \text{ end}; \text{ end};, bs_3, s_2, \epsilon, \epsilon).$$

Here $bs_3 = ((b_1, 0), (b_2, 1), (b_3, 1))$. Bindings b_1, b_2, b_3 and storage state s_2 are shown in Figure 4.

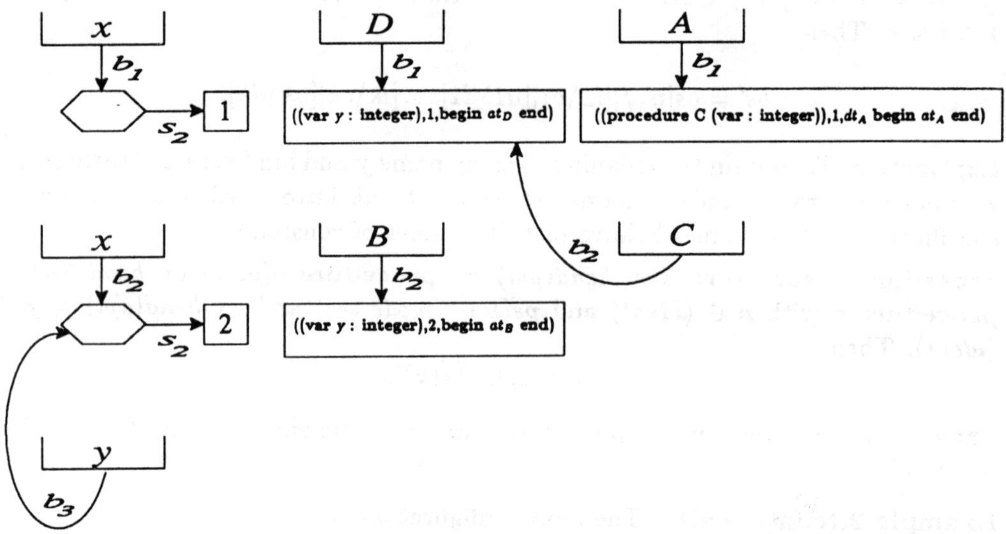

Fig. 4. Binding stack $((b_1, 0), (b_2, 1), (b_3, 1))$ and storage state s_2

Statement **print** x prints $I(bs_3, s_2, x) = s_2(b_1(x)) = 1$. Note that $x \notin Def(b_3)$ and $sv_3 = 1$. Then statement **print** y prints $I(bs_3, s_2, y) = s_2(b_3(y)) = 2$. Finally, assignment $y := y + 1$ increases the value of variable $b_3(y) = b_2(x)$ from 2 to 3. Let us call the new storage state s_3.

Finally, we consider the transition which occurs when returning from a procedure. We merely delete the last member of the binding stack.

(RP)   Returning from a procedure

Let $c = (\mathbf{end};\ \underline{p'}, bs, s, i, o)$.
Then $c' = (p', \overline{bs}, s, i, o)$,
where $\overline{bs} = ((b_1, sv_1), \ldots, (b_{m-1}, sv_{m-1}))$ if $bs = ((b_1, sv_1), \ldots, (b_m, sv_m))$.

Example 2 (continued):   Procedure C is completed and we return to A by deleting $(b_3, 1)$. We are now in configuration

$$c_4 = (A(B);\ \mathbf{end};\ \mathbf{end};\, , bs_4, s_3, \epsilon, (1,2))$$

with $bs_4 = bs_2 = ((b_1, 0), (b_2, 1))$. Bindings b_1, b_2 and storage state s_3 are shown in Figure 5.

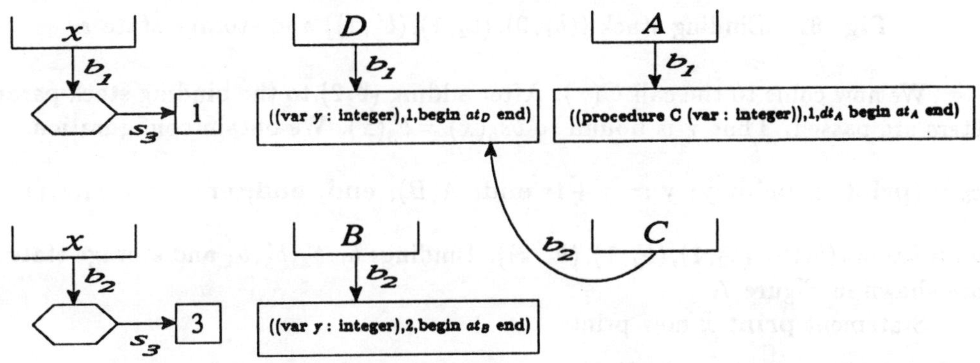

Fig. 5.   Binding stack $((b_1, 0), (b_2, 1))$ and storage state s_3

To execute the call $A(B)$ we first add $(\emptyset, 1)$ to the binding stack. Parameter passing results in C being bound to $bs_4(B) = b_2(B)$, i.e. $b'_3(C) = b_2(B)$. After the declaration section of A and assignment $x := 2$ we obtain configuration

$$c_5 = (C(x);\ A(B);\ \mathbf{end};\ \mathbf{end}; \mathbf{end};\, , bs_5, s_4, \epsilon, (1,2)).$$

$bs_5 = ((b_1, 0), (b_2, 1), (b'_3, 1))$. Bindings b_1, b_2, b'_3 and storage state s_4 are shown in Figure 6.

Configuration c_5 is somewhat surprising. Firstly, procedure B is now declared twice. Of course bodies and parameter lists match, but the binding stacks were different at the declarations. Hence the second components of $b_2(B)$ and $b'_3(B)$ are different! This means that the two incarnations of B access their global variables in a different way. Note also that in the actual environment we can refer to incarnation $b'_3(B)$ using the name B and to incarnation $b_2(B)$ via the name C.

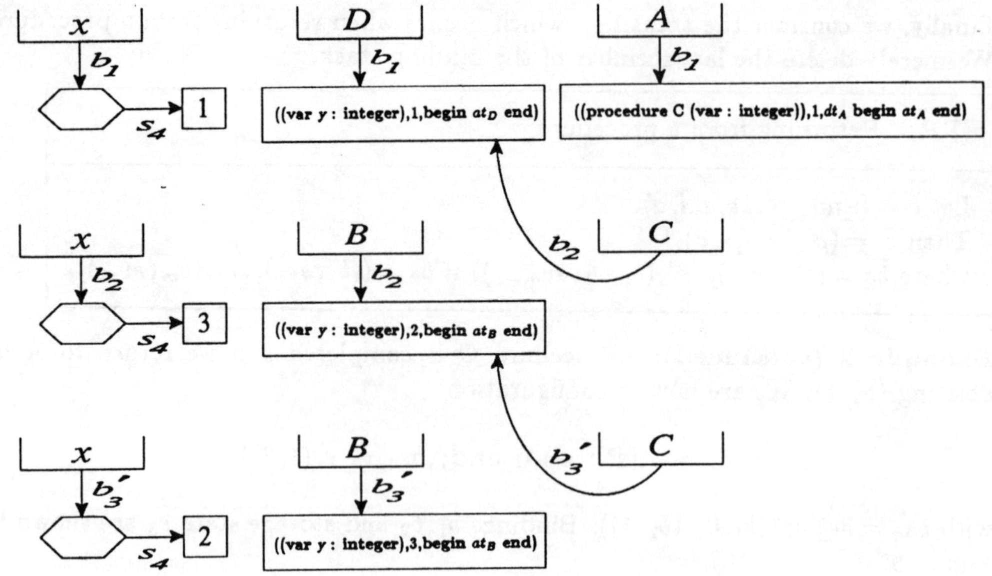

Fig. 6. Binding stack $((b_1, 0), (b_2, 1), (b_3', 1))$ and storage state s_4

We now come to the call $C(x)$. After adding $(\emptyset, 2)$ to the binding stack parameters are passed. Thus y is bound to $bs_5(x) = b_3'(x)$. We obtain configuration

$$c_6 = (\textbf{print } x;\ \textbf{print } y;\ y := y+1;\ \textbf{end};\ A(B);\ \textbf{end};\ \textbf{end};\ \textbf{end};\ ,bs_6, s_4, \epsilon, (1,2))$$

with $bs_6 = ((b_1, 0), (b_2, 1), (b_3', 1), (b_4, 2))$. Bindings b_1, b_2, b_3', b_4 and storage state s_4 are shown in Figure 7.

Statement **print** x now prints

$$
\begin{aligned}
I(bs_6, s_4, x) &= s_4(bs_6(x)) && \text{definition of } I \\
&= s_4(((b_1, 0), (b_2, 1))(x)) && \text{since } x \notin Def(b_4) \text{ and } sv_4 = 2 \\
&= s_4(b_2(x)) && \text{since } x \in Def(b_2) \\
&= 3.
\end{aligned}
$$

Then **print** y prints the value $I(bs_6, s_4, y) = s_4(bs_6(y)) = s_4(b_4(y)) = 2$. Finally we increase variable $b_4(y) = b_3'(x)$ from 2 to 3. On the output tape we now have 1, 2, 3, 2. Continuing the program we find that an output sequence 1,2,3,2,3,2,3,2,...is generated.

Let us suppose that the program-rest in c_5 begins with $B(x)$ instead of $C(x)$. The effect of a call $B(x)$ is to add $(\emptyset, 3)$ to the binding stack bs_5 and parameter passing where y is bound to $bs_5(x) = b_3'(x)$. We obtain configuration

$$c_7 = (\textbf{print } x;\ \textbf{print } y;\ y := y+1;\ \textbf{end};\ A(B);\ \textbf{end};\ \textbf{end};\ \textbf{end};\ ,bs_7, s_4, \epsilon, (1,2))$$

with $bs_7 = ((b_1, 0), (b_2, 1), (b_3', 1), (b_4, 3))$. Bindings b_1, b_2, b_3', b_4 and storage state s_4 are exactly as in configuration c_6, see Figure 7. The only difference between c_6 and c_7, i.e. between bs_6 and bs_7, is the value of sv_4. Statement **print** x now prints

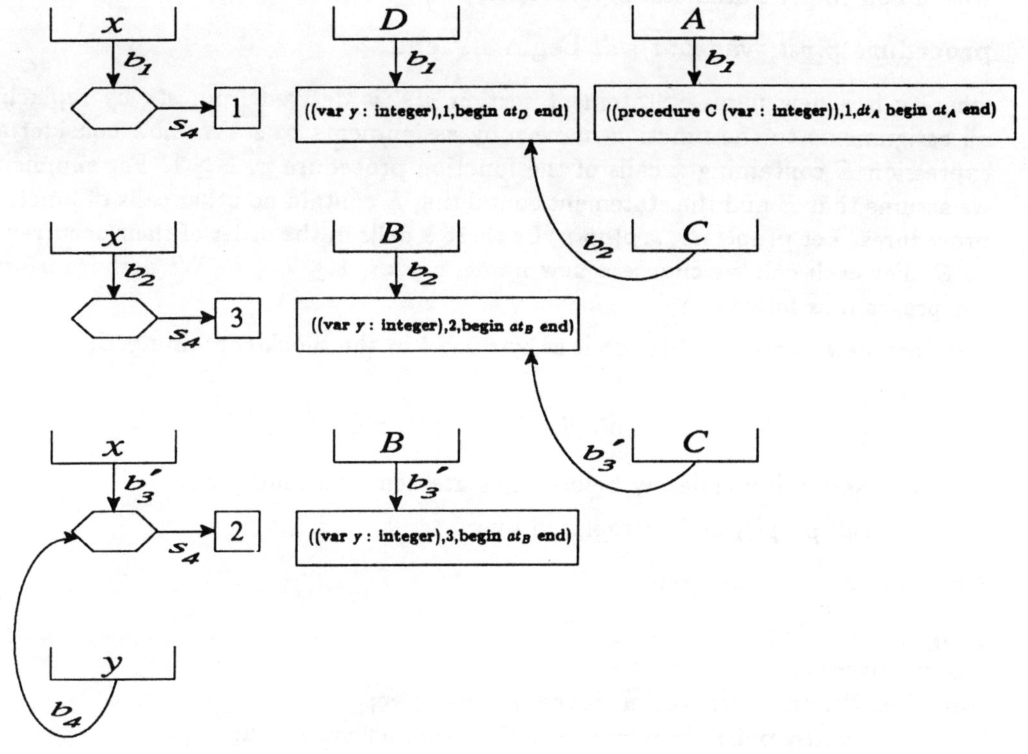

Fig. 7.   Binding stack $((b_1, 0), (b_2, 1), (b'_3, 1), (b_4, 2))$ and storage state s_4.

$$
\begin{aligned}
I(bs_7, s_4, x) &= s_4(bs_7(x)) && \text{definition of } I \\
&= s_4(((b_1, 0), (b_2, 1), (b'_3, 1))(x)) && \text{since } x \notin Def(b_4) \text{ and } sv_4 = 3 \\
&= s_4(b'_3(x)) && \text{since } x \in Def(b'_3) \\
&= 2.
\end{aligned}
$$

Replacing $C(x)$ in A by a call $B(x)$ thus results in an output sequence 2,2,2,... ∎

We must now discuss function procedures. The semantics of the call of function procedures can not be described in the current framework. This is because it must be seen as part of the semantics of expressions since, syntactically, calls of function procedures are factors.

We can proceed in two ways. We could employ the push down automata of Chapter II which evaluate expressions and modify them so that they can also cope with function calls. This approach, although reflecting what is done in practice, is very complex. We therefore prefer a second approach in which we treat function procedures as "syntactic sugar" and reduce them to proper procedures. We only need to introduce a var-parameter of appropriate type, see the examples from Section 6.2. Given a declaration

function $p(psl)$: t; ds **begin** sts **end**

with a non-empty parameter specification list, we replace that declaration by

procedure $p(psl$; **var** $z : t)$; ds **begin** sts' **end**

where z is a new name. Statement section sts' is derived from sts by replacing all assignments to the function name p by assignments to z. We now consider an expression E containing k calls of the function procedure p, $k \geq 1$. For simplicity we assume that E and the statement containing E contain no other calls of function procedures. Let $p(apl1),\dots,p(aplk)$ be these k calls in the order of their occurrence in E. For each call we choose a new name, say xi, $1 \leq i \leq k$. We now transform the program as follows.

- each new name xi is declared as **var** xi: t in the block containing E;

- calls

$$p(apl1, x1); \dots; p(aplk, xk);$$

are inserted immediately before the statement containing E;

- each call $p(apli)$ in E is replaced by xi.

Example 3:   The program

program *funcfunc*;
var y: **integer**;
function *Printandincr*(**var** n: **integer**): **integer**;
       begin print n; $n := n + 1$; *Printandincr* $:= n$ **end**;
begin $y := 0$;
     print *Printandincr*$(y) *$ *Printandincr*(y)
end.

is transformed into

program *funcfunc*;
var y: **integer**; **var** $x1$, $x2$: **integer**;
procedure *Printandincr*(**var** n: **integer**, **var** z: **integer**);
       begin print n; $n := n + 1$; $z := n$ **end**;
begin $y := 0$;
     Printandincr$(y,x1)$;   (∗ prints 0 ∗)
     Printandincr$(y,x2)$;   (∗ prints 1 ∗)
     print $x1 * x2$ (∗ prints 2 ∗)
end.

The function procedure in Example 3 has a so-called "side effect". Whereas functions in the mathematical sense yield a value, function procedures, in addition, can alter the values of global variables and var-parameters. This can lead to surprising effects when evaluating expressions, as shown in the above example. The situation is even worse if push down automata are used to define the semantics.

Then, for example, **print** $y*Printandincr(y)$ prints 0 and **print** $Printandincr(y)*y$ the value 1, since in the second case the pushdown automaton uses for y the value it has on returning from the function procedure. This example shows that side effects can even destroy commutativity of arithmetic operations.

If a programming language permits side effects in function procedures then the semantics must fix an evaluation order for the operands of expressions so that in any environment an expression has a uniquely defined value. The algebraic method in Chapter II did not define this order. Pascal determines an evaluation order from left to right subject to the precedence of operators. "Taking out" the function calls in front of the expression, as in the semantics defined above, differs from the left-right evaluation in Pascal.

All these complications due to side effects in function procedures obviously suggest avoiding them if possible when programming.

The semantics of PROSA is now complete apart from the definition of start and final states. Let $p =$ **program** $n; \; ds$ **begin** sts **end.** be a PROSA program and let $i \in D^*$ be an input sequence. Then

$$in(p, i) = (ds \; sts; \; \textbf{end};\, , ((\emptyset, 0)), \emptyset, i, \epsilon).$$

Thus the program-rest comprises, as before, the declaration and statement sections. Execution is started with a binding stack containing one element and an empty local binding. All variables are undefined, the input tape contains i and the output tape is empty. The set of final states is given by

$$C^f = \{(\epsilon, \epsilon, s, \epsilon, o) \mid o \in D^*, s \in S\}.$$

Thus program-rest, binding stack and input sequence are empty and storage state and output sequence are arbitrary. Function $out : C^f \to D^*$ extracts the output sequence, thus

$$out((\epsilon, \epsilon, s, \epsilon, o)) = o.$$

We have still to show that the context conditions guarantee that there are no type errors in the statement section. Since this is done similar to previous chapters we omit it. Instead, we use the rest of the section to show a further relationship between syntax and semantics, namely the use of procedure identifications to simplify looking up names in binding stacks. The PROSA machine consults the binding stack for each applied occurrence of a name. Proceeding from the actual local binding, it follows the static link until a local binding is found which contains the meaning of the name. *How many pointers to the predecessor have to be followed until the meaning of a name is found?* We will show that this question has a very simple answer (this answer will be very important for the translation of PROSA to RESA in Chapter VII). Let us consider an applied occurrence of x in the body of a procedure q. If x is the name of a formal parameter or of a local variable of q then we find the meaning of x in the actual local binding and do not have to follow any pointer. Otherwise x has a defining occurrence in a procedure q' which contains q. If x is defined in the procedure directly containing q then we must follow one pointer to the predecessor. In the other case we must follow several static links, precisely as many links as the nesting level of procedure q relative to q' indicates. This can be formulated differently. Let (x, pi_1) be the unique name of an applied occurrence of x in q and let pi_2 be the identification of q (procedure identification will usually be shortened to identification). Then precisely $|pi_2| - |pi_1|$ static links have to be followed until the meaning of x is found.

Example 2 (continued): B has procedure identification $(2, 1)$ and A has identification (2). The unique names of the applied occurrences of, for example, x, y, C, B and A in A are $(x, (2)), (y, (2, 1)), (C, (2)), (B, (2))$ and (A, ϵ). Let us go back to Figures 2 to 7. Figure 7 illustrates the situation within B. We do not have to follow a static link to find y. But for x, C and B we need to follow one static link and for A two. Figure 6 shows the situation within the body of A. We do not have to follow any static link to find x, C and B, but we must follow one to find A. The reader should examine the situations in Figs. 2 to 5 in a similar way.   ∎

The relationship between the length of the chain of static links to be followed and the difference between the lengths of the procedure identifications is so important that we formulate it as a theorem.

Theorem 1. *Let x occur in the statement section of a procedure q, let (x, pi') be the unique name of this applied occurrence and let pi'' be the procedure identification of q. Consider a call of q. Let bs be the actual binding stack after parameter passing and executing the declaration section. Then during execution of the body of q*

$$bs(x) = b_{sv^{(d)}(m)}(x).$$

Here $m = |bs|$ is the actual length of the binding stack, $d = |pi''| - |pi'|$ is the difference between the nesting levels and $sv^{(d)}(m)$ is the notation of Definition 2 of Section 6.4.

Proof: For this proof we add an extra concept to the PROSA machine by associating a procedure identification with each local binding in the binding stack. The identification associated with the local binding (b_i, sv_i) is written as pi_i and we define pi_i as follows. By definition $pi_1 = \epsilon$. Procedure calls add local bindings to bs. If we add the local binding (b_{m+1}, sv_{m+1}) to bs in executing a call $p(apl)$ with $bs(p) = (psl, j, R)$ then we define pi_{m+1} as the identification of the body R of p. Remember that sv_{m+1} is set to j.

Example 2 (continued): The situation in Figure 7 results in identifications as shown in Figure 8 .

local binding	$(b_1, 0)$	$(b_2, 1)$	$(b_3', 1)$	$(b_4, 2)$
associated identification	ϵ	(2)	(2)	$(2, 1)$

Fig. 8.   Local bindings and associated identifications in the situation of Figure 7.

Note that b_1 results from the main program, b_2 and b_3' from calls of A and b_4 from a call of C and thus B. This example shows that the identification of the static predecessor of a local binding is precisely the parent of its identification , e.g. $pi_4 = (2,1)$, $sv_4 = 2$ and $pi_2 = (2)$ and analogously $pi_3 = (2)$, $sv_3 = 1$ and $pi_1 = \epsilon$.
∎

Before we continue with the proof of the theorem, we want to show the property illustrated in the example.

Lemma 1. *For all binding stacks* $bs = ((b_1, sv_1), \ldots, (b_m, sv_m))$ *created during the execution of a PROSA program and for the associated identifications* $pi_1, \ldots, pi_m$

a) $pi_{sv_j} = parent(pi_j)$ *for* $2 \le j \le m$;

b) $pi_{sv^{(d)}(m)} = parent^{(d)}(pi_m)$ *for* $2 \le j \le m, d \ge 0$.

Proof: a) We prove part a) by induction on the length of the computation. To do so we show the following stronger assertion.

Claim:

a) $pi_{sv_j} = parent(pi_j)$ *for* $2 \le j \le m$.

b) *For all* j, $1 \le j \le m$ *and all procedure names* $p \in Def(b_j)$: *If* $b_j(p) = (psl, l, R)$ *then* $pi_l = parent(pi(R))$ *where* $pi(R)$ *is the identification of* R.

Proof: Let us first illustrate the claim using our example.

Example 2 (continued):   For procedure name C the second part of the claim can be seen as follows. With $b_3'(C) = (\ldots, 2, \textbf{begin } sts_B \textbf{ end})$, the body has the identification $(2,1)$. Furthermore $pi_2 = (2) = parent((2,1))$ and thus the second part the claim holds. Correspondingly, $b_2(C) = (\ldots, 1, \textbf{begin } sts_D \textbf{ end})$ and hence the body has identification (1). Furthermore $pi_1 = \epsilon = parent((1))$. Thus the second part of the claim holds in this case too. It is intuitively clear that the claim always holds as we define the static predecessor precisely when we process the declaration. The block containing the declaration is just the parent block of the body.
∎

We now prove the Lemma by induction on the length of the computation. It is certainly true for the start configuration. There are precisely four transitions which are relevant for us, processing a procedure declaration, passing a procedure as a parameter, calling of and returning from a procedure. When returning from a procedure the binding stack becomes shorter and by induction hypothesis there is nothing to be shown. Let us now consider a call of a procedure p with $bs(p) = (psl, l, R)$. We add (b_{m+1}, l) with $b_{m+1} = \emptyset$ to the binding stack and define pi_{m+1} as $pi(R)$. Since, by induction hypothesis, $pi_l = parent(pi(R))$ we have a) for $j = m+1$. Since $b_{m+1} = \emptyset$, b) obviously holds for $j = m+1$. We now consider parameter passing, in particular passing a procedure. For part a) there is nothing to be shown. Part b) can be seen as follows. The formal procedure name is bound to a triple (psl, l, R) which has already been bound to a procedure name and thus, by induction hypothesis, satisfies $pi_l = parent(pi(R))$. This shows part b). Finally, we consider the case of processing a procedure declaration. Let, for example, $bs = ((b_1, sv_1), \ldots, (b_m, sv_m))$ be the actual binding stack. Consider processing a declaration of p with body R in body Q of a procedure q. Then $pi(Q) = parent(pi(R))$ since the declaration of p lies in q and $pi_m = pi(Q)$ by definition of pi_i. Furthermore p is bound to a triple $(\ldots, m, R)$ and thus $pi_m = pi(Q) = parent(pi(R))$. In this case, therefore, the induction step is complete and hence part a) of Lemma 1 has been proved. ∎

b) Part b) of the Lemma follows from part a) by induction on d. For $d = 0$ we have $sv^{(0)}(m) = m$ and $parent^{(0)}(pi_m) = pi_m$ and the claim is thus true. For $d > 0$

$$
\begin{aligned}
pi_{sv^{(d)}(m)} &= pi_{sv_{sv^{(d-1)}(m)}} && \text{definition of } sv_{(d)}(m) \\
&= parent(pi_{sv^{(d-1)}(m)}) && \text{according to part a)} \\
&= parent(parent^{(d-1)}(pi_m)) && \text{by induction hypothesis} \\
&= parent^{(d)}(pi_m)
\end{aligned}
$$

which completes the induction step.   ∎

By proving Lemma 1 most of the essential work for the proof of Theorem 1 is accomplished. We now consider an applied occurrence with unique name (x, pi') in procedure p. Let pi'' be the identification of the body of q and let bs be the binding stack resulting from a call of the procedure after parameter passing and execution of the declaration section. Furthermore let $m = |bs|$ be the length of the binding stack and $d = |pi''| - |pi'|$. We must show

$$
bs(x) = b_{sv^{(d)}(m)}(x)
$$

i.e. $x \in Def(b_{sv^{(d)}(m)})$ and $x \notin Def(b_{sv^{(j)}(m)})$ for all $j < d$. First we observe, since we are processing the body of q, that $pi_m = pi''$. The pair (x, pi') is the unique name of an applied occurrence of x in the body of q. Thus by definition of unique names for applied occurrences

1) pi' is a prefix of pi'' and thus $pi' = parent^{(d)}(pi'')$ for some $d \geq 0$.

2) The extended block with identification pi' contains a defining occurrence of x.

3) No extended block with identification pi''' such that pi' is a proper prefix of pi''' and pi''' is a prefix of pi'' contains a defining occurrence of x.

Because of $pi'' = pi_m$, using Lemma 1b, 1) implies $pi' = pi_{sv^{(d)}(m)}$ and thus, by 2), $x \in Def(b_{sv^{(d)}(m)})$. Let $j < d$ and let $pi''' = pi_{sv^{(j)}(m)}$. Then, according to Lemma 1b, $pi''' = parent^{(j)}(pi_m) = parent^{(j)}(pi'')$, i.e. pi''' is a prefix of pi'' and pi' is a proper prefix of pi'''. Because of 3), $x \notin Def(b_{sv^{(j)}(m)})$ and Theorem 1 is proved.   ∎

Theorem 1 is essential for the translation of PROSA to RESA. It facilitates simulating the binding stack in RESA in an obvious way. More about this in the next chapter.

Exercises for 6.4

1) Specify the transitions of the PROSA machine for value and name parameter passing.

2) Introduce const-parameters of record type. Specify the transition of the PROSA machine for parameter passing.

3) Given
```
program exercise 3;
procedure A(const arg: integer; procedure p);
    procedure q;
        begin
            print arg
        end;
    begin p;
        A(arg − 1, q)
    end;
    procedure r;
        var x: integer;
        begin
            x := 1
        end;
(* beginning of the main program *)
begin
    A(5, r)
end.
```

Trace the computation of the PROSA machine for this program.

4) Extend PROSA by constant declarations of the form **const** $\langle def\ ident \rangle = \langle expr \rangle$. Up to now we only permitted standard names to the right of the equality signs. This was quite natural in Chapter III since the PROSA machine must be able to evaluate the expression when executing the declaration.

   a) Specify the transition of the PROSA machine such that the name is bound to the value of the expression in the actual environment.

   b) Specify a suitable context condition which guarantees that the expression in the declaration can be evaluated.

Chapter 7   Translating PROSA into RESA, Part 2

In this chapter we describe how PROSA with procedures is translated to RESA. We have already discussed the translation for PROSA programs without procedures in Chapter V. We now have two new problems in addition to those of Chapter V

1) Procedures permit a very flexible control structure.

2) Procedures demand a more complicated storage administration.

The objective of this chapter is the following theorem.

Theorem 1. *For each PROSA program p_1 there is an equivalent RESA program p_2. Program p_2 can be effectively constructed from p_1 and for all inputs i:*

$$comp_time(p_2, i) \leq c \cdot (1 + comp_time(p_1, i)).$$

c is a constant depending on p_1 but not on i. ∎

To prove Theorem 1 we obviously want to use the results of Chapter V. As in Chapter V, we consider only elementary data types *int* and *bool* and leave the treatment of the other elementary types to the reader. In Chapter V we already showed how to translate PROSA programs without procedures by first translating PROSA programs into primitive PROSA programs and then translating these into RESA. We will proceed likewise in this chapter. Separating the translation into two steps allows us to deal with all special cases within PROSA. Then we can concentrate on just the essentials when translating to RESA. This introductory section is concerned with translating into primitive PROSA. The translation of primitive PROSA to RESA is discussed in Sections 7.1 to 7.3. Section 7.1 examines storage organisation in detail and we show how the binding stack and the storage state of the PROSA machine are reflected in the storage allocation on the RESA machine. Afterwards, in Section 7.2 we describe storage access i.e. how to translate applied names into RESA. In Section 7.3 we specify the actual translation and show which RESA statement sequences must be generated from PROSA statements.

Translating into primitive PROSA (now taking procedures into account) proceeds similarly to Sections 5.4 to 5.8. However, the reduction of multi-dimensional arrays into one-dimensional arrays is more complex because of the possibility of dynamic arrays. In each call an array declared in a procedure can be of a different actual size. Information about the actual form (i.e. the $2k$-tuple of the actual bounds) is needed for generating tests which check whether array indices are within the permissible ranges. Likewise it is necessary to generate array selections in the one-dimensional array representing the multi-dimensional array. For this reason one constructs a so called array descriptor when processing an array declaration. An array descriptor comprises the $2k$-tuple of actual array bounds. In order to construct it we must be able to execute simple statements within the declaration section. Thus we extend PROSA for this chapter by a rudimentary possibility of calculating in the declaration section. A constant declaration now has the form

$$\langle const\ decl \rangle \rightarrow \textbf{const}\ \langle def\ ident \rangle = \langle expr \rangle$$

Condition: The expression contains no local variable names and no calls of function procedures.

The semantics of such a constant declaration is as follows. Let $c = (\textbf{const}\ n = E; p', bs, s, i, o)$ with $n \in \langle ident \rangle$ and $E \in \langle expr \rangle$ be a configuration of the PROSA machine. Then $\delta(c) = (p', bs[n \backslash I(bs, s, E)], s, i, o)$, i.e., n is bound to the value of the expression E in the actual environment.

We now define primitive PROSA.

Definition 1: A PROSA program p is said to be **primitive** if

(1) p uses integer variables only.

(2) There are no type declarations in p and neither pointers nor records are used.

(3) All arrays used in p are one-dimensional and have an index range beginning at 0. Each array selection is of the form $a[i]$ where i is the name of a local variable. Furthermore i has at this point a value which lies within the index range of a.

(4) Print and read statements refer only to simple variables.

(5) Boolean expressions occur only in tests of conditional statements and iteration statements. They are of the form $x = 0$ or $x > 0$. x is a simple variable.

(6) Expressions contain at most one operation symbol.

(7) There is at most one array H: $\textbf{array}[0..\infty]$ **of integer** of infinite size in p.

(8) All array declarations (apart from the declaration of H) are of the form **var** a: $\textbf{array}[0..u]$ **of integer** where u is a constant name declared in the same declaration section as the array. All array parameter specifications are of the form **var** a: $\textbf{array}[l..u]$ **of integer**.

(9) All procedure calls are of the form $n(u_1, \ldots, u_k)$ or n. Here n is the name of a procedure and u_i, $1 \leq i \leq k$, are either names or of the form $a[i]$ or are standard names. ∎

Points (1) to (7) in Definition 1 are the same as those of Definition 2 in Chapter V. However, in addition, we require for array selections that the index is a local variable and do not exclude constant names in (2). Points (8) and (9) determine procedure calls and array declarations. As in Chapter V, we use array H to realise records. Its size must be potentially infinite since the number of records generated during a program run is not known a priori.

We now prove the following theorem.

Theorem 2. *For each PROSA program p_1 there is an equivalent primitive PROSA program p_2 which can be effectively constructed from p_1. For all inputs i:*

$$comp_time(p_2, i) \leq c \cdot (1 + comp_time(p_1, i)).$$

c is a constant depending on p_1 but not on i.

Proof: We proceed in essence as in Chapter V. However, the reduction of multi-dimensional arrays to one-dimensional arrays is more complex. First we eliminate type declarations, records, pointers and boolean variables exactly as described in Sections 5.4 to 5.6. This ensures (1), (2) and (5) and introduces the infinite array H. Next, similar to Section 5.7, we reduce multi-dimensional arrays to one-dimensional arrays. We begin the discussion with array declarations. Then we deal with array parameters of declared procedures, then array parameters of formal procedures and finally array selection.

An array declaration in the declaration section of a procedure p, for instance, is of the form

$$\textbf{var } a : \textbf{array}[E_1..E_2, \ldots, E_{2k-1}..E_{2k}] \textbf{ of integer}.$$

Here E_i , $1 \leq i \leq 2k$ are expressions. We replace this declaration by $2k + 2$ declarations

$\textbf{const } n_1 = E_1; \textbf{ const } n_2 = E_2; \ldots; \textbf{const } n_{2k} = E_{2k};$
$\textbf{const } n = (n_2 - n_1 + 1) * \ldots * (n_{2k} - n_{2k-1} + 1) - 1;$
$\textbf{var } a: \textbf{array}[0..n] \textbf{ of integer}.$

Note that here we use the extension of PROSA. The $2k$-tuple $(n_1, n_2, \ldots, n_{2k})$ is called the **array descriptor** of array a. It describes the k-dimensional structure of the original version of a. We will use the array descriptor later to generate tests for range violations during array selections. After this change we have only one-dimensional arrays. Furthermore their index range starts at 0. We must now take this change into account in the case of parameter passing.

Let

$$\textbf{var } a : \textbf{array}[l_1..u_1, \ldots, l_k..u_k] \textbf{ of integer}$$

be an array parameter in the formal parameter list of a procedure declaration. We replace this specification by (l and u are new names)

$\textbf{var } a: \textbf{array}[l..u] \textbf{ of integer};$
$\textbf{const } l_1: \textbf{integer}; \textbf{ const } u_1: \textbf{integer};$
$$\vdots$$
$\textbf{const } l_k: \textbf{integer}; \textbf{ const } u_k: \textbf{integer}.$

The $2k$-tuple $(l_1, u_1, \ldots, l_k, u_k)$ is called the array descriptor of array parameter a. Again the array descriptor is used later to generate tests for range violations during array selections. In each call of the procedure we replace the actual parameter, for example b, by the sequence

$$b, n_1, n_2, \ldots, n_{2k}.$$

$(n_1, n_2, \ldots, n_{2k})$ is the array descriptor of array b.

Finally, let

$$\textbf{var } : \textbf{array}[\,,\ldots,\,] \textbf{ of integer}$$

specify the mode of a k-dimensional (i.e. there are $k-1$ commas between the square brackets) array parameter in the specification of a procedure parameter. We replace this specification by

$$\textbf{var } : \textbf{array}[\,] \textbf{ of integer};$$
$$\underbrace{\textbf{const } : \textbf{integer}; \ldots; \textbf{const } : \textbf{integer}}_{2k\text{-times}}$$

and thus take into account that now, instead of a k-dimensional array, a one-dimensional array together with its array descriptor is passed. This concludes the discussion of the declaration section and the parameter specifications. We now consider array selections.

Let $a[E_1, \ldots, E_k]$ select a k-dimensional array a. Using the array descriptor, say $(l_1, u_1, \ldots, l_k, u_k)$, of a we first generate tests for range violations

if $E_1 < l_1$ **or** $E_1 > u_1$ **or** $\ldots$ **or** $E_k < l_k$ **or** $E_k > u_k$
then error halt
fi.

Then according to Section 5.7, we compute the index in the one-dimensional version of a which corresponds to $(E_1, \ldots, E_k)$ and store it in a new local variable.

$$i := \sum_{j=1}^{k} \left\{ (E_j - l_j) \prod_{m=j+1}^{k} (u_m - l_m + 1) \right\}$$

Finally we replace $a[E_1, \ldots, E_k]$ by $a[i]$. Thus the transformation of multi-dimensional arrays into one-dimensional arrays is complete and properties (3) and (8) are secured.

Example 1:   A procedure declaration

procedure $p(\textbf{const } c\colon \textbf{integer}; \textbf{ var } A\colon \textbf{array}[l_1..u_1, l_2..u_2] \textbf{ of integer};$
        procedure $q(\textbf{var } : \textbf{array}[\,,\,] \textbf{ of integer}));$
        var $B\colon \textbf{array}[1..8 * y + c, 2..u_1] \textbf{ of integer};$
        begin
          $\vdots$
        $p(17 * y - c, B, q);$
        $A[c, 2] := B[2, y];$
        $q(A);$
          $\vdots$
        end

is transformed into

procedure p(**const** c: **integer**; **var** A: **array**$[l..u]$ **of integer**;
      const l_1, u_1, l_2, u_2: **integer**;
      procedure q(**var**: **array**$[\ ]$ **of integer**; **const**: **integer**;
         const: **integer**; **const**: **integer**; **const**: **integer**));
    const $n_1 = 1$; **const** $n_2 = 8 * y + c$; **const** $n_3 = 2$; **const** $n_4 = u_1$;
    const $n = (n_2 - n_1 + 1) * (n_4 - n_3 + 1) - 1$;
    var i_1, i_2: **integer**;
    var B: $[0..n]$ **of integer**;
    begin

        $\vdots$

      $p(17 * y - c, B, n_1, n_2, n_3, n_4, q)$;
      if $c < l_1$ **or** $c > u_1$ **or** $2 < l_2$ **or** $2 > u_2$ **or**
        $2 < n_1$ **or** $2 > n_2$ **or** $y < n_3$ **or** $y > n_4$
      then error halt
      fi;
      $i_1 := (c - l_1) * (u_2 - l_2 + 1) + 2 - l_2$;
      $i_2 := (2 - n_1) * (n_4 - n_3 + 1) + y - n_3$;
      $A[i_1] := B[i_2]$;
      $q(A, l_1, u_1, l_2, u_2)$;
    end.

The array descriptor of B is (n_1, n_2, n_3, n_4) and that of array A is (l_1, u_1, l_2, u_2). The array descriptor and the size of B are computed by the 5 constant declarations in the declaration section of p. The parameter specification list of p is extended by the four const-parameters l_1, u_1, l_2, u_2. In the call of p the array descriptor of the actual parameter B is passed via these four const-parameters. In the specification of procedure parameter q we replace the mode specification of the two-dimensional array by the mode specification of a one-dimensional array and an array descriptor. When calling q we pass array A and in addition its array descriptor. Finally we modify the two array selections according to Section 5.7. ∎

The rest of the proof is now quite simple. We establish (9) by introducing a new variable for each expression on an actual parameter position not satisfying property (9). The value of the expression is assigned to this variable and then the expression in the actual parameter list is replaced by this variable. Finally properties (4) and (6) are established as in Section 5.8. Note that constant declarations also have to be translated into three-address instructions. In certain circumstances new constant declarations must be added.

Example 1 (continued): Declaration **const** $n_2 = 8 * y + c$ is replaced by

const $l_2' = 8 * y$;
const $l_2 = l_2' + c$ ∎

The proof of Theorem 2 is now complete. ∎

Theorem 2 is one part of Theorem 1. We need only prove the following theorem.

Theorem 3. *For each primitive PROSA program p_1 there is an equivalent RESA program p_2 which can be effectively constructed from program p_1. Furthermore for all inputs i:*

$$comp_time(p_2, i) \leq c \cdot (1 + comp_time(p_1, i)).$$

c is a constant depending on p_1 but not on i. ∎

We have already mentioned that we will prove Theorem 3 and hence Theorem 1 in Sections 7.1 to 7.3. Section 7.3 contains the actual translation into RESA. In order to motivate the reader for the preparatory Sections 7.1 and 7.2, we now give a short sketch of Section 7.3.

One can view a PROSA program as a set of procedures declared in nested or parallel fashion. The main program can also be seen as a procedure, namely as a procedure which is declared and then immediately called. The body of each procedure consists of a declaration and statement section. The body of each procedure will be translated into a RESA program section of its own whose first lines will get the unique name of the procedure as label. To translate the body we proceed, in principle, as in Chapter V. However storage access, in particular for non-local names, is more complex (see Section 7.2). Procedure calls are added as new statements. In a procedure call we first pass parameters and the return address, i.e. the program line where computation must continue after the call is finished, and then jump to the first line of the translated body of the called procedure. After execution of the body we return with the help of the return address to the place of the call and continue the computation there. In this description it remained open where we store parameters and the return address and where local objects of the procedure are held. These questions will be examined in Section 7.1.

7.1 Storage Organisation

The PROSA machine has a binding stack to keep track of the meaning of names and the used variables. This section shows how the binding stack and the PROSA storage state are mapped into the RESA storage state. To keep the description clear we view the RESA storage as two arrays SP: **array**$[0..\infty]$ **of integer** and H: **array**$[0..\infty]$ **of integer** . The heap H which serves to realise records was discussed in Chapter V and need not be mentioned again. Array SP realises the binding stack. Since in this chapter we are only concerned with array SP, we simply identify SP with the storage of the RESA machine, i.e. $SP[i] = ds(i)$ for all $i \in \mathbb{N}$ where ds is the storage state of the RESA machine.

In actual compilers PROSA is translated into RESA in such a way that the generated RESA programs use only initial sections of arrays H and SP, say $H[0]$, $H[1]$, $H[2]$, ... and $SP[0]$, $SP[1]$, $SP[2]$, ... We do not know how big these initial sections are before running the RESA program. Thus arrays SP and H are placed in the (finite) storage of an actual computer as shown in Figure 1. The two sections then grow towards each other. If they meet computation halts because of storage overflow.

$SP[0]$	$SP[1]$	$SP[2]$	$\cdots$	$H[2]$	$H[1]$	$H[0]$
0	1				N-2	N-1

Fig. 1.   Arrays SP and H in the storage of an actual computer. The storage cells have addresses from 0 to $N - 1$.

Array SP is logically divided into so-called **activation records**. Every activation record corresponds to a local binding, see Figure 2, and consists of five parts.

1) pointer to the dynamic predecessor
2) pointer to the static predecessor
3) return address
4) actual parameter
5) local objects

We will describe these parts in turn. Let $c = (pr, bs, s, i, o)$ with $bs = ((b_1, sv_1), \ldots, (b_m, sv_m))$ be a configuration of the PROSA machine. The RESA storage then contains m activation records $AR_1, \ldots, AR_m$. Let l_i be the address of the first storage cell of activation record AR_i and g_i the number of cells in this activation record. We have $l_1 = 0$ and $l_{i+1} = l_i + g_i$ for $i \geq 0$.

Dynamic link: The cell with address l_i contains the value l_{i-1} for $2 \leq i \leq m$ and therefore $ds(l_i) = l_{i-1}$. The content of cell 0 $(= l_1)$ is undefined.

The RESA machine has index registers BFS (**Begin Free Storage**) and BAP (**Begin Active Procedure**) whose contents are named bfs and bap and additional

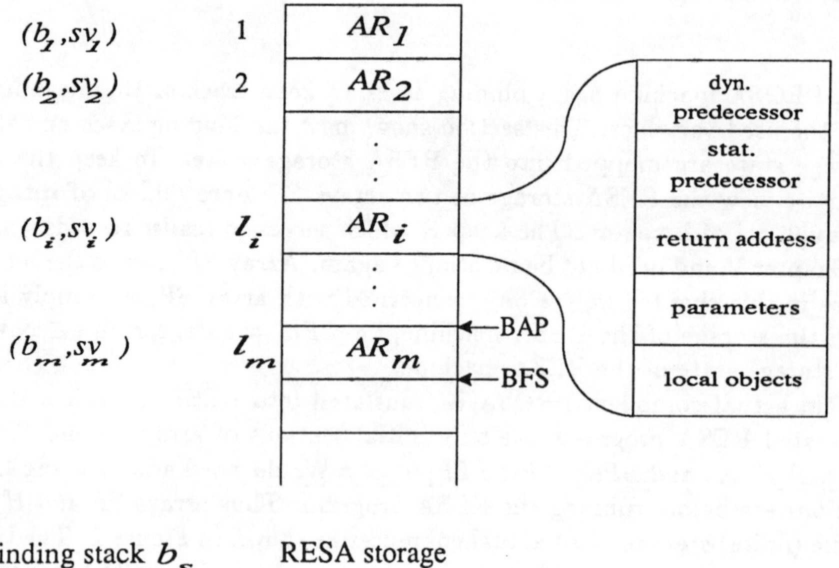

Fig. 2.   Binding stack bs of the PROSA machine and the RESA storage, divided into activation records; l_i is the first cell of activation record AR_i.

instructions LOADBFS, STOREBFS, LOADBAP and STOREBAP. The translation of PROSA to RESA ensures that throughout a generated RESA program we have $bfs = l_m + g_m$ and $bap = l_m$.

Explanation: The RESA storage is organised as a linear list of activation records. The dynamic links connect the activation records, index register BAP points to the "youngest" activation record which corresponds to the active procedure. Index register BFS points to the first cell of the free storage. We can therefore place the next activation record at address bfs when a procedure is called. Returning from a procedure we reset BFS to BAP and BAP to the dynamic link of the active procedure. Thus the activation record of the procedure is freed.

Static link: For $2 \leq i \leq m$ the cell with address $l_i + 1$ contains l_{sv_i}, i.e. $ds(l_i + 1) = l_{sv_i}$. The content of cell 1 $(= l_1 + 1)$ is undefined.

Explanation: The static link corresponds to the pointer in the binding stack. We use it to access global objects.

Return address: For $2 \leq i \leq m$ the cell with address $l_i + 2$ contains the address of the instruction where computation continues on return from the procedure. The content of cell 2 $(= l_1 + 2)$ is undefined.

Explanation: The return address enables return of control to the point after the call.

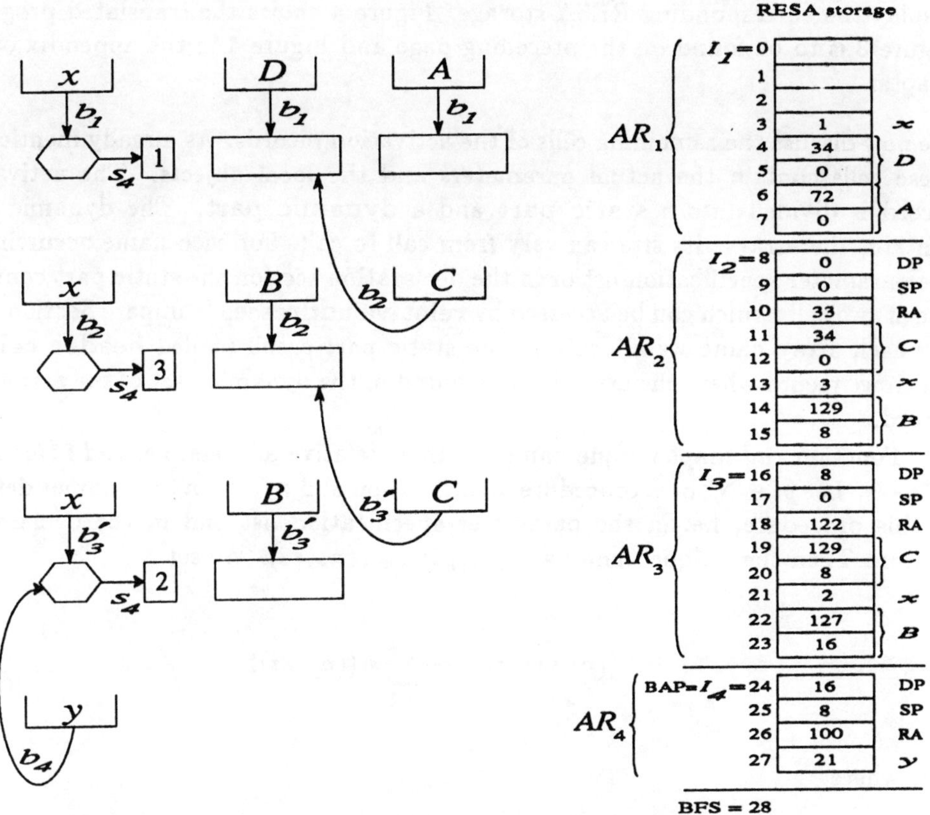

Fig. 3. The binding stack of the PROSA machine is $((b_1, 0), (b_2, 1), (b_3', 1),$ $(b_4, 2))$. The bindings themselves and the storage state are taken from Figure 7 in Section 6.4. The four activation records in the RESA storage extend from cells 0 to 7, 8 to 15, 16 to 23 and 24 to 27. Thus BAP has the value 24 and BFS the value 28. The values of the l_i are $l_1 = 0$, $l_2 = 8$, $l_3 = 16$ and $l_4 = 24$. The value of l_{i-1} is stored in the dynamic link of the activation record AR_i, $i \geq 2$,. The static link of activation record AR_i contains l_{sv_i}, $i \geq 1$; e.g. $ds(l_4 + 1) = l_{sv_4} = l_2 = 8$. As for the return addresses, we refer to Figure 4. Note that AR_1 corresponds to the main program, AR_2 to the call of A in the main program, AR_3 to a recursive call of A in A and AR_4 to the call of C (and thus B) in A. On "returning from AR_4" a call $A(B)$ must be initiated and thus $ds(l_4 + 2) = 100$. On "returning from AR_3" a call of A is completed and thus $ds(l_3 + 2) = 122$ and on "returning from AR_2" the main program is finished and thus $ds(l_2 + 2) = 33$. The contents of the remaining cells of the activation records are explained later.

Example 1 (Continuation of Example 2 from Section 6.4): In Figure 3 we reproduce the binding stack and storage state of Figure 7 from Section 6.4 and display the corresponding RESA storage. Figure 4 shows the translated program. Figure 3 is to be found on the preceding page and Figure 4 in the appendix of the chapter. ∎

We now discuss the remaining cells of the activation records. As already mentioned, these cells contain the actual parameters and the local objects. The activation record is divided into a **static part** and a **dynamic part**. The dynamic part contains the arrays. Its size can vary from call to call. For each name occurring in the parameter specification list or in the declaration section the static part contains one or two cells which can be accessed by **relative addresses** (compare Section 5.3). For each array name we allocate in the static part a cell (called **header cell**) in which we record where the array is to be found in the dynamic part of the activation record.

Function rad maps unique names to their relative address, i.e. $rad : \langle ident \rangle \times \mathbb{N}^* \rightsquigarrow \mathbb{N}$. Let $pi \in \mathbb{N}^*$ be a procedure identification and $n_1, \ldots, n_k$ the names defined in this procedure, i.e. in the parameter specification list and in the declaration section. Then the unique names are $(n_1, pi), \ldots, (n_k, pi)$. We set

$$rad((n_i, pi)) = 3 + \sum_{j=1}^{i-1} si((n_j, pi)).$$

where

$$si((n_j, pi)) = \begin{cases} 1, & \text{if } n_j \text{ is the name of a variable, an array,} \\ & \text{a const-parameter or a var-parameter ;} \\ 2, & \text{if } n_j \text{ is the name of a procedure or of a} \\ & \text{procedure parameter.} \end{cases}$$

$si((n_j, pi))$ is the number of RESA storage cells which we set aside for n_j in the static part of each activation record AR created by a call of the procedure with identification pi. Thus if l is the first cell of the activation record AR we set aside cell $l + rad((n_j, pi))$ for n_j, and, if necessary, the consecutive cell. As the first three cells of each activation record are already used for the dynamic and static links and the return address, the relative addresses start at 3. For each identification pi we use $si(pi)$ to denote the total size of the static part of all defined names in the procedure with identification pi, i.e.

$$si(pi) = \sum \{ si((n, pi)) \mid n \text{ is defined in the procedure with}$$

$$\text{identification } pi \}.$$

Example 1 (continued): Relative addresses are shown in Table 1.

procedure	identification	unique name	relative address
main program	ϵ	(x,ϵ)	3
		(D,ϵ)	4
		(A,ϵ)	6
D	(1)	$(y,(1))$	3
A	(2)	$(C,(2))$	3
		$(x,(2))$	5
		$(B,(2))$	6
B	(2,1)	$(y,(2,1))$	3

Table 1: The relative addresses.

With these relative addresses the association of the storage cells and names listed to the right of the storage cells in Figure 3 becomes apparent. Recall that the activation record AR_1 (AR_2, AR_3, AR_4) corresponds to the main program (to the procedure A, A, B). The contents of the RESA storage cells can now be explained. RESA storage cell $3 = l_1 + rad((x,\epsilon))$ corresponds to PROSA variables $b_1(x)$ and thus contains $s(b_1(x)) = 1$. In the same way cells $13 = l_2 + rad((x,(2)))$ and $21 = l_3 + rad((x,(2)))$ contain the values of variables $b_2(x)$ or $b_3'(x)$, that is 3 or 2. The value of variable $b_2(x)$ can be loaded into the accumulator by the following RESA instruction sequence.

```
LOADBAP    1    loads static link of the current activation record
STORE      IR
LOADIR     5
```

Let us consider cell $27 = l_4 + rad((y,(2,1)))$. y is the name of a var-parameter and is bound during parameter passing to a variable (here $b_3'(x)$). In the cell associated with y we store the address of that RESA storage cell which corresponds to PROSA variable $b_3'(x)$. Thus in our case it is address 21. We call 21 the absolute address of variable $b_3'(x)$. The value of variable $b_4(y)$ can now be loaded using the instructions

```
LOADBAP    3
STORE      IR
LOADIR     0
```

In PROSA terminology, we use cell 27 as a pointer. We do not store the value of variable $b_4(y)$ in it, but the address where this value can be found in the storage.

Next we consider cells 22 and 23. In cell $22 = l_3 + rad((B,(2,1)))$ we store the address of the first line of the translated body of B. According to Figure 4 it is line 129. In cell 23 we store the length of the activation record stack at the declaration of the procedure, that is number $16 = l_3$. Note that $b_3'(B) = (\ldots,3,\ldots)$. Similarly we can understand the contents of all other cells associated with names of procedures or procedure parameters. For example, $b_3'(C) = (\ldots,2,R_B)$ and thus cell 19 contains the address of the first line of the translated R_B and cell 20 contains $l_2 = 8$.

Before we formally define what the individual cells of an activation record contain, we give an example with const-parameters and arrays.

Example 2:

```
program example2;
    var n: integer;
    procedure unusual(const m: integer);
        const d = m; var i: integer;
        var A: array[0..d] of integer;
        var B: array[0..d] of integer;
        procedure p(var C: array[f1..f2] of integer; var x: integer);
            var k: integer;
            begin k := x;
                    C[k] := x; n := x;
            end;
        begin
            i := 0;
            while i ≤ d do A[i] := i; B[i] := i; i := i + 1 od;
            i := 0;
            p(A, B[i])
        end;
    begin read n;
        unusual(n)
    end.
```

The relative addresses for this example are

$$
\begin{array}{lll}
rad((n,\epsilon)) = 3, & rad((unusual,\epsilon))= 4, & \\
rad((m,(1))) = 3, & rad((d,(1))) = 4, & rad((i,(1))) = 5, \\
rad((A,(1))) = 6, & rad((B,(1))) = 7, & rad((p,(1))) = 8, \\
rad((C,(1,1)))= 3, & rad((f1,(1,1))) = 4, & rad((f2,(1,1)))= 5, \\
rad((x,(1,1))) = 6, & rad((k,(1,1))) = 7. &
\end{array}
$$

Suppose the input tape contains 2. Then calling *unusual* in the main program and p in *unusual* immediately after assignment $C[k] := x$ yields the configuration

$$
c = (n := x; \ \textbf{end}; \ \textbf{end}; \ \textbf{end}; \ , \ bs, \ s, \ i, \ o)
$$

with $bs = ((b_1, 0), (b_2, 1), (b_3, 2))$. Bindings and storage state are shown in Figure 5 which also shows the corresponding RESA storage.

The activation record AR_2 consists of $16 = 3 + 7 + 6$ cells, of which the last 6 are elements of arrays A and B. These 6 cells represent the dynamic part of the activation record AR_2. Cell 16 is the first cell of array $b_2(A)$. Cell $16 + i$ plays the role of variable $b_2(A)(i)$, $0 \leq i \leq 2$, and thus contains the value of these variables. We store the initial address of array $b_2(A)$, that is 16, at address $12 = 6 + 6 = l_2 + rad((A,(1)))$. The value of variable $b_2(A)(2)$ is loaded into the accumulator by

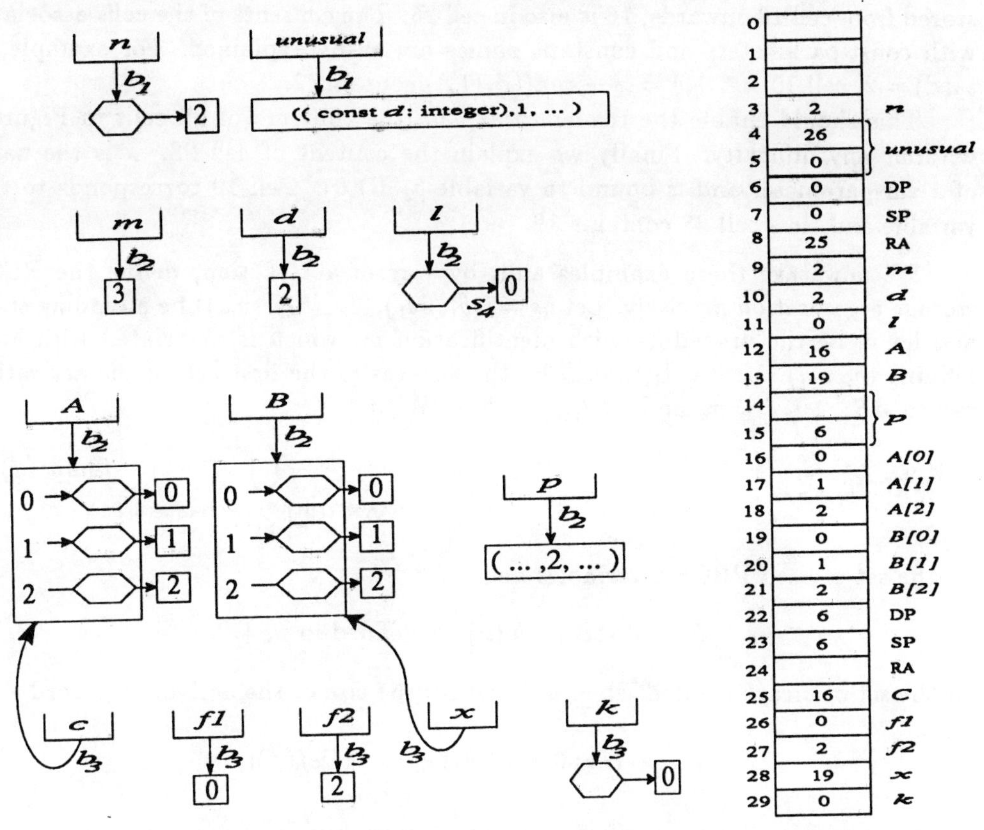

Fig. 5. Binding stack and storage state of the PROSA machine and corresponding RESA storage. Array A occupies cells 16 to 18. Cell $12 = l_1 + rad((A,(1)))$ indicates that the elements of A are located in the storage from cell 16 onwards. Figure 6 in the appendix of this chapter shows parts of the generated RESA program. Cells 14 and 24 can only be filled when the translation is complete.

LOADBAP	1	loads static link of current activation record
STORE	IR	loads initial address of the array
LOADIR	6	
ADDNUM	2	adds index value
STORE	IR	loads value of the variable
LOADIR	0	

The first cell of array B has address 19 and thus cell $13 = 6 + 7 = l_2 + rad((B,(1)))$ contains 19. Furthermore cells $19 + i$ correspond to variables $b_2(B)(i)$, $0 \le i \le 2$.

Consider cell $25 = 22+3 = l_3 + rad((C,(1,1)))$. As $b_3(C) = b_2(A)$ and array $b_2(A)$ is stored from cell 16 onwards, 16 is also in cell 25. The contents of the cells associated with const-parameters and constant names are easily explained. For example, as $b_2(d) = 2$, cell $10 = 6 + 4 = l_2 + rad((d,(1)))$ contains 2.

This should enable the reader to explain the contents of all cells in Figure 5 without any difficulty. Finally we explain the content of cell 28. x is the name of a var-parameter and is bound to variable $b_2(B)(0)$. Cell 19 corresponds to this variable and thus cell 28 contains 19. $\blacksquare$

We now take these examples and, by way of abstraction, define the RESA storage organisation precisely. Let $bs = ((b_1, sv_1), \ldots, (b_m, sv_m))$ be a binding stack and let p_i be the procedure with identification pi_i which is associated with local binding (b_i, sv_i). Let, as before, l_i be the address of the first cell of the activation record AR_i, $1 \leq i \leq m$, and let $l_{m+1} = bfs$. With

$$V_{allocated} = \left(V \cap \bigcup_{1 \leq i \leq m} image(b_i)\right) \cup \bigcup_{f \in \mathbf{ARR} \cap \bigcup_{1 \leq i \leq m} image(b_i)} image(f)$$

for the set of used PROSA variables and

$$F_i = \mathbf{ARR} \cap \{b_i(x) \mid x \text{ defined in } p_i \}$$

for the set of arrays created when p_i is called, the size of the activation record AR_i is

$$l_{i+1} - l_i = 3 + si(pi_i) + \sum_{f \in F_i} |Def(f)|$$

i.e. the activation record consists of three administrative cells (dynamic link, static link, return address), of the cells associated with the names defined in p_i, by way of the relative addresses and of the cells which accommodate the arrays declared in p_i. The last cells represent the dynamic part of the activation record AR_i. In defining the contents of the RESA storage, we first discuss those cells corresponding directly to PROSA variables. These cells obviously contain the value of the corresponding PROSA variables. Formally, we define this relationship by two injective mapping

$$\alpha : V_{allocated} \rightarrow [0..bfs - 1]$$

and

$$\beta : \bigcup_{1 \leq i \leq m} F_i \rightarrow [0..bfs - 1].$$

Mapping α associates a RESA storage cell with each PROSA variable and mapping β maps each array to its initial address. Table 2 shows mapping α for Example 2.

Furthermore $\beta(b_2(A)) = 16$ and $\beta(b_2(B)) = 19$. We call $\alpha(v)$ the **absolute address** of variable v. The following properties hold. We have numbered them so that we can refer to them later. The reader should verify the properties using our examples.

PROSA variable	RESA storage cell
$b_1(n)$	3
$b_2(i)$	11
$b_2(A)(0)$	16
$b_2(A)(1)$	17
$b_2(A)(2)$	18
$b_2(B)(0)$	19
$b_2(B)(1)$	20
$b_2(B)(2)$	21
$b_3(k)$	29

Table 2: PROSA variable and corresponding RESA storage cells for Example 2.

(1) For all $v \in V_{allocated}$ cell $\alpha(v)$ contains the value of variable v, i.e. for all $v \in V_{allocated}$: $s(v) = ds(\alpha(v))$.

(2) If v is bound to a name x declared in p_i then the absolute address of v is determined by the initial address of the activation record and the relative address of x, i.e. for all variable names x declared in procedure p_i with identification pi_i

$$\alpha(b_i(x)) = l_i + rad((x, pi_i))$$

(3) If v is a component of an array $f \in F_i$ then the absolute address of v is determined by the initial address of array f and the index of v in f. Besides, cell $\alpha(v)$ lies in the dynamic part of AR_i, i.e. for all arrays $f \in F_i$ and for all $j \in Def(f)$

$$\alpha(f(j)) = \beta(f) + j \qquad \text{and}$$
$$\alpha(f(j)) \in [l_i + 3 + si(pi_i) \,..\, l_{i+1} - 1]$$

As for storage cells not corresponding to PROSA variables, we have already explained the first three cells of each activation record. For the remaining cells let x be a name in $Def(b_i)$. We now define the content of cell $l_i + rad((x, pi_i))$ and, if x is the name of a procedure or of a procedure parameter, also the content of cell $l_i + rad((x, pi_i)) + 1$.

(4) If x is the name of an array or of an array parameter then cell $l_i + rad((x, pi_i))$ contains the initial address of array $b_i(x)$, i.e.

$$ds(l_i + rad((x, pi_i))) = \beta(b_i(x)).$$

Cell $l_i + rad((x, pi_i))$ is called the **header cell** of array $b_i(x)$.

(5) If x is the name of a const-parameter or is a constant name then cell $l_i + rad((x, pi_i))$ contains the value bound to x under b_i , i.e.

$$ds(l_i + rad((x, pi_i))) = b_i(x).$$

(6) If x is the name of a var-parameter of type *int* then cell $l_i + rad((x, pi_i))$ contains the absolute address of variable $b_i(x)$, i.e.

$$ds(l_i + rad((x, pi_i))) = \alpha(b_i(x)).$$

(7) If x is the name of a procedure or of a procedure parameter and $b_i(x) = (\ldots, j, R)$ then

$$ds(l_i + rad((x, pi_i))) = \text{address of the first line of the translated R}$$
$$ds(l_i + rad((x, pi_i)) + 1) = l_j$$

Binding b_i binds x to a triple consisting of parameter specification list, length j of the binding stack at declaration and body R. The translated body is a RESA program. The address of the first line of this program is stored in the first cell set aside for x in the activation record. In the second cell we store the length of the activation record stack at declaration. In Figure 4 we have $b_1(D) = ((\textbf{var } y : \textbf{integer}), 1, R_D)$ and thus $ds(l_1 + rad((D, \epsilon))) = ds(4) = 34$ and $ds(5) = l_1 = 0$. Note that 34 is the address of the first line of the translated R_D ; see Figure 4 in the appendix of the chapter.

(8) RESA storage cells not belonging to any activation record have no value, i.e.

$$ds(i) = \text{undefined} \quad \text{for } i \geq bfs$$

This corresponds to the definition in PROSA that non-occupied storage cells have no value.

Exercises for 7.1

1) (Continuation of Example 1): In Section 6.4 the reader also finds other configurations of the computation of the program from Example 1. Give the corresponding RESA storage.

2) Determine functions α and β for Figs. 3 and 5. Verify properties (1) to (7).

7.2 Storage Access

Access to variables is achieved in the PROSA machine by consulting the binding stack. How is this realised in RESA programs generated from PROSA programs, i.e. how do we find the storage location which corresponds to a name n? If the name is local in the currently active procedure then its associated storage location can be found in the most recent activation record using the relative address. In the case of a global name, we follow the static links until we reach a local binding in which the name occurs. This binding yields the variable or whatever is bound to the name. From Theorem 1 in Section 6.4 we also know exactly how often we must follow the static links until we reach the right binding. This is precisely d times where d is the difference between the block nesting levels of name n and the currently active procedure. This method is easily accomplished in RESA. Index register BAP contains the initial address of the current activation record. Each activation record has a cell for the static predecessor and thus following the static link is no problem. The corresponding storage cell is found using the relative address. In some examples in Section 7.1 we have already illustrated this method briefly. To be more precise, let $bs = ((b_1, sv_1), \ldots, (b_m, sv_m))$ be a binding stack and s be a storage state of the PROSA machine. Suppose the storage content ds of the RESA machine is determined by bs and s according to Section 7.1.

Lemma 1. *Let $d \geq 0$ be a natural number such that $sv^{(d)}(m)$ is defined. Then the instruction sequence*

$$
\left.
\begin{array}{ll}
\text{LOAD} & \text{BAP} \\
\text{STORE} & \text{IR} \\
\text{LOADIR} & 1
\end{array}
\right\} d\text{-times}
$$

loads the value $l_{sv^{(d)}(m)}$ into the accumulator. We call this instruction sequence StatPred(d).

Proof: Since $bap = l_m$ and $m = sv^{(0)}(m)$ the claim is correct for $d = 0$. Let $d > 0$. After LOAD BAP and $(d-1)$-times STORE IR; LOADIR 1, by induction hypothesis, the accumulator contains $l_{sv^{(d-1)}(m)}$. The instructions STORE IR; LOADIR 1 then load $ds(l_{sv^{(d-1)}(m)} + 1) = l_{sv(sv^{(d-1)}(m))} = l_{sv^{(d)}(m)}$ into the accumulator.   ∎

Theorem 1. *Let $((b_1, sv_1), \ldots, (b_m, sv_m))$ be the currently active binding stack. Let (n, pi) be an applied occurrence of name n in the active procedure. Let the extended body of this procedure have procedure identification pi_m and let $d = |pi_m| - |pi|$ be the difference between the nesting levels.*

a) If (n, pi) is a variable name then the instruction sequence

$$
\begin{array}{ll}
StatPred(d) & \\
\text{ADDNUM} & rad((n, pi))
\end{array}
$$

loads the absolute address $\alpha(bs(n))$ of variable $bs(n)$ and the instruction sequence

$$\begin{aligned} &StatPred(d) \\ &\text{STORE} \qquad\qquad \text{IR} \\ &\text{LOADIR} \qquad rad((n,pi)) \end{aligned}$$

loads the value $s(bs(n))$ of the variable. We call these instruction sequences $LoadAbsoluteAd(n,pi,pi_m)$ and $LoadValue(n,pi,pi_m)$, respectively.

Example 2 (continued): The body of the active procedure in the situation of Figure 5 has procedure identification $(1,1)$. Thus the value of the variable with name (n,ϵ) is loaded by the instruction sequence

$$\left.\begin{aligned} &\text{LOAD} \qquad \text{BAP} \\ &\text{STORE} \qquad \text{IR} \\ &\text{LOADIR} \qquad 1 \\ &\text{STORE} \qquad \text{IR} \\ &\text{LOADIR} \qquad 1 \end{aligned}\right\} StatPred(2)$$
$$\begin{aligned} &\text{STORE} \qquad \text{IR} \\ &\text{LOADIR} \qquad 3 \end{aligned}$$

Note $rad((n,\epsilon)) = 3$. ∎

b) If (n,pi) is the name of a const-parameter or a constant name then the instruction sequence

$$\begin{aligned} &StatPred(d) \\ &\text{STORE} \qquad\qquad \text{IR} \\ &\text{LOADIR} \qquad rad((n,pi)) \end{aligned}$$

loads the value $bs(n)$ bound to n. We call this instruction sequence $LoadValue(n,pi,pi_m)$.

Example 2 (continued): The value $bs(f_2)$ bound to f_2 is loaded by

$$\begin{aligned} &\text{LOAD} \qquad \text{BAP} \\ &\text{STORE} \qquad \text{IR} \\ &\text{LOADIR} \qquad 5 \end{aligned}$$

Note $5 = rad((f_2,(1,1)))$. Of course the value $bs(f_2)$ could also be loaded by instruction

$$\text{LOADBAP} \qquad 5$$

We disregard such optimisations here to avoid unnecessary case distinctions. In actual compilers, however, such optimisations are very important for efficiency reasons. ∎

c) If (n,pi) is the name of a var-parameter of type *int* then the instruction sequence

$$\begin{aligned} &StatPred(d) \\ &\text{STORE} \qquad\qquad \text{IR} \\ &\text{LOADIR} \qquad rad((n,pi)) \end{aligned}$$

loads the absolute address $\alpha(bs(n))$ of variable $bs(n)$. The instruction sequence

```
StatPred(d)
STORE              IR
LOADIR    rad((n,pi))
STORE              IR
LOADIR             0
```

loads its value $s(bs(n))$. These instruction sequences are called
$LoadAbsoluteAd(n,pi,pi_m)$ and $LoadValue(n,pi,pi_m)$.

Example 2 (continued): The instruction sequence

```
LOAD      BAP
STORE     IR
LOADIR    6
```

loads the absolute address of variable $bs(x)$ and

```
LOAD      BAP
STORE     IR
LOADIR    6
STORE     IR
LOADIR    0
```

loads its value.   ∎

*d) If (n,pi) is the name of an array or of an array parameter, then the instruction
sequence*

```
StatPred(d)
STORE              IR
LOADIR    rad((n,pi))
```

loads the start address $\beta(bs(n))$ of array $bs(n)$. We call this instruction sequence
$Loadstartad(n,pi,pi_m)$.

Example 2 (continued): The instruction sequences

```
                              LOAD      BAP
LOAD      BAP                 STORE     IR
STORE     IR      or          LOADIR    1
LOADIR    3                   STORE     IR
                              LOADIR    7
```

load the start address of array $bs(C)$ $bs(B)$.   ∎

*e) If (n,pi) is the name of a procedure or of a procedure parameter and $bs(n) =$
$(\ldots,j,R)$ then the instruction sequence*

```
StatPred(d)                      StatPred(d)
STORE              IR    or       STORE                    IR
LOADIR    rad((n,pi))             LOADIR    1 + rad((n,pi))
```

loads the index of the first line of the translated R, or rather address l_j. This instruction sequence is called *LoadFirstLine*(n, pi, pi_m) or *LoadStatPred*(n, pi, pi_m).

Example 2 (continued):   The instruction sequence

```
LOAD        BAP
STORE       IR
LOADIR       1
STORE       IR
LOADIR       9
```

loads the static predecessor of procedure p, that is $l_2 = 6$.   ∎

f) If (n, pi) is the name of an array or of an array parameter and k is the name of a local variable then the instruction sequence

```
StatPred(d)
STORE                 IR
LOADIR       rad((n, pi))
ADDBAP       rad((k, pi_m))
```

loads the absolute address $\alpha(L(n[k], bs, s))$ of variable $L(n[k], bs, s)$, and the instruction sequence

```
StatPred(d)
STORE                 IR
LOADIR       rad((n, pi))
ADDBAP       rad((k, pi_m))
STORE                 IR
LOADIR               0
```

loads its value. These instruction sequences are called *LoadAbsoluteAd*$(n[k], pi, pi_m)$ or *LoadValue*$(n[k], pi, pi_m)$.

Example 2 (continued):   The absolute address of $C[k]$ is loaded by

```
LOAD        BAP
STORE       IR
LOADIR       3
ADDBAP       7
```

∎

g) If n is the standard name of an integer then

```
LOADNUM    n
```

loads value $c(n)$ of n. This instruction sequence is called *LoadValue*(n, pi, pi_m).

Proof: Let $i = sv^{(d)}(m)$. By Theorem 1 in Section 6.4 we have $bs(n) = b_i(n)$ and $pi = pi_i$, i.e. the meaning of n is found by looking up the bindings after following the static link d steps. Furthermore the identification of the applied occurrence (n, pi) is equal to the identification of the binding reached via the static links.

a) After $StatPred(d)$ and by Lemma 1 we have $ac = l_{sv^{(d)}(m)} = l_i$.
Thus $LoadAbsoluteAd(n, pi, pi_m)$ loads the value

$$l_i + rad((n, pi)) = \alpha(b_i(n)) \qquad \text{by property (2) of Section 7.1}$$
$$= \alpha(bs(n)) \qquad \text{since } bs(n) = b_i(n)$$

Similarly, $LoadValue(n, pi, pi_m)$ loads the value

$$ds(l_i + rad((n, pi))) = ds(\alpha(bs(n))) \qquad \text{as already shown}$$
$$= s(bs(n)) \qquad \text{by property (1)}$$

b) The instruction sequence $LoadValue(n, pi, pi_m)$ loads

$$ds(l_i + rad((n, pi))) = b_i(n) \qquad \text{by property (5)}$$
$$= bs(n) \qquad \text{as } b_i(n) = bs(n)$$

c) The instruction sequence $LoadAbsoluteAd(n, pi, pi_m)$ loads

$$ds(l_i + rad((n, pi))) = \alpha(b_i(n)) \qquad \text{by property (6)}$$
$$= \alpha(bs(n)) \qquad \text{as } bs(n) = b_i(n)$$

and $LoadValue(n, pi, pi_m)$ loads

$$ds(ds(l_i + rad((n, pi)))) = ds(\alpha(bs(n))) \qquad \text{as already shown}$$
$$= s(bs(n)) \qquad \text{by property (1)}$$

d) The instruction sequence $LoadStartAd(n, pi, pi_m)$ loads

$$ds(l_i + rad((n, pi))) = \beta(b_i(n)) \qquad \text{by property (4)}$$
$$= \beta(bs(n)) \qquad \text{as } bs(n) = b_i(n)$$

e) As in b), but with property (7) instead of property (5).

f) The instruction sequence $LoadAbsoluteAd(n[k], pi, pi_m)$ loads the value (compare d)

$$\beta(bs(n)) + s(b_m(k)) = \alpha(bs(n)(s(b_m(k)))) \qquad \text{by property (3)}$$
$$= \alpha(L(n[k], bs, s)) \qquad \text{by definition of } L$$

and the instruction sequence $LoadValue(n[k], pi, pi_m)$ loads

$$ds(\beta(bs(n)) + s(b_m(k))) = ds(\alpha(L(n[k], bs, s))) \qquad \text{as already shown}$$
$$= s(L(n[k], bs, s)) \qquad \text{by property (1)}$$

g) obvious

Theorem 4 solves one half of the compilation problem. We know now which RESA instruction sequences must be generated for storage access and can now easily translate all control structures of PROSA without procedures. It seems advisable for the reader to try this now. In the next section we show how the new control structures are to be translated.

Exercises for 7.2

1) (Optimisation of access to local objects): Check the instruction sequences generated in Theorem 1 and simplify them, if possible, for the special case $d = 0$. In which cases do you find shorter instruction sequences?

2) (Optimisation of access to objects declared in the main program): As Exercise 1, but with $pi = \epsilon$ and d arbitrary.

7.3 Generating RESA Programs

The previous sections determined the relationship between the RESA storage on the one hand, and the binding stack as well as the storage state of the PROSA machine one the other, when PROSA programs are translated into RESA. We already know which RESA instruction sequences load the absolute address or the value of a variable, the initial address of an array and the first line or the static predecessor of a procedure into the accumulator. In this section we discuss the translation proper, i.e. we specify which RESA program is generated from a given PROSA program and show that the properties required in Section 7.1 remain invariant. This guarantees the correctness of the translation.

The body in each procedure declaration and the main program is translated into a sequence of RESA instructions. These program sections are then arranged in arbitrary order and the instructions numbered starting at one. We start in any case with the instruction sequence generated from the main program. The number given to the first instruction of the sequence generated for some procedure p is called **first line** of p. The first line of the main program has therefore number 1, and thus computation of the RESA machine starts with the execution of the first instruction of the main program, as it should. Because the main program can be viewed as the declaration of a procedure which is called immediately, we first discuss procedures in general and then the main program. At this point the reader should recall the instruction repertoire of RESA, in particular, the instructions JUMPAC and CLEARBFS introduced at the end of Section 5.2 in view of Chapter VII.

Example 1 (continued):   Figure 4 in the appendix of this chapter shows the RESA program generated from the PROSA program of Example 2 in Section 6.4. The first lines of procedures D, A, B are 34, 72 and 129. The instruction sequence generated for the main program spans lines 1 to 33 and the instruction sequence generated from A spans lines 72 to 128.   ∎

Example 2 (continued):   Figure 6 in the appendix of this chapter shows parts of the generated RESA program. The main program consists of lines 1 to 25.   ∎

Consider a procedure declaration

$$\textbf{procedure } p(psl); ds \textbf{ begin } sts \textbf{ end}$$

with $p \in \langle ident \rangle, psl \in \langle par\ spec\ seq \rangle, ds \in \langle decls \rangle$ and $sts \in \langle stats \rangle$. The RESA instruction sequence generated from this declaration consists of four parts:

1) instruction to establish the activation record and to set the dynamic link;

2) result of translating the declarations;

3) result of translating the statements;

4) instruction to release the activation record and return jump

These four parts are now discussed in the order 1), 4), 2) and 3).

Instructions to establish the activation record: Let pi be the procedure identification of the extended body of procedure p. The instruction sequence

LOAD	BAP	} set the dynamic link
STOREBFS	0	
LOAD	BFS	} set BAP
STORE	BAP	
ADDNUM	$3 + si(pi)$	allocate the static part
STORE	BFS	of the new activation record

establishes (when procedure p is called in a RESA program) a new activation record of size $3 + si(pi)$ and sets the dynamic link. After this instruction sequence the index register BAP points to the first cell of the new activation record and BFS points to the first free storage cell. Note that as yet we have allocated no space for the arrays declared in the procedure since their size — at least for dynamic arrays — is not known at compile-time. Of course we have set aside a space for the header cell of each array. The space for the array elements themselves is allocated when the declarations are processed (see below). Variable declarations in procedure p have already been taken care of by the activation record. At this point some cells in the newly established activation record have already defined values, namely the dynamic link (this we have just set), the static link, the return address and the cells associated with formal parameters. With the exception of the dynamic link, these cells were set before the call (see below). Together with the instructions generated for the call in the caller, this instruction sequence therefore simulates a

PROSA procedure call, parameter passing and processing variable declarations in the callee.

The correctness of the above instruction sequence is easily seen. The first two instructions obviously set the dynamic link correctly, the next two instructions make the new activation record the active one. Finally, the last two instructions allocate the static part of the new activation record. Furthermore all declarations of variables in p are implicitly processed. Let, for instance, n be the name of a variable declared in p. We then set $\alpha((n,pi)) = bap + rad((n,pi))$. Here bap is the value of BAP at the end of the above instruction sequence. Then requirement (2) is obviously satisfied. Furthermore (1) holds since new PROSA variables have no value, and this, by property (8), is also the case for the RESA storage cells just allocated. Note that the new value of BAP is just the old value of BFS.

Example: Lines 34 to 39, 72 to 77 and 129 to 134 in Figure 4 are generated according to this scheme. Note that an activation record for D (or A or B) consists of 4 (or 8 or 4) lines. Lines 26 to 31 in Figure 6 are generated according to this scheme. An activation record for *unusual* consists of 10 cells plus the cells for the array elements. The cells for the array elements are allocated by the instruction sequence in lines 36 to 45. ∎

Instructions to release the activation record and return jump: After executing the body of a procedure we release the allocated activation record and return to the calling point. The activation record is released by setting BFS to BAP and BAP to the value of the dynamic link of the current activation record and by deleting the contents of all released storage cells. We return to the calling point with the help of the return address.

LOAD	BAP	} BFS := BAP
STORE	BFS	
LOADBAP	0	} load dynamic link
STORE	BAP	} and store in BAP
LOADBFS	2	} load return address
CLEARBFS		} clear released storage cells
JUMPAC		} return jump

The correctness of this instruction sequence is obvious. When executing **end** (=return from a procedure) the PROSA machine removes the topmost binding from the binding stack and continues computation in the calling procedure immediately after the call. Correspondingly, the RESA machine must release the current activation record and return to the caller. Furthermore the content of all released storage cells is erased by the instruction CLEARBFS and thus property (8) is guaranteed.

Example: Compare lines 65 to 71, 122 to 128 and 160 to 166 in Figure 4.

Result of translating the declarations: On entering the procedure, we allocated one or two cells for each name occurring in the parameter specification list or in the declaration section. In the case of formal parameters these cells are already set by the calling procedure. For declared names we must consider procedure declarations, constant declarations and array declarations. No RESA instructions are generated for variable declarations.

Procedure declarations: Let procedure q be declared in procedure p. The PROSA machine binds q to the triple $(\ldots, m, R_q)$ where R_q is the body of q and m is the current length of the binding stack. The activation record of each call of p contains two cells for q which accommodate the initial address of R_q (that is the number of the first line of the instruction sequence generated from R_q) and the static link. We must store l_m in the cell for the static link. This value is available in the index register BAP. Thus we generate the instruction sequence

$$
\begin{array}{lr}
\text{LOADNUM} & \text{start address of } R_q \\
\text{STOREBAP} & rad((q,pi)) \\
\text{LOAD} & \text{BAP} \\
\text{STOREBAP} & rad((q,pi)) + 1
\end{array}
\left.\begin{array}{l} \\ \\ \end{array}\right\} \text{start address of the body} \\
\left.\begin{array}{l} \\ \\ \end{array}\right\} \text{static link}
$$

This instruction sequence obviously establishes property (7) in 7.1.

Example: In Figure 4 lines 5 to 8 correspond to the declaration of D, lines 9 to 12 to the declaration of A and lines 78 to 81 to the declaration of B. Note that 34 is, for example, the first line of D. In Figure 6 lines 5 to 8 correspond to the declaration of *unusual*. ∎

Constant declarations: A constant declaration is of the form

$$
\textbf{const } n_1 = n_2 \text{ } op \text{ } n_3 \qquad \text{or} \qquad \textbf{const } n_1 = n_2
$$

Here n_1 is in $\langle ident \rangle$ and n_2 and n_3 are either in $\langle stand\ name \rangle$ or in $\langle ident \rangle$ or in $\langle ident \rangle [\langle ident \rangle]$. In the last case the selector is a local constant name. We show how to translate a declaration **const** $n_1 = n_2$ op n_3 and leave the simpler case **const** $n_1 = n_2$ to the reader. Let $pi_i, 2 \leq i \leq 3$, be the identification of the applied name n_i (if $n_i = a[k]$ then we take the identification of the array name a). Now the instruction sequence

$$
\begin{array}{lr}
LoadValue(n_3, pi_3, pi) & \\
\text{STOREBFS} & 0 \\
LoadValue(n_2, pi_2, pi) & \\
\text{OPBFS} & 0 \\
\text{STOREBAP} & rad((n_1, pi))
\end{array}
$$

is generated where the instruction sequences $LoadValue(n_3, pi_3, pi)$ and $LoadValue(n_2, pi_2, pi)$ are generated as in Theorem 1 of 7.2. Besides, OPBFS is the instruction corresponding to operator op. Again, the correctness of this instruction sequence is obvious. The value of n_3 is loaded and stored in the first free storage cell. After loading the value of n_2, the operation is applied to it and the stored value of n_3. The result is placed at the relative address of n_1.

Example: Lines 32 to 35 in Figure 6 correspond to the constant declaration **const** $d = n$. ∎

Array declarations: Let

$$\textbf{var } a : \textbf{array}[0..u] \textbf{ of integer}$$

be an array declaration in the declaration section of procedure p where u is a const-parameter of procedure p. We allocate $u + 1$ storage cells for the array elements, starting with the first free storage cell (whose number is in BFS) and store the start address of the array in its header cell.

$$
\begin{array}{lll}
\text{LOAD} & \text{BFS} & \left.\begin{array}{l} \\ \\ \end{array}\right\} \text{set header cell} \\
\text{STOREBAP} & rad((a,pi)) & \\
\text{ADDBAP} & rad((u,pi)) & \left.\begin{array}{l} \\ \\ \\ \end{array}\right\} \begin{array}{l}\text{allocate storage location} \\ \text{for array elements}\end{array} \\
\text{ADDNUM} & 1 & \\
\text{STORE} & \text{BFS} &
\end{array}
$$

Example: Lines 36 to 40 in Figure 6 correspond to the declaration of array A and lines 41 to 45 to array B. Note that the header cell of A has the relative address 6 and the upper bound has relative address 3. ∎

We have yet to show that the above instruction sequence is correct. Let $f \in \textbf{ARR}$ be the array created by the declaration and bound to a. Then the size of the domain of f is of course equal to the number of newly allocated storage cells, since, according to property (5), the value bound to u is in the cell with relative address $rad((u,pi))$ of the current activation record. We set $\beta(f)$ to the value of BFS before executing the instruction sequence and $\alpha(f(i)) = \beta(f) + i$ for $i \in Def(f)$. Then requirements (3) and (4) are definitely satisfied. Furthermore (1) holds since the PROSA variables $f(i)$, $i \in Def(f)$ have no value as yet according to PROSA semantics and the RESA storage cells now allocated have no value according to property (8).

Result of translating the statements: Each statement of the statement section is either an assignment, a procedure call, a print or read statement, or a composite statement. In the last case it is a conditional statement or an iteration statement. The first two cases are discussed in detail, the remaining cases are then routine and are left to the reader. Suppose the identification of the body of the procedure p is pi.

Assignment: An assignment is of the form

$$n_1 := n_2 \text{ } op \text{ } n_3 \qquad \text{or} \qquad n_1 := n_2$$

n_i is either in $\langle stand \; name \rangle$ or in $\langle ident \rangle$ or in $\langle ident \rangle[\langle ident \rangle]$. In the last case the selector is the name of a local variable. We show how to translate an assignment $n_1 := n_2 \text{ } op \text{ } n_3$ and leave the simpler case $n_1 := n_2$ to the reader. Let $pi_i, 1 \leq i \leq 3$, be the identification of the applied name n_i (if $n_i = a[k]$ then the identification of array name a). We generate the instruction sequence

$$LoadAbsoluteAd(n_1, pi_1, pi)$$

STORE	IR1

$$LoadValue(n_3, pi_3, pi)$$

STOREBFS	0

$$LoadValue(n_2, pi_2, pi)$$

OPBFS	0
STOREIR1	0

Here instruction sequences $LoadAbsoluteAd(n_1, pi_1, pi)$, $LoadValue(n_3, pi_3, pi)$ and $LoadValue(n_2, pi_2, pi)$ are generated as in Theorem 1 of 7.2. Besides, OPBFS is the instruction corresponding to operator op. The correctness of this instruction sequence is obvious. First we load the absolute address of n_1 and store it in the auxiliary index register IR1. Then we load the value of n_3 and store it in the first free storage cell. After storing the value of n_2, we apply the operation to it and the stored value of n_3. The result is placed at the absolute address of n_1.

Example: The instruction sequences for all assignments in Figures 4 and 6 are generated according to this scheme. Consider assignment $y := y + 1$ in the body of D (lines 52–64 of Figure 4). Note that y is a formal parameter

LOAD	BAP	load absolute address
STORE	IR	of y and store
LOADIR	3	in IR1
STORE	IR1	
LOADNUM	1	load the second operand
STOREBFS	0	and store temporarily
LOAD	BAP	
STORE	IR	
LOADIR	3	load the first operand
STORE	IR	
LOADIR	0	
ADDBFS	0	Add the temporarily stored second operand
STOREIR1	0	store the result

An optimising compiler would generate a much shorter instruction sequence by making use of the commutativity of $+$ and the double occurrence of y, for example

LOADBAP	3
STORE	IR
LOADIR	0
ADDNUM	1
STOREBAP	3

Procedure Call: Consider a procedure call $q(apl)$ with $q \in \langle ident \rangle$ and $apl \in \langle act\ par\ seq \rangle$ in the body of procedure p. We generate a RESA instruction sequence according to the scheme:

1) parameter passing;

2) setting the static link;

3) setting the return address and jump to first line of q.

For each call of q a new activation record must be allocated and the cells of this activation record must be set as specified in Section 7.1. Allocating the activation record and setting the dynamic link is done by the called procedure itself. Remember that this has been provided for when translating the body. Static link, return address and cells associated with formal parameters are set by the caller. Let (as hitherto) pi be the identification of p, let pi_1 be the identification of the declaring occurrence of q associated with the above call and let pi_2 be the identification of the body of q. Then (q, pi_1) is the unique name of q and pi_2 the identification of the unique names for the formal parameter of q. First we examine parts 2), 3) and then part 1).

Setting the static link: The PROSA machine adds a new local binding $(\emptyset, j)$ to the binding stack when q is called. The index of the static predecessor j is the second component of the triple $bs(q)$, i.e. $bs(q) = (\ldots, j, \ldots)$. Value l_j must be stored in the cell for the static link of the new activation record. According to Theorem 4(e), instruction sequence $LoadstatPred(q, pi_1, pi)$ loads the value l_j into the accumulator. We thus generate the instruction sequence

$$LoadstatPred(q, pi_1, pi)$$
$$\text{STOREBFS} \qquad\qquad 1$$

Example: Lines 23 to 26, 90 to 93 and 108 to 113 in Figure 4 are generated following this scheme. ∎

Setting the return address and jump to first line of q: The PROSA machine prefixes the program-rest with the body R_q of q when q is called. Similarly we must continue computation in the RESA program at the first line of the translation of R_q. According to Theorem 4(e), the instruction sequence $LoadFirstLine(q, pi_1, pi)$ loads the number of the first line of R_q into the accumulator. To call q we need only jump to this line using instruction JUMPAC. Before we compute the first line and jump we store the return address in the corresponding cell of the new activation record.

$$
\begin{array}{rll}
m: & \text{LOADNUM} \quad m + 2(|pi| - |pi_1|) + 6 & \left.\rule{0pt}{12pt}\right\} \text{storing the} \\
m+1: & \text{STOREBFS} \qquad\qquad\qquad\qquad\quad 2 & \left.\rule{0pt}{0pt}\right\} \text{return address} \\
& LoadFirstLine(q, pi_1, pi) & \\
& \text{JUMPAC} &
\end{array}
$$

$$m + 2(|pi| - |pi_1|) + 6:$$

Note that the instruction sequence $LoadFirstLine(q, pi, pi_1)$ comprises exactly $2(|pi| - |pi_1|) + 3$ instructions. Note, furthermore, that the line m where the above instruction sequence starts is known at compile-time. It can be derived from the translated program. The first two instructions, therefore, store the number of the instruction following JUMPAC and thus on returning from procedure q procedure p is continued at the correct place.

Example: Lines 27 to 32, 94 to 99 and 114 to 121 in Figure 4 are generated following this scheme. Let us have a closer look at lines 114 to 121. They are in the body of A (identification (2)) and A is called (identification ϵ).

114:	LOADNUM	$114 + 2(|(2)| - |\epsilon|) + 6$
115:	STOREBFS	2
116:	LOAD	BAP
117:	STORE	IR
118:	LOADIR	1
119:	STORE	IR
120:	LOADIR	6
121:	JUMPAC	
122:		

The return address is, of course, computed by the compiler. The instruction generated in lines 114 is LOADNUM 122.

Parameter Passing: Let *psl* be a sequence of the parameter specifications and *apl* a list of actual parameters. The PROSA machine processes the parameter specification list and the actual parameter list step by step. Thus parameter passing occurs in sequence. We do exactly the same in RESA:

> pass the first parameter
>
> $\vdots$
>
> pass the i-th parameter
>
> $\vdots$
>
> pass the last parameter.

In more detail, let y be an actual parameter. Then y is either a standard name, an identifier or is of the form $\langle ident \rangle [\langle ident \rangle]$. In the last case the selector is a local variable. Let pi' be the identification of the actual parameter. We now give the generated instruction sequence depending on the specification of the formal parameter.

Const-parameter **const** n: **integer**: According to property (5), we must store the value of the actual parameter in the cell of the new activation record set aside for n. Thus we generate the instruction sequence

> $LoadValue(y, pi', pi)$
> STOREBFS $\qquad\qquad rad((n, pi_2))$

As already mentioned above, pi_2 is the identification of the formal parameter. The correctness of this instruction sequence follows immediately from Theorem 4(b).

Example: Lines 11 to 14 in Figure 6 are generated following this scheme. Note that n has relative address 3 and d relative address 3.   ∎

Var-parameter var n: integer: According to property (6), we must store the absolute address of the variable denoted by the actual parameter in the cell of the new activation record set aside for n. Thus we generate the instruction sequence

$$LoadAbsoluteAd(y, pi', pi)$$
$$\text{STOREBFS} \qquad rad((n, pi_2))$$

Correctness of this instruction sequence follows immediately from Theorem 4(c).

Example: In Figure 6 $B[i]$ is passed following this scheme.

```
LOAD      BAP  ⎫
STORE     IR   ⎬ load start address of B
LOADIR    7    ⎭
ADDBAP    5    ⎬ add index value
STOREBFS  6    ⎬ store in new activation record
```

Array parameter n: array$[l..u]$ of integer: According to property (4), we must store the start address of the array denoted by the actual parameter in the cell of the new activation record set aside for n. Thus we generate the instruction sequence

$$LoadStartAd(y, pi', pi)$$
$$\text{STOREBFS} \qquad rad((n, pi_2))$$

Correctness of this instruction sequence follows immediately from Theorem 4(d). Furthermore the actual array bounds have to be passed via the const-parameters l and u. Let y_1, y_2 be the names for the array bounds of y. Then we generate

$$LoadValue(y_1, pi', pi)$$
$$\text{STOREBFS} \qquad rad((l, pi_2))$$
$$LoadValue(y_2, pi', pi)$$
$$\text{STOREBFS} \qquad rad((u, pi_2))$$

Correctness follows again from Theorem 4.

Example: In Figure 6 array A is passed in the call $p(A, B[j])$ according to this scheme.   ∎

Procedure parameter procedure $n(...)$: According to property (7), we must store the first line of the procedure body and the first static link of the procedure denoted by the actual parameter in the two cells of the new activation record set aside for n. Thus we generate the instruction sequence

$$LoadFirstLine(y, pi', pi)$$
$$\text{STOREBFS} \qquad\qquad rad((n, pi_2))$$
$$LoadStatPredecessor(y, pi', pi)$$
$$\text{STOREBFS} \qquad\qquad rad((n, pi_2)) + 1$$

Correctness of this instruction sequence follows immediately from Theorem 4(e).

Example: Lines 15 to 22 in Figure 4 are generated following this scheme.   ∎

At this point we have to comment on calls of formal procedures. Since no names occur in the specifications of the parameter of a formal procedure, we cannot really speak of the relative addresses of formal parameters. We can, however, speak of the relative addresses of the specifications. Then everything said about parameter passing remains valid. During the call $C(x)$ in Figure 4 the actual parameter x is passed to the relative address 3.

This concludes the discussion of translating procedures. We briefly consider the specialities which have to be taken into account in the main program. Neither the dynamic link needs to be set nor do we require the return jump at the end of the main program. Instead of the return jump we generate the instruction HALT which terminates computation of the RESA machine. Theorem 3 and thus Theorem 1 are now proved.

Let us conclude with some remarks concerning actual compilers. Of course everything we have said about them in Chapter V is still valid. But there are a few extras. In particular, actual compilers, would generate much shorter RESA programs than we do. Instructions to access variables are always generated according to the same scheme. There are much shorter instruction sequences, at least for local objects and those declared in the main program. As most accesses are of this sort, it is worth while to deal with these special cases separately.

Exercises for 7.3

1) Give a complete translation of the program in Example 2.

2) Repeat the translation of the program from Example 1 by using the optimisations in exercises 1 and 2 of Section 7.2.

3) Reconsider the translation of an assignment $n_1 := n_2 \; op \; n_3$. Indicate special cases where shorter instruction sequences can be generated.

4) Translate some of the example programs from Section 6.2 to RESA.

5) Optimise parameter passing of array parameters by using the fact that the number 0 is always passed for the lower bound.

Appendix: Figures 4 and 6.

<pre>
First line MP 1: LOADNUM   0   ⎫ establish
               2: STORE   BAP ⎬ activation record
               3: ADDNUM   8   ⎪ for MP
               4: STORE   BFS ⎭
               5: LOADNUM   34   ⎫
               6: STOREBAP   4   ⎬ declaration
               7: LOAD   BAP ⎪ of D
               8: STOREBAP   5   ⎭
               9: LOADNUM   72   ⎫
              10: STOREBAP   6   ⎬ declaration
              11: LOAD   BAP ⎪ of A
              12: STOREBAP   7   ⎭
              13: LOADNUM   1   ⎫
              14: STOREBAP   3   ⎬ x := 1
              15: LOAD   BAP ⎭
              16: STORE   IR   ⎫
              17: LOADIR   4   ⎪
              18: STOREBFS   3   ⎪
              19: LOAD   BAP ⎬ passing D
              20: STORE   IR   ⎪
              21: LOADIR   5   ⎪
              22: STOREBFS   4   ⎭
              23: LOAD   BAP ⎫
              24: STORE   IR   ⎪ set
              25: LOADIR   7   ⎬ static
              26: STOREBFS   1   ⎭ link
              27: LOADNUM   33   ⎫ set
              28: STOREBFS   2   ⎭ return address
              29: LOAD   BAP ⎫ load and
              30: STORE   IR   ⎪ jump to
              31: LOADIR   6   ⎬ first line
              32: JUMPAC   ⎭
              33: HALT   end of program

First line D 34: LOAD   BAP ⎫ set dynamic
              35: STOREBFS   0   ⎭ link
              36: LOAD   BFS ⎫
              37: STORE   BAP ⎪ allocate
              38: ADDNUM   4   ⎬ activation record
              39: STORE   BFS ⎭
</pre>

40:	LOAD	BAP	
41:	STORE	IR	
42:	LOADIR	1	} **print** *x*
43:	STORE	IR	
44:	LOADIR	3	
45:	PRINT		
46:	LOAD	BAP	
47:	STORE	IR	
48:	LOADIR	3	} **print** *y*
49:	STORE	IR	
50:	LOADIR	0	
51:	PRINT		
52:	LOAD	BAP	
53:	STORE	IR	
54:	LOADIR	3	
55:	STORE	IR1	
56:	LOADNUM	1	
57:	STOREBFS	0	
58:	LOAD	BAP	} $y := y + 1$
59:	STORE	IR	
60:	LOADIR	3	
61:	STORE	IR	
62:	LOADIR	0	
63:	ADDBFS	0	
64:	STOREIR1	0	
65:	LOAD	BAP	
66:	STORE	BFS	release
67:	LOADBAP	0	activation record
68:	STORE	BAP	
69:	LOADBFS	2	} load return address
70:	CLEARBFS		} clear released storage cells
71:	JUMPAC		} return jump

First line A	72:	LOAD	BAP	} set dynamic
	73:	STOREBFS	0	link
	74:	LOAD	BFS	
	75:	STORE	BAP	allocate
	76:	ADDNUM	8	activation record
	77:	STORE	BFS	
	78:	LOADNUM	129	
	79:	STOREBAP	6	
	80:	LOAD	BAP	declaration of *B*
	81:	STOREBAP	7	

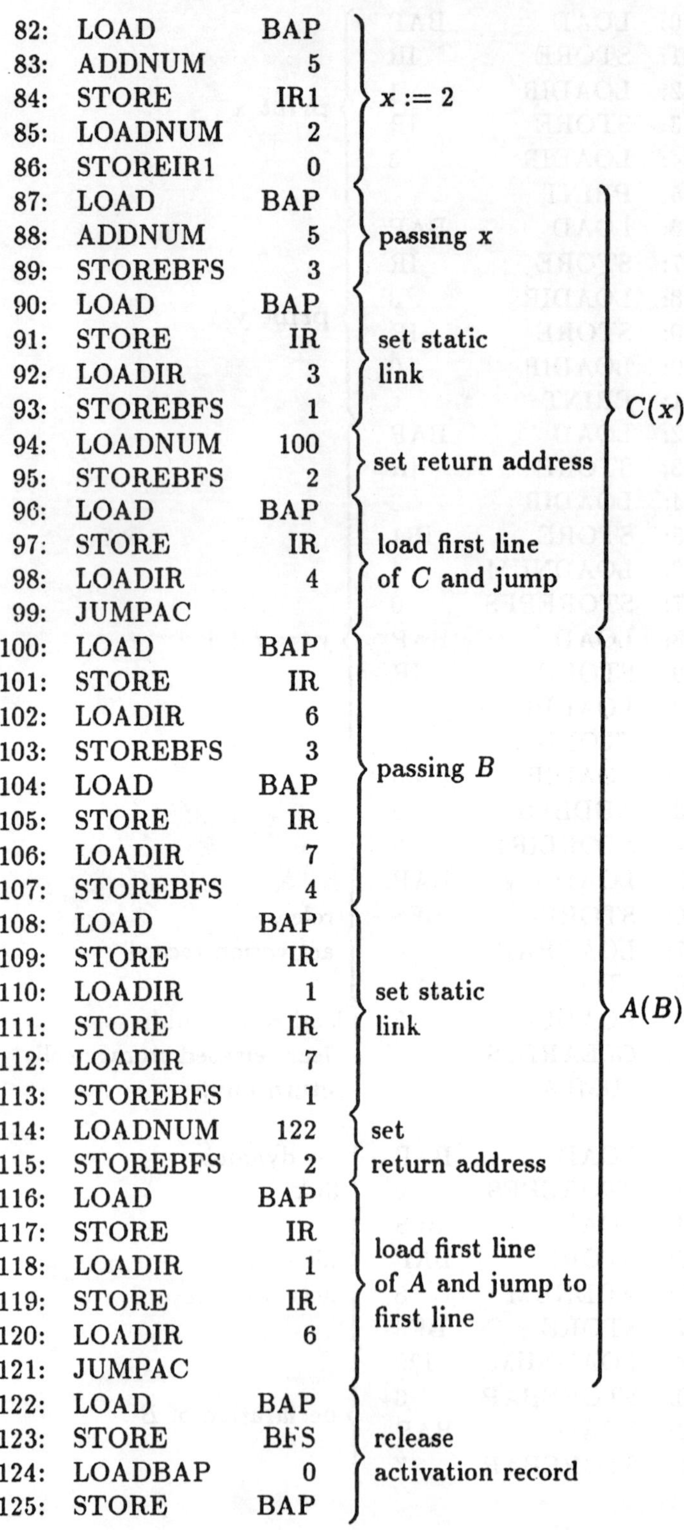

```
 82:  LOAD       BAP   ⎫
 83:  ADDNUM       5   ⎬  x := 2
 84:  STORE       IR1  ⎭
 85:  LOADNUM      2
 86:  STOREIR1     0
 87:  LOAD       BAP   ⎫
 88:  ADDNUM       5   ⎬  passing x
 89:  STOREBFS     3   ⎭
 90:  LOAD       BAP   ⎫
 91:  STORE       IR   ⎬  set static
 92:  LOADIR       3   ⎭  link
 93:  STOREBFS     1
 94:  LOADNUM    100   ⎫  set return address
 95:  STOREBFS     2   ⎭
 96:  LOAD       BAP
 97:  STORE       IR      load first line
 98:  LOADIR       4      of C and jump
 99:  JUMPAC
100:  LOAD       BAP
101:  STORE       IR
102:  LOADIR       6
103:  STOREBFS     3   ⎫  passing B
104:  LOAD       BAP   ⎬
105:  STORE       IR
106:  LOADIR       7
107:  STOREBFS     4
108:  LOAD       BAP
109:  STORE       IR
110:  LOADIR       1      set static
111:  STORE       IR      link
112:  LOADIR       7
113:  STOREBFS     1
114:  LOADNUM    122   ⎫  set
115:  STOREBFS     2   ⎭  return address
116:  LOAD       BAP
117:  STORE       IR
118:  LOADIR       1      load first line
119:  STORE       IR      of A and jump to
120:  LOADIR       6      first line
121:  JUMPAC
122:  LOAD       BAP   ⎫
123:  STORE       BFS   ⎬  release
124:  LOADBAP      0   ⎭  activation record
125:  STORE       BAP
```

The brace spanning lines 82–99 is labelled $C(x)$, and the brace spanning lines 100–121 is labelled $A(B)$.

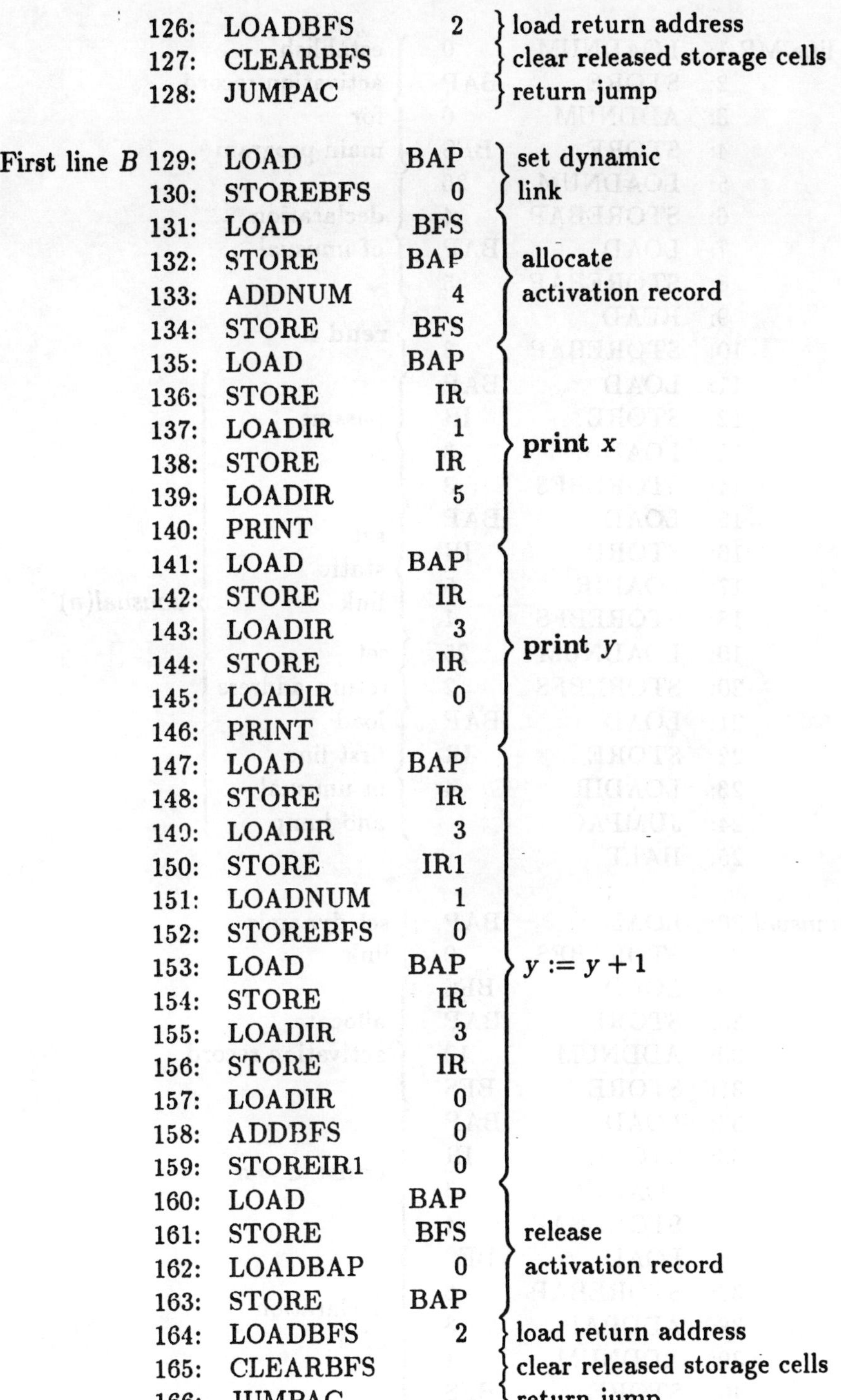

Fig. 4. The program from Example 2 in Section 6.4 translated to RESA. First line of the main program (of the procedures D, A, B) is 1 (34, 72, 129).

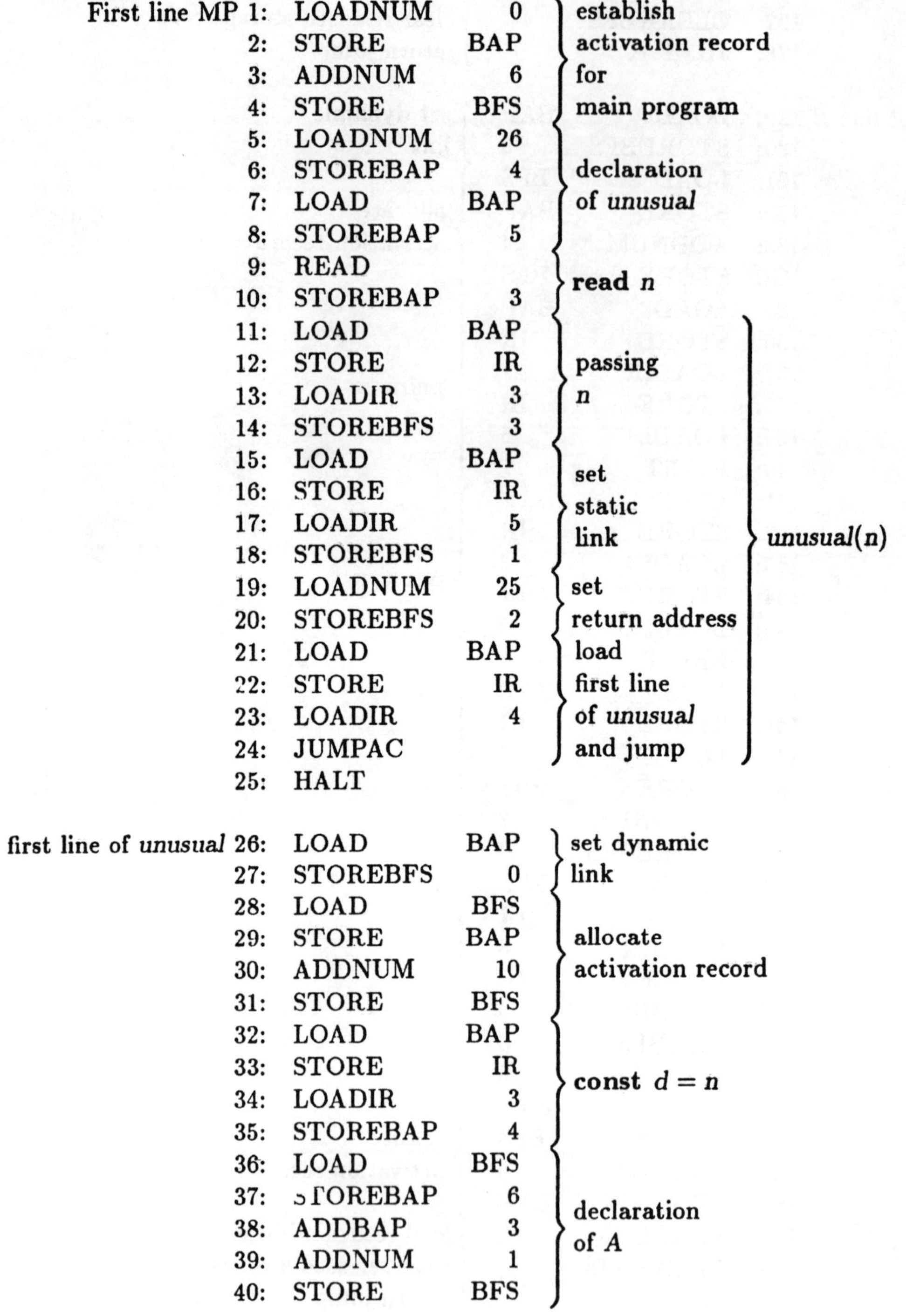

First line MP 1:   LOADNUM   0   establish
            2:   STORE   BAP   activation record
            3:   ADDNUM   6   for
            4:   STORE   BFS   main program
            5:   LOADNUM   26
            6:   STOREBAP   4   declaration
            7:   LOAD   BAP   of unusual
            8:   STOREBAP   5
            9:   READ
           10:   STOREBAP   3   read n
           11:   LOAD   BAP
           12:   STORE   IR   passing
           13:   LOADIR   3   n
           14:   STOREBFS   3
           15:   LOAD   BAP
           16:   STORE   IR   set
           17:   LOADIR   5   static
           18:   STOREBFS   1   link   unusual(n)
           19:   LOADNUM   25   set
           20:   STOREBFS   2   return address
           21:   LOAD   BAP   load
           22:   STORE   IR   first line
           23:   LOADIR   4   of unusual
           24:   JUMPAC   and jump
           25:   HALT

first line of unusual 26:   LOAD   BAP   set dynamic
           27:   STOREBFS   0   link
           28:   LOAD   BFS
           29:   STORE   BAP   allocate
           30:   ADDNUM   10   activation record
           31:   STORE   BFS
           32:   LOAD   BAP
           33:   STORE   IR
           34:   LOADIR   3   const d = n
           35:   STOREBAP   4
           36:   LOAD   BFS
           37:   STOREBAP   6
           38:   ADDBAP   3   declaration
           39:   ADDNUM   1   of A
           40:   STORE   BFS

41:	LOAD	BFS	⎫
42:	STOREBAP	7	declaration
43:	ADDBAP	3	of B
44:	ADDNUM	1	
45:	STORE	BFS	⎭
46:	LOADNUM		⎫
47:	STOREBAP	9	declaration
48:	LOAD	BAP	of p
49:	STOREBAP	10	⎭

$\vdots$

LOAD	BAP	⎫
STORE	IR	
LOADIR	6	
ADDBAP	5	
STORE	IR1	$A[i] := i$
LOAD	BAP	
STORE	IR	
LOADIR	5	
STOREIR1	0	⎭

$\vdots$

LOAD	BAP	⎫	
STORE	IR	passing	
LOADIR	6	A	
STOREBFS	3		
LOADNUM	0	passing	
STOREBFS	4	lower bound	
LOAD	BAP		
STORE	IR	passing	call
LOADIR	4	upper bound	$p(A, B[i])$
STOREBFS	5		
LOAD	BAP		
STORE	IR		
LOADIR	7	passing	
ADDBAP	5	$B[i]$	
STOREBFS	6		

$\vdots$

$\vdots$

Fig. 6: The translated program of Example 2 (in parts). The start address of the translation of the body of p must still be inserted in line 46. However, to do so the program must be completely translated.

Chapter 8   Language Extensions

In this chapter we briefly sketch some further language concepts. Contrary to the previous chapters the discussion will neither be complete nor indeed formal. For details the reader is referred to other literature.

8.1 A Module Concept

In Chapter VI procedures were introduced as a means for functional abstraction. A program section can be turned into a procedure by viewing it as a new syntactic unit. We are mainly interested in the effect of this program section, that is in the semantics of the procedure thus introduced and less in the way this effect is achieved. It is irrelevant for the environment which local objects the procedure manipulates. Consequently, these locally declared objects are not visible nor usable outside of the procedure. Thus functional abstraction turns a program section (essentially a statement list) into a procedure with suitable parameter interface.

In this section a means for **data abstraction** is introduced. Data abstraction enables a new kind of type declaration not yet available in PROSA. The three existing ways of introducing new types, namely by way of record, array and pointer constructs, simply allow the grouping of variables into larger data structures or the use of type-restricted selection. Apart from selection there are no additional operations available for the composite objects in PROSA. Using data abstraction, on the other hand, we can define data types similar to the elementary data types in PROSA. As in their case a data type is characterised by the set of objects of the type and the set of operations applicable to these objects.

As an example we define the data type *string* and use as a basis the corresponding functions in Chapter VI. Of course the example is only of didactic value since data type *string* is already available in PROSA (as one of the five primitive data types). This data type is declared as a **module**. The notation used is PROSA extended by appropriate constructs of the programming language Modula-2.

definition module *Strings*;
(∗ Strings are sequences of symbols. The module provides the functions and procedures listed in the export list ∗)
export
    Empty, Create, CharToString, FirstSymbol, RestWord, Conc, Assignment, String;

    type *String*;

```
    function Empty (const w: String): boolean;
      (* checks for empty string *)

    function Create: String;
      (* creates empty string *)

    function CharToString (const c: char): String;
      (* converts a symbol to a string of length 1 *)

    function FirstSymbol (const w: String): char;
      (* yields first symbol of argument string *)

    function RestWord (const w: String): String;
      (* yields the rest of the argument string without the first symbol *)

    function Conc (const w1: String, const w2: String): String;
      (* yields the concatenation of the two arguments *)

    procedure Assignment (var v: String ; const w: String)
      (* assigns the value of the second argument to the first argument *)
end;

  implementation module Strings;
    type   Word = record Symbol: char; Rest: ↑Word end;
    type   String = ↑Word;
    var p: String;
    function Empty (const w: String): boolean;
    begin
        if w = nil
        then Empty := true
        else Empty := false
    end;
    function Create: String;
    begin
        Create := nil
    end;
    function CharToString (const c: char): String;
    begin
        p := new Word;
        p↑.Symbol := c;
        CharToString := p
    end;
    function FirstSymbol (const w: String): char;
```

$\vdots$

function *RestWord* (**const** *w*: *String*): *String*;

$\vdots$

function *Conc* (**const** *w1*: *String*, **const** *w2*: *String*): *String*;

$\vdots$

function *Copy*(**const** *w*: *String*): *String*;
(* yields a copy of the argument string *)
begin
    if *w* = **nil**
    then *Copy* := **nil**
    else *Copy* := **new** *Word*;
        Copy $\uparrow$ *.Symbol* := *w* $\uparrow$ *Symbol*;
        Copy $\uparrow$ *.Rest* := *Copy*(*w* $\uparrow$ *.Rest*)
    fi
end;
procedure *Assignment*(**var** *v*: *String*; **const** *w*: *String*);
begin
    v := *Copy*(*w*)
end
end;

A module, like procedures, constitutes a relevant unit for the scope of names. Procedures implicitly "import" all names of surrounding units, i.e. these names are visible in the procedure. Within a module, on the other hand, the names of surrounding units are not visible a priori. If such a name is needed it must be quoted in the import-list of the module. Therefore within the module *Strings* no names from its environment are available since there is no import-list. On the other hand, it contains an export-list with names *String*, *Empty*, *Create*, *CharToString*, *FirstSymbol*, *RestWord*, *Assignment* and *Conc*. These names are thus made visible in the surrounding unit, be it a further module or a procedure. Note that the function name *Copy* is not in the export-list. Thus this function can only be called within the module. It serves as an auxiliary function for functions *Conc* and *RestWord*. By exporting the type name *String*, it is possible to declare variables of this type in the environment of the module. All internal properties of such variables, in particular their representation in storage, are concealed in the implementation module and cannot be utilised by the programmer when dealing with objects of type *String*. Thus the implementor of the module can change one realisation of strings for another "equivalent" realisation without influencing the user of the module.

The function *Create* serves to construct empty string-objects. Note that we define a new "elementary" data type but no longer have standard names for objects of this type. If, for example, we would like to construct string *abc*, we would do it by

$$Conc(CharToString('a'), Conc(CharToString('b'), CharToString('c'))).$$

(This involved notation does not invalidate the principle of data abstraction but calls for the introduction of adequate standard names).

As already mentioned, a module falls into two sections, the **public** section (called the definition module in Modula-2) and the **private** section (implementation module). The public section contains a list of all names made known to the outside, the **export-list**, and (partly incomplete) declarations for these names. The private section of the module contains concealed details about names of the public section, that is the complete type and procedure declarations together with further declarations of variables, constants etc. for local use only. In the example we have type declarations *Word* and *String*, the declaration of auxiliary variable p and the complete declarations of all functions of the module. They determine the exact realisation of the new data type.

By distinguishing between public and private sections, it is still possible to check type consistency, whereas implementation details, that is the choice of a special data structure and the realisation of operations which manipulate it, remain concealed from the user of the module. In using the operations he cannot rely on a specific implementation and use its special properties. This can sometimes have a negative effect on computation time but certainly has the following positive effects.

- It is now possible to select another data structure and corresponding operations for the implementation of a data type, without the users noticing it. For example, in a module for data type *set* we could replace an implementation of the data type as a linear list by an implementation in terms of a binary search tree;
- As the semantics of user programs do not depend on implementation details of the module, formal assertions referring to the semantics and thus their proofs become simpler. A user of the above module *Strings* can consider the objects which can be created and manipulated by the functions of the module as sequences of symbols (in the mathematical sense);
- It is now possible to divide a large program working on non-elementary data types into manageable sections and have these parts constructed by a team. Modules with the smallest possible "interfaces", i.e. import/export lists, are obvious tools for that;
- Clearly modules can also be used to translate program units separately and "link" them together later. This makes coordinated program development by groups of programmers possible. Modules can be translated separately and can even be stored in a module library, if the public sections of the modules used are available. Programming languages restrict the "uses" relation between modules in such a way that only directed acyclic graphs can occur.

In conclusion some general remarks about the visibility of names in modules seem appropriate. According to Chapter VI all names in blocks and procedures global to them are visible, if not hidden by a local definition. On the other hand, nothing from within a procedure, in particular its local names, is visible outside of the procedure, and there is no possibility of making such a name known to the outside. This could lead to problems concerning life-time. As the life-time of the incarnation of a procedure, and thus that of its local variables, is properly contained in the life-time of the incarnation of the surrounding program unit, it would be possible to refer from outside to local variables which do not yet or no longer exist.

At the outset, a module (again we follow Modula-2) cannot refer to anything in its environment and vice versa. By way of entering names in the export-list in the public section, we extend their scope and their life-time by the range of the program unit directly containing them, whether it be a procedure or a further module. This in turn can export these names. The scope is extended towards the inside, i.e. to contained program units. In the case of procedures it is extended implicitly as hitherto, in the case of modules explicitly by quotation in the import-list of the module. In nested modules visibility chains can occur leading out of a module to a module further outside and then back into another module tree. There are no life-time problems, as all nested modules together with their local variables begin to exist on entering the surrounding program unit and terminate on leaving this unit.

One problem which arises immediately when modules are developed individually is that of name collision. While inventing names to be exported, the programmer can scarcely anticipate which names the users of the module may use in the future. To resolve name conflicts we use **qualification** of names. This is required already in PROSA when naming record components. The name of the exporting module is prefixed to the exported name. They are separated by a point. In the above example the exported name *Empty*, for example, becomes *Strings.Empty*.

8.2　Polymorphism

We have argued earlier that a type system such as that in PROSA and likewise in Pascal, from which it is borrowed, helps the programmer to discover certain errors at an early stage, namely errors manifesting themselves in wrong typing. PROSA and also Pascal are said to be **statically typed**, because a (very detailed) declaration is given for each name in the program. Using this, a compiler can check the type correctness of programs.

Suppose we want to write a general sorting procedure in Pascal/PROSA, that is a procedure sorting sets of objects of arbitrary type. It is clear how to write a program which either sorts strings in lexicographic or integers in the usual ascending or descending order. Even sets of objects of a fixed record type can be sorted by a program if the sorting key is given. But one cannot write a **general** sorting procedure because in Pascal/PROSA the exact type of the objects to be sorted must be known. It would really be sufficient if one knew that there was a linear ordering on each object domain ever considered. Therefore one would like to be able to write a procedure

```
procedure bubblesort(t: type, var A: array[l..u] of t;
                     function ord(const : t, const : t): boolean)
var i, j: integer;
var a: t;
begin
    i := l + 1;
    while i ≤ l
    do a := A[i];
       j := i - 1;
       while j ≥ l and ord(a, A[j])
       do A[j + 1] := A[j]; j := j - 1
       od;
       A[j + 1] := a
    od
end
```

which we can invoke, for example, with *bubblesort* (**string**, *ls, lexlessequal*) and with *bubblesort* (**integer**, *li, less_usual*). The function procedures *lexlessequal* and *less_usual* are declared in 6.2, Example 1 and Example 10. Procedures, such as *bubblesort* above, are said to be **polymorphic**. A polymorphic procedure is characterised by the fact that its body can be executed with parameters of different types. Polymorphism can be found in most modern functional programming languages such as HOPE, MIRANDA and in ML.

A related concept is the **overloading** of operator symbols. An overloaded operator is one which denotes several operations. When evaluating or translating a term, one has to determine the possible operation denoted by an operator from the types of its operands and perhaps the context. In most programming languages, and in particular in PROSA, the arithmetic operators are examples of overloaded operators.

The operation denoted by the operator $+$ in the assignment $c := a + b$ can be an integer, real or complex addition, but also a string concatenation, depending on the programming language and the types of a, b and c. In Algol 68 and Ada the programmer can introduce additional overloaded operators.

In languages with polymorphic functions and/or overloaded operators the compiler must detect the type of all names and, in the case of overloading, correctly identify the different occurrences of operator symbols. This is achieved by a **type inference** algorithm. It collects type information at defining and applied occurrences of names and operators and checks type compatibility at the same time.

The programming language Ada provides a combination of module concept and polymorphism in the form of **generic packages**. Here a module can have type parameters which can be passed on to the procedures and functions of the module.

8.3 Generalised Control Structures

PROSA programs in Chapter IV used three different control structures, the conditional statement, the while-loop and the sequential composition, represented by a semicolon. In practice this minimal supply of control structures would lead to illegible programs.

If, for example, one has to distinguish between a large number of cases, one is forced to use deeply nested conditional statements. For clarity sake and for more time-efficient implementations, Pascal and other Algol-like languages have introduced a **case-statement**

case v **of**
  w_1: c_1;
  $\vdots$
  w_n: c_n
end

Here w_i represent possible values of the variable v, and c_i are statement sequences which are executed respectively, whenever v has the value w_i at the beginning of the case-statement.

After executing the respective c_i the case-statement is finished. If v has none of the values $w_1, \ldots w_n$, exception handling can be specified in many Pascal-variants although not in standard Pascal. In standard Pascal the case-statement terminates in such a case with an error message.

Some languages feature a generalisation of the conditional statement which encompasses the conditional as well as the case-statement. The basic component is a so-called **guarded command**. It is of the form $G \rightarrow SL$ where G is a boolean expression, called **guard** and SL a list of statements. The sequence SL may only be executed if G is evaluated to *true*. An alternative statement can now be constructed from several guarded commands. The symbol ▯ is used to separate the guarded commands from each other.

if $G_1 \rightarrow SL_1$
  ▯ $G_2 \rightarrow SL_2$
  $\vdots$
  ▯ $G_n \rightarrow SL_n$
fi

Example:
if $x \geq y \rightarrow m := x$
  ▯ $y \geq x \rightarrow m := y$
fi

The semantics of such an alternative statement is as follows. If none of the guards $G_1, \ldots, G_n$ evaluate to *true* the program aborts. Otherwise one of the statement sequences from $SL_1, \ldots, SL_n$ for which the guard is *true* is executed and the alternative statement is finished. Note that alternative statements may introduce **non-determinism** into a program. As the language does not specify which of several statement sequences with true guard is executed, different continuations with probably different results are possible. Thus not all executions of a program with the same input data necessarily end with the same result. In the above example case $x = y$ permits the choice between the two statements $m := x$ and $m := y$. However, in this special case it leads to the same result. The value of this new construct and the following generalised loop construct will be illustrated in the next section when formulating parallel processes.

A generalised loop, let us call it a do-loop, is of the form

$$\textbf{do } G_1 \to SL_1$$
$$\quad \llbracket G_2 \to SL_2$$
$$\quad \vdots$$
$$\quad \llbracket G_n \to SL_n$$
$$\textbf{od}$$

Here G_i and SL_i are defined as above. It describes a form of iteration in which one of the statement lists, whose guard is *true*, is executed in each iteration step. Iteration is complete if none of the guards yield *true*.

Example:

$$\textbf{do } x > y \to x := x - y$$
$$\quad \llbracket x < y \to y := y - x$$
$$\textbf{od}$$

is an iterative version of the Euclidean algorithm to compute the greatest common divisor of natural numbers x and y. The iteration stops if neither of the two guards is satisfied, i.e. $x = y$.

8.4 Parallelism

In Pascal or PROSA only sequential programs can be written, even with all the extensions of the last three sections. These are programs in which precisely one statement is executed at any time. (Note that this sequentiality is a property formulated on the abstraction level of the PROSA machine. Whenever we consider the execution of a PROSA program on the PROSA machine, precisely one transition rule corresponding to a statement type applies. If, on the other hand, we consider the execution of a PROSA program on an actual computer and on another level of abstraction, e.g. the level of a VLSI-chip, there may be potentially a high degree of parallelism. For example, execution of an instruction, loading of operands for the next instruction and loading the next but one instruction may occur simultaneously. But this kind of parallel work is not obvious in the executed program).

In this section we are interested in concepts which permit the description, i.e. the programming of controlled cooperation of several components of a computer system or several processes of an operating system. However, that does not mean to say that several processes actually exist which execute such a "parallel" program. Besides procedures and modules, the proposed language concepts to write parallel programs are an additional useful structuring concept for sequential algorithms. Frequently, a program can be organised as a system of parallel processes rather than a main program with several procedures. This makes proving correctness easier as in the case of modules.

The two principal aspects in designing parallel systems are **communication** and **synchronisation**. It is clear that parallel processes working jointly on the solution of a problem must communicate. This exchange of information can take place by means of shared storage sections, that is by way of global variables, but also by sending messages to each other. In the latter case the parallel processes are de-coupled to a large extent. When processes use shared variables or also shared resources in operating systems, their use, in general, has to be synchronised to facilitate an assertion about the effect of cooperation of these processes. Language concepts have been proposed to ensure exclusive access to global objects by one process at a time. Alternatively, there are language concepts to characterise legal sequences of accesses to such objects. For the first purpose **critical sections** and **monitors** have been proposed. They are the essential language extension of Concurrent Pascal.

We propose a language extension which follows C.A.R. Hoare's **communicating sequential processes** (CSP). This alternative solves the communication as well as the synchronisation problem. CSP uses the guarded commands introduced in Section 8.3. Non-determinism which can be expressed is very welcome here, because frequently a process must be able to process inputs of several other processes where the order in which these processes send portions of input can not be determined in advance. Therefore the behaviour of the other processes appears to be non-deterministic. This non-determinism can be captured in the receiving process by alternative or do statements which establish in the guards whether other processes are ready to send.

In CSP we have a **parbegin-parend** construct similar to the **begin-end** construct of procedures. It marks components to be executed as parallel processes. All these processes start (pseudo) simultaneously and their termination concludes the execution of the whole statement. These processes, running in parallel, may not communicate by shared (global) variables, i.e. they may only read but not alter them. Communication and synchronisation between parallel processes take place by means of simple input/output statements. In an input statement process P indicates a process Q from which it awaits an input, and specifies a (local) variable x of its own in which the input should be stored:

format: $Q\ ?\ x$ Read: the value sent by process Q is stored in x.

Process Q from which input is demanded indicates the receiver, in this case P, and specifies an expression whose value should be communicated:

format: $P\ !\ y + 1$ Read: send the value of $y + 1$ to P

The communication occurs synchronously because execution of one of the processes attempting input or output is stopped until the required partner has reached its output or input statement. Only after passing the information do both participating processes continue to work separately. This type of synchronous communication is also called **rendezvous** . If you consider that at a rendezvous between two people the partner wishing to present a bouquet of flowers does not tie it to a lamp-post and disappear if the other partner does not come, and symmetrically the other partner waits for the bouquet of flowers, this analogy is justified.

It is important that input statements may occur in guards. Such a guard evaluates to *true* only if the partner named there is ready to execute its output statement or input statement. Thus a process which can obtain input from several processes can be described using an alternative or do statement. If input statements occur in the guards of a do statement it terminates if all the processes named in the guards have terminated.

Example 1:   Buffering data between producer and consumer processes which produce or consume data arbitrarily and at possibly different speeds is a problem occurring in many variations in operating systems. If the buffer is of a limited size intermediate buffering de-couples the processes only to some degree. In the sequel we define such a limited buffer with space for ten objects of type *data*. This buffer is defined as a process named *buffer*. Furthermore we have a process *producer* and a process *consumer*. The producer process outputs to the buffer using statements of the form *buffer!* *d*. The consumer process obtains data from the buffer by means of input statements of the form *buffer* ? *d*. The process *buffer* is:

    process *buffer*:
var *buffer*: **array** $[0 .. 9]$ **of** *data*; *in*, *out*: **integer**;
    in := 0; *out* := 0;
    $(* \ 0 \leq out \leq in \leq out + 10 \ *)$

do $in < out + 10$; *producer* ? *buffer* $[in \bmod 10] \rightarrow in := in + 1$;
   (* first one checks if there is space for further producer data
   and if yes, one tests whether *producer* is ready to send.*)
   �‖ $out \leq in$; *consumer* ! *buffer* $[out \bmod 10] \rightarrow out := out + 1$
   (* producer data still in the buffer and the
   consumer demands further data *)
od

Counter *in* represents the number of objects obtained altogether from the producer. Counter *out* represents the total number of objects passed to the consumer. Array *buffer* must be considered as being organised cyclically. In this case *in* mod 10 points to the first free storage location, *out* mod 10 to the storage location whose content will be sent next to the consumers.

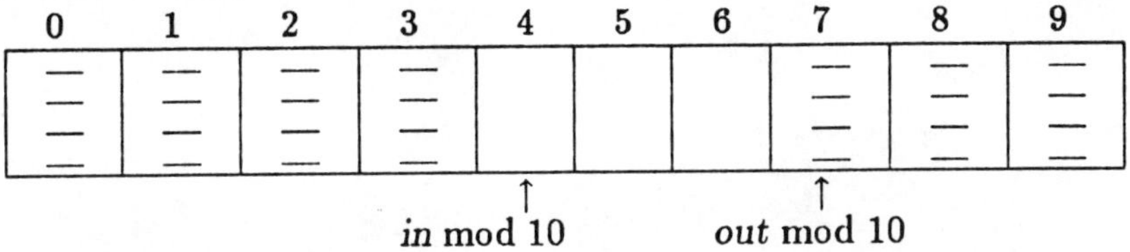

0	1	2	3	4	5	6	7	8	9
=	=	=	=				=	=	=

      ↑   ↑
in mod 10   *out* mod 10

The semicolons in the guards need some explanation. They must be interpreted as a sequential **and**, i.e. as a conjunction where the operands are evaluated in textual order. If the first operand evaluates to *false* the second will not be evaluated at all. Why is this important in our example? Let us consider the do statement with **and** instead of semicolon in the guards.

do $in < out + 10$ **and** *producer* ? *buffer* $[in \bmod 10] \rightarrow in := in + 1$;
   ◻ $out \leq in$ **and** *consumer* ! *buffer* $[out \bmod 10] \rightarrow out := out + 1$
od

The following case may now occur. Process *buffer* tests the first guard, in this case both operands of **and**. Let us assume that the buffer is full, i.e. $in = out + 10$. Evaluating the input statement *producer* ? *buffer*$[in \bmod 10]$ signals "ready to receive" to the producer just the same. If it is ready to send, it is blocked until the process *buffer* actually has space again in its buffer. Similarly, a test of the second guard can block the consumer, if the buffer is empty.

By the way, connecting a producer and a consumer process by means of a buffer of limited capacity occurs very frequently in systems programming. Consider, for example, one of your own PROSA programs as a producer process, and programs using a printer or a terminal for output as consumer processes. Our program will probably produce results much faster than they can be emitted on a terminal or a printer. An intermediate buffer of adequate size administrates the results and passes them on to the output device as required.   ■

How can we extend the PROSA machine so that it can execute programs with parallel processes? On entering a parallel statement, the PROSA machine must create a new PROSA machine for each process of the parallel statement. For each PROSA machine the actual configuration is established. These machines need access to global variables. However, context conditions should check that this access is read only. Furthermore a channel must be set up for each communication direction between two machines whose processes can communicate. This channel corresponds to a named output tape in one machine and a named input tape in another. It must be possible to test if the input tape contains data and if the machine has terminated at the other end. Likewise, each machine must be able to test if some other machine requires input from one of its output tapes. In this way the guards in alternative and do statements can be checked. If all PROSA machines started in parallel have finished the original machine which created them continues.

Index

List of Notations

Special Symbols in the Order of Occurrence

Notation	Section	Notation	Section
$=$	1.1	$\|\,\|$	1.3
$<$	1.1	$\|\,\|_b$	1.3
$\leq$	1.1	$\rightarrow$	1.4
$[\,]_R$	1.1	$\rightarrow^*$	1.4
R^*	1.1	$\xrightarrow[can]{}$	1.4
$\rightsquigarrow$	1.2	$\|$	1.4
$\circ$	1.2	$==$	1.6
$\sqsubseteq$	1.2	δ	1.7
ϵ	1.3	$\Rightarrow$	1.7
Σ^+	1.3	$[x \backslash y]$	3.4
Σ^*	1.3	$\{P\}\,p\,\{Q\}$	3.9
$\leq_{lex}$	1.3	$\Box$	8.3

Symbols in alphabetical Order

Notation	Section	Notation	Section
ARR	4.3.1	G_{pa}	2.2
AR_i	7.1	G_f	2.1
Att	1.6	H	7.1
B, b	3.4	I	1.7
B^A	1.2	in	1.7
BAP, bap	7.1	**INST**	5.1
BFS, bfs	7.1	I_E	2.2
bs	6.4	I_F	2.2
C	1.7	I_p	2.1.2
C^f	1.7	I_T	2.2
$comp_time$	3.8	I_f	2.1.1
$comp_time_M$	1.7	I/O_M	1.7
$Conc$	1.3	$I/O_{M_{PROSA}}$	3.1
D	3.2	L	4.3.2
$Def(F)$	1.2	$L_{G,A}$	1.4
$depth$	1.4	l_i	7.1
DS, ds	5.1	LL(k)	1.4
$frontier$	1.4	LR(k)	1.4
$FV_{c,t}$	3.4	M	1.7
G_p	2.1.2	M_{PROSA}	3.4

Notation	Section	Notation	Section
M_{pa}	2.2	*rad*	5.3
M_f	2.1.1	**REC**	4.3.1
O	1.7	**S**, *s*	3.4
out	1.7	*si*	5.3
parent	1.4	*SP*	7.1
P	1.7	*subst*	1.4
$P(A, B)$	1.2	*subtree*	1.4
PI, *pi*	6.3.1	*sv*	6.4
PR	3.4	**V**	3.4
prefix	1.3	*val*	1.6
PS, *ps*	5.1		

List of Important Nonterminals

⟨act par⟩ 350
⟨act par list⟩ 349
⟨act par seq⟩ 349
⟨app ident⟩ 124
⟨array decl⟩ 209
⟨array par type⟩ 334
⟨array type⟩ 211
⟨ass⟩ 142, 221, 350
⟨block⟩ 333
⟨bound⟩ 212
⟨comp⟩ 211
⟨comp seq⟩ 211
⟨cond⟩ 149
⟨const decl⟩ 135, 208
⟨const decl seq⟩ 208
⟨const decls⟩ 208
⟨decl⟩ 135
⟨decl seq⟩ 135
⟨decls ⟩ 135
⟨def bound seq⟩ 135
⟨def ident⟩ 135
⟨dimensions⟩ 348
⟨elem type⟩ 135, 210
⟨error ⟩ 156
⟨expr⟩ 144, 221
⟨ext funct body⟩ 334
⟨ext proc body⟩ 334
⟨factor⟩ 145, 350
⟨ident⟩ 121
⟨index seq⟩ 219
⟨input⟩ 141
⟨iter⟩ 151
⟨mode⟩ 348
⟨mode seq⟩ 348
⟨name⟩ 142, 218
⟨new stat⟩ 222
⟨output⟩ 141
⟨par spec⟩ 334
⟨par spec list⟩ 334
⟨par spec seq⟩ 334

⟨pointer type⟩ 210
⟨proc call⟩ 307
⟨proc decl⟩ 334
⟨proc decl seq⟩ 334
⟨proc decls⟩ 334
⟨program⟩ 141, 333
⟨ran seq⟩ 211
⟨range⟩ 212
⟨record decl⟩ 209
⟨record type⟩ 211
⟨red array type⟩ 348
⟨simp expr⟩ 145
⟨small type⟩ 210
⟨stand name⟩ 126
⟨stat⟩ 141, 222, 349
⟨stat seq⟩ 141
⟨stats⟩ 141
⟨term⟩ 145
⟨type decl⟩ 209
⟨type decl seq⟩ 209
⟨type decls⟩ 209
⟨var decl⟩ 209
⟨var decl seq⟩ 209
⟨var decls⟩ 209
⟨variable decl⟩ 209